'Health psychology has been at the vanguard of many recent advances practice. This timely textbook offers a thoughtful, state of the art critical around understanding and changing health behaviour. Particularly enco of automatic processes, which are typically overlooked in favour of un behaviours as conscious, deliberative and reasoned. Tapper succeeds ii the real-world by recognising various barriers to translating evidence int practice, including biased interpretation and communication of behavioural science and the spreading of misinformation in the social media age.'
                                                    – Benjamin Gardner, *King's College London, UK*

'Katy Tapper's book covers the research, theory and practice of health psychology and behaviour change in comprehensive detail. She encourages students to develop the critical thinking skills necessary to evaluate contemporary research, whilst also explaining how this can be practically applied to everyday media and online content.'
                                                    – Olga van den Akker, *Middlesex University, UK*

'*Health Psychology and Behaviour Change* is a must-read for all students and others who want to be updated in health psychology and effective interventions for behavioural change.'
                                                    – Jesper Dammeyer, *University of Copenhagen, Denmark*

'This is a comprehensive and lucidly written textbook that makes a compelling case for understanding the relationship between behaviour and health in high-, middle- and low-income societies. In the 21st century, characterized by a high prevalence of communicable and non-communicable diseases, increasing pressures on health care systems, large-scale migration, and unprecedented climate change, this book is a very useful source for students in psychology, health counselling, nursing and related fields. In addition to presenting theory and research associated with important health issues and problems, Dr Tapper also calls attention to criticisms and controversies, thus presenting an important critical perspective.'
                                                    – Ashraf Kagee, *Stellenbosch University, South Africa*

'This fantastic textbook provides a well-organised, succinct and accessible overview of both the scientific evidence in relation to the psychology of behaviour change as well as its practical application in the real-world. This is one of the best textbooks in this area that I have come across and will be an invaluable guide to anyone interested in understanding and changing health behaviour.'
                                                    – Stephan Dombrowski, *University of New Brunswick, Canada*

'This is an excellent modern textbook. It introduces health psychology as an evidence-based and theoretically-grounded science with key contributions to health and wellbeing. Focusing on behavioural change, Dr Tapper illustrates how health psychology interfaces with public health, medicine and other disciplines to address key challenges to population health. The clear focus on critical appraisal and practical skills will encourage students on their path to a career in heath psychology.'
                                                    – Falko Sniehotta, *Newcastle University, UK*

HEALTH PSYCHOLOGY AND BEHAVIOUR CHANGE

From Science to Practice

Katy Tapper

 macmillan international HIGHER EDUCATION

 RED GLOBE PRESS

First published 2021 by
RED GLOBE PRESS

Red Globe Press in the UK is an imprint of Macmillan Education Limited, registered in England, company number 01755588, of 4 Crinan Street, London, N1 9XW.

Red Globe Press® is a registered trademark in the United States, the United Kingdom, Europe and other countries.

ISBN 978-1-137-57948-5 paperback

This book is printed on paper suitable for recycling and made from fully managed and sustained forest sources. Logging, pulping and manufacturing processes are expected to conform to the environmental regulations of the country of origin.

A catalogue record for this book is available from the British Library.

A catalog record for this book is available from the Library of Congress.

The icons that appear throughout this book are printed courtesy of The Noun Project, https://thenoun-project.com/

Printed and bound by CPI Group (UK) Ltd, Croydon, CR0 4YY

Publishers: Luke Block and Jenna Steventon

Assistant Editor: Verity Rimmer

Development Editor: Niki Arulanandam

Cover Designer: Laura De Grasse

Senior Production Editor: Amy Brownbridge

Senior Marketing Manager: Kim Doyle

For my dad, for instilling me with a love of science and for always making me see the other side of the argument.

For my mum, for encouraging me to break the rules.

BRIEF CONTENTS

CONTENTS

Part 2: Theories of Health Behaviour

LIST OF FIGURES AND IMAGES

Figures

Images

LIST OF TABLES

LIST OF BOXES

Hot Topic

Controversial issues that often spark debate within the media or among the general public. Arm yourself with the facts!

Dig a Little Deeper

Material that provides extra breadth or depth. Push yourself further by getting to grips with the ideas in these boxes.

As an Aside

Tangential insights that are simply too good to ignore. Be the most interesting person at the party with these fascinating facts.

Making Connections

Links to material in other chapters. Improve your ability to think both critically and creatively by learning to identify connections between different areas.

Take the Test

Extra detail on a particular test. Bring it to life by seeing how you measure up.

The Great Debate

Questions to get you thinking. Practice developing an argument and using evidence to support it.

Case Study

Real world interventions from around the globe. See how theory and evidence relate to practice.

PREFACE

Credit: Marina Pothos-Tapper.

When I began teaching health psychology in 2006, I wanted my lectures to interest my students. I focussed on behaviour change, in part because that was where my expertise lay, but also because I felt it would be something students could relate to. We're constantly trying to change our own behaviour as well as the behaviour of others. We also find ourselves influenced by the things around us – information, advertising and even architecture – that seem to steer us down a particular path. Behaviour change is relevant, not just to health psychology, but to our everyday lives. This was a topic which would be of use to students beyond the lecture theatre.

In the last decade, it has also become clear how critical behaviour change is for our health. With ever increasing knowledge of how to prevent and treat disease, the weakest link is often behaviour, whether it's eating a healthy diet, getting enough exercise or sticking to a medication regime. The COVID pandemic has also brought behaviour to the fore as we've had to make rapid adjustments to a multitude of habits for the benefit of others as well as ourselves.

It is for these reasons that this book focusses on behaviour change. It is a topic with wide appeal and applicability but also one that is increasingly recognised as key in the fields of health psychology, public health and medicine. This book reflects this new emphasis.

There are other things I'm keen for my students to learn too. In particular, I want them to be more critical consumers of news and information. Young people today grow up in an information saturated world. Almost any question can be answered with the click of a button – though not always with an accurate answer. So, what is important, is not necessarily to have more information, but to have more skills; the ability to think critically about information and the evidence behind it. Health psychology is a great area to teach such skills because we're constantly bombarded with advice about what to eat and how to exercise. In order to evaluate evidence, you need a good understanding of the scientific process, you need to know why certain types of evidence are better than others and you need to be aware of where bias may creep into the literature. The media rarely considers these points, but I want my students to be able to. The next time their doctor recommends a particular course of action, or the government talks about an evidence-based policy, or even when the next goji berry diet is promoted on Instagram, I want my students to be able to evaluate the evidence for themselves. For these reasons, Chapters 10 and 11 cover research methods, bias and misinformation. I also take a more detailed look at some of the latest palaeo-inspired health advice in Chapter 2 and consider vaccine hesitancy in Chapter 12.

I would also like my students to appreciate the complexity of the issues facing the world today and to try to view these from a range of different perspectives. We live in an age where it's easy to see things in black and white, surround ourselves with those who share our views and vilify those who do not. But if there is one thing behavioural science teaches us, it is that people are more likely to change when they feel understood and listened to, not when they feel attacked and judged. One cannot shy away from the fact that health is inherently political, but I believe more progress can be made when we take a collaborative approach. It is easy to get angry but more effective to listen. I have tried to highlight the very complex and interconnected nature of health and health policy in Chapters 2, 3, 4 and 11. Throughout the book, I have also tried my very best to consider issues from all points of view.

Alongside these more general ambitions, there are three additional features of the book that I think are worth highlighting. First, the book has theory at its heart. It is tempting to organise a health psychology book by topic (diet, exercise, alcohol and so on), and certainly this has an intuitive appeal for anyone picking up the book and skimming through it. For most of us, a chapter titled 'Healthy Eating and Weight Loss' sounds far more interesting than one called 'Social Cognition Theories'. But I've avoided organising chapters by topic as I feel this leads to more disjointed learning, with students failing to see the connections between different areas. Rather than acquiring lots of information about particular health behaviours, my hope is that readers acquire knowledge and skills that can be applied across a range of areas. It is for this reason that Part 2 of the book organises material by theory, whilst more detailed information on specific health behaviours has been reserved for the final chapter (Chapter 12). I hope the deeper understanding readers gain from this approach compensates for the slightly less interesting chapter titles!

Second, I've dedicated an entire chapter (Chapter 6) to the discussion of automatic processes. In recent years it has become clear that we simply cannot account for all behaviour using the more traditional health psychology models that tend to emphasise conscious decision-making processes (covered in Chapter 5). An emphasis on decision-making may be especially problematic when it comes to tackling health inequalities whereas strategies that draw on unconscious, automatic processes may prove more fruitful. So even though this is, in parts, a less established literature, throughout the book I have tried to give sufficient weight to theories and techniques that draw on automatic processes.

Third, the final chapter (Chapter 12) includes a series of case studies that look at how different health issues have been tackled across the globe. My aim here is to bring all the material from previous chapters together, to help the reader see it in context and relate it to the real world.

That's all. I hope you enjoy reading this book as much as I've enjoyed writing it.

Katy Tapper
February 2021

ACKNOWLEDGEMENTS

First and foremost, my most heartfelt thanks go to Emmanuel Pothos – thank you for caring about the things that are important to me. (And for the 783 pizzas.) I'm also grateful to Marina and Theo, who probably can't remember a time when I wasn't writing this book – thank you for being interested when I've talked about science and health and thank you for letting me use your photos.

A huge thanks to the team at Red Globe Press – to Paul Stevens for talking me into the project and to Niki Arulanandam for all her careful reading and thoughtful comments. Thank you to Luke Block and Amy Brownbridge for bringing everything together, to Verity Rimmer for tackling permissions and to Ann Edmondson for copy-editing. I am also grateful to the anonymous reviewers whose feedback was critical for shaping the content.

Lastly, thank you to the academic community, for all the excellent research, interesting conversations and constructive criticism. This book is a collaborative effort and I hope I have done the field justice.

Red Globe Press would like to thank the following organisations and individuals for their permission to reproduce or adapt copyrighted material:

Alexandra Heminsley; American Psychological Association; Australian Government Department of Health; Bangor University; Barb D'Arpino; British Film Institute; Cambridge University Press; Cancer Research UK; Centers for Disease Control and Prevention; Cystic Fibrosis Trust; Elsevier; Gapminder.org; Golden Woofs; Guilford Press; Jens Blechert; John Wiley and Sons; Kent State University; Michigan State University Social Norms Program; NIOD; Open International Publishing Ltd; Oxford University Press; Oxford Vaccine Group; Proceedings of the National Academy of Sciences; Public Health England; Public Health England; SAGE Publishing; Sport England; Springer Nature; Susan Michie, Lou Atkins and Robert West; Taylor & Francis Ltd; The British Film Institute; Townsend Centre for International Poverty Research; UNICEF; University of Exeter; US National Library of Medicine; World Health Organization; World Obesity Federation.

INTRODUCTION

INTRODUCTION TO HEALTH PSYCHOLOGY AND BEHAVIOUR CHANGE

Chapter Outline

Toward the end of the Second World War, Dr Henry Beecher, an American anaesthetist, was treating injured soldiers in military field hospitals. Morphine was used for pain relief but was often in short supply. Without morphine, surgery carried the risk of inducing fatal cardiovascular shock. Presented with a young solider with terrible injuries but no morphine, Beecher was understandably worried about his chances of survival. But then something quite unexpected happened – a nurse injected the soldier with a saline solution, a solution which should have had no effect whatsoever. However, to Beecher's surprise, the soldier immediately calmed down, exactly as if he had been injected with morphine. He then underwent surgery, not only avoiding cardiovascular shock, but also reporting little pain (Evans, 2004; **Image 1.1**).

This story shows just how important the mind is when it comes to health. Psychology is the study of mind and behaviour so health psychology is concerned with the relationship between mind, behaviour and health. It strives to understand the psychological factors that influence our health and our experience of illness. However, with improvements in health over the last century, disease is increasingly determined by a person's behaviour. For this reason, this book is particularly concerned with health psychology and behaviour change. In this introductory chapter we will:

- Consider what is meant by the term 'health'.

- Look at the ways in which our understanding of health and illness have changed over time.

- Consider the role of behaviour in health psychology.

- Think about the relative importance of health in our lives.

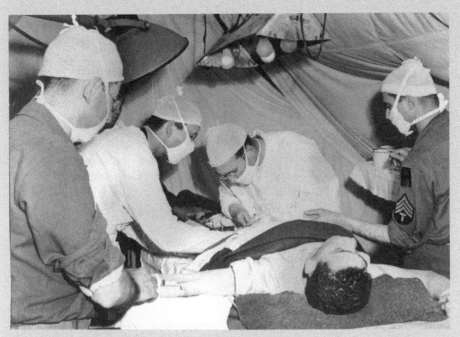

Image 1.1 *A Second World War military field hospital. Beecher's treatment of soldiers in this type of hospital helped formulate his work on placebo effects. Beecher was the first to emphasise the importance of the placebo in relation to both medical research and treatment.*
Credit: Interim Archives/Archive Photos/Getty Images.

WHAT DO WE MEAN BY 'HEALTH'?

What comes to mind when you think of the word 'health'? For what reasons would you describe yourself as 'healthy' or 'unhealthy'? You may find the word has several meanings for you and these may partly be determined by your age, gender, cultural background and whether you are currently experiencing good health or poor health (Benyamini et al., 2003; Blaxter, 1990; Chalmers, 1996; Krause & Jay, 1994; Vaughn et al., 2009).

Blaxter (1990) asked 9,000 members of the British public about what it means to be healthy. She identified nine different themes as follows:

- *Health as not ill* – when a person does not experience any symptoms or does not need to visit a doctor, they are considered healthy.

- *Health despite disease* – a person could be considered healthy when they successfully cope with a chronic condition such as diabetes or arthritis.

- *Health as a reserve* – a person is healthy if they recover quickly from illnesses and operations.

- *Health as behaviour or lifestyle* – a healthy person is one who looks after their health, for example by exercising or eating a good diet.

- *Health as physical fitness* – a person is considered healthy when they are physically strong, fit and athletic or when they have good skin and hair.

- *Health as energy and vitality* – a person is healthy when they feel alert and full of energy and enthusiasm.

- *Health as social relationships* – having good relationships with others and being able to help or care for others means a person is healthy.

- *Health as function* – a person is healthy when they are able to perform their duties without being impeded by physical or mental limitations.

- *Health as psychosocial wellbeing* – having good mental health and feeling happy and relaxed means a person is healthy.

World Health Organization (WHO) – a specialised agency of the United Nations, dedicated to international health. The United Nations (UN) is an international organisation founded in 1945 with the aims of maintaining peace and security, promoting sustainable development, protecting human rights, upholding international law and delivering humanitarian aid. The UN has 193 member states that make financial contributions and agree to abide by the UN Charter.

Thus the concept of health has multiple meanings and is more than just the absence of disease. This idea is captured by the definition of health put forward by the **World Health Organization (WHO)** in 1948. They described health as *'a state of complete physical, mental and social well-being and not merely the absence of disease or infirmity'* (WHO, 1948). This was considered progressive at the time because health-improvement efforts up until that point had largely focussed on the reduction of physical disease. The WHO aimed to shape global thinking about health by introducing the social and mental spheres alongside the physical, highlighting the relevance of economic and social policy. The WHO were also attempting to move towards a more positive definition of health by emphasising wellbeing instead of disease.

However, the WHO definition of health is not without its critics. In particular, the term 'complete' has been questioned, partly because it is difficult to define and measure and partly because it is difficult to achieve (Huber et al., 2011). It implies that to be healthy we need to be functioning perfectly – physically, mentally and socially. For the large majority of us, this would be impossibly hard to achieve. It also runs counter to the natural order of things, where broken hearts and ageing bodies are all part of what makes us human. Huber et al. argue that the WHO definition contributes to an increasing medicalisation of what would previously have been viewed as 'normal', such as the use of antidepressants following loss or disappointment. They also highlight the fact that growing numbers of people suffer from chronic diseases yet lead long, happy lives; to label them as somehow falling short when it comes to health could be viewed as counterproductive and unhelpful. Instead of aiming for a precise definition of health, Huber et al. suggest we should move toward viewing health as a concept; something that would better reflect its more subjective, fluctuating status. Such a concept could be used as a guide, rather than something to succeed or fail at. They propose that health should be conceptualised as 'the ability to adapt and self-manage in the face of social, physical, and emotional challenges'.

Nevertheless, others have defended the original WHO definition and raised concerns about the new concept proposed by Huber et al. (2011). For example, Lewis (2011) argued against Huber's concept of health, pointing out that although many with chronic health conditions cope well, this does not mean they do not suffer. To claim they are healthy would be to dismiss this suffering. He argued that there should be no shame in ill health and that those who are unwell deserve our sympathy and support. Others have suggested that Huber et al. place too much emphasis on the individual and their ability to adapt and self-manage (Shilton et al., 2011). This approach runs the risk that important social factors will be ignored, leading to increases in health inequalities. For example, those living on low incomes or in unsafe and under-resourced neighbourhoods will find it more difficult to adapt and self-manage compared to their more fortunate counterparts. We explore these types of social determinants of health in **Chapter 3**.

HOW HAS OUR UNDERSTANDING OF HEALTH AND ILLNESS CHANGED?

The current debate on health is the latest phase in a long history of changing views of health and illness.

Prehistory

In prehistoric times (prior to around 3000 BC, before the invention of writing), it is difficult to know for sure what people believed. For example, archaeological evidence shows that trepanation, the practice of making a hole in the skull, was widespread (Gresky et al., 2016). It is clear that this was often performed on the living since many of the skulls indicate new bone growth following trepanation (**Image 1.2**). However, the exact reasons for trepanation are uncertain. In some cases it occurs on skulls with other signs of trauma, suggesting it was performed in a belief that it would aid recovery. However, trepanation also appears on remains with no other signs of injury or disease. In these cases, it may have been performed to treat conditions that leave no visible marks, such as migraine or psychological disorders, though it may also have been used as part of a ritual linked to certain spiritual beliefs.

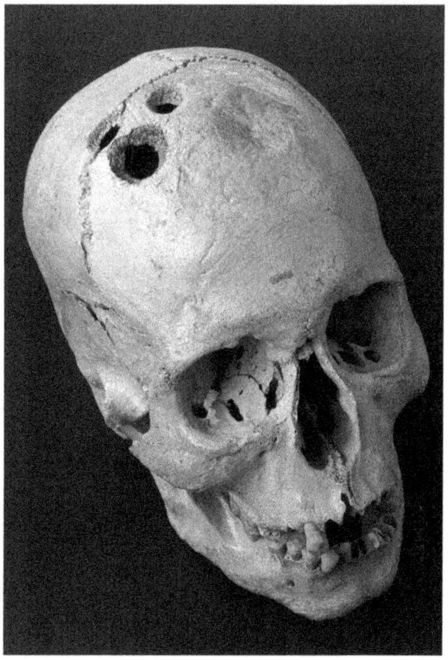

Ancient history

From around 3000 BC we see the rise of a number of different civilisations across the globe, including those found in Mesopotamia (a region of what is now the Middle East), the Indus Valley (now Pakistan and India), Egypt, China and Greece. Although these civilisations developed large bodies of knowledge relating to the diagnosis and treatment of a range of different conditions, their beliefs about the causes of disease were very different from how we understand disease today. For example, in Mesopotamia and Egypt, disease was usually attributed to supernatural causes such

Image 1.2 A skull found in Palestine, from around 2200 BC, with marks of trepanation. The trepanation holes show signs of healing, suggesting the individual survived the procedure.
Source: Bronze Age skull from Jericho, Palestine, 2200-2000. Credit: Science Museum, London. Attribution 4.0 International (CC BY 4.0).

as gods, spirits or demons and treatment often included magical rituals, potions or prayer (Popko, 2018; Porter, 1999).

In the Indus Valley and China, supernatural beliefs were gradually superseded by Ayurvedic medicine and traditional Chinese medicine, both of which view ill health as a result of an imbalance of different elements within the body. In these traditions there was an emphasis on achieving good health through healthy living and treatments were designed to restore equilibrium. Such treatments included massage, sweating and enemas as well as a range of different medicines derived from various animal, mineral and vegetable sources (Porter, 1999).

The Ancient Greeks are generally considered the forefathers of contemporary Western medicine (Porter, 1999). Initially, many Greeks believed that prayer and sacrifice to Asclepius, the god of medicine and healing, could restore good health (**Image 1.3**), until Hippocrates (c.460–377 BC) argued that disease had natural causes, such as environmental factors and diet, rather than supernatural ones, such as punishment from the gods. Hippocrates also introduced the Hippocratic Oath, a code of ethics

Image 1.3 *Asclepius (or Aesculapius), the ancient Greek god of healing and medicine, pictured with his serpent-entwined rod that is still used today as a symbol of medicine. Asclepius had five daughters, including Hygieia, the goddess of health, cleanliness and sanitation, and Panacea, the goddess of universal remedy.*
Source: Aesculapius: the Greek god of healing. Photograph by Alinari, 1900/1920 (?). Credit: Wellcome Collection. Attribution 4.0 International (CC BY 4.0).

for physicians from where the phrase 'First do no harm' originates. Hippocrates applied the concept of 'humors' to medicine. Like the Ayurvedic and Chinese traditions, humorism held that ill health was caused by an imbalance of different elements in the body, in this case, of four different bodily fluids: blood, phlegm, yellow bile and black bile. Humorism was further developed by Galen (129 AD–c. 216 AD), a Greek physician living in Rome. He believed that blood was the dominant humor in the body and therefore the most in need of control. This led to the practice of bloodletting in order to help balance the humors and involved the withdrawal of blood, either by a physician or using leeches. Galen recommended bloodletting for all disorders (even blood loss!) with the exact nature of the condition determining where the blood should be drawn from and the amount that should be taken; the more severe the illness, the greater the quantity let.

The Middle Ages

In Europe, after the collapse of the Roman Empire (AD 476), and throughout the Middle Ages (AD 500–c. 1450), the ideas of Hippocrates and Galen remained popular, and bloodletting continued to be a common treatment carried out by both doctors and barbers. Supernatural explanations for health and illness were also widespread, including astrology, witchcraft and punishment from God. However, with the rise of Christianity, healing and the care of the sick was increasingly seen as one of the duties of the church. The sick made pilgrimages to the shrines of saints and were treated by monks in monasteries with herbs and prayer. This gave rise to the first hospitals.

The Early Modern period

The 1300s marked the start of the Renaissance (or 'Early Modern' period) that began in Florence in Italy and had spread throughout the rest of Europe by the 1500s. This period was characterised by a rediscovery of ancient Greek philosophy, literature and art. It was a period of rapid progress in both the arts and sciences that included the development of the scientific method of experimentation and hypotheses testing. There was also a renewed interest in anatomy and the human body, with the first recorded public human dissection taking place in Northern Italy, in the city of Bologna, in 1315, carried out by Mondino (c. 1270–1326). By the mid-1500s human dissection was routine throughout Europe. As such, there was a huge growth in medical knowledge, and explanations of health and illness increasingly focussed on the body. Also influential at this time was the work of the French philosopher, René Descartes (1596–1650). He considered the mind as separate and distinct from the body (a view termed 'dualism') and thought the body could be likened to a machine. Descartes recommended trying to understand the body by separating it into smaller parts, an approach to scientific understanding called 'reductionism' (Larson, 1999).

The Late Modern period

The Late Modern period (from around the 1800s) saw developments in the understanding of disease. During the early 1800s miasma theory was the most widely held explanation for disease, stating that disease was caused by bad smelling air (miasma) emanating from decomposing organic matter (miasmata). As miasmata decomposed it was thought to release particles into the air, infecting individuals and causing disease. Thus, according to the theory, disease would affect multiple people in the same area, not because it passed from person to person but because they were all breathing in the same air. This theory was gradually replaced in the late 1800s by the germ theory of disease which subsequently led to the identification of many of the organisms that cause ill health. Critical to this change in thinking was the work of John Snow (1813–1858), now considered one of the forefathers of **epidemiology (Box 1.1)**, and of Louis Pasteur (1822–1895), the French biologist who showed that particular microbes caused particular diseases (and from where the term 'pasteurisation' comes; the process of heating milk to kill germs).

> **Epidemiology** – a branch of medicine concerned with the distribution, causes and control of disease in particular populations.

BOX 1.1 UNDERSTANDING OF DISEASE: FROM BAD AIR TO GERMS

AS AN ASIDE

In 1854 there was a severe outbreak of **cholera** in the Soho area of London, killing 127 people in just 3 days and 616 people in total (Porter, 1999). At the time, Soho was overcrowded with both people and animals. It also lacked a proper sewage system, relying instead on cesspits built under homes. But these cesspits were not large enough to support the growing population, and to avoid them overflowing, families would often have their sewage collected and dumped in the River Thames. This contaminated the water supply to the city, leading to outbreaks of cholera.

By talking to those living in the area, John Snow established a link between the incidence of cholera and the use of a particular water pump located on what was then Broad Street (now Broadwick Street). He also observed that workers at a nearby brewery did not contract cholera. They were typically given a daily allowance of beer, which meant they were not drinking water from the Broad Street pump but were instead drinking water that had been boiled as part of the brewing process – something that would have killed any cholera bacteria.

Snow's research managed to convince the local authorities to remove the handle to the pump, at which point the outbreak subsided. It was later discovered that a nearby cesspit had been leaking into the well of the Broad Street pump. However, belief in miasma was so entrenched that government officials rejected Snow's theory about the waterborne transmission of cholera and eventually replaced the pump handle. It was not until later in the century that germ theory became widely accepted.

> **Cholera** – a bacterial infection spread by ingesting food or water that has been contaminated with human faeces containing the bacteria. Cholera causes severe diarrhoea, vomiting and dehydration and, left untreated, kills more than 50% of those infected. With treatment, mortality drops to less than 0.2%. There have been seven recorded cholera pandemics that have killed millions of people across the globe. Cholera is still common in many parts of the world, leading to around 10,000 deaths every year (Clemens et al., 2017; Harris et al., 2012).

CONTEMPORARY MODELS OF HEALTH AND ILLNESS

The biomedical model

In Europe, the renewed focus on the body during the Renaissance led to the development of what we now refer to as the 'biomedical model of disease' (Engel, 1977). This model attributes illness to a single cause located within the body. It is reductionist in that it attempts to explain illness in terms of the smallest possible processes, such as germs and their effect on the body's cells. The model is built on the premise that the cause is always physical in nature; where something cannot be explained in terms of physical causes it should be excluded from the realm of illness and disease. In this way the model is also considered exclusionist. The biomedical model has been critical to the development of modern Western medicine which has in turn proved very successful at treating disease. However, it is not without its limitations.

Challenges to the biomedical model

The case of 'Vance Vanders', reported by Meador (1992), is a good illustration of why the biomedical model can often fall short. Vance Vanders was a 60-year-old man admitted to hospital in Alabama in 1938 by Dr Daugherty. Vanders was weak and emaciated, refusing to eat and insisting he was going to die. His condition continued to deteriorate till he was slipping in and out of consciousness and barely able to talk. Despite running numerous tests, Dr Daugherty could find nothing physically wrong with him. It was only when Vanders was close to death that his terrified wife confided in Dr Daugherty that Vanders had had an argument with a local witch doctor who had waved a foul smelling liquid in his face and told him he had 'voodooed' him and that he would die very soon. He threatened to do the same to his family if he told anyone.

> **Placebo effect** – a beneficial effect brought about by a substance or treatment which cannot be attributed to the properties of that substance or treatment, and is therefore thought to occur due to the person's belief in the substance or treatment. Placebo effects are common in health and medical interventions, but an evidence-based treatment should be able to demonstrate an effect beyond this (see **Box 1.2**).

Dr Daugherty spent several hours that evening mulling over this new information before deciding upon how best to try to help his patient. The next morning he summoned Vanders' family to his bedside and announced he had found the witch doctor and choked him till he'd confessed the secret to his curse. Vanders was dying, Daugherty declared, because the witch doctor had made him breathe in lizards' eggs and now there was a lizard growing inside him, eating the lining of his body as well as any food he ate. With much ceremony he then injected Vanders with a large needle filled with a substance to make him vomit. As Vanders was throwing up into a metal basin, Daugherty discreetly took a live green lizard from his bag and, with sleight of hand, slipped it into the basin. In a loud voice he then announced that the lizard had been removed and the curse lifted.

Vanders fell into a deep sleep. The next morning he woke ravenously hungry and ate a large breakfast of milk, bread, meat and eggs. He regained his strength and weight and was discharged from hospital soon after. He reportedly lived well into his 70s.

This story, along with the description of Beecher's work at the start of the chapter, helps to highlight the limitations of the biomedical model. There was no physical reason for Vanders to lose his appetite and become so ill. So according to the biomedical model, one would not have labelled him as unwell. And yet he nearly died. Likewise, according to the biomedical model, a saline solution should have had no effect on Beecher's soldier's experience of pain. And yet it did. A purely biomedical approach to treatment would likely have ended in the death of both these patients. But in both instances, by taking account of psychological variables, the doctors were able to save their lives.

These types of effects are termed **placebo** and **nocebo effects**. They illustrate the ways in which the mind can influence perception, behaviour and health. They also show how important psychological and social variables are to understanding and promoting health. For example, it was Daugherty's knowledge of witch doctor practices (a social variable) that enabled him to change Vanders' belief that he was going to die (a psychological variable) and ultimately restored Vanders' health (a biological/physical outcome).

> **Nocebo effect** – a harmful effect brought about by a substance or treatment which cannot be attributed to the physical properties of that substance or treatment, and is therefore attributed to the person's belief in the substance or treatment. One of the most common types of nocebo effect may occur where an individual is aware of the potential side effects of a medication they are taking.

With recent advances in neuroscience, one might be tempted to argue that one day we will also be able to explain the mind in physical terms and so do away with the need to refer to psychological variables. Perhaps at some point we will be able to read a person's mind simply by looking at the neuronal connections in their brain. However, even if this were possible, there are important reasons why this type of approach would be limiting.

First, unlike simple machines, humans are not closed systems. Our brains and bodies constantly influence, and are influenced by, our external environment. A snapshot of our brains (or our bodies) will tell us little about what they might encounter the next day, week, month or year. And yet this information is essential if we are to try to maintain good health. In order to know what we might (or might not) encounter, we need to look beyond our physical selves and towards our environment. For example, a doctor may prescribe a particular type of medication for a very elderly patient, but only by considering that patient's psychological status and social support system will they be able to predict whether or not the patient is likely to take the medication as directed.

Second, the type of explanation we select tends to dictate the course of action we subsequently take. If we want to improve someone's health, there are many reasons why we may prefer to try to change their social environment rather than treat their body. Attempting to explain health with reference to just the body, biases treatment toward physical interventions that directly target the body but neglect the mind and environment.

It is for these reasons that, since the 1970s, academics have called for thinking to move beyond a simply biomedical understanding of health and toward a biopsychosocial model, which recognises the role of the psychological and social domains in interaction with the body (Engel, 1977; Matarazzo, 1980).

BOX 1.2 CONTROLLING FOR PLACEBO EFFECTS

MAKING CONNECTIONS

When developing a new drug or intervention, researchers typically need to show that it has benefits that go beyond any placebo effects. In order to achieve this, evaluation studies need to be carefully designed. In drug trials this usually means comparing the real drug with an identical looking pill that contains an inert substance (such as sugar), but in more complex, behavioural interventions, controlling for placebo effects can be more difficult. In **Chapter 10** we look at how studies can be designed to control for placebo effects (as well as other types of bias) and in **Chapter 12** we look at examples of how this has been achieved in relation to different types of interventions.

BOX 1.3 HOW SUSCEPTIBLE ARE YOU TO PLACEBO EFFECTS?

TAKE THE TEST

Certain personality traits seem to predispose people toward experiencing stronger placebo effects. For example, Vachon-Presseau et al. (2018) found that those who reported higher levels of emotional awareness also reported greater pain relief from a placebo. This is just one of a number of different traits that have been associated with a stronger analgesic response to a placebo. Find out how you score on emotional awareness by answering the questions below. Once you've answered the five questions compute a mean by adding up the scores and dividing by 5.

Please indicate how often each statement applies to you generally in daily life	Circle one number on each line					
	Never				**Always**	
1. I notice how my body changes when I am angry.	0	1	2	3	4	5
2. When something is wrong in my life I can feel it in my body.	0	1	2	3	4	5
3. I notice that my body feels different after a peaceful experience.	0	1	2	3	4	5
4. I notice that my breathing becomes free and easy when I feel comfortable.	0	1	2	3	4	5
5. I notice how my body changes when I feel happy/joyful.	0	1	2	3	4	5

Extract, Emotional awareness subscale, taken from Table 2 in the Multidimensional Assessment of Interoceptive Awareness (MAIA) (Mehling et al., 2012).

Vachon-Presseau et al. found that a score of around 2 or less was associated with very little pain relief from a placebo, whereas pain relief averaged around 50% among those who scored 5 or more.

The biopsychosocial model

Health psychologists use the biopsychosocial model to understand health and illness (Engel, 1977; Matarazzo, 1980). While the biomedical model is characterised by mechanistic thinking, where each specific disease or illness is attributed to a single, specific cause, the biopsychosocial model is characterised by contextual, holistic thinking, where disease and illness are a result of a multitude of different, interacting factors, occurring at three different levels of explanation – the biological, the psychological and the social (Schwartz, 1982).

This makes the biopsychosocial model a more complete model of health (though also a more complex one that is potentially more difficult to use, see Suls & Rothman, 2004). This allows for a much wider range of intervention options. As noted above, the way in which we explain a problem tends to guide our approach to solving it. By seeking explanations in the biological, psychological and social domains, the biopsychosocial model can lead to treatments directed at the body, mind and social environment. For example, we can explain obesity with reference to (a) particular genes that predispose a person to gain weight, (b) individual differences in cravings, impulsivity and self-control, or (c) environments that limit opportunities for exercise and make energy-dense foods better value for money. Each of these different explanations would lead to a different type of intervention.

However, what the biopsychosocial model cannot do is weight one explanation over another or help us determine where we should prioritise efforts to improve health (Ghaemi, 2009). Choosing to direct interventions at the biological, psychological or environmental level is often more a matter of social and political values than science. Such choices may also reflect, and influence, the way we attribute responsibility (or 'blame') for particular health conditions. Does a person suffer from overweight because they are lazy or because they are unlucky? Or because they are exploited by big business for profit? Depending on your view, you may be more inclined to invest resources in a particular type of intervention – or to justify not intervening at all.

HEALTH IN THE MODERN AGE: THE IMPORTANCE OF BEHAVIOUR CHANGE

The last century has seen a dramatic decline in infectious diseases, and an increase in chronic, non-communicable conditions such as obesity, diabetes, cardiovascular disease and cancer (Fries, 1983; see **Chapter 2**). Unlike infectious diseases, which are associated with exposure to particular microbes, chronic conditions are influenced by a wide range of different factors, many of which concern behaviours such as diet, exercise, smoking and drinking. Thus over the course of the next century, significant improvements in health may be brought about by interventions that change behaviour in order to help prevent or delay the onset of these diseases or to help manage them when they occur. It is for this reason that this book places a particular emphasis on behaviour change.

However, the importance of behaviour for health extends beyond the behaviour of the 'patient'. Behaviour change is also important in healthcare delivery. For example, every year hundreds of millions of patients around the world acquire infections in hospitals, many of which are life-threatening. Some of these infections could be prevented by healthcare providers cleaning their hands at the right time and in the right way. Effective interventions are needed to change behaviour in order to address this problem (WHO, 2009b, 2011). Likewise, antibiotic resistance is becoming an increasing global concern which will only be tackled by healthcare providers reducing the number of antibiotics they prescribe (*Lancet*, 2014).

More recently, the COVID-19 pandemic has brought to the fore just how important our behaviour is for protecting the health of those around us. From handwashing and social distancing to wearing face masks and self-isolating, we have all had to change our behaviour, not just for our own benefit but for the benefit of the wider community.

Additionally, behaviour change is relevant to our everyday lives. We're constantly trying to exert control over our own behaviour, whether it's eating more healthily, taking more exercise, or mustering up the stamina to meet a deadline. We also try to influence the behaviour of others – children, parents, friends, colleagues. Most jobs include an element of behaviour change too, such as trying to get pupils to behave in the classroom, persuading customers to buy your product, or attempting to get the best out of employees.

Finally, behaviour change is critical to many important challenges facing the world today, climate change being a key example. With a little thought, many of the theories and methods described in this book can be applied to situations beyond health.

HEALTH IN CONTEXT: WHEN HEALTH IS LESS IMPORTANT

Why should we want to improve health? The obvious answer is because it reduces suffering and increases happiness. Health is clearly important in this respect; good health enables us to do the things we want to do, whilst poor health can be limiting and painful. However, we should be wary of pursuing health for its own sake if it comes at the expense of happiness. Many things considered bad for our health bring pleasure (**Image 1.4**) – sweet foods, alcohol, staying up too late. And things that may be good for us can sometimes make us miserable, such as dieting to lose weight. Or they may simply be plain tedious, such as flossing your teeth every night. There's an awfully long list of things we 'ought' to be doing to keep healthy, such as cooking meals from scratch, engaging in different types of exercise, and going for regular check-ups and screenings with doctors, dentists, nurses and opticians. Arguably, if we follow all these recommendations religiously, we may find we have little leisure time left to do the things that really make us happy, such as spending time with family and friends, pursuing exciting hobbies or even putting in extra hours at that dream job.

Thus when thinking about health promotion, it is important to remember that happiness is not always best served by more emphasis on health or longevity. Imagine a woman who dies at 75 having spent her whole life restricting her food intake to maintain a slim figure. Who is to say she has had a better life than her overweight counterpart who dies at 70 having enjoyed a lifetime of laughter over beer and plenty of pizza and ice cream? And should we really insist a man in his 80s quits his cherished cigarette and coffee ritual for the sake of his heart? We cannot know in advance what choices will bring us most happiness, but we should avoid assuming that the healthiest option is always the best. And it is for this reason that we should also avoid passing judgement on those we perceive to be less healthy than ourselves.

Image 1.4 *Happiness is not just about health.*
Credit: Katy Tapper.

CONCLUSIONS – AND SOME WORDS ABOUT THIS BOOK

Health is a woolly concept that is difficult to define. Our understanding of health has also changed over time, along with the most common types of health problems. In modern society, health is often influenced by behaviour, which is in turn determined by biological, psychological and social factors.

The main body of this book starts by looking at the determinants of health. Understanding what causes health and illness can help us understand the types of interventions that are likely to be more or less effective. For example, it will be more difficult to change behaviours that we have a strong evolutionary predisposition towards (**Chapter 2**) or to improve health where it has a clear genetic determinant (**Chapter 4**). And we cannot afford to ignore the role the social environment plays in making certain approaches to behaviour change more or less effective (**Chapter 3**). However, simply identifying different determinants of health is rarely enough to bring about change because different determinants interact in complex ways. For this reason, we also need theory, which we consider in Part 2, in **Chapters 5, 6, 7** and **8**.

In this chapter we looked at the biopsychosocial model of health which states that health is influenced by biological, psychological and social factors. These are considered throughout the following chapters, though certain chapters place more emphasis on some factors than others. When we consider the determinants of health in Part 1, we start by taking a very broad perspective, looking at evolutionary and historical determinants (**Chapter 2**). This chapter encompasses both social and biological influences. We then go on to look at the social determinants of health (**Chapter 3**), which include social and psychological influences. Finally, we narrow our focus down to determinants situated at the individual level (**Chapter 4**), which include biological and psychological factors.

In Part 2, the emphasis of many of the theories we consider, is very much at the psychological level, particularly in **Chapter 5** where we look at social cognition models. In one sense this approach is understandable, given that psychology is concerned with mind and behaviour. But if health psychology is to fully embrace the biopsychosocial model and develop more powerful theories and interventions, it needs to take more account of the social environment. More emphasis is given to social influences in some of the theories covered in **Chapter 6**.

In Part 3 we go beyond theory to look at practice, specifically the development of behaviour change interventions (**Chapter 9**) and their evaluation (**Chapter 10**). These processes are essential if we are to successfully apply what we know about behaviour and behaviour change. Many have argued that, currently, there is too big a gap between science and practice, and too little of what we do as a society is informed by scientific theory or based on good scientific evidence (Henderson, 2012). Thus an understanding of how theory can link to practice is essential. We consider additional reasons for the gap between science and practice in **Chapter 11**. Finally, **Chapter 12** draws everything together in a series of case studies that – hopefully – help illustrate all the different topics that have been covered, as well as providing more detail on specific health issues.

THE GREAT DEBATE

The term 'alternative medicine' is used to refer to treatments that are aimed at healing but which are not based on scientific principles or evidence. They may also be referred to as 'complementary medicine', 'integrative medicine', 'holistic medicine' or 'natural medicine'. Many types of alternative medicine have been shown to be ineffective, in other words, no better than placebo (Ernst, 2019). However, as we've seen in this chapter, placebo effects can be very powerful. What kind of claims should those promoting alternative medicine be allowed to make? Should this vary depending on the type of condition being treated? Do you think similar rules should apply to faith healers?

PART 1

DETERMINANTS OF HEALTH

CHAPTER 2
EVOLUTIONARY AND HISTORICAL DETERMINANTS OF HEALTH

Chapter Outline

The Origin of our Species

Evolution

Hunter-gatherers

The Agricultural Revolution

The Epidemiological Transition

Life Today

Should We Try to Live More Like Hunter-gatherers?

Conclusions

If you've never heard of 'minimalist footwear', you may be mistaken for thinking that the shoes pictured below have come from the set of *The Hobbit* (**Image 2.1**). In fact, they are shoes designed for running, but running as though one were barefoot. Why would anyone want to run long distances (or indeed any distance) barefoot? Fans of this practice argue that we evolved to run without shoes, and that running 'as nature intended' improves speed, strengthens foot muscles, and reduces the risk of injuries (McDougall, 2010).

Image 2.1 *Barefoot running shoes, designed to simulate the experience of running without shoes.*
Credit: Katy Tapper.

The increasing popularity of barefoot running represents just one of many health trends that seek to emulate our hunter-gatherer ancestors, as a means to happier, healthier, longer lives. Whether it's eating raw meat, going to bed at sunset, or carrying your newborn round in a sling all day, proponents of a 'palaeo' lifestyle eschew modern habits for what they view as a more 'natural' existence. The reasoning is persuasive; our species has lived as hunter-gatherers for around 300,000 years, whilst our farming-based lifestyles date back 11,000 years at most. It seems reasonable to argue that we're best suited to a hunter-gatherer way of life. But exactly how healthy were our hunter-gatherer ancestors? What did their daily lives actually look like? And is it really fair to say that the human species has remained completely unchanged over the last 11,000 years?

In this chapter we will:

- Look at how our environment has changed over the course of our species' existence.
- Consider how these changes have influenced our health, the threats to our health, and our health-related behaviours.
- Think about the relationship between our evolutionary history and our health today.
- Consider whether we should all be trying to live more like hunter-gatherers.

THE ORIGIN OF OUR SPECIES

Around 7 million years ago our ape ancestors diverged along two different evolutionary paths. Some became what we today know as chimpanzees and bonobos (pygmy chimpanzees), whilst others, **hominins**, started to walk upright and eventually began using simple stone tools. **Figure 2.1** provides a very approximate timeline of important events in the evolution of our species. Around 300,000 years ago, our own species, Homo sapiens, appeared in Africa (Schlebusch et al., 2017). We had evolved much larger brains than our early ancestors and developed more complex tools and hunting techniques. However, it was not until 11,000 years ago that we started to farm; up until this point we lived as nomadic hunter-gatherers. Arguably then, our bodies and brains may still bear the mark of our hunter-gatherer ancestry. But how much of a mark? First it is helpful to remind ourselves of the mechanics of evolution, before looking at the lifestyles of our hunter-gatherer ancestors.

> **Hominins** – the taxonomic group consisting of modern humans, extinct human species, and all their immediate ancestors from the point of our last common ancestor with chimpanzees and bonobos.

EVOLUTION

Evolution refers to a change in the frequency of a particular gene or genes in a population. This could be the result of random events, for example a natural disaster that happens to wipe out all people with a particular characteristic. Alternatively, evolution could be the result of natural selection.

How does natural selection work? In a nutshell, parents pass down some of their characteristics to their offspring via their genes. If a member of a species survives long enough to reproduce, their characteristics will be more likely to be passed on to subsequent generations. Likewise, if a member of a species has more offspring (and these offspring also survive to reproduce) then these characteristics will be more likely to be passed on to subsequent generations. So any characteristic that helps an organism survive and reproduce will be more likely to occur in later generations and, over time, will become more prevalent in the population. Characteristics that work against survival and reproduction will become less common in a population.

How do new characteristics emerge within a population? Sometimes, when genes are copied from parent to offspring, errors ('mutations') occur. This introduces additional genetic variability into the population. Again, if the characteristics associated with these new genes promote survival and reproduction, they will become more prevalent within the population, if they work against survival and reproduction, they are likely to disappear.

Figure 2.1 The evolution of Homo sapiens

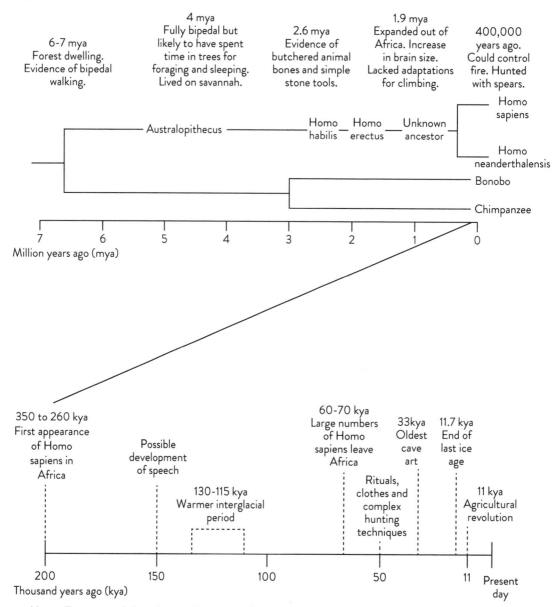

Notes: The top panel shows how we share our evolutionary ancestry with bonobos and chimps.
The bottom panel shows how our species has changed over the last 300,000 years.
Note that both panels are highly simplified – in particular, the human line in the top panel also includes many other branches of extinct species not shown.

In this way, over subsequent generations, the characteristics of a population will change so that it becomes better adapted to the environment it lives in. For example, if fruit is an important source of calories and nutrients for a particular population, but only tall people can reach the fruit from the local fruit trees, the population may gradually become taller over time.

However, a key point to remember is that a population's environment is also changing. In the example above, if the climate gets hotter and all the fruit trees die out, being tall may now be a disadvantage because tall people generally need more calories to survive than their shorter counterparts. And our environment is continually changing. Not only do we have ice ages and temperate periods, but populations migrate. People move from the hot savannah to the cool forest. Or they set out in boats to colonise new islands. So there has never been a point in history in which one could claim that humans were perfectly adapted to their environment. Since the environment is always changing, species are always evolving.

HUNTER-GATHERERS

Hunter-gatherer lifestyle

Although our environment is in constant flux, the rate of these changes varies. Rapid environmental change can represent a challenge to a species because evolution via natural selection is relatively slow, especially for species with long lifespans. As noted above, humans switched from nomadic to settled lifestyles around 11,000 years ago. This switch can be seen as a rapid environmental change; although it may sound like a long time, 11,000 years is actually quite short in evolutionary terms. This raises the question of whether we may still be better adapted to a nomadic lifestyle rather than our modern settled one. Looking at how our hunter-gatherer ancestors lived could therefore give us an indication of what might be a 'healthy' lifestyle; in other words, the type of lifestyle our bodies may be best adapted for.

We can draw on four main sources of evidence to try to figure out how our hunter-gatherer ancestors might have lived:

- We can look at the few remaining contemporary hunter-gatherer groups, for example the Hadza nomads of Tanzania, the Kalahari Bushmen of Southern Africa, or the Aché of South America.

- We can examine fossil records, both of people themselves, and of nearby deposits such as faeces, and also plant remains on teeth and tools.

- We can look at our closest relatives, chimpanzees and bonobos.

- More recently, we have been able to test hypotheses about natural selection by examining our own genes.

These different methods are not without limitations. For example, fossilised evidence is scarce and not necessarily representative of a whole group of hunter-gatherers. Likewise, the lifestyles of contemporary hunter-gatherers are unlikely to have remained completely unchanged over the last ten millennia. Nevertheless, we can still use these different sources of evidence to make inferences about how our ancestors might have lived (Zuk, 2013).

Diet

What did hunter-gatherers eat? It would be a mistake to think that we could identify a 'typical' hunter-gatherer or '**Palaeolithic**' diet. The diets of hunter-gatherers would have varied with both time and place (Milton, 2000). For example, among contemporary hunter-gatherers, the Arctic Eskimos eat a diet that primarily consists of marine mammals (Ho et al., 1972), whilst the Australian aborigines of the Western Desert rely mostly on wild

Palaeolithic – the period in history characterised by hominins' use of primitive stone tools. It extends from 2.6 million years ago to around 10,000 years ago. Sometimes referred to as 'the Stone Age'.

plants (Gould, 1980). Indeed, the success of the human species is believed to be due, in a large part, to its versatility when it comes to food. Being able to find food in a range of different environments would have allowed our ancestors to exploit the different types of habitat found in Africa, and to survive the major changes in climate that took place during hominin evolution (Ungar et al., 2006; Vrba et al., 1995). Arguably, it is our ability to thrive by eating a range of different diets that is one of the hallmarks of our species.

It is also fair to say that there is a great deal we *don't* know about our ancestors' diets, and probably never will (Ungar, 2007). Foods perish and will often leave no trace in the fossil record. Even where we do have fossil evidence, in many instances it is so limited it would be unwise to accept it as representative of an entire species. Since we don't have access to a time machine, there are many details of our ancestors' lives that may forever remain a mystery. However, some things we can be certain of – all plant foods eaten would have been wild rather than cultivated varieties, and any meat eaten would have come from game rather than domesticated animals. From these two details, we can make a number of additional assumptions.

In particular, the wild plant foods that were eaten would have been quite different from what we find on our supermarket shelves today. For example, a wild banana contains lots of large, hard black seeds, whilst a wild avocado contains one very large stone, surrounded by a rather disappointingly thin layer of flesh. As farmers, we have worked quite hard to cultivate varieties of fruit and vegetables that we prefer to eat – sweeter, less bitter, and with less 'waste' in the form of inedible seeds and stones.

Although cultivation has favourably altered the taste and appearance of the plants we eat, it has diminished their nutritional content. Wild plants often have higher concentrations of vitamins and minerals compared to their cultivated cousins, as well as more variation in vitamin and mineral content. They have higher levels of protein and fibre and the presence of small insects and larvae in wild fruit could also be an important source of essential micronutrients for the less squeamish consumer (Milton, 1999).

As well as eating more nutritious plants than we do today, our hunter-gatherer ancestors are also likely to have eaten a wider variety of plant foods. Estimates range from 50 to 100 different species (Zuk, 2013). Given that specific nutrient content varies from plant to plant, this diversity would have made an important contribution to dietary quality (Nagy & Milton, 1979). Nowadays just 30 crops account for 95% of the plants we eat, with much of this consisting of maize, rice and wheat (Harris, 2007). Additionally, most plant food would have been consumed soon after collection. Since many vitamins degrade over time (Kramer, 1977), this represents another reason why plants eaten by our ancestors would have been more nutritious than, for example, our supermarket apples shipped halfway around the globe.

The earliest evidence we have of butchered animal remains is from 2.6 million years ago by Homo habilis (Wrangham, 2013). Fossil records indicate that simple stone tools were being used at this time, and it is thought that their use was linked to an increase in meat consumption (Harris, 1983). Around 800,000 years ago our tools became more sophisticated and we were hunting bigger game (Rabinovich et al., 2008); by 500,000 years ago we were hunting with spears (Wilkins et al., 2012). However, any meat we consumed would have been from wild animals rather than domesticated ones. As such, it would have been much lower in fat than most of the meat we tend to eat today (O'Dea, 1991). For example, a quick online supermarket search shows that venison burgers (from wild meat) contain about 5 grams of fat per 100 grams, whilst their equivalent beef steak burgers (from farmed meat) contain about 13 grams.

By around 800,000 years ago archaeological evidence suggests we may have learned to control fire, at least in some parts of the world (Goren-Inbar et al., 2004). The precise date of this development is difficult to establish, given the natural occurrence of fire and the fact that it makes little mark in the fossil record. So it is possible we were using fire much earlier (Wrangham, 2006). But at whatever point this occurred, it would have been a very significant innovation, providing warmth, protection from predators, and the ability to cook food. However, other than cooking, our food would have been unprocessed and unrefined. In other words, it would have been eaten fresh, with all the fibre, but without any added salt, sugar or fat.

So whilst the diet of our hunter-gatherer ancestors is likely to have varied considerably across both time and place, they certainly wouldn't have been wolfing down crisps, doughnuts and supersized sodas. Compared to what we eat today, we can be reasonably sure that, in general, they would have consumed more fibre, and less sugar, salt, fat and calories. (See **Chapter 12** for today's healthy eating recommendations.)

Physical activity

Our hunter-gatherer ancestors would also have been more physically active compared to most of us today. For example, in the absence of cars and supermarkets, contemporary Aboriginal hunter-gatherers in Australia walk long distances to acquire food. They may dig in hard ground to get to tubers, witchetty grubs and honey ants, or spend time chopping into and climbing trees to reach beehives. Without our handy kitchen appliances, they also need to work hard to gather wood for fires, dig pits for cooking, and to winnow and grind seeds (O'Dea, 1991). Among the Hadza hunter-gatherers of Tanzania, it is estimated that men walk an average of 7.6 miles a day and women 3.9 (Pontzer et al., 2015); US adults are estimated to walk an average of just over 3 miles a day with one-third of the population walking less than 2.5 miles daily (Sisson et al., 2012).

Childrearing

Among contemporary hunter-gatherer populations, the average birth interval is estimated to be 3.7 years (Sellen, 2007). Age of weaning varies both within and between different hunter-gatherer groups, but over three-quarters of babies are still being breastfed long after their second birthday, with most being weaned at around 30 months (Sellen, 2007). Babies tend to be carried by their mother or another carer for most of the day and sleep next to their mother at night. Breastfeeding occurs 'on demand', in other words the baby feeds whenever it chooses, throughout both the day and night. For example, among the !Kung, babies spend 90% of their first year of life in skin-to-skin contact with their mother or another carer. They sleep next to their mother at night and breastfeed an average of four times an hour during the day and at least four times during the night, often without waking the mother. Children are usually breastfed for at least three years (Diamond, 2012). This type of frequent, extended breastfeeding reduces fertility both through lactational amenorrhea (absence of menstruation brought about by frequent breastfeeding) and by increasing energy expenditure; breastfeeding can use more than 600 calories a day and fertility is reduced where a woman has very little body fat (Dewey, 1997; Frisch & McArthur, 1974).

These details are in marked contrast to common practice in many parts of the world today. For example, among wealthy countries less than 20% of babies are still breastfed at 12 months (Victora et al., 2016; see also **Chapter 12**). And whilst infants in Asian countries tend to sleep with their parents, this is less common in North American and European countries, where parents may be encouraged to sleep separately from their newborn[1] and try to limit feeding during the night (Ford, 2006; Mindell et al., 2010; Unicef, 2019). Globally, the mean birth interval is just under 3 years (Molitoris et al., 2019).

Hunter-gatherer adaptations

Food preferences

How did humans evolve in response to this type of environment and lifestyle? A key adaptation would have been the development of preferences for nutrients that were important for the body, but relatively rare in the surroundings, specifically sugar, fat and salt.

Sugar provides a concentrated source of energy; energy that is essential for powering all the body's normal functions, as well as providing fuel for everyday activities and for breastfeeding infants and toddlers. However, concentrated sources of energy are rare in the natural environment. Therefore it would have been advantageous for individuals to expend extra effort to obtain such foods, and to eat more of these, when they got the chance. As such, those who liked the taste of sugar-rich foods, such as honey, may have been at an advantage compared to those who preferred the more common leafy greens and tubers. They may have gained a bit of extra weight that meant they were more likely to survive any subsequent food shortages. It therefore makes sense that a preference for sweet foods became common amongst hunter-gatherer populations.

Fat also represents an important source of energy. In addition, fat helps the body absorb certain vitamins (such as vitamins A, D, E and K) and is a source of essential nutrients that the body can't make itself (such as fatty acids omega-3 and omega-6). Again, fat is less readily available in the natural environment, therefore individuals who were prepared to make an effort to obtain and eat fatty foods, such as nuts and seeds, may have been at an advantage in the survival stakes.

What we refer to as salt, is made up of two minerals: sodium and chloride. Sodium is contained in the extracellular fluid of all of our body's cells. It helps regulate our body fluids and is also needed for muscle and nerve activity. As such, meat is a good dietary source of sodium. Sodium is also found in very small quantities in plant foods. Hunter-gatherer populations living near the sea or salt deposits would have had easy access to sodium. Those who consumed a lot of meat (like the Inuit in the Arctic) would also have had a reasonable intake of sodium. For others however, sodium intake would have been very low. Thus once again, in hunter-gatherer times, individuals with a preference for more salty foods may have fared better.

Today, when we think of the foods we need to eat to keep us healthy, we probably think of foods such as fruit, salads and leafy green vegetables. Why didn't hunter-gatherers develop stronger preferences for these? The answer is that they would have been relatively more abundant in their environment. Thus over and above a general tendency to get hungry, having a strong preference for leaves and tubers would not have conferred much of a survival advantage.

Physical activity

We may also have evolved to avoid unnecessary energy expenditure. Support for such a view comes from a study by Selinger and colleagues (2015). They put people into what

---

1   Health professionals sometimes advise against bed-sharing because of its association with sudden infant death syndrome. However, recent research suggests the two may only be linked in certain contexts, such as where a parent smokes or has been using alcohol. See Ball and Volpe (2013) and Unicef (2019) for further discussion.

they called 'robotic exoskeletons' (leg braces), that increased the energy costs of their normal gait. What they found was that people very quickly started walking in an 'abnormal' way in order to minimise energy expenditure. They suggest this type of flexible motor control would help keep energy expenditure to a minimum across a range of different situations – learning new tasks, adapting to new terrains, and compensating for injury. Again, this makes sense from an evolutionary perspective; our ancestors who stored a bit of extra energy, rather than burned it all off, would have had more energy available to support survival and reproduction.

Hunter-gatherer health and life expectancy

Life expectancy at birth amongst our hunter-gatherer ancestors is estimated to have been around 22 years (Gage et al., 2012). This seems very low compared to global life expectancy today; in 2016 it was 72 years (WHO, 2020c). However, it is important to remember that such figures are averages and may conceal large variations among individual members of a group. In particular, the low life expectancies of pre-industrial populations will be heavily skewed by high rates of infant and juvenile mortality (death before the ages of 1 and 15, respectively). For example, Hadza life expectancy at birth is 32.5 years, but infant and juvenile mortality rates are 21% and 46% (Blurton Jones et al., 1992, 2002). Thus if a person survives till adulthood they have a good chance of living to a reasonable age. Indeed, there are many Hadza who live well into their 70s and sometimes their 80s (Marlowe, 2010).

Amongst contemporary hunter-gatherers the main causes of death are acute infectious and parasitic diseases (Blurton Jones et al., 2002; Hewlett et al., 1986; Howell, 2000). Without the advantages of modern medicine, an ailment that might be easy for us to treat could prove serious for a hunter-gatherer. For example, diarrhoea is a common symptom of many bacterial, viral and parasitic infections, and can result in severe dehydration. This is easily treated with simple rehydration solutions or, if necessary, by administering fluids directly into the body via a drip. But without access to such treatments, dehydration from diarrhoea can quickly prove fatal. Indeed, even today diarrhoea is the second leading cause of death in children under the age of 5 (WHO, 2017a). Accounts of contemporary hunter-gatherer groups also report it as a frequent cause of death among both children and adults (Hewlett et al., 1986; Howell, 2000). Other common causes of death among contemporary hunter-gatherers include childbirth, accidents and violence (Blurton Jones et al., 2002; Hewlett et al., 1986; Howell, 2000).

Today, the leading causes of death are from **non-communicable diseases**, in other words, non-infectious diseases that are often (but not always) influenced by what some have called 'lifestyle-related' factors such as smoking, diet and exercise. This contrasts with the near absence of such diseases in hunter-gatherer populations (Howell, 2000). To a certain extent, this is because we have done such a good job of tackling infectious diseases – since everyone has to die of something, a reduction in deaths from infectious diseases will inevitably result in a relative increase in deaths from other causes.

However, this is only part of the story, since when we look at some of the key risk factors for one of our biggest killers, coronary heart disease, we see clear differences between those living in modern societies and those from hunter-gatherer groups. For

> **Non-communicable disease** – a disease that cannot be passed from person to person but is often influenced by everyday behaviours such as diet and exercise (though see **Box 2.1**). Sometimes known as chronic or degenerative diseases, they tend to show slow progression so that the individual may live with symptoms of the disease for many years. As a result, they can be quite costly in terms of healthcare. The four main types of non-communicable disease are cardiovascular disease, chronic respiratory disease, cancer and diabetes.

Cholesterol – a fatty substance known as a 'lipid' that is important for the normal functioning of the body. Cholesterol is produced in the liver but is also obtained from some types of food. It is carried in the blood by proteins ('lipoproteins'). There are two types of lipoproteins. Low-density lipoproteins (LDL) carry cholesterol to the cells. If there is too much of this type of 'bad' LDL cholesterol it can be deposited on the artery walls, leading to atherosclerosis (a narrowing of the arteries). By contrast, high-density lipoproteins (HDL) pick up excess cholesterol and carry it back to the liver to be broken down or excreted. This type of cholesterol, HDL cholesterol, is referred to as 'good' cholesterol as it reduces the amount of 'bad' cholesterol in the blood.

example, in Europe 54% of adults have high **cholesterol** and around 30–45% of the population have hypertension (sustained high blood pressure; Mancia et al., 2013; WHO, 2020e). Blood pressure also tends to rise with age (Whelton, 1994). Globally, 1 in 3 people are considered overweight or obese and 1 in 11 have **diabetes** (Ng et al., 2014; WHO, 2020a). By contrast, amongst hunter-gatherer groups there is little evidence of hypertension, blood pressure shows little age-related change, and cholesterol levels are low (Barnicot et al., 1972; Gurven et al., 2012; Stevenson, 1999). When individuals from such groups adopt a modern diet and lifestyle, they quickly show increases in blood pressure and cholesterol as well as levels of obesity, diabetes and heart disease. This suggests that hunter-gatherers' lower rates of heart disease are linked to their lifestyle and that, although we have a higher life expectancy, in many ways we can be considered less healthy.

THE AGRICULTURAL REVOLUTION

A change in lifestyle

Around 12,000 years ago things started to change (Burroughs, 2005). In particular:

• The climate had become both warmer and less variable.

• In some regions, climate change may have reduced the yields of wild foods.

• A drier climate had started to bring people, plants and animals in closer contact with one another, on the banks of rivers.

• Hunter-gatherers started to have more offspring than they could sustain through hunting and gathering. The reasons for this growth in population are unclear but may have been due to more frequent use of settlements that reduced the distances over which young children had to be carried.

These changes prompted a gradual shift to agriculture. Around 11,000 years ago, in different parts of the world, people began to cultivate crops such as wheat, barley and lentils, and to keep animals such as sheep and goats. This coincided with a switch from a more nomadic lifestyle to one in which people lived in settled agricultural communities. The earliest evidence of such communities comes from an area known as the Fertile Crescent in what is now the Middle East, though there is evidence of early agriculture being independently developed in other parts of the world too, for example 9,000 years ago in the Yangzi and Yellow River Basins (now part of China). Over time, agriculture spread across the globe, for example reaching Britain around 6,000 years ago, Southern India around 4,500 years ago and South Africa around 2,000 years ago (Diamond, 1998; Diamond & Bellwood, 2003; Sadr, 2003).

This dramatic change in lifestyle is known as the 'agricultural revolution' (or sometimes the Neolithic revolution) and set us down the road to the complex societies we know today. A permanent settlement allows one to store food surpluses, which in turn means there may be sufficient food to allow some people to devote their time to activities other than food production. Thus with the emergence of settled communities comes the appearance of people with expertise in areas such as metalwork, building construction and written communication. It is this ability to specialise and build expertise that has led to some of our greatest achievements and discoveries – Shakespeare and Da Vinci, space exploration and vaccines – not to mention everyday comforts such as hot showers, cosy duvets and films on demand. So why did anthropologist Jared Diamond (1987) once describe agriculture as 'the worst mistake in the history of the human race'?

Increased inequalities

Diamond argued that agriculture led to large inequalities in wealth and power. With the ability to store food, it becomes possible to accumulate food stores, and for these food stores to be unfairly distributed between individuals. Land ownership also becomes possible once the population is no longer moving from place to place. Again, this leads to disparities between individuals, which in turn mean differences in the ability to accumulate food, wealth and power. Thus we see the emergence of class divisions, with the elite becoming better off, but the majority becoming poorer.

Adverse effects on health

Diamond also argued that agriculture was detrimental to our health. Although we might have been able to increase our overall calorie intake, by eating a much less varied diet there was more malnutrition and a greater risk of starvation as a result of crop failure. For example, skeletal remains from ancient Egyptian populations show that the introduction of agriculture coincided with a significant reduction in height, most likely due to malnutrition (Zakrzewski, 2003).

There was also an increase in infectious diseases and parasites. Settled living brings us into more contact with waste products. This promotes the development of diseases spread by faecal-oral transmission. Cholera, for example, is spread by water and food that has been contaminated with faeces containing cholera bacteria (**Chapter 1**). Increased contact with domesticated animals leads to more opportunities for diseases to spread from them to us. And finally, increases in population size mean that certain diseases can be sustained within the population. For example, most people exposed to the measles virus develop immunity to it. This means they cannot catch it a second time. As such, the virus can only be sustained in a population with a high enough birth rate for there to be a continual supply of susceptible individuals; measles can only be sustained in populations greater than around 250,000 people (Gay, 2004).

Disease, as well as other physiological stressors such as malnutrition, impairs the formation of tooth enamel, so examining the tooth remains of our ancestors is one way of inferring their health. The teeth of ancient Egyptian populations show impaired tooth enamel formation with the introduction of agriculture, suggesting a general decline in health when they stopped hunting and gathering and started farming (Starling & Stock, 2007).

Nevertheless, despite these detrimental effects on health, agriculture was still associated with higher fertility and lower childhood mortality (Sellen & Mace, 1997; 1999). Thus the switch to farming led to a large increase in the world's population, from around 5 million 10,000 years ago, to 7.8 billion today.

Diabetes – a condition that causes a person's blood sugar (glucose) level to become too high. Type 2 diabetes is the most common type. It occurs when the body's cells become resistant to insulin or where the pancreas doesn't produce enough insulin. Insulin is a hormone that helps glucose get from the blood to the body's cells, which they need for energy. Overweight and obesity are one of the main risk factors for type 2 diabetes. Type 1 diabetes occurs where the immune system attacks the cells in the pancreas making them unable to produce insulin. Type 1 diabetes tends to be hereditary and develops earlier in life than type 2. Both types of diabetes may result in the individual feeling tired, thirsty and with an increased need to urinate. High glucose levels can also damage organs, leading to vision loss, kidney failure, nerve damage and loss of blood supply to limbs. The latter can result in gangrene that may require amputation. Since diabetes can lead to atherosclerosis (clogging of the arteries) it also increases the risk of heart disease and stroke.

Pandemic – an epidemic that has spread to a number of different countries and/or continents such that there is simultaneous worldwide transmission. Definitions vary. For example, the World Health Organization uses the term conservatively, only when there have been sustained community-level outbreaks within at least three countries across at least two different regions of the world and where transmission can no longer be contained (Lancet Infectious Diseases, 2020; WHO, 2009a).

Epidemic – the widespread occurrence of an infectious disease throughout a given population. This can be distinguished from an outbreak of disease which is smaller than an epidemic and refers to an increase in the number of expected cases in one specific area. It can also be distinguished from endemic which refers to an infectious disease that is sustained at a particular level within a population.

Bubonic plague – a bacterial infection that causes flu-like symptoms and swelling of lymph nodes (buboes). It can also result in gangrene in the toes, fingers, lips or nose, as a result of insufficient blood supply, causing these areas to turn a greenish brown or black. Bubonic plague is caused by infection of the lymphatic system after being bitten by an infected flea. Untreated, bubonic plague results in the death of 50–90% of those infected, usually within about ten days. When treated, for example with antibiotics, the death rate is reduced to around 5–15% (Prentice & Rahalison, 2007). The 14th-century bubonic plague pandemic is often referred to as 'The Black Death' and is estimated to have killed 25 million people (Benedictow, 2004).

THE EPIDEMIOLOGICAL TRANSITION

After the initial transition to agriculture, our health did eventually improve. For example, fossil records show that Ancient Egyptians began to regain their stature and to show fewer tooth enamel defects (Starling & Stock, 2007; Zakrzewski, 2003). Similarly, over the course of many centuries, rates of infectious diseases also declined. This change in the main causes of death from infectious to chronic diseases is referred to as the 'epidemiological transition'. Omran (1971) suggested three stages to this transition:

- *The age of pestilence and famine*, when life expectancy is low and variable, ranging from 20 to 40 years.

- *The age of receding pandemics*, during which mortality declines, the population grows, and life expectancy at birth steadily increases from about 30 to 50 years.

- *The age of degenerative and man-made diseases*, during which mortality continues to decline before stabilising at a relatively low level, and life expectancy at birth increases until it exceeds 50 years.

The age of pestilence and famine

The age of famine and pestilence can be said to describe patterns of health and disease for much of our post-hunter-gatherer history (Omran, 1971). For example, there have been three recorded **pandemics** of **bubonic plague**, in the 6th century, 14th century and 19th century, all with devastating effects.

There have also been numerous plague **epidemics,** such as the 1665 Great Plague of London that killed around 80,000 people within seven months (Byrne, 2012). During this time, the wealthy deserted London, victims and their families were locked in their homes, and carts carried corpses away to be buried in large pits (**Image 2.2**). Similarly, it is estimated that 1 million people died during the Irish potato famine in the late 1840s, when a disease affecting potato crops destroyed what was a staple part of the diet for a large proportion of the population (Ross, 2002). More recently, the 1918–1919 influenza pandemic (sometimes called 'Spanish flu') is thought to have killed between 20 and 50 million people (WHO, 2018f).

The age of receding pandemics

Over the past 100–150 years there has been a marked decline in deaths from infectious disease. McKeown (1976) identifies four possible reasons:

1. The co-evolution of parasites and hosts (in other words, the tendency for diseases to become less virulent and hosts to become more resistant).

2. Improvements in sanitation, such as cleaner water and better sewage disposal.

Image 2.2 *Costume worn by plague doctors in Europe in the 17th, 18th and 19th centuries. In keeping with miasma theory (Chapter 1), the beak was filled with herbs and spices that were thought to help purify the air and prevent infection.*
Source: A physician wearing a 17th-century plague preventive costume. Watercolour. Credit: Wellcome Collection. Attribution 4.0 International (CC BY 4.0).

3. Advances in medicine, such as the development of **antibiotics** and vaccines (**Chapter 12**).

4. Improvements in nutrition and standards of living.

Gage (2005) also notes the possible contribution of advances in medical knowledge, such as germ theory (**Chapter 1**), that may have had important influences on behaviours such as handwashing. Whilst the relative contribution of these different factors is uncertain, it is generally accepted that improvements in medicine played a smaller role, since these occurred after rates of infectious disease had already shown significant declines (Gage, 2005). For example, life expectancy at birth in the UK had reached 48 years by 1900 (Matarazzo, 1984), even though Fleming did not discover **penicillin** until 1928 and antibiotics were

Antibiotics – agents that inhibit or kill the growth of bacteria. They are not effective against viruses such as the common cold or influenza. Antibiotics are used to help treat a wide variety of diseases such as tuberculosis and typhoid. However, their overuse has led to increased antibiotic resistance, in other words, the evolution of new strains of bacteria against which antibiotics are ineffective. Sometimes referred to as 'superbugs', these bacteria mean diseases such as tuberculosis, that were once treatable, may now, once again, prove fatal.

Penicillin – a group of antibiotics discovered by Alexander Fleming in 1928. Penicillin started being used to treat infections in 1942.

Smallpox – a highly contagious disease that leads to a high fever, fatigue and a rash of blisters. Smallpox is caused by a virus that is contracted when tiny droplets of infected saliva are breathed in (for example after an infected person has sneezed or coughed), or when a person touches infected bodily fluids, such as skin blisters. Smallpox has affected humans for thousands of years; Pharaoh Ramses V was thought to have died of smallpox over 3,000 years ago in Ancient Egypt. Smallpox kills approximately 30% of infected individuals and also leads to blindness and scarring. In the 1950s there were an estimated 50 million cases of smallpox each year. A vaccine was introduced in the early 1800s, which became compulsory in Britain in 1853. In 1967 the World Health Organization launched a campaign to eradicate the disease and in 1979 declared that this had been achieved.

Cardiovascular disease – diseases of the heart and circulation, including coronary heart disease, stroke, heart attack and angina. These diseases are caused by a narrowing of the arteries due to a build-up of fatty material on their walls (atherosclerosis). This makes it more difficult for blood to be delivered to the heart. Pieces of fatty material may also break away from the arteries and cause blood clots. When these block the arteries that supply blood to the heart, they can cause a heart attack; when they block arteries to the brain, they can cause a stroke.

not introduced until the 1940s. Likewise, whilst Jenner created the first **smallpox** vaccination in 1796, vaccines did not become widely available until the 1920s.

This reduction in infectious diseases continued throughout the 20th century. Coupled with an increase in life expectancy, this has led to the emergence of chronic diseases as the most common cause of death, placing us firmly in Omran's (1971) age of degenerative and man-made diseases.

LIFE TODAY

Causes of death

So what does our health look like today? As shown in **Figure 2.2**, the leading causes of death are now from non-communicable diseases, such as **cardiovascular disease, cancer** and **chronic respiratory disease**. The proportion of deaths from non-communicable diseases has increased from 58% in 1990 to 73% in 2017. By contrast, deaths from communicable, maternal, neonatal and nutritional diseases showed a relative decline from 33% in 1990 to 19% in 2017. Deaths from injuries also showed a relative decline from 9% in 1990 to 8% in 2017. The only exception to this pattern is deaths from sexually transmitted diseases (predominantly HIV/AIDS) which showed an increase from just over 1% to just under 2% (IHME, 2020).

Why are we seeing increases in deaths from non-communicable diseases? As Gage et al. (2012) note, everyone must die of something, so if other risks decline, then deaths from non-communicable diseases will go up even if one's risk remains constant. Improvements in diagnosis may also have contributed towards an apparent increase in incidence. However, regardless of the relative changes in rates of different diseases, it is clear from **Figure 2.2** that non-communicable diseases now account for the greatest number of deaths. Since non-communicable diseases are often influenced by our everyday behaviours, arguably the biggest threat to our health today is not from infections or accidents, but from our way of life (though see also **Box 2.1**).

Non-communicable disease and rising obesity

Part of the reason for the increase in non-communicable diseases may be due to rising levels of overweight and obesity. As well as being associated with increased mortality, these are also linked to health conditions, such as type 2 diabetes, hypertension, coronary heart disease, stroke and cancer (Kopelman, 2007; Whitlock et al., 2009; see also **Chapter 12**). Over the last three decades there has been a dramatic increase in worldwide levels of overweight and obesity; in 2013, more than 1 in 3 adults were considered overweight or obese (Ng et al., 2014).

Figure 2.2 Leading causes of death globally in 1990 (top) and 2017 (bottom)

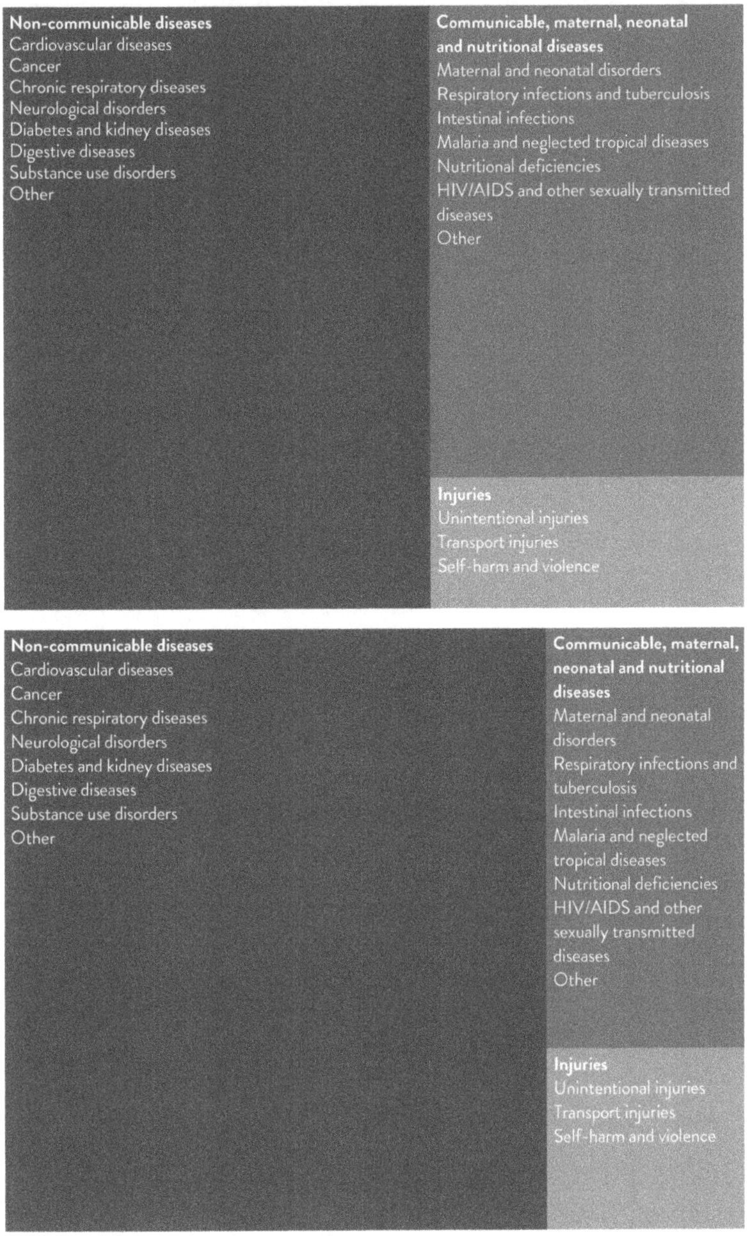

Non-communicable diseases
Cardiovascular diseases
Cancer
Chronic respiratory diseases
Neurological disorders
Diabetes and kidney diseases
Digestive diseases
Substance use disorders
Other

Communicable, maternal, neonatal and nutritional diseases
Maternal and neonatal disorders
Respiratory infections and tuberculosis
Intestinal infections
Malaria and neglected tropical diseases
Nutritional deficiencies
HIV/AIDS and other sexually transmitted diseases
Other

Injuries
Unintentional injuries
Transport injuries
Self-harm and violence

Non-communicable diseases
Cardiovascular diseases
Cancer
Chronic respiratory diseases
Neurological disorders
Diabetes and kidney diseases
Digestive diseases
Substance use disorders
Other

Communicable, maternal, neonatal and nutritional diseases
Maternal and neonatal disorders
Respiratory infections and tuberculosis
Intestinal infections
Malaria and neglected tropical diseases
Nutritional deficiencies
HIV/AIDS and other sexually transmitted diseases
Other

Injuries
Unintentional injuries
Transport injuries
Self-harm and violence

Note: The size of each box reflects the proportion of deaths.

Source: Institute for Health Metrics Evaluation. Used with permission. All rights reserved.

Cancer – where the cells in a specific part of the body show abnormal growth, resulting in a lump or tumour. In some cases tumours are non-cancerous (benign) and do not spread. Where a tumour is cancerous (malignant) it can spread to other parts of the body (metastasis), interfering with their function. Screening programmes are designed to identify malignant tumours in their early stages, so they can be treated in order to prevent metastasis. There are over 200 different types of cancer, many of which are influenced by factors such as diet, exercise and smoking.

Chronic respiratory diseases – diseases of the airways and lungs. These include chronic obstructive pulmonary disease (COPD), lung cancer, asthma and hay fever. COPD refers to lung diseases such as chronic bronchitis and emphysema. In these conditions the airways of the lungs have become permanently narrowed, usually as a result of smoking. This can lead to breathlessness, a persistent cough, and frequent chest infections.

CHAPTER 2

BOX 2.1 THE ROLE OF MICROBES IN NON-COMMUNICABLE DISEASE

DIG A LITTLE DEEPER

Although we think of non-communicable diseases as non-infectious, recent research suggests this distinction may not be quite as clear cut as we once believed – it seems that the trillions of microbes living both on and inside our bodies (our microbiome) may also play a role in the development of certain non-communicable diseases.

Most of these microbes are actually good for our health. For example, they help us digest food, support our immune system and suppress the growth of more harmful bacteria (Becattini et al., 2017; Hooper et al., 2012). We get our first dose of healthy microbes at birth, via the birth canal, breastmilk and skin-to-skin contact with caregivers. And although the general make-up of a person's microbiome tends to stabilise in early childhood, it continues to be influenced by environmental factors such as the foods we eat and the microbes we come in contact with during our daily lives (Nicholson et al., 2012; Wu et al., 2011). Indeed, you may have seen adverts for certain food products touting the benefits of the 'friendly bacteria' (or 'probiotics') they contain. These aid digestion and grow in unprocessed, fermented foods such as certain types of yoghurt, sauerkraut, kimchi and kefir. (However, not all probiotics will survive the journey through the stomach to the intestine.)

Some have argued that certain aspects of modern life – antibiotics, sanitation, processed foods and a less varied diet – have led to a loss of gut microbiome diversity and that this may be having a negative impact on our health (Eisenstein, 2020). For example, Hadza hunter-gatherers have been shown to have much more diverse gut microbiota than their urban dwelling counterparts (Schnorr et al., 2014). Researchers have also found links between gut microbiota and a wide range of different health conditions, including gastric cancer, diabetes, heart disease, and even anxiety and depression (Menni et al., 2018; Peirce & Alviña, 2019; Sharma & Tripathi, 2019; Wroblewski et al., 2010).

One interesting line of research concerns the role of gut microbes in obesity. There is evidence to suggest that certain microbes may increase the amount of energy extracted from food, making some people more susceptible to weight gain. Researchers have also managed to make germ-free mice gain or lose weight simply by introducing gut microbiota from other mice that are either obese or lean (Castaner et al., 2018; Turnbaugh et al., 2006). This raises the possibility that obesity may at some point be treated using faecal transplants, with processed stool from a healthy, lean donor being transferred into the gastrointestinal tract of someone suffering from obesity (Kootte et al., 2017). (Faecal transplants are already used to treat recurrent infection with a particular strain of bacteria that cause diarrhoea; van Nood et al., 2013.)

Another potentially important area of research has shown links between gum disease and Alzheimer's (a form of dementia), highlighting the possible importance of tooth brushing and flossing over and above healthy teeth and gums (Dominy et al., 2019).

However, these are new areas of research with most findings to date based on observational studies (**Chapter 10**) looking at associations between particular microbes and certain health conditions. As such, it is difficult to rule out the possibility that the health condition led to changes in microbiota rather than vice versa. Although there has been some experimental work, which provides better evidence of causality, this has mostly been carried out with mice which means we can't be certain we'd see the same effects in humans.

Nevertheless, a causal link has been more firmly established in relation to cervical cancer and the human papillomavirus (HPV) that is transmitted during sex. This research has led to the development of a vaccine for HPV that is now used in many countries as part of routine vaccination programmes (see **Chapter 12**).

BOX 2.2 ARE YOU A HEALTHY WEIGHT?

Body mass index, or BMI, is calculated by dividing a person's weight (kg) by the square of their height (m²). It is used to determine whether someone has a healthy weight; those with a BMI of under 18.5 are considered **TAKE THE TEST** underweight, whilst those with a BMI of over 25 are considered overweight. A BMI of over 30 is considered obese, and over 40 as morbidly obese. (These cut-offs are reduced among those of South Asian descent because of a higher risk of diabetes.) You can use **Figure 2.3** to find out which weight category you fall into – simply follow the appropriate lines for your weight and height to see where they intersect. Alternatively, you can find a link to a BMI calculator at macmillanihe.com/tapper-health-psychology.

Figure 2.3 Calculate your BMI

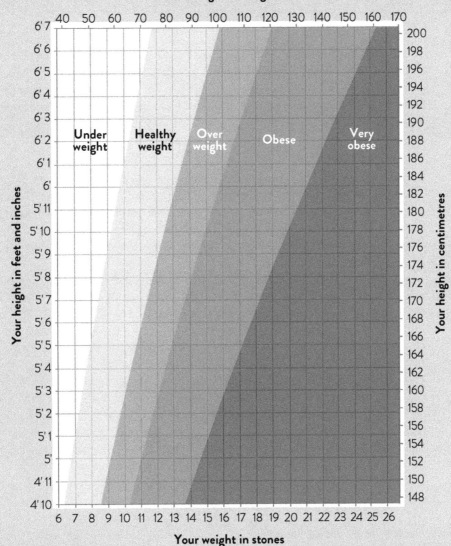

CHAPTER 2

However, BMI is not without its limitations:

- It is not terribly accurate for people who are very tall or very short, being more likely to categorise a healthy tall person as overweight and a healthy short person as underweight.

- It fails to differentiate between muscle and fat, so people with a lot of muscle may fall into the overweight category even when they have very low levels of body fat.

- It does not give any indication of the distribution of fat on a person; fat stored on the waist and chest is more problematic than fat stored on the hips and thighs.

For these reasons, some people prefer a measure of waist-to-hip ratio or waist circumference. However, obtaining an accurate measure of someone's hips and waist is a little more tricky – and arguably more intrusive – than simply measuring their height and asking them to hop on the scales. Another alternative is bioelectrical impedance, where a safe electric current is passed through the body to measure resistance (body fat shows more resistance than lean body mass or water). However, this measure may be influenced by levels of hydration as well as recent exercise or food consumption. For these reasons, BMI remains the most widely used index of obesity.

Obesity is defined as an excess of body fat, so at a proximal level, it can be seen to be the result of an imbalance between energy intake and expenditure; if we take in more energy than we burn off, we will put on weight. So what's caused the average energy balance to change over the last three decades? Have we all just got lazier and greedier? Or is there something else going on?

An obesogenic environment

Egger and Swinburn (1997) suggest these increases in obesity are a result of a range of different changes to our environment that encourage us to eat more and move less (**Table 2.1**). For example, average portion sizes in restaurants, fast food outlets and supermarkets have all got bigger (Young & Nestle, 2012). These are often accompanied by promotions and special offers that persuade us to consume more – free drinks refills, buy one get one free, all you can eat buffets.

At the same time, innovations that save us time and effort – washing machines, online shopping, and conveniently located car parks and lifts – collectively combine to reduce the amount of exercise we get in an average day (Egger et al., 2001; James, 1995). Work has changed too; it is estimated that in the 1960s, 50% of workers in the US had a physically active job, with this figure dropping to 20% in 2006 (Church & Martin, 2018).

Assuming that 1 lb (0.45 kg) of body weight equates to around 3,500 kcal, an excess intake of just 50 kcal a day could lead to weight gain of 5lbs (2.3 kg) a year – an extra stone (6.4 kg) in just under 3 years (Hill et al., 2003). As discussed previously, until relatively recently in our evolutionary history it made sense for us to stock up on high-calorie foods when we could, and to avoid burning calories unnecessarily. Thus, we could say it is in our nature to be both 'lazy' and 'greedy'. As such, rather than being a result of lifestyle 'choices', obesity may be better viewed as an inevitable outcome of what Egger and Swinburn call an 'obesogenic environment'.

The energy expenditure puzzle

However, more recent research has questioned the extent to which obesity is linked to reduced energy expenditure. For example, Pontzer et al. (2012) measured daily energy

CHAPTER 2

Table 2.1 Examples of environmental influences on food intake and physical activity

Level of influence	Physical environment		Social environment		Economic environment	
	Food	Activity	Food	Activity	Food	Activity
Micro	• Types of food available: • at home • at school • at work • in local shops • in local restaurants and takeaways	• School space, facilities and equipment • Availability of: • a garden • safe streets for walking and cycling • local parks and leisure facilities • cars and bicycles	• Family eating habits and attitudes • Peer group eating habits and attitudes • Attitudes shaped by advertising	• Family, peer group and school practices and attitudes toward: • exercise • sport • leisure activities • TV and digital devices • transport • safety	• Household income • Subsidised food at school and work • Home grown food	• Cost of clubs, classes, leisure facilities and equipment • Availability of subsidies
Macro	• Food advertising • Regulations relating to food sales and advertising • Food portion sizes and macro- and micronutrient content • Regulations relating to food portion sizes and macro- and micronutrient content	• Labour saving innovations • Transport system and policies • Education policies and school curriculums • Crime • Weather	• Traditional diet • Foods from immigrant populations • Cultural attitudes towards food and eating	• Cultural attitudes towards exercise, sport and leisure activities • Fear of crime	• Food subsidies and taxes • Food prices • Food promotions • Regulations relating to food prices and promotions	• Transport costs • Transport-related taxes and subsidies • Investment in parks, leisure facilities and active travel

Source: Inspired by Egger & Swinburn (1997).

expenditure and physical activity levels among Hadza hunter-gatherers over a period of 11 days. As expected, compared to adults in Europe and the US, the Hadza were more physically active. But, contrary to expectations, they did not expend more energy. Other research has also shown a weak relationship between levels of physical activity and energy expenditure. (Increased physical activity seems to be associated with increased energy expenditure only among those who are very sedentary or who have a greater body fat percentage; Pontzer et al., 2016; Pontzer, 2018.)

There are two likely explanations for this lack of association. The first is that after we have been more physically active, we tend to reduce our levels of 'non-exercise activity thermogenesis' (NEAT), in other words, everyday activities that burn energy such as housework, walking, talking, standing and even fidgeting (Levine, 2004). Indeed, there is evidence to support the idea that people compensate for vigorous bouts of exercise with subsequent reductions in NEAT energy expenditure (Paravidino et al., 2016; Thivel et al., 2013).

A second explanation is that the body compensates for energy expended on physical activity by reducing energy expended on non-essential physiological functions such as immune and stress responses and reproductive readiness. Pontzer (2018) argues that we have evolved to maintain energy expenditure within a narrow range. To ensure we stay within the limits of this range, our body compensates for increases in physical activity by downregulating physiological activity. This also helps explain why moderate levels of exercise are good for health – because they prevent excessive physiological activity. For example, the immune response is associated with inflammation, and chronic inflammation has been linked to conditions such as cardiovascular disease, diabetes and cancer as well as poorer mental health (Silverman & Deuster, 2014; Wu et al., 2014). Conversely, too much exercise may be detrimental for health because essential functions are compromised, leading to, for example, an increased frequency and severity of infections, reduced fertility, and a loss of libido (Schnohr et al., 2015).

As such, although rising levels of non-communicable disease may be linked to reductions in physical activity, increased levels of obesity may be more related to increased caloric intake than to reduced energy expenditure. (See also **Box 2.1** for an additional explanation for rising obesity.)

Infectious diseases: epidemics and pandemics

Although non-communicable disease is now responsible for more ill health around the world, we are still at risk of high rates of mortality from outbreaks of infectious disease. Some of these are re-emerging diseases, such as cholera and bubonic plague. However, others are new diseases that emerge when pathogens mutate into new strains or where they cross species from animals to humans (a process termed 'zoonosis'). The latter accounts for around 70% of all new human pathogens (WHO, 2018f). New diseases represent a particular challenge because the scientific community will not have had time to develop effective treatments or vaccines and because the population will have had no previous exposure to the pathogen so are likely to have little natural immunity.

Over the last 30 years we have seen an increase in the number of outbreaks of disease (Smith et al., 2014). This has been linked to certain aspects of modern society that also increase the risk of these outbreaks turning into epidemics or pandemics and affecting large numbers of people. In particular:

- The world's population has increased from 3.7 billion in 1970 to 7.8 billion in 2020. It is expected to reach around 11 billion by 2100, before levelling off (United Nations, 2015, 2019; World Bank, 2019). This growth has created more opportunities for the emergence of new diseases.

- In 1970 just 37% of the world's population were living in urban areas compared to 55% in 2018. This is projected to increase to 68% by 2050 (United Nations, 2018). Urbanisation brings people into closer contact with one another, making it easier for a new disease to spread through a population.

- In 1970 a total of 310 million people travelled by air. This figure was 4.2 billion in 2018 (World Bank, 2019). Increased air travel means new outbreaks of disease have the potential to spread round the globe faster. This is especially the case where they originate in wealthier countries with higher levels of international travel.

However, advances in science and medicine mean we are also now better equipped to tackle outbreaks of disease and, once we take into account population growth, we find that outbreaks of disease per capita (per person) have actually declined (Smith et al., 2014).

In other words, we are still less likely to catch an infectious disease than we were 30 years ago.

One key development in infectious disease prevention is vaccination. For example, in 1980 just 22% of 1-year olds had received at least one important vaccination, but this figure had risen to 88% by 2016 (Rosling, 2018). We look at vaccination in more detail in **Chapter 12**.

Another important development is increased international surveillance and cooperation. For example, the International Health Regulations are a governing framework for global health security that has been signed by 196 countries. These regulations were revised in 2005 to take account of the increased risk presented by international trade and travel. They require countries to report events that represent a potential public health emergency of international concern. They also require countries to collaborate with one another to develop systems to rapidly detect, prevent and contain disease outbreaks before they spread internationally. Although the 2005 revision of this framework is not without shortcomings (Gostin et al., 2015), its very existence reflects levels of global cooperation in the world today, which would have been hard to imagine 100 years ago.

The International Health Regulations are coordinated by the World Health Organization which also provides recommendations on how to respond to health emergencies. They identify five key response phases to prevent and manage epidemics and pandemics (WHO, 2018f). These are as follows:

1. *Anticipation.* Prior to the detection of a new disease, anticipation involves identifying the most likely threats and planning for potential outbreaks.

2. *Early detection.* This means having systems in place so that healthcare workers can recognise and report diseases that have the potential to become epidemic. Healthcare workers should also reduce the risks of transmission through measures such as patient isolation.

3. *Containment.* This is used as soon as the first case is identified in order to prevent disease spread. It includes contact tracing where all persons who have come into contact with an infected person are traced and either tested for the disease, asked to self-isolate or asked to monitor themselves for symptoms. Where they test positive or show symptoms, their contacts are also traced.

4. *Control and mitigation.* Once the disease has reached epidemic or pandemic levels, and containment is no longer possible, measures are introduced to reduce rates of infection and mortality and to limit wider health, social and economic impacts. Such measures may include school and workplace closures, cancellation of mass gatherings, public transport restrictions, social distancing, and controls on movement.

5. *Elimination.* This describes a situation where the disease is sufficiently controlled to prevent an epidemic. Surveillance and control measure should continue to prevent its re-emergence. In some instances, *eradication* may be achieved, for example through the use of a vaccine.

Nevertheless, despite these measures, pandemics may be difficult to avoid completely; history shows they tend to occur every 10–50 years (WHO, 2018f). **Table 2.2** details pandemics of the 20th and 21st centuries.

Table 2.2 Pandemics of the 20th and 21st centuries

Date	*Common name	Pathogen type	Origins	Mode of transmission	Estimated deaths	World population[a]
1918–20	Spanish flu	Influenza virus	Unknown	Respiratory droplets	20 to 50 million[b]	1.8 billion
1957–58	Asian flu	Influenza virus	Birds	Respiratory droplets	1 to 4 million[b]	2.9 billion
1961 onwards	Cholera	Bacterial	A mutated strain of the cholera bacterium found in water	Faecally contaminated water	5 to 7 million[c]	3 to 7.8 billion
1968–69	Hong Kong flu	Influenza virus	Birds	Respiratory droplets	1 to 4 million[b]	3.5 to 3.6 billion
1981 onwards	HIV	Retrovirus	Chimpanzees	Specific bodily fluids	38 million[d]	4.5 to 7.8 billion
2009–2010	Swine flu	Influenza virus	Pigs	Respiratory droplets	100,000 to 400,000[b]	6.8 to 6.9 billion
2020 onwards	COVID-19	Coronavirus	Possibly bats via pangolins	Respiratory droplets	> 1.5 million as of December 2020[e]	7.8 billion

Notes: *To avoid unnecessary negative impacts on trade, tourism, travel and animal welfare, and to avoid causing offence, the World Health Organization now recommends that new human diseases are not named after people, places or animals (WHO, 2015b).
[a]Roser et al., (2019); [b]WHO (2018f); [c]Ali et al., (2015); Zuckerman et al., (2007); [d]WHO (2019c); [e]WHO (2020h)

SHOULD WE TRY TO LIVE MORE LIKE HUNTER-GATHERERS?

As a species, our gene pool, and our health, is constantly changing in response to our environment and our behaviour, as well as advances in modern medicine (**Box 2.3**). However, in recent years there has been a fashion for 'palaeo'-inspired lifestyles and popular health advice, based on the assumption that these offer a more 'natural' way of life, better suited to our evolutionary history. In this section we examine the evidence behind some of these claims.

Grains and dairy

In the mid-1980s, Eaton and colleagues argued that there was a mismatch between our genes and our environment that was responsible for the rise in non-communicable diseases (Eaton & Konner, 1985; Eaton et al., 1988). They suggested that whilst our genetic make-up hadn't really changed over the last 50,000 years, our environment was radically different compared to what it had been 11,000 years ago. Examining the diets of contemporary hunter-gatherer groups, they concluded that our ancestors would have been consuming a diet that was primarily based on meat and vegetables, in contrast to modern diets that include a substantial amount of grains and dairy.

Later referred to as the 'evolutionary discordance hypothesis' (Konner & Eaton, 2010), this idea inspired a number of palaeo-style diets, such as the stone age diet, the paleo diet and the primal blueprint diet to name but a few. All these diets claim that eating more meat and cutting out grains and dairy will lead to both weight loss and health benefits.

BOX 2.3 ALTERING OUR GENE POOL: MODERN MEDICINE AND HUMAN EVOLUTION

Modern medicine is providing us with more and more opportunities to alter our gene pool (Zampieri, 2017). For **HOT TOPIC** example, increased use of Caesarean section (where a baby is delivered through a cut in the mother's abdomen) may inadvertently be increasing the *need* for Caesarean section (Mitteroecker et al., 2016). Obstructed labour, where a baby gets stuck during delivery, occurs in around 3–6% of births. Without medical care, it frequently results in the death of the infant or the mother or both. The high rates of obstructed labour are thought to arise because of selection pressures for (a) larger infant body weight (which correlates with greater survival and a reduced risk of disease) and (b) narrower pelvises in women (which reduce the risk of pelvic floor disorders). Natural variability in both these traits results in some cases of 'fetopelvic disproportion', where the pelvic canal is not wide enough for the baby's head. Caesarean sections have been used regularly in wealthier countries since the 1950s and 1960s, significantly reducing deaths from obstructed labour. However, reducing these deaths (of babies with larger heads and mothers with narrower pelvises) is estimated to have led to an increase in rates of fetopelvis disproportion of up to 20%.

Conversely, prenatal screening tests for congenital health conditions and developmental disorders may lead to parents terminating pregnancies that test positive. This may result in a reduction in the numbers of people in society with these conditions. However, where people suffering from a particular condition tend not to have children themselves, increased rates of termination would not alter the gene pool or the frequency with which such conditions occur in pregnancy. A similar line of reasoning applies to treatments for many chronic conditions; they will only alter the gene pool where they change the likelihood of the person having children. Fertility treatment would fall into this category whilst heart bypass surgery would probably not.

Finally, gene editing allows for the possibility of making direct modifications to our genes that could, in principle, be passed on to subsequent generations. This brings with it a range of new scientific and ethical questions. We discuss gene editing in more detail in **Chapter 4**.

However, it is wrong to say we have not evolved over the last 50,000 years. Whilst the rate of evolution may be relatively slow amongst smaller populations, as a population gets larger, so the rate of evolution can speed up. This is because evolution relies on random gene mutations that turn out to be beneficial. With a small number of people, there is only a small chance of a particular mutation occurring within one generation, but with a larger population, there is a greater chance, simply because of the greater number of offspring. For example, it is estimated that prior to the agricultural revolution, favourable mutations were occurring approximately every 100,000 years, but following the agricultural revolution, the larger population meant they were occurring around every 400 years (Cochran & Harpending, 2009).

Two areas where we have clearly evolved in the last 11,000 years are in terms of our ability to digest grains and dairy. To digest dairy, we need to produce an enzyme called 'lactase'. All mammals produce lactase at birth, but this disappears later in life in most humans and all non-human mammals. Lactase persistence (the ability to continue producing lactase throughout life) is a genetically determined trait found in 35% of people, mostly from Northern Europe, the Middle East and parts of Africa. Genome analysis indicates that this trait has spread through the population as a result of natural selection. In other words, it conferred an advantage that increased the individual's chances of successful reproduction.

Our ability to digest the starch in grains also depends on us having copies of certain genes that control the production of an enzyme called 'amylase'; the more copies we have of this gene, the better we're able to digest starch. Again, genome analysis indicates that humans have evolved in order to better digest starch; amongst populations with historically high levels of starch consumption, the majority of individuals have six copies of the gene. This proportion is lower amongst populations that have historically consumed lower levels of starch (Perry et al., 2007). More recent evidence also indicates that we were consuming grains long before we turned to agriculture (Henry et al., 2011; Revedin et al., 2010).

Thus the idea that humans have not evolved to eat grains and dairy seems misguided. Indeed, in a more recent revision of their Palaeolithic-informed dietary recommendations, Konner and Eaton have included low-fat dairy products and whole grains (Konner & Eaton, 2010).

Raw food

What about 'raw foodism'? This is the idea that we should only eat uncooked, unprocessed foods. Proponents claim that eating a raw food diet leads to an array of health benefits – more energy, less need for sleep, a better memory, and an improved immune system. Cooking, they claim, destroys important enzymes, vitamins and the 'life force' (Stevens, 2010). Irrespective of the slightly *Star Wars*-like references, the idea behind this notion has an intuitive appeal. No other animals cook their food, so why should we? Are we adapted to eat a raw food diet?

Not so, according to Richard Wrangham (Carmody & Wrangham, 2009; Wrangham & Conklin-Brittain, 2003; Wrangham & Carmody, 2010). He argues that cooking is what made us who we are today. Cooking food increases the energy we can derive from it. It makes starch, protein and meat easier to digest. This means we extract more energy from our food, and use less energy breaking it down. Cooking also kills bacteria, meaning we get ill less often, avoiding the energy costs of fever. According to Wrangham, these energy savings not only enhanced survival and reproduction, but also allowed for the development of the larger brains that make us human.

Although others have questioned the link between cooking and brain development (Leonard et al., 2012), it certainly seems to be the case that we are adapted to eat at least some of our food cooked. All groups of contemporary hunter-gatherers employ some form of cooking (Wrangham & Conklin-Brittain, 2003), and research shows that a diet high in raw foods is associated with weight loss and, in women, amenorrhea (Koebnick et al., 1999). We simply cannot extract sufficient calories from a 100% raw food diet.

Calorie restriction

However, there is another school of thought that states that calorie restriction is good for our health. It has been argued that in the past we would have experienced periods of short food supply. Rather than reproduce during these times (which would mean increased energy costs from pregnancy and an additional mouth to feed) it would have been more advantageous for our bodies to expend energy on repair and maintenance, warding off diseases in the hope that we would be fit enough to reproduce when food was plentiful again. Some argue that calorie restriction helps stimulate this process of repair, which in turn increases longevity.

Research in this area began in the 1930s when McCay et al. (1935) found that male (but not female) rats placed on nutrient adequate, calorie restricted diets lived longer than their non-calorie restricted counterparts. Since then this effect has been replicated in species ranging from fruit flies and roundworms, to mice and fish (Barrows & Kokkonen, 1982; Weindruch et al., 1986).

Such findings were the inspiration for the creation of the Calorie Restriction Society in the 1990s (www.crsociety.org) as well as the publication of books such as *The 120 Year Diet* and *The Longevity Diet*. Calorie restriction advocates recommend consuming primarily nutrient-dense, calorie-sparse foods in order to reduce calorie intake whilst still consuming adequate levels of vitamins, minerals and other essential nutrients in the belief that this will lead to better health and a longer life.

But humans are not mice and findings from calorie restriction research with primates are less clear cut. Given primates' longer life spans, such research is also less common. The two largest, best controlled studies in this area, both set up in the 1980s, provide contradictory findings. Rhesus monkeys in Wisconsin placed on a 30% calorie restricted diet in young adulthood lived longer than those allowed to eat as much as they liked (Colman et al., 2014). However, among monkeys at the National Institute of Ageing in Maryland, although some health benefits were observed, there were no equivalent effects in terms of lifespan (Mattison et al., 2012). Researchers have speculated on the reasons for the disparity and suggested that one of the key differences between the studies is that whilst the non-calorie restricted Maryland monkeys were fed a healthy diet, the equivalent Wisconsin monkeys were fed 'ad-libitum' (freely) and consequently ate a more unhealthy diet, containing much higher levels of sucrose. This has led some researchers to suggest that the beneficial effects of calorie restriction tend to occur, not because calorie restriction is beneficial, but rather because the tendency to overeat among those eating an unrestricted diet has negative effects on health and longevity (Maxmen, 2012; Sohal & Forster, 2014). They question whether the benefits found in short-lived species, such as rodents, generalise to long-lived species, such as humans.

Obviously, conducting such a study with humans would be tricky, both practically and ethically. There are several alternative approaches:

- We can conduct cross-sectional observational studies (**Chapter 10**). In other words, examine longevity amongst groups who are already practising calorie restriction.

- We can use surrogate measures in place of longevity, for example disease-related risk factors and markers of ageing. These are more likely to show up over a much shorter timescale. This makes it easier to conduct longitudinal studies, where measures are taken both before and after individuals embark upon a change in diet.

- Surrogate markers also allow for the possibility of randomised controlled trials (**Chapter 10**), in which the effects of calorie restriction on individuals randomly assigned to follow that type of diet are compared to a control group.

However, it is important to bear in mind that surrogate outcomes will not necessarily map onto disease outcomes, as disease risk factors do not predict disease with 100% accuracy. For example, whilst raised cholesterol levels increase the risk of heart disease, the relationship is far from perfect – some individuals with low cholesterol will develop heart disease, whilst others with high cholesterol will not. Thus it is possible that a treatment may influence a risk factor, but have no effect on the related disease.

When it comes to cross-sectional studies of calorie restriction and longevity, the elderly population of the Japanese island of Okinawa supports a link between the two. They are some of the longest-lived people in the world, with a relatively high proportion remaining fit and healthy well beyond the age of 100. Traditionally, they also practise 'hara hachi bu', eating until they are only 80% full, resulting in an intake of approximately 11% fewer calories than would normally be recommended for body weight maintenance (Willcox et al., 2007). Nevertheless, the correlational nature of these data make it difficult to rule out other factors, for example, there may be something particular about the genetic make-up of the Okinawans that results in them living such a long life (Bendjilali et al., 2014).

The same is true of cross-sectional studies examining those who choose to practise calorie restriction. Whilst data suggest this may be correlated with a range of positive health markers (Holloszy & Fontana, 2007), it is difficult to separate out the effects of other important variables in such studies. For example, it is likely that those who choose to stick to a calorie restricted diet are those who are already more interested in good health, and thus more likely to engage in a range of other important health-related behaviours such as getting plenty of exercise, and not smoking. Those who eat calorie restricted diets also tend to eat diets that are very healthy; they tend to consume lots of vegetables, nuts, low-fat dairy products and lean meat, whilst avoiding refined and processed foods. As such, it is unclear whether the benefits come from the calorie restriction per se or from the types of foods they are eating (Rizza et al., 2014).

Other studies have used longitudinal methods to examine the effects of switching from a 'normal' diet to a calorie restricted diet. Again, whilst effects on health generally seem positive, most of these have been conducted with people suffering from overweight or obesity (Lefevre et al., 2009; Piacenza et al., 2015; Snel et al., 2012). Thus we are back to the Wisconsin monkey problem; calorie restriction may be preferable to an unhealthy diet, but for those of a healthy weight, does it have any benefits over and above a balanced healthy diet? Are there benefits which are important enough to outweigh reported adverse effects? These include hunger, reduced fertility and libido, decreased bone mass, and low mood (CR Society, 2020). Not to mention the time and expense needed to ensure the diet still contains adequate intakes of essential nutrients.

Intermittent fasting

A slightly less extreme version of calorie restriction is intermittent fasting, during which a person refrains from eating for set periods of time (such as every other day). This purports to have the same health benefits but without the disadvantages. Part of the thinking behind intermittent fasting is that rather than eating three square meals a day, our ancestors evolved to cope with feast-famine cycles, where periods of poor food supply would have alternated with periods of food abundance (Chakravarthy & Booth, 2004; Diamond, 2003). A period of fasting is thought to both reduce body fat and, similar to calorie restriction, stimulate cellular repair (Horne et al., 2015).

Intermittent fasting has been popularised in recent years by the fast diet (also known as the 5:2 diet; Mosley & Spencer, 2013). This diet encourages people to eat normally five days a week, but substantially reduce calorie intake on the other two days. The authors claim that as well as helping people lose weight, fasting has substantial health benefits, such as reduced risk of age-related diseases (for example cancer), increased insulin sensitivity (reducing the risk of obesity, diabetes, heart disease and cognitive decline), and improved mood and wellbeing.

Research on intermittent fasting has shown promising results, in terms of a range of different markers of health as well as weight loss among those suffering from overweight and obesity (Cho et al., 2019; de Cabo & Mattson, 2019; Freire, 2020; Horne et al., 2015; Welton et al., 2020). However, it should be noted that some of this research has been restricted to rodents whilst trials examining weight loss in humans have tended to be small, of short duration and limited to young and middle-aged adults. This makes it difficult to know whether people would be able to adhere to intermittent fasting over longer periods of time, whether effects would be maintained over time or whether they would generalise to other age groups such as older adults. Thus further research is needed before we can confidently recommend intermittent fasting for all.

BOX 2.4 WHEN IT COMES TO DIETING, HOW DO WE KNOW WHAT WORKS?

MAKING CONNECTIONS

Diets such as the paleo diet and the fast diet are often promoted with real-life examples of people who claim their lives have been transformed. Whilst such stories can be persuasive, how can we be sure the person wouldn't have lost just as much weight (or felt just as good) on a completely different diet? How do we know they're not one of only a very small number of people who benefited? A randomised controlled trial is generally considered the most reliable way of establishing whether a particular treatment works. We look at randomised controlled trials in **Chapter 10**.

Barefoot running

At the start of the chapter we introduced the idea of barefoot running, another palaeo-inspired, health-related trend. We can be fairly sure our hunter-gatherer ancestors were not wearing swoosh-adorned, triple-density, dynamically supported running shoes. So do we need them? Or would we be better off 'au naturel' when it comes to running and other forms of exercise?

Expensive cushioned sports shoes have been promoted as a way to avoid injury, the assumption being that injury usually results from the impact of the feet hitting a hard surface, and that cushioning reduces this impact. However, there is little evidence to support this claim. Indeed, prior to the 1970s runners ran in much more minimal footwear but did not suffer from greater rates of injury (Jenkins & Cauthon, 2011; Richards et al., 2009). Researchers have speculated that humans evolved to run long distances in order to compete with other scavengers or to pursue prey. In particular, long distance running may have enabled persistence hunting, the practice of tracking a prey until it reaches exhaustion and can run no further (Bramble & Lieberman, 2004; Liebenberg, 2006).

To date, there is little evidence to indicate, one way or another, whether barefoot running should be recommended over shod running (Hollander et al., 2017). However, research does show that people have a tendency to run in slightly different ways, depending on whether or not they are wearing shoes. Lieberman et al. (2010) compared the running styles of five groups of long distance runners; those from the USA who had always worn shoes, individuals from Kenya who had grown up without wearing shoes but now wore shoes, runners from the USA who had grown up wearing shoes but now ran barefoot, or with minimal footwear, and Kenyan teenagers who had either never worn shoes or always wore shoes. The results showed that those who were used to wearing shoes tended to land on the heel when running (regardless of whether they were asked to run with or without shoes). By contrast, those who had grown up without shoes, or who had switched to barefoot running tended to land on the forefoot. Because the forefoot provides more cushioning than the heel, this results in lower impact. This research would seem to suggest that we do not need the latest padded footwear in order to go running. Though whether barefoot running actually reduces the risk of injuries is a question that has yet to be answered.

CONCLUSIONS

Arguably, we are healthier now than we have ever been – certainly for those of us lucky enough to have been born in a wealthier country. Our lives are very different from our hunter-gatherer ancestors, or pre 20th century counterparts. We may worry about the pain and inconvenience of an upset stomach or nasty cut but they don't usually become matters of life and death. Mums-to-be may get anxious about childbirth but we tend to assume there will be a healthy baby at the end of it. Most of us enjoy clean water and flushing toilets. We get vaccinated against disease and wash our hands before eating. We name our children shortly after they're born, rather than waiting to see if they survive an inevitable smallpox infection. We live safe in the knowledge that doctors, hospitals and emergency services are on hand to help us in the event of accident or ill health. Whilst things may have deteriorated after we switched from a nomadic lifestyle to a settled one, they have certainly improved dramatically in the last century. If global life expectancy is anything to go by, now at an astonishing 72 years (WHO, 2020c), life has never been so good. We should feel truly privileged.

However, as well as this quantitative increase in life expectancy, the big health challenges we face have also undergone a qualitative change; from trauma, famine and infectious disease to, more recently, chronic, non-communicable disease. In this respect, we might argue that our hunter-gatherer ancestors lived healthier lifestyles than we do today. They ate food that was low in sugar, salt and fat, they didn't eat too many calories, they exercised, and they didn't drink alcohol or smoke. We would be even healthier today if we lived a little more like this. Happily, these are things that would seem to be within our power to change. Unlike fighting the Black Death or figuring out how to successfully perform a Caesarean, the solution appears easy – we simply need to change our behaviour. Eat better, get more exercise, quit smoking and cut back on the alcohol. Unfortunately, things aren't quite so simple. Whether you're a person struggling to lose weight, or a government trying to increase fruit and vegetable consumption, behaviour change is *really* hard. In this chapter we have seen how our evolutionary history can make it difficult for us to eat healthily and get enough exercise. In the next two chapters we look at how social and individual differences can also influence our health and health-related behaviours.

Was the agricultural revolution really 'the worst mistake in history' (Diamond, 1987)? Would you rather be a hunter-gatherer or a modern city dweller? Would your answer differ if you were a poor person living in a poorer nation? What about if you were an environmental activist?

THE GREAT DEBATE

SOCIAL DETERMINANTS OF HEALTH

Chapter Outline

Health Inequalities Between Countries

Health Inequalities Within Countries

Social Determinants of Health Behaviours

Income Inequality and Health

Implications for Intervention

Conclusions

How do the circumstances a person is born into influence their health and life expectancy? Do wealthier people live longer? The image below shows Prince George, heir to the British throne, aged two. His prospects for a long and healthy life are pretty good. He'll be able to afford the best healthcare and an excellent education. There's little danger of unemployment either. We can also see his mother, Kate Middleton. She's crouching down to his level, following his gaze, trying to see the world through her little boy's eyes. She looks happy and relaxed, the archetypal patient, loving mother. We can't quite see her in this picture, but just to the right is George's great grandmother, Queen Elizabeth II, in a lime green outfit, celebrating her 90th birthday. George's great-great grandmother, the Queen Mother, lived to the age of 101.

Image 3.1 *Catherine, Duchess of Cambridge enjoys watching the Royal Air Force flypast with Prince George from the balcony of Buckingham Palace.*
Credit: Max Mumby/Indigo / Contributor.

How might George's prospects differ if he'd been born into a different family? We can probably all agree he'd suffer poorer health growing up as a street child in India. But what if he'd been born into a different family in Britain? One where his parents were a little too distracted by the threat of unemployment to have the patience to really listen to what he was trying to say, or to read him bedtime stories. Would this affect his health? And what if he'd been born into a well-off British family, one that could afford private healthcare and education, but were not quite as wealthy as royalty? Would his health and life expectancy be any worse? Or perhaps he'd be better off without the pressure of public life?

The social determinants of health refer to the economic and social conditions that influence health. So this chapter is all about how the country, society and family you're born into influence your health and life expectancy. More specifically, in this chapter we will:

- Examine differences in life expectancy between high- and low-income countries as well as the reasons for these differences.

> **Gross domestic product (GDP)** – the total value of goods produced and services provided in a country during one year (see also **Box 3.1**).

- Look at health inequalities within countries, focussing on the relationship between socioeconomic status and health.

- Think about the social influences on health-related behaviours.

- Consider whether more equal societies lead to better health for all.

> **GDP per capita** – average GDP per person. A country's GDP will be heavily influenced by the size of its population. GDP per capita takes this into account by dividing the GDP of a country by its population. This gives a better indication of the income of a country relative to its population.

HEALTH INEQUALITIES BETWEEN COUNTRIES

Life expectancy

Table 3.1 shows life expectancy in 2018, in the ten countries with the highest life expectancies and the ten with the lowest life expectancies. The table also shows **gross domestic product** (GDP) per capita for each of these countries as well as rank according to **GDP per capita**.

As we can see from **Table 3.1**, there are substantial differences in life expectancy between countries. For example, life expectancy in Japan is more than 30 years longer than life expectancy in Central

Table 3.1 Life expectancy (in years), GDP per capita (in US dollars) and rank according to GDP per capita, for countries with the highest and lowest life expectancies in 2018

Highest life expectancy				Lowest life expectancy			
Country	Life expectancy	GDP per capita	GDP per capita rank	Country	Life expectancy	GDP per capita	GDP per capita rank
Japan	84.2	39,290	29	Equatorial Guinea	58.4	10,144	71
Liechtenstein	83.7	165,028	1	Guinea-Bissau	58.0	778	177
Switzerland	83.6	82,829	4	South Sudan	57.6	1,120	168
Spain	83.3	30,324	37	Cote d'Ivoire	57.4	1,716	149
Singapore	83.1	64,582	9	Somalia	57.1	315	194
Italy	82.9	34,489	31	Nigeria	54.3	2,028	145
Norway	82.8	81,734	5	Sierra Leone	54.3	534	187
Israel	82.1	41,720	27	Chad	54.0	728	180
Australia	82.7	57,396	13	Lesotho	53.7	1,299	162
Iceland	82.7	73,368	7	Central African Republic	52.8	476	191

Source: World Bank (2019).

African Republic. It is also clear that those countries with the highest life expectancies have much higher incomes than those with the lowest. For example, GDP per capita is US$82,829 in Switzerland but just US$315 in Somalia. What are the reasons for this relationship?

BOX 3.1 GENDER BIAS IN THE DATA

HOT TOPIC

We rely on data to draw conclusions about the world around us, make predictions about the future, and design effective solutions to pressing problems. But what if these data only accurately represent half the world's population?

Criado Perez (2019) argues that much of the data we rely on is drawn from the lives of men rather than women. This is not necessarily because of overt discrimination against women, but rather because it is often men who collect the data or design the solutions and, like the rest of us, they are inclined to see the world from their own point of view. Bias can also arise because of beliefs about data from women being too complex or variable to easily collate or interpret.

For example, GDP is designed to reflect a country's productivity and refers to the total value of goods and services produced in that country. But it is restricted to goods and services that are paid for. This means that the work involved in caring for children or elderly relatives or looking after a home (traditionally 'women's work') are not included in the figures. It is as if this work does not count as 'real work'. But if people start paying for childcare and cleaners and buying takeaway and ready meals instead of cooking from scratch, the GDP of the country will go up because money is changing hands, even though no extra work is being done, it is simply being shifted to a different person.

A similar bias occurs in biological and medical data where women may be excluded from studies and trials. This stems in part from historical views of the male body as the default body. For example, a 2008 analysis of over 16,000 images from 12 textbooks recommended by the most prestigious universities in Europe and North America found that there were three times as many male bodies as female bodies (Plataforma SINC, 2008). Exclusion of women from research studies has also been justified by the fact that their reproductive cycles mean they experience more hormonal variation. Whilst it is true that this could result in data that are more difficult to interpret, it is hardly a good reason to ignore half the population.

Indeed, because women's bodies are different from men's, this type of bias has very real effects on women's health. If we don't understand the way different diseases, drugs and interventions affect women, we will be less well equipped to treat them. For example, the classic signs of a heart attack – pain in the chest and left arm – are more likely to be absent in women than in men, which can lead to delayed treatment and worse outcomes (Khamis et al., 2016).

Criado Perez (2019) calls not only for a more systematic inclusion of women in scientific and medical research, but also for it to become standard practice to disaggregate data by gender, to make it easier to identify and explore differences between men and women.

Healthcare

Arguably, the differences in life expectancy between high- and low-income countries are not surprising. Good healthcare comes at a price. Money is needed to pay for the building and upkeep of hospitals and clinics. Healthcare professionals must be trained and paid. Equipment has to be purchased, as do vaccines and medicines. Transport is needed to get people to clinics and hospitals, and healthcare professionals to people. Poorer countries are less likely to be able to afford such things. For example, a survey of health facilities in Sierra Leone found that, on average, they did not have nearly half of 12 important antibiotics and around 12 of 17 medicines considered essential for the treatment of non-communicable diseases (WHO, 2015a). A similar picture emerges in relation to childbirth; in wealthier countries nearly all births are attended by an appropriately trained health professional and maternal mortality is very low; between 3 and 10 deaths per 100,000 births for the high-income countries listed in **Table 3.1**. By contrast, in poorer countries fewer births benefit from such expertise, and this is reflected in higher levels of maternal death. For example, in Somalia just 9% of births are attended by skilled personnel and for every 100,000 births, 732 mothers die (WHO, 2016c).

Living conditions

As described in **Chapter 2**, a person's health is influenced not just by the healthcare they receive, but also by the environment they live in. For example, where a community has no access to clean drinking water or has to use nearby fields as a toilet area, disease will spread more easily. If they are provided with clean drinking water, handwashing facilities and safe sewage disposal, their health is likely to improve. But, as with healthcare, these types of environmental improvements cost money. As such, we see large differences in deaths attributed to environmental factors between high- and low-income countries. For example, in the wealthier countries of Europe, deaths attributed to unsafe water, sanitation and lack of hygiene stand at 5 for every 100,000 people. In Africa, where many of the world's poorest countries are located, the figure is 45 per 100,000 and reaches over 100 per 100,000 in some countries such as Central African Republic, Democratic Republic of the Congo and Angola (WHO, 2016c).

As noted previously, it is not surprising to find that a county's income influences its ability to provide both healthcare and a healthy living environment, and that these, in turn, impact upon the health of the population.

Education

A third factor that is critical for health is education. There have been remarkable improvements in education over the last two centuries, and even within the last 50 years. For example, in 1970, a total of 66% of the world's population could read and write; by 2016, this figure had reached 86% (Roser & Ortiz-Ospina, 2018).

Nevertheless, there are still more than 60 million children of primary school age not in education (around 9%) with many of these living in low-income countries and regions. For example, in sub-Saharan Africa, 1 in 5 primary-aged children are not in school, compared to 1 in 55 in Hong Kong, 1 in 69 in New Zealand and 1 in 165 in the UK (Roser & Ortiz-Ospina, 2020).

Gender disparities

In many countries, accessing education is more difficult for girls than for boys. This is particularly the case in sub-Saharan Africa, Northern Africa and Western Asia where girls may experience a range of different barriers to education (UNESCO, 2019; see also **Image 3.2**). These include the following:

- Social norms that view the primary role of females as housewives and caregivers, placing a higher value on the education of boys.

- Textbook content, curricular and teacher instruction that reinforce these norms (such as women being less suited to work outside the home).

- Greater involvement in paid or unpaid domestic work making school attendance difficult.

- Child marriage (often to ensure economic security), followed by domestic responsibilities and norms that confine girls to their homes.

- Laws and school rules that prohibit attendance by pregnant girls and young mothers.

- The threat of sexual violence, both at school and travelling to and from school.

- A lack of single-sex toilets (with doors and locks) and sanitation facilities (such as soap and water for handwashing) that are needed for menstrual hygiene.

Education and health

Education is critical because it influences the knowledge and behaviour of individuals. Someone who knows it is important to wash their hands after going to the toilet (and who follows this advice) is less likely to get sick than a person who is unaware of the connection between germs and disease.

Interestingly, the effects of education on health appear to be linear (Lutz & Kebede, 2018). This means there does not seem to be a threshold above which more education has no additional health benefits. Academics have suggested that part of the reason for the linear relationship may be that education not only improves understanding of basic healthcare principles, but also increases a person's confidence and skills to both seek and comply with modern preventive and curative healthcare solutions (Cleland, 2010). Put simply, a more educated person is more likely to seek the advice of a healthcare professional and is more likely to follow the advice they are given.

Mothers' education and child health

A parent who understands the importance of basic hygiene, immunisation and the role of good nutrition in infant and child development will also be better equipped to raise healthy children. Indeed, there is a clear association between a mother's level of education and the health of her children. For example, median levels of **stunting** are 39% among children born to mothers with no education, whilst this figure drops to 23% among mothers who have completed at least secondary school education (WHO, 2016c).

Image 3.2 *Malala Yousafzai who in 2012, at the age of 14, was shot in the head by the Taliban in Pakistan after speaking out against attacks on girls' education. Malala survived and in 2014 was awarded the Nobel Peace Prize for her struggle for children's right to an education. You can find out more about Malala's life in her biography I am Malala and on the webpage for her charity, The Malala Fund, that works to ensure that girls everywhere complete 12 years of safe, quality education (www.malala.org).*
Credit: Richard Stonehouse / Stringer.

Stunting – low height relative to age as a result of poor nutrition and frequent infections during childhood. Stunting affects an estimated 23% of children worldwide (WHO, 2016c) and is frequently used as a marker of malnutrition. Malnutrition impacts on cognitive development and educational achievement as well as physical health.

Similarly, women's level of education shows a linear relationship with child mortality, with every additional year of education being associated with a reduction in child mortality of 9.5% (Gakidou et al., 2010).

One of the things that is so interesting about the effect of education on child mortality is that it seems to be much larger than that which can be achieved by increasing the GDP of the country (Gakidou et al., 2010; Lutz & Kebede, 2018). This means that countries that prioritise education can achieve higher life expectancies despite low income levels. Conversely, countries that focus only on economic growth, with little investment in education, will not see equivalent benefits for health (Caldwell, 1986). For example, Cuba is an outlier when it comes to life expectancy. It is a middle-income country with a GDP per capita of $8,822. And yet life expectancy stands at nearly 79 years, longer than some high-income countries such as the United States and Saudi Arabia. One possible explanation is that Cuba spends a relatively high proportion of its GDP, around 13%, on education. This compares with around 5% in the United States and Saudi Arabia. In stark contrast is oil-rich Equatorial Guinea (see **Table 3.1**) which has a higher GDP per capita than Cuba ($10,144) but a much lower life expectancy of 58 years. Equatorial Guinea is estimated to be spending around 2% of GDP on education (World Bank, 2019).

Education and wealth

There are also likely to be indirect effects of education on health that come about via improvements in wealth. An individual who is educated is likely to earn a higher income. Likewise, population level improvements in education lead to increases in productivity and employability, which are in turn linked to national economic growth (Unicef, 2015).

However, it would be disingenuous to pretend that education is free. Whilst education may increase wealth it also requires wealth. In order to educate its population, a country needs to be able to build and maintain schools, provide equipment such as textbooks and pencils, and pay for the training and salaries of teachers. Additionally, families need to be able to support their child through school; a child that is at school is an extra mouth to feed that is not earning an income. Nevertheless, the data suggest that where there is money to spend, education, particularly the education of girls, is a wise investment.

Economic growth and shrinking inequalities

Although there are still inequalities between different parts of the world, it is important to acknowledge the progress that has been made in tackling poverty and poor health, particularly in the last 50 years. For example, as shown in **Figure 3.1**, in 1970, 38% of the global population were living in extreme poverty and countries tended to be either 'rich' or 'poor' (often referred to as 'developed' or 'developing'). However, by 2015 the percentage of the population living in extreme poverty had dropped to 10% with most of the world's population (around 5 billion people) now living in what are best described as middle-income countries. These include many countries in Asia with very large populations (such as India and China) that would have been described as developing nations 30 years ago.

HEALTH INEQUALITIES WITHIN COUNTRIES

In the last section we argued that health inequalities between countries are largely (but not completely) driven by differences in income that influence key factors such as healthcare, living conditions and education. In this section we continue this line of argument, showing how health inequalities within countries are also closely related to differences in income and education. However, it is important to note that health inequalities cut across other

Figure 3.1 Changes in world poverty and income from 1970

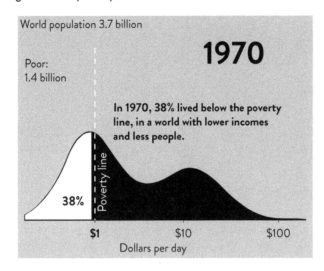

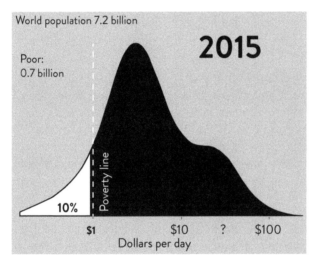

Source: Gapminder.com. Used and adapted under the terms of the Creative Commons BY 4.0 licence. www.gapminder.org/downloads/human-development-trends-2005.

groups too, such as gender and ethnicity. It is beyond the scope of this chapter to provide a detailed exploration of all group differences in health, though there is often substantial overlap between the underlying causes. We consider this briefly toward the end of this section when we think about ethnicity and discrimination.

The relationship between socioeconomic status and health

Within countries, health is closely linked to **socioeconomic status** (SES; also referred to as socioeconomic group). For example, **Table 3.2** shows how deaths from cardiovascular disease in Australia increase as one moves from lower to higher socioeconomic groups. This relationship holds true for both men and women over the course of 16 years during which there were overall declines in

Socioeconomic status (SES) – the social standing or class of an individual or group, generally measured as a combination of education, income, wealth and/or occupation. (Though note that these individual variables are not always highly correlated and researchers have warned against using them interchangeably; Braveman et al., 2005).

Table 3.2 Deaths from cardiovascular disease per 100,000 Australian men and women, between 2001 and 2016, grouped by socioeconomic status

Social group	Women				Men			
	2001	2006	2011	2016	2001	2006	2011	2016
1 (lowest)	229	189	165	139	334	263	239	207
2	218	190	160	129	314	267	218	185
3	219	173	145	118	304	245	203	163
4	207	165	127	108	291	219	172	146
5 (highest)	191	147	123	104	271	195	160	136
Ratio (lowest/highest)	*1.20*	*1.29*	*1.34*	*1.33*	*1.23*	*1.35*	*1.49*	*1.52*

Source: Australian Institute of Health and Welfare (2019).

deaths from cardiovascular disease. For example, the figures show that in 2016, men in the lowest socioeconomic group were 1.52 times more likely to die from cardiovascular disease compared to men in the highest socioeconomic group. The equivalent ratio for women was 1.33.

The Whitehall studies

This kind of association between health and socioeconomic status has been found in a very wide range of studies, including two large prospective cohort studies (see **Chapter 10**) conducted with British civil servants. Known as the 'Whitehall' studies, after the street in London along which many government departments and ministries are located, these studies were set up to explore relationships between occupation and disease. Whitehall I began in 1967. It recruited over 18,000 men aged 40 to 64 years, classified them into four different grades according to their type of employment, and tracked them over a 25-year period. The data showed that the lower the grade, the more likely the individual was to die during the study period. Indeed, those in the lowest grades (for example messengers, porters and other unskilled manual workers) were three times more likely to die than those in the highest grade (Marmot et al., 1984; Marmot & Shipley, 1996).

Whitehall II was established in 1985 and continues to track its participants today. It recruited over 10,000 individuals aged 35 to 55 years, one-third of whom were women. These data also show an association between occupational grade and mortality; over a 24-year period those in the lowest grade were 1.6 times more likely to die compared to those in the highest grade (Stringhini et al., 2010).

What is particularly interesting about the data from these studies is that they show a linear relationship between occupation type and health. It is not just those at the very bottom of the ladder who suffer more ill health; even those near the top have worse health outcomes than those at the very top. What accounts for this gradient? In the previous section we saw how poorer countries were less able to afford things like good healthcare and clean living environments. However, this does not seem a very likely explanation when it comes to British civil servants. Indeed, it is probably safe to assume that they all have access to clean drinking water, flushing toilets and a doctor when they need one. So why does the relationship between socioeconomic status (SES) and health persist?

Cause or effect?

There are three possible ways of accounting for the relationship between SES and health (**Figure 3.2**):

a) SES could influence health. For example, having a higher income could mean access to better healthcare. This explanation has been labelled the *social causation hypothesis*.

b) Health could influence SES. For example, those who are healthier may be more able to get a better education and a better job, whilst those who become ill may have difficulty keeping up with schoolwork or holding on to a better job. This account has been labelled the *health selection hypothesis*.

c) SES and health could be correlated only because of their association with a third, underlying variable. For example, certain personality traits such as conscientiousness may influence both educational achievement and health leading to an association between the two, despite the absence of any causal connection. This explanation is termed the *indirect selection hypothesis*.

Figure 3.2 Explanations for the correlation between socioeconomic status and health

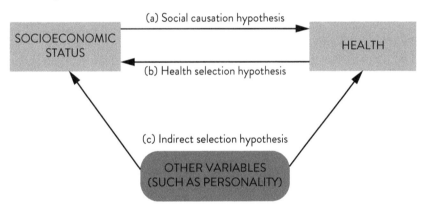

One challenge for those wishing to distinguish between these three possibilities is that it is a little tricky to conduct experimental work in this area; indeed, it is simply not possible to take a set of individuals and randomly assign them to different types of occupation. As a result, it is more difficult to establish direction of causality and to control for other variables (such as personality) that may be related to both SES and health. Nevertheless, with a large enough sample it is possible for observational study designs to control for the influence of other variables using statistical methods. Whilst such data cannot provide conclusive evidence of causality, they can provide sufficient evidence for us to make statements about likely causal links (see **Chapter 10** for further discussion of study design).

This is exactly how the Whitehall studies were designed and data from these, along with similar studies, have given us some insight into the complex relationships between these variables. For example, data from Whitehall II showed that over a 10-year period, disease risk factors in adulthood (such as obesity and high blood pressure) did not consistently predict promotion whereas lower adult occupational position did predict adverse changes in a number of disease risk factors. These results provide support for the social causation

CHAPTER 3

hypothesis as opposed to the health selection hypothesis, at least in relation to disease risk factors among British civil servants.

However, using the Whitehall data, researchers have also found that hospitalisation during childhood, and a lower birth weight, predicted a lower occupational position, providing support for the health selection hypothesis at younger ages (Elovainio et al., 2011). Indeed, a systematic review of studies that have contrasted the social causation and health selection hypotheses found support for both (Kröger et al., 2015). Yet other research has found support for the indirect selection hypothesis (Foverskov & Holm, 2016).

Thus it seems that a number of different causal pathways may be responsible for the relationship between SES and health and it is possible that different pathways may be more or less influential at different stages of life. But what are the mechanisms underlying these pathways? It is relatively easy to see why poor health could interfere with educational attainment, earning power or promotion at work, but why might the latter influence health? In the remainder of this section we consider four different ways in which we can try to account for the effects of SES on health: access to healthcare, working and living environment, health-related behaviours and stress.

Access to healthcare

Access to healthcare seems like a good candidate for explaining the link between SES and health; surely the more money you have, the better the healthcare you can afford?

Low- and middle-income countries

This would certainly be the case for low- and middle-income countries where good healthcare may not be affordable for those with less money, either because of the direct costs of healthcare and medicines, or because of indirect costs such as travelling to a faraway hospital or clinic.

The United States

Income and access to healthcare are also linked in the United States (a high-income country) because healthcare is paid for via health insurance, and health insurance is purchased by employers, the individual or the state. This means that those with better jobs or more money tend to have better insurance, whilst some people, typically those from lower socioeconomic backgrounds, may have no insurance at all.

Research shows that US citizens with no health insurance are more likely to die compared to those who are insured (Wilper et al., 2009). In 2007 it was estimated that 46 million Americans had no health insurance (Wilper et al., 2009). This figure dropped after President Barack Obama introduced the Affordable Care Act (sometimes referred to as 'Obamacare') in 2010, aimed at increasing the quality and affordability of health insurance. Nevertheless, in 2018, census data indicated that 27.5 million people were still uninsured, representing 8.5% of the population (United States Census Bureau, 2019). The United States is the only high-income country without nearly **universal health coverage** (Rice et al., 2014).

> **Universal health coverage** – a system in which all citizens have access to the preventive, curative, rehabilitative and palliative healthcare they need, without incurring financial hardship. Universal health coverage is a priority objective of the World Health Organization.

Other high-income countries

In all other high-income countries, money is generally not a barrier to basic, essential healthcare. For example, in the UK, the National Health Service (NHS), established in 1948, operates on the principle that healthcare should be free at the point of delivery. Indeed, research shows that those in lower socioeconomic groups often access NHS services more frequently than those in higher socioeconomic groups (Britton et al., 2004). Nevertheless, inequalities may still occur because of relative differences in the availability and quality of services in different geographical areas (Asaria et al., 2016).

Inequalities may also arise because of differences in the behaviours of patients and health professionals. For example, in Australia, researchers found that men from disadvantaged socioeconomic areas were less likely to be prescribed **statins** compared to those from wealthier areas (Stocks et al., 2004). The authors suggested this may be because better educated patients were more likely to request statins. Alternatively, doctors, who were predominantly male, middle-aged and middle class, may have identified more strongly with their better-off patients in a way that made them more likely to prescribe statins. Similarly in Canada, researchers found that, although those from lower socioeconomic backgrounds had relatively more family doctor and hospital appointments, they accessed less specialist care. The authors suggested they may have been less likely to have been referred to specialist care, possibly due to differences in patient and/or doctor behaviour (Veugelers & Yip, 2003).

> **Statins** – a class of drugs that help lower blood cholesterol levels. They are prescribed to reduce the incidence of heart disease and the risk of heart attack and stroke amongst certain populations.

Thus access to good quality healthcare does appear to contribute to health inequalities in high-income countries, though the extent of its impact will vary depending on the type of healthcare system and the way in which it is implemented.

Living conditions

Low- and middle-income countries

In low- and middle-income countries, family income will make a substantial difference to a person's living conditions. For example, the poorest families may go to the toilet in the forest or fields with no fresh water supply and the threat of snake and insect bites. With more money they may be able to build a pit latrine, though this still risks contaminating water supplies and crops, and flies may spread bacteria from faeces to food. An outhouse with a deeper, covered latrine reduces these risks. The wealthier will be able to afford an indoor flushing toilet as well as cleaning products (**Image 3.3**). Those with less money may also rely on an open fire for cooking and heating that causes indoor air pollution that damages the lungs. With more money they may be able to afford a stove and cleaner fuel. The wealthiest may have an integrated stove and oven connected to a national gas or electricity supply.

High-income countries

Whilst people in high-income countries enjoy more uniformly better living conditions than those in low- and middle-income countries, there are still within-country differences that can contribute to differences in health. For example, low socioeconomic neighbourhoods tend to be situated in areas with more traffic and industrial facilities and have been shown to have higher levels of air pollution. Housing in low SES areas may also contain more allergens, for example from pests such as mice and cockroaches, and pollutants from gas stoves and heaters. These factors have been linked to an increased prevalence and severity of **asthma** among children from low SES backgrounds (Schreier & Chen, 2012).

> **Asthma** – a chronic respiratory condition that inflames and narrows the airways of the lungs, causing difficulty in breathing.

Image 3.3 *Different types of toilets in Africa for families on different incomes: a field in Malawi (top left), a pit latrine in Burundi (top right), an outhouse in Tanzania (bottom left), an indoor flushing toilet in South Africa (bottom right). You can find more pictures of homes from around the world, belonging to families on different levels of income, at Dollar Street on https://www. gapminder.org/dollar-street.*

Top left: Zoriah Miller for Dollar Street, Top right: Johan Eriksson for Dollar Street, Bottom left: Angie Skazka for Dollar Street, Bottom right: Robin Timmermans for Dollar Street.

Source: Free photographs from Gapminder.com, shared under the CC BY licence.

The environment a person lives in can also influence health less directly by promoting or discouraging certain behaviours. For example, low SES neighbourhoods tend to have fewer supermarkets and more fast food restaurants and it is possible this type of food environment increases the risks of obesity and a poor diet, particularly among those with less education (though the evidence is mixed; Black et al., 2014; Burgoine et al., 2016; Cobb et al., 2015; Larson et al., 2009).

Similarly, lower SES neighbourhoods tend to have fewer exercise facilities and green spaces (Estabrooks et al., 2003; Powell et al., 2006). Again, although researchers have yet to fully disentangle associations between green space and health, there is some evidence to suggest that access to exercise facilities and specific types of green space (such as well-maintained parks) help promote physical activity and reduce BMI (Coombes et al., 2010; Cummins & Fagg, 2012; Gong et al., 2014; Gordon-Larsen et al., 2006; Lachowycz & Jones, 2011). Indeed, longitudinal studies have found that children who live in greener neighbourhoods are less likely to become overweight (Bell et al., 2008; Sanders, 2015).

CHAPTER 3

Working conditions

In all countries, individuals from lower socioeconomic groups may be exposed to more dangerous or unhealthy working environments. For example, the 2015 European Working Conditions Survey found that 23% of workers in the European Union reported that their health was at risk because of their work, for instance as a result of repetitive hand and arm movements, carrying or moving heavy loads, exposure to loud noise or vibrations from machinery, or from handling chemicals or infectious materials (Eurofound, 2015a). People working in lower skilled occupations, such as mining and construction labourers, refuse workers, agricultural workers or machine operators, are more likely to be exposed to such risks (Eurofound, 2015b). In high-income countries, although work-related fatalities are rare, they tend to occur exclusively in those working in lower skilled occupations (Health and Safety Executive, 2016).

Health-related behaviours

Although healthcare and living and working conditions may explain some of the differences in health between the wealthiest and poorest members of a society, it is more difficult to see how they can account for differences in health that occur toward the top end of the SES scale. Recall that in the Whitehall studies, even the well-paid, well-educated civil servants in professional and executive roles were more likely to die than those slightly higher up the ranks, in charge of running government departments (Marmot et al., 1984). Why might this be the case?

As described in **Chapter 2**, health-related behaviours such as diet and exercise increase the risk of non-communicable diseases. Thus health-related behaviours are an obvious place to look when attempting to explain the socioeconomic gradient in health. Do those from lower SES groups have less healthy lifestyles?

The answer to this question is a tentative 'yes'. In many countries, those in lower socioeconomic groups tend to have higher intakes of saturated fat, added sugar and salt, they tend to eat fewer fruit and vegetables, engage in less physical activity and are more likely to smoke (Cappuccio et al., 2015; Clare et al., 2014; De Irala-Estévez et al., 2000; Gidlow et al., 2006; Mullie et al., 2010; Office for National Statistics, 2016). They are also more likely to suffer from overweight or obesity (Devaux & Sassi, 2011; Stamatakis et al., 2010). The one exception to this trend is alcohol consumption, which is often higher among those in higher SES groups (Bonevski et al., 2014; NHS, 2015).

Research also suggests that these differences in lifestyle make a significant contribution to the socioeconomic gradient in health. For example, using data from Whitehall II, Stringhini et al. (2010) looked at the extent to which differences in smoking, alcohol consumption, diet and physical inactivity could account for the relationship between SES and mortality over a 24-year period. They found that these four behaviours explained 72% of the association. A similar pattern has been found in the US where, over a 10-year period, smoking, alcohol consumption and physical inactivity accounted for 68% of the association between SES and mortality (Nandi et al., 2014).

In some countries, health behaviours seem to account for a much smaller proportion of the SES gradient in health. For example, research in France found that health behaviours only accounted for 19% of the association between SES and mortality (Stringhini et al., 2011). Comparing this with the findings from the Whitehall study, the authors suggested the discrepancy may be because SES differences in smoking, diet and activity were much greater in Britain than in France. For example, high rates of smoking in France means there is less variation between SES groups. As smoking rates start to fall, they are likely to fall more rapidly among higher SES groups. This in turn would strengthen the association between SES and health, widening the gap in life expectancy among those from high versus low SES groups.

These findings prompt a further question – why is there an association between SES and health-related behaviours? We consider this later in the chapter, in the section titled *Social determinants of health-related behaviours*.

Stress

Another explanation for the SES gradient in health relates to stress. Stress occurs when we encounter a challenging situation and is characterised by an emotional response (such as a feeling of anxiety) as well as a physical response (such as the release of cortisol into the bloodstream).

An adaptive response to physical threats

The stress response would have originally evolved to help us deal with threats in our environment. If a hunter-gatherer encounters a hungry lion, they can try to fight it off, or they can take flight and run for their life. This is what is known as the 'fight-or-flight' response, and both behaviours will be more effective if a greater proportion of the body's available energy is diverted to the muscles. As such, if we come across a hungry lion, our body responds by releasing a range of different hormones into the bloodstream that help get energy to the muscles and prepare our body for action. More specifically:

- Energy storage is blocked

- Stored energy is converted to glucose and released into the blood stream

- Heart rate and blood pressure are increased to distribute energy faster

- Blood clotting function is increased to help avoid excessive blood loss in case of injury

- Physiological processes such as digestion, growth, tissue repair and immune function are supressed since they are not immediately needed.

Social threats

These days we are unlikely to encounter a hungry lion whilst picking up our weekly groceries. However, as well as exhibiting a stress response to physical threats, we also show a stress response to situations that threaten our social status. Dickerson and Kemeny (2004) reviewed over 200 laboratory studies that examined physiological stress responses to psychological variables. They found that tasks that resulted in the largest stress response had two key features:

- They represented a *social-evaluative threat* – participants' performance could be judged negatively by others

- They were *uncontrollable* – participants' efforts had little effect on the outcome.

For example, a particularly stressful task may be one in which a participant is asked to perform a cognitive task or speech in front of an audience during which they are given false feedback that they are performing badly. Thus however hard the participant tries, they are unable to avoid the negative evaluations of others. As well as producing the largest stress response among participants, such tasks also resulted in the most extended stress response.

Whilst this type of acute stress does not generally present a problem for healthy individuals, difficulties can arise when people are exposed to such stressors over prolonged periods. In other words, they are exposed to chronic stress that leads to sustained activation of the stress response.

Stress at work

What types of situations might lead to chronic stress and why might we see a social gradient in such situations? One such area is occupation. Karasek and Theorell (1990) describe how different types of occupation result in different levels of stress. They suggest that jobs vary along two key dimensions: the amount of demands the job places on the individual and the level of control the person has over how they cope with those demands. Jobs that involve high demand and low control (high strain jobs) will be the most stressful. Examples include assembly line worker, construction worker, factory garment stitcher and waiter. Jobs that have low demands but high control (low strain jobs) will be the least stressful. Examples include architect, accountant, dentist and computer programmer. Thus, according to this model, many lower socioeconomic occupations are likely to be more stressful than many higher socioeconomic occupations.

Data collected in Whitehall I and II support the view that those in lower employment grades tend to have lower levels of job control (though not necessarily lower demands; Bosma et al., 1997; Kuper & Marmot, 2003; Marmot et al., 1997). **Meta-analyses** have also shown that higher job strain is associated with an increased incidence of cardiovascular disease (Kivimäki et al., 2012; Schnall et al., 1994). Whether this is because job strain has a direct impact on cardiovascular risk factors (such as blood pressure and cholesterol levels) or whether it influences disease via behavioural risk factors (such as diet and smoking) is less clear (Nyberg et al., 2013). Nevertheless, job strain does seem to increase the risk of diabetes, probably by contributing to disturbances in glucose metabolism (Nyberg et al., 2013). Data from the Whitehall studies also suggest that job strain accounts for some of the SES gradient in coronary heart disease (Bosma et al., 1997; Kuper & Marmot, 2003; Marmot et al., 1997).

> **Meta-analysis** – an analysis that combines data from multiple independent studies that have all examined the same research question. The results are considered more reliable than the results of any single study (see **Chapter 10** for further discussion).

Stress at home

Those from lower socioeconomic groups are also likely to suffer from lower levels of control at home. Using data from Whitehall II, researchers asked individuals to rate the extent to which they agreed with the statement 'At home, I feel I have control over what happens in most situations' (Chandola et al., 2004). They found that low control predicted higher rates of coronary heart disease among women, but not men. This effect was independent from the effects of occupational stress and heart disease risk factors (blood pressure, diabetes, smoking, exercise and obesity). Additionally, being in a household with more financial difficulties was associated with lower control at home among women. As such, the authors suggested that control at home may be one of the mechanisms underlying the social gradient in coronary heart disease among women; those from lower socioeconomic backgrounds may have less material and psychological resources which in turn make it more difficult to cope with household and family responsibilities, leading to a low sense of control.

Stress beyond work and home

Other researchers have also described how individuals from lower socioeconomic backgrounds experience lower levels of control and higher levels of stress across many aspects of their lives, ranging from the communities they live in, to their status in society (Baum et al., 1999; Whitehead et al., 2016). Consistent with these findings, research has shown that those from lower socioeconomic backgrounds have higher levels of stress hormones (Cohen et al., 2006).

Gender and stress: 'fight-or-flight' or 'tend-and-befriend'?

Taylor and colleagues note that research into the fight-or-flight response has been largely conducted with males (see **Box 3.1**). They argue that although males and females may experience a similar physiological response to stress, females are more likely to respond with patterns of behaviour they describe as 'tend-and-befriend' (Taylor et al., 2000; Taylor, 2006). They suggest that, traditionally, females have been more involved in the care of offspring and, from an evolutionary perspective, responses to threat that would have increased the chances of survival for both mother and offspring would have been advantageous. Both fight and flight would have been difficult and risky for a pregnant mother or one looking after a baby or young child. Instead, Taylor and colleagues propose that more effective strategies would have been to hide from danger and to group together with others for safety. Hiding from danger requires offspring that are quiet, hence the 'tending' response that functions to achieve this. Grouping together with others requires the development and maintenance of social networks, hence the 'befriending' response.

BOX 3.2 HOW STRESSED ARE YOU?

What's the best way of measuring stress? If someone asked you to rate your stress on a scale of 1 to 5, what would you say? And what would you base your estimation on? You **TAKE THE TEST** might think about how stressed you've felt over the past couple of weeks compared to how stressed you've felt at other points in your life. But perhaps, compared to most, your whole life has been relatively stress-free. In which case, although our measure may be useful for tracking the ups and downs in your levels of stress, it won't be so helpful if we want to compare you with someone else.

A more objective way of assessing stress is to measure the body's stress response. This can be achieved by taking physiological measures, for example samples of saliva, blood or urine, that can be used to estimate levels of stress hormones in the body. However, such measures can be relatively costly, time-consuming, and invasive. An alternative approach is to look at the circumstances of a person's life that are believed to be associated with stress (such as level of control in the workplace) or life events that are assumed to elicit stress. Holmes and Rahes' (1967) social readjustment rating scale (SRRS) is one such measure. It lists 43 significant life events, such as switching jobs or getting married, and asks respondents to report on whether or not they have experienced these over the previous 12 months. Different events are given different 'life change units' according to the extent to which they are likely to be disruptive. For example, death of a spouse is given a value of 100, divorce 73 and marital separation 65. Going on holiday is given a value of 13. The higher the person's total score, the higher the risk of stress-related illness. You can have a go at the test at **macmillanihe.com/tapper-health-psychology**.

However, the SRRS is not without its limitations. Would your interpretation of 'change in frequency of arguments' be the same as someone else's? Is a 'change in residence' going to elicit the same amount of stress for everyone? (Are you moving to a detached house in the country or a hostel for the homeless?) Might some people relish the challenge of a new job, and others approach it with trepidation? What about everyday sources of stress such as financial worries, a difficult commute to work, or noisy neighbours keeping you awake at night?

Social support

Laboratory studies have supported the tend-and-befriend theory, showing that the provision of social support prior to a stressful event attenuates stress-related cortisol and cardiovascular responses among both men and women (Ditzen et al., 2007; Heinrichs et al., 2003). These findings are in line with a wide body of research that shows that social support is associated with better health. For example, a meta-analysis of 148 studies, with over 300,000 participants, examined the relationship between social support and mortality (Holt-Lunstad et al., 2010). The authors distinguished between two types of social support:

- Functional support – benefits received (or perceived to be received) from social relationships, such as emotional or tangible support.

- Structural support – the existence and interconnectedness of social networks, for example marital status and number of social contacts.

The strongest effects were for structural measures, particularly those relating to social integration. Overall, those with more social support had a 50% increase in the likelihood of survival over 7.5 years, an effect comparable to quitting smoking. These findings led the authors to recommend that health professionals screen for and target social connections in a similar manner to other health-related behaviours such as smoking and obesity.

But is there a socioeconomic gradient in social support? A number of studies do indeed show that those from higher socioeconomic groups have higher levels of social support compared to those from lower socioeconomic groups. For example, they are more likely to be married and to have more friends (House et al., 1988; Taylor & Seeman, 1999). However, research examining the extent to which such differences can help account for SES differences in health have produced mixed findings, with only some studies indicating a meditational effect, with SES influencing support and support influencing health (Matthews et al., 2010). Analysis of data from Whitehall II showed that differences in structural social support explained around a quarter of the association between SES and mortality among men but did not account for the relationship among women (Stringhini et al., 2012). Thus although structural social support is clearly important for health, the extent to which it can account for the SES gradient in health has yet to be firmly established.

Social status and immune function

A final explanation for the SES gradient in health is that socioeconomic position may have a direct effect on health via immune function. Research with female rhesus monkeys has shown that manipulating their social hierarchies (by introducing new females into established groups) has an effect on their immune function. Lower status monkeys have immune systems that are very aggressive, causing inflammation in the body that, in humans, could increase the risks of heart disease, diabetes and mental health problems. The researchers found that changes to a monkey's place in the social hierarchy could improve or worsen their immune function (Snyder-Mackler et al., 2016). Although human societies are more complex than the rhesus monkey hierarchies, this study identifies a plausible mechanism via which SES position could impact upon health in humans.

Structural racism – the ways in which societies foster discrimination via mutually reinforcing systems, such as those relating to housing, education, employment and criminal justice. These systems in turn reinforce discriminatory beliefs and the unequal distribution of resources (Bailey et al., 2017).

Ethnicity, discrimination and health

As noted at the start of this section, in many countries we see variations in health across ethnicity as well as SES, with people from certain ethnic groups suffering from poorer health. For example, in the US, life expectancy among those who are Black is 75.6 years compared to 79 years among those who are White (Bailey et al., 2017). Although genetic differences mean certain diseases are more common among some ethnicities (see **Chapter 4**), overall health inequalities are more likely to be the result of social factors. In particular, a history of **structural racism** may mean that some ethnic groups are more likely to occupy lower paid jobs and experience poorer living conditions which directly expose them to greater health risks and higher levels of stress. For example, in the UK, people from Black, Asian and Minority Ethnic (BAME) groups are more likely to live in overcrowded households and suffer from greater material deprivation (Raisi-Estabragh et al., 2020). Likewise, in the US, 26% of those who are Black live below the poverty line, compared to 10% of those who are White (Bailey et al., 2017). People from ethnic minorities may also suffer from poorer health because of higher levels of stress that occur as a direct result of stigma and discrimination (Berger & Sarnyai, 2015; Paradies et al., 2015).

BOX 3.3 STIGMA AND DISCRIMINATION

In many countries, certain groups suffer from stigma and discrimination. This may be because of their ethnicity, gender, occupation, health status or appearance. In this **MAKING CONNECTIONS** chapter we have looked at discrimination based on gender (in relation to education) and ethnicity (in relation to living and working conditions). However, stigma and discrimination influence health through multiple pathways. For example, in **Chapter 12** we consider weight stigma and look at how this may increase levels of stress, leading people to eat more. We also look at an intervention in India that helped tackle discrimination against sex workers (**Case Study 11**). Reading these sections alongside one another may help you think about the different ways in which stigma and discrimination can lead to poorer health.

SOCIAL DETERMINANTS OF HEALTH BEHAVIOURS

A little earlier in this chapter we saw how part of the association between SES and health is likely brought about by SES differences in health-related behaviours. For example, those from lower SES groups are more likely to smoke and are less likely to eat a healthy diet and be physically active. This requires further exploration. Why are people from lower SES groups less likely to lead healthy lifestyles? In this section we look at three possible explanations: knowledge, early life experiences, and cognitive resources. While these are far from the only explanations, they have been selected as important areas that also represent potential targets for intervention. As you read through later chapters in this book, other potential explanations may also occur to you.

BOX 3.4 CAPABILITY, OPPORTUNITY OR MOTIVATION?

MAKING CONNECTIONS

In this chapter we refer to a range of different behaviours that contribute to inequalities in health. In **Chapter 9** we look at the COM-B model that states that for a person to change their behaviour, they must have the capability, opportunity and motivation to do so. Identifying which of these elements are present and which are absent can help determine which types of behaviour change strategies are likely to be effective. As you go through the examples in this chapter, you might like to consider which of these three key elements – capability, opportunity or motivation – seem most critical, and how you might address these in an intervention.

Knowledge

As discussed above, education has a positive influence on health-related behaviours, because it increases knowledge of the causes of good health and ill health and promotes engagement with modern healthcare solutions. The better educated may also be better equipped to request the healthcare resources they need and follow the advice they are given (Stocks et al., 2004; Veugelers & Yip, 2003; see also **Box 3.5**). But in a country where health warnings are emblazoned in black and white across cigarette packets, to what extent can unhealthy behaviours be attributed to a lack of knowledge?

Key health promotion messages

Chamberlain and O'Neil (1998) examined this issue by interviewing smokers in New Zealand from both high and low SES groups. They found no difference between the two in terms of their understanding of the health consequences of smoking; all participants showed a clear understanding of the relationship between smoking and diseases such as lung cancer and emphysema. Similarly, in the US, Narevic and Schoenberg (2002) asked a random sample of Kentucky residents to state what they thought was the most

BOX 3.5 EHEALTH LITERACY

DIG A LITTLE DEEPER

Health literacy refers to the skills required to access, use and understand health information. As well as being able to engage with advice from health professionals and follow instructions on medicines, these days the internet is increasingly used as an important source of information. However, the internet also contains a lot of nonsense! Thus successful use requires the consumer to consider the source of the information as well as its content. Norman and Skinner (2006) suggest that ehealth literacy entails six essential skills including traditional literacy and health literacy, but also media literacy that involves metacognitive processes used to take account of the social and political contexts that influence the messages that are delivered. Research shows that more educated individuals have higher levels of ehealth literacy (Neter & Brainin, 2002). Thus the internet may serve to reinforce socioeconomic inequalities in health.

important reason for the high rates of heart disease in Kentucky. Irrespective of level of education, most people were aware that smoking and poor diet were major risk factors.

Thus, it appears that regardless of socioeconomic status, or level of education, many people are aware of key health promotion messages, such as 'smoking is bad for you' or 'eat more fruit and vegetables'.

More complex behaviours

However, when issues become more complex, differences begin to emerge. For example, Wood et al. (2010) interviewed mothers from a socioeconomically deprived community in Wales about their understanding of healthy eating recommendations. Although mothers were aware of the link between poor diet and ill health and were familiar with government recommendations such as eating a balanced diet and plenty of fruit and vegetables, their knowledge of nutrition was often superficial and standard advice was sometimes misunderstood. For example, out of the 46 mothers interviewed, only 3 mentioned whole grain or brown foods and only 2 made reference to the importance of cooking methods (such as grilling rather than frying or steaming rather than boiling). Some reported confusion over the fact that drinks promoted as 'natural' could also be high in sugar, or they had difficulty understanding the distinctions between different types of fat (such as unhealthy saturates found mainly in animal products and healthy polyunsaturates found mainly in vegetable products). Some thought that a 'balanced diet' meant you could balance junk foods with good foods (rather than balance foods from all the major food groups).

Misunderstandings, and lack of knowledge, are not restricted to more deprived groups. If you were advised by your doctor to reduce your salt intake, would you know how to go about this? You might remove the salt shaker from your table and stop adding salt to your cooking, but would you realise that most of your salt comes from processed foods such as bread, cheese and meat products? Are you aware that even products such baked beans, breakfast cereals and tomato ketchup can be high in salt? Do you know that salt can also be labelled as 'sodium' or 'sodium chloride' on food packaging? And that you need to multiply the figure for sodium by 2.5 to get the amount of salt?

If you were not aware of these facts then you are not alone. Even very well-educated people have limited knowledge of dietary salt or how to interpret food labels (Land et al., 2014; McLean & Hoek, 2014; Okuda et al., 2014). Thus for behaviours such as smoking, where advice consists of a clear and easy distinction between a specific healthy behaviour (not smoking) and a specific unhealthy behaviour (smoking), lack of knowledge is unlikely to explain SES differences. This may also be true of messages that are difficult to map onto specific behaviours, such as reducing salt intake. In these cases, very few people may have the necessary knowledge to achieve such an outcome, so once again, differences in knowledge are unlikely to explain SES differences in behaviour. However, for other behaviours that fall somewhere in between, such as eating more fibre or reducing saturated fat, it is possible that level of education helps explain some of the association with SES.

Early life experiences

So if knowledge cannot account for SES differences in behaviours such as smoking, what can? One possibility is that early life experiences shape our personality, which in turn influences behaviour later in life.

Life-history theory

Early life experiences are a key feature of life-history theory. This theory draws on the principles of evolution to provide an account of how and why organisms allocate resources to competing life tasks (growth, body maintenance and reproduction) in order to maximise survival and reproduction (Ellis et al., 2009). Although we may be inclined to view behaviours such as smoking and unsafe sex as maladaptive, once we consider them from an evolutionary perspective, and take account of the context in which they occur, they can start to make more sense.

According to life-history theory, different behaviours are more or less advantageous in different types of environment. If we live in an environment that is both dangerous and has limited resources, there is a good chance we will not live very long. In this case, from an evolutionary point of view, it makes most sense to prioritise reproduction in order to ensure our genes are passed on before we die. By contrast, in an environment that is both safe and has plenty of resources, we are probably better off delaying childbirth in order to first invest in our own fitness. When we do finally reproduce, since our children are less likely to die, it makes sense to have fewer of them, but to invest more in each one.

In life-history theory these two different types of strategy are labelled as 'fast' and 'slow' respectively and are related to a number of other differences in behaviour. In particular, as well as earlier puberty, reproduction and a greater number of offspring, a fast life strategy is associated with a greater tendency to take risks and prioritise immediate gratification over longer term rewards. This seems perfectly reasonable. If you are not sure whether you will live into your 30s, risking your life for a large, immediate gain becomes more worthwhile. Likewise, why worry about lung cancer in your 50s if you are unlikely to ever reach that age? Especially if smoking provides a boost to your social status (and access to potential sexual partners) right now. Indeed, Nettle (2010) presents a mathematical model to illustrate how health preventive behaviours are of less benefit to those in lower socioeconomic positions.

By contrast, a slow life strategy is linked to less risky behaviours and more investment in long-term outcomes. In a stable, resource-abundant environment, this makes more sense. If you are likely to live into your 70s there is more time to invest in your own personal fitness before reproducing.

This is not to imply that teenagers sit down and weigh up their relative chances of successfully reproducing if they quit school early or pursue a career in medicine. Rather, research shows there are critical periods in childhood that influence life strategy. Simpson and colleagues looked at how childhood environment influenced later sexual and risky behaviours. They examined both the harshness of the environment, defined by SES, as well as the unpredictability of the environment, assessed by recording changes in the mother's employment status, changes in residence and changes in cohabitation (male romantic partners moving in or out). They found that at age 23, individuals who had experienced more unpredictable environments in the first 5 years of life subsequently had more sexual partners, engaged in more aggressive and delinquent behaviours (such as stealing and substance abuse) and were more likely to be associated with criminal activity (such as speeding, drug possession and prostitution). Exposure to harsh environments or unpredictability in later childhood (between the ages of 6 and 16) had no significant effect on these outcomes (Simpson et al., 2012).

Temporal discounting

These effects can be explained, at least in part, by differences in **temporal discounting**, risk taking and tendency to approach temptation (Griskevicius et al., 2013). These in turn may be

> **Temporal discounting** – sometimes called delay discounting, delay of gratification or future orientation, this refers to the tendency to prefer smaller, more immediate rewards over larger, more distant ones (see **Chapter 7**).

influenced by the person's sense of control; those from poorer backgrounds perceive environmental threats as less controllable than those from wealthier backgrounds (Mittal & Griskevicius, 2014). Research has also shown that a person's upbringing interacts with their current environment such that when resources are scarce, people from higher SES backgrounds tend to become less impulsive, more risk averse and approach temptations more slowly, whilst the reverse is true for those from lower SES backgrounds (Griskevicius et al., 2013).

Locus of control

The importance of a sense of control in childhood has been highlighted in other research too. Bosma and colleagues found that men and women in the Netherlands who grew up in families of low SES were more likely to have an external **locus of control** and a negative coping style. In other words, they were more likely to believe that events in their life were controlled by external factors over which they had little influence, and they were less likely to respond to difficult situations with active, problem-focussed coping (see **Chapter 4**). These particular personality traits predicted self-reported adult health independently of adult SES. The authors suggest that because children in lower SES families have parents with less money and education they are less likely to develop a sense of mastery and control over their lives, which leads to these specific personality traits (Bosma et al., 1999)

Subsequent research has also confirmed the importance of childhood locus of control on adult health-related behaviours; Gale et al. (2008) found that those with a more internal locus of control at age 10 were less likely to suffer from overweight or obesity aged 30. Locus of control at age 10 was higher among children with parents from higher SES backgrounds. Whitehead et al. (2016) suggest that these types of low control beliefs that are socialised in childhood influence adult health-related behaviours via a number of pathways including increased uncertainty about the future, which leads to behaviours that prioritise the present over the future, and low **self-efficacy** that limits success at behaviour change.

> **Locus of control** – the extent to which an individual feels they can control the events that affect them; a person with an external locus of control feels events are determined by external factors over which they have little influence, a person with an internal locus of control believes events are primarily determined by their own actions (see **Chapter 4**).

> **Self-efficacy** – a person's belief in their ability to perform a specific task or achieve a particular outcome (see **Chapter 4**).

Cognitive resources

Another way in which we can account for SES differences in health-related behaviours is via reduced cognitive resources. Mullainathan and Shafir (2013) argue that having too little of something has specific psychological effects that interfere with a person's ability to manage other aspects of their life. They suggest these effects can occur in relation to anything a person has a severe shortage of (such as time, social contact or food), though for those on very low incomes, this is likely to be money.

According to Mullainathan and Shafir (2013), when we have too little of something it captures our attention. This has the advantage of focussing our energies on addressing this need; we are more proficient at making judgements related to this shortage and less distracted by unrelated concerns (Shah et al., 2012, see also Shah et al., 2002). For example, when faced with a shortage of time, such as an approaching deadline, we become more productive; with a shortage of money, we show a greater awareness of the price of goods and are better at making price comparisons and recalling price information (Ariely & Wertenbroch, 2002; Binkley & Benjnarowicz, 2003; Goldin & Homonoff, 2013;

CHAPTER 3

Rosa-Diaz, 2004). However, this increased engagement comes at a cost, which is the neglect of other concerns that are unrelated to the shortage or that are relevant only in the more distant future. Mullainathan and Shafir argue that this effect stems from the fact that most of our cognitive resources are expended on addressing the shortage, which means we have less cognitive resources available for other tasks (Shah et al., 2012).

This effect is nicely illustrated in a study by Mani and colleagues who looked at poverty and cognitive performance among Indian sugarcane farmers. Sugarcane farmers receive most of their income once a year, after harvest. This means they tend to experience poverty in the months prior to harvest, as their savings are running out, but are better off after harvest when they receive their annual payment. Mani and colleagues compared cognitive function among these farmers before and after harvest. They found that their performance was significantly impaired before harvest, when they were poorer, compared with after harvest, when they were wealthier. This effect did not seem to be due to differences in time availability, nutrition, work effort, or stress. Rather, the authors argue, it was because poverty-related concerns drew on cognitive resources, leaving less available for other tasks. The difference in cognitive performance was the equivalent of approximately 13 IQ points, and nearly as disruptive as losing a full night's sleep (Mani et al., 2013).

Mullainathan and Shafir (2013) describe how this depletion of cognitive resources can help account for the fact that the poor in low-income countries are less likely to engage in a range of health protective behaviours such as getting their children vaccinated, washing their hands after using the toilet, or treating their water before drinking it. The same may also be true of the poor in high-income countries whose most pressing concerns may be how to pay the bills at the end of the week, not whether they are eating five portions of fruit and vegetables a day, or remembering to take the medication that has been prescribed to them by their doctor.

INCOME INEQUALITY AND HEALTH

At the start of this chapter, when comparing population health between countries, we saw how important money is; the poorest countries have the lowest life expectancies, the wealthiest countries the highest. But what about when a country has sufficient wealth to provide all the basics such as clean drinking water, healthcare and education? *Within* countries, SES and health tend to follow a gradient; even someone who is well off is likely to have slightly poorer health than someone who is very well off. Does the same pattern occur between countries?

Figure 3.3 shows the relationship between GDP per capita and life expectancy among high-income countries.[1] As you can see, population level income does not appear to be related to population level health.

In the late 1980s and early 1990s Richard Wilkinson published a series of articles suggesting that what mattered for health in rich countries was not absolute wealth but relative wealth (Wilkinson, 1990, 1992). In other words, countries with large gaps between rich and poor (high-income inequality) have poorer health than countries with smaller gaps between rich and poor (low-income inequality). In 1996 two articles were published in the prestigious *British Medical Journal* (*BMJ*) that supported this view; both showed that in the United States, between-state differences in income inequality were related to differences in mortality (Kaplan et al., 1996; Kennedy et al., 1996). The papers were

---

1   Defined by the World Bank as having a gross national income per capita of $12,535 in 2019 (World Bank, 2020b).

Figure 3.3 The relationship between GDP per capita ($) and life expectancy in high-income countries in 2019

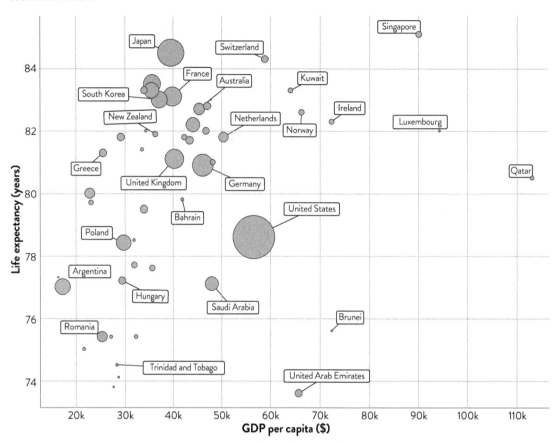

Notes: The size of the bubble represents the relative size of the population. Selected countries have been labelled.

Source: Created using free data and software from Gapminder.com, shared under the CC-BY licence.

accompanied by an editorial that described the income inequality hypothesis as a 'big idea' and highlighted the importance of the findings as follows:

> The more equally wealth is distributed the better the health of that society ... Measures [to redistribute wealth] would be more likely to be effective than measures that increased overall wealth but also increased inequalities – [the latter are] exactly the measures advocated over the past 10–20 years in Britain, the United States, and many other countries. (Smith, 1996)

The editorial highlights the political implications of the findings. Those on the left of the political spectrum tend to advocate wealth redistribution. They believe that those with more money should pay more taxes so these can be used to improve the living standards of those with less. Those on the right tend to feel that such an approach is inefficient; the process of redistributing money in itself is costly and we can't necessarily trust government to spend our cash wisely. Critically, those on the right also tend to believe that higher taxes act as a disincentive; the wealthiest take up residence elsewhere, big businesses decide it is more profitable to open offices and factories in other countries. According to the right, this means higher unemployment and less wealth for the country overall, so that in absolute terms, everyone gets poorer, including the poor. Allow for big profits, they claim, and all of society benefits.

You can see why the income inequality hypothesis is so controversial. What it is saying, essentially, is that if we allow the rich to get richer, it has a detrimental effect on the health of the whole population, even if there has been no change in the living standards of the poor.

Unsurprisingly this research has been hotly debated in both the academic and popular press. In 2009 Wilkinson and Pickett published a book called *The Spirit Level* which claimed that income inequality had an adverse effect, not just on health, but a range of other social problems such as teenage pregnancy, illiteracy and violence (Wilkinson & Pickett, 2010). The book has been widely cited by British politicians on the right as well as the left (Cameron, 2009; Miliband, 2010). However, the book has not been without its critics, with some accusing Wilkinson and Pickett of 'cherry picking' (selectively choosing) their data (Snowdon, 2010).

So, what is the evidence for the relationship between income inequality and health? And how do its proponents account for the association?

Explanations for effects

Social comparison

Earlier in this chapter we saw how social-evaluative threats cause stress. Wilkinson and Pickett (2006; 2010) draw on a similar literature to account for the relationship between income inequality and health; as the gap between rich and poor gets larger, so stress caused by social comparisons increases. If all our friends and neighbours enjoy designer clothes and exotic holidays, we may feel somewhat inadequate with our high street sweaters and camping trips in the rain. We are likely to feel even worse if we are unable to afford any new clothes or holidays. According to Wilkinson and Pickett, this is a source of stress that impacts negatively on our health.

Earlier in this chapter we also described research that showed that a monkey's rank within its social group could influence its immune function (Snyder-Mackler et al., 2016). The same may be true of humans and it is possible that a larger gap between rich and poor results in a larger effect on immune function.

Image 3.4 With increasing inequalities, we tend to see reductions in trust and social cohesion. This image shows spikes placed in a luxury housing complex in London, designed to deter homeless people from sleeping in the area. Credit: ullstein bild / Contributor.

Trust and social cohesion

Wilkinson and Pickett (2006, 2010) also argue that income inequalities are detrimental to health because they undermine trust and **social cohesion (Image 3.4)**. Trust and social cohesion are believed to be good for health because people who trust others and are socially integrated tend to live longer, whilst those who are more distrustful and more isolated are more likely to die prematurely

Social cohesion – the willingness of members of a society to cooperate with one another in order to bring about benefits for all members. In research studies, social cohesion is sometimes assessed using questions about trust.

(Barefoot et al., 1998; House et al., 1988; see also Giordano & Lindström, 2016). A lack of trust and social cohesion may also have additional adverse effects on health, for example, by increasing fear of crime (De Jesus et al., 2010; Stafford et al., 2007).

Kawachi and Kennedy (1997) argue that reduced social cohesion leads to increased residential segregation, with the better off isolating themselves in affluent communities that have more money to spend on public services and amenities such as schools, community centres and playgrounds. By contrast, those who are less well off are increasingly concentrated in poorer neighbourhoods with fewer amenities, more crime and under-resourced schools. This type of segregation and reduced social cohesion can also erode support for wealth redistribution (Kearns et al., 2014).

There is some research to support the view that income inequality influences health via reductions in trust and social cohesion. For example, Kawachi et al. (1997) looked at income inequality in 39 states in the US. They found that those who lived in states with higher levels of income inequality were less likely to be members of civic associations (such as church groups, sports groups and professional societies) and reported that they were less likely to trust others. These in turn were associated with higher mortality. Similarly, Elgar (2010) examined associations between income inequality, trust and health across 33 countries. He found that higher income inequality was associated with lower life expectancy and higher mortality and that these relationships were partly mediated (explained by) by differences in trust.

Social capital

Kawachi et al. (1997) also argue that a lack of social cohesion may contribute to a lack of **social capital**, which may further exacerbate the negative effects of stress, poverty and isolation. For example, in a community with high social capital, an elderly person living on their own may benefit from community efforts that lead to social events, a local environment that is better cared for, and initiatives, such as a neighbourhood watch scheme, that reduce crime. In a community with low social capital the same person may have even less social contact, be more likely to have an accident in neglected streets and be more fearful of crime. Research has found mixed evidence for relationships between income inequality, social capital and health (Jen et al., 2010; Meijer et al., 2012; Poortinga, 2006; 2012; Snelgrove et al., 2009).

> **Social capital** – the networks of relationships between individuals in a society that promote reciprocity and help bring about benefits for all members. Social cohesion and trust are sometimes viewed as one component of social capital.

Political ideology

An alternative (though not mutually exclusive) hypothesis is that income inequality reflects a political ideology that is associated with under-investment in public resources and welfare spending; the same governments that put in place policies that allow income inequalities to grow are the same governments that tend to cut public spending. According to this argument income inequality does not have a causal effect on population health, rather the two both come about as a result of particular government policies. Support for this argument comes from the United States where the association between state-level income inequality and mortality was partly accounted for by the level of local government expenditure on public services such as education and health (Dunn et al., 2005).

Measuring income inequality: the Gini coefficient

In order to evaluate the relationship between income inequality and health, we first need a way of assessing income inequality. Although there are several different ways of going about this, the most frequently used measure is the **Gini coefficient**. As well as comparing income inequality between countries, we can also use this coefficient to determine how income inequality has changed over time within a country. As shown in **Figure 3.4**, since the early 1980s, the Gini coefficient in many high-income countries has risen.

Do these increases in inequality matter? If they are accompanied by increases in wealth for everyone (with associated improvements in, for example, education, healthcare and leisure facilities) then perhaps increased inequality is the price we have to pay for overall improvements in health and wellbeing. What is the evidence that income inequality has adverse effects on health, over and above the effects of low income?

> **Gini coefficient** – a measure of inequality within a country. The measure gives a score from 0 to 1 where 0 indicates a population in which, after taxes and transfers, everyone receives the same income whilst 1 indicates a population in which, after taxes and transfers, all the income goes to just one individual.

Figure 3.4 Gini coefficient since 1970 in selected* high-income countries

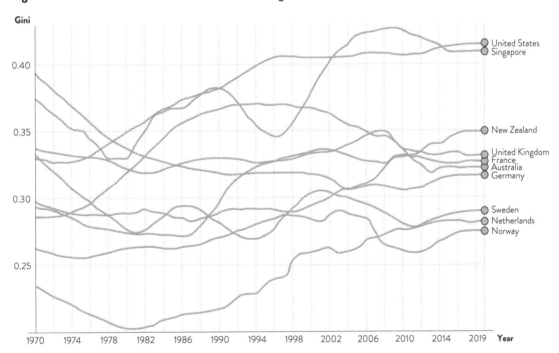

Note: *For the sake of clarity, only a small number of high-income countries are shown. You can explore data for other countries via **macmillanihe.com/tapper-health-psychology**.

Source: Created using free data and software from Gapminder.com, shared under the CC-BY licence.

Evidence for effects

In 1992 Wilkinson published research showing a significant correlation between life expectancy and income inequality and suggested that mortality tended to be lower in countries with a more egalitarian distribution of wealth (Wilkinson, 1992). However, Wilkinson's analysis relied on data from just nine countries and was criticised for the way it assessed income inequality (percentage of income received by the least well-off 70% of families, unadjusted for family size; Judge, 1995). Nevertheless, in 1996 two further research articles were published that supported the income inequality hypothesis; Kaplan et al. (1996) and Kennedy et al. (1996) both showed that state differences in income inequality in the United States were related to state differences in mortality.

However, in 2001, Lynch and colleagues looked at the relationship between income inequality and health in 16 high-income countries (Lynch et al., 2001). They found inconsistent associations between income inequality and a range of different health outcomes and no relationship between income inequality and life expectancy. Their research also highlighted some of the difficulties with this type of country-level cross-sectional analysis. For example, with only 16 countries the removal or addition of just one country can heavily influence the strength of any relationship. With such small numbers it is also difficult to control for cultural differences between countries that may be related to health outcomes. For example, people in Southern European countries are more likely to eat a Mediterranean diet which is associated with lower levels of heart disease (Estruch et al., 2013; Kunst et al, 1998).

Four additional studies in 2002 looked at relationships within the US, Copenhagen and Japan and also failed to find support for the income inequality hypothesis (Muller, 2002; Osler et al., 2002; Shibuya et al., 2002; Sturm & Gresenz, 2002). This caused some to suggest that the relationship may be specific to the US and may only occur because of the link between individual-level income and health (Mackenbach, 2002). In other words, income inequality effects may have emerged simply because populations with large inequalities are likely to have a larger proportion of people living in poverty.

However, more recently, Kondo and colleagues conducted a meta-analysis of both cross-sectional and prospective cohort studies (Kondo et al., 2009). They also employed multilevel analysis, in order to separate out effects on health associated with (a) individual-level income and (b) population-level income inequality. They found that income inequality *was* associated with an increased risk of both premature mortality and poor self-rated health. They also found support for a threshold effect; evidence that the relationship between income inequality and health only begins to emerge once Gini coefficients reach 0.3. This may be part of the reason for the inconsistencies within the literature.

Although the overall size of the income inequality effect was modest, Kondo and colleagues note that because it applies to such large numbers of people (whole populations) its potential impact is quite substantial. For example, they estimate that reducing the Gini coefficient to below 0.3 in 30 high-income countries could prevent over 1.5 million deaths annually. Nevertheless, they also note that their data do not enable them to rule out the possibility that the effects simply reflect other features of societies that influence health, such as political ideology or race relations. For this reason, it looks as though the controversy over income inequality and health is set to continue.

BOX 3.6 EVIDENCE-BASED POLICY

MAKING CONNECTIONS

The nature of the relationship between wealth and health has important political implications. To what extent is government policy influenced by research findings? Do policy makers weigh up evidence in an impartial manner, uninfluenced by their values and political biases? What about those carrying out the research? In **Chapter 11** we look at these questions and think about some of the challenges for evidence-based policy.

IMPLICATIONS FOR INTERVENTION

In 1999 the UK Department of Health published 'ten tips for better health' (DoH, 1999). These give evidence-based advice about health-related behaviours such as eating, being physically active, and making time to relax in order to manage stress. However, whilst these are all sound advice, they place responsibility for health squarely at the door of the individual. They assume we are all equally well equipped to de-stress and manage our behaviour.

In response to these tips, academics published a series of alternative tips (**Table 3.3**; Townsend Centre for International Poverty Research, 1999). Also based on research evidence, they draw attention to the fact that many of the important influences on our health are beyond our control. This shifts responsibility for health away from just the individual and encourages us to look towards society, particularly government, to help improve public health. For example, an individual may have little ability to avoid stressful low-paid manual work, but government legislation designed to improve working conditions and set minimum levels of pay might help alleviate some of the negative effects on health.[2]

Table 3.3 Ten tips for better health, put forward by England's Chief Medical Officer – and alternative tips proposed by academics from the Townsend Centre for International Poverty Research

Chief Medical Officer's ten tips for better health	Alternative tips
Don't smoke. If you can, stop. If you can't, cut down.	Don't be poor. If you are poor, try not to be poor for too long.
Follow a balanced diet with plenty of fruit and vegetables.	Don't live in a deprived area. If you do, move.
Keep physically active.	Don't be disabled or have a disabled child.
Manage stress by, for example, talking things through and making time to relax.	Don't work in a stressful low-paid manual job.
If you drink alcohol, do so in moderation.	Don't live in damp, low-quality housing or be homeless.
Cover up in the sun, and protect children from sunburn.	Be able to afford to pay for social activities and annual holidays.
Practise safer sex.	Don't be a lone parent.
Take up cancer screening opportunities.	Claim all benefits to which you are entitled.
Be safe on the roads: follow the Highway Code.	Be able to afford to own a car.
Learn the First Aid ABC: airways, breathing and circulation.	Use education as an opportunity to improve your socioeconomic position.

Source: DoH (1999); Townsend Centre for International Poverty Research (1999). Reproduced with permission.

At face value this type of intervention sounds like the remit of sociologists and policy makers rather than psychologists, but such issues are relevant for psychologists too. Given you are reading this book, you are probably sufficiently future oriented to have sacrificed a few immediate pleasures in order to study hard and achieve a good education. But it would be a mistake to assume that everyone sees the world as we do. For example, a well-meaning health psychologist may wonder why their intervention works wonderfully on middle-class professionals but falls flat when rolled out to blue-collar factory workers. Since those from lower SES groups tend to also be those who engage in the least healthy behaviours it is important to understand why this is the case.

Similarly, an anti-smoking campaign that draws attention to the horrors of lung cancer might work well in a nice middle-class school with aspirational children considering careers in medicine or banking; it may have less success with children from a deprived council estate

---

2   Whether there is an economic cost to such legislation, for example in terms of deterring outside investors or making it harder for small businesses to survive, and how such costs stack up against the financial benefits of a healthier population, is a debate we shall leave for the economists.

who have learned to place more value on the here and now. An intervention that taps into the things that are currently of most concern to these children may work better. Is there some way of linking smoking abstinence to immediate access to other sources of status?

Likewise, trying to educate parents about how to read nutritional labels and reduce their child's sugar intake may be a losing battle when all that parent's mental efforts are devoted to figuring out how they're going to pay rent at the end of each month. Is there an alternative form of intervention that avoids taxing the parent's already stretched cognitive resources? Could we do something that utilises their increased attention towards money, making healthy choices less expensive than unhealthy ones? Or perhaps we would be better off targeting the child instead?

We look at specific interventions in more detail in **Chapter 12**, and at theories of behaviour change in **Chapters 5 to 8**. As you go through these chapters, you may like to think about how appropriate these interventions and theories are for people from different social groups.

CONCLUSIONS

The time, place and family you're born into has an enormous impact on your health and life expectancy. Whilst the largest effects occur between rich and poor countries, even within wealthy countries such circumstances make a difference.

Prince George, who we met at the start of the chapter, might not enjoy such good health if he was being brought up near a busy, polluted main road by a single parent with an unstable lifestyle and little interest in education. How might his health compare in a household that is affluent, but not quite as prestigious as royalty? Assuming stability in his early years, the extent to which he develops and experiences a sense of control would seem to be key. Without knowing all the details of Prince George's life, we can only speculate about how this might differ for royalty relative to the rest of us. Any child that is supported in their attempts to manipulate the world around them may be more likely to develop an internal locus of control and an active coping style that will benefit their health in later years. But regal status may also buy influence that other wealthy individuals cannot necessarily achieve, whether it's access to the schools and university of your choice or knowing you have the ear of the prime minister. To what extent might such factors influence health? And how might they be balanced by other areas in which those of royal birth may experience less control? The average commoner rarely has to cope with intrusive paparazzi and private pictures that circulate the globe.

Whilst these particular questions may seem a little trivial, what is not trivial is that, rightly or wrongly, there are very real differences in the resources, power and influence that people from different walks of life experience, and these differences have very tangible effects on health.

Marjorie is a single mother of four children, all of whom have different fathers. She relies on state benefits. She has never had a job and has no intention of getting one. Should taxpayers' money be used to support Marjorie's way of life? How might increases or reductions in benefits impact upon the health of her children, both now and in the future? Are child benefits a good investment? Are there other things the government could do to improve the health and life chances of Marjorie's children?

THE GREAT DEBATE

INDIVIDUAL DETERMINANTS OF HEALTH

Chapter Outline

Genetics

Gene-based interventions

Personality

Personality-based interventions

Cognitive variables

Conclusions

For her eighth birthday, Marina was very excited to receive two pet gerbils. You can see them pictured below, a black one she called Midnight and a grey one she called Lightning (**Image 4.1**). Midnight and Lightning are brothers, from the same litter.

One of the first things Marina noticed about her gerbils was how different they looked from one another. Lightning is small and grey, with big eyes and ears and long whiskers. Midnight has soft, silky black fur and is a bit larger than Lightning. Indeed, one might even describe him as plump. Because they are siblings, they share approximately 50% of their genes. It's probably safe to assume their difference in colour is due to differences in genes that determine fur type. But what about their difference in weight? In **Chapter 2** we saw how certain environments promote weight gain, but Midnight and Lightning have experienced a shared environment, so environmental influences seem an unlikely explanation.

One possibility is that there are genetic differences between Midnight and Lightning that influence their physiology, which in turn influence their weight. Perhaps Midnight stores fat more easily than Lightning, or Lightning has a faster metabolism. However, as Marina got to know her gerbils better, she noticed how different they were in personality. Midnight never passes up an opportunity for a sunflower seed. He's also quite content to snooze in the crook of her arm, whilst she obligingly strokes his nose. All in all, he's one pretty chilled creature.

Image 4.1 *Midnight (left) enjoying a peanut. Lightning (right), on the lookout for adventure.*
Credit: Katy Tapper.

Lightning, on the other hand, has more of a take-it-or-leave-it attitude to sunflower seeds. He's likely to be found racing around, digging tunnels and shredding cardboard tubes, with a kind of furious enthusiasm that seems to imply he has *far* more important things to do than simply eat or sleep. So another explanation for their difference in weight is that Midnight eats more and moves less, whilst Lightning eats less and moves more. But why? What are the pathways from genes to behaviour?

In this chapter we look at individual differences, from the biological to the psychological, and the ways in which these differences influence health. More specifically we will:

- Look at the ways in which our genes directly influence our health, causing or predisposing us toward certain health conditions.

- Think about the ways in which our genes influence health indirectly, through their effects on personality and behaviour.

- Examine less stable cognitive variables that may be influenced by both personality and environment.

- Consider the implications of these fields for interventions designed to improve health.

GENETICS

Our genes have a profound effect on our health. In this section we consider the nature of these effects. However, in order to do so, it is first important to understand a little more about what exactly genes are and how they are passed on from parents to offspring.

The relationship between body and genes can be summarised as follows:

- Our body is a collection of different types of cells.

- Each of these cells contains a nucleus that in turn contains 46 chromosomes (23 pairs).

- These chromosomes are made up of DNA (deoxyribonucleic acid).

- DNA consists of molecules called 'nucleotides' that are made up of sugar, phosphate and a chemical base, all arranged in a double helix structure (see **Figure 4.1**).

- The chemical base can be one of four different types; adenine (A), guanine (G), cytosine (C) or thymine (T).

It is the order of these chemical bases that acts as a code or set of instructions for building and maintaining the body; a little like the letters of the alphabet can be rearranged to form words and sentences, and to convey meaning.

Figure 4.1 The structure of DNA

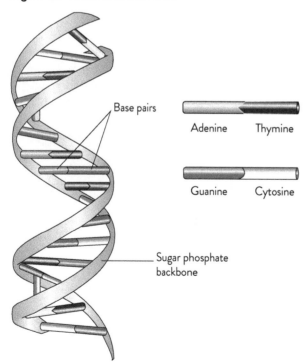

Base pairs

Adenine   Thymine

Guanine   Cytosine

Sugar phosphate backbone

Note. DNA comprises a series of chemical bases, attached to a sugar phosphate backbone. The double helix structure was discovered by Watson and Crick in 1953.

Source: US National Library of Medicine. Reproduced with permission.

Genes are regions of DNA that determine the **phenotype** of a living organism and can vary in size from a few hundred DNA bases to more than 2 million. Most biological traits are polygenetic, in other words they are influenced by many different genes.

> **Phenotype** – an organism's observable characteristics, for example its appearance, physiology and behaviour.

Genes are also the way in which biological traits are passed from parent to offspring. Recall that each cell in the body contains 23 pairs of chromosomes. One chromosome of each pair will have been inherited from the father and one from the mother and each will contain their own version of every gene. These different versions are called 'alleles'. If the alleles from the mother and father are identical they are referred to as homozygous, if they are different they are referred to as heterozygous. Sperm and egg cells are formed by a process known as 'meiosis', in which cells divide to form new cells with just one randomly selected chromosome from each pair. This means the sperm and egg cells have just 23 chromosomes in total and will vary from each other according to the chromosomes they contain. When an egg is fertilised the chromosomes in the egg and sperm come together to form a new set of 46 chromosomes, half from the mother and half from the father.

It is this passing of chromosomes and genes from parent to child that gives some health conditions a hereditary component. In other words, we find they tend to run in families.

When genes have a direct effect on health: cystic fibrosis

One example of a hereditary condition that has a direct effect on health is cystic fibrosis. Cystic fibrosis leads to the build-up of thick, sticky mucus in the lungs and digestive system. As a result, the individual may experience difficulty breathing, have frequent chest infections and, because mucus blocks the flow of digestive juices, they may also suffer from malnutrition, poor growth in childhood and physical weakness. Cystic fibrosis is a progressive condition, which means it gets worse over time; the lungs tend to become damaged and may eventually stop working. Currently, only about half of all people diagnosed with cystic fibrosis live beyond 40 (though advances in medical care mean that babies born with the condition today are likely to live longer).

Cystic fibrosis is an inherited condition which occurs because of a mutation on a particular gene that controls the movement of salt and water through cell walls. However, this version of the gene is recessive. In other words, it only expresses itself if there are two versions of the mutation, one on the chromosome inherited from the father and one on the chromosome inherited from the mother. If there is just one version of the mutation the individual is considered a carrier of the condition but will not suffer from it. What this means in practice is that a baby is only at risk of suffering from cystic fibrosis if both parents carry the genetic mutation, and even then a baby will only have a 1 in 4 chance of inheriting both copies of the mutation and suffering from the condition (see **Figure 4.2**). Approximately 1 in 25 individuals of European descent are carriers of the cystic fibrosis mutation (Cystic Fibrosis Genetic Analysis Consortium, 2005; see **Box 4.1**).

Figure 4.2 Chances of suffering from cystic fibrosis where both parents are carriers of the gene

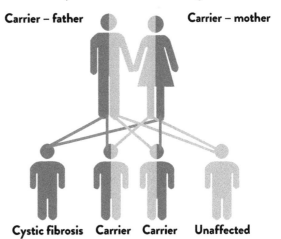

Carrier – father   Carrier – mother

Cystic fibrosis   **Carrier**   **Carrier**   **Unaffected**

Note: If both parents carry the cystic fibrosis gene, their children have a 25% chance of suffering from cystic fibrosis, a 50% chance of being a carrier, and a 25% chance of being unaffected.

Credit: Cystic Fibrosis Trust. Reproduced with permission.

BOX 4.1 WHY DO LETHAL GENE MUTATIONS PERSIST IN A POPULATION?

AS AN ASIDE

Cystic fibrosis is thought to have been around for at least 11,000 years (Wiuf, 2001). But if two copies of the gene are so bad for health (meaning the sufferer is less likely to live long enough to have children) we would expect the mutation to gradually disappear. So how can we account for the fact that it has persisted and spread through the population?

The answer may be that a single copy of the gene actually confers a survival advantage. Research has shown that those who carry the gene have some resistance to tuberculosis, because tuberculosis bacteria need a nutrient that is not made by those with the cystic fibrosis mutation (Tobacman, 2003). Thus, those who were cystic fibrosis carriers, but not sufferers, would have been more likely to survive a tuberculosis epidemic and pass the mutation on to their children. This interpretation is consistent with the fact that Europe suffered from a particularly severe outbreak of tuberculosis between 1600 and 1900, causing 20% of all deaths, and that today cystic fibrosis is more prevalent among those of European descent (Poolman & Galvani, 2016). The cystic fibrosis mutation also seems to provide some resistance against cholera, again meaning the mutation is more prevalent in regions where cholera is or was endemic (Withrock et al., 2015; see **Chapters 1 and 2**).

Similar explanations have also been put forward to account for other potentially fatal hereditary diseases. For example, sickle cell anaemia is associated with sickle-shaped red blood cells that do not live as long as normal red blood cells and are also more likely to become stuck in blood vessels. The condition can lead to heart disease, stroke, organ damage and increased bacterial infection (Rees et al., 2010). Like cystic fibrosis, a person will only suffer from the disease if they have two copies of the sickle cell gene mutation. Research shows that having just one copy of the mutation offers some protection from malaria, a potentially fatal infectious disease spread by mosquitoes in tropical countries (Williams et al., 2005). This is consistent with the fact that sickle cell anaemia is most common in sub-Saharan Africa where deaths from malaria are at their highest (Murray et al., 2012; Rees et al 2010).

When genes predispose toward health conditions: breast cancer

In other instances, a person's genetic make-up may predispose them toward a particular disease, rather than directly cause it. This is true of breast cancer, the most common form of cancer among women.

Rates of breast cancer tend to be higher in wealthier countries, particularly those in Western Europe and North America. For example, for a woman in the United States, the lifetime risk of developing breast cancer is around 12%. In other words, 1 in 8 women will develop breast cancer during their life (Siegel et al., 2016; Stewart & Wild, 2014). This high incidence has led many countries to introduce screening programmes, designed to identify breast cancer at an early stage, before it becomes symptomatic. However, as discussed in **Box 4.2**, screening comes with its own risks.

Smoking, overweight and alcohol increase a woman's risk of developing breast cancer whilst breastfeeding and physical activity exert a protective effect (Beral et al., 2002; Macacu et al., 2015; Michels et al., 2007; Monninkhof et al., 2007). However, by far

BOX 4.2 TO SCREEN OR NOT TO SCREEN?

HOT TOPIC

Screening programmes are used to detect undiagnosed disease in individuals who are asymptomatic (in other words, they have no disease symptoms). The aim is to identify disease early, so it is easier to treat. Like other preventive measures, such as visiting the dentist or taking regular exercise, this all sounds eminently sensible. So why did the Swiss Medical Board recommend their country's breast screening programme be abandoned?

A good screening test is one with both high sensitivity (able to correctly identify a person with the disease) and high specificity (able to correctly identify someone without the disease). But screening tests are rarely perfect so can lead to false negatives (failing to identify the disease) and false positives (identifying disease where there is none).

Breast screening is carried out in order to detect cancers in their very early stages, when they are too small to be felt or seen. It means offering women above a certain age regular mammograms (breast X-rays). The Swiss Medical Board argued that breast screening results in too many false positives (Biller-Andorno & Jüni, 2014). This means women are called back for repeat mammograms and biopsies which cause unnecessary worry. In some instances, women are diagnosed and treated for benign breast cancers that would never have caused them any harm. They may undergo unnecessary surgery, radiotherapy and chemotherapy. Data suggest that for every 1,000 women screened annually for a decade, 0.3 to 3.2 will have life-saving treatment, 490 to 670 will have at least one false alarm, and 3 to 14 will undergo unnecessary treatment (Welch & Passow, 2014). As such, the Swiss Medical Board concluded that screening is not cost-effective and that its harms outweigh its benefits.

Similar controversy exists over screening men for cancer of the prostate (a gland that lies just below the bladder and secretes fluid that helps make up semen). A blood test can be used to measure the amounts of prostate specific antigen (PSA) in the blood, with raised levels being a possible sign of prostate cancer. However, the PSA test is not terribly accurate, showing both poor sensitivity and poor specificity (Thompson et al., 2014; Wolf et al., 2010). It also cannot distinguish between fast-growing, aggressive cancers, and more common slow-growing cancers that are unlikely to ever cause any problems. Testing can therefore lead to overdiagnosis and over-treatment. For example, one trial estimated that 1,410 men would need to be screened and 48 cases of cancer would need to be treated in order to prevent just one death (Schröder et al., 2009). Other trials have failed to find any reduction in deaths from prostate cancer as a result of screening programmes (Ilic et al., 2013). Since side effects of treatment for prostate cancer can be significant, for example urinary incontinence and reduced sexual function (Donovan et al., 2016), again one could argue that the harms do not outweigh the benefits.

the biggest risk factors are being older and having a family history of breast cancer (Beral et al., 2001; McPherson et al., 2000). The latter illustrates the important role genetics plays in the aetiology (cause) of this disease. This is also highlighted by the identification of specific genetic mutations that have been shown to be important. For example, mutations on the BRCA1 and BRCA2 genes increase the risk of breast cancer from 12% to 57% and 49% respectively (Chen & Parmigiani, 2007).

CHAPTER 4

So unlike cystic fibrosis, which is directly determined by a particular genetic mutation, with breast cancer the relationship between genes and disease is more complex; whether or not a woman develops breast cancer will depend on interactions between genes, environment and behaviour. We now turn to another condition that, at first glance, may seem to be more linked to behaviour than genes.

Complex gene-health relationships: obesity

Obesity runs in families. If a child belongs to a family of healthy weight individuals, their chances of obesity are less than 5%. But if a child belongs to a family that suffers from obesity, the likelihood that they will also suffer from obesity rises to over 25% (Garn et al., 1981).

However, this information does not tell us much about the cause of obesity; children could be similar to their parents and siblings, either because of shared genes or because of shared environment (or a combination of the two). In an attempt to untangle these influences Börjeson compared similarities in fat and body weight between monozygotic and dizygotic twins (Börjeson, 1976). Monozygotic ('identical') twins are twins that are formed when a single fertilised egg splits in two, resulting in two separate embryos that develop into two separate foetuses. Because such twins originated from the same sperm and egg, they have the same chromosomes and genetically they are nearly identical.[1] By contrast, dizygotic twins ('non-identical' or 'fraternal' twins) occur when a woman releases two eggs at ovulation and these are both fertilised by two different sperm. Thus although such twins would have shared a womb, genetically they will be no more similar than ordinary siblings. In other words, they will share, on average,[2] 50% of their genes. This means that if genes play a role in obesity we would expect monozygotic twins to suffer from more similar levels of obesity compared to dizygotic twins.

This is exactly what Börjeson found, leading him to conclude that genetic factors do play a role in obesity. Since this study, other research has indicated that between 40% to 70% of variation in body mass index (BMI) within a population is the result of genetic differences (Ramachandrappa & Farooqi, 2011).

But how do genes influence obesity? Are there genes that directly cause obesity, like the genetic mutation that causes cystic fibrosis? Or is the relationship more like that between genes and breast cancer? In other words, do genes predispose a person to obesity rather than directly cause it? Since Börjeson's twin study in 1976 we have seen huge advances in the field of genetics that are helping us answer such questions.

Monogenic obesity

One important discovery is that there are a number of different single gene mutations that result in obesity (Farooqi & O'Rahilly, 2005). This type of obesity is referred to as 'monogenic obesity', meaning that a variant of a single gene exerts a strong effect on the phenotype, resulting in a very close relationship between genotype and phenotype. Such instances are often associated with hormonal disorders and typically result in severe obesity that occurs shortly after birth or early in childhood. For example, leptin is a hormone that helps regulate hunger and satiety (feelings of fullness). Individuals with mutations in genes associated

---

1 They are not 100% identical as genetic mutations may occur after the fertilised egg has split in two (Li et al., 2014).

2 On average, because the chromosomes we inherit from our mother and father are selected at random, so in theory two siblings could end up inheriting exactly the same chromosomes or completely different ones. This means that some siblings will be more genetically similar than others, but *on average* we would expect similarity to be around 50%.

with leptin synthesis or secretion may suffer from **congenital** leptin deficiency. Although such individuals tend to be a normal weight at birth, they display constant food-seeking behaviour, hyperphagia (excessive appetite and eating) and impaired satiety. As a result they show rapid weight gain and severe early-onset obesity (Funcke et al., 2014). They can be successfully treated with daily injections of leptin (Paz-Fiho et al., 2011).

> **Congenital** – a disease or physical abnormality present from birth.

Syndromic obesity

Genetic variation can also result in what is known as 'syndromic obesity', where obesity is accompanied by specific learning disabilities and developmental abnormalities (Mutch & Clément, 2006). These syndromes can arise from specific genetic mutations or chromosomal abnormalities. They differ from monogenic obesity in that the same phenotype may arise in different individuals via different genetic mutations or abnormalities. Thus whilst there is still a direct relationship between genes and obesity, the ways in which we categorise monogenic and syndromic obesity differ; the former is categorised according to the specific gene mutation, the latter according to the syndrome.

Prader-Willi syndrome is the most common syndromal cause of obesity (Mutch & Clément, 2006). It is characterised by distinctive facial features, learning difficulties, lack of sexual development, restricted growth, reduced muscle tone (hypotonia) as well as hyperphagia. It occurs due to abnormalities on a specific chromosome that arise purely by chance.

However, both monogenic and syndromic obesity are very rare. For example, Prader-Willi syndrome occurs in just 1 in 25,000 births (Mutch & Clément, 2006) and congenital leptin deficiency is so rare that only a handful of cases have been reported (Wasim et al., 2016). Thus, neither can account for the fact that around 13% of the world's population now suffers from obesity (WHO, 2016a).

> **Glycogen** – a substance that is stored in the body and readily converted to glucose when the organism needs energy. Energy is also stored in the body in the form of fat.

Polygenic obesity

More than 95% of all instances of obesity can instead be described as 'polygenic' (Huvenne & Dubern, 2014). In other words, they are the result of the effects of a number of different genes. In isolation these genes may each have a relatively small effect on weight, but where someone carries a large number of genes that promote weight gain, the cumulative effect can be quite large.

Some of these differences may be physiological. For example, some people may less readily convert dietary fat to energy. This means that when eating a high fat diet, **glycogen** stores are depleted, which in turn stimulates appetite and energy intake, leading the person to consume more (Astrup, 2011). Additionally, researchers have identified a particular gene variant associated with a slower **metabolism**. This variant is more common in people with severe early-onset obesity compared with those of a healthy weight. However, it has only been found in just over 2% of people with severe obesity (compared to 1% of the population), again meaning that although it may contribute to obesity, it is far from the only explanation (Pearce et al., 2013).

> **Metabolism** – all the chemical reactions within cells and living organisms that sustain life, such as repairing cells, breathing and digesting food. The amount of energy the body needs to carry out these processes is referred to as the 'basal metabolic rate' (BMR). It takes more energy to maintain muscle than fat so those with a higher muscle to fat ratio will have a higher BMR (or 'faster' metabolism). People with overweight will also have a higher BMR as more energy is needed to maintain a larger body. Diets that severely restrict calories can reduce BMR because the body breaks down muscle for energy.

But are these types of physiological differences the whole story? Recall our two gerbils, Midnight and Lightning. They have distinct personalities that influence both their willingness to sit quietly and their propensity to eat sunflower seeds. Might we see similar differences in people? Could genes influence weight gain and obesity because of their effects on eating and activity?

A wide range of studies suggest that people differ in the extent to which they respond to food cues. For example, people vary in the degree to which they direct their attention toward images of food, salivate in the presence of palatable foods and choose food rewards over other incentives (Aspen et al., 2012; Epstein et al., 1996; Hendrikse et al., 2015; Saelens & Epstein, 1996; Tapper et al., 2010). Some people also eat much faster than others (Llewellyn et al., 2008). In many instances these differences correspond to differences in weight, with those who suffer from overweight or obesity being more responsive to food cues than their healthy weight counterparts. More recently, research with children has suggested that this type of food responsiveness may have a hereditary component, in other words it may be influenced by a person's genes (**Image 4.2**) (Carnell et al., 2008; Carnell & Wardle, 2008).

Image 4.2 *When offered a serving of grated cheese, Theo decided he would much prefer the whole block. Young children are very variable in their responses to food and this has been shown to have a genetic component.*
Credit: Katy Tapper.

Similarly, research has also shown that people differ in the extent to which they perceive or respond to feelings of fullness (satiety). For example, research has found differences in people's ability to perceive internal bodily sensations, such as their own heartbeat and gastric sensations ('interoceptive awareness'), with lower interoceptive awareness predicting a higher BMI (Herbert et al., 2013; Herbert et al., 2012). Again, research with children indicates that satiety responsiveness has a genetic component (Carnell et al., 2008; Carnell & Wardle, 2008; Llewellyn et al., 2014; Maillard et al., 2015; Wardle et al., 2008).

So it seems that our genes can influence our response to food and eating. But what about energy expenditure? Are there genetic differences that could account for Lightning's seeming inability to sit still? Humans show substantial individual differences in energy expenditure. This is partly a result of differences in spontaneous physical activity

(SPA), for example voluntarily choosing to participate in an exercise class, play a sport, or go for a walk. This type of exercise participation seems to be influenced by a person's genes. For example, one study conducted with over 85,000 twins across seven different countries (including Australia, Norway and the Netherlands) suggested that genetics accounts for between 48% and 71% of the variability between individuals in exercise participation (Stubbe et al., 2006). Although the specific mechanisms underlying such an effect have yet to be identified, the authors of this study suggested that they could be the result of differences in personality traits such as conscientiousness, differences in physiology that influence the extent to which people find exercise rewarding or aversive, and/or differences in exercise ability, for example in strength and endurance, which in turn may influence positive feelings of mastery and competence when engaging in exercise.

However, energy expenditure is also influenced by non-exercise activity thermogenesis (NEAT). As described in **Chapter 2**, NEAT refers to energy that is expended for all activities apart from eating, sleeping and voluntary exercise (Levine, 2003). This ranges from behaviours such as walking to work and mowing the lawn to fidgeting and spontaneous muscle contraction. Research shows that after eating excess calories, some people are more likely to compensate for this by increasing NEAT, whilst others are not. Those who show this compensation are more resistant to weight gain (Levine et al., 1999). Similarly, individuals with obesity show lower levels of NEAT compared to those who are lean. The fact that this tendency does not change when a person with obesity loses weight, or when someone who is lean gains weight, suggests that it has a genetic component (Levine et al., 2005). Indeed, a gene linked to increased NEAT has now been identified in mice (Sakkou et al., 2007).

Thus, whether or not someone suffers from obesity is, to some degree, influenced by their genes (**Box 4.3**). However, it is rarely the case that genes directly cause obesity. Instead, the pathways from genes to body weight are both numerous and complex, often mediated by behaviours such as our response to food and our tendency to expend energy.

BOX 4.3 BLAMING YOUR GENES: EFFECTS OF GENETIC DETERMINISM ON WEIGHT STIGMA AND WEIGHT LOSS-RELATED BEHAVIOURS HOT TOPIC

People who suffer from obesity are often perceived as lazy and lacking in self-discipline (Puhl & Heuer, 2009; Teachman et al., 2003). As a result, they frequently experience stigmatisation and discrimination (see **Chapter 12**).

So could we reduce weight stigma by increasing public knowledge of the genetic influences on obesity? The answer to this question seems to be a tentative 'possibly' (Hilbert, 2016). However, such an approach may also have a downside; a belief in genetic determinism seems to be associated with a more fatalistic attitude that could lead to both sufferers and healthcare providers feeling that efforts to control weight are futile (Dar-Nimrod & Heine, 2011; Dar-Nimrod et al., 2014).

Epigenetics

From the literature described so far, it is clear that our genes influence both our health and our health-related behaviours. However, over the last couple of decades, new findings have emerged that suggest that the relationship between genes and health is even more complex than we first thought. This is highlighted in the following example.

In September 1944, toward the end of the Second World War, the German administration blocked the transport of food and fuel supplies to the western Netherlands. This, together with an unusually harsh winter that froze canals and prevented the movement of barges, led to severe food shortages and widespread famine. As food stocks in cities ran out, official rations in some areas dropped to under 500 calories a day, forcing people to eat sugar beet and tulip bulbs and burn furniture to keep warm. Some townspeople walked for several days in snow or rain to try to buy food for their families from farmers. Many lost their lives doing so. Overall, around 4.5 million people were affected by what has become known in the Netherlands as the *Hongerwinter* (Hunger winter, **Image 4.3**). It is estimated that at least 10,000 people died as a direct result of malnutrition and many more from related causes (Banning, 1946).

Image 4.3 *Toward the end of the Second World War, millions of people in the Netherlands suffered from malnutrition, the effects of which are still being felt generations later. This picture was taken during April/May 1945, following air drops of food by the Allies. It shows a woman and her daughter gathering bits of food that have fallen from trucks transporting the air drops.*
Credit: Image Bank WW2 - NIOD, www.niod.nl.

Inevitably, some women were pregnant, or became pregnant, during the time of this famine and data collected from these women and their children have been used to look at the effects of prenatal exposure to famine on later health. These data show that those who were conceived during the famine were more likely to suffer from worse health later in life. For example, they showed poorer glucose tolerance (which increases the risk of type 2 diabetes) and higher levels of obesity and coronary heart disease (Painter et al., 2006; Ravelli et al., 1976, 1998; Roseboom et al., 2000). This in itself is perhaps unsurprising; it shows that a person's later health can be adversely affected if they fail to receive sufficient nutrients during their development in the womb. However, what was surprising was that these children's own children, who were never exposed to any famine, were also more likely to suffer from poor health (Painter et al., 2008; though see also Veenendaal et al., 2013). This raises the possibility that environmental influences (such as famine) can somehow leave marks upon a person's genes, and that these marks can then be passed on to subsequent generations.

Other research supports this view that our environment and our behaviour can indeed affect our genes, and that these effects can influence the health of future generations. For example, harvest records from an isolated community in northern Sweden have been used to show that access to greater quantities of food in the years just before puberty was associated with a reduced lifespan among grandchildren. This effect was sex-specific; men's diet influenced the longevity of their grandsons whilst women's diet influenced the longevity of their granddaughters (Pembrey et al., 2006). Similarly, a survey of British couples who gave birth in the early 1990s showed that men who started smoking before the age of 11 had sons who were heavier than average at age 9 (Pembrey et al., 2006).

This field of research is termed **epigenetics**. Laboratory work has shown that the mechanism underlying such effects consists of biological markers placed on an individual's genes during their development or lifetime. These markers influence the way in which these genes are expressed. They function a bit like on-off switches or volume knobs, turning the effects of genes up or down,

> **Epigenetics** – the study of changes in gene function that are heritable but which do not involve a change in DNA sequence.

or switching them on or off entirely. Although most of these markers are wiped clean prior to or just after conception, a small percentage remain, where they are passed on to future generations. It is this type of 'transgenerational' epigenetic effect that is thought to be responsible for the effects of nutrition and smoking on subsequent generations, as described in the studies above.

CHAPTER 4

BOX 4.4 EPIGENETICS AND NATURAL SELECTION

MAKING CONNECTIONS

In **Chapter 2** we saw how natural selection has shaped the biology and psychology of our species. Why might epigenetic effects be advantageous for a species? In what types of circumstances might they enhance the survival or reproduction of an individual? To what extent are these circumstances relevant today?

Other research has shown how epigenetic effects can also influence our psychological make-up. Weaver et al. (2004) compared rat pups from two different types of mothers: 'attentive' mothers, who spent a long time licking, grooming and feeding their babies in the first few weeks of life, and 'inattentive' mothers, who engaged in less of this behaviour. The pups of inattentive mothers display higher levels of stress in adulthood, for example in novel environments they are slower to eat and spend less time exploring. They also exhibit increased physiological responses to stress. Weaver et al. examined the genes that regulate stress sensitivity and found that in the pups of inattentive mothers the DNA in these genes were methylated, in other words, the genes had been epigenetically marked. When they switched pups and mothers at birth, they still found that those pups who had been looked after by the inattentive mothers had evidence of epigenetic marking on the genes that regulate stress, suggesting that the critical variable was the pups' environment – how they were treated by their mother – rather than the genes they had inherited. Weaver et al. (2006) later went on to remove the epigenetic marks by injecting the pups of inattentive mothers with a drug that removes methyl. They found that these pups grew up to behave like the pups of attentive mothers, displaying lower levels of stress.

These experiments show how early experiences could influence a person's response to stress in later life. Indeed, those with a history of child abuse tend to display an altered stress response and recent research has found evidence of epigenetic marking among such individuals (McGowan et al., 2009).

Such findings are revolutionising the way we think about the effects of genes and environment on health and behaviour. In particular, if transgenerational epigenetic effects are firmly established in humans, the implications are profound. They mean that the lifestyle decisions your grandparents made could be influencing your health today. Likewise, the decisions you make could influence not only your health, but also the health of your children and your children's children. They mean that the impact of war, poverty and pollution could echo down the generations for many years to come. And they raise the possibility that recent increases in conditions such as obesity and diabetes could be the result of events that occurred a century ago. At the moment such possibilities are largely speculation, but at the very least the field of epigenetics seems set to change the way we view the relationship between genes, health and behaviour.

BOX 4.5 EPIGENETICS AND HEALTH INEQUALITIES

MAKING CONNECTIONS

In **Chapter 3** we looked at the different ways in which upbringing and environment could lead to inequalities in health. How might epigenetic effects also contribute to health inequalities?

Genes, sex and ethnicity

As well as varying between individuals, genes also vary across sex and ethnicity, making particular groups more or less susceptible to different diseases. For example, females tend to have a stronger immune system than males. This means females are less likely to die from infectious diseases in infancy, are less likely to suffer from non-reproductive malignant cancers, such as lung, bowel and stomach cancer, and have a greater antibody response to vaccines (making vaccines more effective). However, it also means females are more susceptible to autoimmune diseases (where the immune system attacks the body) such as rheumatoid arthritis and multiple sclerosis (Klein & Flannagan, 2016).

In this chapter we have also seen examples of how those from different parts of the world are more likely to suffer from different diseases because of a history of particular selection pressures within the environment. For example, cystic fibrosis is more prevalent among those of European descent whilst sickle cell anaemia is most common in sub-Saharan Africa (**Box 4.1**).

However, these genetic differences should not blind us to the social influences on health that so often co-vary with both sex and ethnicity. In **Chapter 3** we saw how our health is influenced by a wide range of social factors including living conditions, occupation, stress and social status. Arguably such factors have a much larger impact than genes on the differences in health we see across both gender and ethnicity.

GENE-BASED INTERVENTIONS

Given the advances in our understanding of the relationships between genes and health, how is this influencing modern medicine? In this section we look at some recent developments in gene-based interventions. These fall into three broad categories:

- Interventions that change a person's genes (gene therapy)

- Interventions that identify those at risk of a particular disease to allow them to receive specific treatments (genetic screening)

- Interventions that are tailored to match the genetic profile of the individual in order to maximise their efficacy (personalised medicine).

Gene therapy

Gene therapy involves 'fixing' a specific gene mutation. One way of achieving this is to add new healthy genetic material to a person's cells. This can be achieved via a **retrovirus**. Retroviruses introduce genetic information into cells when they infect them so scientists have used them as a means of transporting healthy DNA into the body. **Liposomes** have also been used for DNA transportation as they fuse with the outer membrane of cells, which means any DNA they are carrying gets released into the cell. This technique was used in a trial with cystic fibrosis patients; over a 12-month period, those who, every month, inhaled a vaporised solution containing DNA-carrying liposomes showed a small but significant improvement in lung function compared to those who inhaled an inert saline solution (Alton et al., 2015).

Another form of gene therapy is gene editing (or genome editing). Rather than simply inserting additional genetic material into cells, gene editing involves disabling sections of DNA or cutting them out and inserting replacement sections. This technique was used successfully in the UK in 2015 to cure an 11-month-old baby girl of **leukaemia** (Reardon, 2015). Trials with other cancer patients are currently underway. As well as treating disease, in principle this technique could also be used to prevent genetic disorders by modifying genes in embryos.

Mitochondrial replacement therapy is used to prevent children from inheriting genetic disorders caused by mutations in the **mitochondria**, which are highly aggressive and fatal. Mitochondria contain a very small amount of DNA, which makes up just 37 genes (compared to the 23,000-odd contained in the chromosomes in the cell nucleus). However, harmful mutations on these genes can interfere with the cells' ability to make energy which can in turn result in fatal disorders such as Leigh syndrome that typically results in death within two to three years. Unlike the DNA contained in the chromosomes, mitochondrial DNA is passed down through the maternal line only. This means that although a son may inherit a mitochondrial disorder from his mother, he would not pass it on to his children.

Mitochondrial replacement therapy involves removing the nucleus from an egg or fertilised embryo and placing it in a donor egg (with healthy mitochondria) from which the nucleus has been removed. Where this donor egg comes from a third person, in effect this creates a three-parent baby (albeit with the third parent contributing a minuscule amount of DNA, and none that influences appearance or personality). The world's first three-parent baby was born in Mexico in 2016 (Zhang et al., 2016). In 2016 the UK also became the first country to formally approve the use of mitochondrial replacement therapy.

> **Retrovirus** – a virus is an infectious agent, 100 times smaller than a single bacteria cell. Unlike bacteria, viruses can only reproduce inside the living cells of other organisms. A retrovirus is a particular type of virus that can alter the chromosomal DNA of the host cell.

> **Liposome** – a minute spherical sac of phospholipid molecules, containing a droplet of water.

> **Leukaemia** – cancer of the white blood cells.

> **Mitochondria** – energy producing structures situated in cell fluid, outside the cell nucleus.

Genetic screening

As noted previously, genetic testing can be used to determine whether a person carries specific genes that will influence their likelihood of having a child with a genetic disorder (such as cystic fibrosis) or of their chances of developing a particular disease themselves (such as breast cancer). Some prenatal screening tests are routinely carried out for those considered at high risk of specific single-gene disorders. For example, pregnant women

In vitro fertilisation (IVF) – a process in which an egg is fertilised by a sperm outside the body. ('In vitro' means 'in glass'.)

Huntington's disease – a progressive disease that destroys brain cells resulting in both physical and mental difficulties.

in England who are at high risk of being a sickle cell carrier (see **Box 4.1**) are all offered screening via a blood test. If both parents are carriers, they may then decide to conduct further tests to determine whether or not the foetus has the disease and, if this is confirmed, make a decision about whether or not to continue with the pregnancy. Alternatively, if couples opt for **in vitro fertilisation** (IVF), embryos can be screened before implantation.

Genetic screening may also be used to determine whether someone is at increased risk of developing a particular disease, such as those carrying the *BRCA1* mutation for breast cancer. In some cases, this may lead a person to take preventive action. For example, women who test positive for the *BRCA1* mutation may undergo a double mastectomy (surgical removal of the breast) even in the absence of any disease. This reduces the risk of breast cancer by around 90% (Rebbeck et al., 2004).

However, in other cases there may be little a person can do to prevent a particular disease. For example, it is possible to test for the gene that results in **Huntington's disease** but, as there is no known cure for Huntington's, the person needs to think carefully about whether or not they want this information. Symptoms typically first appear between the ages of 30 and 50 but can develop earlier. Death usually occurs 15 to 20 years from first symptoms. Huntington's is caused by a dominant gene mutation which means a child has a 50% chance of inheriting the disease from an affected parent.

But what about diseases for which lifestyle-related behaviours play a significant role? Could informing someone that they are at increased risk for such a disease encourage them to, for example, quit smoking, do more exercise or lose weight? Whilst relatively few studies have been conducted in this area, to date the evidence suggests that, although such information might increase a person's intention to change, it seems to have little effect on their actual behaviour (Marteau et al., 2010; Meisel et al., 2015).

Genes and personalised medicine

Because genes vary from person to person, and can also influence an individual's response to drugs, many people end up taking medications that do not benefit them. For example, Nexium is a widely prescribed medicine for heartburn, but data suggest it is helpful for just 1 in 25 people (Gralnek et al., 2006; Schork, 2015). This is neither cost-effective nor good for the patient, who may end up suffering side effects in the absence of any benefit. Personalised medicine, sometimes called stratified medicine or precision medicine, aims to identify which individuals will respond to which drugs or therapies so that a person's treatment can be better tailored to their unique needs.

BOX 4.6 N-OF-1 TRIALS

MAKING CONNECTIONS

Standard trials, used to evaluate the effects of particular drugs or interventions, typically recruit hundreds or thousands of people. However, such trials generally focus on the *average* response to the intervention, which means that if only a small number of people benefit (or do not benefit) such an effect may be difficult to identify. An alternative approach is n-of-1 trials in which an intervention is tested on just one individual but with a much larger number of measures. We look at n-of-1 trials in **Chapter 10**.

Recent advances in genetics offer new opportunities for personalised medicine and a number of diagnostic tests are currently being used, particularly in relation to cancer treatment, to help identify patients who are more likely to benefit from particular drugs (Luo et al., 2016). Nutrition is another field that has much to gain from personalised medicine; an idea that is explored in **Box 4.7**.

BOX 4.7 DO YOU HAVE VEGETARIAN GENES? THE NEW SCIENCE OF NUTRIGENOMICS

AS AN ASIDE

Would you benefit from turning vegetarian? Or from including more fish in your diet? Should you be eating more whole grains? Or trying to limit your intake of dairy? In **Chapter 2** we saw how our evolutionary history means we are better suited to diets that include plenty of fruit and vegetables and limited amounts of sugar, salt and fat. However, we also saw how the diets of our hunter-gatherer ancestors would have varied, depending on where they lived; those living near the sea would have eaten more fish whilst those living inland would have enjoyed a wider variety of plants. This variation seems to have led to a range of different genetic adaptations that still exist in our species today. This in turn means that when it comes to population-level dietary advice, it can be difficult to go beyond very general recommendations.

One example of this type of variation is in genes that affect the synthesis of long-chain omega-3 fatty acids. Long-chain omega-3 is used in cell membranes throughout the body and seems to be particularly important for brain function and heart health (Nichols et al., 2010). But too much omega-3 can interfere with the overall balance of fatty acids within the body.

Long-chain omega-3 is found in oily fish (such as salmon, mackerel and sardines) and, in much smaller quantities, in red meat and eggs. It can also be synthesised in the body from medium-chain omega-3 found in plant oils such as flaxseed, walnuts and canola oil. However, different gene variants affect the efficiency with which the body is able to make this conversion.

The evolution of these different gene variants seems to have been driven by the diets of our ancestors. For example, the Inuit population of Greenland, who eat plenty of fish, lack gene variants that aid this conversion; without fish in their diet they may struggle to obtain sufficient quantities of long-chain omega-3. By contrast, among vegetarian communities in India, a high proportion of people can more efficiently convert medium-chain omega-3 to long-chain; thus they can get sufficient long-chain omega-3 from a plant-based diet. These types of 'vegetarian genes' have also been found in other parts of Asia, East Africa and Southern Europe. They seem to be less common in Northern Europe and North America (Gross, 2017).

However, without knowing our individual genetic make-up, we cannot know whether we would be more suited to a vegetarian diet or to one that includes fish. The same can be said of grains and dairy (see **Chapter 2**). Nutrigenomics is a new field of study that explores these types of relationships between genes, diet and health. It is possible that at some point in the future we may be able to receive specific dietary advice tailored to our own unique genetic make-up.

CHAPTER 4

Personality – in psychology, personality refers to stable patterns of thoughts, feelings and behaviours that differ from person to person (Funder, 2001). Research may also refer to personality-related variables as 'trait variables' or 'dispositional traits'.

Temperament – individual differences in emotional, motor and attentional reactivity, as well as differences in self-regulation processes that moderate reactivity (Rothbart & Derryberry, 1981). These differences can be present from birth and are determined by one's genes (Posner et al., 2007).

PERSONALITY

So far, this chapter has shown how our genes influence both our physiology and our tendency to behave in specific ways, which in turn influence our health. However, our genes also play a role in the development of **personality**, since personality is thought to result from both experience and **temperament** (Rothbart, 2007). Personality can also influence health and health-related behaviours. Although we touched on this in our discussion of polygenic obesity, we now take a more detailed look at the ways in which different personality traits have been linked to better or worse health.

Models of the personality-health relationship

In psychology there is a long history of using personality traits to predict health outcomes such as mortality or the incidence of coronary heart disease. However, perhaps a more interesting question to ask is why such traits are linked to health. Do they affect our responses to stressful situations or change the likelihood that we will follow health-related advice? Do they influence the way we interpret events or is it simply that personality and health are both the result of some other underlying variable?

Wiebe et al. (2010) identify three key models that aim to account for the effects of personality on health (**Figure 4.3**):

(a) *Transactional stress-moderation model.* This model states that our personalities shape the way we respond to stress, in terms of how we appraise stressful events (for example as a challenge or a threat) and how we cope with them (see section on *Coping*). These psychological responses influence the intensity, frequency and duration of the physiological stress response, for example in relation to blood pressure, heart

Figure 4.3 The different pathways via which personality may influence health

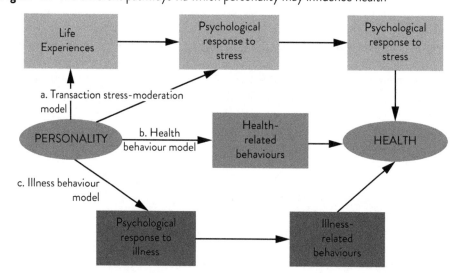

rate and the release of hormones (such as cortisol). These physiological responses impact upon our health (see **Chapter 3**). According to this model, our personalities also influence the type of life experiences we have. For example, a person who is high in hostility may experience more interpersonal conflict and lower levels of social support, which may increase their levels of stress.

(b) *Health behaviour model.* According to this model, our personalities influence the extent to which we engage in health-promoting behaviours (such as exercise) versus health-damaging behaviours (such as smoking).

(c) *Illness behaviour model.* This model states that our personalities influence the way we respond when we perceive ourselves to be ill. For example, whether we visit a doctor and take medication we are prescribed. These behaviours will in turn influence our health.

In the sections that follow, we look at examples of selected personality traits and their relationships with health. Although this selection is not exhaustive, it represents some of the most well-researched variables and serves to illustrate the models described above.

Type A personality and hostility

In the 1950s two cardiologists set out to investigate the effects of different types of behaviour patterns on the incidence of coronary heart disease. They grouped men according to the type of behaviour they displayed: driven, competitive and achievement oriented (Group A) versus laid-back and relaxed (Group B). They found that the incidence of coronary heart disease was seven times higher among the men in Group A compared to those in Group B (Friedman & Rosenman, 1959). This finding led to a programme of research in the 1970s and 1980s into the association between what became known as Type A and Type B personalities on mortality and heart disease. Whilst initial research seemed to support an association between Type A personality and coronary heart disease (Rosenman et al., 1976), a subsequent meta-analysis of ten prospective studies failed to find any links (Myrtek, 2001). However, other reviews identified one aspect of Type A behaviour that did appear to be more influential for health – that of hostility (Matthews, 1988). Thus subsequent research in this area has tended to shift in focus from Type A behaviour to hostility.

Hostility can be defined as a negative attitude toward others. It includes cynicism and mistrust of others as well a tendency to attribute others with hostile intent (Smith et al., 2004). Research has shown that higher levels of hostility are risk factors for both the development of coronary heart disease and premature mortality, particularly among men (Chida & Steptoe, 2009; Miller et al., 1996). Why might this be the case? Smith et al. (2004) proposed a number of explanations that draw on both the transactional stress-moderation model as well as the health behaviour model. They concluded that there was some evidence to support these interpretations but that the strength of the evidence varied.

Neuroticism

Neuroticism is one of the Big Five personality traits (**Box 4.8**). Like hostility, some studies have found that higher levels of neuroticism predict higher mortality, particularly from cardiovascular disease (Mroczek & Spiro, 2007; Roberts et al., 2007; Shipley et al., 2007; Terracciano et al., 2008). (Note that other studies have found more mixed evidence; Chapman et al., 2011.) A wide range of reasons have been put forward to explain these associations, including explanations that map onto both the transactional stress-moderation model and the health behaviour model.

CHAPTER 4

BOX 4.8 THE BIG FIVE

DIG A LITTLE DEEPER

One of the most well-known theories of personality is the five-factor theory (McCrae & Costa, 1987, 2008). Sometimes referred to as the 'five-factor model' or the 'Big Five', it states that individuals vary along five broad dimensions as follows:

1. *Openness to experience.* A desire for variety, novelty and change; a need for intellectual stimulation.
2. *Conscientiousness.* A tendency to be organised, reliable and hard-working.
3. *Extraversion.* A preference for the company of others and a tendency to seek social stimulation.
4. *Agreeableness.* The extent to which a person is cooperative, helpful and trusting.
5. *Neuroticism.* A person's tendency to experience negative emotions such as depression, anxiety and guilt.

These personality traits can be easily recalled using the acronym *OCEAN*. Although there is evidence to suggest that environmental influences play a role in the development of these traits (Caspi et al., 2005), a person's genes also seem to be important. For example, Bouchard and Loehlin (2001) estimated that half of all variability in the Big Five factors could be accounted for by hereditary effects. **Box 4.9** explores the notion that certain environmental pressures may have resulted in different populations evolving different temperaments.

In terms of the the transactional stress-moderation model, neuroticism is characterised by more intense emotional reactions to events, so one explanation for the negative relationship between neuroticism and longevity is that those who are high in neuroticism experience greater levels of stress when they encounter difficult events. They may also be more likely to perceive events as threatening or stressful. This interpretation is supported by studies in which individuals have kept diaries recording the daily problems they experience, as well as their fluctuations in mood. Data from these studies show that those higher in neuroticism tend to report more daily problems and also experience larger and longer lasting changes in mood as a result of these problems (Suls & Martin, 2005).

In terms of the health behavior model, another possible explanation is that those who are high in neuroticism engage in more health-damaging behaviours as a means of coping with the negative emotions they experience. For example, research has shown that those who are high in neuroticism are more likely to smoke and, when they do smoke, they tend to smoke more (Almada et al., 1991; Goodwin & Hamilton, 2002; Grekin et al., 2006; Lerman et al., 2000). Neuroticism has also been linked to an increased risk of alcohol abuse and dependence (Almada et al., 1991; Grekin et al., 2006; Larkins & Sher, 2006). Evidence that these types of health-damaging behaviours can explain some of the relationship between neuroticism and poorer health comes from a 3-year longitudinal study of 1,788 American men that showed that cigarette smoking (but not alcohol consumption) partially mediated the effects of neuroticism on mortality (Mroczek et al., 2009).

BOX 4.9 PERSONALITY, NATIONALITY AND DISEASE

AS AN ASIDE

We are all familiar with national stereotypes. From the British stiff upper lip to the hot-blooded Italian lover, many of our stereotypes may have their roots in literature and films rather than reality. But research suggests that people living in different parts of the world do indeed show differences in personality (Schmitt et al., 2007). Why might this be? As strange as it may sound, one possible explanation is that these differences have arisen in part because of geographical differences in levels of infectious disease.

When we come into contact with a pathogen, such as a bacterium or virus, our body produces an immune response. This is one way in which we have evolved to protect ourselves from disease. However, we also seem to have evolved different psychological and behavioural responses to reduce the extent to which we come into contact with pathogens in the first place. Termed the 'behavioural immune system', such responses range from feelings of disgust to xenophobia, and may also extend to personality traits (Schaller, 2011).

For example, a person who is highly extraverted is likely to come into contact with a greater number of people. This may be beneficial in terms of increased opportunities for social exchange and reproduction. However, it may also expose them to more potential pathogens. Likewise, a person who is high in openness may be more likely to form new, advantageous relationships and make novel discoveries but may also put themselves at increased risk for disease transmission. Schaller and Murray (2008) looked at personality and infectious disease across 71 geopolitical regions and found evidence to suggest that geographical variation in these particular traits may be an adaptation to disease; in regions with historically high levels of infectious disease, the population reported lower levels of extraversion and openness to experience.

This link between personality and disease is further supported by Vedhara et al. (2015). They found that the genes that trigger inflammation (an immune response that helps the body fight infection) tend to be more active among those showing higher levels of extraversion. In other words, extraverts may be better equipped to fight disease. However, whether a better immune system leads one to be more extraverted or whether being more extraverted helps one develop a better immune system has yet to be established.

Conscientiousness

Another personality trait that has been linked to health is conscientiousness (see **Box 4.8**); people who are higher in conscientiousness tend to live longer (Friedman et al., 1995; Kern & Friedman, 2008; Roberts et al., 2007; Terracciano et al., 2008; Turiano et al., 2015). As per hostility and neuroticism, the health behaviour model can be used to explain this relationship because conscientiousness is associated with a tendency both to avoid health-risk behaviours and to engage in health-promoting behaviours. For example, people who are high in conscientiousness are less likely to smoke, abuse drugs, eat an unhealthy diet, drink heavily, or engage in risky sex or risky driving (Bogg & Roberts, 2004). They are also less likely to suffer from obesity or be sedentary, but are more likely to exercise and adhere to medical regimes (Allen et al., 2016; Brickman et al., 1996; Jokela et al., 2013;

Rhodes & Smith, 2006). Support for this model comes from Turiano et al. (2015) who followed a national sample of over 6,000 US adults over a period of 14 years. They found that heavy drinking, smoking and waist circumference significantly mediated (explained) the relationship between conscientiousness and mortality.

However, it is unlikely that this is the whole story; whilst health behaviours do seem to account for some of the relationship between conscientiousness and longevity, they do not seem to account for it all. For example, in the longitudinal study by Turiano et al. (2015), health behaviours explained 42% of the relationship between conscientiousness and mortality, leaving 58% unaccounted for. One possibility is that the relationship is also partially mediated by occupation. In **Chapter 3** we saw how important occupational status is for health, and conscientiousness predicts higher occupational attainment, even after controlling for IQ and socioeconomic status (Roberts et al., 2007). This account is consistent with the transactional stress-moderation model which states that personality influences the type of life experiences we have.

BOX 4.10 EFFORTFUL CONTROL

MAKING CONNECTIONS

Temperament varies along a range of different dimensions including positive emotionality, negative emotionality and effortful control (Hampson, 2012; Rothbart, 2007). Positive emotionality can be seen as a precursor to extraversion, negative emotionality to neuroticism, and effortful control to conscientiousness. Effortful control, also termed 'constraint', refers to a person's ability to inhibit their behaviours. Whilst some view this ability as a relatively fixed, stable trait, others consider it as more variable. We look in more detail at theories of effortful control, or 'willpower' in **Chapter 7**.

Approach and avoidance

Some researchers distinguish between approach and avoidance temperaments that refer to innate differences in our response to pleasant versus unpleasant events. At a very basic level an animal will attempt to obtain rewards (such as food) and avoid punishment (such as pain) and it is individual differences in these two fundamental processes that underpin a number of models of personality.

One of the most influential models in this area is reinforcement sensitivity theory (RST) (Corr, 2008; Gray, 1982; Gray & McNaughton, 2000). RST states that there are three principal systems that determine emotion, motivation and learning, which in turn help form our personalities. These are as follows:

1. *The behavioural approach system (BAS).* The BAS relates to our sensitivity to reward. It is concerned with appetitive stimuli, determining the ways in which we seek out and respond to reward.

2. *The behavioural inhibition system (BIS).* The BIS is concerned with the detection and resolution of goal conflict, for example in situations where there is the possibility of reward, but also of punishment. The BIS is responsible for feelings of anxiety, worry and rumination.

3. *Fight-flight-freeze system (FFFS).* This system is responsible for our response to immediate danger. It is associated with feelings of fear (but not anxiety).

These three systems can be considered independent in that a person may show high or low sensitivity in all three or just one or two. The systems often work together to influence behaviour.

Reward sensitivity and health-related behaviours

So how do these systems relate to health? Most work in this area has focussed on their influence on health-related behaviours (in line with the health behaviour model described above). The BAS is relevant in this respect because many behaviours that are potentially damaging to health – eating high fat foods, drinking alcohol, smoking – have a high reward value. Thus we might expect those with a more sensitive BAS to engage in more of these types of behaviours.

There is some evidence to support this notion. For example, research has shown that higher reward sensitivity is associated with a higher alcohol intake, more binge drinking, a greater likelihood of being a smoker, and more frequent use of cigarettes, cigars or chewing tobacco (Feil & Hasking, 2008; Franken & Muris, 2006; Loxton & Dawe, 2001; O'Connor et al., 2009; Tapper et al., 2015; Voigt et al., 2009).

Sensitivity to reward also seems to be associated with eating. Research suggests that those with a higher sensitivity to reward are more responsive to appetising foods and food cues, are more likely to overeat, express a greater preference for foods high in fat and sugar, and show a higher intake of dietary fat (Beaver et al., 2006; Davis et al., 2007; Rollins et al., 2014c; Tapper et al., 2015; Tapper et al., 2010). However, the relationship between reward sensitivity and BMI is more complex. Davis and Fox (2008) found a curvilinear relationship between the two; for healthy weight individuals and for those suffering from overweight, higher reward sensitivity was associated with a higher BMI, suggesting that reward sensitivity was promoting a tendency to eat more calories. By contrast, among those with obesity there was actually a negative association between reward sensitivity and BMI, suggesting that those with a lower sensitivity to reward were consuming more calories.

These findings are consistent with what has been termed 'reward deficiency syndrome' (Blum et al., 1996); the idea that some people have underactive brain reward systems and may compensate for this by consuming larger quantities of palatable foods (or drugs or alcohol) in order to get the same level of pleasure as someone with a more typical brain reward system. The reward circuits in the brain are regulated by the neurotransmitter dopamine and neuroimaging has found that individuals with obesity have fewer dopamine receptors compared to their healthy weight counterparts (Wang et al., 2001). According to reward deficiency theory, such differences are due to a specific variant of a gene that controls dopamine receptors, and thus can be seen as relatively stable (Blum et al., 1996). However, since eating (and other pleasurable behaviours) releases dopamine in the brain (Schultz et al., 1997; Stice et al., 2013) it is also possible that overeating among people with obesity causes a reduction in the number of dopamine receptors as a compensatory response. We look in more detail at dopamine and addiction in **Chapter 8**. In the meantime, the possibility that certain personality types are at increased risk of addiction is considered in **Box 4.11**.

Behavioural inhibition and health-related behaviours

The BIS has also been linked to health-related behaviours in a similar manner to that of neuroticism, in that the individual engages in health-damaging behaviours as a way of coping with negative emotions. Specifically, a more active BIS may be associated with more anxiety (Corr, 2008) which may lead individuals to try to cope with this by

CHAPTER 4

BOX 4.11 IS THERE SUCH A THING AS AN ADDICTIVE PERSONALITY?

HOT TOPIC

Gastric bypass surgery is increasingly being used to treat obesity. However, anecdotal reports suggest that an unintended side effect of such treatment may be addiction to alcohol, painkillers, or even exercise (Blum et al., 2011; Sogg, 2007; Wendling & Wudyka, 2011). It is as if these people, no longer able to consume large quantities of food, turn to alternative substances or behaviours in order to satisfy an overwhelming need for pleasure. Is there something about the make-up of such individuals that underlies this phenomenon? Could they be described as having addictive personalities?

To a certain extent, the answer to this question depends on how we define addiction – an issue we return to in **Chapter 8**. It is also important to note that gastric surgery does not inevitably result in other addictive behaviours. For example, it is estimated that less than 3% of those who undergo gastric surgery develop an alcohol dependence problem (Ertelt et al., 2008). This finding is in keeping with other research that suggests that, rather than there being a specific 'addictive personality', a range of different factors may predispose a person to addiction.

For example, one line of research suggests that certain genes predispose a person to becoming addicted to specific substances such as alcohol or tobacco (Li & Burmeister, 2009). However, the same genes that predispose addiction to one substance do not necessarily predispose addiction to other substances. Indeed, a mutation associated with nicotine dependence has been shown to protect against addiction to cocaine (Grucza et al., 2008). Such findings contrast with reward deficiency syndrome that suggests that one particular genetic mutation tends to be common to all addictive behaviours (Blum et al., 1996).

Others have suggested that certain personality traits may be linked to a greater likelihood of addiction. For example, a meta-analysis suggests that individuals who are high in disinhibition, low in conscientiousness, and low in agreeableness may be more prone to substance use disorders (Kotov et al., 2010).

So whilst this area is still very much a source of debate among academics, it seems likely that there is not just one specific personality trait that leads inevitably to addiction.

engaging in behaviours such as drinking alcohol, overeating and smoking. In support of this interpretation, a more active BIS has been associated with more drug use and a poorer diet (Tapper et al., 2015; Voigt et al., 2009).

However, another possibility is that a more active BIS could act as a protective factor. This may occur as the result of a desire to avoid potentially risky or aversive consequences (such as becoming intoxicated or having a hangover), or because of greater levels of anxiety experienced in response to health promotion information (that may in turn help promote behaviour change; see protection motivation theory, **Chapter 5**). In support of this view, some studies have found lower levels of alcohol consumption and binge drinking amongst those with a more active BIS, as well as lower levels of substance abuse among female (but not male) youths (Franken & Muris, 2006; Knyazev et al., 2004; Tapper et al., 2015).

How can we understand these seemingly contradictory findings? One possibility is that sensitivity to reward and punishment interact with coping style to influence behaviour. We consider coping style in the next section.

CHAPTER 4

BOX 4.12 ARE YOU HIGH IN REWARD SENSITIVITY?

TAKE THE TEST

A number of different measures have been used to assess reward sensitivity. The reinforcement sensitivity theory of personality questionnaire (RST-PQ) reflects the most recent revisions to the underlying theory (Corr & Cooper, 2016). The questionnaire contains 65 items with scales relating to FFFS, BIS and BAS. The BAS is further divided into subscales relating to reward interest (openness to new experiences and opportunities that may be rewarding), goal-drive persistence (maintenance of motivation when the reward is not immediately available), reward reactivity (feelings of pleasure upon obtaining a reward) and impulsivity (rapid 'capture' of a reinforcer). Reward interest and goal-drive persistence are more concerned with the early stages of reward attainment; identifying rewards and planning how to achieve them. By contrast, reward reactivity and impulsivity relate to the later stages of the process when the organism comes into contact with the reinforcer. You can see how you compare to others on these factors by taking the test via **macmillanihe.com/tapper-health-psychology**.

Coping

Coping refers to the ways in which a person attempts to deal with the difficulties they face. Whilst some have suggested that coping style varies from situation to situation (Lazarus & Folkman, 1984) others have argued that it is more stable, reflecting an aspect of personality (Beutler et al., 2003). Compared to other personality traits however, coping style does appear to be less stable over time, and only modestly heritable (Jang et al., 2007; Murberg et al., 2002). Thus one possibility is that certain personality traits or temperaments influence coping style, but that coping is also subject to significant environmental influences (Carver & Connor-Smith, 2010; Jang et al., 2007).

Different types of coping styles have been distinguished from one another in a wide variety of ways (Carver & Connor-Smith, 2010). One of the most frequently employed distinctions is between problem-focussed coping and emotion-focussed coping (Carver et al., 1989):

- *Problem-focussed coping* is where a person proactively engages in specific behaviours in an attempt to solve the problem, for example they may put together a plan of action or seek the advice of others.

- *Emotion-focussed coping* is where a person concentrates their energies on regulating the emotions that the problem has elicited, for example they may seek emotional support from a friend, try to reframe the problem as something positive or turn to drugs or alcohol to help dampen their feelings.

Another commonly used distinction is engagement versus disengagement coping (Carver & Connor-Smith, 2010):

- *Engagement coping* (also referred to as 'approach coping') involves proactively dealing with the problem or the related emotions.

- *Disengagement coping* (also referred to as 'avoidance coping') is aimed at escaping either the threat or the emotional response, for example through avoidance or denial.

Research suggests that, in general, problem-focussed coping is associated with better psychological and physical health, whilst avoidance coping is linked to poorer psychological and physical health (Moskowitz et al., 2009; Penley et al., 2002; Roesch et al., 2005). However, it would be a mistake to assume that there was one particular style of coping that was always more adaptive than others; what is helpful in one situation may not be helpful in another. For example, problem-focussed coping may be beneficial in situations where the outcomes can be changed (such as managing diabetes) but less so in uncontrollable situations (for example, upon a diagnosis of terminal cancer).

As mentioned previously, research has also shown how coping style may interact with other personality traits to influence health-related behaviours. For example, in a study with adolescents, Hasking (2006) found that a more active BAS predicted higher alcohol consumption, but only among those with an avoidant coping style. Hasking suggested that whilst sensitivity to reward and punishment could be viewed as distal (distant) predictors of behaviour, coping strategy could be viewed as a more proximal (immediate) predictor.

Locus of control

As described in **Chapter 3**, locus of control refers to the extent to which a person feels they have control over events that affect them. Developed by Rotter in the 1950s and 1960s, the theory distinguishes between an internal locus of control, in which the person believes the events in their life are primarily a result of their own actions, and an external locus of control, in which they believe events are outside their control, being instead a result of chance, fate, or the influence of more powerful others (Rotter, 1966).

In **Chapter 3** we saw how children with a more external locus of control tended to report poorer health as adults and were more likely to suffer from overweight or obesity at age 30 (Bosma et al., 1999, Gale et al., 2008). Other researchers have looked more specifically at health locus of control and how this may relate to health-related behaviours. Health locus of control is the extent to which a person believes their health is primarily determined by their own behaviour, by powerful others, or by chance. A recent meta-analysis found that a more internal health locus of control predicted more positive perceptions of health status but was only very weakly related to health behaviours (Cheng et al., 2016). The authors suggested that more behaviour-specific control beliefs may better predict health-related behaviours. We look at two such concepts, self-efficacy and perceived behavioural control, later in this chapter.

Interpreting research on personality and health

Although researchers have identified some interesting links between personality and health, there are also reasons to be cautious about some of the findings. In brief, these are as follows:

- *Reliance on correlational data* – this makes it difficult to establish cause and effect. It is the same difficulty we encountered in **Chapter 3** when examining the effects of socioeconomic status on health. For cross-sectional studies it means we cannot be sure of the direction of causality and for both prospective and cross-sectional studies we cannot rule out the possibility that relationships occur simply because of links with other underlying variables.

- *Use of self-report measures* – self-report measures of health, illness and behaviour may be subject to bias and will not always reflect actual health, illness or behaviour.

- *Small effect sizes* – even where a particular personality trait does seem to predict a particular health outcome, the effect may be too small to be considered very important. Other predictors, such as socioeconomic status or behaviour, may represent much more important predictors.

- *Bias on the part of researchers* – this may be introduced because of practices such as the selective reporting of data, or *p*-hacking (see **Chapter 11**). Bias may be more likely to occur when research is funded by organisations that would benefit from particular findings. For example, the tobacco industry funded much research into the effects of Type A personality on heart disease and cancer, hoping to detract from the role of tobacco (Petticrew et al., 2012).

However, many of these issues are not specific to personality research but instead apply across the field more generally. For this reason, we do not discuss them at length here, but consider them in more detail in **Chapters 10 and 11**.

PERSONALITY-BASED INTERVENTIONS

In principle, the types of personality-based health interventions we could develop mirror the gene-based interventions we described above. In other words, they could:

- Attempt to change a person's personality
- Screen people for certain personality traits to identify those who would most benefit from intervention
- Tailor interventions to suit a person's personality in order to maximise effects.

However, in practice, links between personality and health may often be too weak to make such interventions worthwhile. Nevertheless, there may still be some scope for personality-based interventions. In this section we consider whether personality change is feasible, as well as look at some possibilities for tailored interventions.

Can we change personality?

As discussed above, certain aspects of a person's personality seem to predict their health. It therefore follows that if we could change a person's personality, we might also be able to improve their health. But, as noted previously, one of the characteristics of a personality trait is that it is relatively stable over time. So can personality change?

There is good evidence to show that personality traits do indeed slowly change over the course of a person's life with people generally becoming more agreeable, confident, conscientious and emotionally stable (Roberts et al., 2006). This raises the possibility that personality could also be modified though intervention.

One area of intervention in which measures of personality are often taken is in relation to clinical therapies aimed at improving mental health. A recent meta-analysis of such studies provides tentative evidence that therapy can, to some degree, influence personality, particularly in terms of reducing neuroticism and increasing extraversion, with most changes occurring within the first month of therapy (Roberts et al., 2017). However, the extent to which this type of clinical intervention impacts upon physical health has yet to be fully explored.

Personality and personalised medicine

In principle, personality assessment could be used to ensure interventions are tailored in a way that is likely to be most effective for the individual. In particular, there is increasing evidence that health-related messages are more effective when their content or presentation is matched to the characteristics of the person. For example, Thompson and Haddock (2012) found that narrative persuasion (persuasion that occurs through storytelling) was more effective at changing attitudes to cervical screening

> **Need for affect** – a tendency to seek out and become involved in situations that elicit strong emotions (Maio & Esses, 2001).

> **Need for cognition** – a tendency to engage in and enjoy effortful cognitive activities (Cacioppo et al., 1996).

and organ donation among those with a higher **need for affect** and a higher **need for cognition**. By contrast, rhetorical persuasion (persuasion based on facts) was more effective at changing attitudes among those with low need for affect and cognition. Similarly, Williams-Piehota et al. (2004) found that communications emphasizing individual responsibility for health were more effective at promoting uptake of mammograms among women with an internal health locus of control, whilst communications emphasizing the role of the healthcare provider were more effective among women with an external health locus of control (see also Williams-Piehota et al., 2005). The rise in digital technologies may afford new opportunities for this type of health promotion tailoring.

COGNITIVE VARIABLES

Personality traits are considered to be relatively stable over time and thus quite difficult to change. However, another way in which individuals vary from one another is in terms of their attitudes and beliefs. These are often referred to as 'cognitive variables' and are generally considered less stable than personality traits and more open to influence. As such, they can represent an important target for intervention. For example, if we can change a person's attitude or increase their self-efficacy, this might just be sufficient to change their behaviour. In this section we review a selection of cognitive variables that feature widely in both models of behaviour change (**Chapter 5**) and behaviour change interventions (**Chapter 12**).

Attitudes

An attitude can be described as an evaluative judgement, based on cognitive, affective and behavioural information (Maio et al., 2019). In other words, we may have a positive or negative attitude toward something, and this evaluation is influenced by our beliefs and feelings as well as our previous behaviours. The term 'attitude' is used to refer to judgements about a very broad range of entities, from the US president, to the place we grew up, to whether or not we like sugar in our tea.

Intuitively, we expect attitudes to influence behaviour. If we believe that cycling to work is good for health and are excited by the thought of whizzing past queues of stationary traffic, we will be more likely to cycle to work. On the other hand, if we believe that cycling to work will mean breathing in dangerous traffic fumes and are anxious about the prospect of being knocked down by a car, we are unlikely to cycle unless we really have to. Research bears out our intuitions; attitudes can influence behaviour (Albarracín et al., 2001; Armitage & Conner, 2001; Glasman & Albarracin, 2006; Kraus, 1995; McEachan et al., 2011).

So how do we change attitudes? There is no simple answer to this question. In principle, attitudes could be changed by targeting their cognitive, affective or behavioural components, in other words, by changing relevant beliefs, feelings and behaviours (Maio et al., 2019). However, there are many different ways in which this might be achieved, and many other factors that may influence the efficacy of such approaches. In **Chapters 5, 6, 7 and 8** we look in more detail at a number of different theoretical models relevant to attitude change.

CHAPTER 4

Values

Values are concepts or beliefs that relate to desirable end-states or behaviours, but which transcend specific situations. Thus they are more general than attitudes and can help guide behaviour over a much broader range of situations (Schwartz, 1992; Schwartz et al., 2012). For example, if someone has a favourable attitude toward fruit and vegetables it may lead them to eat plenty of fruit and vegetables. However, if someone values their health, not only may they try to eat plenty of fruit and vegetables, they may also try to exercise, refrain from smoking and drink in moderation.

Values are thought to be universal in nature, reflecting key aspects of human psychology linked to evolved needs for both security and exploration. Important values include tradition (preserving cultural, family or religious traditions), personal security (safety in one's immediate environment), hedonism (pleasure and sensuous gratification) and achievement (success according to social standards) (**Figure 4.4**). Although health can also be viewed as a value (Tapper et al., 2012, 2014), its meaning seems to vary both between people and across cultures (Schwartz et al., 2012). For example, for some it may be linked to personal security (in terms of disease avoidance) whilst for others it may be more closely associated with achievement (in terms of being fit and healthy).

Different people will place more or less importance on different values. Values can also conflict with one another, even within the same person. For example, the desire to maintain good health may conflict with values relating to the pursuit of pleasure. Value conflicts can also be a barrier to evidence-based health policy, an issue we explore in **Chapter 11**.

Figure 4.4 Proposed circular motivational continuum of 19 values with sources that underlie their order

Source: Schwartz et al., 'Refining the theory of basic individual values', *Journal of Personality and Social Psychology*, 103(4), 663, 1 October 2012, doi.org/10.1037/a0029393, © American Psychological Association. Reprinted with permission.

Outcome expectancies

Outcome expectancies are beliefs about what might happen as a result of a particular behaviour (Bandura, 1986). Because they are beliefs, they can be seen to relate to the cognitive component of attitudes. However, they are more specific than attitudes since they are directed at the consequences of behaviours only. These consequences may be physical, social or self-evaluative. For example, outcome expectancies relating to joining an exercise class may include feeling fitter (a physical consequence), approval from others (a social consequence) and a sense of achievement (a self-evaluative consequence). These consequences may be positive (feeling relaxed afterwards) or negative (feeling self-conscious during the class), long term (avoiding diabetes) or short term (getting less out of breath climbing stairs).

Both positive and negative outcome expectancies have been shown to predict intentions and behaviour, with some studies suggesting that self-evaluative outcome expectancies (expectancies that relate to emotions) are most influential (Dijkstra et al., 1999; Gellert et al., 2012; Hankonen et al., 2013; Williams et al., 2005).

As with attitudes, there are many possible ways of changing outcome expectancies. In **Chapter 5** we see them appear in a number of models of health behaviour and in **Chapter 12** we will look at how they relate to behaviour change interventions.

Self-efficacy

Self-efficacy has similarities with locus of control. However, it is much more specific than locus of control, referring to one's belief in one's ability to perform a certain action or achieve a particular outcome (Bandura, 1997). From school performance to career success, research shows that those with higher self-efficacy tend to be more motivated, work harder, and persist for longer in the face of difficulties (Spurk & Abele, 2014; Zimmerman, 1995). This means they're more likely to reach their goals. For example, studies looking at the effects of different weight loss programmes have found that a person's confidence in their ability to change their diet and take up more exercise is one of the best predictors of weight loss success (Teixeira et al., 2015).

The apparent effect of self-efficacy on performance is nicely illustrated in research conducted by Hutchinson and colleagues. They recruited volunteers to take part in an experiment on handgrip strength. After completing a practice test, the volunteers were given fabricated feedback in order to either enhance or undermine their confidence; some were congratulated and told their performance was particularly good, and some were informed that their handgrip strength was very weak compared to their peers. Others received no feedback at all. The volunteers were then asked to perform the handgrip test for as long as they possibly could. The results showed that those who had received positive feedback persevered for an average of 2 minutes and 53 seconds, whilst those who had been told they were not very good, or who had received no feedback, gave up more quickly, after an average of 2 minutes and 13 seconds. What's more, these differences were consistent with changes in self-efficacy computed from measures taken before and after the practice test; those who'd been given positive feedback became more confident they could perform the handgrip test for a longer period of time whilst those who'd been given negative feedback showed a reduction in confidence. Those who'd received the positive feedback also reported finding the task less strenuous and more enjoyable (Hutchinson et al., 2008).

In the above study self-efficacy was improved by building feelings of mastery and competence; participants were led to believe they had performed well at the task. According to social cognitive theory (which we look at in more detail in **Chapter 5**), these types of 'mastery experiences' are one of the best ways of improving self-efficacy (Bandura, 1998). In practice, when trying to change behaviour, this may mean that self-efficacy can be improved by setting smaller, intermediate goals, which are realistic to achieve. However, according to social cognitive theory, vicarious experience and verbal persuasion can be important too. For example, if you see others around you reach their goals, you may feel encouraged that you could do the same. This is especially true where you see yourself as similar to those who have succeeded. Likewise, words of praise and encouragement from others can also help boost confidence.

Nevertheless, others have questioned the extent to which self-efficacy is causally related to behaviour change. French (2013) notes that self-efficacy is also predicted to increase as a consequence of successful behaviour change (in other words, as a result of mastery experiences). Thus in some studies it can be difficult to determine whether observed changes in self-efficacy have caused the observed changes in behaviour or whether they have arisen as a consequence of it. Additionally, interventions designed to increase self-efficacy may inadvertently be influencing other important variables too, such as whether one formulates specific plans. It may be that formulating plans leads to both behaviour change and increased self-efficacy, but that self-efficacy has no influence on the behaviour. In order to investigate such possibilities, French recommends more carefully constructed studies that take measures of self-efficacy immediately following the manipulation, but prior to any opportunity to engage in the behaviour (as in the experimental study described above, conducted by Hutchinson et al., 2008). This would help rule out the possibility that self-efficacy change occurs only as a consequence of behaviour change. He also recommends taking measures of other relevant variables, such as planning, to help rule out alternative explanations. Finally, he highlights the potentially important role that self-efficacy may play in maintaining behaviour change as well as initiating it.

Perceived behavioural control

Perceived behavioural control is very similar to self-efficacy and, as noted above, also overlaps with the concept of locus of control. It refers to a person's perception of the extent to which they can exercise control over their behaviour and incorporates both internal factors (such as summoning up sufficient motivation to attend an exercise class) and external factors (such as having the means to get to an exercise class). These factors may sometimes be referred to as personal and environmental barriers, respectively.

There is evidence to show that perceived behavioural control predicts behaviour and intentions (Armitage & Conner, 2001). Again, it is a construct that features in many models of health behaviour, which we review in **Chapter 5**.

CONCLUSIONS

One of the key characteristics of life on earth is its diversity. This diversity occurs not just between species but also within them, even between members of the same family. The two gerbils we met at the start of the chapter, Midnight and Lightning, showed surprising differences in both appearance and behaviour despite being so closely related. If such differences can occur in gerbils, raised in a relatively stable environment, over a fairly short lifespan, it's little surprise that humans, with their widely diverging environments and lifestyles, can vary so much from one another.

Diversity is good. It's nature's way of ensuring that at least some members of a species survive, irrespective of whatever catastrophe may be just around the corner. But these differences also mean differences in health; they mean some of us experience much better health than others. And if we're interested in improving health, we may wish to try to reduce a little of this variation, or at least use it to our advantage. Whilst theories of personality have been around since the time of Hippocrates, it is only in the last couple of decades that we've really begun to understand our genes and how they influence our health and behaviour. Our knowledge in this field is changing from day to day, bringing new possibilities for health intervention.

In the three chapters in Part 1, we've looked at the determinants of health across both time and place (**Chapters 2 and 3**) and between groups and individuals (**Chapters 3 and 4**). Hopefully it has become clear that there is significant overlap across these factors. For example, the country a person lives in will influence their individual attitudes towards health and health-related behaviours. If they have ancestral roots in that country, it may also have exerted an effect on their genes. Likewise, some of the differences in health we see between different socioeconomic groups may be explained by differences in cognitive variables such as self-efficacy and outcome expectancies. Health also varies across other groups, such as age, gender, ethnicity and religion. Although it is beyond the scope of this book to explore all these group differences in detail, many will be linked to variables we have explored in these chapters, such as social status, social support, attitudes and values.

Hopefully these chapters have also served to highlight the complexity of health – it has multiple determinants, all interacting with one another in multiple ways at different levels, from individual beliefs and attitudes to global influences on economic wealth. This shows the importance of taking a multidisciplinary approach to health – intervening at just one level is likely to be less effective than intervening at multiple levels, drawing on the expertise of, to name but a few, biologists, economists and geographers, as well as psychologists. Thus, whilst this book focusses on the psychology of behaviour change, it is important to remember that this particular approach represents just one small part of a very large and complex system.

Prenatal screening tests can lead to a reduction in the numbers of people born with health-related conditions such as cystic fibrosis as well as developmental disorders such as Down syndrome. Do you think prenatal screening tests are a good idea? Would your opinion differ if you suffered from one of these conditions? How might a reduction in the incidence of such conditions influence society's attitudes to those affected by them? If we had the ability to screen for any characteristic, where would you draw the line? (Or wouldn't you?)

THE GREAT DEBATE

PART 2

THEORIES OF HEALTH BEHAVIOUR

CHAPTER 5

SOCIAL COGNITION THEORIES OF BEHAVIOUR AND MOTIVATION

Alexandra Heminsley, pictured below, had never been 'the sporty type'. At school she was curvy and clumsy, playing the fool in sports class to deflect from her inability to hit a tennis ball or use a hockey stick. As a young adult she was of the firm opinion that she 'couldn't run' and, other than a few half-hearted attempts to take up yoga or join a gym, her early 20s were marked by a distinct lack of exercise. And yet by her mid-30s she had four marathons under her belt. So what brought about this dramatic change in lifestyle?

In Alexandra's account of her transformation (Heminsley, 2014) we can identify some of the factors we considered in **Chapter 4**; her first forays into running seem to have been prompted by expectations that it would help her sleep better and improve her mental health. Her confidence in her ability to run also seems to have been boosted by words of encouragement from her father and brother. Indeed, her father, a marathon runner himself, told her in no uncertain terms that she could run if she tried. Losing a bit of weight early on was also an unexpected bonus. But there were barriers she had to overcome too; the disbelief and amusement of some of her friends, her fear of being spotted – sweaty-faced and exhausted – by someone she knew, and, of course, the temptation of a warm bed and a good novel on a cold winter's morning.

However, to *really* understand why people change their behaviour we need to do more than just identify a string of different influences. Did Alexandra's father's opinion boost her confidence more than her friends' comments diminished it? What

Image 5.1 *Alexandra Heminsley, transformed from 'not sporty' to marathon runner.*
Credit: Alexandra Heminsley. Used with permission.

difference did her father's expertise make? How did she manage to get over her self-consciousness and resist her warm bed? We need to know when different factors promote behaviour change, and when they do not. We need to know whether some factors are more important than others and how they interact. We also need to understand *why* they work. As such, we need theory. In this chapter we will:

- Think about why theory is important and what makes a good theory.
- Look at a selection of social cognition theories of behaviour and motivation.
- Examine the evidence for these theories.
- Consider their limitations.
- Explore similarities and differences between theories.

THE IMPORTANCE OF THEORY

Why is theory so important? As noted above, theories are essential for a full understanding of health behaviour and behaviour change. Imagine you were trying to get your partner to eat more fruit and vegetables. You have a long discussion about why eating fruit and vegetables is so important. You describe how they reduce the risk of cancer and heart disease, you explain how easy it is to eat a couple more portions every day and you refer to government statistics showing how most people eat far more fruit and vegetables than your partner. Hey presto, your partner starts eating more fruit and vegetables. Brilliant! But would this approach work with your uncle, who lives alone, smokes a pack of cigarettes a day, and has never taken much interest in his health? What about your three-year-old nephew who has simply decided that all green things are 'yucky'? If we don't understand how particular factors influence behaviour, we will have little idea about whether or not they will work for other people or in other contexts. We won't know whether we can use the same approach for other types of health behaviours or whether the effect is likely to endure or be short-lived. On a larger scale, this lack of knowledge can become very expensive and time-consuming if a government-funded intervention fails to work as expected. For this reason, in order to effectively change health-related behaviours, we need to understand how behaviour change works. In short, we need theory.

Criteria for a good theory

So what makes a good theory? Good theories must be able to explain what we see around us. But they should also do more than this. Experts in behaviour change have identified a set of nine criteria by which theories can be judged (Davis et al., 2015). These are as follows:

1. *Explanatory power* – as noted above, a good theory is one that can account for observations.

2. *Testability* – a good theory should be able to generate predictions so that it can be tested.

3. *Clarity of constructs* – there should be evidence for the independence of the constructs identified in the theory.

4. *Relationships between constructs* – these should be clearly described.

> **Construct** – in the context of a theory, a construct is an explanatory variable that cannot be directly observed. For example, we cannot directly observe a person's attitude towards smoking, but we might use this construct to help explain why they do or don't smoke, or whether they intend to quit.

5. *Measurability* – there should be a way of measuring the constructs.

6. *Descriptions of causality* – the theory should describe mechanisms of change.

7. *Parsimony* – the theory should not be more complicated than it needs to be.

8. *Generalisability* – there should be evidence that the theory applies across different contexts, populations and behaviours.

9. *Evidence base* – there should be empirical support for the theory.

When thinking about behaviour change interventions, we can also add an additional criterion:

10. *Identification of behaviour change techniques* – the extent to which the theory identifies specific strategies that will be effective at influencing theory constructs, in order to change behaviour.[1]

From a health promotion point of view, such information is critical as we need to be able to *change* behaviour, not just predict it.

BOX 5.1 EVALUATING THEORY

In this chapter we use the criteria detailed above to help evaluate the theories we look at. You can take a similar approach to the theories described in **Chapters 6, 7** and **8**, using these criteria to help you critically evaluate the theories.

MAKING CONNECTIONS

Types of theory

In this chapter we look at social cognition theories of health behaviour. These are theories in which a person's cognitions (or thoughts) intervene between the observable external environment and the person's behaviour. In this way, a person's behaviour is driven by their perceptions of reality, rather than reality itself (Conner & Norman, 2015). As such, if we know more about these thoughts, we will be better able to predict and influence behaviour. These types of social cognition theories contrast with the theories we examine in **Chapter 6**, that reflect more automatic processes, and those discussed in **Chapters 7 and 8**, that are more concerned with emotion.

The social cognition theories described in this chapter are further divided into continuum theories and stage theories. Continuum theories are those that describe a number of different constructs (typically types of thought, such as beliefs about benefits or barriers) that are added together in order to predict a person's intention or behaviour (Sutton, 2015). The likelihood of someone behaving in a particular way can thus be viewed as varying on a continuum. (For example, someone with strong beliefs about the positive benefits of a particular behaviour, who also perceives few barriers, is more likely to carry out that behaviour than someone who holds weak beliefs about benefits and perceives many barriers.) Where an intervention is based on a continuum theory, it would be developed to target the determinants (the constructs) specified in that theory.

---

1 Arguably this is encompassed by 'descriptions of causality', except such descriptions could be limited to links between constructs (such as attitudes and intentions) which will be less helpful from a health promotion perspective.

By contrast, stage theories conceptualise behaviour (and behaviour change) as a process (as opposed to a one-off event), with different types of cognitions being important at different stages of this process. This means that interventions based on stage theories require different strategies for people at different stages (Sutton, 2015).

We also look at self-determination theory in this chapter. This is slightly different from the continuum and stage theories because of its focus on motivation. Thus, it is arguably more concerned with feelings than with thoughts. However, it is included in this chapter because of its emphasis on the cognitive processes that influence these feelings.

Lastly, it is important to note that there are a huge number of different social cognition theories and it is beyond the scope of this book to examine them all. However, in practice a very small number of theories tend to dominate the field. These include the health belief model, the theory of planned behaviour, social cognitive theory, the transtheoretical model and self-determination theory (Davis et al., 2015). Because these theories are so widely used, they are examined in detail in this chapter. To this list we also add protection motivation theory, because it relates to a popular health promotion strategy (use of fear), and the Rubicon model of action phases, because it underpins implementation intentions, a widely used behaviour change technique that we look at in **Chapter 6**.

CONTINUUM THEORIES

In this section we look at the health belief model, the theory of planned behaviour, protection motivation theory and social cognitive theory (see **Box 5.2** for an explanation of 'model' versus 'theory'). Many of the constructs used in these theories, such as attitudes and self-efficacy, were reviewed in **Chapter 4**. We will look at each of these theories in turn and highlight some of the key ways in which they do, or do not, meet our criteria of a good theory.

BOX 5.2 WHAT'S THE DIFFERENCE BETWEEN A THEORY AND A MODEL?

DIG A LITTLE DEEPER

A theory refers to a set of generalised statements aimed at explaining a particular phenomenon. According to West and Brown (2013), a theory aims to explain and predict with reference to the existence or operation of entities that have not been observed. For example, constructs such as 'attitudes' and 'self-efficacy' cannot be directly observed, so any account that refers to these to explain behaviour would be viewed as a theory. By contrast, a model represents a system, object, or set of events, but does not explain them. For example, a model might describe how increasing the price of alcohol is associated with a reduction in binge drinking. We can directly observe both the price of alcohol and levels of binge drinking. The model provides a description but not an explanation. Once we start talking about why the increase in price influences behaviour, for example with reference to outcome expectancies, we get into the realms of theory. In practice however, the boundary between theories and models is often quite blurred and the two terms tend to be used interchangeably within psychology. As such, readers should not make inferences based on whether something has been labelled a theory or a model. In this book, for the sake of continuity, the use of the term 'theory' versus 'model' is based on that used by the relevant author. However, according to West and Browns' definition, all of the 'models' described in this chapter should really be viewed as theories.

The health belief model

Imagine a middle-aged, overweight, overworked surgeon. His health is important to him, but all his energies are focussed on keeping up with his job. He works long hours at the hospital and spends much of his spare time reading journal articles to try to stay abreast of the latest developments in his field. Of course he is aware of the links between diet and heart disease, and knows he should really lose some weight, but his food is a source of great pleasure and his wife likes to indulge him with hearty home-cooked meals. One evening, after a particularly stressful day in surgery, he suffers from severe chest pain. He is rushed to hospital with a suspected heart attack. It turns out to be bad indigestion. Nevertheless, the incident prompts him to take action. He starts to walk to work rather than drive, he asks his wife to reduce the amount of fat and salt in their food, and he resolves to select more salad options at the hospital cafeteria.

In this example, our surgeon was well aware of the links between diet, exercise and heart disease. He'd likely witnessed the devastating consequences of a heart attack in some of his own patients and he would have known that his weight placed him at greater risk. Yet it wasn't until he had a suspected heart attack that he actually took action. How can we make sense of this sudden change in behaviour?

The model

The health belief model was developed to explain such effects; to understand what prompts someone to take action to prevent disease or ill health (Rosenstock, 1974). It draws on expectancy-value theories of decision-making that take account of an individual's expectations about the outcome of a particular course of action, as well as the value they place on that outcome (Maiman & Becker, 1974). The key components of the model can be seen in **Figure 5.1**. Of particular importance are:

- Threat perception
- Behavioural evaluation
- Cues to action.

Threat perception refers to one's beliefs about how susceptible one is to the disease or illness and how severe the consequences of the disease or illness would be. These work together to influence the perceived threat and likelihood of action. For example, a person might believe they have bad teeth and are therefore quite likely to suffer from tooth decay, but if that person does not view fillings and dentures as much of a problem, they may not be inclined to take much action to prevent tooth decay. In other words, although they may believe they are susceptible to tooth decay, they do not believe this particular outcome is very severe.

Behavioural evaluation refers to the person's beliefs about the action they have to take in order to avoid the disease or illness; these comprise beliefs about the perceived benefits of the action (*Will regular flossing be effective at helping prevent tooth decay?*) as well as perceived barriers and costs (*How do I know if I'm flossing properly? Have I got time to floss every day?*). Again, these work together to influence the likelihood of the person taking action to protect their health.

These constructs are also influenced by what are referred to as 'demographic variables' (such as age, gender and ethnicity), 'sociopsychological variables' (such as personality and socioeconomic status) and 'structural variables' (such as knowledge about, or prior contact with, the disease).

However, according to the health belief model, even where a person believes they are at risk, that consequences would be severe, and that the benefits of action outweigh the barriers and costs, they may still fail to act. This is where a cue to action may help prompt

Figure 5.1 The health belief model

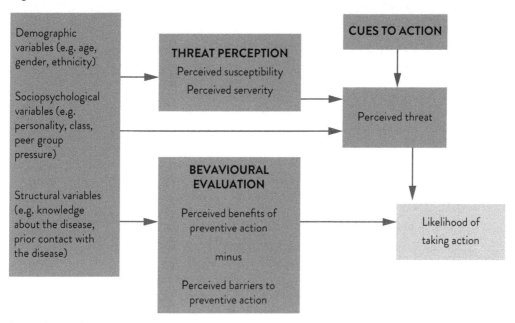

Source: Adapted from Rosenstock, 1974, with the permission of SAGE Publishing.

the individual to change their behaviour. So in our example of the surgeon, he already held beliefs that were compatible with altering his lifestyle but it took a specific event, in this case a suspected heart attack, to actually elicit the change in behaviour.

A cue to action need not be quite so dramatic though. It could be reading a magazine article, receiving a reminder letter about an overdue dental check-up, or simply noticing that one's trousers are a little tighter than they used to be. The important feature of these cues to action is not that they change the information you have, or the value you place on your health, rather they simply trigger an action. Indeed, they will only prompt action where the individual already holds certain beliefs relating to the threat of the disease or illness and the action that needs to be taken to avoid it.

In subsequent versions of the model, authors have suggested that additional constructs be added. For example, Becker et al. (1977) incorporated health motivation to refer to the value the individual places on their health (such as whether or not health is important to them and their readiness to be concerned about health matters). Likewise, Rosenstock et al. (1988) suggested the inclusion of self-efficacy (one's belief in one's ability to perform an action, see **Chapter 4**). However, most research employing the health belief model has tended to focus on threat perception, behavioural evaluation and, to a lesser extent, cues to action (Zimmerman & Vernberg, 1994).

The evidence

If the health belief model is accurate, we should be able to use it to predict who is likely to take action and who is not. In other words, measures of key constructs (such as perceived susceptibility and severity) should correlate with behaviour. A number of studies have examined just this, in relation to behaviours ranging from condom use and influenza vaccinations to weight loss and smoking cessation (Carpenter, 2010; Harrison et al., 1992; Janz & Becker, 1984). However, many of these studies use cross-sectional study designs and retrospective measures that are arguably problematic as tests of the model (see **Box 5.3**).

BOX 5.3 TESTING THEORIES OF BEHAVIOUR CHANGE: CROSS-SECTIONAL, PROSPECTIVE AND EXPERIMENTAL STUDY DESIGNS

DIG A LITTLE DEEPER

Theories of health behaviour have often been tested using cross-sectional study designs where measures of cognitive variables and behaviour are taken simultaneously. Measures of behaviour in such studies also tend to be retrospective, for example they may ask a person to report on their behaviour during the previous week or month. This is problematic as people can engage in post-hoc justification of their behaviour. For instance, someone who has unprotected sex may subsequently downplay the risks in their mind. Additionally, some cognitive variables may change because the individual has taken action to protect their health (Janz & Becker, 1984). For example, a person may feel they are less susceptible to an illness once they have modified their behaviour, and barriers may be perceived as smaller once they have been overcome.

By contrast, prospective longitudinal studies take measures at different time points, in line with the ways in which theory variables are assumed to influence one another. So if perceived susceptibility is thought to influence behaviour, one would take the measure of susceptibility at an earlier point in time than the measure of behaviour. If the model is accurate, higher levels of perceived susceptibility should correlate with a greater likelihood (or higher level) of the protective behaviour. Where theories of behaviour assume sequential ordering between variables and outcomes, prospective studies are a far better test than cross-sectional studies.

However, both cross-sectional and prospective studies are a type of observational study design that relies on correlational analyses. These contrast with experimental study designs where variables are manipulated so their effects on behaviour can be measured. With appropriate controls, experimental studies allow us to more confidently conclude that a change in a particular construct or outcome occurred as a result of a change in a particular predictor. Unfortunately, when it comes to testing social cognition theories, experimental study designs are less common than observational designs (Hagger & Chatzisarantis, 2015; Sniehotta et al., 2014). As such, although there may be evidence to support a particular model, it may not necessarily be the best evidence. We consider study design and research methods in more detail in **Chapter 10**.

A meta-analysis conducted by Carpenter (2010) identified 18 studies that used prospective designs. Carpenter found that, as predicted by the model, variables relating to severity, barriers and benefits were all significantly related to the likelihood of performing the relevant behaviour. Benefits and barriers were the strongest predictors with correlations of 0.27 and 0.30, respectively. Severity showed a weaker correlation of 0.15. Susceptibility, on the other hand, was unrelated to behaviour ($r = 0.05$). Although Carpenter's results relied on a relatively small number of studies, he concluded that the weakness of susceptibility and severity as predictors meant the model was not accurate. He recommended that future work should test for more complex relationships between the variables.

Cues to action were not included in Carpenter's (2010) analysis since there were insufficient prospective studies that had measured this variable. This may be because cues to action can refer to such a wide range of different factors, making them difficult to measure. Since cues to action are thought to influence threat perception alongside susceptibility and severity, this may be one reason for the weaker relations between these two variables and behaviour in Carpenter's analysis. Studies that have examined the effects of particular cues to action on behaviour provide mixed evidence (Abraham & Sheeran, 2015). Likewise, fewer studies have examined the extent to which demographic, sociopsychological and structural variables predict susceptibility, severity, benefits and barriers. Again, whilst some studies that have looked at such variables do provide support for associations (Abraham & Sheeran, 2015) the lack of specificity in the model makes this aspect difficult to test.

Key limitations

The health belief model succeeds in identifying several key variables that appear to be important predictors of behaviour. It has also been used to inform the development of a wide range of successful health interventions (Abraham & Sheeran, 2015; Sohl & Moyer, 2007). Nevertheless, it does have a number of important limitations, some of which are detailed below:

- *Clarity and measurability of constructs* – some of the constructs are not clearly defined and have been operationalised in different ways by different researchers (Harrison et al., 1992). This is particularly true of cues to action that can encompass a very wide range of events. Whilst some of these, such as a letter from a dental practice, may act as a simple reminder, others, such as illness of a family member, could be influencing perceptions of susceptibility and severity. There is little in the model to help researchers distinguish between such possibilities. This makes this part of the model very difficult to measure and test.

- *Relationships between constructs* – although constructs are linked to one another in the model, the nature of these relations is often vague. In particular, it is not clear whether some variables are more important than others or how they may interact with one another. For example, it is unclear whether susceptibility and severity scores should be simply added up or multiplied by one another (the latter would be more consistent with the expectancy-value theories the model draws on; Fishbein & Ajzen, 1975). Likewise, the model states that barriers should be subtracted from benefits but it is unclear whether this refers to number of benefits and barriers or some measure of their perceived importance; irrespective of how beneficial you may believe a particular action to be, just one insurmountable barrier will prevent you from engaging in that behaviour.

- *Identification of behaviour change techniques* – the model predicts that change in key cognitive variables will result in change in behaviour. However, it does not provide any indication of how one might go about changing these variables. What are the most effective ways of influencing a person's threat perception and behavioural evaluation?

- *Empirical evidence* – as noted above, while there is good evidence to indicate that some of the constructs are related to behaviour, consistent support for the relevance of all the constructs is lacking, at least in terms of the relationships set out by the model.

- *Explanatory power* – there are a number of variables that are thought to be important predictors of behaviour change that are not included in the model. These include self-efficacy, social support, habits and intention (Bandura, 1997; Greaves et al., 2011; Lara et al., 2014; McEachan et al., 2011; Neal et al., 2011; Olander et al., 2013; Ramchand et al., 2017; Sokol & Fisher, 2016). Additionally, the model says little about the role of rewards in behaviour change; the fact that we can act to achieve positive health outcomes as well as avoid negative ones.

The theory of planned behaviour

The theory of planned behaviour[2] addresses some of the limitations of the health belief model (Azjen, 1991, 2005). Like the health belief model, it employs an expectancy-value framework that takes account of both outcome expectations and the value that is placed on them. However, unlike the health belief model it includes components that are more clearly related to intention, self-efficacy and the influence of others. It is also more explicit about the ways in which these different constructs interact with one another.

The theory

The theory of planned behaviour is illustrated in **Figure 5.2**. Key constructs are:

- Attitudes

- Subjective norms

- Perceived behavioural control

- Intention.

Like the health belief model, a person's outcome expectations are considered to be important. However, in this case the theory is explicit about the fact that any measure of outcome expectancy should be weighted by the value the individual places on that outcome. For example, a person might expect reduced alcohol intake to lead to weight loss. However, if that person does not value weight loss, the strength of their belief about

Figure 5.2 The theory of planned behaviour

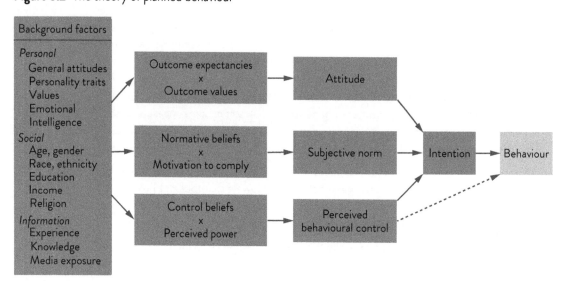

Source: Ajzen, I., *Attitudes, Personality and Behaviour* © 2005. Adapted with the kind permission of Open International Publishing Ltd. All rights reserved.

---

2   An earlier version, called 'the theory of reasoned action', was developed in the 1970s (Fishbein & Ajzen, 1975) but was subsequently extended to include perceived behavioural control and at this point was renamed the theory of planned behaviour (Ajzen, 1991, 2005).

the link between alcohol and weight loss will have no impact on their attitude toward their alcohol intake. Put another way, there would be little point trying to persuade someone that reducing alcohol intake is helpful for weight loss, if losing weight is not important to them. According to the theory, different weighted outcome expectancies are then summed to form the person's attitude toward the behaviour, either positive or negative.

Unlike the health belief model, the theory of planned behaviour also includes key constructs that relate to social pressures to behave in a particular way. Normative beliefs refer to the individual's beliefs about what others do, and about what others will think of them if they do or do not perform the behaviour in question. For example, will others think you are odd for sticking to soft drinks all night? Or will they applaud your self-restraint? Again, these beliefs are weighted by the value the individual places on them; their motivation to comply. If someone else's opinion is important to you, you are more likely to be influenced by their views; if they are someone you have little regard for, it probably won't matter to you what they think. According to the theory, relevant weighted normative beliefs are then added together to form the individual's subjective norm.

As mentioned previously, the theory of planned behaviour also takes account of self-efficacy. Termed 'perceived behavioural control', this refers to both internal control factors (how much willpower or self-control the individual believes they are able to exercise), and external control factors (whether there are factors beyond the person's control that they feel unable to influence). Again, beliefs about relevant control factors are weighted by the extent to which the person feels they are influential and these values are then added together to form the construct of perceived behavioural control.

According to the theory of planned behaviour, attitudes, subjective norms and perceived behavioural control combine to determine the person's intention to perform the relevant behaviour. Behavioural intention is causally related to whether or not they actually perform the behaviour. However, a key feature of the theory is that perceived behavioural control will also predict behaviour directly, bypassing intention. So it may be the case that we have every intention of performing a particular behaviour but factors beyond our control ultimately prevent us from doing so. For example, we may intend to stick to soft drinks all night, but ultimately fail to resist the allure of half-price cocktails. Alternatively, we may intend to engage in some early morning exercise but find the swimming pool closed for refurbishment. This link is shown as a dotted line in Figure 5.2 to reflect the fact that it depends on the accuracy of the individual's perceptions of control. (In this particular instance, perceived behavioural control is being used as a proxy for actual control.)

The relative importance of attitudes, subjective norms and perceived behavioural control is thought to vary across different situations and behaviours. So in some cases it may be that attitudes are the most important predictor of behaviour whilst in other cases subjective norms may be more influential.

Finally, background factors such as personality, socioeconomic status and previous experience are thought to exert their effect on behaviour via attitudes, subjective norms and perceived behavioural control.

The evidence

McEachan et al. (2011) conducted a meta-analysis of over 200 prospective studies that used the theory of planned behaviour to predict health-related actions. They found that, taken together, attitudes, subjective norms and perceived behavioural control accounted for 44.3% of the variance in intention, with the best predictors being attitudes and perceived behavioural control. Intention and perceived behavioural control accounted for 19.3% of the variance in behaviour. They also looked at whether the strength of these associations varied depending on the type of behaviour and found that the theory of planned behaviour was best at predicting physical activity and dietary behaviours, accounting for 23.9% and 21.2% of variance, respectively. It was not as good at predicting safe sex, detection behaviours (such as breast self-examination), engagement in risk behaviours (such as speeding or smoking) or abstinence behaviours (such as refraining from smoking). The variance accounted for in these types of studies ranged from 13.8% to 15.3%.

Key limitations

The theory of planned behaviour has arguably been the most dominant theory of health-related behaviour for the last three decades (Sniehotta et al., 2014). In some ways this is not surprising; empirical support is relatively high compared to models such as the health belief model. Nevertheless, it has been subject to criticism, with academics debating over whether it may be time to retire the theory or whether it can still make a useful contribution to the field (Ajzen, 2014; Sniehotta et al., 2014). It is probably fair to say that some of the criticisms levelled at the theory have been convincingly refuted. For example, some have argued that it fails to take account of the way in which the performance of a particular behaviour can influence subsequent cognitions about that behaviour (McEachan et al., 2011; Sutton, 1994). However, as Ajzen (2014) points out, this is a misunderstanding resulting from the fact that the graphic representation of the theory is generally simplified and such links omitted; by contrast, the text describing the theory is quite clear about the fact that the consequences of a behaviour can feed back into the person's beliefs and in this way influence future intentions and actions (Fishbein & Ajzen, 2010). Similarly, whilst some have suggested the theory focusses exclusively on rational reasoning, ignoring the role of unconscious influences (Sheeran et al., 2013), Ajzen (2014) has countered that behavioural, normative and control-related beliefs may arise via a wide range of irrational and unconscious processes (in addition to rational ones). Nevertheless, the theory of planned behaviour does have a number of limitations that are more difficult to defend against. Some of these are outlined below:

- *Identification of behaviour change techniques* – as noted previously, the utility of a theory of behaviour change depends not just on whether it can accurately *predict* behaviour, but also on whether it can help us *change* behaviour. To assess this we need to go beyond simply looking at correlations between different constructs, and find out what happens when we attempt to change those constructs. Far fewer studies of the theory of planned behaviour have attempted to do the latter, and those that have, have not always provided support for the theory (Hardeman et al., 2002; Sniehotta et al., 2014). For example, manipulations targeting specific constructs have not always been successful at changing those constructs, and when they have, these changes have not always translated into changes in intention and behaviour (McCarty, 1981; Sniehotta, 2009). Ajzen and Fishbein have argued that such studies are often poorly designed; for example, measures may not properly capture constructs, or researchers may fail to target the most relevant variables (Ajzen, 2014; Fishbein & Ajzen, 2010). Nevertheless, it is still the case that the theory fails to provide any information about how one might successfully influence the key constructs. Ajzen (2014) contends that the theory of planned behaviour was developed to explain and predict people's intentions and behaviour, not as a theory of behaviour change. However, if we are evaluating it in terms of its utility for health promotion, the lack of detail here is an important shortcoming.

- *Explanatory power (the intention-behaviour gap)* – although the theory of planned behaviour can predict behaviour to some extent, there is still a large amount of variation, around 80%, that it does not account for (McEachen et al., 2011). This is often referred to as the 'intention-behaviour gap' and is generally the result of 'inclined abstainers'; those who intend to perform a behaviour but fail to do so (Orbell & Sheeran, 1998). In some cases, this may be attributed to events that occur after intentions have been assessed, that result in subsequent changes to both intentions and behaviour (Ajzen, 2014). However, it seems unlikely that such instances account for all the unexplained variance. This in turn suggests there are important influences on behaviour that are not captured by the theory.

- *Explanatory power (mediation via intentions and perceived behavioural control)* – according to the theory, behaviour is mediated via intentions and perceived behavioural control. In other words, interventions that change behaviour will do so by changing intentions and/or perceived behavioural control. However, there are plenty of examples within the literature of instances in which we can bring about a change in behaviour without changing intentions or perceived behavioural control. We explore such approaches in **Chapter 6** (see **Box 5.4**).

BOX 5.4 THE ROLE OF INTENTIONS

MAKING CONNECTIONS

Many social cognition theories of behaviour emphasise the importance of intentions in behaviour and behaviour change. Changing intentions in order to change behaviour can be viewed as a reflective or controlled process. In other words, we are consciously aware of our intentions and the extent to which they guide our behaviour. But to what extent do we actually need to change intentions to change behaviour? **Chapter 6** looks at theories of behaviour change that place more emphasis on the role of automatic processes. In other words, they propose that we can influence a person's behaviour without them even necessarily being aware of it, let alone making a conscious decision to change.

- *Explanatory power (emotions)* – emotions are included in the theory of planned behaviour as part of the outcome expectancies construct; if one expects a particular behaviour to make one feel a certain way, either good or bad, this will influence one's attitude toward the behaviour. However, research suggests outcome expectancies is too broad a construct to adequately capture some of the more nuanced distinctions between different types of emotion. Research also suggests that emotions have a much more complex relationship with intentions and behaviour than that described by the theory of planned behaviour. For example, Conner and colleagues looked at the role of emotion in relation to blood donation (Conner et al., 2013a). Their data supported a distinction between cognitive attitudes, affective attitudes, anticipated negative affect and anticipated positive affect. In other words, these appeared to be separate constructs, able to vary independently from one another. Such distinctions are not captured well by the theory of planned behaviour that would group anticipated positive and negative affect together as outcome expectancies, and cognitive and affective attitudes as simply attitudes. (See **Box 5.5** for a more detail on the difference between affective attitudes and anticipated affect.) Even more problematic for the theory was that anticipated positive affective reactions, anticipated negative affective reactions and cognitive attitudes were *simultaneous* predictors of intention. Likewise, intentions, perceived behavioural control and anticipated positive affective reactions were *simultaneous* predictors of actual blood donation. Recall that the theory of planned behaviour states that outcome expectancies influence intention (and behaviour) *via* attitudes. However, the data from this study suggest that outcome expectancies that relate to emotions can have a *direct* influence on both intentions and behaviour. Thus in this instance, the theory of planned behaviour does not provide a good explanation of the data.

BOX 5.5 HOW DO YOU FEEL ABOUT IT? DISTINGUISHING BETWEEN AFFECTIVE ATTITUDES AND ANTICIPATED AFFECT

DIG A LITTLE DEEPER

As noted in **Chapter 4**, attitude research has long distinguished between cognitive attitudes (beliefs) and affective attitudes (feelings; Maio et al., 2019). However, more recently researchers have made a distinction between affective attitudes and anticipated affective reactions (Giner-Sorolla, 2001). Whilst affective attitudes refer to one's feelings about a particular behaviour (or other attitudinal object), anticipated affective reactions refer to feelings that are expected to *follow* from the performance or non-performance of the behaviour (rather than feelings that may occur *during* behavioural performance or non-performance). For example, we may feel wonderful whilst tucking into the delicious starter and bread rolls at a fancy restaurant, but thoroughly disappointed when we realise we've spoilt our appetite for the main course. These two constructs also tend to be characterised by different types of feelings; hedonic emotions such as pleasure and excitement during the behaviour (or non-behaviour), self-conscious emotions such as guilt, regret or satisfaction afterwards.

- *Explanatory power (socioeconomic status and other demographic variables)* – the theory states that the impact of all external variables on behaviour is mediated via theory of planned behaviour constructs. In other words, factors such as age, gender and socioeconomic status exert their effects on behaviour by influencing cognitions such as attitudes and intentions. However, research tends to show partial rather than full mediation (Godin et al., 2010; McMillan et al., 2009), suggesting external variables also influence behaviour via mechanisms other than those identified by the theory of planned behaviour. As such, the theory may be too simplistic a depiction. In particular, in **Chapter 3** we saw how poverty can reduce the cognitive resources a person has available for anything other than their most urgent problems (Mani et al., 2013; Mullainathan & Shafir, 2013). This is advantageous as it means all their attention is focussed on their most pressing needs. For example, if a person receives an unexpected bill that means they face eviction from their home at the end of the month, avoiding eviction would become a priority. As such, it seems unlikely they would spontaneously expend additional cognitive resources mentally adjusting a whole series of attitudes and intentions they previously held prior to receiving the bill (for example, in relation to dental check-ups, exercise, losing weight or eating more healthily). And yet they may now be much less likely to engage in these behaviours. Of course, they may report lower intentions to engage in such behaviours if questioned, but arguably such questions would be simply prompting them to consider and adjust their intentions (see **Box 5.6**). Other research also suggests socioeconomic status may moderate the relationship between intentions and behaviour, with those from lower socioeconomic backgrounds showing weaker links between the two (Conner et al., 2013b). Again, this type of relationship is not captured by the theory of planned behaviour.

BOX 5.6 THE QUESTION-BEHAVIOUR EFFECT: SIMPLY ASKING SOMEONE ABOUT THEIR INTENTIONS CAN INFLUENCE THEIR BEHAVIOUR

AS AN ASIDE

To fully test the theory of planned behaviour, one needs to measure intentions. However, an important difficulty here is that simply asking someone about their intentions to perform a particular behaviour can make them more or less likely to perform that behaviour (Rodrigues et al., 2015; Wilding et al., 2016).

This effect was first demonstrated in the 1980s by Sherman (Sherman, 1980), who asked people to indicate how likely they would be to perform a socially desirable behaviour (collecting money for charity) or an undesirable behaviour (such as singing over the telephone). He found that those who had been asked to indicate their intentions were subsequently more likely to perform the desirable behaviour and less likely to perform the undesirable behaviour. This effect has since been replicated in areas ranging from consumer behaviour to health (Wilding et al., 2016). It has also been used as an intervention in its own right, to try to promote behaviours such as blood donation and the uptake of vaccinations and health checks (Conner et al., 2011; Godin et al., 2008).

But how does it work? Several explanations have been put forward. Sherman (1980) proposed a processing fluency account. He suggested that the question elicits a mental simulation of the behaviour; when the individual is subsequently presented with an opportunity to act, they access this mental simulation, which makes it easier for them to behave in accordance with it. An alternative explanation is that the question increases the accessibility of relevant attitudes (Dholakia, 2010). When faced with a choice of whether or not to act, these attitudes are then more readily brought to mind, meaning the person is more likely to be influenced by them. Finally, a third explanation draws on the theory of **cognitive dissonance** (Festinger, 1957). According to this explanation we are motivated to behave in ways that are consistent with our beliefs and opinions. Thus, having expressed an intention to behave in a particular way, we are subsequently motivated to do so in order to limit any cognitive dissonance that may arise from a discrepancy. The evidence for these different explanations is reviewed by Wilding and colleagues (Wilding et al., 2016).

Cognitive dissonance – a feeling of mental discomfort that occurs when a person simultaneously holds two or more contradictory beliefs, ideas or values. According to cognitive dissonance theory, people strive for internal psychological consistency and so are motivated to reduce cognitive dissonance by adjusting either their thoughts or their behaviour (Festinger, 1957).

CHAPTER 5

- *Generalisability* – some have argued the theory is best at predicting behaviour among young, healthy, affluent individuals (McEachan et al., 2011; Sniehotta et al., 2014; Sniehotta et al., 2013). In other words, those who are least in need of behaviour change interventions. Research examining the moderating effects of socioeconomic status is certainly in keeping with this view; as noted above, those from lower socioeconomic backgrounds may show weaker links between intention and behaviour (Conner et al., 2013b). Again, from a health promotion point of view, this significantly limits the utility of the theory.

Protection motivation theory

The 1980s saw the beginning of the HIV pandemic, the virus that leads to AIDS (see **Chapter 12**). In Britain, this prompted the government to launch its 'Don't Die of Ignorance' campaign to raise awareness of the disease and promote safe sex. This featured an erupting volcano, an ominous soundtrack and a tombstone being chiselled with the word 'AIDS' (**Image 5.2**). The campaign was deliberately designed to shock viewers into taking notice and taking action.

Image 5.2 *A tombstone chiselled with the word 'AIDS' that appeared on British television screens in the late 1980s as part of a campaign to promote safe sex.*

Credit: 'AIDS – Monolith' is Crown copyright and is reproduced with the permission of The British Film Institute under delegated authority from The Keeper of Public Records.

Are scare tactics a good idea when it comes to health promotion? We could try to understand the potential impact of such a campaign using the health belief model, or the theory of planned behaviour. Alternatively, we could use protection motivation theory, a theory developed specifically for understanding the effects of communications designed to elicit fear.

The theory

Protection motivation theory is based on the fear-drive model that states that when a communication elicits fear in the viewer, they are motivated to reduce that fear and so inclined to follow the advice that is provided. However, if no advice is provided (or if following the advice fails to reduce fear) the viewer will instead attempt to avoid or deny the content of the communication (Janis, 1967; see also disengagement coping, **Chapter 4**). Although the theory was originally developed to help understand the effects of fear (Rogers, 1975), it was later extended to provide a more general account of persuasive communications (Rogers, 1983). Key components of the theory are:

- Threat appraisal
- Coping appraisal
- Protection motivation.

As shown in **Figure 5.3**, according to protection motivation theory, behaviour is directly influenced by a construct called 'protection motivation'. This in turn is determined by the individual's 'threat appraisal' and their 'coping appraisal'.

Figure 5.3 Protection motivation theory

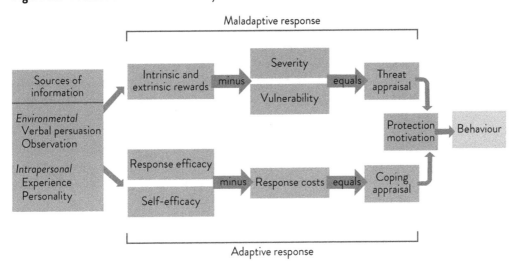

Source: Adapted from Rogers (1983) with the permission of Guilford Press.

Threat appraisal relates to the maladaptive response. In our AIDS example, this would refer to unprotected sex. According to the theory, threat appraisal is a result of the intrinsic and extrinsic rewards of the unsafe (or unhealthy) behaviour, after subtracting perceptions of severity and vulnerability. Intrinsic rewards of unprotected sex might include enhanced pleasure and spontaneity whilst extrinsic rewards could, in principle, include things like social approval or payment. Severity refers to how bad the potential consequences of the unsafe behaviour are. This was clearly targeted in the Don't Die of Ignorance campaign; one of the key messages was that AIDS kills and there is no known cure. Vulnerability refers to how at risk the person believes they are. Again, this was a target of the British campaign. A common misperception at the time was that the disease was restricted to gay men and intravenous drug users; the advert and accompanying billboard posters aimed to correct this with the words 'Gay or straight, male or female, anyone can get AIDS from sexual intercourse'.

Coping appraisal refers to the person's beliefs about the adaptive response, in this case the use of a condom. Coping appraisal is computed from the degree of response efficacy and self-efficacy, minus any response costs. Response efficacy relates to how effective the individual believes the action would be, self-efficacy to their confidence in carrying out the action, and response costs to any undesirable consequences of carrying out the action. These feature less in the Don't Die of Ignorance campaign. The television advert does not even mention condoms, but instead urges the viewer to protect themselves by reading a relevant leaflet (which was subsequently delivered to all households). Although the billboard posters do identify the adaptive response ('Protect yourself, use a condom') they do not give any information designed to reassure the viewer that condoms would be effective (response efficacy), inform viewers how to use condoms (self-efficacy) or tackle perceptions of barriers, such as ease of purchasing or reduced pleasure (response costs). The leaflet provides much more detailed information but takes a similar approach. There is a lot of emphasis on increasing perceptions of severity and vulnerability, but little information on condom use. It simply urges the reader to 'always use a condom' as this will 'reduce the risk of catching the virus'. It goes on to add that it is best to use water-based lubricating gels with condoms as oil-based gels can weaken the rubber, but then simply adds '*Ask your chemist for advice.*' Thus, according to protection motivation theory, the Don't Die of Ignorance campaign would have been more effective had it more explicitly targeted viewers' beliefs about using condoms (the adaptive response). (Visit **macmillanihe.com/tapper-health-psychology** to see the Don't Die of Ignorance leaflet.)

As noted previously, protection motivation theory was originally developed to account for the effects of fear-based appeals, such as the Don't Die of Ignorance campaign (Rogers, 1975). However, its later extension (Rogers, 1983) referred to additional external events that could elicit the cognitive processes described in the theory. These external events included not just other types of persuasive communications, but also observation of others, personal experience and personality. (Whilst the notion of personality as a 'source of information' is not elaborated upon by Rogers, one could assume that rather than being a source of information per se, it instead influences cognitive processing by *interacting* with other sources of information. For example, those with certain personality traits may be more resistant to verbal persuasion than others.)

The evidence

Two meta-analyses have examined the extent to which protection motivation variables predict intentions and behaviour (Floyd et al., 2000; Milne et al, 2000). These generally provide support for the predictive utility of the constructs, with coping appraisal variables (particularly self-efficacy) being better predictors than threat appraisal variables. However, these analyses showed that, like the theory of planned behaviour, protection motivation theory is better at predicting intention than behaviour. Additionally, these meta-analyses drew on studies that employed a wide range of designs including cross-sectional as well as prospective and experimental designs. As discussed in **Box 5.3**, the interpretation of data from cross-sectional studies can be particularly problematic.

Also as noted previously, from a health promotion perspective, we are more interested in the extent to which a theory can help us change behaviour, rather than just predict it. Studies that have attempted to manipulate protection motivation theory constructs have generally had more success at changing cognitions relating to threat appraisal than cognitions relating to coping appraisal. However, with the exception of response costs, medium-to-large effects have still been observed for the latter (Milne et al., 2000). Norman et al. (2015) also provide a narrative review of experimental and intervention studies that have examined effects on intention and behaviour. These show support for the notion that we can influence intentions and behaviour via protection motivation theory constructs, again showing better effects for intention relative to behaviour. These studies also suggest that increases in self-efficacy may have the largest effects on intention. These findings are consistent with other research that has highlighted the importance of self-efficacy in fear appeals (see **Box 5.7**).

Key limitations

Some of the limitations of protection motivation theory are similar to those already outlined for the health belief model and the theory of planned behaviour, whilst others are more specific. These limitations include (but are not restricted to) the following:

- *Clarity of constructs* – some have argued that it can be difficult to distinguish between the rewards of a maladaptive behaviour and the costs of an adaptive behaviour (Abraham et al., 1994). For example, increased spontaneity may be one of the rewards of unprotected sex whilst reduced spontaneity may be a cost of using a condom. Are these

BOX 5.7 SHOULD WE BE USING FEAR TO TRY TO CHANGE PEOPLE'S BEHAVIOUR?

A wide variety of health promotion campaigns try to elicit fear. Such campaigns are typically concerned with behaviours such as drink driving, binge drinking, speeding, safe sex and smoking. However, the wisdom of such an approach has been questioned.

HOT TOPIC

In this chapter we look at protection motivation theory, though a number of other theories are also concerned with the effects of fear on behaviour. These include the extended parallel process model (Witte, 1992), the stage model of processing of fear-arousing communications (de Hoog et al., 2007) and terror management theory (Goldenberg & Arndt, 2008). These theories make a range of different predictions about the relationship between fear and behaviour, and also about the role of self-efficacy. For example, while some suggest a linear relationship between fear and behaviour (Witte & Allen, 2000), others predict a curvilinear relationship, with high levels of fear being less effective, or even counterproductive (Janis & Feshbach, 1953). This is because high levels of fear are thought to elicit defensive reactions, where the viewer attempts to manage discomfort by, for example, avoiding the message or engaging in other strategies such as denial or suppression (van 't Riet & Ruiter, 2013). Likewise, some theories predict an interaction between fear and self-efficacy, such that fear will only be effective at motivating behaviour change when self-efficacy is also successfully targeted, or when the target population already has high self-efficacy for the behaviour in question. Again, whilst some theories predict that a lack of self-efficacy will simply result in no effects, other theories suggest that in these circumstances fear may be detrimental, eliciting defensive reactions. For example, terror management theory states that where self-efficacy is low there will be a decoupling between intention and behaviour, such that although fear may positively impact upon intentions, it may have the opposite effect on behaviour, with individuals engaging in more risky actions as a means of escaping self-awareness (Peters et al., 2013).

However, despite the widespread use of fear appeals in public health, there are very few studies that have rigorously tested the above hypotheses (Peters et al., 2013). Some meta-analyses provide reassurance. For example, they have failed to find any evidence to support a curvilinear relationship between fear and behaviour, instead suggesting a positive linear relationship (Witte & Allen, 2000) or a relationship that is linear up to a point, after which increasing levels of fear are no more effective, but are not counterproductive (Tannenbaum et al., 2015). Meta-analyses have also tended to show that whilst fear appeals are more effective when they include efficacy statements, they are still effective even without efficacy statements (Tannenbaum et al., 2015). However, these meta-analyses are based on a limited number of studies, with outcomes that include attitudes and intentions, as well as behaviour. When analysis is restricted to studies that have measured behaviour, an interaction between efficacy and threat emerges, such that fear only results in behavioural change when self-efficacy is high (Peters et al., 2013). These findings are in line with neurocognitive and eye-tracking studies that have shown that attention is diverted away from threatening information among populations for whom it is most relevant (Kessels et al., 2010, 2011, 2014).

These meta-analyses have also been restricted to experimental studies in which participants are typically required to engage with whatever message is presented to them. In real life the audience is at liberty to switch television channels, immediately bin a leaflet that arrives through the letterbox or simply divert their attention away from uncomfortable billboards and magazine adverts. A meta-analysis of real-world HIV prevention interventions that employed fear appeals concluded that, although use of fear increased perceptions of risk, it actually decreased knowledge and condom use (Earl & Albarracín, 2007).

Hastings et al. (2004) have also raised concerns over the ethics of imposing upsetting images on viewers. As well as questioning the morality of actively trying to cause people anxiety and distress they also highlight a number of potentially damaging consequences. For example, children may inadvertently be exposed to distressing images, parents may prevent children from walking to school because of road safety fears, and vulnerable adults, who may feel unable to quit smoking, may suffer from increased anxiety, with further negative effects on their wellbeing. This in turn may serve to widen health inequalities. Hastings et al. suggest that the use of positive emotions such as humour, empathy and hope are better alternatives to fear.

really two separate factors that both independently influence protection motivation? The theory implies that someone could perceive the rewards but not the costs, or vice versa. Is this really the case?

- *Explanatory power (self-efficacy)* – some studies have found that self-efficacy directly influences behaviour, independently from intention (Levy et al., 2008; Plotnikoff et al., 2009a; Plotnikoff et al., 2009b; Plotnikoff et al., 2010; Tavares et al., 2009; Tulloch et al., 2009). However, protection motivation theory does not include a direct link between self-efficacy and behaviour, instead assuming that self-efficacy influences behaviour via intentions ('protection motivation').

- *Explanatory power (past behaviour)* – one of the best predictors of future behaviour is past behaviour (Conner & Armitage, 1998). Past behaviour could influence future behaviour either consciously, for example via intentions, or unconsciously, in the form of habits (Ouellette & Woods, 1998). Whilst protection motivation theory could account for the former (past behaviour could initiate the appraisal processes detailed in the model) it cannot account for the latter, which would require a direct link between past behaviour and future behaviour. We considering the role of habits and automatic processes in **Chapter 6**.

- *Generalisability* – the success of public health campaigns, such as Don't Die of Ignorance, rely on people paying attention to them. However, the extent to which people attend to such communications outside the laboratory is unclear and protection motivation theory does not help us predict who will and will not attend to such information. As such, the extent to which the theory can account for the effects of real health promotion campaigns is unclear.

Social cognitive theory

One of the key criticisms of the social cognition theories we have looked at so far is that they tell us little about how we might influence the constructs that are believed to predict intention and behaviour. As such, we might question their utility for the development of behaviour change interventions. A theory that addresses some of these concerns is social cognitive theory (Bandura, 1986, 1997).

The theory

The key constructs of social cognitive theory are:

- Goals
- Outcome expectancies
- Self-efficacy
- Socio-structural factors.

The ways in which these constructs are believed to relate to one another is shown in **Figure 5.4**.

Figure 5.4 Social cognitive theory

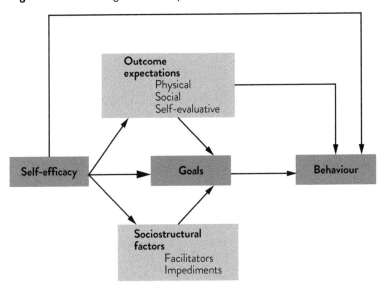

Source: Bandura, A. (2009). Reproduced with permission from John Wiley & Sons.

According to social cognitive theory, behaviour is directly influenced by goals, outcome expectancies and self-efficacy. Goals may be either distal or proximal, with proximal goals being very similar to the concept of intentions used in other social cognition theories. In social cognitive theory, goals are necessary for behaviour change but are not sufficient. In other words, one's behaviour would not change in the absence of a relevant goal, but it could fail to change even if one had formed a goal.

Outcome expectancies are beliefs about what might happen as a result of a particular behaviour (see **Chapter 4**). They may be short term or long term, positive or negative. They include beliefs about physical outcomes, social outcomes and self-evaluative outcomes. As well as influencing behaviour directly, outcome expectancies also influence goals.

Self-efficacy plays a central role in social cognitive theory, directly influencing every other construct. Self-efficacy is one's belief in one's ability to perform a specific action or achieve a particular outcome (see **Box 5.8** and **Chapter 4**).

Finally, socio-structural factors exert their effects on behaviour via goals. These socio-structural factors may be things that impede action, such as lack of access to exercise facilities, or things that facilitate action, such as the opening of a new cycle path.

BOX 5.8 DO YOU FEEL ABLE TO EAT PLENTY OF FRUIT AND VEGETABLES?

TAKE THE TEST

How confident are you in your ability to eat plenty of fruit and vegetables? Mainvil et al. (2009) set out to develop a questionnaire to assess just this among New Zealand adults, aged 25 to 60 years. They began by conducting focus groups, targeting those at risk for poorer health outcomes, and encouraging them to discuss situations in which they found it easy and difficult to eat fruit and vegetables. The themes that emerged were used to develop a set of questionnaire items that were then checked for face validity by a nutrition researcher before being tested on a group of individuals from low- to middle-income backgrounds, to check their understanding of the items. Finally, after some minor wording and order changes they sent their 79-item questionnaire to 350 New Zealand adults, randomly selected from a nationally representative sample. The questions asked them to rate their confidence in their ability to eat fruit and vegetables, for example with items such as 'I can eat vegetables even when I have to prepare them myself' and 'I can eat fruit as a snack at least once a day'. A total of 228 individuals returned the questionnaire. If you recall, self-efficacy is meant to relate to specific actions (see **Chapter 4**). In keeping with this, the results showed that self-efficacy for eating fruit was distinct from self-efficacy for eating vegetables. Also, in line with theory, both these sub-scales showed positive correlations with intake ($r = 0.30$ for fruit and $r = 0.34$ for vegetables). You can test your own self-efficacy for eating fruit and vegetables at **macmillanihe/com/ tapper-health-psychology**.

Looking at **Figure 5.4**, we can see there are three natural points of intervention for those wishing to change behaviour: outcome expectancies, self-efficacy and socio-structural factors. Assuming we can accurately identify relevant socio-structural factors, in principle these are relatively easy to target; for example, we can simply create more exercise facilities and ensure people are able to access them. (Of course, in practice this is not simple at all, but the key difficulty here is in terms of implementing the intervention, not identifying what it should consist of.) However, outcome expectancies and self-efficacy are a little trickier. How do we influence these more elusive constructs that reside in the minds of those whose behaviour we are trying to change?

This is one of the strengths of social cognitive theory; it clearly describes the factors that influence outcome expectancies and self-efficacy and so provides an easier starting point for the development of behaviour change interventions. According to the theory, outcome expectancies are influenced by both direct experience and by observation of others. For example, if we observe another person return from a run, happy and smiling, enthusing about what a wonderfully de-stressing and mood enhancing experience it was, we might start to think that perhaps we too could enjoy the same benefits from running.

Similar factors are at play when it comes to self-efficacy; again it can be influenced by personal experience (sometimes termed performance accomplishments or mastery experiences) and by observing others (vicarious experience), especially others we perceive as similar to ourselves. For example, we may think to ourselves, '*If non-sporty Alexandra Hemingsley can run a marathon, then perhaps I can too.*' Self-efficacy can also be influenced by verbal persuasion (such as words of encouragement from those around you) as well as emotional arousal (we tend to feel more confident in our abilities when we are in a good mood, less confident when we are feeling down). According to the theory, personal experience is most effective at influencing self-efficacy, followed by vicarious experience, then verbal persuasion and lastly emotional arousal.

The evidence

There is substantial evidence to support a link between self-efficacy and behaviour change. For example, self-efficacy has been identified as one of the best predictors of weight loss success, medication adherence, condom use, physical activity and fruit and vegetable consumption (Langebeek et al., 2014; Rovniak et al., 2002; Teixeira et al., 2015; Van Duyn et al., 2001; Widman et al., 2014; Williams & French, 2011; though see also Olander et al., 2013). Nevertheless, as discussed in **Chapter 4**, French (2013) notes that such research is often designed in a way that makes it difficult to distinguish between cause and effect. He suggests that an alternative explanation for such findings is that increased self-efficacy occurs as a *result* of behaviour change. Or alternatively that both self-efficacy and behaviour may change independently as a result of a third variable, such as **action planning**. More experimental work would be needed to really tease apart these different possibilities.

> **Action planning** – the creation of a detailed plan of all the actions that need to be taken in order to achieve a specific goal.

In terms of techniques that increase self-efficacy, there is evidence to suggest that verbal persuasion and activities aimed at promoting experiences of success are effective (Hyde et al., 2008; Prestwich et al., 2013; Williams & French, 2011). Such findings are in line with social cognitive theory. Stress management has also been shown to be associated with improved dietary self-efficacy (Prestwich et al., 2013), a finding that is consistent with the notion that self-efficacy is influenced by emotional arousal. However, other techniques, such as action planning, have been shown to be associated with increased self-efficacy too (Olander et al., 2013; Williams & French, 2011) and such findings are more difficult to explain using social cognitive theory.

Fewer studies have tested other aspects of social cognitive theory, and where they have, support has tended to be weaker compared to the support for self-efficacy. For example, Young and colleagues conducted a systematic review of 44 studies examining social cognitive theory in relation to physical activity (M.D. Young et al., 2014). They found that social cognitive theory accounted for 31% of the variance in physical activity. However, whilst self-efficacy and goals were consistently associated with physical activity, outcome expectations and socio-structural factors were not. They also found that the amount of variance explained was moderated by methodological quality, with studies of higher quality explaining a greater proportion of variance in physical activity. They recommended that researchers aim to assess all constructs of the theory and ensure they do so with reliable scales. Luszczynska and Schwarzer (2015) also reviewed studies examining social cognitive theory in a range of different domains and came to a similar conclusion; that more high-quality studies were needed to confirm associations between other social cognitive theory constructs, as well as provide accurate estimates of their effects on behaviour.

> **Social norms** – rules of behaviour that are considered acceptable to a particular society or group. We look at social norms in more detail in **Chapter 6**.

Key limitations

As noted above, one of the major strengths of social cognitive theory is the fact that it describes the ways in which important constructs are influenced. This makes it attractive for those wishing to develop behaviour change interventions. Nevertheless, the theory is not without limitations. These include the following:

- *Explanatory power (mediation via goals, self-efficacy and outcome expectancies)* – similar to the theory of planned behaviour, a limitation of social cognitive theory is that all behaviour is thought to be mediated via goals (similar to intentions), self-efficacy (similar to perceived behavioural control) and outcome expectancies. Like the theory of planned behaviour, social cognitive theory assumes all behaviour change is under explicit, conscious control. As mentioned previously, we will consider alternative perspectives in **Chapter 6**.

- *Explanatory power (past behaviour)* – like protection motivation theory, social cognitive theory fails to account for research that suggests that much of our behaviour is habitual, performed outside conscious awareness (Wood et al., 2002). Again, we explore habits and automatic processes in **Chapter 6**.

- *Explanatory power (social norms)* – research suggests that **social norms** can have a powerful influence on behaviour (Burger & Shelton, 2011; Burger et al., 2010; Cialdini et al., 1990; Schultz et al., 2008). Whilst these are a component of the theory of planned behaviour (in the form of subjective norms) they are not explicitly addressed in social cognitive theory. Although one could argue they are encompassed by outcome expectancies, one could also take the view that they warrant separate consideration because they have such an important influence on behaviour. Additionally, it would be difficult to account for the effects of descriptive norms (norms that describe what others do) using outcome expectancies.

Continuum theories: summary

In this section we looked at four different continuum models: the health belief model, the theory of planned behaviour, protection motivation theory and social cognitive theory. Each of these theories have their own specific strengths and weaknesses. However, one weakness common to them all is that they do not really address the issue of behaviour change maintenance. Whilst some health-related behaviours involve a one-off performance (such as undergoing a screening test or getting a vaccination), many involve repeated performance over extended periods of time (such as being physically active or eating healthily). Continuum models assume the person simply cycles through the same process over and over again. But is this really the case? Are the factors that determine whether a person initiates a behaviour exactly the same as those that help them repeat it over time? In the next section we turn to stage theories that are more concerned with behaviour change over time.

STAGE THEORIES

Have you ever managed to successfully change your behaviour? Have you gone on a diet, taken up more exercise, or started studying harder? Was it a sudden decision or something you had mulled over for a while? Did your behaviour change overnight or was it a more gradual process in which you became increasingly convinced it was the right thing to do, and more certain of the actions you needed to take?

As noted above, one of the criticisms of the theories we've looked at so far is that they do not really capture the fact that behaviour change may often be better viewed as a process. For example, in a group of smokers, some may have absolutely no desire to quit, some may be thinking about quitting and others may have decided to quit the following week. Intuitively, we can see that these people are quite different from one another and might benefit from different strategies. We might highlight the dangers of smoking to the individual with no desire to quit but offer more practical help to the person who plans to quit next week. Continuum theories would distinguish between such people in terms of their attitudes or intentions or levels of self-efficacy, but they would still all be categorised as smokers. Stage theories have been developed to better capture the process of behaviour change and to more explicitly address the qualitative differences between people who have all still yet to change their behaviour.

Stage theories have four key features (Weinstein et al., 1998). These are as follows:

1. A classification system to define different stages

2. Stages that are ordered

3. Common barriers to change facing people within the same stage

4. Different barriers to change facing people in different stages.

According to stage theories, people must pass through each stage in order to reach the endpoint (that is, either behaviour change or behaviour change maintenance). They cannot skip stages but they may go back stages and will not necessarily reach the endpoint. According to stage theories, different types of strategies will be relevant for people at different stages.

Stage theories include the Rubicon model of action phases (Achtziger & Gollwitzer, 2008; Gollwitzer, 1996), the transtheoretical model (Prochaska & DiClemente, 1983; Prochaska et al. 1992, 2008; Prochaska & Velicer, 1997), the precaution adoption process model (Weinstein et al., 2008), the health behaviour goal model (Maes & Gebhardt, 2000) and the model of pathways to treatment (Scott et al., 2013). As noted previously, it is beyond the scope of this book to review all social cognition theories. In this section we look at the Rubicon model of action phases, because it underpins **implementation intentions**; an important behaviour change technique we examine in **Chapter 6**. We also look at the transtheoretical model because it is the most commonly used stage model (Davis et al., 2015).

> **Implementation intention** – a type of action plan that specifies when, where and how a behaviour will be performed.

The Rubicon model of action phases

Imagine an ambitious young designer working for an advertising agency at their spacious out-of-town offices. She cares about her health, but her job is desk-based, and she works long hours. She struggles to find the time to exercise. She hates her commute to work too. Although it's not far, the traffic makes the drive frustratingly slow. Some days she has difficulty finding a parking spot which makes her late and puts her in a bad mood. She wonders whether she should cycle instead.

The model

The Rubicon model of action phases was developed to capture the types of processes that may take our aspiring young designer from thinking about cycling to actually cycling. It distinguishes between goal setting (the process of deciding to pursue a particular goal) and goal striving (the process of trying to achieve that goal) (Achtziger & Gollwitzer, 2008; Gollwitzer, 1996). These two processes are reflected in the model as two different stages:

- A motivational or deliberative stage

- An implementational or volitional stage.

These stages are further divided into four phases that map onto different tasks that have to be addressed before the person moves on to the next phase. These stages and phases are depicted in **Figure 5.5**.

Crossing the Rubicon – to pass a point of no return. The Rubicon refers to a river in the north of Italy that once marked the boundary between Italy and Cisalpine Gaul. In 49 BC Julius Caesar led an army south over the river toward Rome. Crossing the river was considered a declaration of war, making conflict inevitable.

A key part of the model is the process of **crossing the Rubicon**, which marks a switch from deliberation to firm commitment to action. In the first predecisional phase the person considers the possible long-term and short-term outcomes of action, both positive and negative. They also think about the likelihood of the outcomes and whether they have the necessary time and resources to pursue them. So in our example, the designer may weigh up the potential benefits of cycling (such as improved health and reduced frustration) with its potential costs (such as a longer commute, safety concerns and a need to change clothes at work). However, it is also assumed that people will have many different desires and wishes so a single desire (such as improved health) will not be considered in isolation but instead weighted against competing desires (such as career progression). Where a desire is weighted highly, it needs to be transformed into a concrete

Figure 5.5 The Rubicon model of action phases

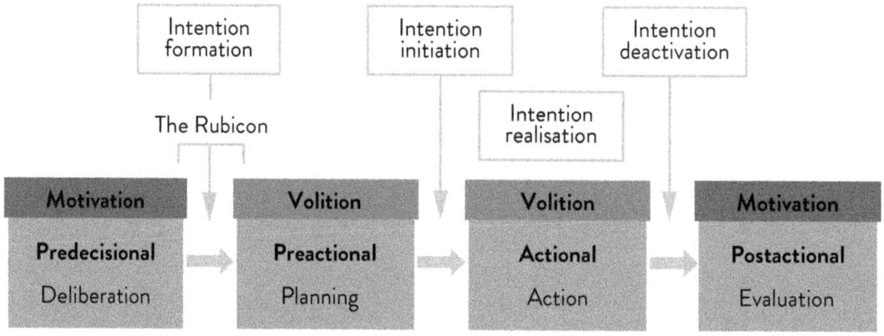

Source: Achtzinger, A. & Gollwitzer, P.M., 'Motivation and volition in the course of action' in J. Heckenhausen and H. Heckenhausen (eds.) *Motivation and Action*, Cambridge University Press, New York, USA. Copyright © 2008. Adapted with permission from Cambridge University Press.

goal (in this case, cycling to work) before the person moves to the next stage (crosses the Rubicon). This process is referred to as 'intention formation'.

The four different phases are also associated with different styles of thinking or 'mindsets'. The characteristics of both the phases and the mindsets are summarised in **Table 5.1**.

The evidence

The Rubicon model is relatively new compared with some of the other theories we have looked at in this chapter, and it has been subject to fewer evaluations. However, some aspects of the model, such as the existence of different mindsets, have been supported with experimental evidence. For example, studies have shown that those in a deliberative mindset have a wider breadth of visual attention, are more likely to process task-irrelevant information, process information relating to outcome desirability and feasibility in a more objective manner, and are less likely to take risks (Büttner et al., 2014; Fujita et al., 2007; Gagné & Lydon, 2001; Gollwitzer & Kinney, 1989; Keller & Gollwitzer, 2017; Puca, 2001; Taylor & Gollwitzer, 1995).

Table 5.1 Key characteristics of different phases and mindsets in the Rubicon model of action phases

Stage	Phase	Mindset	Examples
Motivational	*Predecisional* – the desirability and feasibility of the potential goals are assessed.	*Deliberative* – the person is concerned with information relating to the outcomes of different goals, and the likelihood of achieving them.	Works out how long it would take to cycle to work. Reads articles about the safety risks versus health benefits of cycling on busy roads.
Volitional	*Preactional* – the person decides how best to achieve their goal, for example by making a specific plan.	*Implemental* – there is a focus on information that is relevant to task performance. If action plans need to be formulated the individual will be receptive to information that relates to when, where and how they should act. They will be less receptive to incidental information that may be relevant to the goal but less relevant to task performance, for example goal desirability and feasibility.	Notices bicycle racks near the office. Decides to buy a bike at the weekend and cycle to work on Monday. Uses a map to plan a route. Ignores local news headlines about a cyclist being hit by a car.
Volitional	*Actional* – the person carries out their plans.	*Actional* – the person is focussed on their actions, attending only to aspects of the self and environment that help sustain these. They will be less receptive to information that might distract them.	Cycles to work and finds a convenient place to lock the bike. Takes little interest in the work email about plans to expand the car park.
Motivational	*Postactional* – the results of the action are assessed against the goal. The goal may be deactivated, abandoned, adjusted or retained but with renewed efforts to achieve it.	*Evaluative* – the person attends to information that helps them assess the outcome and its desirability, comparing this with what they had anticipated.	Notices she sleeps better at night and arrives at work feeling happier. Dislikes having to carry clothes and spend time in the office changing. Decides to restrict cycling to days when she can dress more casually and it's not raining.

BOX 5.9 FOCUSSED ATTENTION

MAKING CONNECTIONS

According to the Rubicon model, an implemental mindset is associated with focussed attention and shielding from the distractions of competing goals (Achtziger & Gollwitzer, 2008). How does this relate to the literature on cognitive resources that we looked at in **Chapter 3**?

Key limitations

One of the strengths of the Rubicon model is that it does not stop at predicting intentions but also aims to account for the processes involved in converting intentions to action. Given the gap between intentions and behaviour (McEachen et al., 2011; Orbell & Sheeran, 1998) this is important, and the model has led to a large body of valuable work on implementation intentions. We look at implementation intentions in **Chapter 6**. In the meantime, two key limitations of the Rubicon model are as follows:

- *Clarity of constructs and relationships between constructs* – whilst the Rubicon model describes the types of information that are important in the deliberative phase, it is less clear about how these different variables are weighted against each other or how they combine to lead to intention formation.

- *Identification of behaviour change techniques* – as with many of the theories described in this chapter, the Rubicon model tells us little about how we might best influence the deliberative processes in the predecisional phase to ensure the Rubicon is crossed and desires are converted into intentions.

Transtheoretical model

One of the most commonly employed theories of behaviour change is the transtheoretical model (Prochaska & DiClemente, 1983; Prochaska et al., 1992, 2008; Prochaska & Velicer, 1997). For example, in a review of behaviour change theories, Davis et al. (2015) found that the transtheoretical model was used in 33% of the articles they identified, compared to 13% and 11% for the theory of planned behaviour and social cognitive theory, respectively. So what makes the transtheoretical model so popular? And is it worthy of its status as the most widely used theory of behaviour change?

The model

Like other stage models, the transtheoretical model divides the behaviour change process into a series of discrete stages. These are as follows:

1. *Precontemplation* – the individual is not thinking about changing their behaviour. They may be in denial and may report low self-efficacy and more barriers to change.

2. *Contemplation* – the individual is thinking about changing their behaviour within the next six months but has yet to make a commitment to take action. They may report fewer barriers to change and more benefits. They may seek out more information but still underestimate their susceptibility to the health threat.

3. *Preparation* – the individual has decided to change their behaviour within the next month. They start setting goals and making concrete plans. They may set unrealistic goals or underestimate their ability to succeed.

4. *Action* – the individual carries out the relevant behaviour or behaviours.

5. *Maintenance* – the individual continues to maintain the behavioural change (for example, abstain from smoking or participate in more exercise).

6. *Termination* – the behaviour has been changed permanently and no longer requires thought or effort on the part of the individual. (Only relevant for certain types of behaviour, such as quitting smoking.)

According to the model, movement through the stages from precontemplation to termination is unlikely to be linear as people will relapse and so generally recycle through stages several times before successfully changing their behaviour. But success is not guaranteed; they may also get stuck at a particular stage and fail to progress. Three sets of factors influence the individual's progression from one stage to the next:

- *Decisional balance* – the individual's awareness of the pros (advantages) of changing relative to the cons (disadvantages).

- *Self-efficacy and temptation* – the individual's confidence in their ability to perform the relevant behaviour and to resist temptations.

- *Processes of change* – the strategies the individual engages in, in order to help them progress to the next stage. These strategies are drawn from a range of different theories, hence the name 'transtheoretical' for the model. They include five cognitive-affective processes:

  » seeking out new information

  » experiencing negative emotions, such as fear and anxiety

  » relating behaviour change to one's self-identity

  » considering the impact of the behaviour on one's social or physical environment

  » making a firm commitment to change
  and five behavioural processes:

  » seeking and using social support

  » substituting the unhealthy behaviour with healthier alternatives

  » increasing rewards for the healthy behaviour and decreasing rewards for the unhealthy behaviour

  » removing cues to engage in the unhealthy behaviour and adding cues or reminders to engage in the healthy behaviour

  » relating behaviour change to social norms.

The model states that at different stages, different factors will be more or less effective at moving individuals on to the next stage. For example, to progress from precontemplation to contemplation, the pros of changing must increase. So for a smoker to start thinking about quitting, the benefits of quitting must go up. Perhaps they meet a new partner who dislikes them smoking. Conversely, to progress from contemplation to action, the cons of changing must decrease. For a smoker, this could be access to nicotine patches that help reduce their cravings. Thus from an intervention perspective, it is better to highlight the benefits of change for those at a precontemplation stage, but address the downsides of change for those at the contemplation stage.

   We would also expect to see differences in the use of processes of change. According to the model:

- Those in the contemplation stage will spend more time seeking information.

- Those in contemplation and action stages will be more likely to relate behaviour change to self-identity.

- Those in the action stage will be more likely to use strategies relating to behavioural substitution, rewards, cues and reminders, and social norms.

Self-efficacy will determine the individual's willingness to engage in processes of change and we would expect to see self-efficacy increasing relative to temptations as the person moves through the stages from precontemplation to action.

The evidence

The transtheoretical model has been tested using both cross-sectional and prospective study designs to compare people at different stages and to track transitions through stages (for a review, see Sutton, 2015). However, the strongest tests of stage models are experimental studies that compare the effects of 'stage-matched' versus 'stage-mismatched' interventions. In other words, interventions that use strategies that either should, or should not, help move the person to the next stage. It is these studies that we look at in this section.

One such study that failed to support the model was carried out by Dijkstra et al. (1998). They grouped over 1,000 smokers into four different stages:

- immotives – not planning to quit or cut down within the next 5 years
- precontemplators – planning to quit within the next year to 5 years
- contemplators – planning to quit within the next 6 months
- preparers – planning to quit within the next month.

The smokers received individually tailored letters that either provided them with:

a) information on the consequences of smoking and quitting smoking (designed to increase the pros and reduce the cons of quitting)

b) information about coping skills (aimed at enhancing self-efficacy)

c) both types of information

d) no information.

They then assessed the smokers' stages 10 weeks later. They predicted that immotives would respond to outcome information only, preparers to self-efficacy information only, and precontemplators and contemplators to both types of information. However, there were no significant differences in stage progression between those who had received information that was matched to their stage and those who had not.

In a subsequent study of smoking, Dijkstra et al. (2006) categorised smokers as either in the precontemplation, contemplation, preparation or action stage and randomly assigned them to receive one of three different types of information letters relating to either:

a) positive outcome expectancies (predicted to be most effective in precontemplation and preparation)

b) negative outcome expectancies (predicted to be most effective in contemplation and preparation)

c) self-efficacy (predicted to be most effective in the action stage).

Consistent with the transtheoretical model, they found that more individuals in the stage-matched interventions progressed, compared to those in the mismatched conditions (45% versus 26% respectively).

However, other studies of smoking have failed to show any benefits of matched interventions over mismatched interventions (Aveyard et al., 2006; Quinlan & McCaul, 2000). The same is true for a study on fruit intake (de Vet et al., 2008) and for one on physical activity (Blissmer & McAuley, 2002). Sutton (2015) concludes that, taken together, these studies provide little support for the transtheoretical model.

Key limitations

Like the Rubicon model, the transtheoretical model has an intuitive appeal; the notion of people being at different stages of change seems to tally with our everyday experience. However, theories need to do more than just appeal to our common-sense understanding, and the transtheoretical model has some important limitations. These include (but are not limited to) the following:

- *Evidence base* – as described above, many experimental tests of the model have failed to support its predictions with respect to stage-matched versus mismatched interventions.

- *Relationship between constructs* – like the Rubicon model, although the transtheoretical model identifies variables that are important for moving people through the different stages, it doesn't specify how these are weighted against each other or whether they interact with one another (Sutton, 2015).

- *Measurability and explanatory power* – the model provides clear guidelines on how individuals should be categorised into different stages. However, the validity of such criteria has to be questioned; why should someone planning to change within 30 days be qualitatively different from someone planning to change in 32 days? Some have argued that although people vary in their desire to change, such variation should be viewed as continuous (as conceptualised in continuum theories) rather than as discrete stages that are qualitatively different from one another (Sutton, 2001; West, 2005; 2006).

- *Explanatory power* – the model cannot account for the fact that people often decide to change their behaviour in the absence of any planning, and that such attempts are not always doomed to fail (Larabie, 2005; West & Sohal, 2006). It is also inconsistent with data showing that intentions can change over very short periods of time (Hughes et al., 2005).

Stage theories: summary

We looked at two different stage theories in this section: the Rubicon model of action phases and the transtheoretical model. Whilst the transtheoretical model has been popular with both researchers and practitioners, the absence of empirical support means its continued use cannot really be justified. The Rubicon model is newer and has been subject to less evaluation.

Compared to continuum theories, stage models may better capture processes involved in the maintenance of behaviour. However, like continuum theories, they tend to emphasise rational decision-making and have been criticised for failing to fully account for the role of emotions in behaviour change. In the next section we turn to theory that is more concerned with feelings.

THEORIES OF MOTIVATION

Motivation can be viewed as a desire to achieve a particular outcome, which in turn helps drive behaviour. When we talk about being motivated to do something, we tend to refer to instances associated with a particular feeling, not just a set of beliefs. For example, we can all probably think of occasions in which we've done something rather reluctantly; we may report that although we behaved in accordance with our beliefs, we lacked motivation.

The theories we have looked at so far have all included constructs relating to motivation. For example, attitudes, outcome expectancies and beliefs can all influence desire. However, as noted above, these theories place more emphasis on rational decision-making. For example, it is hard to see how many of these theories could distinguish between behaviours that come from the heart and those that are performed under duress, and yet such distinctions may be critical when it comes to maintaining behaviour over the long term (Deci & Ryan, 2000, 2008; Ryan, 2009; Ryan & Deci, 2000). The theory we consider in this section, self-determination theory, has a more specific focus on human motivation.

Self-determination theory

Not all academics would identify self-determination theory as a social cognition theory. However, it is included in this chapter because of its reference to cognitive evaluation, where a person's thoughts and perceptions determine the effects of their environment on their behaviour. As described at the start of the chapter, this type of process is a key feature of social cognition theories. Nevertheless, other aspects of self-determination theory arguably have more in common with the theories described in **Chapters 6 and 7** and you may like to think about how you would categorise it.

The theory

Self-determination theory aims to account for human motivation and behaviour via a combination of innate psychological needs, cognitive processes, environmental influences and individual differences (Deci & Ryan, 2000, 2008; Ryan, 2009; Ryan & Deci, 2000). It consists of five sub-theories:

- organismic integration theory
- basic psychological needs theory
- cognitive evaluation theory
- causality orientations theory
- goal contents theory.

1. Organismic integration theory

Organismic integration theory states that human motivation is either autonomous or controlled (**Table 5.2**). Autonomously motivated behaviours include those that are intrinsically motivated, where the person performs the behaviour simply because they enjoy doing so (**Image 5.3**). Such behaviours are linked to greater creativity and productivity and are more likely to be maintained over the long term. At the other end of the spectrum, controlled motivation includes behaviours that are extrinsically motivated. These are performed only because of external rewards or punishments. They are associated with feelings of compliance and will only be maintained for as long as the rewards or punishments are in place. Between these two extremes lie two other types of autonomous motivation (integrated regulation and identified regulation), and one other

Table 5.2 Types of motivation together with the regulatory processes they are associated with

Type of motivation	Motivation sub-type	Regulatory process	Example
Autonomous	Intrinsic	Interest, enjoyment, satisfaction	Playing football because you enjoy it.
	Integrated regulation	Congruence, synthesis with self	Taking regular exercise because you see yourself as someone who keeps fit.
	Identified regulation	Personal importance, valuing	Going to an exercise class because it is important to you to lose weight.
Controlled	Introjected regulation	Internal rewards and punishments	Going to an exercise class to avoid feeling guilty about letting down a friend.
	External regulation	Compliance, external rewards and punishments	Playing sport at school because you have to (non-participation will result in detention).

Image 5.3 *Playing football, simply because you enjoy it, is an example of an intrinsically motivated behaviour.*
Credit: Getty Images/Cultura RF/Ben Pipe Photography.

type of controlled motivation (introjected regulation). As described in **Table 5.2**, these are associated with different regulatory processes.

2. Basic psychological needs theory

What leads to a behaviour being more intrinsically motivated? Here, self-determination theory draws on basic psychological needs theory and states that the more a behaviour meets our innate psychological needs for competence, autonomy and relatedness, the more it will be intrinsically motivated. In other words, we need to feel we are good at the things we do (competence), are at liberty to make our own decisions (autonomy), and are understood, cared for and valued by others (relatedness). If a behaviour promotes such feelings it is more likely to become intrinsically motivated. For example, someone who decides to try out their workplace football game and finds themselves scoring the winning goal to cries of delight and admiration from their colleagues may very well decide to play again the following week.

3. Cognitive evaluation theory

Cognitive evaluation theory refers to the ways in which external events are interpreted by the individual and come to influence their perceptions of competence, autonomy and relatedness. Returning to our workplace football example, how might our new player's interpretation of events differ if she was the recently appointed new head of department, brought in to scrutinise workload, pay and promotions? She may be inclined to suspect that perhaps the goalie had not really been trying his hardest, and to wonder about the sincerity of her colleagues' expressions of praise and admiration. In this case, her winning goal and colleagues' reactions may be less likely to promote feelings of competence and relatedness and she may be less inclined to play again.

Cognitive evaluation theory has also been used to explain the effects of rewards on motivation. For example, children who are told they will receive a reward for engaging in an activity they already enjoy (such as painting) subsequently show reduced interest in that activity (Lepper et al., 1973). This has been termed the 'overjustification effect' and is thought to occur as a result of the person inferring that they are performing the behaviour in order to achieve the reward, not simply because they enjoy the activity. As such, when the reward is no longer in place, they cease to engage in the activity. This effect does not occur for verbal rewards (praise) or when a tangible reward is unexpected (Deci et al., 1999; Tang & Hall, 1995). This may be because the effect of rewards on behaviour is determined by the ways in which they are perceived; where they undermine feelings of autonomy (as may often be the case for expected, tangible rewards) they will reduce intrinsic motivation, but where they promote feelings of competence (such as when given as marks of achievement) they are likely to increase intrinsic motivation (Deci et al., 1999; Tang & Hall, 1995).

4. Causality orientations theory

Self-determination theory further refers to causality orientations theory to take account of individual differences in the types of opportunities that are sought and the ways in which external events are interpreted (Deci & Ryan, 1985; Hagger & Chatzisarantis, 2011). There are three types of causality orientations: autonomy, controlled and impersonal.

- A person with an autonomy orientation will seek out situations that allow for greater self-direction, initiative and enjoyment and will be more likely to interpret extrinsic rewards as affirmation of competence.

- Someone with a control orientation will select situations that are more regulated by social controls and rewards. For example, pay and status may be important determinants of job choice. They will be more likely to interpret events as controlling, reacting with either compliance or defiance.

- A person with an impersonal orientation will view themselves as lacking in competence and will have little faith in their ability to achieve desired outcomes. They may be anxious about entering new situations and have a tendency to do things the way they've always been done.

These three orientations are not mutually exclusive, in other words, most people vary in their levels of all three types of orientation, rather than falling into just one category. Causality orientations are slightly different from the concept of locus of control (see **Chapter 4**; Rotter, 1966) as one could have an internal locus of control but still have either an autonomy or control orientation. However, Deci and Ryan (1985) note that, developmentally, an external locus of control may be one of the determinants of an impersonal causality orientation.

5. Goal contents theory

The last sub-theory, goal contents theory, states that intrinsic goals, such as those relating to intimate relationships, personal growth or the community, are compatible with our basic psychological needs and so foster health and wellbeing. On the other hand, extrinsic goals relating to external indicators of worth, such as wealth, reputation or fame, do not tend to enhance wellbeing, even when one is successful at attaining them (Kasser & Ryan, 1996; Niemiec et al., 2009). The theory also relates to the way in which goals are framed; those framed in terms of intrinsic outcomes tend to be better adhered to than those framed in terms of extrinsic outcomes (Vansteenkiste et al., 2006).

The evidence

Three meta-analyses have examined self-determination theory in relation to health contexts. Chatzisarantis et al. (2003) reviewed 21 studies that applied self-determination theory to exercise, sport and physical education. They found that intrinsic motivation was most strongly associated with intentions and also mediated the effect of perceived competence on intentions. Nearly a decade later Teixeira et al. (2012) also reviewed studies that had examined exercise and physical activity in relation to self-determination theory. Across 66 studies they found support for a positive relationship between more autonomous forms of motivation and greater exercise engagement. Finally, Ng et al. (2012) reviewed 166 studies that had examined self-determination across a range of different healthcare and health promotion contexts. Consistent with self-determination theory, they found that healthcare settings that supported autonomy were associated with higher patient/client feelings of autonomy, competence and relatedness. These, together with more autonomous motivation, predicted better mental health as well as higher levels of health-related behaviours.

Key limitations

Self-determination theory enjoys widespread popularity, being applied across a broad range of domains from education to management to health (Cerasoli et al., 2014; Hagger & Chatzisarantis, 2015). Arguably, it has been subject to less criticism compared to other social cognition theories. However, it is not without limitations. These include the following:

- *Explanatory power (automatic versus controlled processes)* – unlike many other social cognition theories, self-determination theory does not include a construct relating to intention. This means there is more scope for incorporating effects relating to automatic processes into the model. Nevertheless, the model does not distinguish between these different pathways, and in its current form cannot always provide a full account of all observations. For example, research suggests that in some instances, automatic motivation predicts behaviour independently from reflective (controlled) motivation (Keatley et al., 2013). Likewise, research has shown that automatic processes can influence motivational orientation, which in turn influences behaviour (Levesque & Pelletier, 2003).

- *Utility for health behaviour change* – self-determination theory is a theory of motivation. As such it is not necessarily going to be relevant for all areas of health behaviour change. For example, compared to social cognitive theory or protection motivation theory, it may be less useful for an agency designing a nationwide health promotion campaign. This is because it is less able to make specific predictions about the types of information and messages that would be most effective. Also, for behaviours that do not need to be maintained over time (such as a one-off vaccination), type of motivation matters less. This is not necessarily a criticism of the theory itself, but rather a recognition of the limits of its scope. In **Chapter 9** we look at how one might go about selecting an appropriate theory for use in an intervention.

CRITIQUE OF SOCIAL COGNITION THEORIES

We have made some comparisons between theories in earlier sections. We have also considered some of the limitations of each theory. In this section we draw out key similarities and differences between theories and highlight limitations that tend to apply across all the theories.

Similarities and differences

Table 5.3 shows how the theories compare with one another across both key constructs and key issues. As shown, most include a construct or constructs related to intention, even if they are not labelled as such. This is also true of self-efficacy and outcome expectancies.

Previously, we highlighted the identification of behaviour change techniques and maintenance of behaviour change as important issues for any theory of behaviour change. **Table 5.3** details where important behaviour change techniques are identified by each theory and compares the ways in which maintenance of behaviour change is addressed. The table also shows how the Rubicon model is the only model that takes account of the relative importance of a specific outcome. We have finite time and, as described in **Chapter 3**, we also have finite cognitive resources (Mullainathan & Shafir, 2013; Shah et al., 2012); irrespective of how important we believe a set of different goals to be, we are unlikely to be able to simultaneously adjust our behaviour in a multitude of different ways.

Limitations

The theories we examined in this chapter have all made an important contribution to our understanding of health-related behaviours and our efforts to promote good health. In particular, they identify some of the key influences on behaviour such as intention, motivation, self-efficacy and beliefs about outcomes. In this section we consider important limitations that can be applied to most, or all, of the theories we have looked at.

Automatic processes

A recurring criticism we have encountered across all the theories is that they tend to focus on conscious, controlled processes and fail to address the role of automatic processes, including habits. For example, the continuum theories assume that all behaviour is mediated via conscious processes such as intentions, self-efficacy or beliefs about outcomes; both the stage models we looked at refer to factors that involve conscious processing, such as evaluating goals and outcomes, and action planning; self-determination theory, whilst allowing more scope for automatic processes, makes no distinction between conscious and automatic pathways. This absence of reference to automatic processes reduces the explanatory power of these theories. In **Chapter 6** we look in more detail at the role of automatic processes.

Emotions

As one might expect from the name, social cognition theories tend to emphasise cognitive influences over affective influences. For example, many theories assume that people engage in a rational weighing up of the relative costs and benefits of a particular course of action. However, research suggests that emotion may often have greater sway over our behaviour than reason (Lawton et al., 2009). Note that this criticism is less relevant for self-determination theory where feelings of autonomy, competence and relatedness play a key role in motivating behaviour.

Social factors

The theories are limited in the extent to which they can account for the effects of social factors, such as socioeconomic status or the environment a person lives in. On one level this is understandable; these are psychological theories not sociological ones, so the focus is on the individual not society. However, as we saw in **Chapter 3**, a person's position in society can influence, not just their everyday experiences, but also the ways in which

Table 5.3 Ways in which different constructs and issues are addressed in a selection of social cognition theories

	Health belief model	Theory of planned behaviour	Protection motivation theory	Social cognitive theory	Rubicon model of action phases	Transtheoretical model	Self-determination theory
Construct							
Intention	x	Intention	Protection motivation	Goals	Goals	Maps onto the preparation, action and maintenance stages.	x
Self-efficacy	Perceived barriers to action	Perceived behavioural control	Self-efficacy	Self-efficacy	Relates to processes that occur in the predecisional phase.	Self-efficacy	Overlaps with the construct of competence.
Outcome expectancies	Captured via constructs relating to perceptions of disease consequences and benefits of action.	Outcome expectancies. (Also encompassed by normative belief in terms of anticipated approval/disapproval.)	Related to intrinsic and extrinsic rewards, response efficacy and response costs.	Outcome expectancies	Relates to processes that occur in the predecisional phase.	Captured via decisional balance. (Also encompassed by the process of change strategy – considering the impact of the behaviour.)	x
Issue							
Maintenance of behaviour change	Assumes the person repeatedly cycles through the same process.	Assumes the person repeatedly though the same process.	Assumes the person repeatedly cycles though the same process.	Assumes the person repeatedly cycles though the same process.	Addressed in the postactional phase.	Includes a distinct maintenance phase.	More autonomous behaviour is more likely to be maintained.
Identification of behaviour change techniques	x	x	Provision of information about disease severity and susceptibility. Advice on how one can protect oneself and how effective this protection will be.	Strategies that build personal experience or involve the observation of others will be particularly effective.	Informed the development of implementation intentions.	Techniques are identified in the five behavioural processes of change (for example, social support, rewards and cues).	Effective techniques may include verbal praise and certain types of reward. Punishment will undermine long-term behavioural change.
Evaluates goals in context	x	x	x	x	Goals are weighted against competing goals.	x	x

CHAPTER 5

they interpret and process information. Even where social factors are referred to, such as in social cognitive theory, their relationships with other variables are likely to be more complex than is depicted. For example, social cognitive theory states that socio-structural factors influence behaviour via goals. However, in practice such factors may influence behaviour directly or may moderate links between variables, for example the link between intention and behaviour.

Additionally, as noted above, social cognition theories tend to assume a rational decision-making process. But deliberating over the pros and cons of one course of action relative to another is arguably a luxury available only to those with sufficient time and cognitive resources. As discussed in **Chapter 3**, those suffering from financial hardship, or experiencing other types of severe stress, may be particularly short of cognitive resources. As such, their behaviour may better reflect automatic processes, rather than those described in social cognition theories.

There is a political aspect to such models too; by identifying the causes of behaviour as stemming from internal cognitive events, it tends to place the responsibility for change with the individual, prompting the development of interventions that target people's beliefs and expectations at the expense of those that tackle social issues such as low incomes, unsafe neighbourhoods and a lack of employment opportunities.

Personality and individual differences

As with social factors, most of the theories fail to take account of the ways in which personality and other individual differences might influence different variables or moderate the relations between them. For example, in **Chapter 4** we introduced the idea that personality affects health because of its influence on health-related behaviours (the health behaviour model). However, the precise nature of this influence may vary:

- In some cases, this may be because of direct links between personality and behaviour. For example, high sensitivity to reward may have a direct effect on one's diet (Beaver et al., 2006; Davis et al., 2007; Rollins et al., 2014c; Tapper et al., 2010, 2015).

- In other cases, effects may be mediated via social cognition variables. For example, conscientiousness has been found to predict increased mammography uptake in women under the age of 50, in part because those who are more conscientious are less likely to view cost as a barrier (Siegler et al., 1995).

- In yet other instances, personality may moderate the relationship between social cognition variables. For example, conscientiousness is associated with stronger intention-behaviour links in relation to exercise (Rhodes et al., 2002).

Of the theories we have examined in this chapter, self-determination theory is the only one that incorporates personality variables in any detail. As long as social cognition theories fail to account for these types of individual differences, it is likely they will be limited in the extent to which they can be used to successfully change behaviour. Social cognition theories describe the 'average' person, but in reality there may be no single person who actually fits this description (Johnston & Johnston, 2013).

Critique: summary

As detailed at the start of this chapter, theory is critical when it comes to developing behaviour change interventions. Whilst some theories are much more popular than others (Davis et al., 2015), these are not necessarily those with the best evidence. Care should be taken when selecting a theory to ensure it is suitable for the behaviour in question;

an issue we will return to in **Chapter 9**. In particular, one might question whether one theory can apply to all health behaviours; there are many theories that are specific to particular behaviours such as smoking cessation or dieting and in some instances these more specialised theories may be more appropriate (see **Box 5.10**). It should also be noted that theories can be combined to address all relevant aspects of the target behaviour.

BOX 5.10 HOW MANY THEORIES OF BEHAVIOUR CHANGE ARE THERE?

DIG A LITTLE DEEPER

In this chapter we've looked at just a handful of different theories of behaviour change. It would be a mistake to assume this is a comprehensive list. Indeed, this is really just the tip of the iceberg. For example, Davis et al. (2015) identified a total of 83 theories specifically relating to behaviour change (see also Michie et al., 2014). In addition to these there are also numerous other theories of emotions, drives and cognitive processes that may not explicitly refer to behaviour change but are nonetheless still relevant.

CONCLUSIONS

Alexandra Heminsley managed to transform her lifestyle from one of exercise avoidance to regular running. This was very much a conscious decision. She thought hard about her reasons for wanting to get more exercise, listened carefully to her father's words of encouragement and took note of the benefits she experienced. Many others have made similar changes, whether it's quitting smoking, eating a healthier diet or simply taking better care of their teeth. The social cognition theories we've looked at in this chapter can help us understand the factors that prompt people to make such changes and, more importantly, help us develop interventions to improve public health.

However, social cognition models are not the whole story; the explanations they provide are far from perfect and leave a lot of behaviour change (or lack of change) unaccounted for. In particular they are less able to explain behaviours that occur outside of conscious decision-making processes; the things we do, or fail to do, without really thinking about it. It is to this area that we turn in **Chapter 6**.

Does the end justify the means when it comes to public health? Is it okay to scare people into trying to change their behaviour? Are there particular circumstances in which this could never be justified? Are there other circumstances in which it would definitely be justified?

THE GREAT DEBATE

HABITS AND OTHER AUTOMATIC PROCESSES

Chapter Outline

Have a quick look at the pictures below.

Image 6.1 *Which picture captures your attention?*
Credit (left): Maciej Rusek.
Credit (right): Whitney Wright.

Which image did you look at first? The one on the left, or the one on the right? Why? Because of the way they were set out on the page, or because of their content? What initial thoughts and feelings flashed through your mind? A pleasurable feeling associated with the taste of chocolate chip cookies? Or perhaps a more uncomfortable thought about needing to eat more healthily?

Chances are, whichever picture you looked at first, and whatever thoughts or feelings sprung to mind, you had little control over these events. Indeed, you may not even really have been aware of them and may have struggled to answer the questions that followed. However, these types of automatic processes can still have an important influence on our behaviour. In this chapter we will:

- Consider what we mean by 'automatic processes'.
- Think about different types of interventions that draw on automatic processes.
- Explore research on habits as an example of a behaviour that uses automatic processing.
- Look at techniques designed to train specific automatic associations.
- Look at techniques that draw on automatic processes to cue specific behaviours.

AUTOMATIC VERSUS CONTROLLED PROCESSING

When was the last time you bought a hot drink from a coffee shop? Did you place your order without much thought, asking for the same thing you always have? Or did you spend ages studying the menu, unable to decide between the skinny latte and the caramel frappuccino? What about the last time you bought margarine? Did you stop to compare products on price and ingredients? Or simply grab the one you usually buy?

According to dual-processing theories, we have two different information-processing systems in the brain (Evans, 2008). The first is an unconscious, rapid, automatic system. This is the system we rely on when carrying out behaviours with little thought (such as picking up the margarine we usually buy). The second is a conscious system that is slower and more deliberate. We use this system when making more thoughtful decisions (such as comparing the saturated fat content of margarine in order to select between alternatives). The key features of these different processing systems are shown in **Table 6.1**.

Table 6.1 Key characteristics of automatic versus controlled processing systems

Automatic processing	Controlled processing
Unconscious/preconscious	Conscious
Relatively fast	Relatively slow
Not under voluntary control	Under voluntary control
Low effort	High effort
High capacity	Low capacity
Associative	Rule-based
Perceptual	Reflective
Holistic	Analytical
Default process	Deliberate

In this chapter, we use the terms 'automatic' versus 'controlled' processing to describe these two systems (Schneider & Shiffrin, 1977), mainly because habit theory (which forms a key part of this chapter) draws heavily on the concept of automaticity. Nevertheless, a number of other different names have been used to describe similar processes (such as impulsive versus reflective and implicit versus explicit) and you may come across these terms in the literature.[1]

Some researchers have applied dual-processing theories to health behaviours in order to try to integrate automatic (impulsive) behaviours with the more controlled (reflective) processes described in **Chapter 5**. **Box 6.1** provides a brief overview of this area.

BOX 6.1 DUAL-PROCESSING ACCOUNTS OF HEALTH BEHAVIOUR

DIG A LITTLE DEEPER

Dual-processing accounts of health behaviour combine the types of controlled (reflective) processes we looked at in **Chapter 5**, with pathways relating to automatic (or impulsive) influences. Hofmann et al. (2008) propose a framework for integrating these two different pathways. This framework refers to:

a) Reflective (controlled) influences on behaviour (like those described in **Chapter 5**).

b) Impulsive (automatic) influences on behaviour (like those described in this chapter).

c) Situational and dispositional moderators that shift the balance between the reflective and impulsive influences. Situational moderators include some of those discussed in **Chapter 3** (such as stress and cognitive resources) whilst dispositional moderators refer to personality traits, like some of those described in **Chapter 4** (such as reward sensitivity and effortful control).

The framework is outlined in **Figure 6.1**.

Figure 6.1 A framework for predicting health-related behaviours from reflective and impulsive influences

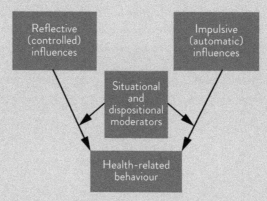

Source: Adapted from Hofmann et al. (2008) with permission from the authors and from Taylor & Francis Ltd, www.tandfonline.com.

---

1   Alternative terms used to describe automatic versus controlled processes include (respectively): implicit/explicit (Reber, 1993); system 1/system 2 (Stanovich & West, 2000), heuristic/analytic (Evans, 2006); intuitive/analytic (Hammond, 1996); impulsive/reflective (Strack & Deustch, 2004); associative/rule-based (Sloman, 1996); stimulus bound/higher order (Toates, 2006); experiential/rational (Epstein, 1994).

> Thus, depending on both the person and their situation, their behaviour may be more influenced by reflective/controlled processes or by impulsive/automatic influences. A key part of this framework is the idea of willpower, as this can help shift the balance toward more reflective influences. We explore the concept of willpower in more detail in **Chapter 7**.
>
> Examples of dual-processing models that you may like to explore include the reflective impulsive model (Strack & Deutsch, 2004), the prototype/willingness model (Gibbons et al., 2003, 2015) and the goal conflict model of eating (Stroebe et al., 2008).

However, whilst many theorists view automatic and controlled processing as reflecting separate, independent systems, others have argued that this is a misrepresentation and that mental processes are best viewed as varying on a continuum across a range of different, independent features (such as those listed in **Table 6.1**; Moors & De Houwer, 2006).

This view is consistent with Hollands et al. (2016), who examined the extent to which health behaviour change interventions work via conscious versus unconscious processes (a characteristic typically associated with controlled and automatic processing, respectively; see **Table 6.1**). They describe how behaviour may be a mix of conscious and unconscious processing depending on whether the individual is aware of:

- the external stimulus or intervention
- their behaviour
- the causal link between the stimulus and their behaviour.

For example, on their way to the supermarket a person may see a health promotion advert relating to heart disease. If the supermarket is out of their usual type of margarine, they may end up selecting a reduced-fat brand instead. Perhaps they'd taken an interest in the advert and had specifically decided to try to reduce the fat in their diet. Or maybe they only glimpsed the advert from the corner of their eye. Although they would still have made a conscious decision to select the reduced-fat margarine, they may have been unaware of the advert's influence on their behaviour. In other words, their choice of margarine may have been determined by both conscious (controlled) and unconscious (automatic) processes.

Thus any intervention or behaviour may draw on a range of different conscious and unconscious processes and how one labels that intervention or behaviour depends on the level at which it is analysed. For these reasons, it would be hard to argue that all the behaviours and intervention strategies covered in this chapter fulfil all the criteria for automatic processing. However, it is likely they all use some degree of automatic processing – certainly more so than the social cognition models we looked at in **Chapter 5**.

TRAINING VERSUS CUEING INTERVENTIONS

Papies (2016b) suggests that two different types of health intervention can be based on automatic processes: interventions that target the individual's response to cues that elicit behaviour (training interventions) and interventions that target the cues themselves (cueing interventions). She notes that training interventions typically require one-on-one interactions with the individual that may limit the extent to which they can be applied to larger populations. By contrast, cueing interventions rely on changes to the environment that mean they could more easily reach a much wider audience.

These different types of intervention may also both influence and reflect the ways we view health-related behaviours such as smoking, exercise and healthy eating. Does a person eat an unhealthy diet because they make poor choices? If so, we may need interventions that change the person. This is the implicit assumption made by the social cognition models we looked at in **Chapter 5**. It also relates to some of the literature we reviewed in **Chapter 4**. On the other hand, we may argue that a person's unhealthy diet is a product of the environment they live in. In this case we should be developing interventions aimed at changing environments. We looked at literature supporting this view in **Chapter 2** and **Chapter 3**. In practice, drawing on both types of approach may be the most effective way of improving population health. However, you might like to think about the ways in which different governments emphasise, and justify, one type of approach over another.

In **Chapter 3** we also saw how those from lower socioeconomic groups may experience more stress and financial hardship which may occupy their thinking, leaving fewer cognitive resources available for less urgent matters (such as healthy eating and exercise). As shown in **Table 6.1**, automatic processing is quicker and less effortful than controlled processing. It is also the default type of processing that we tend to rely on in times of stress. As such, an intervention that influences behaviour via automatic processes may be more helpful for reducing health inequalities. This may be particularly true of cueing interventions that target the environment. It may be less true of training interventions since a person would need to invest a certain amount of time and effort in order to engage with the training.

This approach contrasts with that taken by the social cognition models described in **Chapter 5**. As discussed in Chapter 5, a limitation of such models is their reliance on controlled processing. This means that related interventions may widen health inequalities because they will only be effective at influencing those with sufficient time and energy to reflect on their behaviour and act on their intentions.

Before turning to techniques associated with training and cueing interventions, we first look at habits. Arguably, habits represent one of the most important ways in which automatic processes influence health-related behaviours.

HABITS

Have you ever left your house in the morning and been unable to remember whether or not you'd locked the front door? Perhaps you were so unsure you felt compelled to go back and check. Or perhaps you've arrived at work still clutching the letter you had meant to post on the way? Are you just really forgetful or is something else going on?

The examples described above all involve behaviours that have been carried out with little thought or attention. If you'd been thinking about locking your door as you'd done it, you would likely have remembered afterwards. Similarly, if you had been paying attention to your route as you walked to work, you would probably not have forgotten to post your letter. Both instances involve behaviours that have likely been carried out multiple times, in almost exactly the same way; you lock the door every time you leave the house, you take exactly the same route to work. These actions have become so well rehearsed you can perform them automatically, with little thought or attention. You might describe them as habits.

What are habits?

Habits can be defined as 'learned sequences of acts that have become automatic responses to specific cues and are functional in obtaining certain goals or end-states' (Verplanken & Aarts, 1999, p. 104; see also Gardner, 2015). We can break this definition down into four key characteristics:

1. learned sequences of acts

2. automatic

3. responses to specific cues

4. functional in obtaining certain goals or end-states.

We will consider each of these features in turn.

1. *Habits are 'learned sequences of acts'*. In other words, a habit does not necessarily involve a single response, but may comprise a series of actions. So habits can be short or long. A habit may be as simple as turning off the hall light as you go upstairs to bed or it could be much longer. Making yourself a cup of tea in the morning may involve filling the kettle, turning it on, reaching for a mug from the cupboard, retrieving a teabag from a different cupboard, putting it in the mug, pouring boiling water onto the teabag, getting milk from the fridge and a teaspoon from the drawer, lifting the teabag from the tea and placing it in the bin, pouring in some milk and giving it a stir (**Image 6.2**). This habit consists of around ten separate actions that are likely performed in roughly the same sequence.

2. *Habits are automatic.* Automatic processes have distinct qualities (see **Table 6.1**). For example, they usually occur outside of awareness, are mentally efficient, unintentional, and difficult to control (Bargh, 1994). Habits do not necessarily always display all these features, but they generally display at least some of them. For example, we may lock our front door or turn off a light without even really being aware that we are doing it. Whilst making a cup of tea we might be thinking about something entirely different; our actions are mentally efficient which allows us to think about other things in parallel. In some instances, habits may be unintentional and difficult to control. For example, we may end up taking the same route to work even though we'd intended to go a different way in order to post a letter.

Image 6.2 *Making a cup of tea is an example of a habit that involves a relatively long sequence of acts, such as retrieving milk from the fridge and finding a teaspoon for stirring. However, because habits tend to be performed automatically, we may give little conscious thought to any of these actions.*
Credit: Calum Lewis.

3. *Habits are responses to cues.* These cues may be environmental events, such as the alarm clock going off in the morning, being in a certain location or being with a certain group of friends. Alternatively, they may be internal events such as a pang of hunger or a certain thought. The cue may also be a combination

CHAPTER 6

of events (Adriaanse et al., 2009; Ji & Wood, 2007; Wood, 2017). For example, walking past the convenience store on the way home from work may only prompt chocolate purchasing behaviour when it is also accompanied by a feeling of low mood. However, in each case it is the cue, or specific combination of cues, that is responsible for eliciting the habit.

4. *Habits are functional in obtaining certain goals or end-states.* Recall that habits are *learned* sequences of acts. The reason we originally learned the sequence of acts would have been to achieve a desired outcome; we learn how to make a cup of tea because we enjoy drinking tea in the morning, we learn how to get to work because we want to get paid. So in many instances habits serve a useful purpose; they help us achieve certain goals in a mentally efficient manner. However, just because habits develop in order to obtain goals does not mean they always continue to serve such goals. Indeed, as illustrated by our letterbox example, habits are usually insensitive to changes in goals (Wood & Rünger, 2016). We look at this insensitivity in more detail later on page 152.

Additionally, Gardner (2015) distinguishes between two different types of behaviour that involve habits:

- Behaviours that are habitually initiated, where the decision to engage in a particular behaviour is carried out automatically.

- Behaviours that are habitually performed, where the execution of the behaviour is automatic.

For example, you may be in the habit of going for a run first thing every morning, but may vary the route you take each day. Thus whilst you may automatically put on your running shoes and step out the door, you may then devote more conscious thought to the run itself, deliberating over what route to take and how long to run for. Conversely, your running efforts may be more sporadic and it may take some mental effort to persuade yourself to go for a run. However, once you step out the door, you may take exactly the same route, leaving your mind free to think about something entirely different. Of course there is also a third possibility; that both your decision to run and the run itself are habitual. This means that the distinction between habitual initiation and habitual performance can result in three qualitatively different types of habits:

- Habits that are habitually initiated but consciously performed.

- Habits that are consciously initiated but habitually performed.

- Habits that are habitually initiated and habitually performed.

How do habits develop?

> **Operant conditioning** – also called instrumental conditioning. A type of learning in which the likelihood of a particular behaviour reoccurring is increased when it leads to a desirable outcome ('reinforcement') and reduced when it leads to an undesirable outcome ('punishment').

Recall the definition we discussed above: a habit develops when someone initially performs a behaviour, or sequence of behaviours, in response to a specific cue, in order to achieve a particular goal or end-state. **Operant conditioning** means that where the desired outcome is achieved, the person is likely to repeat the same behaviour or behaviours when in the presence of the relevant cue or cues. Each time this reoccurs there is repeated co-activation of neurons associated with the cue and the response, which strengthens the links between them to the extent that eventually the cue comes to elicit the behaviour automatically without the need for goals (Neal et al., 2012; Wood & Neal, 2007). This process is referred to as 'direct cuing' (Wood & Neal, 2007; see also Wood & Rünger, 2016).

However, habit associations may also arise via 'motivated cueing' (Wood & Neal, 2007). In this case **classical conditioning** means that particular cues become associated with specific rewards to the extent that the cues elicit a representation of the reward that helps motivate behaviour. Thus we can also distinguish between different types of habits, according to the ways in which they have developed:

- Habits that occur because of direct cueing and are unlikely to be associated with any strong feelings (such as putting on your seatbelt when you get into a car).

- Habits that also involve motivated cueing and are more likely to be associated with feelings of desire (such as always having a biscuit with your mid-morning cup of tea).

> **Classical conditioning** – also called Pavlovian conditioning or respondent conditioning. A process by which the repeated pairing of a neutral stimulus with a biologically important stimulus (such as food) results in the previously neutral stimulus eventually eliciting the same response as the biologically important stimulus. For example, if you always buy a chocolate bar when the train refreshment trolley comes by, the mere sight of the train refreshment trolley could make your mouth water.

BOX 6.2 HABITS, AUTOMATICITY AND ADDICTION

MAKING CONNECTIONS

Behaviours such as smoking and drinking are sometimes referred to as habits. However, in some instances they may be qualitatively different from other habits (such as making a cup of tea or brushing your teeth) because of their addictive qualities. In **Chapter 8** we see how automatic processes are also thought to play a key role in addiction.

However, not all behaviours that are repeatedly performed in a consistent context develop into habits. If a person employs planning or decision-making whilst performing a behaviour (such as when a doctor examines a patient), this seems to inhibit habit formation (Gillan et al., 2015). Conversely, habit learning seems to be enhanced when behaviour is rewarded on an interval schedule, in other words, when a person is rewarded for performing a behaviour only some of the time, not all of the time (Dickinson, 1985). Wood and Rünger (2016) suggest this may be because it allows cue-response associations to form in the absence of any association with the outcome.

As a result, habit formation is highly variable, with some behaviours never becoming habits despite frequent repetition, and others taking varying lengths of time to develop. This is nicely illustrated in a study by Lally et al. (2010). They asked 96 individuals to select an eating, drinking or physical activity-related behaviour to carry out on a daily basis in the same context for a 12-week period. Activities selected ranged from 'eating a piece of fruit with lunch' to 'running for 15 minutes before dinner' (p. 1000). They also asked participants to complete daily measures of the extent to which they performed their chosen behaviour automatically. Only around half of participants performed the behaviour consistently enough for it to become a habit. Statistical models using the automaticity measures also indicated that the time taken for the behaviour to become a strong habit would likely have ranged from 18 to 254 days, with a median time of 66 days.

How prevalent are habits?

Wood et al. (2002) set out to examine how much of our daily behaviours can be viewed as habits. They asked over 200 students to carry a diary and a watch with them over a period of two days. The watch was set to chime every hour, at which point the students were asked to record their behaviours, thoughts and emotions, and to rate each behaviour on a number of dimensions. Habits were defined as behaviours performed 'just about every day' and 'usually in the same location'. Using this definition, Wood et al. found that 43% of behaviours were labelled as 'habits', with behaviours relating to hygiene, appearance, sleeping and waking most likely to be classified as 'habitual'.

However, you may have noticed a slight inconsistency in the definition of habits employed by Wood et al. (2002) and the definition we looked at previously. Wood et al. defined habits according to their frequency and consistency but, as noted above, a key characteristic of habits is that they exhibit features of automaticity. It is possible to think of examples of behaviours that are repeated frequently, in stable contexts, but which are unlikely to be carried out automatically. For example, a Shakespearean actor may perform in the same play, on the same stage, night after night, but as he delivers his final heart-wrenching soliloquy one would assume he isn't simply thinking about what he is going to have for supper. As noted previously, if a person engages in more conscious, controlled processing as they perform a behaviour, this tends to inhibit habit formation (Gillan et al., 2015).

Thus it is possible that the estimate of 43% obtained in the study by Wood et al. (2002) is an overestimate. Nevertheless, it illustrates the ubiquity of habits in everyday life. It also raises the important question of how best to measure habits in everyday life.

Measuring habits

One of the most commonly employed measures of naturally occurring habits is the Self-Report Habit Index (SRHI) (Verplanken & Orbell, 2003; see **Box 6.3**). This measure comprises 12 items that tap into perceptions of automaticity (items 2, 3, 4, 5, 6, 8, 9, 10), frequency (items 1, 7, 12) and self-identity (item 11).

BOX 6.3 HOW STRONG ARE YOUR HABITS?

To what extent is eating fruit a habit for you? Or snacking on biscuits? How about walking to work or brushing your teeth? The Self-Report Habit Index (SRHI; Verplanken & Orbell, 2003) is one way of assessing this. It is most accurate **TAKE THE TEST** when used in relation to a specific behaviour carried out in a specific context, such as eating fruit with breakfast or snacking on biscuits whilst studying (Sniehotta & Presseau, 2012).

Identify your habits by answering the questions below. Responses should be provided on a 7-point scale ranging from 1 (*agree*) to 7 (*disagree*).

(Behaviour X) is something:

1 ... I do frequently.
2 ... I do automatically.
3 ... I do without having to consciously remember.
4 ... that makes me feel weird if I do not do it.
5 ... I do without thinking.

6 ... would require effort not to do it.

7 ... that belongs to my (daily, weekly, monthly) routine.

8 ... I start doing before I realise I'm doing it.

9 ... I would find hard not to do.

10 ... I have no need to think about doing.

11 ... that's typically 'me'.

12 ... I have been doing for a long time.

Item scores are reversed so that high values indicate stronger habits. They are then summed to give a total score ranging from 12 to 84. A score of under 48 means the behaviour is probably not a habit (Lally et al., 2010), whilst higher scores suggest the behaviour is more likely to be habitual.

Source: Verplanken and Orbell (2006). Reprinted with permission from John Wiley and Sons.

However, although the SRHI is widely used (Gardner, 2015), it has been subject to a number of criticisms, as follows:

- *Absence of reference to cues* – Sniehotta and Presseau (2012) argue that the scale fails to take account of the central role that cues play in defining a habit. For example, a person may automatically eat biscuits in one context (such as with an afternoon cup of tea) but always make a conscious decision to eat them in another context (for example when served at a weekly staff meeting). Thus any rating of the extent to which 'biscuit eating' is habitual would conflate two qualitatively different behaviours. As such, Sniehotta and Presseau suggest the scale should be modified to refer to the context as well as the behaviour, for example 'Eating biscuits when I have my afternoon cup of tea...'.

- *Inclusion of items relating to behavioural frequency* – Sniehotta and Presseau (2012) also argue that although frequent repetition of a behaviour may lead to habit formation and may also occur as a result of habit formation, it is not an essential feature of a habit since the frequency with which a habit occurs will always depend upon the extent to which the relevant cues are encountered. Just because one behaviour occurs more frequently than another does not necessarily mean it represents a stronger habit; as noted above, it is possible for a behaviour to be frequently repeated without developing into a habit.

- *Inclusion of an item relating to identity* – similarly, both Sniehotta and Presseau (2012) and Gardner and colleagues suggest that the item relating to identity (item 11) is redundant since identity is also not a defining characteristic of a habit (Gardner, 2015; Gardner et al., 2012a).

- *Failure to distinguish between habit initiation and performance* – finally, Gardner (2015) notes that the scale does not distinguish between habit initiation (deciding to carry out the behaviour) and habit performance (actually carrying out the behaviour). They suggest this limitation can be addressed with more clear specification of the target behaviour, for example '*Choosing* to eat biscuits...' as opposed to '*Eating* biscuits...'.

These limitations have led some researchers to assess habits using only items on the SRHI that clearly relate to automaticity. For example, Gardner et al. (2012b) use just four items from the SRHI (items 2, 3, 5 and 8) to form their Self-Report Behavioural Automaticity Index (SRBAI). However, as discussed by Gardner (2015), all attempts to measure habits have been limited in one respect or another. For example, the SRBAI, in focussing solely on automaticity, may fail to distinguish between automatic behaviours that have developed through repetition (in other words, habits) and those that have arisen via other processes (such as via implementation intentions, see page 159). Gardner and Tang (2014) have also questioned the extent to which people can accurately report on processes and behaviours that tend to be carried out with little conscious awareness.

Key characteristics of habits

Habits have a number of interesting features that have important implications for behaviour change interventions. These features have been demonstrated through a range of different empirical studies, including an ingenious series of studies using stale popcorn.

Habits are resistant to changes in attitude

A key characteristic of habits is that they are resistant to changes in attitude. In the first of the stale popcorn studies, Neal et al. (2011) recruited participants to take part in what they thought was research examining personality and movie interests. They were given a bottle of water and a box of popcorn, and had 15 minutes to sit back and enjoy some audio-visual entertainment. However, some of these participants watched movie trailers in a cinema whilst others watched music videos in a meeting room. Additionally, whilst some were given delicious, freshly popped popcorn, others received popcorn that was somewhat stale and chewy, having been popped seven days previously. After the trailers and videos were over, participants were asked to indicate how frequently they ate popcorn in the cinema (a measure of habit strength) and how much they liked the popcorn they had just eaten (a measure of attitude toward the popcorn). The researchers also weighed the amount of popcorn they'd eaten. The results are shown in **Figure 6.2**.

Figure 6.2 Percentage of popcorn eaten during (a) 15 minutes of movie trailers in a cinema and (b) 15 minutes of music videos in a meeting room

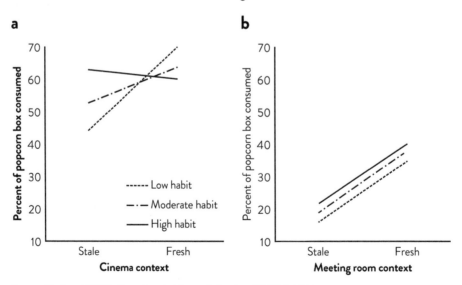

Source: Neal et al. (2011). Reproduced with permission from SAGE Publishing.

Figure 6.2(a) shows that in the cinema context those with weak popcorn eating habits ate more of the fresh popcorn than the stale popcorn. This is unsurprising and consistent with the fact that all participants reported liking the fresh popcorn significantly more than the stale popcorn. However, those who frequently ate popcorn in the cinema (those with strong popcorn eating habits) ate just as much stale popcorn as fresh popcorn, *despite* later reporting that they had not really liked the stale popcorn. Thus their popcorn eating habit was resistant to a shift in attitude; they still performed the behaviour, even though the outcome was no longer as valuable.

Habits can be disrupted by shifts in cueing

If we turn to **Figure 6.2(b)**, we can see what happened when the study took place in a meeting room rather than a cinema. Here, irrespective of the strength of participants' popcorn eating habits, they ate significantly more of the fresh popcorn than the stale popcorn. The switch in context, from cinema to meeting room, disrupted participants' habits so that not only did they now eat less popcorn overall, their behaviour was also influenced by their attitude to the popcorn (in other words, whether or not they liked the taste). A critical part of the habit cue (being in a cinema) was missing, so the behaviour of eating popcorn was not elicited automatically but was instead under conscious control.

Habits can be disrupted by interrupting the execution of the behaviour

In a second popcorn study, Neal et al. (2011) were interested in what would happen in the cinema context if they made participants eat with their non-dominant hand. In other words, right-handed people had to eat with their left hand, and left-handed people had to eat with their right hand. They found that, as in the previous study, those with strong popcorn eating habits who ate with their dominant hand consumed just as much of the stale popcorn as the fresh popcorn. However, those that ate with their non-dominant hand were influenced by the taste of the popcorn and ate less stale popcorn than fresh popcorn. These findings illustrate how a habitual behaviour can also be disrupted and brought under conscious control, when part of the response (in this case eating with the dominant hand) is blocked.

Attentional resources are needed to inhibit a habit

Another important feature of habits is that, whilst attentional resources are not required to perform the habitual behaviour, they are required to inhibit it. For example, Baxter and Hinson (2001) used a dual-task procedure to assess attentional allocation among novice and experienced smokers. They asked them to perform a reaction time task on the computer (a task that requires concentration) whilst also performing one of four different behaviours:

- not smoking (no cigarettes or cigarette-related items were visible), referred to as 'baseline'
- smoking
- pseudosmoking (pretending to smoke but not inhaling)
- holding a lit cigarette over an ashtray.

As shown in **Figure 6.3**, the results showed that experienced smokers had slower reaction times when they were holding the cigarette or pretending to smoke, suggesting that these tasks drew on attentional resources, disrupting their performance on the reaction time task. By contrast, their performance when actually smoking was equivalent to their performance when no cigarettes were available, suggesting they were able to smoke automatically, without it requiring attentional resources. The novice smokers showed slower reaction times when smoking or pretending to smoke. This suggests that the action of smoking was not yet automatic for the novice smokers and required some attentional resources.

Figure 6.3 Mean reaction time (+ standard error of the mean) for experienced and novice smokers across four smoking conditions

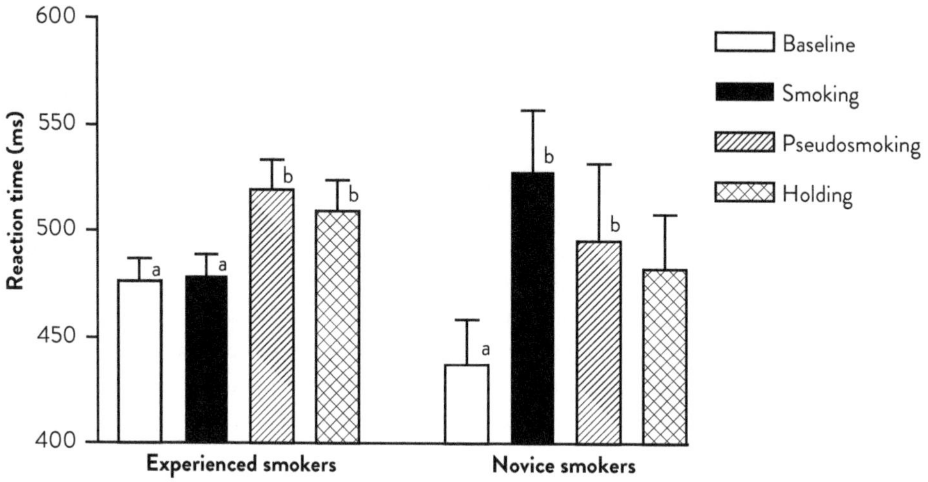

Note: Within each group, means having different letters differed at $p < .5$ or better (two tailed).
Source: Baxter, B. W., & Hinson, R. E. (2001). Is smoking automatic? Demands of smoking behavior on attentional resources. *Journal of Abnormal Psychology*, 110(1), 59. Copyright © 2001, American Psychological Association. Reproduced with permission.

Habits influence attention to new information

Habits may also impact upon the extent to which a person attends to new information relating to the target behaviour (Verplanken & Wood, 2006). For example, Verplanken et al. (1997) asked individuals to decide whether to travel by bus, car, bicycle or foot for a series of hypothetical journeys. To help with their decisions they were provided with information display boards containing further details about each of the four different travel options. The authors found that those with strong habits relating to a particular mode of travel searched for less information than those with weak habits. Individuals with strong habits also sought out the most information around the type of travel mode they usually selected, suggesting a confirmatory bias. These two factors suggest that behaviour change interventions based around the provision of new information may be less successful at changing behaviours that represent strong habits. (Astute readers may notice similarities between these findings and research relating to the distinction between deliberative and implemental mindsets that we looked at in **Chapter 5**.)

Habits may moderate the relationship between intentions and behaviour

In **Chapter 5** we considered the intention-behaviour gap; the fact that although we may intend to behave in a particular way, we often fail to do so. Some research suggests that the more a behaviour is a habit, the weaker its relationship with intention (Gardner et al., 2011). This would make sense in light of the fact that, as discussed above, habit performance tends to occur without the involvement of either goals or attitudes (Neal et al., 2011, 2012; Wood & Neal, 2007). Thus we would expect habits to be relatively resistant to shifts in intention. However, not all studies have found such a relationship; some have shown no effect of habit strength on intention-behaviour correlations (Gardner et al., 2012b) whilst others have shown effects in the opposite direction, with stronger habits being related to an increased association between intention and behaviour (de Bruijn et al., 2012; Gardner et al., 2011; Rhodes & de Bruijn, 2010).

Gardner (2015) suggests that these inconsistent findings may in part reflect the design of these studies since they tend to examine instances in which intentions, habits and behaviour are all congruent. For example, a study may examine intention-behaviour relationships among gym-goers with weak, moderate or strong intentions to go to the gym, but may not include those who intend to quit the gym (those whose behaviour runs counter to their intentions). Because habits are formed by the repetition of goal-directed behaviours, we would expect them to show a fairly close correspondence with intention; the stronger a person's intention, the more they are likely to have repeated a particular behaviour, which may in turn have led to a stronger habit. Thus a more meaningful test of moderation by habits may be to examine instances in which intentions have shifted so that they are at odds with habits. For example, someone in the habit of walking to work may decide they now wish to cycle. The extent to which their intention to cycle predicts their cycling behaviour may be moderated by the strength of their walking habit. (Note, however, that two studies that have included these types of counter-intentional habits in relation to binge drinking and mode of travel-related behaviours have still failed to find this type of interaction; Gardner et al., 2012a; Murtagh et al., 2012).

Stress promotes a reliance on habits

Finally, stress seems to encourage a reliance on habits. This may be in part because stress impairs the more cognitively demanding forms of information processing needed for decision-making. However, it could also be the result of an adaptive mechanism that, in challenging circumstances, promotes the use of well-rehearsed behaviours with a track record of success (Schwabe & Wolf, 2013; Wood & Rünger, 2016).

Intervention: breaking bad habits

Habits are of paramount importance for health psychology. As described above, they drive a large proportion of our everyday behaviours, impacting upon diet, physical activity, dental care and smoking. The unique characteristics of habits mean that a healthy habit can help sustain health-promoting behaviours over extended periods, but an unhealthy habit can be very difficult to break. In this section, and the section that follows, we look at the ways in which we can use our understanding of habits to inform health promotion interventions.

Cue avoidance

Since habits are elicited by specific cues, one approach to breaking bad habits is simply to avoid the cues that elicit them. This is sometimes termed 'cue avoidance' or 'stimulus control'. For example, a person who is trying to lose weight, and is in the habit of buying a croissant on the way to work every day, may decide to take a different route to work in order to avoid the bakery. However, the problem with simply avoiding the relevant cue is that it may not change the underlying cue-response association, and continuously avoiding cues may be unsustainable. For example, when our dieter reaches their weight loss goal they may revert back to their normal commute because it is far more convenient. When the relevant cue is encountered again (in this case the bakery), the croissant eating habit may re-emerge.

Life events

Cue avoidance may therefore be more successful where changes in context can be made permanent; for example, where someone is undergoing a significant life event that is likely to naturally disrupt habits, such as changing job, moving house, or having a baby. This approach has the added advantage of compelling the person to consciously consider their behaviours, which can in turn allow them to be more guided by attitudes and goals. For example, if you move to a new city for a new job you need to make a whole set of decisions about how you are going to organise your day, such as how you will travel to work, what you will eat for lunch and whether you will navigate your way around the office building using the lift or the stairs. This can present an opportunity for the person to align their behaviour more closely with their values, attitudes and goals. This type of effect is illustrated in a study by Verplanken et al. (2008) who looked at the way in which university employees travelled to work. They found that those who had recently moved, and also expressed concern for the environment, were less likely to drive to work compared to those who had not recently moved or who expressed less concern for the environment. In other words, moving house provided an opportunity for people to behave in a way that was more consistent with their values.

We can also see these processes at work in government-led initiatives designed to promote healthier and more environmentally friendly behaviours. For example, in the United States new city residents may be provided with a temporary free bus pass to try to encourage them to get into the habit of using public transport rather than the car (Verplanken & Wood, 2006). Similarly, many governments have legislated against smoking in workplaces and public areas, forcing people to abandon habits such as smoking at their desk, or whilst out for a drink with friends in the evening.

Vigilant monitoring

An alternative way of breaking bad habits is through vigilant monitoring. This is where someone watches carefully for the target response in order to prevent its performance. Quinn et al. (2010) examined this approach in two diary studies that looked at a range of everyday habits individuals were trying to supress, such as snacking when stressed, biting nails and procrastinating when trying to study. They found that vigilant monitoring was the only approach that was successful in controlling strong habits. Attempting to avoid relevant cues was not successful, leading the authors to conclude that this was because it was not always possible for the person to accurately identify the cues that triggered their behaviour. A third experimental study showed that vigilant monitoring was successful, not because it reduced the strength of the habit, but because it increased conscious, intentional control of the behaviour, enabling the person to override their automatic response. However, this highlights one of the key drawbacks of this approach; it is effortful and requires a degree of self-regulation, or 'willpower'. This means it is only likely to be successful where the person has sufficient self-regulatory resources and may be difficult to sustain over time; where people have low levels of self-control, they are more likely to fall back on habits (Neal et al., 2013). We look at theories of willpower and self-regulation in **Chapter 7**.

Counter-conditioning

A technique that might improve the success of vigilant monitoring is counter-conditioning. This is where the habitual behaviour is not simply supressed but is instead replaced with an alternative behaviour. In this way the person may learn to associate the cue with a behaviour that is incompatible with the habit and may eventually form a new, more desirable habit. For example, someone may have a piece of chewing gum every time they feel like smoking a cigarette. However, although this has been proposed as a possible approach, it has yet to be rigorously tested in the context of habitual behaviours (Quinn et al., 2010; van 't Riet et al., 2011; Wood & Neal, 2007).

Point-of-decision prompts

Another strategy that may help prompt awareness of habits, and thus also promote behaviour change, is the use of point-of-decision prompts (also referred to as 'situational cues' or 'environmental reminders'). These are notices or objects placed at the location that cues the target behaviour (Lally & Gardner, 2013). For example, prompts placed at lifts and escalators have been shown to increase stair use (Soler et al., 2010; **Image 6.3**). Whilst the effect of such reminders may diminish over time (as people habituate to their presence), it is possible their effects may be sustained for long enough to allow people to develop new habits (Tobias, 2009). Alternatively, Lally and Gardener (2013) suggest that replacing initial reminders with new reminders (in other words, the same message but with different imagery and/or phrasing) may help overcome this type of habituation and reduce the risk that it occurs prior to the development of new habits.

Intervention: creating good habits

If bad habits are hard to break, then good habits should be easy to sustain. As such, it would seem sensible to try to turn health-promoting behaviours into habits. How

Image 6.3 *A point-of-decision prompt in the library at Kent State University. The eye-catching display on the elevator doors suggests you 'Save your time, use the stairs' whilst the footprints on the floor lead the way to the stairwell.* Credit: Kent State University.

might we go about this? As noted above, habits develop when the same behaviour is repeated in the same context, though this type of repetition will not always lead to habit formation. Lally and Gardner (2013) identify four factors that can aid the development of automaticity; rewards, consistency, simplicity and clarity of cues. These are described below.

Rewards

Lally and Gardner (2013) suggest that habit development may be undermined where someone anticipates receiving an immediate, external reward for their behaviour since this will strengthen response-outcome associations, leading them to perform the behaviour in order to achieve the reward. Recall that, by contrast, habits are characterised by strong cue-response associations with responses performed even when any outcome is removed or devalued. Thus Lally and Gardner suggest avoiding consistent, immediate rewards when trying to develop a habit. If some initial rewards are deemed important to help establish the behaviour, these should appear random in timing and size to reduce the perception that they are contingent on the performance of the behaviour (see also Wood & Neal, 2009). For example, a parent trying to instil a vegetable eating habit in their child could offer varying levels of praise as an occasional reward. (See **Chapter 12** for further discussion of the use of rewards in this context.)

CHAPTER 6

Consistency

To promote habit development, a person should aim to always (or nearly always) perform the target behaviour upon encountering the relevant cue. And ideally only the target behaviour should be performed in response to this cue so as not to dilute the cue-response association. For example, to promote a stair climbing habit at work, a person should consistently take the route to the stairs (rather than the lift) when they encounter the relevant part of the building. However, such a habit may be weakened if this part of the building also leads to other frequently visited areas, such as the bathrooms or a cafeteria.

Simplicity

The target response should also be as simple as possible. Whilst relatively complex behaviours can show features of automaticity (Wood et al., 2002), Lally and Gardner (2013) argue that behaviours that require high levels of flexibility may be more likely to remain under conscious rather than automatic control. They suggest that for these types of complex behaviour sequences (such as cooking a healthy meal) it may be more sensible to focus on turning the initiation of the behaviour into a habit rather than the entire behaviour sequence. For example, when thinking about what to eat in the evening, one could get into the habit of taking out a pre-prepared list of healthy meal options. It would be easier to make this behaviour habitual than the behaviours that come later in the sequence, such as selecting a meal, finding the appropriate recipe, checking one has the right ingredients in the cupboard and so on.

Clarity of cues

Finally, cues that are more salient and more readily identified will be more effective at supporting habit formation. Lally and Gardner (2013) argue that this means that it will be easier to insert a new behaviour into a routine at a 'large task boundary' (where one task is complete and another is about to start), rather than within the middle of a task (see also Judah et al., 2013). For example, if you always make a cheese sandwich to take with you to work, and want to get into the habit of also packing an apple, it would be easier to get the apple after making the cheese sandwich rather than whilst making it, even though the former may seem more efficient if you keep the apples in the fridge next to the cheese. This is because retrieving the cheese will already function as a strong cue for slicing it up and putting it in the sandwich so the behaviour of selecting an apple will be competing with an existing, well-established response. By contrast, your behaviour after making the cheese sandwich may be more variable (less habitual), so it should be easier to link the cue of 'cheese sandwich completion' with a new 'apple retrieval' behaviour.

BOX 6.4 MOTIVATION, INTENTION AND THEORY SELECTION

MAKING CONNECTIONS

The strategies described in these sections – on making and breaking good and bad habits – typically assume the person wants to change their behaviour. However, this will not always be the case. As such, a behaviour change intervention may need to target motivation or intention as well as habits. This is where the social cognition models we looked at in **Chapter 5** can be helpful. It also shows how it can be a good idea to combine different theories when designing behaviour change interventions. In **Chapter 9** we look at frameworks designed to help with the selection of appropriate theories according to the target behaviour and population.

An additional technique that can help with habit formation is the use of implementation intentions. However, since implementation intentions have been used so extensively in health psychology, and because they have generated such a large body of research, we consider them in detail in a separate section below.

Changing habits through training and cueing

Most of the strategies outlined above, in relation to breaking and making habits, can be seen as training interventions. This is because they focus on breaking or creating specific cue-response associations. In most cases these types of strategy will initially require a substantial amount of effort and commitment from the individual.

However, where strategies target a habit cue, they can be viewed as cueing interventions. These include strategies relating to cue avoidance, life events and point-of-decision prompts. Some of these will require effort from the individual to implement (such as where they need to actively change their behaviour or environment to avoid certain cues). But others are likely to require less cognitive resources and willpower, such as where governments introduce legislation or point-of-decision prompts.

We now turn to implementation intentions, another type of training intervention related to habit theory.

IMPLEMENTATION INTENTIONS

What are implementation intentions?

Implementation intentions are a type of action plan in which a person specifies when, where and how they will perform a particular behaviour (Gollwitzer, 1993; 1996; 1999; Michie et al., 2013). Unlike goal intentions, which identify a particular outcome, implementation intentions describe a specific action that will help one achieve that outcome. For example, a goal intention might be 'I'm going to get fitter' whilst an implementation intention might be 'If it is a weekday morning, and I have just got out of bed, then I will do 10 minutes of yoga.' The implementation intention specifies the time (a weekday morning), the place (the bedroom) and the action (10 minutes of yoga). Implementation intentions work best when formulated using an 'If...then...' structure, since this more closely corresponds to the way in which the behaviour is performed. In other words, the cue (when and where) is encountered prior to the action (how) being completed (Oettingen et al., 2000).

Evidence for the effects of implementation intentions

Despite their apparent simplicity, implementation intentions can be a very effective tool for promoting behaviour change (Gollwitzer & Sheeran, 2006). In particular they have been shown to be helpful for achieving **approach related health goals**. For example, implementation intentions have been shown to help people increase their physical activity and fruit and vegetable consumption, engage in breast and testicular self-examination, increase their contraception use and improve their dental care. In some instances, they have also been shown to promote medication adherence (Adriaanse et al., 2011; Bélanger-Gravel et al., 2013; Martin et al., 2011; Pakpour et al., 2016; Prestwich et al., 2015; Schüz et al., 2009).

Approach related goals - goals that involve the introduction of a new behaviour or behaviours, or an increase in the level of a specific behaviour.

Avoidance related health goals - goals that involve the reduction, elimination or avoidance of specific behaviours.

Implementation intentions can also help people achieve **avoidance related health goals**. For example, implementation intentions have been shown to help reduce consumption of dietary fat, promote smoking cessation and abstinence and reduce alcohol intake (Arden & Armitage, 2012; Armitage, 2007, 2009, 2016; Armitage & Arden, 2008, 2012; Chatzisarantis & Hagger, 2010; Conner & Higgins, 2010; Elfeddali et al., 2012; Hagger et al., 2012a; Hagger et al., 2012b; Murgraff et al., 1996; Rivis & Sheeran, 2013; van Osch et al., 2008a; Vilà et al., 2017; Webb et al., 2009; though see also Higgins & Conner, 2003; Armitage et al., 2011). However, the evidence here is slightly more mixed, with some studies showing significant benefits and others not. For example, Webb et al. (2009) found that implementation intentions reduced smoking among those with weak or moderate smoking habits but not among those with strong smoking habits. Similarly, Hagger and colleagues found that implementation intentions were helpful for reducing alcohol consumption only among heavy drinkers (Hagger et al., 2012a). In a separate study they also found that implementation intentions were helpful for reducing alcohol consumption among students from the UK and Estonia but not from Finland (Hagger et al., 2012b).

Findings from studies aimed at reducing unhealthy snacking are even more mixed with some studies showing positive effects and others showing no effect (Adriaanse et al., 2011). Adriaanse et al. suggest that these discrepancies may in part be the result of differences in the format of the implementation intentions employed. In particular, when applied to unwanted behaviours, three different types of implementation intention can be formed (Gollwitzer et al., 2005). For example, imagine a person who always buys a bar of chocolate on their way home from work but is trying to eat more healthily. The three different types of implementation intention they might use are shown in **Table 6.2**. These different types of plans may be more or less effective in different circumstances (Parks-Stamm et al., 2010).

Table 6.2 Examples of different types of implementation intention that could be used to reduce an unwanted response of buying chocolate

Type of implementation intention	Example
	If I am on my way home from work and pass the corner shop, then I will...
Response to inhibit the unwanted behaviour is specified.	...not buy a bar of chocolate.
Response to ignore the cue is specified.	...ignore the corner shop.
Cue for the unwanted behaviour is linked to a new, desired behaviour.	...buy a piece of fruit.

An additional factor that may influence the efficacy of avoidance-related implementation intentions is the extent to which they have been tailored to the individual. Relevant cues for a specific behaviour are likely to vary substantially from person to person, so pre-formulated implementation intentions that are simply provided to the individual may fail to identify the correct (or most important) cue. The importance of identifying the right cue is illustrated in a study by Adriaanse et al. (2009). They asked participants to formulate implementation intentions aimed at replacing an unhealthy snack with a healthy snack. Some participants were asked to identify situational cues, such as being with friends or on a visit, whilst others were asked to identify motivational cues, such as feeling bored or in order to be sociable. Compared to a control condition, only participants who had formed implementation intentions specifying motivational cues changed their snacking behaviours.

The issue of factors that influence the efficacy of implementation intentions (moderate their effects) is an important one, and something we will look at in more detail on page 162.

How do implementation intentions work?

We've now seen how effective implementation intentions can be when it comes to changing behaviour, but how do they work? As discussed in **Chapter 5**, it's important we understand how particular techniques work, in order that we may successfully extend them to new situations and to different populations.

Implementation intentions are underpinned by the Rubicon model of action phases (Achtziger & Gollwitzer, 2008; Gollwitzer, 1996). In **Chapter 5** we saw how social cognition models are better at predicting intention than behaviour. This is because they tend to focus on *motivation* for behaviour change. By contrast, implementation intentions are designed to target the person's *ability* to change, in other words, the volitional stage of behaviour change. They aim to reduce the intention-behaviour gap by overcoming problems of:

- Intention activation (when we forget to perform the target behaviour, or our priorities change).

- Intention elaboration (when we fail to think through exactly how we will achieve our goals).

Implementation intentions are thought to address these difficulties via two key mechanisms; increasing the cognitive accessibility of relevant situational cues and increasing the automaticity of the behaviour. These types of underlying mechanisms, that help explain the links between two variables, are also referred to as **mediators**. We look at each of these mediators in turn, before considering an additional possibility; that implementation intentions also work by enhancing the person's memory for the behaviour.

> **Mediator** – a variable that explains the relationship between an independent variable and a dependent variable. Mediators are concerned with why an effect occurs.

Increased cognitive accessibility of relevant situational cues

Increased cognitive accessibility of relevant situational cues refers to the fact that implementation intentions help people recognise good opportunities to act. Identifying a particular situation or cue within an implementation intention makes its representation more readily available in the mind, which in turn makes the actual cue easier to notice and attend to (Aarts et al., 1999; Achtziger et al., 2012). For example, forming an implementation intention that begins 'If I am passing the supermarket on my way to work…' makes the person more likely to notice the supermarket on their way to work instead of walk straight past it, lost in thoughts about the day ahead.

Increased automaticity of the behaviour

The second mechanism via which implementation intentions are thought to influence behaviour is by increasing the strength of the relationship between the cue and the response in the person's mind. This means that when the person encounters the cue, they are likely to perform the behaviour in a more automatic fashion (Webb & Sheeran, 2008). In this way, implementation intentions are believed to lead to behaviour that is a little like habits. In other words, the behaviour is not the result of controlled deliberation but rather it is simply elicited by the cue with relatively little conscious thought. However, the

CHAPTER 6

difference between habits and implementation intentions is that in the former the cue-behaviour association is developed through repetition, whilst in the latter it occurs because the person has consciously linked the two in their mind.

More recently, Martiny-Huenger et al. (2017) have referred to simulation theories of cognition to help account for the effects of implementation intentions. Simulation theories of cognition (also called theories of grounded cognition; Barsalou, 2008) state that thinking or hearing about particular objects or events activates the same sensory and motor areas in the brain as those that are elicited when we actually encounter those objects or events. As such, Martiny-Huenger et al. suggested that the formation of an implementation intention is accompanied by neural activity in the brain associated with the perception of the event (the relevant cue) as well as neural activity in motor areas associated with the response. Since they are activated together, the links between the two areas become strengthened so that when the individual subsequently encounters the actual cue, the related motor areas are also activated, increasing the likelihood that the person will perform the intended behaviour. Although Martiny-Huenger et al. did not look at actual neural activity, they found evidence to support the view that implementation intentions create these types of direct perception-action links.

Enhanced memory for the behaviour

Nevertheless, other research has suggested that implementation intentions may do more than simply strengthen cue-response associations. Papies et al. (2009) asked participants to form an intention to behave in a way that deviated from their normal routine (to return to an office from the laboratory via the cafeteria, rather than directly). They asked some participants to form implementation intentions relating to this behaviour, some to perform a computer-based task that taught them to associate the relevant cue with the behaviour, and some (those in the control condition) to perform an unrelated associative learning task. They found that both forming implementation intentions and completing the computer task resulted in an immediate increase in the actual behaviour (relative to the control condition). However, one week later this effect was only maintained in the implementation intention group. These results suggest that the effects of implementation intentions are not simply brought about by learned cue-response associations. Instead, the authors speculate that implementation intentions may be better at helping the individual to mentally simulate the behaviour, which may in turn help them better consolidate it in memory.

Moderator – a variable that influences the relationship between an independent variable and a dependent variable. For example, it may strengthen or weaken the relationship or may even alter its direction from positive to negative or vice versa. Moderators are concerned with when an effect occurs (under what circumstances and for what type of person). Moderators may be qualitative (such as male or female) or quantitative (such as level of stress).

When do implementation intentions work?

Another important question to answer is *when* implementation intentions work. In other words, do they work all of the time, for all people, or is it the case that they work better in certain types of situations and for certain types of people? We refer to such factors as **moderators**.

A wide range of different factors have been examined as potential moderators of implementation intentions, though for many of these there is still insufficient evidence to draw any firm conclusions (Prestwich & Kellar, 2014). Here we look at a selection.

Motivation/intention

The moderator with the best evidence base is motivation/intention. Implementation intentions are more effective when the person is motivated to perform the behaviour (Prestwich & Kellar, 2014;

Prestwich et al., 2015). For example, van Osch et al. (2008b) asked parents in the Netherlands to form implementation intentions to encourage them to apply sunscreen to their children. However, they found that the implementation intentions were only effective at increasing sunscreen use among parents who were already highly motivated to use it. Likewise, Prestwich et al. (2003) found that implementation intentions designed to promote exercise were most effective when combined with a task aimed at increasing motivation to exercise. As discussed previously, such findings are consistent with the Rubicon model of action phases (**Chapter 5**) that states that behaviour change will only occur when the person is both motivated to change and has the ability to change (Achtziger & Gollwitzer, 2008; Gollwitzer, 1996).

Ease of behaviour

Some research suggests that when a behaviour is very easy, implementation intentions will be less helpful because the person will not need any additional assistance. In other words, motivation alone will be sufficient to bring about change (Prestwich et al., 2015). For example, Gollwitzer and Brandstätter (1997) asked students to identify easy and difficult personal goals they wanted to achieve over the Christmas break. Without an implementation intention, difficult goals were achieved in 22% of cases, but this figure increased to 62% when an implementation intention was used. However, easy goals were often achieved even without an implementation intention (78% of the time) and the addition of an implementation intention resulted in a much smaller further improvement (to 84%).

Nevertheless, Dewitte et al. (2003) later suggested that the effect in the above study may have occurred simply because of a ceiling effect with easy goals. In other words, with easy goals there was often no room for improvement. By contrast, in their studies where all goals were sufficiently difficult to avoid a ceiling effect, they found that implementation intentions were *not* less effective for relatively easy goals. Taken together, these findings suggest that the effect of goal difficulty on the relationship between implementation intentions and behaviour may show a stepped relationship rather than a linear one. In other words, implementation intentions may not be helpful for very easy goals, due to a ceiling effect, but once goals get sufficiently difficult to avoid this ceiling effect, increasing goal difficulty may not increase the helpfulness of implementation intentions. (Though note that Dewitte et al. also found that implementation intentions were not effective at increasing the likelihood of achieving certain types of difficult goals, suggesting that the relationship between these variables may actually be even more complex.)

Self-regulatory ability

Another way of thinking about behavioural difficulty is to consider the ability of the individual rather than the characteristics of the behaviour; what seems easy for one person may be less easy for another. Put another way, implementation intentions may be more useful for those who tend to struggle to put plans into action and less useful for those who find this easier. In support of this view, Allan et al. (2013) found that implementation intentions relating to the completion of an online diary were only helpful among those identified as poor planners. Similarly, implementation intentions tend to show larger effects among groups who have more trouble regulating their behaviour, such as those suffering from heroin addiction, a brain injury, or schizophrenia (Gollwitzer & Sheeran, 2006). However, given that most research on implementation intentions has been conducted with university students (Gollwitzer & Sheeran, 2006), who are presumably already relatively good at self-regulation, further research with community and clinical samples would be helpful to more fully explore the effects of self-regulatory ability.

Habits

Implementation intentions may be less effective at changing behaviours that represent strong habits. For example, Webb et al. (2009) asked high school smokers (aged between 17 and 21) to form implementation intentions relating to how they would avoid smoking in situations that normally prompted smoking (for example when their friends were smoking). One month later they took measures of how many cigarettes the pupils were smoking per day. They found that compared to a control group, implementation intentions were effective at reducing smoking among pupils with weak or moderate habits but not among those with strong habits. Similar results have also been found in relation to physical activity (Maher & Conroy, 2015).

Engagement and plan specificity

Research shows that when asked to form implementation intentions, not everyone will do so. For example, Michie et al. (2004) found that 37% of pregnant women who intended to attend antenatal screening chose not to form an implementation intention when prompted. Likewise, Armitage (2009) found that 46% of those asked to generate implementation intentions to reduce their alcohol intake failed to generate them and that this lack of engagement moderated the effect of the intervention on behaviour. However, engagement did not moderate effects where participants were asked to simply select and copy out an implementation intention from a choice of three provided by the researcher, suggesting that in this case, simple exposure to specific implementation intentions was more important than whether or not the person generated the details themselves.

Additionally, even where people do attempt to form an implementation intention, they will not necessarily form it as instructed (specifying exactly when, where and how they will perform the target behaviour). For example, de Vet et al. (2011b) asked individuals to form up to three implementation intentions designed to increase their level of physical activity. However, they found that over 30% of people failed to form even one specific implementation intention. In other words, although they wrote down a plan relating to physical activity, it was too vague to really be considered an implementation intention. The authors also found that the more specific the person's implementation intentions, the higher their levels of physical activity two weeks later.

Similar effects of specificity were found in a study conducted by Ziegelmann et al. (2006). They asked patients in an orthopaedic rehabilitation clinic to form implementation intentions to increase their physical activity. However, half of these patients formed these implementation intentions on their own, whilst the other half were assisted by an interviewer. Those who were assisted by the interviewer formed more specific plans and also reported higher levels of physical activity six months later. Greater implementation intention specificity has also been associated with higher rates of smoking abstinence (van Osch et al., 2010), though findings are less consistent for condom preparatory behaviours (such as buying and carrying condoms; de Vet et al., 2011a).

Number of implementation intentions

In some instances, greater effects on behaviour are observed where a greater number of implementation intentions are formed. For example, Wiedemann et al. (2012) asked participants to form between one and five implementation intentions to increase their fruit and vegetable consumption. They found that the more implementation intentions the person formed, the greater their increase in consumption. Similar results have been obtained for physical activity (Wiedemann et al., 2011).

However, both the above studies looked at the initiation of new behaviours. When it comes to breaking habits, forming a larger number of implementation intentions may be less successful. For example, Verhoeven et al. (2013) found that whilst forming one implementation intention to reduce unhealthy snacking was effective, forming three (each relating to different cues and different behaviours) was not effective. A second study suggested that the single implementation intention was effective because the link between the cue and the desired behaviour was stronger than the link between the cue and the original, unwanted, habitual behaviour. However, when there were three implementation intentions all relating to the same goal, they suffered from interference from one another such that the cue-response associations were not strong enough to replace the original cue-response associations relating to the unwanted behaviour. In other words, forming three implementation intentions diluted their effects to the extent that none were successful. A similar effect has been shown to occur where a second implementation intention is formed as a 'Plan B'. In other words, an alternative behaviour is specified in relation to the same cue (Vinkers et al., 2015).

Forming implementation intentions about multiple different goals has also been found to be less effective than forming an implementation intention about a single goal (Dalton & Spiller, 2012). However, in this case the reduction in effect seems to occur because the multiple implementation intentions highlight the difficulties of achieving multiple goals and so undermines the person's commitment to those goals. As such, framing the goals as more manageable may help counteract this effect.

Types of implementation intention interventions

As can be seen from the literature reviewed so far, there is a wide range of different ways in which implementation intentions can be employed. Some of the most commonly used variations are shown in **Table 6.3**. (See Prestwich et al., 2015 for an alternative taxonomy and for further discussion of some of these variants.)

Volitional help sheets

Whilst we have already encountered many of the variations detailed in **Table 6.3**, it is worth highlighting several important variants that we have not yet come across. In particular, volitional help sheets may be especially useful for health interventions. These list a range of specific cues on one side of the page and a list of responses on the other. The person is then asked to select a cue that is appropriate for them and to link it to a response by drawing a line between the two. Thus the help sheets have the advantage of being relatively easy for participants to engage with whilst also ensuring that cues and responses have been clearly specified (see *Engagement and plan specificity* section). They also require minimal resources, making them a potentially cost-effective way of delivering an intervention to large numbers.

Volitional help sheets have been shown to be effective at promoting both approach-related behaviours, such as increasing physical activity and fruit consumption, as well as avoidance-related behaviours, such as reducing binge drinking, alcohol consumption, smoking, speeding and stress-related unhealthy snacking, as well as aiding weight loss (Armitage & Arden, 2010, 2012; Armitage, 2008, 2015a, 2015b; Armitage et al., 2014, 2017; Brewster et al., 2015; O'Connor et al., 2015).

Action planning versus coping planning

Some authors distinguish between action planning and coping planning. The former refers to implementation intentions used to help initiate an action (such as when and where

Table 6.3 Implementation intention (II) variations

Feature	Variations			
Type of prompt	Individual is simply prompted to form an II	Individual works with an interviewer who helps them form an appropriate II	Individual is asked to form an II by linking cues and responses that they have been provided with ('volitional help sheet')	Individual is provided with an II
Type of cue	External	Internal: bodily sensation	Internal: cognition	Internal: emotion
Type of response	Avoid: specifies that a target response will not be carried out	Avoid: specifies that the cue will be ignored	Avoid/approach: specifies that an unwanted response will be replaced with a wanted response	Approach: specifies that a new response will be performed
Response content	Refers to a behaviour	Refers to a cognition		Refers to an emotion
Number of IIs formed within the same session	One	Multiple: relating to the same goal, specifying the same cue but alternative responses	Multiple: relating to the same goal, specifying different cues for the same response	Multiple: relating to the same goal, specifying different cues and different responses	Multiple: relating to different goals
Number of II sessions	One		More than one: original IIs repeated	More than one: additional IIs formed
Reminders	None		One or more	
Other intervention components	None: IIs are used on their own		One or more: IIs are used in combination with other behaviour change strategies (for example, targeting motivation)	

a person will exercise). By contrast, the latter refers to implementation intentions that help a person identify potential barriers to a behaviour and plan how to overcome these. For example, someone may anticipate feeling too tired to exercise and plan to ignore this feeling and start exercising straight away. Research shows that whilst action planning may be useful for initiating a behaviour, coping planning may be more helpful for maintaining that behaviour over time. For example, research with cardiac patients undergoing rehabilitation showed that those who engaged in coping planning were more likely to still be exercising several months after discharge (Sniehotta et al., 2005, 2006).

Digital reminders

The increased use of digital technologies over the last decade has also given rise to new ways for individuals to be reminded of their implementation intentions without the need for another person. For example, Prestwich et al. (2009) used text messages to remind people of their implementation intentions, whilst Tapper et al. (2014) developed a fully automated web-based intervention that prompted individuals to develop (and review) implementation intentions and then emailed them reminders of these one, two and four days later.

With social cognition theories

Whilst some studies have used implementation intentions in isolation, others have combined them with additional intervention strategies drawn from social cognition theories (such as those described in **Chapter 5**). For example, Milne et al. (2002) tried to increase exercise participation in undergraduate students by combining implementation intentions (IIs) with a health education leaflet. The leaflet was based on protection motivation theory (PMT) and provided information about coronary heart disease as well as the benefits of exercise. They randomised students into three groups:

- a PMT only group who were asked to read the leaflet

- a PMT plus II group who were asked to read the leaflet and, one week later, were also asked to form an implementation intention relating to when and where they would exercise in the following week

- a control group who were simply asked to read the opening three paragraphs of a novel.

Self-report measures of exercise were taken over a two-week period and showed that only those in the PMT plus II group increased exercise relative to the control group; 91% of those in the PMT plus II group exercised at least once, compared to 38% and 35% in the control and PMT only groups respectively.

This intervention has a solid foundation in theory. Recall that in **Chapter 5** we looked at the Rubicon model of action phases, that states that behaviour change has two distinct stages; a motivational stage, in which the individual makes a decision to pursue a particular goal, and a volitional stage, in which they consider how they will actually achieve that goal. Thus, according to this model, behaviour change is most likely to occur where the person is both motivated and has also made a specific behaviour change plan. The study carried out by Milne et al. (2002) targeted both these stages; the leaflet was designed to increase motivation whilst the implementation intentions were designed to target volition. Thus the results are consistent with the Rubicon model; we would not necessarily expect to see behaviour change with an intervention that targeted motivation alone, without also addressing volition (the leaflet on its own had no effect). However, where we combine these two elements, we see an increase in the target behaviour (the leaflet plus the implementation intentions increased exercise participation).

Nevertheless, observant readers may have spotted a key limitation to this study; it does not tell us what happens if we use implementation intentions on their own. We are assuming that the PMT component served a useful purpose, boosting participants' motivation to change their behaviour. Indeed, the study also showed that the leaflet significantly increased participants' intentions to exercise. However, since there was no condition that used implementation intentions in isolation, we cannot be certain that they would not have worked just as well on their own, without the leaflet.

Indeed, other studies have found that implementation intentions can successfully change behaviour, even in the absence of strategies targeting motivation. For example, Armitage (2004) asked company employees to form implementation intentions relating to how they would eat a low-fat diet in the next month. Compared to those who had not formed implementation intentions, these participants subsequently reported reduced intake of both saturated fat and total fat. In this study it is probably safe to assume participants already had a reasonable idea of *how* to reduce their fat intake. It is likely they were also already motivated to do so. As such, it was not necessary to complicate the intervention by including additional components designed to increase knowledge and motivation. This example highlights the importance of considering the characteristics of the target population when developing an intervention; an issue we return to in **Chapter 9**.

With mental contrasting

Finally, recent research suggests a promising new approach to behaviour change may be to combine implementation intentions with mental contrasting. Mental contrasting is where a person is asked to imagine, in detail, the positive outcomes associated with achieving a specific goal. They are then asked to imagine, again in detail, the things that might stand in the way of them achieving this goal. In other words, they contrast their desired future with their present reality (Oettingen, 2012). This technique is thought to help motivate people to pursue their goals, by helping them create a mental link between future desired outcomes and present obstacles. As such, when obstacles are encountered, the desired outcomes come to mind and help motivate behaviour. Research also suggests mental contrasting helps change the meaning of certain situations, so they become viewed as obstacles, which in turn prompts the individual to try to overcome them. Additionally, mental contrasting is thought to support the formation of appropriate implementation intentions by helping the person identify the most important obstacles (Adriaanse et al., 2010).

Although this is a relatively new area of research, mental contrasting with implementation intentions has been shown to be helpful for increasing physical activity, promoting fruit and vegetable consumption, improving study behaviours and reducing unhealthy snacking (Adriannse et al., 2010; Christiansen et al., 2010; Saddawi-Konefka et al., 2017; Stadler et al., 2010).

Summary

As noted above, implementation intentions represent a type of training intervention because they are designed to change the person's response to cues that elicit behaviour. We now turn to strategies that use (a) cognitive bias modification and (b) evaluative conditioning. Strategies based on these can also be viewed as training interventions because they aim to alter a person's response to specific cues. However, implementation intentions draw on habit theory and the Rubicon model of action phases. By contrast, strategies that use cognitive bias modification draw on theories of attention and motor control whilst strategies that use evaluative conditioning draw on theories of conditioning. We consider cognitive bias modification in the next section and look at evaluative conditioning in the section that follows.

COGNITIVE BIAS MODIFICATION

Cognitive bias modification refers to techniques designed to alter a person's mental associations in the hope that these will, in turn, extinguish or reverse their automatic, biased responses to particular cues. Two areas that have generated a lot of interest are those concerned with altering biases in attention and those concerned with altering automatic tendencies to approach particular stimuli.[2] We consider each of these areas in turn.

Attention and attentional bias modification

As we go about our daily lives we're bombarded with a huge array of different sights, sounds, smells and physical sensations. We see words and images plastered across billboards and buses, our smartphones ping and vibrate with new notifications, and flashy adverts attempt to divert our attention as we browse the news on the internet. Which of these things do we look at and process and which do we ignore?

---

2 For useful reviews of cognitive bias modification interventions see Cristea et al (2016) and Jones et al (2017).

Our attention is thought to be controlled by two different systems: a voluntary, 'top-down', goal-directed system in which we decide where we are going to direct our attention, and an involuntary, 'bottom-up', stimulus-driven system in which our attention is automatically captured by particular stimuli (Theeuwes, 2010). These two systems can be seen to correspond to the automatic and controlled processing systems outlined at the start of the chapter (see **Table 6.1**).

What types of stimuli capture our attention automatically? First, our attention seems to be drawn to stimuli that have particularly salient characteristics. For example, stimuli that appear suddenly or unexpectedly, that are novel or that differ significantly from their surroundings in terms of features such as colour or size (Theeuwes, 1994, 2010; **Image 6.4**).

Second, our attention seems to be captured by emotional stimuli, especially those that are relevant to our needs and goals (Bar-Haim et al., 2007; Brosch et al., 2007, 2008; Pool et al., 2016; Sander et al., 2005). In particular, we seem to be drawn to things in our environment that we associate with reward (Anderson et al., 2011). For example, when you looked at the two pictures at the start of the chapter (**Image 6.1**), chances are that the cookies held your attention more than the pile of chopped wood. This is because your previous interactions with cookies are likely to have led to more pleasure than your previous interactions with piles of chopped wood.

Image 6.4 Many smartphone apps capture our attention with brightly coloured notification icons.

Credit: Karsten Winegeart.

The tendency for a person's attention to be captured and/or held by particular types of stimuli is termed 'attentional bias' (Field et al., 2016). Attentional biases can be influenced by both state and trait variables. For example, attentional bias toward palatable foods is higher among those who are hungrier and also among those who are more sensitive to reward (see **Chapter 4**; Tapper et al., 2010; see also Anderson, 2017; Anderson et al., 2011; Field et al., 2016; Pool et al., 2015).

Attentional biases are considered important because of their relationship with behaviour. For example, in the laboratory they have been shown to automatically activate relevant motor response plans, reduce inhibitory processing, and influence decision-making (Anderson, 2017). Outside the laboratory, some studies have shown that attentional bias toward drug-related stimuli predicts a relapse amongst those in treatment for addiction (Marissen et al., 2006). Such findings have led researchers to explore the possibility of developing interventions aimed at modifying attentional biases in order to influence behaviour. For example, Field and Eastwood (2005) recruited heavy social drinkers and used a computer-based task to train half of them to direct their attention toward alcohol-related cues (such as pictures of alcohol or of people drinking alcohol) and half to direct their attention away from alcohol-related cues. Those who had been trained to direct their attention toward the alcohol cues reported a greater urge to drink and, when given the opportunity, also drank a greater quantity of beer.

However, as evidence in this area has grown, so it has become apparent that the promising effects described in some of these studies are not necessarily very robust. For example, Christiansen et al. (2015) reviewed studies in the area of addiction and concluded that there was no convincing evidence that attentional bias assessed in the clinic predicted later relapse, or that attempts to modify attentional bias could reduce the risk of relapse.

CHAPTER 6

Likewise, Field et al. (2016) examined research on obesity and addiction. They concluded that attentional bias does not consistently predict future drug use or food intake. Similarly, whilst experimentally inducing attentional bias seems to increase cravings and consummatory behaviour, it is less clear whether training people to direct their attention away from relevant cues can reliably reduce cravings and intake. This especially seems to be the case where training occurs in a clinical or laboratory setting but effects are measured outside the laboratory or clinic in the daily lives of participants. On the basis of their review, Field et al. suggest that, rather than being a stable phenomenon, attentional bias is determined by the person's current motivational state, which will fluctuate over time. They suggest that rather than having a direct causal influence on behaviour, it may have a smaller, indirect effect that occurs due to links between attention and craving. As such, attempts to modify attentional bias will be most beneficial where they take place outside the laboratory setting, when cravings are at their strongest. They suggest that smartphone apps may be one way of delivering such training (see Kerst & Waters, 2014). We look at craving in more detail in **Chapter 7**.

Automatic action tendencies

As well as automatically capturing our attention, certain cues in our environment may also automatically elicit an approach response, in other words, a tendency to move toward them. For example, in a computer-based task, Field et al. (2008) found that heavy drinkers were faster at moving toward, rather than away from, alcohol-related images. That is, they displayed an approach bias. This approach bias was also positively correlated with self-reported levels of alcohol craving. Similar findings have been described in relation to cigarettes, cannabis and high-calorie foods (Batterink et al., 2010; Field et al., 2006; Mogg et al., 2005).

Such findings have led researchers to develop training interventions aimed at reducing this type of automatic approach bias, in the hope that this will in turn influence behaviour. The types of tasks employed in these training interventions can broadly be described as targeting approach-avoidance or developing cue specific inhibitory control.

Approach-avoidance training

In approach-avoidance training (also called cue avoidance training) a person is trained to avoid problematic cues and approach alternative, non-problematic (or neutral) cues. For example, Wiers et al. (2010) trained male students who were consuming risky levels of alcohol (at least 15 units a week) to avoid alcohol-related cues and approach soft drink-related cues. This was achieved using a computer-based task in which participants were asked to push or pull a joystick away from or toward them in response to a range of different alcohol- and soft drink-related images presented on the screen. These pushing and pulling actions were associated with the image getting smaller or larger respectively to create a sensation of the viewer moving away from or toward the image. In a control condition, participants were trained to approach the alcohol-related pictures and avoid the images of soft drinks.

Although the training procedure had no overall effect on the amount of alcohol participants later drank, when analyses were restricted to those who were 'successfully' trained (who became faster at either pulling or pushing the alcohol-related images toward or away from them) there were significant effects; those who became better at avoiding alcohol cues drank less beer compared to those who became faster at approaching alcohol cues. Thus the results suggested that approach-avoidance training might have potential as an intervention aimed at altering automatic action tendencies. (Though with the important caveat that the training in this particular study was only successful for a sub-set of people and there was no measure of alcohol consumption outside the laboratory.)

Subsequent research employing approach-avoidance training has since demonstrated effects outside the laboratory, in terms of reduced rates of relapse among recovering alcoholics at a one-year follow-up and fewer cigarettes smoked by psychiatric inpatient smokers at three months (Eberl et al., 2013; Machulska et al., 2016). Following a meta-analysis of 18 studies examining approach-avoidance training for consumption behaviours (alcohol use, cigarette smoking and unhealthy eating), Kakoschke et al. (2017) concluded that it was effective at both reducing approach bias and changing behaviour.

However, others have been more cautious. For example, Becker et al. (2018) highlight the possibility of publication bias (the fact that research showing significant effects is more likely to be published than research showing non-significant effects, see **Chapter 11**). They also argue that in many of the studies participants in control conditions were trained to approach the consumption-related cues (see the Wiers et al., 2018, study described above). This means that subsequent differences between intervention and control participants could be due to increased approach behaviour among control participants rather than reduced approach behaviour among intervention participants. (Though see also Kakoschke et al., 2018, who argue that such control conditions are likely to reflect participants' existing approach biases.)

Cue specific inhibitory control

Other researchers have developed what have been termed 'cue specific inhibitory control' interventions where training is aimed at developing the ability to stop, change or delay a behavioural response to a specific type of cue. Commonly employed tasks include the Go/No-Go task and the Stop Signal task.

In Go/No-Go tasks, participants are presented with images relating to the behaviour of interest (for example a glass of beer) as well as neutral images (for example an empty glass) and are required to make or withhold a response (such as pressing a key) depending on the presence of a 'go' or 'no-go' cue (for example, one of two different letters presented in one of the corners of the picture). Training a person to withhold a response to specific types of image is achieved by pairing them with more no-go cues (Houben et al., 2012).

By contrast, Stop Signal tasks require participants to make judgements about a range of different images and to indicate this by making a particular response (such as pressing a key on a keyboard). For example, they may be shown a series of images of drinking glasses and be asked to indicate whether the glass is full or empty. However, in the presence of an additional cue (such as an auditory noise) they are required to inhibit this response (Houben et al., 2012). Again, training is achieved by pairing concern-related images with the inhibition-related cue.

Stop Signal tasks differ from Go/No-Go tasks in terms of the point at which the response-related cues are presented; in the Go/No-Go task these are presented simultaneously with the image, meaning the person has to refrain from initiating a response. In the Stop Signal task the response-related cue is presented after a short time delay, meaning the person has to cancel an initiated response (Schachar et al., 2007).

Meta-analyses of studies employing cue specific inhibitory control training have concluded it has small but significant effects on food and alcohol consumption in the laboratory, with larger effects produced by Go/No-Go training compared to Stop Signal training (Allom et al., 2015; Jones et al., 2016). More recent research suggests that the benefits of Go/No-Go training may also extend beyond the laboratory (Lawrence et al., 2015; see **Case Study 1, Chapter 12**).

Interestingly, effects of Go/No-Go training on behaviour do not seem to arise as a result of improved top-down inhibitory control. Instead, it seems more likely that repeated association between the appetitive stimuli and response inhibition reduces automatic approach tendencies as a result of a devaluation of the appetitive stimuli. In other words, the appetitive stimuli become viewed as less attractive (Chen et al., 2016; Veling et al., 2017; see also Stice et al., 2016). However, it is important to note that some studies have failed to find support for this proposed mechanism and the extent to which it can account for longer term effects of training on behaviour has also yet to be established (Di Lemma & Field, 2017).

EVALUATIVE CONDITIONING

Evaluative conditioning is the change in liking for a stimulus that occurs as a result of it being repeatedly paired with another liked or disliked stimulus (De Houwer et al., 2005). Evaluative conditioning has been used in laboratory studies to try to both increase health-protective behaviours and reduce health-damaging behaviours.

For example, Ellis et al. (2015) used evaluative conditioning to change people's affective responses to condoms. They asked participants to take part in what they thought was a computer-based attention task. However, for some participants this included the repeated pairing of images of wrapped and unwrapped condoms with a range of different positively valenced words and images, such as the word 'terrific' or a picture of a chipmunk (**Image 6.5**). They then measured participants' feelings about condoms using the prompt 'When I think about using condoms, it makes me feel....' followed by seven positive words and seven negative words (such as 'joy' or 'angry'). Participants rated their agreement with each description on a 9-point scale. The researchers also examined participants' behaviour by offering them the opportunity to take a number of health-related items away with them at the end of the study, supposedly as part of a university health promotion campaign.

Image 6.5 *Researchers have increased people's positive feelings towards items such as condoms, by pairing pictures of them with other positively valenced images, such as this one.*
Credit: Barb D'Arpino.

The items consisted of condoms as well as hand sanitiser, granola bars and wellness centre pamphlets. Results showed that those who had seen the condom images repeatedly paired with positive words and images reported more positive feelings towards condoms. Those who regularly used condoms also took more condoms at the end of the study.

By contrast, Legget et al. (2015) used evaluative conditioning to try to reduce liking for unhealthy foods. They did this by pairing images of high-calorie foods with images likely to elicit disgust (such as a cockroach on a slice of pizza or vomit in a dirty toilet). The disgust-evoking images were presented subliminally. In other words, they were flashed up on the computer screen so fast participants were unable to consciously report what they had seen. The researchers found that this procedure reduced participants' reported desire to eat the high-calorie foods.

Other researchers have used similar procedures to increase reported preferences for healthy foods, intentions to eat healthy foods and selection of fruit over an alternative snack (Bui & Fazio, 2016; Walsh & Kiviniemi, 2014). Although effects outside the laboratory, over more extended periods, have yet to be examined in a controlled manner, it is possible that a number of different health promotion campaigns draw on evaluative conditioning (see Case Studies 4 and 8 in **Chapter 12**). Though note that similar effects may also arise via other mechanisms such as goal priming, discussed in the next section (see Hollands & Marteau, 2016).

How does evaluative conditioning work? A number of explanations have been put forward to account for effects (Hofmann et al., 2010). Some of these state that evaluative conditioning occurs as a result of the formation of automatic associations between the stimuli. For example, the implicit misattribution model states that associations arise because the feeling that is evoked by the liked/disliked stimulus is misattributed to the neutral stimulus (Jones et al., 2009). By contrast, the propositional model states that evaluative conditioning occurs as a result of the person consciously forming a rule about the co-occurrence of the stimuli which in turn leads to a belief that the neutral stimulus shares some of the properties of the liked/disliked stimulus (Mitchell et al., 2009). The propositional model suggests the involvement of a conscious, explicit process and is consistent with the fact that evaluative conditioning effects tend to be stronger when people are aware of the relationship between the stimuli (Hofmann et al., 2010; see also Shanks, 2010). Nevertheless, in line with association formation accounts, effects can sometimes still occur even in the absence of awareness (Hofmann et al., 2010), as illustrated by the study described above that used subliminal disgust-evoking images (Legget et al., 2015). Thus it is possible that several different processes may lead to evaluative conditioning (Jones et al., 2010).

BOX 6.5 USING EVALUATIVE CONDITIONING TO CHANGE ATTITUDES

MAKING CONNECTIONS

Many of the social cognition theories we looked at in **Chapter 5** incorporated constructs relating to attitudes. However, as noted, a common limitation of these theories is that they often fail to specify how one might go about changing attitudes. Recall that attitudes comprise beliefs, feelings and behaviours (see **Chapter 4**). Thus evaluative conditioning offers one possible way of changing the affective component of attitudes. You may like to think about whether some of the other strategies described in this chapter could also influence constructs discussed in **Chapter 5**.

Summary

As noted previously, evaluative conditioning can be viewed as a type of training intervention. We now turn to techniques that are better described as cueing interventions: the use of priming, social norms and environmental proximity and defaults. Unlike the strategies reviewed so far, these techniques do not aim to train specific automatic associations. Instead, they alter cues in the environment to exploit existing automatic associations and processes.

PRIMING

Priming occurs where exposure to a stimulus activates not only the mental representation of that stimulus, but also mental representations of related objects, actions and/or concepts. This increased activation in related areas then influences the individual's responses, without them being aware of this influence. In other words, although the person may be aware of the stimulus, they are not aware of its influence on their behaviour (Bargh, 2016).

A variety of different types of priming effect have been identified (Förster et al., 2007). For example, perceptual priming occurs as a result of perceptual similarity between two stimuli, which means that exposure to a word such as 'sofa' may make a person more likely to respond with a visually similar word, such as 'software' in a subsequent task. By contrast, semantic priming occurs because of connections that stem from the meanings of the stimuli. For example, exposure to a word such as 'pet' may increase the speed at which a semantically related word such as 'cat' is recognised. Priming effects have also been found to extend beyond computer-based tasks to behaviours that are more relevant to everyday life, such as product selection, food consumption and prosocial behaviours (Karremans et al., 2006; Papies & Hamstra, 2010; Shariff et al., 2016). These types of priming effects are often referred to as 'behavioural priming'.

Behavioural priming has been the subject of extensive research and debate. Some of this has arisen from failures to replicate certain influential findings in the area. This has led researchers to question the reliability of the effects (Doyen et al., 2012; Yong, 2012) but also to suggest they may be sensitive to differences in the target population, for example in relation to state differences (such as hunger) and demographic differences (such as level of education; Cesario, 2014; Forwood et al., 2015).

Researchers have also debated the mechanisms responsible for behavioural priming effects. One explanation, referred to as the 'perception-behaviour link', is that behavioural priming occurs as a result of associations between environmental stimuli and specific behaviours. As a result, perceiving these stimuli activates not only mental representations of the stimuli, but also mental representations of the behaviour they are associated with. This increased activation makes the behaviour more likely to occur (Bargh et al., 1996; Dijksterhuis & Bargh, 2001).

Goals – behaviours or end-states that are associated with reward and are supported by knowledge structures relating to both relevant contexts and ways in which the goal can be achieved (Papies, 2016b). Goals may be short-term hedonic goals, such as quenching thirst, or long-term investment goals, such as losing weight (Papies, 2016b). Importantly, the activation of one goal can result in the inhibition of other goals (Shah et al., 2002; see also Stroebe et al., 2008).

Goal priming

An alternative explanation for behavioural priming is that it occurs because environmental stimuli are associated with specific **goals**. Perception of these stimuli thus activates these goals that in turn elicit behaviours aimed at achieving them (Custers & Aarts, 2005; Papies & Aarts, 2016). This is referred to as 'goal priming'.

A meta-analysis of 133 behavioural priming studies contrasted these two explanations (Weingarten et al., 2016). The results showed that effects of priming were stronger when the person valued the outcome of the behaviour. This suggests the involvement of goals;

if a behaviour is activated due to direct links between environmental stimuli and the behaviour, the value the person places on the behaviour or its outcome will have no effect on the likelihood of it being performed. However, if the stimuli influence behaviour via goal activation, we would expect effects to occur only where that goal is important to that person. For example, priming a goal such as weight loss will have little effect on behaviour for those who have no interest in losing weight. Although Weingarten et al. found support for both perception-behaviour priming and goal priming, the results indicated that goal-priming effects were both stronger and more likely to persist over time. These findings suggest that goal priming probably exerts a stronger influence over our behaviour.

In practice, it may not always be possible to establish whether a priming effect occurs as a result of goal priming or perception-behaviour links (Förster et al., 2007). However, a number of studies suggest that goal priming can influence health-related behaviours. For example, Veltkamp et al. (2009) found that priming drink-related words increased soda consumption among participants, but only when they were fluid deprived. Similarly, Karremans et al. (2006) found that priming participants with the name of a branded drink increased the likelihood of them subsequently choosing that drink, but only if they were thirsty. These are examples of primes that activate hedonic goals of quenching thirst. Given the ubiquitous nature of fast food advertising, such effects may be commonplace in everyday life, possibly prompting us to consume a more unhealthy diet than we might otherwise (Cohen, 2008).

However, goal priming can also be used to activate long-term investment goals, such as healthy eating or weight loss. For example, individuals who were handed a recipe flyer for a low-calorie, healthy pasta dish as they entered a supermarket subsequently purchased fewer unhealthy snacks (Papies et al., 2014). In this case, the recipe flyer likely activated concepts of healthy eating and/or weight loss that then influenced purchasing behaviours. Consistent with goal priming, the recipe cards only reduced unhealthy snack purchases among those suffering from overweight or obesity. (Although participants paid attention to the flyer when they received it, they reported that they had not been aware of its influence on their behaviour. As such, it can be viewed as a prime, rather than a prompt.) In a similar study, Papies and Hamstra (2010) found that individuals who were concerned about weight management ate fewer free snack samples in a local store when a poster promoting a low-calorie recipe was displayed on the door.

On the basis of these and related findings, Papies (2016b) argues that goal priming may be a useful tool for encouraging healthier behaviours. She suggests five principles for use with goal priming to maximise its effects. These are as follows:

1. Target individuals that value the goals that are being primed.

2. Identify and refer to the specific motivations underlying the goal, for example weight loss goals may be driven by a desire to improve one's appearance or to maintain good health.

3. Prime positive outcomes to be achieved (such as good health) rather than negative outcomes to be avoided (such as disease).

4. Use primes that attract attention (see page 169) and employ them as close as possible to the point at which the critical goal-relevant decision is being made (for example, in a menu).

5. Avoid barriers that may prevent the target behaviour, such as lack of knowledge (for example, how to reduce salt intake) or lack of availability (such as the absence of healthy options on a menu).

Nevertheless, despite the promising results in this area, it is also important to note that further research is needed to establish the extent to which goal priming can bring about benefits for the wider population. For example, Forwood et al. (2015) note that much of the research examining priming effects on food choice or intake has been conducted with groups who are unlikely to be representative of the general population (such as university students who tend to be younger and more educated). Their research showed that priming healthy eating goals increased preferences for fruit only among more educated participants, raising the possibility that priming interventions could inadvertently increase health inequalities (see **Chapter 3**).

SOCIAL NORMS

Social norms are informal rules about what is considered acceptable behaviour for members of a particular group or society. The focus theory of normative conduct (Cialdini, 2012; Cialdini et al., 1991) distinguishes between two main types of social norms:

- *Injunctive norms* (sometimes termed prescriptive norms) are perceptions of what most people approve or disapprove of.

- *Descriptive norms* (sometimes termed informational norms) are perceptions of what most people actually do in a given situation.

Injunctive norms and descriptive norms are not always the same. For example, in many societies there is an injunctive norm relating to littering; most people are likely to believe that others would disapprove of them dropping litter. However, in some situations (a street party, a carnival, a picnic area in summertime) we see a lot of litter, leading to a perception (a descriptive norm) that in this situation most other people leave litter.

According to Cialdini (2012), injunctive norms influence behaviour by signalling social rewards and punishments, whereas descriptive norms work by providing information about what is likely to be a good decision; if everyone else is doing it, it is probably worth doing too. Thus descriptive norms represent a mental shortcut, saving the person the time and effort of weighing up pros and cons in order to decide on a sensible course of action. Others have suggested that descriptive norms may also be followed in order to promote or signal affiliation with a social group or even to liberate individuals from perceived social pressure (Higgs, 2015; Miller & Prentice, 2016; Robinson et al., 2014b).

Research shows that one can influence behaviour by highlighting either injunctive norms or descriptive norms (Cialdini et al., 1990). The use of the latter may sometimes be viewed as a nudge (see **Box 6.6**). However, their different characteristics mean they may be more or less effective in different situations. In particular, where there are high levels of an undesirable behaviour (or low levels of a desirable behaviour), highlighting a descriptive norm will likely be ineffective or even counterproductive. For example, Sieverding et al. (2010) highlighted low participation rates in cancer screening using the message '*only one fifth of men (only 18%!) have undergone a standard early-detection cancer examination*'. This resulted in men reporting that they would be *less* likely to attend cancer screening within the next 12 months. In such situations, reference to an injunctive norm would be preferable (Cialdini et al., 2006).

Thus descriptive norms should only be used when the behaviour one is trying to promote is more common than the less desirable behaviour. Descriptive norms will also be more effective when the comparison group is similar to the target audience, both in terms of demographics (such as age and gender) as well as their situation (such as studying at a particular university; Cialdini, 2012). Additionally, since processing descriptive norms is thought to be less cognitively effortful than processing injunctive norms, they may be more effective when a person's cognitive resources are limited (Cialdini, 2012).

Descriptive norms have been used to promote a range of different health-related behaviours including stair climbing, safe sex, sun protection and reduced drink driving

BOX 6.6 NUDGES AND CHOICE ARCHITECTURE

HOT TOPIC

The terms 'choice architecture' and 'nudges' were first coined by Thaler and Sunstein in their influential book *Nudge*. 'Choice architecture' refers to the design features of an environment that influence the choices people make in that environment. Choice architecture is never neutral, it will influence our behaviour one way or another. As such it makes sense to design it in ways that influence our choices for the better. This is where 'nudges' come in. A 'nudge' is defined as 'any aspect of the choice architecture that alters people's behaviour in a predictable way without forbidding any options or significantly changing their economic incentives' (Thaler & Sunstein, 2008, p. 6). Thus a key feature of a nudge is that whilst it makes a particular choice more likely, the individual still feels at liberty to choose something different. For example, placing fruit near the till at a cafeteria may make people more likely to select a piece for dessert, but they are still free to choose a chocolate bar if they prefer. Thus positioning the fruit in this way would count as a nudge. By contrast, banning chocolate from the cafeteria would restrict people's freedom to choose. Thus whilst it would change the choice architecture it would not count as a nudge.

Nudges can be viewed as a form of what Thaler and Sunstein (2008) call 'libertarian paternalism'. This is the idea that governments can guide people toward better choices, without taking away their freedom to choose. This approach has become popular with some governments due to emerging evidence that it may be more acceptable to the general public than alternative approaches (Petrescu et al., 2016). For example, it can be contrasted with the use of legislation to enforce or prohibit certain behaviours (such as wearing seatbelts or not smoking in public places) that can sometimes lead to governments being accused of acting like a 'nanny state', restricting people's rights and liberties.

However, some have argued that the concept of nudging lacks clarity and has been inconsistently applied to different types of intervention. This in turn has hindered attempts to systematically examine the evidence for this approach, meaning that at present we know little about the long-term effects of nudges on health-related behaviours and population health (Hollands et al., 2013; Marteau et al., 2011). As such, some researchers have started reconceptualising this area as interventions that alter aspects of what they term the 'physical micro-environment', in other words, settings people use for specific purposes, such as shops, restaurants and bars. By developing a clear definition and typology they aim to help researchers categorise research studies according to consistent characteristics and to establish what works and what does not (Hollands et al., 2017).

(Burger & Shelton, 2011; Chernoff & Davison, 2005; Perkins et al., 2010; Reid & Aiken, 2013). Much research has also focussed on reducing alcohol consumption among young people. This was thought to be a particularly promising area for the use of descriptive norms because research suggests young people often overestimate the amount of alcohol their peers consume (Franca et al., 2010; McAlaney & McMahon, 2007; Neighbours et al., 2006). Thus descriptive norms can potentially be used to correct this misperception and, in doing so, hopefully also change behaviour.

Social marketing – the application of techniques drawn from commercial marketing to campaigns aimed at influencing behaviour that benefits either the individual or society as a whole (for a useful review of social marketing in public health see Grier & Bryant, 2005).

For example, DeJong et al. (2006, 2009) developed a **social marketing** campaign called *Just the Facts* in which posters, newspaper adverts and other media channels were used to deliver messages to university students regarding the percentage of their peers who drank less than a certain number of drinks. For example, '*67% of Northwest University students have 4 or fewer drinks when they party*'. The figures were derived from surveys conducted at the university in question.

However, one potential problem with these types of messages is what has been termed the 'boomerang effect'; the fact that those who engage in lower than average levels of the undesirable behaviour may actually show an increase (Schultz et al., 2007). One way to avoid this may be to use a combination of descriptive and injunctive norms, targeting those whose behaviour is less desirable than average with descriptive norms and those whose behaviour is more desirable than average with injunctive norms (Schultz et al., 2007). Whilst this would be difficult to achieve through mass media, it could be accomplished through the use of tailored feedback to individuals, provided in response to an initial assessment (see Neighbours et al., 2004).

Another way of tackling the boomerang effect is to simply avoid any reference to specific levels of the target behaviour. For example, in Wales, where most students were drinking more than recommended levels, Moore et al. (2013) had to be careful to avoid normalising hazardous drinking. As such they focussed their descriptive norm messages on the mismatch between people's perceptions and average consumption. They achieved this through the use of messages such as: '*Those around you are drinking less than you think: students overestimate what others drink by 44%*' and '*How much do you think the average female first year student drinks? Halve it. It really is less than you think.*' These, and similar messages, were printed on posters, coasters, drinking glasses and leaflets in university halls of residence (see also **Image 6.6**).

Image 6.6 In this image, a descriptive norm has been used to try to reduce risky drinking among university students. It avoids the boomerang effect because the target behaviour (eating before or whilst drinking) does not refer to a specific quantity.

Credit: 2016 Michigan State University Social Norms Program, Data: 2015 Fall Celebration Survey, N=1,040.

However, despite the appeal of such interventions, they do not always bring about significant changes to behaviour (e.g. DeJong et al., 2009; Moore et al., 2013). Indeed, a review found there was little evidence to indicate that social norms-based interventions could significantly reduce alcohol misuse among university and college students. It concluded that where significant effects had been found, they were likely to be too small to be of real practical benefit (Foxcroft et al., 2015).

More recently, descriptive norms have been used to try to change eating-related behaviours. A number of laboratory-based studies have shown how descriptive norms can influence both the amount of food consumed as well as choice of one food over another (Robinson et al., 2014b). For example, Robinson et al., (2014a) found that for low consumers of fruit and vegetables, a descriptive norm was more effective at increasing vegetable consumption than a health message. The descriptive norm stated '*Most students eat more vegetables than you'd expect. A lot of people aren't aware that the typical student eats over three servings of vegetables each day (according to a 2011 study).*' In this study, despite reference to a specific quantity ('*over three servings of vegetables*') the message did not result in a boomerang effect, but instead simply had no effect on high consumers of fruit and vegetables.

However, most research into social norms and eating has been conducted in the laboratory, with young, healthy weight, educated females (Robinson et al., 2014b). Thus the extent to which these promising findings might generalise to eating outside the laboratory, among those who are more representative of the general population, is less clear. Nevertheless, one field study suggests there may be reason for optimism: Thomas et al. (2017) found evidence to indicate that a norm-based message could increase vegetable consumption in the workplace. Over a two-week period they displayed posters in workplace restaurants that stated '*Most people here choose to eat vegetables with their lunch.*' This increased sales of meals with vegetables from 62% to 64%, which further rose to 67% after the posters had been removed.

Thus whilst social norms represent a promising, and potentially very cost-effective approach to health promotion, it is clear that effects are likely to vary depending on a range of different factors such as:

- type of behaviour (for example, risky versus health promoting)
- content of the message (such as descriptive versus injunctive norm)
- mode of delivery (for instance, social marketing versus personalised feedback)
- target population (for example, cohesive group with a strong social identify versus less cohesive group).

More research is needed to identify when social norms can be used to good effect and when they are likely to achieve very little or may even be counterproductive.

BOX 6.7 DESCRIPTIVE NORMS AND THE THEORY OF PLANNED BEHAVIOUR

MAKING CONNECTIONS

You may recall from **Chapter 5** that the theory of planned behaviour refers to 'normative beliefs'. When weighted by motivation to comply, these make up the person's 'subjective norms', which help predict intentions. In the theory of planned behaviour, normative beliefs refer to the person's beliefs about what others will think of them if they do or don't perform the behaviour in question. Thus they can be viewed as the equivalent of injunctive norms. Rivis and Sheeran (2003) showed that descriptive norms could also help predict intentions over and above attitudes, subjective norms and perceived behavioural control (in other words, existing theory of planned behaviour variables). As such they suggested that the theory of planned behaviour could be extended to include descriptive norms as an additional predictor of intention.

EASE OF BEHAVIOUR

As discussed in **Chapter 2**, from an evolutionary perspective it often makes sense to conserve rather than expend valuable energy and resources. Consistent with this view, when faced with a choice, humans often take the path of least resistance. This means that changes to our environment or 'choice architecture' (**Box 6.6**) can influence our behaviour in predictable ways.

Proximity

Proximity, in particular, has a significant effect on behaviour. The nearer we are to something, the less effort it takes to interact with it, so the more likely we are to do so. Thus by making unhealthy foods and drinks less accessible and healthy foods and drinks more accessible, we could potentially improve food choice. Indeed, experimental research has shown that the more effort required to obtain a food, the less likely a person is to make that effort (Goldfield & Epstein, 2002; Salvy et al., 2009). Field studies indicate that such effects also occur outside the laboratory (Bucher et al., 2016).

For example, Baskin et al. (2016) looked at the effect of proximity of snacks to beverages in the workplace. They found that when snacks were placed nearer the drinks station (approximately 2 metres away), 20.5% of employees took a snack. However, when snacks were placed further away (approximately 5.5 metres), only 12.2% took a snack. Similarly, Rozin et al. (2011) looked at the amounts of salad selected at a self-service salad bar. They found people selected less salad when it was made slightly more difficult to reach (by increasing its distance from them by around 25 cms) or slightly more difficult to serve (by presenting it with tongs rather than a spoon).

Defaults

Another way in which ease of behaviour can be manipulated is through the use of defaults. Defaults refer to outcomes that occur when a person fails to make a choice. Since it is easier not to take action, an outcome is likely to occur more frequently when it is set as the default. For example, in some countries such as Australia, Germany and the United States, people have to sign an **organ donation** register to indicate that they would be willing to donate their organs in the event of their death. In other countries, such as England, Wales, France and Spain, consent is assumed unless the person has registered their preference for their organs not to be donated. In other words, organ donation is the default option that occurs when no action is taken. These different policies can result in presumed consent rates of nearly 100% in countries where organ donation is the default option. This compares to explicit consent rates of around 5–30% where non-donation is the default (Johnson & Goldstein, 2003).

> **Organ donation** – where an individual donates an organ. This may occur for research purposes, though in most instances it involves the removal of healthy organs and tissues that are then transplanted into another person. Some organs, such as kidneys, can be donated by a living donor but most organs can only be donated after a person has died. Organs only survive outside the body for a few hours so need to be transplanted quickly. Across the globe there are more people on organ waiting lists than there are organ donors and many people die whilst waiting for a transplant (Howard, 2007).

The effect of defaults can be seen to be underpinned by status quo bias, our tendency to disproportionately stick with existing choices or behaviour (Samuelson & Zeckhauser, 1988). Status quo bias can, in turn, be explained by transition costs; the fact that the cost of switching (or the cost of deciding whether it is worth switching) may exceed any benefits actually gained from switching. However, transition costs cannot always account for status quo bias and additional explanations have been put forward (Samuelson & Zeckhauser, 1988). These include loss aversion (the fact that individuals weigh potential losses as more important than potential gains; Tversky & Kahneman, 1992) as well as regret avoidance (the fact that people feel greater regret for negative outcomes that result from new actions than for negative outcomes that result from taking no action; Kahneman & Tversky, 1982).

CONCLUSIONS

We are not always rational creatures, carefully weighing up the pros and cons of each and every decision. Indeed, this would be a terribly inefficient way of going about our daily lives. Instead, we carry out many actions with very little thought, sometimes barely even aware of the reasons for our choices. This means there is enormous potential for health interventions that target such automatic processes and in recent years we have seen growing interest in this field.

These interventions tend to be one of two types: they may either work with the individual, attempting to create or break specific mental associations (training interventions), or they may manipulate the environment, changing the cues that elicit particular behaviours (cueing interventions). The latter may be particularly important in relation to health inequalities. As discussed in **Chapter 3**, those from lower socioeconomic groups tend to experience higher levels of stress and reduced cognitive resources. Thus they may be less likely to benefit from interventions that require sustained motivation or controlled decision-making. By contrast, they may be just as sensitive to environmental interventions that elicit certain behaviours automatically. As such, these interventions may be less likely to widen health inequalities.

THE GREAT DEBATE

The idea of nudging has proved popular with many governments (**Box 6.6**). However, nudges may have limited impact against the well-financed marketing strategies used by the food industry (Marteau et al., 2011). This has led some to argue that legislation is needed to tackle rising levels of obesity, similar to the ways in which it has been used to combat smoking (see **Chapter 12**). However, legislation can be unpopular with the public (**Chapter 11**). When is government justified in introducing legislation in relation to behaviours such as eating, smoking and drinking? How could it make legislation more acceptable? Should there be limits to what industry can and cannot do to persuade us to buy their products? How might we create an environment in which industry interests align with the health and wellbeing of the population?

CHAPTER 6

7

CRAVING, WILLPOWER AND SELF-REGULATION

Chapter Outline

Craving

Willpower

Self-regulation

Conclusions

Try searching for the term 'craving' in the health and lifestyle section of any online bookstore and you'll get a sense of just how often this word is used in relation to anything we'd like to do less of, from smoking cigarettes and drinking alcohol to eating sugary foods and using smartphones. These books promise to help you 'beat', 'cure' or 'conquer' your cravings, the underlying assumption being that if we could just get rid of our cravings we could live happily ever after in cigarette-/sugar-/smartphone-free bliss (**Image 7.1**).

So what exactly do we mean when we talk about cravings? And how might we strengthen our willpower in order to overcome them? Or are there other ways of managing cravings that are a little less effortful? In this chapter we will:

Image 7.1 *The concept of craving is often central to self-help books aimed at helping people live healthier lifestyles.*
Credit: Kyaw Tun.

- Think about experiences of craving and how craving relates to behaviour.

- Examine theories of craving and the ways in which they can inform intervention.

- Explore the concept of willpower and its relevance for behaviour.

- Consider different ways of measuring willpower.

- Look at theories of willpower and their implications for behaviour change interventions.

- Draw on relevant theory to think about how we might best regulate our behaviour over time.

CRAVING

What is craving and how does it relate to behaviour?

Craving is typically defined as an intense, conscious desire, usually to consume a specific food or drug (Drummond, 2001; May et al., 2015; Pelchat, 2002; Tiffany & Wray, 2012). Some academics also distinguish between tonic craving and cue-induced craving (Drummond, 2000). The former is defined as craving in the absence of external cues, that is thought to reflect abstinence (for example, a cigarette craving that occurs as a result of nicotine deprivation), whilst the latter occurs as a result of exposure to cues previously associated with the substance or behaviour (for example, a cigarette craving that occurs in a particular setting even when the individual is not nicotine deprived). However, in practice many episodes of craving may represent a combination of both these factors rather than just one or the other.

Another way to get an insight into the concept of craving is to listen to people's accounts of what craving feels like. Below is one person's experience of craving coffee:

> When I get to work in the morning, I almost always have an intense urge to have a cup of coffee. Sometimes it comes to me almost like I am talking to myself – "I must get a cup of coffee before I do anything else". Sometimes I look at my coffee cup and imagine it is filled with coffee. Sometimes my mouth feels dry, and I can imagine what it will be like to have a drink. I get these thoughts and feelings whether or not I have already had a cup at home, and I find it hard to concentrate on anything else without getting that cup of coffee first. (May et al., 2004, p. 447)

This description certainly meets the definition of craving provided above; the person describes an intense, conscious desire ('an intense urge') to consume a specific substance (coffee). It also appears to be an instance of cue-induced craving since it occurs irrespective of whether or not the person has already had a cup of coffee at home. However, there is more than that. They describe vividly imagining the sight and taste of the coffee and they report having difficulty in concentrating on anything else. These additional features are explored in two theories of craving we consider in this chapter: the elaborated intrusion theory of desire and the grounded cognition theory of desire.

Does craving have a causal influence on behaviour? Some would argue not. For example, according to the cognitive processing model of addiction, craving occurs when something blocks the execution of an automatic action plan (see **Chapter 8**). As such, rather than being causally related to behaviour, cravings simply reflect underlying cognitive processes, which in turn means that interventions directly targeting craving reduction should have limited effect on behaviour. However, most other theories of craving (and addiction) state that cravings do influence behaviour. This view is supported by reviews showing that drug craving predicts relapse episodes in substance use and food cravings predict both eating and weight gain (Boswell & Kober, 2016; Serre et al., 2015). As such, if we can reduce a person's cravings this should make it easier for them to change their behaviour.

We now consider some of the key explanations and theories of craving as well as their implications for intervention.

Conditioning-based explanations of craving

Conditioning-based explanations of craving draw on Pavlovian conditioning. (Recall that Pavlovian conditioning is also called classical or respondent conditioning, see page 149, for a definition.) There are two different types of conditioning effects that could account for craving (Skinner & Aubin, 2010; Tiffany & Conklin, 2000). These are as follows:

- *Conditioned incentive effects.* (Sometimes called Pavlovian appetitive conditioning.) These occur where relevant cues are repeatedly paired with substance use. This means these cues can come to elicit physiological responses associated with substance use.

These are experienced as craving and motivate the person to use the substance in order to experience its pleasurable effects. Thus substance use that stems from conditioned incentive effects can be viewed as being positively reinforced (see page 218 for a definition of positive reinforcement). For example, if a person always buys and eats a bar of chocolate whenever they travel by train, cues associated with train travel (such as the distinct style of seating) may eventually come to elicit insulin and salivary responses that the person will experience as a food craving.

- *Conditioned withdrawal effects.* In this case specific cues are repeatedly paired with substance withdrawal so that the cues alone eventually come to elicit a withdrawal response. A feeling of craving arises as a result of a desire to escape these unpleasant withdrawal symptoms. As such, the relevant behaviour is negatively reinforced (see page 218 for a definition of negative reinforcement). For example, since one cannot smoke on an aeroplane, being on an aeroplane may repeatedly precede nicotine withdrawal so that eventually simply boarding a plane may elicit withdrawal symptoms and a craving for cigarettes, even if the person has just recently had a cigarette.

The evidence

There is evidence to support both conditioned incentive and conditioned withdrawal effects. For example, the eponymous Pavlov (1927) showed that dogs salivated in response to a buzzer that had previously been paired with the presentation of food. Likewise, O'Brien et al. (1977) found that individuals addicted to heroin showed a conditioned withdrawal response (reduced skin temperature, increased heart rate, increased respiration) when exposed to a tone and a peppermint fragrance that had previously been associated with heroin withdrawal. But are these physiological responses accompanied by feelings of craving? Here the evidence is much weaker. For example, Tiffany and Conklin (2000) reviewed studies examining self-reports of craving and autonomic reactions (such as heart rate, salivation and sweat-gland activity) among individuals with alcohol use disorder. They found that very few of these studies reported significant correlations between cue elicited autonomic reactions and craving (see also Bongers & Jansen, 2015; Jansen et al., 1992).

Nevertheless, other research has shown the emergence of feelings of desire or craving in the presence of cues previously associated with the consumption of a rewarding substance. For example, individuals who repeatedly consumed a milkshake in a specific virtual reality environment (such as a Japanese martial arts dojo) later reported greater desire for milkshake when re-exposed to that environment (van den Akker et al., 2013; see also Jansen et al., 2016). There is also some evidence to suggest that emotional eating (the tendency to overeat in response to certain emotions) may be underpinned by Pavlovian conditioning; Bongers and Jansen (2015) used a range of different stimuli (such as music, movie scenes and pictures) to repeatedly induce a negative or neutral mood in participants before giving them either chocolate to eat or nothing to eat. Ratings of desire for chocolate were subsequently higher following the type of mood induction (negative or neutral) in which they had previously been given chocolate.

Thus Pavlovian conditioning does seem to play a role in craving even though craving may not stem from conditioned physiological responses. Pavlovian conditioning may also depend on the person being consciously aware of the link between the cue and the outcome (Lovibond & Shanks, 2002; van den Akker et al., 2013; Weidemann et al., 2016), which in turn suggests the involvement of higher-order cognitive processes. This allows for the possibility that Pavlovian conditioning leads to craving as a result of its influence on cognitive processes (such as reward expectations) rather than its influence on physiological responses. With this in mind, we now turn to two theories of craving that place more emphasis on cognitive processes.

The elaborated intrusion theory of desire

Take a look at **Image 7.2**. If you happen to be reading this on a cold, wet, winter's day, in a slightly frazzled, overworked state of mind, you may find yourself dreaming about a summer holiday. You may start to imagine the warm sun beating down on your skin, the soft sand between your toes and the cool water rippling gently round your ankles. Perhaps you can hear the breeze whispering in the trees behind you. Maybe you picture yourself stretched out on the sand, drifting off into a peaceful doze, or swinging gently in a hammock, iced cocktail in your hand and absolutely nothing to do all day except relax.

Image 7.2 *Are you craving sunshine? The elaborated intrusion theory of desire suggests that the processes underlying cravings for food and drugs are the same as those that underlie other desires such as a desire for a holiday.*
Credit: Ishan @seefromthesky on Unsplash.

On the other hand, if you've just come back from a summer holiday, if it's blistering hot outside, or if you happen to live in warmer climes and can see a beach like this from your kitchen window, then you might appreciate the picture from an aesthetic point of view but it may not prompt you to imagine the sensations of sun and sea on your skin and it may not elicit any feelings of longing.

The elaborated intrusion theory of desire was developed to explain these types of feelings as well as cravings for food and drugs (Kavanagh et al., 2005; May et al., 2012; 2015). What distinguishes it from other theories is that it suggests that the same processes underlie all desires and cravings, whether they are for chocolate cake, a glass of wine, or a holiday in the sunshine.

Intrusive thoughts

Like conditioning models of craving, the elaborated intrusion theory maintains that the initial source of cravings is learned associations between specific external or internal cues and the object of desire. According to the theory, these cues automatically trigger transitory, intrusive thoughts. For example, a feeling of fatigue may prompt us to think about coffee, a magazine advert may remind us we wanted new shoes, whilst an attractive person eating lunch at the next table may lead to thoughts of sex (or sandwiches, or both). Most of the time these thoughts simply come and go, in other words, they are transitory (though they may still influence our behaviour by biasing our choices). However, in some instances these thoughts will be elaborated on and, according to the theory, it is this elaboration that is experienced as desire or craving.

Elaboration

Elaboration involves higher-order cognitive processes (such as memory and attention) whereby the person seeks additional information relating to the intrusive thought. This information may be sought from external sources (the environment) or internal sources (such as feelings and memories). This information is then retained and manipulated in working memory and is typically used to construct vivid sensory images relating to the object of desire and its acquisition. Elaboration of intrusive thoughts occurs when:

- the thought elicits a powerful affective reaction
- the thought elicits a sense of deficit
- the person is experiencing negative affect (because this will increase their sense of deficit).

For example, if you feel rested and relaxed, having recently returned from a sunny holiday, you may have simply glanced at the picture of the beach, been reminded of your holiday, then continued reading. However, if you are feeling stressed and fed up, and in desperate need of a holiday and a bit of sunshine, the intrusive thought about a holiday that the beach picture elicited may have been accompanied by a stronger feeling of deficit, which may in turn have led you to dwell on the picture a little longer. You may have sought additional information from external sources by looking for more detail in the picture (*Are those shadows of trees in the foreground? I wonder if you could stay in the huts on the horizon?*) and from internal sources (such as recalling the sensation of warm sand beneath your toes). This information would have helped you to imagine, in rich and vivid detail, what it would feel like to be on holiday.

Because of the similarity between mental imagery and real cues, elaboration leads the person to experience some of the pleasure or relief associated with obtaining the real object of desire. This is experienced as desire or craving and may initially be pleasurable but is subsequently aversive because it draws attention to the difference between the person's current state and their desired state. It is this aversive state that motivates behaviour.

As noted above, elaboration involves the manipulation of sensory images, which means it uses working memory. Because working memory has limited capacity it competes with other cognitive tasks, which in turn means that when engaged in elaboration it is difficult to concentrate on other things.

Termination of elaboration

Elaboration (and thus craving) can be terminated in several different ways:

1. If the object of desire is acquired and the craving is satisfied, further thoughts no longer elicit strong feelings and so are not elaborated. For example, if you feel like an ice cream, buy a big ice cream and eat it, thoughts of ice cream lose their appeal.

2. You may be forced to divert your attention to a competing cognitive task. For example, if you're strolling along, dreaming of ice cream and realise you've taken a wrong turn, you will need to create a mental representation of where you are, where you need to be, and how you're going to get there. This will use visual working memory and so prevent you elaborating on ice cream (thus interrupting your ice cream craving).

3. You may decide to divert your attention to a competing cognitive task. For example, you may decide you really ought to be thinking about what you wanted to buy rather than dreaming of ice cream and so make a conscious decision to start planning your purchases instead of thinking of ice cream.

4. Your attention may be diverted to an alternative object of desire. Passing a cocktail bar, you may realise that what you'd like even more than ice cream is a large pina colada topped with cherries and watermelon. Hence you stop thinking about ice cream and start thinking about pina coladas.

Effects on behaviour

According to elaborated intrusion theory, cravings influence behaviour. When you are craving something, you are motivated to try to satisfy that craving. However, the effects of craving on behaviour will be moderated by the following:

- *Availability.* When acquisition is very easy or very difficult, craving will be less predictive of behaviour. For example, if you have a bowl of chocolates on your desk, you may be inclined to eat them whilst you work, even though you have very little desire for them. By contrast, if you have no chocolates on your desk, or in your house, and the nearest shop that sells chocolate is five miles away, you may not end up eating chocolate, however strong your craving.

- *Competing incentives.* Craving will be less predictive of behaviour when competing incentives are high. For example, if you are trying to lose weight and have your weekly 'weigh in' at your local slimming club the next day, this may be sufficient to enable you to resist the chocolates on your desk even in the context of a strong craving.

- *Skills.* Craving will be less predictive of behaviour where a person has the relevant skills to resist, for example where they are good at exercising self-control. In other words, they have good willpower (an issue we explore later in this chapter).

The evidence

There is evidence to support many of the key predictions made by the elaborated intrusion theory (for a review, see May et al., 2015). For example, elaboration has been shown to increase desire, subjective reports of craving frequently refer to imagery, and more vivid imagery tends to be associated with stronger craving (Drobes & Tiffany, 1997; Kavanagh et al., 2009; Maude-Griffin & Tiffany, 1996; May et al., 2004).

The theory also predicts that any task that occupies visual working memory should reduce cravings, as it will prevent elaboration. This is an important prediction because of its implications for intervention and the effect has been demonstrated in a number of different studies that have used tasks ranging from guided imagery and dynamic visual noise to clay modelling and playing games that rely on visuo spatial skills (Andrade et al., 2012; Hamilton et al., 2013; Kemps & Tiggemann, 2007, 2013; Kemps et al., 2008; Knäuper et al., 2011; Skorka-Brown et al., 2014, 2015). For example, Skorka-Brown et al. (2014) asked students to report on what, if anything, they were craving and to rate their level of craving. They then randomly allocated participants to one of two conditions. In the experimental condition participants were asked to spend three minutes playing a game of 'Tetris'. Tetris is a computer game in which the player has to move a series of different shaped blocks in order to fit them into gaps so they take up the least amount of space. Thus, a little like a jigsaw puzzle, the game requires visual working memory as the player has to visualise and mentally adjust the pieces to figure out where to place them. In the other (control) condition, participants were asked to wait for Tetris to load. However, unknown to these participants, in this condition the computer game was designed not to load and simply ended, three minutes later, with a message saying 'Load Error'. All participants then rated the level of their cravings. Of the 121 participants who took part in this study, 80 reported craving something (58 were craving a particular food or drink, 10 caffeine and 12 nicotine). Among these participants there was a significant reduction in craving over time (that is, they reported weaker cravings at the end of the study than at the start) but, importantly, consistent with the elaboration intrusion theory, this decline was significantly greater among those who had played Tetris.

In a similar vein, Harvey et al. (2005) found that getting participants to engage in a visual imagery task (such as imagining the appearance of a rainbow) was significantly better at reducing food cravings compared to an equivalent auditory task (such as imagining the sound of a telephone ringing). They interpreted this as showing that food cravings are primarily visual rather than auditory in nature.

Thus there is good evidence to support some of the key predictions of the elaborated intrusion theory. However, it is also worth highlighting research by Morewedge et al. (2010) who showed that imagined food consumption can sometimes *reduce* rather than increase desire for that food. They asked participants to *repeatedly* imagine eating a particular food (for example, eating 33 chocolates, one at a time) and found that these participants subsequently ate less of this food when presented with it and also displayed less desire for the food (in other words, they were less willing to expend effort to obtain it). Morewedge et al. concluded that because mental imagery tends to elicit similar neural responses to actual perception (Decety & Grèzes, 2006; Kosslyn et al., 2001), the repeated imagined consumption led to **habituation** to the food (in the same way that actually eating 33 chocolates would reduce your desire for them). They contrasted this with the process of **sensitisation** that may occur when imagining a single exposure to a food (McSweeney & Swindell, 1999). In this case the person may imagine biting into the food just once or twice, rather than repeatedly, which may lead to an increase in desire (see also Kappes & Morewedge, 2016). The theory we now turn to, the grounded cognition theory of desire, places even more emphasis on the similarities between mental imagery and perception.

> **Habituation** – where repeated or extended exposure to a stimulus reduces an organism's physiological and/or behavioural response toward it. For example, after eating lots of crisps you may be less inclined to eat more crisps but still keen to eat chocolate.

> **Sensitization** – where a single or repeated exposure to a stimulus increases an organism's physiological and/or behavioural response toward it. For example, eating just one crisp will likely increase your desire for them (it is usually easier to not eat any crisps than to eat just one or two then stop). This is the logic behind appetisers at restaurants; they are designed to whet your appetite and increase your desire for food.

The grounded cognition theory of desire

The theory

The theory of grounded cognition (sometimes referred to as situated cognition) is a very broad theory that aims to explain cognition, perception and motivation as well as desire and craving (Barsalou, 2008; Papies & Barsalou, 2015; Papies et al., 2017). It states that as we go about our daily lives we develop 'situated conceptualisations' that contain information about all the different situations we encounter. These situated conceptualisations integrate information across a wide range of different modalities, including information about the setting, objects within the setting, physical actions, relevant goals, cognitive and affective responses and physiological states. As well as acquiring situated conceptualisations through our own experience we can also acquire them vicariously by observing others.

In any given situation, the best matching situated conceptualisation becomes active. Any aspect of a situation can activate a situated conceptualisation and the best match is selected according to Bayesian principles; in other words, on the basis of it having occurred frequently in the past and being a good fit with the current situational cues. A process called 'pattern completion' then produces inferences about what is likely to happen. Again, any aspect of a situated conceptualisation can be used for pattern completion. This pattern completion involves partially reinstating the neural activation from the active situated conceptualisation. This means that situated conceptualisations can be superimposed on top of the current situation, influencing the person's perception and experience of the current event. Pattern completion also includes simulating interacting with objects we encounter, which can result in feelings of desire and craving.

For example, a trip to the beach on a hot summer's day may activate a situated conceptualisation that has developed through previous trips to the beach on a hot summer's day. These may have typically involved ice cream so pattern completion may activate areas in the brain associated with eating ice cream and in this way elicit feelings of desire for ice cream. Likewise, simply viewing a picture of an ice cream will activate a situated conceptualisation relating to ice cream and the person will simulate interacting with it. This could include simulating its sweet flavour, cold temperature and soft, melting texture. The presence of other situational cues (such as the weather and feelings of hunger) will determine the exact situated conceptualisation that is activated. This in turn will determine the extent to which these hedonic properties are simulated; you may have more experience of enjoying ice cream in hot weather when you are hungry compared to cold weather right after you've indulged in hot chocolate. In other words, aspects of the current situation (such as the weather and feelings of hunger) will influence the situated conceptualisation that is selected (for example, eating ice cream in hot weather when hungry versus eating/not eating ice cream in cold weather when not hungry). This in turn will determine the type of pattern completion (simulated interaction with the ice cream that is pleasurable versus simulated interaction with the ice cream that is neutral) which will then determine the presence or absence of feelings of desire or craving (see **Image 7.3**).

Image 7.3 *According to the grounded cognition theory of desire, this picture will make you more likely to want to eat ice cream if current situational cues (such as the weather or feelings of hunger) match previous instances in which you have enjoyed eating ice cream. It will also make you more likely to want to eat ice cream if you are right-handed than if you are left-handed. This is because the picture more closely matches a right-handed person's experience of eating an ice cream. This makes it easier to simulate eating the ice cream, which in turn elicits desire.* Credit: GG LeMere.

Explanatory power and evidence

One of the strengths of grounded cognition theory is that the situated conceptualisations help it account for a wide range of different influences on desire, from social norms and goal priming to implementation intentions and habits (Barsalou, 2016; Best & Papies, 2017; Papies, 2016a, see also **Box 7.1**). In other words, it has good explanatory power.

BOX 7.1 A GROUNDED COGNITION THEORY EXPLANATION OF HABITS

MAKING CONNECTIONS

In **Chapter 6** we looked at habits and how they are thought to arise from cue-response associations. The grounded cognition theory offers a slightly different perspective on habits, suggesting they emerge from situated conceptualisations rather than isolated cue-response associations (Best & Papies, 2017).

The theory states that as a behaviour is carried out, so that behaviour, and the cues associated with that behaviour, are integrated into the most closely related existing situated conceptualisation. If a particular behaviour is carried out repeatedly in the same context, connections between the behaviour and these particular cues are strengthened. This means that when these cues are subsequently encountered, they activate a situated conceptualisation that includes the behaviour. A process of pattern completion means the behaviour may be performed automatically.

However, since situated conceptualisations integrate a wide range of different cues across multiple different experiences, and because the process of pattern completion means situated conceptualisations also *influence* current experience, the habitual behaviour could also be activated indirectly even in the absence of the critical cues or cues. This is because the critical cue or cues may be inferred due to their association with the active situated conceptualisation. In other words, habit performance is not dependent on the occurrence of just one specific cue or set of cues but can occur more flexibly in response to a range of different cues that are linked to the habitual behaviour via situated conceptualisations. This can help explain why a habitual behaviour may even be performed in a novel environment. For example, a person may still automatically stir sugar into their tea even when they are visiting a new tea shop for the first time, the sugar is a different colour to their normal variety, they are drinking from an unfamiliar cup and the spoon is a peculiar shape.

There is also good evidence to support some of the theory's key predictions. In particular, research using behavioural, physiological and neurological measures shows that people do spontaneously simulate interacting with objects they encounter (Papies et al., 2017). Additionally, this simulation seems to be causally related to feelings of desire. For example, when people are shown images of food that facilitate the simulation of eating (such as a bowl of yoghurt with a spoon facing toward the participant's dominant hand) they report more spontaneous eating simulations and state that they would be more likely to purchase the food (see **Image 7.3**). However, when the motor simulation is prevented, for example by asking participants to squeeze a small object in their hand, these effects are eliminated (Elder & Krishna, 2012).

Additionally, there is evidence to support the prediction that cueing different situated conceptualisations will influence a person's perception and experience (due to situated conceptualisations being superimposed onto current experiences). For example, soup labelled 'low salt' is perceived as less salty, the same wine labelled as more expensive is experienced as more pleasant, and smoked salmon ice cream is rated as more pleasant and less salty when labelled as 'frozen savoury mousse' (Liem et al., 2012; Plassmann et al., 2008; Yeomans et al., 2008).

Controlling cravings

We now consider the implications of these different theories of craving for interventions designed to change behaviour, either by reducing cravings or by increasing desire for healthy options.

Nicotine replacement therapy

A good place to start is with nicotine replacement therapy (NRT). Nicotine is the chemical found in cigarettes that makes them addictive (see **Chapter 12**) and NRT is used to help manage withdrawal symptoms that occur when someone is attempting to quit smoking. This is achieved by delivering nicotine into the blood stream via, for example, a nicotine patch (a small plaster placed on the skin), chewing gum, lozenges, a nose spray or an inhaler. There is good evidence that NRT increases the rate of quitting by 50% to 60% (Hartmann-Boyce et al., 2018). However, as we have seen in this section, whilst NRT may help alleviate tonic craving (craving associated with withdrawal) it would not eliminate cue-induced craving. All the theories of craving we have looked at would predict that a smoker would likely still experience some cigarette cravings even when using NRT.

Cue avoidance

According to the theories we've looked at, in principle cravings could be eliminated by simply avoiding the cues that elicit them. However, in practice this may be difficult to achieve. This is particularly true from the perspective of grounded cognition theory where multiple different cues may be associated with the target behaviour in the form of situated conceptualisations. Although cue avoidance is sometimes recommended as a strategy for managing behaviour (Wansink & Chandon, 2014), others have argued that it is flawed because it fails to address the more important underlying cause of cravings (the cue-response association; Brewer et al., 2013). Indeed, some have argued that this type of approach is responsible for difficulties in the maintenance of behaviour change (Jansen et al., 2011). For example, someone on a strict diet, drinking meal replacement milkshakes at lunchtime instead of eating in the work cafeteria may lose weight over the short term but may find it difficult to sustain this weight loss when they revert back to cafeteria lunches and experience the same cravings at the dessert counter.

Response prevention

Another way to tackle cravings is to repeatedly prevent the relevant behaviour when the craving occurs. According to conditioning theories of craving, this would eventually extinguish the cue-response association since the cue would no longer predict the behaviour. According to elaborated intrusion theory, this would reduce intrusive thoughts, and according to grounded cognition theory, it would modify situated conceptualisations. This approach is used in cue exposure and response prevention where the person is exposed to cues that elicit cravings but the target behaviour is prevented (Jansen et al., 2011). Care should be taken to match exposure to situations that typically elicit cravings in the person in everyday life, for example taking account of the specific craved item, location, time of day and mood state. Exposure to the relevant cues should also be sustained until the craving dissipates. A similar mechanism may underlie some of the effects found with mindfulness-based interventions (Tapper, 2018). Here people are typically provided with a range of different metaphors and exercises to encourage them to notice, fully experience and 'accept' difficult thoughts and feelings rather than try to avoid or control them.

However, this approach may be less effective for those wanting to lose weight. Unlike drugs or cigarettes, it is not possible to quit food, and although one could quit certain types of foods (such as sugary and high fat foods), this may not be desirable from a social or quality of life point of view. As such there will be a continued strengthening of certain cue-response associations. Nevertheless, a diet that restricts frequency of consumption of craved foods is likely to be more effective at reducing cravings than one that limits the serving sizes of these foods. This is because fewer eating occasions will mean a smaller range of different cues that are associated with eating, which will in turn mean fewer cues that elicit craving (Apolzan et al., 2017).

Visuospatial tasks

Unlike conditioning-based theories, elaborated intrusion theory additionally predicts that loading working memory with visuospatial tasks will be effective at reducing craving strength. As described above, there is considerable evidence to support this. However, it is less clear what the long-term effects of such a strategy would be on craving frequency since it is the cravings themselves that are targeted rather than the Pavlovian associations that lead to the intrusive thoughts and cravings in the first place. If loading working memory helps prevent the response (such as eating or smoking), it is possible this would also eventually reduce the frequency of intrusive thoughts and likewise the frequency of cravings. Some indication of the possible long-term effects of this type of approach come from Hsu et al. (2014). They developed a smartphone app that prompted people to engage in visual imagery every time they experienced a craving for a snack. Compared to those who simply tracked their snacking, over a one-week period the imagery app led to significant reductions in both unhealthy snacking and reported strength of cravings for unhealthy snacks. However, there was little evidence to suggest it reduced craving frequency within the one-week timeframe.

Mindfulness-based decentering

Grounded cognition theory also has other implications for intervention. In terms of reducing craving strength, it is possible that a mindfulness-based strategy called 'decentering' may be effective. Decentering involves seeing one's thoughts, feelings and bodily sensations as transient events that are separate to oneself (Tapper, 2017b, 2018). Applying this strategy may help reduce the believability of mental simulations and in this way reduce the extent to which they elicit desire. For example, Papies et al. (2015) asked students to view a series of pictures (including some of high-calorie foods) and to observe their reactions to these pictures as passing mental events. They subsequently reported lower food cravings compared to those who had been asked to view the pictures in a relaxed manner. However, although there is some evidence that decentering may reduce cravings, further research is needed to rule out other explanations for these effects, such as working memory load (Papies et al., 2015; Schumacher et al., 2017; Tapper, 2018; Tapper & Turner, 2018).

Promoting desire for healthy foods

Grounded cognition theory also has implications for promoting desire for, and enjoyment of, healthy foods (Best & Papies, 2017; Papies et al., 2017). For example, it suggests that marketing that provides cues associated with previously rewarding experiences will strengthen simulations of reward and in doing so increase desire. These cues could be context-related (such as cues associated with summer holidays when promoting fruits such as watermelon) or they could be related to the sensory properties of the food itself (such as imagery or descriptions associated with smell, taste and texture). As well as promoting desire (Krishna et al., 2014), this type of imagery may also enhance taste perception since the situated conceptualisations that are activated (for example arising from previous experiences of biting into a slice of crisp, cool, juicy watermelon) are superimposed onto the current experience (Elder & Krishna, 2010).

Imagery that facilitates mental simulation of consumption (such as a spoon with a bowl of muesli or a hand holding an apple) may also more effectively elicit desire. However, one should be wary of using health labels that may undermine food enjoyment, for example promoting an item as lower in sugar or salt may lead the person to experience it as insufficiently sweet or salty. Indeed, simply labelling a food as 'healthy' could, for some people, activate situated conceptualisations associated with the consumption of unpalatable foods or feelings of self-denial.

Summary

The different theories we've reviewed in this section have slightly different implications for intervention. However, there is also much overlap. In particular, all the theories predict that response suppression (preventing yourself from carrying out the relevant behaviour) would, over time, lead to reductions in craving. But how easy is it to supress one's behaviour in the presence of a strong craving? This type of strategy requires a substantial amount of willpower, or self-control, a concept we explore in the next section.

WILLPOWER

As noted above, one way of coping with cravings is to simply try to resist them through sheer willpower. Indeed, the notion of willpower is central to our beliefs about perseverance, achievement and even strength of character. However, it remains a rather elusive concept. It is not something we can see and, unlike feelings of craving, not something we tend to experience directly, unless perhaps in its absence. In this section we will look in more detail at what we mean by willpower, how we can measure it and the way in which it is conceptualised according to different theories. Finally we consider the varied implications of these theories in relation to techniques and interventions one might use to try to improve willpower.

What is willpower and why is it important?

Willpower, or self-control, is the ability to override one response, making an alternative response possible (**Image 7.4**). The alternative response aligns with the person's ideas about how something should or should not be and may reflect goals, values, ideals, norms, morals, laws or the expectations of others. By contrast, the response that is overridden is associated with automatic or impulsive behaviour. For example, we may refrain from engaging in a behaviour that provides immediate pleasure (such as dozing in the sunshine) but carries long-term costs (such as failing to meet a deadline). Exercising self-control is viewed as a conscious choice that feels effortful (Baumeister & Vohs, 2016; Baumeister et al., 2007).

Image 7.4 *Sugar the Golden Retriever from Golden Woofs, demonstrating exceptional self-control as she inhibits the impulse to wolf down the treat, which in turn allows her to balance it on her nose (which presumably aligns with the expectations of her owner).*

Source: Reprinted with permission from www.sugarthegoldenretriever.com/2010/09/10sec-trick-n-treat-dog-treat-on-my/.

The ability to exercise self-control underpins a wide variety of behaviours essential to everyday life. For example, studying for an exam usually means delaying pursuits that are more immediately pleasurable, trying to lose weight typically involves resisting tempting high-calorie foods, and buying a house often means saving money for a deposit rather than spending it all at the weekend. As such, higher levels of self-control have been linked to a range of positive outcomes across the lifespan. For example, Moffitt et al. (2011) followed a cohort of 1,000 children from birth to the age of 32 years. They found that higher levels of childhood self-control predicted better physical health, lower substance dependence, improved wealth and lower levels of criminal offending. These effects were independent from cognitive ability and socioeconomic background. Similarly, in a longitudinal study with over 21,000 people, children with higher levels of self-control were subsequently less likely to smoke as adults and, if they did take up smoking, smoked fewer cigarettes, were more likely to quit and less likely to relapse. Again, these effects were independent of socioeconomic background and cognitive ability as well as psychological distress, gender and parental smoking (Daly et al., 2016). Such findings have prompted researchers to suggest that interventions targeting self-control could bring about significant benefits for public health, wealth and happiness (Moffitt et al., 2011; Schlam et al., 2013).

Measuring willpower

A huge array of different measures has been used to assess willpower. Duckworth and Kern (2011) categorised these into four types:

- *Self-report questionnaires* – where the person reports on their own levels of self-control.

- *Informant-report questionnaires* – where someone else (such as a parent or teacher) reports on a person's levels of self-control.

- *Delay tasks* – tasks in which the person has to make a real or hypothetical choice between a smaller, immediate reward or a larger, delayed reward.
- *Executive function tasks*[1] – these are tasks where conscious, controlled processing is used to override automatic responses. They include some of the tasks we looked at in **Chapter 6**, such as the Stop Signal task and the Go/No-Go task.

Duckworth and Kern (2011) identified over 104 different self- and informant-report questionnaires, 4 different types of delay tasks and 12 different types of executive function tasks. In addition to these, other researchers have used a range of different laboratory-based behavioural measures (see section on Willpower as a muscle), though some have questioned the validity of these. Below we look at a small selection of some of the most widely used report and delay measures.

Self- and informant-report measures

Informant-report questionnaires often use teachers, parents or other caregivers to report on a child's level of self-control, whilst self-report questionnaires are more commonly employed with teenagers and adults. These types of measures demonstrate good convergent validity (they correlate with one another and with other measures of self-control) and have also been shown to predict a wide range of outcomes thought to be related to self-control, including academic achievement, wealth, criminal activity, substance dependence and physical health (Duckworth & Kern, 2011; Duckworth et al., 2010; Moffitt et al., 2011; Tsukayama et al., 2010). An example of one of the most frequently used self-report questionnaires, the Self-Control Scale, is described in **Box 7.2**.

BOX 7.2 HOW STRONG IS YOUR WILLPOWER?

The Self-Control Scale is a 36-item questionnaire designed as a broad measure of self-control (Tangney et al., 2004). There is also a Brief Self-Control measure comprising just 13 of the items contained in the full scale. Higher scores on the **TAKE THE TEST** Self-Control Scale have been shown to correlate with better academic performance, less binge eating, less alcohol abuse, and better relationships and interpersonal skills (Tangney et al., 2004). You can take the brief version of the test by rating how much each of the following statements reflects how you typically are. You should rate these items on a scale of 1 ('Not at all') to 5 ('Very much').

1. I am good at resisting temptation.
2. I have a hard time breaking bad habits. (R)
3. I am lazy. (R)
4. I say inappropriate things. (R)
5. I do certain things that are bad for me, if they are fun. (R)
6. I refuse things that are bad for me.
7. I wish I had more self-discipline. (R)

---

1 Executive function is also studied as a separate line of research in its own right and not simply as a measure of self-control.

8. People would say that I have iron self-discipline.

9. Pleasure and fun sometimes keep me from getting work done. (R)

10. I have trouble concentrating. (R)

11. I am able to work effectively toward long-term goals.

12. Sometimes I can't stop myself from doing something, even if I know it is wrong. (R)

13. I often act without thinking through all the alternatives. (R)

Items followed by '(R)' should be reverse scored (if you put down '1' you should convert this to '5', if you put down '4' you should convert this to '2' and so on). All ratings should then be summed to give a total score from 13 to 65. A higher score indicates a higher level of self-control. In a sample of over 600 North American undergraduate students (who were presumably already relatively high in self-control), the mean score on the Brief Self-Control measure was 39 with around 68% of students scoring between 31 and 48 and 95% of students scoring between 22 and 56 (Tangney et al., 2004).

Delay of gratification task (aka the 'marshmallow test')

One of the best-known delay-type measures of willpower is probably the delay of gratification task (sometimes referred to as the 'marshmallow test' due to the fact that the original studies were carried out with marshmallows). In a delay of gratification test a child is presented with a treat (for example a marshmallow) and a bell. The child is told that the adult will leave the room and if they can wait until the adult returns they will receive two of the treats. Alternatively, if they ring the bell the adult will come back straight away but they will only receive one treat. Once the adult has ensured the child has fully understood the instructions they leave the room and time how long the child is able to wait (usually up to a maximum of 15 minutes). Although the child generally expresses a preference for two treats rather than one, they are usually unable to wait and end up ringing the bell before the 15 minutes is up. The length of time the child is able to wait is the measure of self-control or willpower.

Performance on the delay of gratification task correlates with teacher and caregiver ratings of self-control (Duckworth et al., 2013). It has also been shown to predict a wide range of other measures and behaviours in adolescence and adulthood that are thought to relate to self-control. These include performance on cognitive aptitude tests, academic achievement, social competence, planning ability, impulsivity, BMI and overweight status (Duckworth et al., 2013; Eigsti et al., 2006; Mischel et al., 1988; Schlam et al., 2013; Seeyave et al., 2009; Shoda et al., 1990, though see also Watts et al., 2018). These types of longitudinal associations are consistent with other evidence suggesting that ability to delay on the gratification task reflects a relatively stable trait (Casey et al., 2011). Performance has also been shown to be independent from intelligence and reward-related impulses (Duckworth et al., 2013).

However, performance on the delay of gratification task also seems to be moderated by children's expectations about their likelihood of receiving the rewards if they wait. Kidd et al. (2013) manipulated children's beliefs about an adult researcher by having them fulfil or break promises about going to fetch better art supplies and more stickers. In a subsequent delay of gratification test, administered by the same researcher, children delayed for an average of 12 minutes when the researcher had kept their promise but an average of just 3 minutes when they had not. Similar findings have been obtained by Michaelson and Munakata (2016) who found that children were less likely to delay when they had observed the researcher lie or behave dishonestly.

The authors of these studies suggest that although the delay of gratification test may partly reflect a child's level of self-control, it could also be influenced by social trust and their expectations about the reliability of their environment. If their experience of adults is one of broken promises and misplaced trust, arguably they are wise to take whatever is on offer then and there rather than wait for an extra treat that may never materialise. This is consistent with other research that has shown that children with absent fathers (who tend to be less trusting than children in two-parent families; Wentzel, 1991) show shorter wait times in the delay of gratification paradigm (Mischel, 1961). Thus low levels of social trust and an unreliable worldview may account for some of the longitudinal associations found between delay of gratification and later outcomes. An alternative interpretation is that the development of self-control is directly influenced by factors related to social trust and environmental predictability. Such a view is more in keeping with life-history theory that we looked at in **Chapter 3**. (See also **Box 7.3**.)

BOX 7.3 SELF-CONTROL ACROSS CULTURES

AS AN ASIDE

One of the criticisms of research in psychology is that it is often carried out by Western researchers using Western participants. This means that our understanding of concepts such as self-control can be biased towards Western views and Western practices. In particular, Western cultures tend to be individualist, viewing the self as a unique, independent and autonomous agent, capable of exercising control over their environment. By contrast, Eastern cultures tend to be collectivist, emphasising the needs and goals of the group over and above those of the individual. They view the self as interdependent rather than independent and as more malleable and context specific. Lamm et al. (2018) suggest those from individualist cultures may be more inclined to act on the basis of their feelings because feelings are thought to represent the 'true' self. On the other hand, those from collectivist cultures may be more likely to view the context and the needs of others as the primary determinants of their behaviour, rather than their own emotions.

Lamm et al. (2018) also argue that these cultural differences shape parenting practices and the development of self-control. For example, rural Cameroonian Nso children tend to live in extended families of three or more generations with lots of children. There is a strict social hierarchy defined by age, gender and social status and children are expected to respect and obey their elders, care for younger children and develop social responsibility. Parenting involves instructing, controlling and training the child (Lamm et al., 2015). However, German middle-class children tend to live in smaller families with just one or two parents and one or two children. Parenting tends to be child-centred with parents encouraging their children to express their intentions, emotions and preferences (Keller, 2007).

Children from Eastern cultures tend to perform better on measures of self-control compared to their Western counterparts (e.g. Keller et al., 2004; Oh & Lewis, 2008; Sabbagh et al., 2008). For example, Lamm et al. (2018) compared German middle-class and Cameroonian Nso children on the delay of gratification task. The Nso children were able to delay significantly longer than their German peers with the majority of Nso children waiting the full 10 minutes for the researcher to return. They also displayed few signs of frustration and fewer distraction behaviours (such as singing or averting their attention away from the treat). This was despite the fact that the Nso children seemed to value the treat just as much as the German children – for example they smiled and reached for it when it was first presented, said they preferred two treats to one, and ate the treats immediately upon receiving them.

Lamm et al. (2018) suggest that the German children may experience conflict in the task as they are socialised to view themselves as independent agents able to exert control over their environments. The task may make them feel like they lack control over the situation, which may be experienced as unpleasant and lead them to try to compensate for this lack of control by engaging in self-determined activities aimed at cooling down the positive affect associated with the treat. By contrast, Nso children are taught to prioritise the social functioning of the group over and above their own emotions. Waiting for the treat aligns with this goal and this view of the self as interdependent. As such, it is possible they experience less conflict and negative emotion during the task. However, more research would be needed to confirm this interpretation and to fully understand the development of self-control in individualist versus collectivist cultures.

Delayed discounting

Another commonly employed delay-type measure is the delay discounting task (Green et al., 1994). The delay of gratification task is only suitable for children aged from around 3 to 5 years as younger children find the test too difficult whilst older children find it too easy (though it has been adapted for 10-year-olds; see Duckworth et al., 2013). The delay discounting task operates on similar principles to the delay of gratification task but uses hypothetical rewards instead of real ones. This means the content can be made suitable for adults. For example, a person may be asked whether they would prefer £500 today or £1,000 in a year's time. If they choose the immediate reward, the value of the delayed reward in the next trial is increased, whereas if they select the delayed reward the value of the immediate reward in the next trial is increased, and so on. This means it is eventually possible to compute a 'discounting curve' for the person that summarises the relative 'cost' they attribute to delays of various lengths. The steeper the curve, the more they devalue rewards when they are delayed, showing a preference for smaller, immediate rewards.

The extent to which a person discounts monetary rewards has been shown to positively correlate with the extent to which they discount other rewards (such as food, alcohol, cigarettes, heroin, books, music CDs and DVDs; Charlton & Fantino, 2008; Odum, 2011). This, together with the fact that people show a similar response on different versions of the test (alternate reliability) and on the same version of the test administered at different points in time (test-retest reliability), suggests it reflects an underlying trait (Odum, 2011). However, rate of discounting does seem to change across the lifespan, with children showing steeper curves than younger adults who in turn show steeper curves than older adults (Green et al., 1994; Reimers et al., 2009). Rate of discounting also varies according to type of reward with rewards that serve a direct metabolic function (such as food, alcohol and drugs) being discounted more steeply than other rewards such as money, books or DVDs (Charlton & Fantino, 2008).

Greater discounting of delayed rewards (a steeper curve) is associated with increased engagement in addictive behaviours as well as increased severity of addiction (Amlung et al., 2017). For example, smokers show greater discounting than non-smokers (Bickel et al., 1999), smokers who show greater discounting are more likely to relapse during a quit attempt (MacKillop & Kahler, 2009) and adolescents who show greater discounting are more likely to take up smoking (Audrain-McGovern et al., 2009). Similarly, people who eat unhealthy diets, or who suffer from overweight or obesity, also show greater discounting, whilst those attempting to lose weight tend to lose more weight if they show lower discounting (though these effects only tend to emerge when using food-based rather than monetary rewards; Barlow et al., 2016). Additionally, discounting rates have been linked to other health-related behaviours such as risky sexual behaviour, safety belt use, health screening, dental visits, exercise and adherence to medical advice (Axon et al., 2009; Bradford, 2010; Chesson et al., 2006; Daugherty & Brase, 2010).

BOX 7.4 DELAY DISCOUNTING AND SOCIOECONOMIC STATUS

MAKING CONNECTIONS

In **Chapter 3** we looked at possible explanations for the relationship between lower socioeconomic status and poorer health. Bickel et al. (2014) suggest that delay discounting might mediate this relationship. They propose that decision-making is determined by two competing neurobehavioral systems: an impulsive system that promotes the selection of immediate rewards and an executive system that favours long-term outcomes and helps inhibit impulses. (This can be viewed as a dual-system model, see **Chapter 6**.) According to Bickel et al., factors that are more likely to occur among those from lower socioeconomic backgrounds, such as stress or a lack of cognitive resources (see **Chapter 3**), lead to dysfunction in the executive system that results in a tendency to choose immediate over long-term rewards. This account is consistent with research showing that those from lower socioeconomic groups show higher rates of discounting (Reimers et al., 2009).

We now look at the ways in which these different measures have been used to inform and test different theories of self-control.

Willpower as cool cognition: the hot/cool framework

Using the delay of gratification paradigm, Mischel and Baker (1975) found that children's ability to exercise self-control was associated with, and could be improved by, specific strategies. Drawing on these findings, Metcalfe and Mischel (1999) proposed a theory of hot and cool cognition to account for the ways in which cognition and emotion interact to influence self-control.

The theory

According to this theory, cool cognition is complex, reflexive and slow (similar to controlled processing, see **Chapter 6**). It is also diminished by stress. The cool system is responsible for self-control and is represented in the brain by what Metcalfe and Mischel refer to as 'cool nodes' that comprise verbal or non-verbal descriptions and have extensive interconnections with other cool nodes.

By contrast, hot cognition is concerned with quick, emotional processing and is under the control of stimuli in the immediate environment (similar to automatic processing, see **Chapter 6**). It is simple, reflexive and fast, and it is accentuated by stress. This system is represented in the brain by 'hot spots' that consist of fragments of feeling and connect directly to output responses. Hot spots do not connect to other hot spots but do connect to a corresponding cool node, allowing spots and nodes to activate one another and the two operating systems to interact. However, chronic selective activation of either the hot or cool system will result in a tendency for that system to dominate.

According to Metcalfe and Mischel (1999), the hot system is the default state; when it is dominant, exposure to 'hot' stimuli elicits automatic responses. For example, a child under the influence of the hot system will be unable to wait for the treat. So how could we enhance willpower according to this theory?

Strategies for improving self-control

Metcalfe and Mischel identify six strategies that can be used to improve self-control, which they group into three different types according to the ways in which they work. These are as follows:

1. Strategies that work by decreasing activation of the hot spots in the brain that lead to the impulsive action. Such strategies include:

   a. Obscuring the stimulus

   b. Not attending to the stimulus.

2. Strategies that work by shifting the balance of activation away from the relevant hot spot in the brain to other irrelevant hot or cool networks in the brain. This could be achieved by:

   a. Physically presenting distractors

   b. Internally activating non-relevant cool or hot system networks (in other words, thinking of something else).

3. Strategies that work by enhancing cool system control of the hot spot. This could be achieved by:

   a. Presenting the cool rather than the hot properties of the stimulus

   b. Thinking about the cool rather than the hot properties of the stimulus.

The first two types of strategy include things that most of us naturally learn to do from a young age. For example, three- to five-year-olds who do better on the delay of gratification task tend to spontaneously avoid looking at the treat (for example by deliberately looking away, or covering their eyes with their hands). Or they attempt to distract themselves (for example by singing or creating games with their hands or feet; Mischel et al., 1989). However, the third type of strategy is less intuitive as it involves continuing to attend to and think about the treat but doing so in a slightly different way.

The effect of this third type of strategy on self-control was demonstrated in a study carried out by Mischel and Baker (1975) with three- to five-year-old children using the delay of gratification task. They presented half the children with marshmallows and half with pretzels. They also assigned the children to one of five different groups and gave each of these groups slightly different instructions to follow whilst waiting for the adult to return. The type of instructions they were given are shown in **Table 7.1.**

Table 7.1 Type of instruction and average length of time children were able to wait for a treat when asked to think about the hot or cool properties of a treat that was either in front of them ('relevant') or out of sight ('irrelevant')

Condition	Example instructions for those waiting for marshmallows	Delay time (in minutes)
Control	None.	8.44
Hot properties of relevant treat	Think about the sweet taste of marshmallows and their soft, chewy texture.	5.60
Hot properties of irrelevant treat	Think about how crunchy and salty pretzels are.	16.82*
Cool properties of relevant treat	Think about how marshmallows are white and puffy like clouds or white and round like the moon.	13.51*
Cool properties of irrelevant treat	Think about how pretzels are long and brown like logs or round and tall like a telephone pole.	4.46

Note: *Significantly different from the control condition.
Source: Mischel & Baker (1975).

Table 7.1 also shows the length of time children were able to wait in the different conditions. Where children were not given any instructions about what to think about, on average they managed to wait nearly 8½ minutes before ringing the bell. However, they were able to wait significantly longer when instructed to think about the cool properties of the treat that was in front of them (the 'relevant' treat) or when instructed to think about the hot properties of the treat that was not in front of them (the 'irrelevant' treat). (Trying to think about the cool properties of a treat that was not in front of them was less successful, possibly because this task was too difficult.)

These findings support Metcalfe and Mischels' (1999) theory of hot and cool cognition and suggest that avoidance and distraction are not the only ways of resisting temptation; instead self-control can also be enhanced by thinking about the tempting object in a different way, a technique sometimes termed 'reappraisal'. We now turn to an alternative theory of self-control that has very different implications for how we might resist temptations.

Willpower as a muscle: the limited resource model

How often have you started your day full of good resolutions to work hard, eat healthily and resist the lure of social media and extended coffee breaks? Only to find that by the middle of the afternoon you've already spent an hour checking status updates and are now contemplating messaging a friend to see if she wants to get chocolate with you. Most of us would probably agree we're usually better at exercising self-control in the morning compared to later in the day, whether that means concentrating on work, making a difficult phone call, resisting a particular website or sticking to a diet.

This everyday experience forms the basis of the limited resource (or strength) model of self-control, developed by Baumeister and colleagues (Baumeister & Heatherton, 1996;

CHAPTER 7

Baumeister & Vohs, 2016; Baumeister et al., 2007). The central thesis of this theory is that self-control is a single, finite resource that is needed for a wide range of different behaviours and gets used up in the process. This means that as the day goes on, we have less resource available and find it increasingly difficult to exercise self-control, particularly if we have been engaged in demanding tasks throughout the day. Willpower is likened to a muscle (**Image 7.5**) because it:

- Tires with use
- Gets stronger with practice
- Uses glucose as fuel.

Image 7.5 *Is willpower like a muscle? The limited resource model of self-control states that willpower is like a muscle because it tires with use, gets stronger with practice and uses glucose as fuel. However, other research suggests you may be able to improve your willpower simply by not believing that willpower is a limited resource.*

Credit: Edgar Chaparro.

Tiring with use

Baumeister and colleagues use the term 'ego depletion' to refer to the idea that a person will perform more poorly on a task that requires self-control if they have already engaged in other tasks that need self-control. They demonstrated this effect across a series of experiments in which participants' ability to exercise control was assessed under two different conditions: after they had already engaged in a task requiring self-control, or after they had engaged in a task that did not require self-control (Baumeister et al., 1998; Muraven et al., 1998). Since self-control was assumed to be important for a wide variety of different behaviours, the studies employed a very diverse set of tasks that ranged from physical stamina and emotion regulation to persistence at problem solving and resisting temptation. However, consistent with the ego depletion hypothesis, the experiments all showed that participants performed more poorly on a second task when they had already engaged in a task assumed to require self-control. For example, compared to participants who were asked to refrain from eating radishes for five minutes (a task assumed to need no self-control), participants who had to refrain from eating freshly baked cookies (a task assumed to need self-control) were subsequently quicker to quit when trying to solve puzzles (a task also assumed to need self-control). Likewise, those who were asked to supress their emotions whilst watching funny or sad video clips (a task assumed to require self-control) subsequently solved fewer anagrams (a task also assumed to require self-control) compared to those who had not been asked to supress their emotions whilst watching the video clips (assumed to require no self-control).

Strengthening with practice

Baumeister and colleagues also suggest that, like a muscle, willpower can be strengthened with practice and a number of studies have supported this view (Finkel et al., 2009; Gailliot et al., 2007b; Muraven, 2010a, 2010b; Muraven et al., 1999; Oaten & Cheng,

2006a, 2006b; see also Inzlicht & Berkman, 2015 for a review and Miles et al., 2016 for a null finding). For example, Muraven (2010a) recruited individuals wanting to quit smoking and asked them to complete a daily task for a period of two weeks prior to their quit date. For some people this task was something that required them to practise self-control (avoiding eating sweets or carrying out exercises with a handgrip), whilst for others the task did not require significant levels of self-control but helped rule out possible effects of repeatedly engaging in an exercise (solving simple maths problems twice a day) or becoming more aware of self-control behaviours (making a note in a diary of any occasion when they resisted temptation). The results showed that a month after their quit date 27% of those who had been assigned to the sweets and handgrip conditions had managed to maintain smoking abstinence compared to just 12% of those assigned to the maths and diary conditions.

Glucose as fuel

Finally, Baumeister and colleagues have also compared willpower to a muscle by proposing that it uses glucose as fuel and that ego depletion is the brain running out of fuel. This glucose depletion hypothesis was based on observations that the brain uses extra glucose when working hard, self-control failures are more likely to occur when glucose levels are low (or glucose cannot be effectively processed, such as in diabetes), and providing glucose improves self-control (Baumeister & Vohs, 2016; Gailliot & Baumeister, 2007). It was also supported by findings from a series of nine experimental studies conducted by Gailliot et al. (2007a). They found that (a) tasks requiring self-control resulted in a drop in blood glucose levels, (b) lower blood glucose levels after an initial task requiring self-control were associated with poorer performance on a subsequent task requiring self-control, and (c) consuming a glucose drink eliminated the ego depletion effect. The glucose depletion hypothesis was further bolstered by other research showing that equivalent effects on ego depletion were not obtained with artificially sweetened drinks (Masicampo & Baumeister, 2008; McMahon & Scheel, 2010; Wang & Dvorak, 2010).

However, there are conceptual problems with the idea that the brain runs out of fuel and that this is responsible for ego depletion (Beedie & Lane, 2012; Kurzban, 2010). In particular, Kurzban (2010) points out that the amount of additional energy used by the brain for self-control-related tasks is likely to be so small that effects on overall blood glucose levels will be negligible. For example, it is estimated that the brain as a whole uses about a quarter of a calorie per minute (Clarke & Solokoff, 1998). Over a 5-minute task this would equate to just 1.25 calories, though the specific part of the brain involved in any one particular task would use far fewer calories than this. Thus even if the brain was using additional calories from working extra hard the amounts would still be incredibly small. By contrast, running for 5 minutes at a 9-minute-mile pace would burn an estimated 60 calories (Ainsworth et al., 2000), but moderately intense aerobic exercise of up to 60 minutes tends to *improve* performance on a number of self-control-related tasks (e.g. Hillman et al., 2009; Tomporoski, 2003). Indeed, studies conducted subsequent to Gailliot et al. (2007a) failed to replicate their finding that tasks requiring self-control resulted in a drop in blood glucose levels (Molden et al., 2012). Additionally, Beedie and Lane (2012) cite evidence indicating that our bodies have evolved to be able to supply energy to the brain both quickly and effectively. For example, during starvation or malnutrition the brain is the only organ that does not show weight loss (Mora, 1999), and even during intense muscular activity glucose supply to the brain is prioritised over supply to the muscles (Wilmore et al., 2008). Thus there is little evidence to support the idea that ego depletion occurs due to the brain running out of fuel.

From limited resource to energy conservation

In light of these criticisms, and in response to alternative mechanisms proposed by others (Beedie & Lane, 2012; Evans et al., 2016), Baumeister and Vohs (2016) revised the glucose depletion aspect of their theory, stating instead that ego depletion may reflect selective allocation of glucose. Specifically, in the absence of any awareness of absolute levels of glucose in the body, a central governor system recognises when glucose is being used in self-control-related tasks and seeks to conserve glucose – unless other factors indicate that self-control should continue to be a priority. This revised explanation is actually more comparable to a muscle since muscles tend to feel fatigued long before they are no longer able to function (Evans et al., 2016). This explanation also helps account for the fact that research shows that simply swishing one's mouth with a glucose drink for five seconds then spitting it out (rather than ingesting it) is sufficient to counteract the ego depletion effect (Molden et al., 2012; Hagger & Chatzisarantis, 2013). Baumeister and colleagues suggest that in this case the perception of glucose signals the availability of additional energy in the near future which is sufficient for the body to continue to allocate resources to self-control (Baumeister & Vohs, 2016).

The idea that ego depletion reflects an attempt to conserve energy (rather than energy reserves that have been completely exhausted) is also more in keeping with research showing that the effects of ego depletion can be moderated by a range of different factors, including mood and motivation (for reviews see Baumeister & Vohs, 2016 and Hagger et al., 2010). For example, Tice et al. (2007) found that ego depletion was counteracted when participants received a surprise small gift or watched a funny video, suggesting that being in a positive mood encourages a person to continue to exert self-control. Similarly, ego depletion effects appear to be weaker when a person perceives the task to be more intrinsically rather than extrinsically motivated (see **Chapter 5**; Graham et al., 2014) or when payment is tied to performance (Muraven & Slessareva, 2003).

Criticisms and controversy

The limited resource model of willpower has been highly influential, generating a huge number of studies across a wide range of disciplines (Friese et al., 2019). It has also been widely cited in the media and is the subject of several popular science books (Baumeister & Tierney, 2011; McGonigal, 2012). However, before you start stockpiling glucose drinks to get you through exam revision, it is important to look at recent research that has questioned the reliability of some of the findings.

First, although a meta-analysis of 83 studies (comprising 198 independent tests) found evidence to support an ego depletion effect (Hagger et al., 2010), a re-analysis of these data, together with a subsequent meta-analyses, concluded that there may be no effect at all (Carter et al., 2015; Carter & McCullough, 2014). How could different authors come to such radically different conclusions? And how could there be so many studies showing significant ego depletion effects if such an effect does not exist?

The main reason for these discrepancies is publication bias. Publication bias refers to the fact that both researchers and journal editors are more likely to publish studies that show significant effects rather than those that show null effects. This means that the published literature is not representative of the field and will likely overestimate effects or even give the impression of an effect where there is none. (We look at this and related issues in more detail in **Chapter 11**.) There are statistical techniques that can be used to estimate publication bias when conducting meta-analyses but Carter and colleagues argued that Hagger et al. (2010) had not used the most up-to-date methods and had also not made a sufficient effort to track down and include unpublished data (for example by contacting academics in the field).

A second key reason for the different findings relates to inclusion criteria. Carter et al. (2015) argued that the validity of many of the tasks used to manipulate or measure self-control has not been established (in other words, it is not clear that they really do manipulate/measure self-control) and that meta-analyses should be restricted to studies using only the most frequently employed manipulations and measures, as these would likely be the most valid ways of operationalising self-control. This meant their subsequent meta-analysis included a smaller number of tests compared to the original meta-analysis conducted by Hagger et al. (2010); 116 compared to 198, and these were more homogeneous in terms of manipulations and measures.

In addition to the revised analyses conducted by Carter and colleagues, a large pre-registered trial of the ego depletion effect (conducted with over 2,000 participants across 23 different laboratories), failed to find significant results (Hagger et al., 2016). A pre-registered trial is one in which the study methods and hypotheses are published prior to data collection; a relatively new innovation in psychology designed to help address the problem of publication bias (see **Chapter 11**).

These, together with other findings, have prompted more academics to question both the existence of a reliable ego depletion effect and the limited resource model. For example, Job and colleagues found that ego depletion (and the effects of glucose on ego depletion) only occurred among those who believed willpower was a limited resource (Job et al., 2010, 2013, 2015a). They suggested that amongst such people, exerting self-control activates a rest goal that in turn influences their behaviour.

Similarly, Savani and Job (2017) found a reverse ego depletion effect among Indian participants. In other words, they performed *better* on a self-control-related task after having just completed a strenuous (as opposed to non-strenuous) task. This effect was mediated by cultural beliefs; whilst people from Western societies tend to believe that exerting mental effort is depleting, Indian participants are more inclined to view it as energising. Savani and Job state that, to their knowledge, only one other study on ego depletion has compared Westerners with non-Westerners and this also showed no ego depletion effect among non-Western (Asian) participants (Seely & Gardner, 2003). As such, Savani and Job suggest that ego depletion effects are actually rooted in cultural beliefs rather than representing a universal psychological phenomenon (see also **Box 7.1**).

Baumeister and colleagues remain committed to the limited resource model of self-control, providing arguments to counter those who question the existence of ego depletion and offering alternative interpretations of findings that apparently contradict the limited resource account (Baumeister et al., 2018; Baumeister & Vohs, 2016; Cunningham & Baumeister, 2016). For example, they suggest that whilst motivation and beliefs may counteract effects where ego depletion is mild, effects are likely to re-emerge where ego depletion is severe (for example for very strenuous tasks or where tasks are sustained over long periods; Vohs et al., 2012). Attempting to provide a balanced analysis of the arguments for and against the existence of ego depletion, Friese et al. (2019) concluded that whilst it is clear that publication bias has led to an overestimate of effects, the extent and nature of the publication bias is unknown so, at this point, it is difficult to draw any firm conclusions about either the existence or the non-existence of ego depletion. Only time (and efforts to reduce bias in subsequent research) will tell. As mentioned, we consider the issue of bias in research in more detail in **Chapter 11**.

Willpower as motivation: the process model

In response to some of the difficulties with a limited resource view of self-control, Inzlicht and colleagues proposed an alternative – that self-control could instead be seen as a form of motivation.

The theory

The process model of self-control (also called the shifting priorities model of self-control) states that we evolved to balance a need for exploitation with a need for exploration, that is, exploitation of established sources of reward versus exploration of possible new sources of reward (Inzlicht & Schmeichel, 2012; Inzlicht et al., 2014; Milyavskaya & Inzlicht, 2017). This is adaptive because it prevents a person from investing too much time on a single source of reward that may result in missed opportunities for other (potentially larger) rewards. For example, continuing to harvest berries from a known food source for too long may lead to one missing the game congregating just over the horizon. Thus although continuing to harvest berries represents a gain in terms of the acquisition of increasing amounts of food, it also represents a cost in terms of possible missed opportunities that may have led to the acquisition of even larger amounts of food (or sources of food that would still be available once the berries were no longer in season). According to the process model, we prefer an optimal trade-off between these benefits and costs that means that too long spent on exploitation goals (tasks associated with work, that we feel we have to do, that involve suppressing and inhibiting desires) will increase motivation for exploration goals (tasks associated with leisure, that we engage in because we want to).

In practice this means that when we have engaged in 'have-to' tasks, our motivation to continue to engage in 'have-to' tasks declines. At the same time, our motivation to engage in 'want-to' tasks increases, resulting in a corresponding increase in the value of rewarding stimuli and an increase in approach motivation. Thus we experience a shift in motivational priorities that may be perceived as fatigue and that makes it increasingly difficult to continue to engage in 'have-to' tasks. It is this switch in motivation that results in a decline in performance on 'have-to' tasks and has been labelled 'ego depletion' in other research.

According to the process model this shift in motivation also leads to shifts in attention; attention toward cues signalling control declines whilst attention toward cues signalling reward (such as money or food) increases. (The changes in attention may then also intensify the changes in motivation.) Both changes in motivation and attention may undermine self-control. Specifically, self-control failure may either occur because motivation to inhibit responses is low and/or motivation to pursue reward-related stimuli is high, or it may occur simply

Figure 7.1 The process model of self-control. Exercising self-control leads to shifts in motivation and attention that make it more difficult to continue exercising self-control.

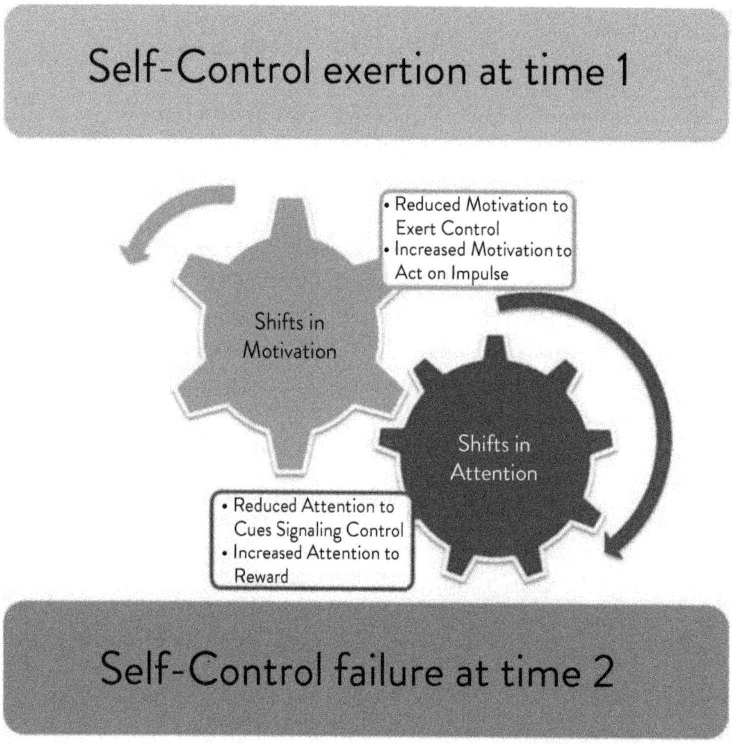

Source: Inzlicht, M. & Schmeichel, B.J. (2012). Reprinted with permission from SAGE Publishing.

because the person has not attended to control-related cues and so failed to notice that self-control was needed (**Figure 7.1**).

Explanatory power and evidence

Although there is currently little direct evidence that self-control failure is mediated by changes in motivation, priorities or goals (Baumeister and Vohs, 2016; Inzlicht & Schmeichel, 2016), arguably this view of self-control provides a more parsimonious account of existing data showing that self-control is enhanced by factors such as incentives and intrinsic motivation (Graham et al., 2014; Muraven & Slessareva, 2003). There is also some evidence to show that tasks that require self-control do result in increased attention toward reward-related stimuli. For example, Schmeichel and colleagues found that, compared to participants who were asked to spend six minutes writing a story, those who spent six minutes writing a story but without using the letters 'A' or 'N' were subsequently better at detecting dollar signs in a series of pictures (a symbol associated with reward) but not percent signs (a symbol not associated with reward) (Schmeichel et al., 2010).

The process model is also consistent with something called the 'self-licensing effect'. This is where self-control failure occurs, not because the person is unable to control their impulses, but rather because they find some way of justifying their behaviour (De Witt Huberts et al., 2012). For example, a person on a diet might justify eating an ice cream with the fact that they are on holiday. They may do this even when they have spent the entire day relaxing in the sunshine. Such instances suggest low motivation rather than depleted self-control resources.

BOX 7.5 SELF-CONTROL AS A TRAIT VARIABLE

MAKING CONNECTIONS

The models described in this chapter, particularly the limited resource and process models, tend to conceptualise self-control as something that fluctuates and is also quite malleable. However, other research suggests that individual differences in levels of self-control are quite stable over time (Casey et al., 2011) suggesting that genes and early environmental influences may be important (as well as other aspects of the environment that remain stable over time, see **Chapter 3**). Such differences may be captured by questionnaire measures (see **Box 7.2**) or other measures such as the delay of gratification test. They can then be used to predict health-related behaviours and outcomes. Thus one can view self-control as a trait variable, similar to those we looked at in **Chapter 4**, such as conscientiousness and locus of control. In Chapter 4 we noted that, from the point of view of intervention, research that identifies environmental rather than genetic influences on behaviour is arguably more useful. In a similar manner, models that emphasise the variable rather than the fixed nature of self-control may also be more helpful.

Improving willpower

The three different theories described above have different implications for intervention. If you were devising an intervention to improve self-control (or, indeed, thinking about how you might improve your own self-control) you would take a slightly different approach depending on the theory you referred to. If you equate willpower with cool cognition (Metcalfe & Mischel, 1999) you might encourage a person to change their environment to reduce exposure to tempting stimuli and you might provide a number of different strategies to help distract them from tempting stimuli and/or to get them to focus on the cool properties of the stimuli. You might also encourage them to practise exercising self-control in a range of different domains on the assumption that this would help increase the dominance of cool system networks relative to hot system networks. Additionally, you may think about measures to reduce stress since stress is thought to increase reliance on hot cognition.

If you view willpower as a limited resource (Baumeister & Heatherton, 1996; Baumeister & Vohs, 2016; Baumeister et al., 2007) you might still get a person to practise exercising self-control since, like a muscle, willpower is thought to strengthen with practice. However, since willpower is also believed to be limited, over the short term this may be detrimental, drawing on precious reserves. As such, this type of approach may only be appropriate for an intervention with long-term goals. For shorter term outcomes one might want to focus on just one goal at a time, trying to limit other factors that use self-control. For example, a person wanting to quit smoking may be advised to attempt this whilst on holiday rather than when studying for exams. As with the cool cognition model, attempting to limit stress may also be beneficial to the extent that stressful situations may use up willpower and because being in a good mood can counteract ego depletion. Tasks requiring willpower (such as exercises) or that involve exposing oneself to temptation (such as grocery shopping) would be best scheduled for the morning when reserves of willpower are higher. Frequent breaks between difficult tasks would be recommended. A novel strategy associated with the limited resource model would be the consumption of glucose, for example in the form of sugary drinks and snacks – though such a strategy would definitely be less desirable in terms of dietary and dental health!

However, other research suggests that in demanding situations willpower could be improved simply by *not* viewing it as a limited resource (Job et al., 2010, 2013, 2015b). For example, Job et al. (2015b) assessed students' theories about willpower and then tracked their self-control and academic performance over the course of a 10-week term. They found that for students who faced high demands, having a non-limited theory predicted better time management, less procrastination, less unhealthy eating and less impulsive spending. For those with a heavy course load, having a non-limited theory was also associated with higher grades, an effect that was mediated by reduced procrastination.

Such findings are more consistent with the process model (Inzlicht & Schmeichel, 2012; Inzlicht et al., 2014; Milyavskaya & Inzlicht, 2017). If you referred to this theory when thinking about willpower improvement, you would emphasise strategies that target motivation and attention (Milyavskaya & Inzlicht, 2017). In particular you might try to shift the values of indulgence- versus control-related behaviours in favour of control. This could be achieved either by increasing the value of self-control or decreasing the value of indulgence. For example, the value of self-control could be increased by providing external rewards or by identifying personally relevant reasons for self-control that would increase intrinsic/autonomous motivation (see **Chapter 5**) and help turn 'have-to' goals into 'want-to' goals. Indeed, people who show higher levels of self-control are more likely to identify autonomous reasons for pursuing their goals (Converse et al., 2019). Motivation for indulgence could be reduced by removing some of its value, for example by imposing costs such as fines for smoking in public places.

Adjusting the amount of effort needed for carrying out indulgence- versus self-control-related behaviours may also be helpful as this will contribute to the relative value of each option. So self-control could be improved by making the desired behaviour easier to perform and/or the indulgent behaviour more difficult. For example, fruit could be made more easily accessible and chocolate harder to reach. The effort needed to carry out a desired behaviour could also be reduced through the use of implementation intentions (see **Chapter 6**).

Finally, according to the process model, self-control could be improved by enhancing monitoring of, and attention to, control-related cues. These might help improve self-control because self-control failures may sometimes occur, not because of a lack of motivation, but because of reductions in attention toward control-related cues. This could be addressed by providing feedback (Wan & Sternthal, 2008). For example, alerts could be used to inform a person when they have spent too long on social media or in a sedentary position.

For the most part, the strategies described above relate to instances in which we need to exercise self-control over a relatively short period of time. We tend to think of willpower as something that requires a short, sharp burst of effort, such as working late to meet a deadline or resisting the leftover dessert in the fridge. However, a healthy lifestyle generally requires efforts that are sustained over time, whether it's maintaining one's weight or sticking to an exercise plan. For this we turn to the concept of self-regulation.

SELF-REGULATION

Self-regulation is a slightly broader concept than self-control (although these terms are sometimes used interchangeably). It refers to a person's ability to regulate their behaviour over time, in order to achieve certain goals. For example, someone trying to lose weight needs to monitor and adjust their food intake over an extended period (not just decline chips on a couple of occasions). Successful self-regulation means drawing on a range of different strategies. These might include strategies described in **Chapter 6** (such as implementation intentions) as well as those outlined above, in relation to both craving and self-control. Thus self-regulation refers to the ways in which a person employs such strategies over time, in pursuit of their goals. It can encompass strategies that rely on effortful self-control (such as resisting tempting foods) as well as those that draw on automatic processes (such as developing healthy habits or removing tempting foods from your environment). In health psychology the most widely used theory of self-regulation is control theory, which we look at in this section along with its implications for intervention.

Control theory

The theory

Control theory has its origins in cybernetics, the scientific study of control in people, animals and machines (Carver & Scheier, 1982). A key feature of this theory is a feedback loop that helps the person adjust their behaviour in order to achieve a particular goal. According to the theory, the process of self-regulation consists of the following steps:

1. The person sets a goal.
2. They monitor their behaviour or other relevant outcome.
3. This monitoring provides them with feedback which allows them to compare their current state with their desired state.
4. Where there is a discrepancy between their current and desired states, they take action to resolve this discrepancy by:
   » Adjusting their behaviour and/or
   » Adjusting their goal, for example to make it more realistic.
5. They return to step 2 of the process.

For example, someone who is trying to lose weight might weigh themselves every morning, comparing their current weight with their target weight for that week. They then use this information to inform their behaviour during the course of the day; if they have exceeded their weight loss goal for the week they may allow themselves a little extra indulgence; if it looks like they are going to fail to meet their weight loss goal they might try to further limit their food intake. Or, they may adjust their weekly weight loss goal to something slightly less ambitious.

The evidence

The theory predicts that certain techniques will be key to successful self-regulation. These include setting goals, monitoring behaviour, obtaining feedback from that behaviour and reviewing behaviour and goals. Several meta-analyses indicate that these techniques do help people modify their behaviour. For example, Michie et al. (2009) examined the effectiveness of different behaviour change techniques in 122 interventions designed to promote healthy eating and physical activity. Interventions that used self-monitoring alongside at least one other technique derived from control theory were significantly more effective than other interventions. Similarly, Dombrowski et al. (2012) reviewed dietary and physical activity interventions for obesity. They also found that interventions with techniques related to control theory (particularly self-monitoring) were associated with significantly greater weight loss.

Improving self-regulation

Tracking devices

Both control theory and several meta-analyses indicate that self-monitoring is particularly important for self-regulation. Self-monitoring has been made all that much easier in recent years with the rise of digital technology. Not only is it possible to keep a daily log of your weight on your smartphone, you can use various devices to automatically count your steps, time your sleep and extract calorie information from food labels. Never has it been easier to track your own behaviour.

So is all this tracking helpful? A number of meta-analyses indicate that apps and devices that track behaviour can help people be more physically active, lower blood pressure, lose weight, and reduce energy intake (Bravata et al., 2007; Brickwood et al., 2019; Cooper et al., 2018; El Khoury et al., 2019; Franssen et al., 2020; Lewis et al., 2015; Lynch et al., 2020). Research has also shown that those who have successfully managed to maintain significant weight loss for more than a year are more likely to be tracking their weight, diet or exercise compared to the general population (Goldstein et al., 2017).

However, according to control theory, we would not really expect tracking to be helpful in isolation. Participants in the above studies were likely also using additional strategies encompassed by control theory, such as goal setting, reviewing behaviour and goals, and adjusting behaviour. According to control theory, a person is only going to be able to successfully self-regulate where they have the skills and opportunity to adjust their behaviour and where they are sufficiently motivated to do so. Regardless of how often a person weighs themselves, they may find it difficult to lose weight if they are unaware of the calorie content of different types of foods or if they find it too hard to limit their food intake.

Such caveats are illustrated in a randomised controlled trial that looked at the effects of a calorie counting app (MyFitnessPal) among primary care patients with overweight or obesity (Laing et al., 2014). Logins dropped sharply after the first month and most participants did not use the app regularly, often reporting that it was too tedious or they were too tired or stressed. Over a six-month period the app had no effect on weight loss. The authors concluded that although participants had reported an interest in losing weight, they may not have been sufficiently motivated to invest the necessary time and effort needed to track calorie intake. Thus whilst an app or device that tracks behaviour can be a useful tool, it needs to be accompanied by additional strategies in order to successfully promote behaviour change.

Effortless self-regulation

Other research has also suggested that successful self-regulation often results from the use of strategies that draw on automatic processes rather than processes that require effortful self-control. For example, Milyavskaya and Inzlicht (2017) looked at students' daily experiences of temptations and effortful self-control over the course of a semester. They found that the extent to which a person exercised self-control had no effect on goal achievement. Rather it was the person's experience of temptations in general that was more influential; those who experienced more temptations felt more fatigued in the evenings which led to them making less progress toward their goals. These findings suggest that removing temptations from one's environment is the key to better self-regulation, rather than strengthening willpower. This view is consistent with the concept of effortless self-regulation[2] put forward by Fujita (2011) that refers to goal achievement through the use of strategies that draw on automatic processes (see also Duckworth et al., 2016).

CONCLUSIONS

Craving is part of what makes us human. It serves a useful function, directing our attention and behaviour toward things that help us fulfil our biological needs (see **Chapter 2**). However, sometimes cravings can go awry, threatening both our physical and mental health. This is especially the case among the ubiquitous temptations of modern society. Learning how to exert and strengthen willpower is one means of managing these cravings and of allowing us to prioritise long-term outcomes over immediate pleasures. Successful self-regulation can also help us maintain healthy behaviours over time. However, exercising willpower is effortful and likely to be more difficult when cognitive resources are in short supply (see **Chapter 3**). An alternative approach is to try to manage our environments to ensure they limit temptations and support healthy habits.

In this chapter we've seen how important self-control and self-regulation are for maintaining healthy behaviours. But can you have too much of a good thing? Is it possible for someone to exercise too much self-control? Or too much self-regulation? How might self-control and self-regulation relate to quality of life? And are there times when less is more?

THE GREAT DEBATE

---

2   Labelled as 'self-control' by Fujita, illustrating the varied ways in which the terms 'self-control' and 'self-regulation' are employed in the literature. In keeping with the definitions used in this chapter (where self-control/willpower is defined as effortful), we use the term 'effortless self-regulation'.

Chapter Outline

What Does it Mean to be Addicted?

Theories of Addiction

Conclusions

In 2008 soul singer and songwriter Amy Winehouse won five Grammy awards for best new artist, song of the year, best female pop vocal performance, best pop vocal album and record of the year (**Image 8.1**). She performed via satellite from London. This was a night beyond many artists' wildest dreams, a once-in-a-lifetime event that most of us can only ever fantasise about. But according to one of her friends, Amy sadly observed that the evening was 'so boring without drugs' (Gay-Reese et al., 2015). Three years later, at the age of just 27, she was dead from alcohol poisoning.

What makes drugs so appealing and so difficult to resist? Was there something about Amy's personality or lifestyle that led to her addictions? And how do cravings for drugs differ from cravings for other substances such as sugary foods? In this chapter we will:

- Look at how experts have attempted to define and diagnose addiction.

- Review some of the most widely used theories of addiction.

- Consider the ways in which theory can help us understand and treat addictive behaviours.

Image 8.1 *Singer and songwriter Amy Winehouse who died of alcohol poisoning at the age of just 27 after a lifelong battle with addiction.*
Credit: Chris Christoforou/Redferns/Getty Images.

WHAT DOES IT MEAN TO BE ADDICTED?

The term 'addiction' crops up frequently in everyday life. We hear reports of celebrities suffering from addictions to heroin or cocaine. We may know of people who are addicted to cigarettes or who drink heavily every night. Perhaps we even talk about someone being addicted to their smartphone or joke that we are addicted to a particular flavour of ice cream. But what does the term actually mean? Can we only become addicted to certain types of drugs or can we become addicted to food too? What about certain types of behaviour? We have all heard of people who struggle with gambling but what about shopping or sex or computer games? Or reading, or running or travel? What makes one thing an addiction and another a passion?

Definitions of addiction

There has been much debate around how we should define addiction. One of the more recent and comprehensive definitions comes from West and Brown (2013). They define addiction as:

> *a chronic condition involving a repeated powerful motivation to engage in a rewarding behaviour, acquired as a result of engaging in that behaviour, that has significant potential for unintended harm.... Someone is addicted to something to the extent that they experience this repeated powerful motivation.* (p. 15)

If we unpick this definition, we can identify five concepts relating to motivation, reward, repetition, acquisition and unintended harm.

1. *Motivation.* Central to West and Brown's understanding of addiction is the person's experience of a 'powerful motivation'. This differs from other definitions of addiction (such as Kerr, 1884) that refer to physical dependence (a state in which the body has adapted to a particular substance so that abstinence results in unpleasant physiological withdrawal symptoms). Thus West and Brown's definition does not limit addiction to substance use but allows for its application to other behaviours such as gambling, shopping and exercise. It also means that for the millions who believe they can't function properly without their morning cup of coffee, few are likely to be viewed as addicts, regardless of how wretched they might feel.

2. *Reward.* The behaviour must also be rewarding. In other words, (at least initially) it should bring pleasure. This helps distinguish addiction from conditions where someone is motivated to engage in a behaviour as a means of relief from mental or physical discomfort. Such conditions might include excessive cleaning in obsessive compulsive disorder or purging in bulimia. It also helps distinguish addiction from instances in which a person is on medication for pain relief or relief from symptoms such as depression or anxiety.

3. *Repetition.* The feeling of motivation must be chronic. According to West and Brown, a person is not addicted to a substance or behaviour where they only experience this motivation in particular situations. This means that the social smoker, who longs for a cigarette whilst out with friends, but not at other times of the day, would not be considered addicted, however hard that habit may be to break.

4. *Acquisition.* The behaviour must be 'acquired as a result of engaging in that behaviour'. In other words, it is the person's experience that leads to addiction. So someone dreaming of finding a cure to cancer or being the first female American president would not be considered addicted. However single-minded they may be, they have yet to experience the thrill of realising their ambition so, according to West and Brown, it is not addiction that is driving their behaviour.

5. *Unintended harm.* Finally, according to West and Brown, the behaviour must be dysfunctional. This is an interesting idea as it brings with it a degree of subjectivity. It is easy to view some behaviours as having the potential for unintended harm; the smoker is unlikely to want die of lung cancer and the gambler probably does not want to lose their family home. But what about the 'workaholic' or fitness fanatic whose personal relationships are falling apart? Are we less likely to describe them as addicted because their behaviour is making a useful contribution to society or benefiting their health? It also raises the possibility of cultural shifts in what we define as addiction as we acquire new knowledge about what is good and bad for our health. According to this view, in the 1940s, when no one was aware of the harmful effects of tobacco, heavy smokers would not have been considered addicted. Could we see the appearance of coffee cessation services in two decades time?

However, West and Brown's (2013) definition is not the only one. An alternative definition by Heather (2016) states that:

a person is addicted to a specified behavior if they have demonstrated repeated and continuing failures to refrain from or radically reduce the behavior despite prior resolutions to do so or if they would have demonstrated such failures under different personal or environmental circumstances (p. 3)

Arguably this view of addiction is easier to apply since it places more emphasis on observed behaviour ('repeated and continuing failures to refrain') rather than relying on the idea of 'powerful motivation' that may be difficult to identify. (At what point do we decide that feelings of motivation are 'powerful' as opposed to 'normal'?) However, by applying the concept of repetition to behaviour rather than motivation it allows for a much broader range of behaviours to be viewed as addictions. For example, in contrast to West and Brown, social smokers who repeatedly fail to refrain from smoking with friends, but experience no motivation to smoke at other times, would be viewed as addicted. In terms of type of behaviour, like West and Brown, Heather also makes no reference to drugs so his definition allows for extension to non-drug-related behaviours. His definition also captures the notion of unintended harm through reference to 'different personal or environmental circumstances'. However, there is no mention of reward, which makes it more difficult to differentiate between addictive behaviours and other impulse control disorders such as obsessive compulsive disorder or instances where behaviour is driven by negative reinforcement such as pain relief.

> **Diagnostic and Statistical Manual of Mental Disorders (DSM)** – a handbook published by the American Psychological Association that sets out standard criteria for the classification of mental disorders. It was first published in 1952 and is updated as new evidence emerges. The fifth edition was published in 2013. The DSM is widely used by both researchers and practitioners though it has been criticised for cultural bias, for the medicalisation of what should be viewed as normal distress, and for relying too much on symptoms as opposed to underlying mechanisms and aetiology.

Addiction according to the DSM-5

In contrast to the above, the **Diagnostic and Statistical Manual of Mental Disorders** (DSM-5; American Psychiatric Association, 2013) avoids labelling any condition as an addiction. This is partly because of difficulties in defining addiction but also because of the negative connotations associated with the term. Instead, the DSM-5 refers to 'substance-related and addictive disorders'. This includes reference to 'substance use disorders' which are what we might typically view as addiction. According to the DSM-5, a key feature of these are a change in brain circuits that persists beyond detoxification and leads to repeated relapse and intense craving when the individual encounters drug-related stimuli. Diagnosis of a substance use disorder is based upon evidence of clinically significant impairment or distress that results from any of the following:

- *Impaired control* – such as strong cravings or unsuccessful efforts to cut down
- *Social impairment* – such as failure to fulfil major obligations at school, work or home
- *Risky use* – for example, risks of injury or risks to health
- *Pharmacological effects* – consisting of tolerance (such as a need for increased amounts to achieve the same effects) and withdrawal (specific physiological symptoms associated with withdrawal from that substance).

The DSM-5 also refers to 'substance intoxication' and 'substance withdrawal'. The distinction between a substance use disorder, intoxication and withdrawal allows for the diagnosis of other clinical conditions relating to substance use that do not represent an addiction. For example, someone could be suffering from alcohol intoxication, or alcohol withdrawal symptoms, in the absence of an addiction to alcohol.

There are separate diagnoses for alcohol, cannabis, hallucinogens, inhalants, opioids, sedatives/anti-anxiety drugs, stimulants and tobacco. However, because these substances affect the body in different ways, there are some differences between them. For example, for caffeine there are diagnoses relating to intoxication and withdrawal but not substance use disorder. In other words, according to DSM-5, people do not become addicted to caffeine even though it has distinct physiological effects that can also lead to withdrawal symptoms. Likewise, there are no diagnoses relating to intoxication for tobacco or withdrawal for hallucinogens and inhalants.

Within the overarching heading of 'substance-related and addictive disorders', there is also a category called 'non-substance-related disorders', intended to cover what we would view as behavioural addictions. However, the only disorder currently contained within this category is gambling disorder. This is because, according to the DSM-5, there is not yet sufficient evidence to establish diagnostic criteria for other potential addictions such as gaming, shopping or exercise.

Summary

The definitions of addiction we've explored in this section, together with the diagnostic criteria described in the DSM-5, give us a sense of what it means to be addicted to something and where we might draw the line between addiction and desire (**Box 8.1**). The DSM-5 refers to the effect of addictive substances on brain circuits, making it clear there can be a physical component to addiction. However, both our definitions of addiction focussed on the psychological aspects, which means they can be applied more broadly, for example to behavioural addictions as well as addictions to substances. But what causes addiction? And why might one person become addicted to alcohol or cigarettes whilst another does not? For a more complete understanding of addiction, we need to turn to theory.

BOX 8.1 CAN WE BECOME ADDICTED TO SUGAR?

Tonia Buxton, cook, food writer and mother of four, won't let her children eat birthday cake, or other foods containing sugar. **HOT TOPIC**

'Sugar has the same effect on the brain as cocaine,' she explained in an interview, 'they go crazy, they're running around and then they're coming down and then they want more, and another hit and another hit, so you're better off not having any.' (Barr, 2018)

CHAPTER 8

The idea that we can become addicted to sugar, or to food more generally, is a view increasingly being endorsed in the popular press and held by the general public (Lee et al., 2013; Ruddock et al., 2015; Ruddock & Hardman, 2017). But how much truth is there in it? Can sugar really be compared to cocaine? And is it wise to start diagnosing people as food addicts?

According to the definitions of addiction we've explored in this chapter, eating sugary foods could, in theory, meet the criteria for addiction. For example, a person may experience a powerful motivation to eat sugary foods, and this motivation may be chronic and acquired as a result of eating sugary foods. They may experience pleasure when eating high sugar foods even though they may be damaging their health (in terms of, for example, weight gain and risk of diseases such as diabetes). Thus, using the definition provided by West and Brown (2013), a person could be considered addicted to food in the same way that a person may be considered addicted to other behaviours such as online gaming, gambling, shopping or sex. But does this justify comparing sugar to cocaine? Does sugar have physiological effects equivalent to cocaine and other addictive drugs?

Gearhardt et al. (2011a) argue that the modern food environment includes foods engineered to be 'hyperpalatable', that is, foods with much higher levels of fat, sugar, salt, flavours and additives compared to what one would typically find in 'traditional' foods such as fruit, vegetables and nuts. For example, on average, an apple contains 19g of sugar whilst an ice cream cone contains 34g; a serving of chicken contains 0.16g of salt whilst a serving of pizza contains 2.31g. We have evolved to find these 'hyperpalatable' foods more rewarding than 'traditional' foods (see **Chapter 2**) and, according to Gearhardt et al., they share many features with addictive drugs. For example, they activate similar reward pathways in the brain, can lead to the downregulation of dopamine receptors in the brain (receptors associated with reward) and can elicit withdrawal and tolerance responses (Avena et al., 2008; Gearhardt et al., 2011b; Johnson & Kenny, 2010).

However, Rogers (2017) disagrees with this view. He points out that because addictive drugs tap into the same processes that evolved to help motivate adaptive behaviour, such as eating, inevitably there will be similarities between our responses to food and our responses to addictive drugs. According to Rogers, these similarities include craving, bingeing and tolerance. However, he argues that addictive drugs have more potent effects on the brain and highlights the fact that some of the research used as evidence for food addiction consists of studies with rats in relatively unstimulating environments with only intermittent access to sugar and/or food. This is unlikely to be a good parallel with most human experience where food and sugar are plentiful, alongside other sources of pleasure such as shopping opportunities, smartphones and television.[1]

As we've seen in this chapter, addiction is a fuzzy concept. It doesn't describe a discrete, unitary phenomenon, such as whether or not a person has blue eyes, but rather a much vaguer and more variable collection of features, more akin to whether someone has short hair; some people definitely have short hair, others definitely do not, and then there are a set of people who are more difficult to categorise. So it is with addiction; some might argue a person is addicted to sugar, others would disagree. Perhaps the more useful debate here is not whether one can become

---

1   Though, see Nettle et al., 2017 for an interesting discussion of the effects of food insecurity on obesity

addicted to sugar, but what would be the implications of such a label? What purpose would it serve?

Gearhardt et al. (2011a) believe labelling sugar as addictive would be beneficial for public health. Drawing parallels with the tobacco industry they argue that it would help shift responsibility away from the individual, instead placing the onus on government to introduce legislation to reduce consumption. Such legislation could include taxation and restrictions on marketing and accessibility. For example, many governments subsidise sugar, which means sugary foods are often cheap. They also tend to be easily accessible (for example in vending machines) and frequently marketed to children and teenagers (Powell et al., 2007).

On the other hand, Rogers (2017) argues that such a label could undermine people's attempts to reduce their sugar intake by promoting a belief that consumption is very difficult to control (see also **Box 4.3**). He also suggests it could lead to expectations of negative withdrawal effects which could in turn increase the experience of such effects. The influence of expectations on perception in eating and appetite is well documented and can be accounted for by grounded cognition theory (**Chapter 7**). Nevertheless, there may also be some benefits to identifying oneself as a food addict (such as helping to alleviate feelings of guilt and shame) and researchers are exploring both the short- and long-term advantages and disadvantages of such a label (Ruddock & Hardman, 2017).

THEORIES OF ADDICTION

There are an enormous number of theories of addiction, many of which take very different approaches to the subject (West & Brown, 2013). At one end of the spectrum, neurobiological theories tend to view addiction as a brain disease, focussing on the effects of drugs on the central nervous system and individual differences that make some people more susceptible to addiction than others. Seeing addiction as a disease suggests the behaviour is beyond the control of the individual and points towards pharmacological and neurological treatments. There is a danger that this view could lead to a fatalistic acceptance of the condition and a lack of investment in population-based policies and behavioural interventions (Hall et al., 2015).

By contrast, other theories view addiction as a conscious choice that arises out of a rational analysis of costs of benefits. Some of the social cognition models we looked at in **Chapter 5** fall under this heading. For example, the health belief model, the theory of planned behaviour, protection motivation theory and the transtheoretical model have all been applied to addictive behaviours. Viewing addiction as a conscious choice more naturally leads one to look at a person's environment to explain their actions and to develop more psychological and environmental interventions to try to alter their behaviour (see **Case Studies 8 and 9** in **Chapter 12**). However, in some instances this view of addiction may also lead people to feel a person has 'chosen to be an addict', and so are less deserving of help. For example, Morse (2016) argues that Anglo-American criminal law leans toward this view of addiction, holding 'addicts' morally responsible for their actions, leading to more punitive sentencing.

However, most theorists would probably agree that neither of these extreme views are accurate; a person suffering from an addiction is rarely unable to control any of their behaviour, but neither are they simply making choices consistent with their

CHAPTER 8

preferences. Segal (2016) takes the middle ground stating that addiction is a 'neurally based malfunctioning of choice-making systems that has the potential to cause great distress' (p. 461). In this way he acknowledges the influence of both decision-making and biological influences.

It is far beyond the scope of this chapter to provide a comprehensive review of all theories of addiction. Instead, we examine a small selection, chosen because they have been widely applied or offer an interesting perspective. Whilst some of these theories (such as the self-medication model and incentive-sensitisation theory) have been developed in relation to addictive substances, others (such as PRIME theory) have been used to account for both substance and behavioural addictions.

The self-medication model

One potential explanation for drug use is that it helps the person manage uncomfortable emotions. For example, a glass of wine at the end of the day may unwind office tensions whilst a couple of beers at a party might ease social anxiety. Likewise, shooting up heroin first thing in the morning could temporarily obliterate painful feelings of shame or memories of traumatic events.

Negative reinforcement – where the rate of a behaviour increases because it leads to the removal of an aversive event or stimulus ('escape') or it results in the avoidance of an aversive event or stimulus ('avoidance'). Negative reinforcement is a component of operant conditioning (also called instrumental conditioning).

Positive reinforcement – where the rate of a behaviour increases because it leads to a desirable event or stimulus. Positive rein-forcement is a component of operant conditioning (also called instrumental conditioning).

The theory

This view of drug use is formalised in the self-medication model of addiction. This model was put forward not as a complete theory of addiction, but rather as an account designed to complement other perspectives (Khantzian, 1997). It states that much substance use is driven, not by the pleasure that drugs provide, but rather by relief from, or control of, unpleasant feelings. In other words, substance use is often initiated and maintained as a result of **negative reinforcement** rather than **positive reinforcement**.

According to this model, biological and/or psychological predispositions mean that certain people struggle to regulate their emotions and relationships. For example, they may feel overwhelmed by painful emotions or they may have difficulty labelling or experiencing certain emotions. This psychological difficulty may be present at a clinical level (such as schizophrenia or major depression) or at a non-clinical level (such as low mood or simply feeling isolated). In many instances this may stem from trauma experienced early in life. If such a person also has an impaired ability to anticipate harm or danger they are more likely to try to escape from these unpleasant states by 'self-medicating' with a drug. It is this combination of poor affect regulation and impaired danger recognition that makes a person vulnerable to substance abuse. According to the theory, drugs help relieve psychological suffering.

The self-medication model also predicts that the drug or drugs a person takes depend upon the types of emotions they are trying to avoid or control. The person may experiment with a range of different drugs, before discovering that one type is especially effective at making them feel better. This means that different people will gravitate towards different drugs, depending on their psychological difficulty. For example, according to Khantzian (1997), alcohol and other central nervous system depressants tend to soften psychological defences so may be taken to reduce feelings of isolation. On the other hand, opiates reduce feelings of anger so may be used to counter such emotions and their effects. As the person develops a tolerance for the drug so these effects diminish. If a person successfully quits the drug they may still be prone to relapse as they may recall the initial relief they originally experienced upon first taking the drug.

The evidence

Empirical support for the self-medication model is mixed. Consistent with the model's predictions, there is substantial comorbidity between psychopathology and substance use disorders (in other words, they often occur together). For example, among those with schizophrenia, approximately 40–50% also suffer from a substance use disorder and rates of smoking are two to four times higher compared to the general population (Blanchard et al., 2000; de Leon et al., 2002; Diwan et al., 1998; Hughes et al., 1986; Kumari & Postma, 2005). Likewise, alcohol use disorder is often comorbid with mood disorders and with social anxiety disorder (Davidson et al., 1993; Grant et al., 2009). However, these types of associations do not necessarily mean the substance abuse occurred as a result of the psychopathology. For example, in a longitudinal study, Fergusson et al. (2009) found more evidence to support a causal model in which problems with alcohol led to an increased risk of major depression rather than vice versa. Other research indicates that genetic and environmental influences increase the risk of *both* major depression and alcohol use disorder (Kendler et al., 1993, 2003; Prescott et al., 2000). In other words, *part* of the reason for the co-occurrence of depression and alcohol abuse is because of underlying factors that increase the risk of both, rather than a strong causal relationship between the two.

Darke (2013) reviewed evidence for the self-medication model in relation to heroin users. He found that it supports the view that trauma and psychopathology play a causal role in heroin addiction. For example, he noted that:

- Around one-third of heroin users had at least one substance-dependent parent (Conroy et al., 2009; Coviello et al., 2004).

- Parents of heroin users have higher levels of psychopathology (Ravndal et al., 2001; Rossow & Lauritzen, 2001).

- Heroin users report experiencing high levels of parental conflict, separation or absence (Conroy et al., 2009; Rossow & Lauritzen, 2001).

- One-third to one-half of heroin users will have experienced childhood sexual abuse and similar proportions will have experienced physical abuse (Conroy et al., 2009; Wu et al., 2010; see also Heffernan et al., 2000).

- More than half of heroin users will have experienced neglect or emotional abuse (Conroy et al., 2009; Wu et al., 2010).

- As adults, around three-quarters meet the criteria for at least one comorbid non-substance use psychiatric disorder (Cacciola et al., 2001)

- Nearly 1 in 3 heroin users will have attempted suicide (Darke et al., 2007).

Research has also shown that pre-existing psychopathology increases the risk of heroin use whilst treatment for post-traumatic stress disorder reduces drug use (but not vice versa; Hahesy et al., 2002; Hien et al., 2010; Martins et al., 2009).

However, heroin users nearly always use a wide range of different drugs. Before starting to use heroin they will usually have tried tobacco (typically starting at 12 to 14 years of age), before moving on to alcohol (at 13 to 14 years), cannabis (at 14 to 16 years), methamphetamines and cocaine (at 17 to 19 years) and heroin at around 20 years (Darke, 2011). It then usually takes around 18 months for irregular use to turn to dependency. But once they become addicted to heroin, they do not tend to quit other drugs. Most heroin users will be smokers, around 25% will be alcohol dependent, more than half will use cannabis, one-fifth to one-half will use cocaine or methamphetamine and one-third to one-half will use benzodiazepines (Darke, 2011). Thus heroin users tend to take a wide range of pharmacologically distinct drugs, in other words, drugs that are depressants as well as those that are stimulants. This contradicts the self-medication model that predicts that individuals gravitate to certain types of drugs that best address their underlying psychopathology.

Thus Darke (2013) concludes that whilst there is evidence to support the view that trauma and psychopathology play a causal role in heroin dependence, the pattern of drug use is more consistent with a general attempt to use as many drugs as possible in order to escape negative affect through intoxication, rather than select particular drugs because of their specific effects. Darke also notes that not every episode of drug use will be an attempt to self-medicate; whilst self-medication may lead to heroin dependence, use may then be maintained by other factors such as neurological changes and relief from withdrawal symptoms.

Blanchard et al. (2000) looked at possible explanations for high rates of substance use disorders among those with schizophrenia. Again they found no evidence to support the drug specificity predicted by the self-medication model. Although those with schizophrenia have higher rates of drug use compared to the general population, the pattern of drug use is similar, with alcohol being most frequently used, followed by cannabis and then stimulants. This pattern is also found in other mental health disorders. Additionally, they found no evidence to indicate that more negative symptoms were associated with greater substance use. In light of their review, Blanchard et al. proposed an alternative affect regulation model in which certain personality traits associated with schizophrenia (negative affectivity/neuroticism and disinhibition/impulsivity) are also linked to a maladaptive coping style which in turn leads the person to attempt to regulate their emotions and their response to stress through the use of drugs (see **Chapter 4** for discussion of personality and coping styles).

Thus whilst there is limited evidence to support the drug specificity component of the self-medication model, research does seem to indicate that a history of trauma and psychopathology predicts substance abuse. This is consistent with the model's predictions that drugs are used to avoid or control unpleasant emotions. However, although the model makes a useful contribution to our understanding of substance abuse, as noted by Khantzian (1997), it was never intended to be a complete account and cannot explain all aspects of addiction. In particular, it has difficulty explaining instances in which drug addiction occurs in the absence of distress or the fact that many people with histories of trauma and/or psychopathology do not go on to become addicted to drugs even though most will have come into contact with addictive substances, such as alcohol or cigarettes. For a slightly broader theory of addiction we now turn to opponent process theory.

Opponent process theory

The theory

According to opponent process theory, addiction is driven by the same processes that underpin our responses to all stimuli that elicit an affective response, whether that response is positive or negative (Solomon, 1980; Solomon & Corbit, 1974). The theory states that the brains of mammals are designed to maintain homeostasis (a state of equilibrium). This leads to what is termed a 'hedonic contrast effect'; when a stimulus provokes a primary hedonic response (for example, a feeling of pleasure, pain, fear or anxiety) other processes are automatically elicited in the autonomic nervous system that are designed to counteract this effect and reduce the intensity of these feelings. For example, a feeling of happiness associated with achieving a good grade in an exam or eating ice cream on a hot summer's day will set in motion processes in the central nervous system designed to counteract these emotions. Likewise, feelings of despair upon discovering you have failed all your exams, or fear at encountering an angry dog on a country path will elicit central nervous system processes designed to bring your mood back to a more neutral level.

The first process, elicited in response to the stimulus, is called the 'a-process' whilst the second opponent process, elicited in response to the a-process, is called the 'b-process'. The a-process occurs rapidly in response to the stimulus and is proportionate in intensity and length; one chocolate truffle will elicit a small, relatively brief feeling of pleasure, finding out you secured your dream job will lead to more intense feelings of pleasure that are sustained over a longer time period. By contrast, the b-process is much slower in initiation but also much slower to dissipate, so lasts for a longer period of time compared to the a-process. Panels A2 and A3 of **Figure 8.1** show the time course of these two processes in relation to the stimulus.

Figure 8.1 The time course of the a- and b-processes in opponent process theory

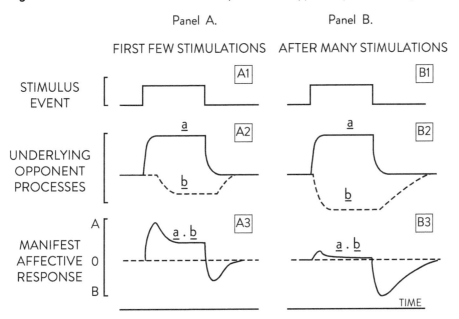

Note: When a stimulus elicits an affective response (a; Panel A2), this results in processes designed to counteract this effect (b; Panel A2). This means that the person's feelings show an initial peak, followed by a plateau that is equal to the a-process minus the b-process (Panel A3). The a-process closely tracks the stimulus, so when the stimulus is removed the a-process ceases. However, the b-process takes longer to dissipate (Panel A2) resulting in a withdrawal stage during which the individual experiences feelings that contrast with their initial response to the stimulus (Panel A3). Where a person is repeatedly exposed to a stimulus (Panel B) the b-process is strengthened (Panel B2) so the person experiences dampened initial reactions to the stimulus (a-b) but stronger feelings of withdrawal (Panel B3).

Source: Solomon, R. L., & Corbit, J. D. (1974). An opponent-process theory of motivation: I. Temporal dynamics of affect. *Psychological Review*, 81(2), 119. Copyright © 1974 by American Psychological Association. Adapted with permission.

This hedonic contrast effect also results in a hedonic habituation effect. This is a period of adaptation during which the affective response declines and reaches a steady state, even where the intensity of the stimulus remains the same. This is shown in section

A3 of **Figure 8.1** and occurs because the affective response is a sum of both the a- and b-processes. However, because of the delay in onset of the b-process there is an initial peak in affective response representing the influence of the a-process in isolation.

The time course of the affective response can be illustrated by imagining you have found yourself face to face with an angry dog. Your initial reaction may be one of intense fear and heightened heart rate. However, following this initial reaction, even though the dog may remain in the pathway, growling at you menacingly, it is likely that your heart rate will lower slightly and your feelings of fear subside a little. Your heart rate will still be elevated and you may still feel very frightened, but not quite as frightened as that very first moment you set eyes on the dog. If the dog eventually runs away (the stimulus is removed) the a-process (that resulted in the feeling of fear) would dissipate very quickly. However, the b-process (elicited as an automatic reaction to the a-process) would take longer to subside. This means that after the dog has run away, and your fear has vanished, the b-process will still be at work, leaving you with a feeling opposite to fear, for example a feeling of relief.

This is the pattern we see in response to many drugs. There may be an initial high or rush associated with the a-process, followed by a more sustained feeling of euphoria as the b-process kicks in and counteracts some of the effects of the a-process. However, as the drug wears off, only the b-process remains, resulting in unpleasant feelings associated with withdrawal. For example, a night of heavy drinking may be accompanied by much merriment but followed by an unpleasant headache and feelings of low mood the next day.

According to opponent process theory, with repeated exposure to the stimulus, the b-process gets both stronger and more sustained. It also becomes quicker to initiate. By contrast, the a-process does not change. This means that a stimulus that initially resulted in a pleasant feeling eventually elicits a much weaker pleasant feeling but a stronger aversive or withdrawal response (see **Figure 8.1,** Panel B). According to the theory, this is what we see in drug addiction. Initially drug use may be positively reinforced by the rush and euphoria that occurs due to the a-process. However, with repeated use we see these pleasurable feelings decline whilst aversive feelings associated with withdrawal get stronger and last for longer. These aversive feelings include feelings of craving (**Chapter 7**). The user may then start to take drugs to alleviate these negative withdrawal symptoms since drug use will elicit the a-process that will counteract the b-process. The user may also take increasing amounts of the drug in an attempt to experience the pleasure they felt when they first used the drug. Hence we have a model of drug addiction that starts with positive reinforcement (taking drugs for the rush and euphoria) but may eventually be controlled by negative reinforcement (taking drugs to alleviate unpleasant withdrawal symptoms and cravings). Over time, if not used, the b-process will get weaker. This means that someone who has stopped using drugs may once again experience the rush and euphoria if they start using them again.

Previously neutral stimuli that precede the peak b-process may also become associated with withdrawal symptoms via classical or Pavlovian conditioning (see page 149 for a definition). These stimuli may then elicit craving and prompt the person to re-expose themselves to the stimulus in order to avoid the upcoming aversive withdrawal state. For example, the sight of an empty cigarette packet may frequently precede nicotine withdrawal and thus eventually come to elicit feelings of craving even when the person is not nicotine deprived. In this way drug use may become controlled by attempts to avoid negative affect rather than escape it (see earlier definition of negative reinforcement, page 218) that in turn may result in increasingly shorter gaps between episodes of drug use. These conditioned stimuli may also continue to elicit feelings of craving even after a user has quit a drug.

According to opponent process theory, someone could become addicted to any stimulus that is capable of eliciting intense pleasure and is followed by an opponent process that is relatively sustained. This means the theory can be used to account for behavioural addictions as well as drug addiction. Solomon and Corbit (1974) speculate that some pleasures (including some drugs, such as cannabis) may have no opponent process (in other words, the associated a-process does not arouse a b-process) so it would not be possible to form an addiction to these. They suggest that aesthetic pleasures (such as music and art) may fall into this category. They also suggest that stimuli that result in a relatively short b-process will not be addictive since the negative feelings associated with the b-process will disappear relatively quickly meaning it is never necessary to re-expose oneself to the stimulus in order to alleviate these aversive feelings. They speculate that the taste of food could be an example of a stimulus that has a short b-process.

Limitations

Although opponent process theory can account for a number of important features of addiction, some have argued that it places too much emphasis on withdrawal as a key motivator of behaviour and that this is not always consistent with the research evidence (Robinson & Berridge, 2003). For example, drug withdrawal symptoms typically peak one to two days after drug use cessation, but susceptibility to relapse tends to continue to increase for several weeks or months beyond this (Grimm et al., 2001). Additionally, although opponent process theory suggests that withdrawal symptoms may be elicited by conditioned stimuli, others have argued that escape from withdrawal is an insufficient explanation for the powerful feelings of craving still experienced by many individuals long after they have successfully managed to abstain from drug use (Robinson & Berridge, 2003).

Incentive-sensitisation theory

Aims and key insights

In contrast to opponent process theory, incentive-sensitisation theory was specifically developed to explain drug craving and aims to account for several important features of drug addiction (Berridge & Robinson, 2016; Robinson & Berridge, 1993, 2001, 2003, 2008). These include the following:

- Drug craving and relapse can occur among those recovering from addiction, even after long periods of abstinence when any physical withdrawal symptoms would have disappeared. For example, one year after treatment for drug addiction, around 40–60% of individuals will have failed to remain abstinent (McLellan et al., 2000). This suggests drug craving and relapse are underpinned by something other than simple physiological withdrawal.

- Not everyone who uses addictive drugs becomes addicted. For example, only around 30% of those who take cocaine go on to become addicted (Berridge & Robinson, 2016). Indeed, most of us have probably tried at least one addictive drug in our lives, such as alcohol, but most likely relatively few of us are addicted to these substances.

Incentive-sensitisation theory accounts for these and other observations with two key insights:

- **'Wanting'** (or craving) is different from 'liking'
- Brain dopamine systems (that underpin 'wanting') can be sensitised to drugs and drug-related cues.

'Wanting' – in incentive-sensitisation theory quotation marks are used to refer to 'wanting' that is triggered by reward-related cues. This type of 'wanting' is associated with activation of reward circuits in the brain and is distinct from wanting that relates to a cognitive desire or goal, such as wanting to get good grades (Berridge & Robinson, 2016).

CHAPTER 8

Theory and evidence

It may seem natural to link 'wanting' and liking; we tend to want things because they bring us pleasure. Indeed, both wanting and liking were once believed to be regulated by brain dopamine systems since these systems are activated by rewards. However, research has contradicted such assumptions. For example, whilst dopamine suppression reduces amphetamine and cocaine users' desire for these substances, it does not appear to reduce the pleasure they experience upon using them (Leyton et al., 2005). Similarly, the reduced brain dopamine levels experienced by patients suffering from **Parkinson's disease** do not seem to impact upon the pleasure they experience from food (Sienkiewicz-Jarosz et al., 2013; see also Hardman et al, 2012). Additionally, neuroimaging studies have shown that changes in brain dopamine transmission tend to correlate with changes in ratings of desire for drug and food rewards rather than changes in ratings of liking (Evans et al., 2006; Smith et al., 2016).

> **Parkinson's disease** – a degenerative disorder of the central nervous system that affects the motor system. The main symptoms include involuntary shaking of particular parts of the body, slowness of movement and stiff, inflexible muscles. These symptoms get progressively worse with time and may eventually result in severe disability. Parkinson's is caused by the death of brain cells in a region of the midbrain called the 'substantia nigra'. This leads to insufficient levels of dopamine in this area.

We know now that 'wanting' and liking are mediated by independent brain substrates. 'Wanting' is controlled by dopamine in the mesocorticolimbic systems in the brain, whilst liking is linked to a number of hedonic hotspots distributed throughout the brain that respond to neurotransmitters such as opioids and endocannabinoids.

According to incentive-sensitisation theory, addictive drugs sensitise the reward circuits in the brain without impacting upon liking. This means the drug becomes increasingly 'wanted' or craved without it delivering any additional pleasure when consumed. Indeed, the person may habituate to the effects of the drug so that, paradoxically, the pleasure experienced may decline over time whilst feelings of desire for it increase. Thus, according to incentive-sensitisation theory, addiction occurs as a result of excessive increases in 'wanting', without any increase in liking. This leads to compulsive drug seeking and taking behaviours that may occur even where the person has a strong desire to abstain and does not necessarily even anticipate pleasure from drug use (**Image 8.2**).

Image 8.2 As a person becomes addicted to cigarettes, so their desire for them increases, even though the pleasure they get from them may decline.
Credit: Julia Engel.

The other key insight from incentive-sensitisation theory is that brain dopamine systems responsible for 'wanting' can be sensitised to drugs and drug-related cues. This sensitisation process occurs through the development of Pavlovian associations between a cue for the drug (such as the sight of a cigarette packet) and the drug itself (in this case cigarettes). Pavlovian conditioning (also called classical or respondent conditioning, see page 149 for a definition) states that through repeated association, a previously neutral cue (in this case a cigarette packet) will eventually come to elicit some of the same responses as the unconditioned cue (in this case the cigarette). Incentive-sensitisation theory goes beyond this by stating that during this process incentive salience is attributed to the cognitive representation of the conditioned cue (the cigarette packet). Cues that acquire incentive salience:

- Elicit an approach response ('Pavlovian conditioned approach behaviour')
- Elicit 'wanting' for the unconditioned reward ('Pavlovian instrumental transfer')
- Function as rewards themselves (as reinforcers, 'conditioned reinforcement').

Thus, the attribution of incentive salience makes both the conditioned cue (the cigarette packet) and the reward (the cigarette) more attractive and 'wanted'. The person is more likely to notice and approach such cues in their environment (such as cigarette packets in a sales display) and these cues also elicit 'wanting' for the reward (in this case either unconscious 'wanting' or conscious feelings of craving for a cigarette; Wyvell & Berridge, 2000; 2001).

The attribution of incentive salience to important environmental cues occurs in everyday life to a range of different types of cue. If you recall, in **Chapter 6** we saw how our attention is captured by stimuli that are relevant to our goals and needs. For example, most people will display an attentional bias for highly palatable foods, particularly when they are hungry (Tapper et al., 2010). Thus in everyday life the attribution of incentive salience to particular cues serves a useful function, drawing our attention toward potentially rewarding opportunities and motivating us to pursue them. However, drug use turns into drug addiction when the neural systems that attribute incentive salience become sensitised to specific drug-related cues. This means these cues trigger *excessive* incentive motivation that leads to compulsive drug seeking and using behaviour. This occurs because addictive substances enhance dopamine transmission and dopamine is the neurotransmitter responsible for the attribution of incentive salience. As the reward circuits in the brain become sensitised to the drug, cues relating to that drug elicit a greater dopamine response in the reward circuits, which in turn increases feelings of wanting or craving for the drug, but not necessarily feelings of pleasure upon obtaining it. These changes are long lasting and may even be permanent, which means that someone who has successfully quit a drug may still experience cravings even though they may no longer be physically dependent on it.

Importantly, incentive salience strength will depend not just on the strength of associations between the cue and the reward, but also on states that heighten dopamine reactivity in the reward circuits in the brain. This is because dopamine magnifies incentive salience attributed to environmental stimuli (Anselme, 2016; Berridge, 2012; Robinson & Berridge, 2013). This means that 'wanting' and craving may be intensified by stress, excitement, relevant physiological deprivation (such as nicotine deprivation in the case of cigarette craving) and drugs that increase dopamine transmission (for example, alcohol or cannabis may accentuate cravings for food or other drugs). Because rewards release dopamine in the brain too, this can also help explain why it may sometimes be difficult to stop at just one chocolate, one glass of wine or, for the user, one line of cocaine. Additionally, environmental cues exert some control over dopamine release so that incentive salience will be stronger in contexts in which the reward has previously been experienced, and much weaker in novel environments (Robinson & Berridge, 2008). For example, the sight of a cigarette packet is likely to elicit a stronger desire for a cigarette when seen in a context the person associates with smoking (such as their kitchen table) as opposed to a context in which they have never smoked (such as a lecture theatre). This is one reason why studying craving in the laboratory can be difficult, since it is an

CHAPTER 8

environment that is unlikely to be familiar for most people, let alone one in which they have previously indulged in their favourite food or drug.

Finally, research indicates that some people may sensitise more easily whilst others are more resistant. This helps account for the fact that some people can use drugs for long periods without becoming addicted whilst others may become addicted quite quickly. Genetic factors, gender, levels of specific sex hormones and the presence of stress-related psychopathologies (such as depression and post-traumatic stress disorder) all seem to contribute to an increased vulnerability to sensitisation (Becker et al., 2012; Franklin et al., 2011; Hutchison et al., 2008; Moeller et al., 2013).

Although incentive-sensitisation theory was originally proposed to account for drug addiction, more recently the authors have suggested that similar processes may underlie behavioural addictions, particularly among those who are susceptible to sensitisation-related brain changes, though the exact mechanisms are as yet unclear (Berridge & Robinson, 2016). In support of this view they refer to Parkinson's patients who receive dopamine-stimulating medications in order to compensate for low levels of dopamine. Around 15% of these patients develop what appear to be behavioural addictions to activities such as gambling, sex, or shopping (Callesen et al., 2013; O'Sullivan et al., 2009). This suggests that hyper-stimulation of dopamine-related systems in the brain is not just associated with drug craving but can also lead to compulsive motivations to engage in a diverse set of non-drug-related behaviours. These compulsive motivations tend to disappear once medication is stopped.

BOX 8.2 STRESS, CRAVING AND DOPAMINE

In **Chapter 3** we saw how those from lower socioeconomic groups tend to experience more stress, which may help account for the socioeconomic gradient in cardiovascular disease. An additional consequence of stress is that it can activate the dopamine system in the brain (Belujon & Grace, 2015) and so may increase attribution of incentive salience to environmental cues. In this way it may exacerbate cravings and increase the likelihood of relapse among those who have managed to quit addictive substances.

MAKING CONNECTIONS

The cognitive processing model

All the theories we have looked at so far emphasise the role of desire in drug use; addictive behaviours are thought to be motived by a desire to obtain a pleasurable state (positive reinforcement) or to avoid a negative one (negative reinforcement). In other words, there is an assumption that drug use is primarily driven by cravings and urges. This assumption was challenged by Tiffany who noted that drug use and relapse were not always preceded by urges or cravings (Tiffany, 1990; Tiffany & Carter, 1998; Tiffany & Conklin, 2000). For example, he cited research by Miller and Gold (1994) who surveyed over 300 individuals who had been treated in a drug rehabilitation programme. Only 7% of those who had relapsed since discharge selected craving (out of a list of nine possible reasons) as the primary cause.

In light of these and other similar findings, Tiffany suggested that the psychological processes underpinning drug use behaviour were not necessarily the same as those that elicited drug use urges and cravings and that compulsive drug use was not caused by cravings. Instead, he proposed that automatic processes may play a key role in drug use behaviour and developed the cognitive model of drug urges to account for these (Tiffany, 1990). This model later became known as the 'cognitive processing model' (Tiffany, 1999; Tiffany & Conklin, 2000). (Note that we discussed automatic processing in **Chapter 6** and you may find it helpful to go back and remind yourself of the key features of automatic versus controlled/conscious processing.)

The theory

According to the cognitive processing model, because of a history of repetition, both drug acquisition and drug use behaviours can become automatic. As a result, they are usually carried out in a fast and efficient manner, often with little awareness. They are also difficult to control. The model states that procedures for carrying out these automatic behaviours are stored in memory in the form of action schemata or action plans. These action plans contain all the necessary information for the initiation and coordination of complex sequences of drug use behaviour. Specifically they include:

- Representations of stimuli (or combinations of stimuli) that elicit particular behaviours (such as a morning alarm prompting a person to smoke).

- Representations of procedures for carrying out specific behaviours (such as lighting a cigarette).

- Information about the coordination of shorter actions into longer action sequences. (For example, to smoke a cigarette a person must join together a series of shorter actions: locating their packet of cigarettes, taking a cigarette from the packet, putting the cigarette in their mouth, locating a lighter, lighting the cigarette, inhaling and so on.)

- Alternative action sequences that may be initiated in the event of minor obstacles. (For example, if a person's lighter fails to light, they may shake it and try again.) These variations may be contained within the action plan and so also enacted automatically with little conscious awareness.

- Information relating to two types of physiological responses: responses that support specific parts of the action sequence (such as pupil dilation when lighting the end of a cigarette) and responses associated with drug tolerance that occur in anticipation of drug intake, in response to stimuli associated with intake (such as changes in heart rate).

Not all drug use behaviour will become automatic. As with habits (see **Chapter 6**), drug acquisition and consumption behaviours that are frequently repeated in the same context will be more likely to become automatic. This means we are more likely to see automaticity in relation to drugs that are legal and more readily available (such as cigarettes) compared to those that are illegal and more difficult to obtain (such as heroin). For example, if a person constantly needs to find new ways to obtain money to buy heroin, heroin acquisition is unlikely to ever become automatic. Likewise, if a person needs to plan where to inject their heroin in order to avoid discovery, consumption may also not be elicited automatically (though once consumption is initiated, subsequent behaviours may be performed automatically, see **Chapter 6** for the distinction between habitual initiation and habitual performance). Thus according to the cognitive processing model, drug acquisition and use will vary in the extent to which it is automatised, though it is likely that at least some components of drug consumption will come under the control of automatic action plans.

CHAPTER 8

In contrast to drug use behaviours, urges and cravings are thought to arise via non-automatic cognitive processing that occurs when something blocks the action plan. This may occur as a result of environmental conditions (such as the person running out of cigarettes) or because a person is actively employing conscious processing in an attempt to inhibit the action plan (for example if they are trying to quit smoking). According to the cognitive processing model, relapse among abstinent drug users occurs when their conscious processing is insufficient to inhibit the automatic execution of the drug use action plan. This may often coincide with drug use urges and cravings, but relapse may also occur in the absence of urges and cravings if the person fails to activate conscious processing. For example, if they encounter cues associated with drug use when their conscious attention is directed toward another task (they are distracted) the cues may automatically elicit drug use behaviour in the absence of any urges or cravings. In other words, they may relapse without even really being aware of it.

Tiffany (1990) suggests that stress and negative affect may make relapse more likely because they tend to engage conscious processing and so compete with the conscious processing needed to inhibit action plans. Similarly, Tiffany suggests that alcohol impairs conscious processing which helps explain why many abstinent smokers relapse when they have been drinking (in addition to the fact that alcohol is frequently associated with smoking and so may also automatically elicit smoking-related action plans).

Implications for intervention

The cognitive processing model offers an interesting perspective. According to the model, it is automatic processing that is at the heart of addiction rather than operant conditioning (positive reinforcement and/or negative reinforcement). This contrasts with most other theories (and, indeed, the DSM-5) that emphasise the importance of craving and conscious motivational processes. According to the cognitive processing model, craving is something that occurs when action plans have been blocked, not something that is causally related to behaviour. This means that medications aimed at reducing cravings (such as nicotine patches) will be ineffective. Instead, treatment should be aimed at either reducing exposure to cues that elicit action plans (which may be difficult to achieve on a permanent basis) or trying to protect or enhance the conscious processing resources that are required to inhibit action plans. For example, this may include stress reduction or training designed to enhance cognitive capacity. There is some overlap between Tiffany's notion of conscious processing resources and theories of willpower (**Chapter 7**).

PRIME theory of motivation

Unlike the theories we have looked at so far, PRIME theory was developed as a general theory of motivation, rather than a specific theory of addiction (West & Brown, 2013). In other words, although it has primarily been used in the context of addiction, it was developed in order to explain all aspects of behaviour and behaviour change. It was also developed in response to what the authors saw as a problem within the field of addiction research: that there is a plethora of theories but each only manages to account for just one aspect of addiction rather than being able to explain the whole phenomenon. For example, the self-medication model can explain why some people with histories of trauma or psychopathology become addicted to drugs but it cannot explain why others with similar histories do not, or why those who are not suffering from distress may use drugs. Likewise, incentive-sensitisation theory can account for the strong feelings of craving experienced by former drug users but cannot explain why some people decide to quit and others do not. PRIME theory was born out of dissatisfaction with the traditional model of theory development within psychology (see **Box 8.3**). It emphasises explanatory power over specificity of predictions (see **Chapter 5**) and attempts to provide a comprehensive account of the wide range of different factors and processes that influence our behaviour. It does this by drawing on a range of existing theories and explaining how the different constructs interact with one another, with a view to being able to also incorporate new theories and evidence as they emerge. As such, PRIME theory may be best viewed as a conceptual framework or very broad, high level theory.

BOX 8.3 THE PROBLEM WITH TRADITIONAL THEORY DEVELOPMENT AND TESTING IN PSYCHOLOGY

DIG A LITTLE DEEPER

According to West and Brown (2013), rather than aiming for a comprehensive account of a particular phenomenon, theories in psychology are often developed in order to draw attention to particular ideas or increase our understanding of the role of quite specific factors. Whilst this may be a worthwhile aim, they argue that it may also impede scientific progress because these theories tend to be developed without reference to existing theories in the field or to what is commonly known about the field (what West and Brown call the 'big observations', see below). This approach to theory development leads to the existence of a large number of theories that each account for some, but not all, of the important observations. For example, in **Chapter 5** we evaluated a number of different theories against a range of criteria and found that many of the theories lacked explanatory power. In other words, they were unable to explain some of the important observations in the field. Or they had weak generalisability, only being able to account for behaviour in very specific contexts or among specific populations.

This problem is exacerbated by the fact that it can be difficult to refute theories. This occurs for a number of reasons:

- As highlighted in **Chapter 5**, many theories do not specify constructs with sufficient precision to allow them to be measured, which in turn makes it difficult for the theory to be falsified.

- Even where a construct can be measured, measurement may not be sufficiently precise or reliable to allow one to be confident the theory has been disproved; the author of the study may be more likely to put their results down to measurement error rather than theory error.

- Even where we can reliably and precisely measure a particular construct or outcome, the type of statistics traditionally employed in psychology (null hypothesis significance testing) makes it difficult to conclude that there is an absence of effect (see **Chapter 11**). Again, this makes it more difficult to refute a prediction made by a particular theory.

As a result of these factors, theories tend not to be disproved and discarded but instead simply fall in or out of fashion. And rather than replacing theories with better, more comprehensive theories, we instead see an increasing number of different theories, each with its own particular strengths and weaknesses, each viewing the phenomenon from a slightly different perspective.

The existence of a large number of theories all purporting to explain the same phenomenon is particularly problematic when it comes to developing interventions. As we shall see in **Chapter 9**, interventions should ideally be based on theory. But faced with dozens of different theories, which do you choose? More often than not you may simply end up picking the theory you are most familiar with or the one you find most appealing. If there were just one theory that reflected our current best understanding, the choice would be easier and the intervention might be more successful. In **Chapter 9** we look at a more systematic approach to theory selection when developing behaviour change interventions.

Aims

PRIME theory aims to account for all the 'big observations' in the field of addiction (see **Box 8.3**). Brown and West (2013) identify these big observations as follows:

- Some drugs and activities are more addictive than others.
- Addiction takes repeated exposures to develop but then tends to remain at a stable level with further exposure.
- Some individuals and groups are more susceptible to addiction than others.
- Many people suffering from an addiction are able to spontaneously stop engaging in the relevant behaviour, but few are able to remain abstinent on a permanent basis.
- Withdrawal symptoms tend not to be strongly related to relapse.
- Certain situations increase the likelihood of relapse.
- Certain types of interventions and treatments for addiction are more successful than others.
- Different addictive drugs show different types of consumption patterns among the general population (for example, alcohol is widely used, heroin is not).
- Different addictive drugs show different temporal patterns of use (for example, alcohol tends to be consumed during leisure hours whilst smoking may occur at regular intervals throughout the day).

The theory

As noted above, PRIME theory emphasises explanatory power and aims to account for these observations by integrating a range of different theories. It states that at any given moment our behaviour is driven by our strongest wants and needs. Wants refer to anticipated pleasure or satisfaction whilst needs refer to relief from mental or physical discomfort. The strength of our wants and needs is in turn determined by a number of interacting subsystems that correspond to the PRIME acronym:

- *P: plans* (conscious intentions)
- *R: responses* (behaviour, comprising starting, stopping or modifying actions)
- *I: impulses/inhibitory forces* (motivational forces that compel a person to behave in a particular way, consciously experienced as urges or cravings)

- *M: motives* (mental representations with associated feelings of attraction or revulsion, consciously experienced as desires)
- *E: evaluations* (beliefs about what is good or bad).

Figure 8.2 shows how these subsystems interact with one another and with the external and internal environments in order to influence behaviour ('responses'). The external environment can have a direct influence on all five subsystems as well as the internal environment. The internal environment can also directly influence, and be influenced by, all of the subsystems. Important aspects of the internal environment include:

- *Drives* – biological needs, such as the need to eat or drink.
- *Emotional states* – including generalised emotions, such as feelings of happiness and sadness, as well as targeted emotions, such as liking and disliking.
- *Arousal* – for example whether we are tired or alert.

Both drives and emotional states are influenced by, and can influence, level of arousal.

To explain behaviour (the response subsystem), we need to refer to the other four subsystems as well as the internal and external environment. Although the acronym is 'PRIME', it can also be helpful to order these four non-behavioural subsystems from least to most complex; impulses, motives, evaluations then plans (see **Figure 8.2**).

Figure 8.2 The motivational system according to PRIME theory. The external environment, the internal environment and impulses/inhibitory forces directly influence our behaviour whilst plans, evaluations and motives have an indirect influence

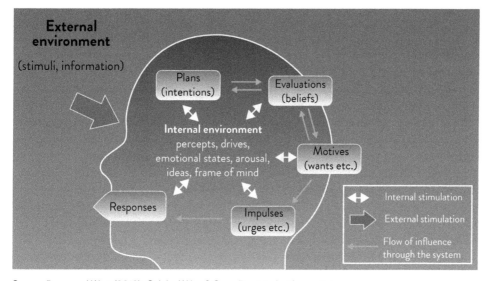

Source: Brown and West (2013). © John Wiley & Sons. Reprinted with permission.

According to PRIME theory, our behaviour is directly influenced by our internal and external environments and by our impulses. At the simplest level this involves reflexes; if someone squirts water in your face (an external stimulus) you will react with an involuntary blink (a response) to protect your eyes. Impulses/inhibitory forces are slightly more complex and may be influenced by a combination of internal and external stimuli as well as motives. For example, a drive (an internal stimulus) is influenced both by internal physiological stimuli and by external stimuli that draw attention toward or away from these internal stimuli. To illustrate, food deprivation will lead to a drive to eat (an internal stimulus), which may be amplified upon smelling good food (an external stimulus) or supressed when juggling a hectic schedule of meetings (external stimuli). Drives can lead to impulses (an inclination to act in a particular way) but, consistent with the cognitive processing model (see page 226), we only become aware of an impulse when it is not immediately translated into action, at which point it is experienced as an urge.

BOX 8.4 CRAVING IN THEORIES OF ADDICTION

MAKING CONNECTIONS

In **Chapter 7** we looked at several different theories of craving. Since craving is also central to addiction, the theories described in this chapter can help extend our understanding of craving. For example, according to opponent process theory craving occurs alongside withdrawal symptoms as part of the b-process. According to incentive-sensitisation theory craving is underpinned by dopamine systems in the brain. PRIME theory asserts that cravings are consciously experienced urges that directly influence behaviour. By contrast, the cognitive processing model states that cravings only emerge when an automatic action plan is interrupted and that they have no influence on behaviour.

Our behaviour may also be influenced by plans, evaluations and motives, but only indirectly, via impulses/inhibitory forces or via our internal environment. For example, a desire (motive) to avoid a fine may lead to an inhibitory force that prevents a person from lighting up a cigarette in a smoke-free zone. However, a state of nicotine deprivation may lead to a drive that may in turn generate a competing impulse to smoke. The resulting behaviour (smoking or not smoking) will be determined by whichever is stronger, the impulse to smoke, generated from the drive (that occurs as a result of nicotine deprivation), or the inhibitory force generated from the desire (motive) to avoid a fine. A motive may also influence impulses via the internal environment. For example, the prospect of a fine may create a feeling of anxiety (an internal event) that generates an inhibitory force that prevents smoking. Similarly, the internal environment may influence motives: feelings of nicotine deprivation and anxiety about a fine may result in conflicting desires (motives) about smoking or not smoking. When there are competing motives, the motive with the stronger valence will succeed in generating an impulse or inhibitory force.

Evaluations refer to our beliefs about what is good and bad. They influence behaviour via motives. They can also influence motives via the creation of emotional states (part of the internal environment). For example, if one believes that smoking is bad for health this may lead to a desire (motive) to avoid smoking. This belief may also lead to feelings of anxiety about one's health. These feelings (internal environment) may generate an additional desire (motive) to abstain from smoking. Like motives, it is possible for competing evaluations to co-exist. For example, a person may believe that smoking is bad for health but also that it reduces anxiety. This type of conflict (called cognitive dissonance, see page 117) is aversive and the individual will try to resolve it by supressing or changing particular beliefs. If a belief can be changed without creating new conflicts this is usually the preferred solution. If not, belief suppression may occur.

Finally, planning is the most complex subsystem and refers to our conscious intentions to behave in a particular way. Plans involve a mental representation of the relevant action or actions, a representation of the starting conditions, and a feeling of commitment toward carrying out the action or actions. Plans may be made in relation to behaviours that are carried out immediately, or in the more distant future. For a plan to influence behaviour it needs to be recalled at the appropriate moment in order for it then to generate a motive. Once this motive has been generated it will combine or compete with other motives to influence impulses and inhibitory forces. However, plans can also influence behaviour by influencing the internal environment. For example, a plan to lose weight that is made public to others may generate anxiety about public failure if it is not kept. These feelings of anxiety may then generate inhibitory forces when one encounters chocolate, chips and other high-calorie foods.

Thus impulses/inhibitory forces, motives, evaluations and plans represent increasingly complex subsystems that allow for increasing levels of flexibility in terms of behavioural control. However, this increased complexity is accompanied by less direct links to behaviour; for evaluations and plans to influence behaviour they need to generate motives that are stronger than competing motives generated from other sources. This means it is easier, and more likely, for our behaviour to be influenced by our motives and impulses than by our plans and evaluations.

(Note that the above is a very brief overview of some of the key features of PRIME theory; readers are directed to West and Brown, 2013, for a more detailed description.)

BOX 8.5 PRIME THEORY AND DUAL-PROCESSING MODELS

MAKING CONNECTIONS

In **Chapter 6** we discussed dual-processing accounts of cognition that state that we have two distinct ways of processing information: via a fast, automatic, unconscious system or via a conscious, reflective system that is slower and more deliberative. In keeping with these accounts, PRIME theory distinguishes between automatic and reflective processes. For example, the influence of external stimuli (such as information) on beliefs would be considered reflective whilst the influence of internal stimuli and impulses/inhibitory forces on behaviour would be considered automatic. However, whilst dual-processing accounts state that there are two independent systems directly influencing behaviour, PRIME theory holds that reflective processes can only influence behaviour *via* automatic processes (in other words, via the internal environment or via impulses/inhibitory forces).

Implications for understanding and treating addiction

So how can PRIME theory help us understand addiction? And what are the implications for intervention? According to PRIME theory, addiction occurs because of abnormalities in the motivational system. Importantly, addiction can occur as a result of different kinds of abnormalities. In other words, it does not have one single underlying cause or set of causes.

These abnormalities can be seen as falling into one of three main types:

1. Abnormalities in the person's social or physical environment that lead to strong pressures to engage in the activity. For example, smoking may be viewed as 'normal'

or 'cool' or as a means of coping with stressful living or working conditions. Such factors broadly correspond to the type of literature we looked at in **Chapter 3** on the social determinants of health.

2. Abnormalities in the motivational system of the person that mean they are more susceptible to addiction. For example, they may have very high sensitivity to reward or an avoidant coping style. These factors broadly correspond to the type of literature we looked at in **Chapter 4** on the individual determinants of health. They will also influence, and be influenced by, the person's social or physical environment.

3. Abnormalities in the motivational system that arise because of the addictive behaviour, such as those described in incentive-sensitisation theory, earlier in this chapter.

We can also see how other theories of addiction place more or less emphasis on these different types of abnormality. For example, the self-medication model focuses on individual abnormalities, though with these being at least partly determined by the person's upbringing, in other words, their social environment. On the other hand, opponent process theory and incentive-sensitisation theory are more concerned with abnormalities that arise as a result of the addictive behaviour. PRIME theory states that addiction may be underpinned by any of these abnormalities, or any combination of them, and it draws on different theories of addiction to explain abnormalities in specific parts of the motivational system.

Thus, according to PRIME theory, addiction may actually be best viewed as a symptom rather than a single, unitary disorder, since it can occur as a result of a range of different underlying abnormalities. As such, no single intervention or treatment is going to be effective for all instances of addiction. Instead, treatments and interventions should be tailored to the underlying causes. A parallel may be drawn here with medicine where different medical conditions may have similar symptoms; although a doctor may prescribe something to alleviate the symptoms best practice would be to attempt to identify and treat the underlying disease. Indeed, as noted above, a common criticism of the DSM-5 is that it organises mental disorders according to symptoms rather than causes.

In terms of intervention, PRIME theory states that all interventions must, ultimately, translate into either reduced impulses to engage in the target activity or increased inhibitory forces to abstain from it. Educational interventions that target rational, cognitive processes (such as those emphasised in some of the social cognition models described in **Chapter 5**) will only be successful where these translate into motives or emotions that can influence the impulse/inhibitory force subsystem. Thus they represent weaker interventions than those that more directly target emotions and desires. PRIME theory also states that motivation is best viewed as a highly responsive system that balances inputs from a large number of different sources, rather than a series of discrete stages that people move through. As such, according to PRIME theory, the most successful interventions will simultaneously target as many different relevant factors as possible rather than attempt to match interventions to hypothetical stages as recommended by stage models of behaviour change (see **Chapter 5**) – whilst tailoring an intervention in relation to the underlying abnormalities might be considered helpful, tailoring according to 'stage' would not.

CONCLUSIONS

Amy Winehouse achieved enormous success in her professional life but still suffered from devastating addictions. Whilst this type of severe addiction might typically be treated by a clinical psychologist, health psychologists play a central role in relation to both nicotine and alcohol (see **Chapter 12**). Given these are both highly addictive, a good understanding of the psychology of addiction is essential.

However, as we've seen in this chapter, the concept of addiction is not clear cut. Its definition is widely debated and relevant theory points to a range of different underlying mechanisms that seem to make addiction both more or less likely as well as more or less severe. One can also argue that we should be viewing addiction as a symptom, rather than a disease in its own right, and focus our energies on identifying and treating the underlying problems that are most relevant in each particular situation.

Should addictive drugs be legalised? How might legalisation impact upon use, addiction and population health? What legislation or policies would you put in place to accompany legalisation? Would you legalise some substances but not others? If so, on what basis? Should cigarettes and alcohol be made illegal? What might be the potential benefits and costs of such changes? Which groups in society would have most to gain or lose? Would there be a widening in health inequalities or a reduction?

THE GREAT DEBATE

PART 3

BEHAVIOUR CHANGE IN PRACTICE

DEVELOPING BEHAVIOUR CHANGE INTERVENTIONS

Chapter Outline

Intervention Development

Evaluation Frameworks

Conclusions

Illicit drugs are often smuggled into prisons and used by inmates. This is a concern because shared needles can lead to the spread of infectious diseases such as HIV and hepatitis C. A person who leaves prison addicted to drugs may also be more likely to engage in theft and violent crime and less likely to be able to hold down a job. As such, it's in society's best interests to try to limit drug use in prisons. One obvious solution to this problem is to employ random mandatory drug testing with sanctions for those who test positive, such as loss of prison earnings or extra days added to a sentence. This approach is used around the world today, in order to help encourage those suffering from an addiction to engage in rehabilitation programmes and to deter others from taking up drugs whilst in prison.

Image 9.1 *Drug use can be a problem in prisons but mandatory testing may lead inmates to switch to harder drugs such as heroin.*
Credit: Paweł Czerwiński.

However, not all 'obvious solutions' turn out as expected. Research in England and Wales suggests that the introduction of mandatory drug testing may actually increase the use of harder drugs such as heroin (Gore et al., 1996). Why? Probably because some prisoners switch from cannabis to heroin because there is less chance of it being picked up by testing; cannabis can be detected in urine for up to three weeks after use whilst opiates can typically only be detected for two or three days.

This example highlights the risks associated with simply opting for what looks like an obvious solution to a social problem. Well-meaning interventions can have unintended outcomes that may mean the intervention does more harm than good. This in turn emphasises the importance of rigorously evaluating interventions to determine whether or not they are working as intended. It also draws attention to the need to use existing theory and evidence to develop interventions that have the best chance of bringing about positive change. Additionally, the fact that drug testing in prisons was rolled out across England and Wales, despite the worrying data, shows that science is not the only factor that influences government decisions on health and social policy. We look at issues relating to intervention evaluation and use in **Chapters 10 and 11**. In this chapter we focus on intervention development. In particular we will:

- Discuss different approaches to intervention development.

- Consider the advantages and disadvantages of these different approaches.

- Look at some of the ways in which evaluation can be integrated into the development process.

INTERVENTION DEVELOPMENT

Most real-world interventions that target behaviour are likely to be 'complex' interventions. This contrasts with medical interventions that are more likely to be considered 'simple'. An intervention may be described as complex for any of the following reasons:

- It has a number of interacting components.

- It aims to change more than one behaviour, or the behaviour that needs to change is difficult to change.

- It targets more than one group or more than one level within an organisation.

- There are a number of different key outcomes.

- It has a degree of flexibility that allows for some tailoring for different individuals or groups or for different settings or contexts.

There are no clear distinctions between simple and complex interventions, and interventions will vary in the extent to which they are considered complex, with some clearly being more complex than others.

Craig et al. (2008) describe the main steps in the development and evaluation of a complex intervention as follows:

1. Intervention development

   » Identification and/or development of underpinning theory or theories

   » Examination of the evidence base for similar interventions (this may include a **systematic review**)

> **Systematic review** – a type of literature review that uses objective, transparent methods to try to provide a complete and unbiased summary of all the evidence relating to a particular research question. Systematic reviews should adhere to the PRISMA (Preferred Reporting of Items for Systematic Reviews and Meta-Analyses) guidelines.

» Identification of key processes and outcomes (such as the expected relationships between intervention components, mediators, moderators and outcomes).

2. Feasibility testing

   » Testing of procedures

   » Estimation of participant recruitment and attrition

   » Calculation of the sample size needed for a full evaluation.

3. Evaluation

   » Assessment of effectiveness

   » Assessment of processes of change

   » Assessment of cost-effectiveness.

4. **Implementation**

   » Dissemination

   » Monitoring

   » Conduct of long-term follow-ups.

> **Implementation** – the adaption and use of evidence-based interventions in real-world settings in order to improve population health.

Although these steps are, to a certain extent, followed in a linear fashion, there may also be substantial cycling back to earlier stages. In particular, both the feasibility and evaluation stages may bring to light issues that make it necessary to move back a stage, for example to look for a more appropriate theory or to pilot a modified intervention. Likewise, even after a successful intervention has been rolled out, changing circumstances can mean it becomes out of date and loses efficacy. As such it may be necessary to return to the start of the process in order to develop a new or modified intervention. Thus the process of intervention development and evaluation is best viewed as iterative rather than linear.

As noted above, the development phase involves identifying (or developing) relevant theory. However, this may be easier said than done. In **Chapter 5** we reviewed a number of different social cognition theories, all relevant to health behaviour change, in **Chapter 6** we went on to look at theories relating to automatic processes whilst in **Chapters 7 and 8** we considered yet more theories, this time concerned with craving, willpower, self-regulation and addiction. Out of the myriad theories available (which far exceed those covered in this book), how should you go about selecting the best one for your intervention?

There are a number of different frameworks available to support this process, including the Behaviour Change Wheel, Intervention Mapping and MINDSPACE (of which the latter could be considered an intervention in its own right, aimed at changing the behaviour of those developing and implementing government policy). We will look at each of these in turn. We will also consider three other approaches; developing an intervention directly from a specific theory or theories, adapting an existing intervention and developing an intervention based on practical expertise.

The Behaviour Change Wheel (BCW)

The Behaviour Change Wheel (BCW) (Michie et al., 2011, 2014) is arguably one of the most comprehensive approaches to intervention development as it draws on extensive taxonomies of both theoretical constructs and behaviour change techniques, and provides step-by-step guidance on how to use these to develop an intervention. It identifies three main stages to the process: (a) understand the behaviour, (b) identify the intervention possibilities, and (c) decide on the intervention content and mode of delivery. Within these three stages are eight separate steps as follows:

(a) Understand the behaviour

   1. Define the issue in behavioural terms

   2. Select the target behaviour or behaviours

   3. Specify the target behaviour or behaviours in more detail

   4. Identify what needs to change in the person or their environment, using the COM-B model and, potentially, the Theoretical Domains Framework (TDF)

(b) Identify the intervention possibilities

   5. Identify intervention functions, potentially using the APEASE criteria

   6. Identify policy categories, potentially using the APEASE criteria

(c) Decide on the intervention content and mode of delivery

   7. Select behaviour change techniques using the BCT taxonomy and, potentially, the APEASE criteria.

   8. Decide on the mode of delivery, potentially using the APEASE criteria.

We will consider each of these steps in turn.

Step 1. Define the issue in behavioural terms

The first step to developing a behaviour change intervention is to identify the behaviour you want to change. This may sound obvious but it is easy to fall into the trap of thinking of an intervention in terms of non-behavioural outcomes and forget to identify the behaviours needed to reach these outcomes. For example, you may be interested in developing an intervention to promote weight loss. However, whilst weight loss may be your key outcome measure, it is not a behaviour. Rather, it is the result of a number of other possible behaviours such as cutting out high-calorie snacks, reducing serving sizes and/or increasing exercise. Thus it is important to identify which behaviour, or set of behaviours, the intervention is going to try to change.

Step 2. Select the target behaviour or behaviours

As described above, a desired outcome may involve a number of different behaviours and it is important to decide which of these the intervention is going to target. Additionally, further thought may lead to the identification of yet more behaviours that could be targeted. For example, imagine you decide to try to get people to swap high-calorie snacks for fruit as part of an intervention aimed at weight loss. This sounds straightforward but may actually depend on other behaviours. Suppose a person usually has a mid-morning snack at work. If they bring it in from home, they would need to have fruit available at home, which brings in another behaviour – whoever does the grocery shopping for the household would need to ensure they bought sufficient fruit. Alternatively the person may usually buy their mid-morning snack from a worksite cafeteria or vending machine. In this case the behaviour is dependent on fruit being available at these places or the person changing where they usually go to buy their mid-morning snack. Although one might not want to explicitly target all these behaviours, identifying them helps ensure the most promising behaviours are selected.

   The selection of the target behaviour or behaviours should be informed by:

- *The potential impact of changing the behaviour.* For example, limiting consumption of high-calorie foods may result in substantial reductions in calorie intake and so be likely to promote weight loss. However, taking the stairs rather than the lift at work may result in very little additional energy expenditure so may be less important to target.

CHAPTER 9

- *The extent to which it may be possible to change this behaviour.* For example, if a worksite cafeteria does not sell fruit, and there are no other alternative venues for lunch, it may be difficult to get someone to start eating fruit at lunchtime.

- *The extent to which changing the behaviour may bring about changes to other important behaviours.* For example, asking someone who never buys fruit to eat a piece of fruit at breakfast could lead them to start buying fruit and eating it at other times of the day as well. They may also start replacing some high-calorie snacks and desserts with fruit. On the other hand, asking someone to simply cut out their mid-morning high-calorie snack may result in them being extra hungry at lunchtime which in turn could lead them to consume more total daily calories than had they eaten their mid-morning snack. (See also spillover and spillunder effects; Galizzi & Whitmarsh, 2019; Krpan et al., 2019.)

Step 3. Specify the target behaviour or behaviours in more detail

The details to consider include:

- *Who* will be performing the behaviour

- *What* they will be doing

- *When* they will be doing it

- *Where* they will be doing it

- *How often* they will be doing it

- *With whom* they will be doing it.

Specifying the behaviour(s) in more detail can influence Step 2, the selection of the target behaviour(s) (see above). It can also help clarify later steps.

Step 4. Identify what needs to change in the person or their environment

This is where theory comes in. Theory is used to identify the mechanisms you are going to target in order to bring about the behavioural change. Whilst it might be tempting to skip this step and move directly onto the intervention itself, as discussed in **Chapter 5**, theory is important for understanding behaviour, and understanding behaviour is important for the development of behaviour change interventions. Specifically, behaviour change interventions should be underpinned by theory because:

- The intervention is likely to be more effective (Glanz & Bishop, 2010; Noar et al., 2007; Prestwich et al., 2014; Taylor et al., 2012; Webb et al., 2010). Using theory can improve intervention effectiveness by helping to identify:

  » the behaviour change strategies most likely to be effective

  » the type of individuals the intervention should target

  » the ways in which the intervention may be tailored to particular individuals.

  Having said that, evidence is not always consistent and the relationship between theory use and intervention success will also depend on the strength of the underlying theory, whether the most appropriate theory has been selected, and the extent to which the theory has genuinely informed the intervention (Davis et al., 2015; Michie & Prestwich, 2010; Prestwich et al., 2014).

- If the intervention is not successful it will be easier to identify the reasons for lack of success and to address these reasons in subsequent interventions.

- It will be easier to successfully adapt the intervention to other behaviours, contexts and populations.

The Behaviour Change Wheel incorporates theory into the process of intervention development through the use of the COM-B model (Michie et al., 2011) and with the additional optional component of the Theoretical Domains Framework (TDF) (Cane et al., 2012). The COM-B model uses broad constructs to identify areas that need to change in order to change the target behaviour. For closer links to theory, the COM-B model can also be used to help identify the type of theory or theories that may be relevant. The TDF identifies relevant theoretical constructs that are more specific than those used in the COM-B. Again, these constructs can then either be used directly to help determine the content of the intervention (as per Step 5) or they can be used to help identify relevant theory that can then be used to help guide intervention development.

The COM-B model

COM-B stands for capability, opportunity, motivation, behaviour. According to the model, a behaviour will not occur unless all of the first three elements are present. Each of these elements can also be further sub-divided into two types as follows:

- Capability – the person must be able to perform the behaviour
    - i. Physical capability – they must have the physical skill, strength or stamina.
    - ii. Psychological capability – they must have the relevant knowledge or psychological skills, strength or stamina.
- Opportunity – there must be the opportunity to perform the behaviour
    - i. Physical opportunity – there should be the necessary time and resources as well as an accessible location. Aspects of the physical environment may also facilitate or cue the behaviour.
    - ii. Social opportunity – the behaviour should be socially acceptable. Aspects of the social environment may also facilitate or cue the behaviour.
- Motivation – the person should be motivated to perform the behaviour
    - i. Reflective motivation – refers to motivation that involves plans and evaluations. (Plans and evaluations are defined in PRIME theory in **Chapter 8**. The theories in **Chapter 5** tend to draw on reflective motivation.)
    - ii. Automatic motivation – refers to motivation that involves automatic processes such as emotional reactions, desires, impulses, inhibitions, drive states and reflex responses. (These relate to the impulses, inhibitory forces, motives, drives and emotional states referred to in PRIME theory. The theories in **Chapter 6** tend to harness automatic motivation.)

These three elements interact with one another, and with behaviour, as shown in **Figure 9.1**. For example, if a person learns how to ride a bicycle, this may increase their motivation to cycle rather than drive to work. If a new employee cycle scheme makes it possible for that person to purchase a bicycle, this may also increase their motivation to cycle to work. However, regardless of how much a person may want to cycle to work, this will not happen unless they are capable of riding a bicycle and have access to a bicycle; motivation can only influence capability and opportunity via behaviour (that is, learning to ride a bicycle and purchasing a bicycle). Importantly, as noted above, for the behaviour to occur (cycling to work) there needs to be the capability (being able to cycle), the motivation

Figure 9.1 The COM-B model. For a behaviour to occur there must be the capability, opportunity and motivation.

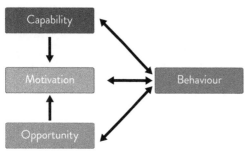

Source: Michie et al., 2011. Reproduced with permission from Springer Nature.

(wanting to cycle) and the opportunity (having access to a bicycle and suitable cycle path). If one of these elements is missing, the behaviour will not occur.

As mentioned above, the COM-B model is used to help identify the elements that need to be modified in order for a particular behaviour to change. For example, an organisation trying to encourage employees to cycle to work could use the COM-B model to identify what needs to change and then develop an appropriate intervention. So it may be that employees would like to cycle to work (they are motivated) but do not have access to a bicycle or a secure place to store it during the day (opportunity). Thus an intervention that builds new employee bicycle shelters and subsidises the cost of buying a bicycle may be effective at changing behaviour. Alternatively it may be that most employees lack confidence about cycling through busy city traffic (capability) in which case city cycling training sessions may be helpful. Or, if employees lack motivation rather than opportunity or capability, the organisation may want to focus on strategies aimed at increasing motivation, such as promotional material highlighting the pleasures and benefits of cycling. Identifying areas that need to change may require some research. For example, employees could be asked to take part in interviews or focus groups or to complete questionnaires. An example of the sort of questionnaire that could be used is shown in **Box 9.1**. Further guidance on conducting this type of behavioural analysis can be found in Michie et al. (2014). Additionally, **Box 9.2** provides another example of the way in which the COM-B model has been applied in practice.

BOX 9.1 WHY DON'T YOU DO MORE EXERCISE?

The COM-B-Qv1 (Michie et al., 2014), or a variation of this questionnaire, can be used where people have insight into, and are willing to share, their reasons for the relevant **TAKE THE TEST** behaviour. In this example the questionnaire has been adapted for use in relation to 'doing more exercise'. However, bearing in mind the importance of specifying target behaviours in detail (page 242) you might like to think about a more specific type of exercise relevant to you, such as walking to work, starting an evening exercise class, or playing a sport at the weekends. Alternatively you could consider these questions in relation to a completely different behaviour, such as having an alcohol-free day, eating less meat or using a reusable water bottle instead of buying plastic ones. The questionnaire is as follows:

What do you think it would take for you to do more exercise? (Circle any of the items on the list that you think apply; you can circle as many or as few as you think appropriate. Some of the items may look strange but that is just because we need to include anything that might possibly apply to some people.)

For each item you circle please also say why you think it might be important for you. (Examples have been provided.)

For me to do more exercise, I would have to...

Capability		
	Item	*Example*
1.	...know more about why it was important.	Have a better understanding of the benefits of doing more exercise.
2.	...know more about how to do it.	Have a better understanding of effective ways of doing more exercise.
3.	...have better physical skills.	Learn how to perform a particular type of exercise or take part in a particular type of sport.
4.	...have better mental skills.	Learn strategies for overcoming obstacles to exercising.
5.	...have more physical strength.	Build up more muscles for exercise.
6.	...have more mental strength.	Get better at resisting the temptation not to exercise.
7.	...overcome physical limitations.	Find safe ways of exercising with a health condition or injury.
8.	...overcome mental obstacles.	Find ways of addressing anxiety about exercising.
9.	...have more physical stamina.	Be able to keep up with an exercise class.
10.	...have more mental stamina.	Be able to sustain effort during an exercise class.
Opportunity		
	Item	*Example*
11.	...have more time to do it.	Create dedicated time during the day to exercise.
12.	...have more money.	Be given or earn funds to pay for exercise classes.
13.	...have the necessary materials.	Be given or purchase exercise-related clothing or equipment.
14.	...have it more easily accessible.	Have easier access to exercise facilities.
15.	...have more people around me doing it.	Be part of a 'crowd' who are exercising.
16.	...have more triggers to prompt me.	Have more reminders to exercise at strategic times.
17.	...have more support from others.	Have family or friends encouraging me to exercise more.
Motivation		
	Item	*Example*
18.	...feel that I want to do it enough.	Feel more of a sense of pleasure or satisfaction from exercising.
19.	...feel that I need to do it enough.	Care more about the negative consequences of not exercising.
20.	...believe that it would be a good thing to do.	Have a stronger sense that I should be exercising more.
21.	...develop better plans for doing it.	Have clearer and better developed plans for doing more exercise.
22.	...develop a habit of doing it.	Get into a pattern of exercising without thinking about it.
Other		
	Item	
23.	Something else (please specify).	

Reproduced from Michie et al. (2014) with the permission of the authors.

By looking at the items you circled on this questionnaire it should be possible to identify what would need to change in order for you to do more exercise (assuming you have accurate insight into the reasons for your behaviour). For example, it may be that you are sufficiently motivated and capable but lack opportunity. Or perhaps you have sufficient opportunities to exercise but lack motivation and capability.

CHAPTER 9

BOX 9.2 HOW CAN GOVERNMENTS REDUCE COMMUNITY DISEASE TRANSMISSION? APPLYING COM-B TO COVID-19

HOT TOPIC

During the COVID-19 pandemic, governments around the world have used a range of different strategies to try to reduce community disease transmission. These have had varying degrees of success. Where might they have got things right and wrong? And what does the science of behaviour change tell us about the types of strategies that are likely to be effective?

Once we've identified the specific behaviours that need to change (as per steps 1 to 3 of the Behaviour Change Wheel) we can use the COM-B model to identify the types of behavioural determinants we may want to target. More specifically, for each behaviour we want to change, we need to consider whether people have the necessary capability, opportunity and motivation, and to target intervention efforts where these may be lacking (see West et al., 2020 for a comprehensive analysis). The COM-B model can also point us in the direction of relevant theory.

For example, it may be that people are already motivated to wash their hands after using public transport, and that they have the opportunity to do this (in terms of access to handwashing facilities and/or hand sanitising gel). However, they also need to know how to wash their hands effectively to ensure they are completely clean and which types of hand sanitising gels are effective. In other words, capability will be important. As such, educational campaigns providing information may be helpful.

Most adults are likely to know how to use a tissue when coughing or sneezing (capability). However, if they do not have a tissue to hand, they will lack the opportunity. To address this, they will need to remember to carry tissues with them when they go out. Being able to remember something relates to capability – being able to convert intentions into actions. Strategies such as implementation intentions and point-of-decision prompts may be helpful (**Chapter 6**). For example, a box of tissues could be placed next to the house keys.

In some cases, people may lack the opportunity to socially distance, depending on their living and working environments (**Chapter 3**). In particular, it may be more difficult for those from lower socioeconomic backgrounds to socially distance even where they have both the skills (capability) and motivation. Opening up more green spaces (such as golf courses and school playing fields) could provide more opportunities for people to stay socially distanced whilst exercising and engaging in leisure activities.

Avoiding touching the face may be difficult because of a lack of capability. We tend to touch our faces automatically so although a person may want to avoid touching their face, they may struggle to do so. Here we could draw on habit theory (**Chapter 6**) to think about providing people with effective strategies for breaking habits, such as counter-conditioning (engaging in a behaviour that is incompatible with the habit). For example, people could be encouraged to hold items (such as small coins) in each hand whilst out in public, to make it more difficult for them to touch their face.

For all the above behaviours, motivation will be important. However, COM-B distinguishes between reflective motivation and automatic motivation, whilst PRIME theory (**Chapter 8**) suggests that automatic motivation will have a stronger influence on behaviour than reflective motivation. So whilst communications emphasising the rational arguments for engaging in these behaviours may be an effective way of influencing reflective motivation, it will also be important to target automatic motivation. This could be achieved via communications that elicit particular emotions (for example drawing on protection motivation theory, **Chapter 5**, or evaluative conditioning, **Chapter 6**) as well as the use of strategies designed to build habits (**Chapter 6**).

Additionally, it will be important to think about the most effective ways of delivering these interventions to ensure they reach as wide an audience as possible (see Step 8 of the Behaviour Change Wheel). Where certain groups or communities are considered more at risk (either of disease transmission or from the disease itself) a more targeted approach could be employed.

Once this type of behavioural analysis has been completed one can either move on to Step 5 or, for closer links to theory, one can employ the Theoretical Domains Framework (TDF) (Cane et al., 2012).

The Theoretical Domains Framework (TDF)

The TDF was developed to try to simplify and integrate the large number of behaviour change theories in order to make them more accessible to those developing interventions. It helps users design interventions that are informed by current theory whilst also allowing them to bypass the tricky process of selecting any one particular theory or theories. The vast number of theories of behaviour change makes it difficult to sufficiently and comprehensively understand them all in order to be able to weigh up the relative strengths and weaknesses of each one and select the most appropriate. Indeed, the majority of behaviour change interventions draw on an extremely limited set of theories and choice of theory may often be more influenced by what is currently most widely used or what the researcher is most familiar with, rather than what is most appropriate or has the most evidence (Davis et al., 2015; see also **Box 8.3**).

In order to achieve this aim, the TDF identifies 84 key theoretical constructs drawn from theories of behaviour change and groups these into 14 different domains (see Cane et al., 2012). Some of the 14 domains map onto more than one COM-B component. For example, the domain of skills may refer to physical skills or psychological skills. Likewise, the domains of role and identity, and optimism may refer to either reflective or automatic processes. Some of the TDF constructs also appear in more than one TDF domain. For example, the construct of beliefs is relevant to beliefs about capabilities as well as beliefs about consequences. Similarly, action planning appears under goals as well as behavioural regulation. However, if you have identified the components of behaviour that are relevant using the COM-B model, this can help you narrow down the theoretical constructs in the TDF that you may want to target with your intervention. Most (but not all) of these constructs can be viewed as mechanisms of action (that is, mediators) that need to be changed in order to bring about a change in capability, opportunity or motivation which will in turn help change behaviour. Thus the next step is to decide how to try to change the TDF constructs that have been identified. Or, if you have omitted the TDF, how to increase the facets of capability, opportunity and/or motivation identified as relevant by the COM-B.

Step 5. Identify intervention functions

The Behaviour Change Wheel uses the term 'intervention functions' to refer to broad categories of ways in which an intervention can change behaviour. This is slightly different from the actual techniques that are used in an intervention because each technique could serve several different functions. For example, providing information about the health consequences of a behaviour (such as the possibility of catching a sexually transmitted disease as a result of unprotected sex) is best viewed as a behaviour change technique. However, it could influence behaviour both by increasing knowledge and by eliciting negative feelings associated with the behaviour, that is, by both education and persuasion. The nine intervention functions of the Behaviour Change Wheel are listed below, with examples:

1. *Education* – such as providing information about the benefits of eating fruit and vegetables.

2. *Persuasion* – such as using an image of a lung that has become diseased as a result of smoking.

3. *Incentivisation* – for example, stating that new mothers will receive shopping vouchers for breastfeeding.

4. *Coercion* – such as stating that people will be fined for smoking in a particular location.

5. *Training* – for example, teaching a person how to use a condom.

6. *Restriction* – such as prohibiting the sales of cigarettes in vending machines.

7. *Environmental restructuring* – such as building cycle paths.

8. *Modelling* – for example, having a character in a television drama get a vaccination.

9. *Enablement* – for example, providing nicotine replacement therapy for smokers trying to quit.

The COM-B components and/or TDF domains identified in Step 4 are used to pick out the intervention functions that are likely to be effective for changing behaviour (see Michie et al., 2014).

At this point you may have identified rather a lot of intervention functions, which in turn means there may be a lot of different potential strategies for your intervention. It may not be feasible (or indeed desirable) to use all these functions so you may need to be selective. But on what basis should you select intervention functions? One approach is to use the APEASE criteria and select functions that meet/score highly on these criteria (**Table 9.1**). Once you have decided which function or functions to focus on, you can then move on to Step 6 if there are options to influence policy, or Step 7 if it is not going to be possible to influence policy or if it will only be possible to influence one type of policy.

Table 9.1 The APEASE criteria that can be used to evaluate and select functions and behaviour change techniques (BCTs) when developing an intervention

APEASE criteria	Description
Affordability	How much will it cost? Can it be achieved within the constraints of the budget?
Practicability	Can it be delivered as intended to the target population? (Practicability is sometimes referred to as feasibility.)
Effectiveness and cost-effectiveness	How effective is it? In other words, how much will it change behaviour in a real-world context? Or what is the likely effect size? (Note that effectiveness is different from efficacy, see page 260.) How cost-effective is it? In other words, what is the ratio of costs to benefits? (See **Box 9.4**.)
Acceptability	What are **stakeholders**' views? Do they view it as appropriate or do they have objections? (See **Box 9.3**.)
Side effects/safety	Are there any adverse side effects or unintended outcomes that cause harm?
Equity	What effect will it have on social and health inequalities? Will they widen or reduce? Or will it have no impact?

Stakeholders – individuals, groups and organisations that may influence or be influenced by the intervention. The most important stakeholders for an intervention are probably those the intervention is aimed at. Other stakeholders include those involved in developing, commissioning and delivering the intervention as well as those who may be affected by the intervention even though it is not directed at them.

Source: Adapted with permission from Michie et al. (2014).

BOX 9.3 INTERVENTION ACCEPTABILITY

MAKING CONNECTIONS

One of the APPEASE criteria (**Table 9.1**) states that an intervention should be acceptable to stakeholders. In **Chapter 11** we look at barriers to the adoption and use of evidence-based interventions. These include some (but not all) of the reasons why people (including government) may find an intervention unacceptable. **Case Studies 2, 7 and 8 (Chapter 12)** also provide examples of interventions where acceptability has been problematic.

BOX 9.4 CALCULATING COST-EFFECTIVENESS

DIG A LITTLE DEEPER

The cost-effectiveness of an intervention is calculated by dividing its cost by a measure of the health gains it brings. The measure of health gain will vary depending on the intervention, and could refer to things like incidents of disease averted, number of fatalities prevented or years of life gained.

For example, an intervention aimed at preventing **spina bifida** by increasing folic acid intake among women trying to conceive could quantify health gains in terms of the reduction in incidents of spina bifida. In this case a cost-effectiveness analysis would give an indication of the cost of preventing one case of spina bifida.

Note that this is different from effectiveness. A very intensive intervention may increase folic acid supplementation from 25% to 60% but it may be costly to implement. A less intensive intervention may be much cheaper but only increase supplementation to 40%. Thus it may

Spina bifida – a birth defect where the backbone and membranes around the spine are not completely closed. It is thought to be caused by a combination of genetic and environmental factors. Taking folic acid supplements pre-conception and during the first 12 weeks of pregnancy has been shown to significantly reduce the risk of spina bifida.

be less effective but more cost-effective. This difference reflects the fact that there can often be a proportion of the population that are 'hard-to-reach' and tend to be less responsive to health interventions. Increasingly intense interventions may be needed to change the behaviour of this group that in turn increases the cost of the intervention and in doing so reduces the cost-effectiveness. A decision to prioritise cost-effectiveness over effectiveness may have implications for inequalities, since populations that are harder to reach are often those from more deprived backgrounds experiencing poorer physical and psychological health (see **Chapter 3**).

Step 6. Identify policy categories

As noted above, this step need only be included if there is the possibility of influencing more than one type of policy. This step serves to identify the types of policy changes that could best support the identified intervention functions. The seven possible policy categories are listed below with examples:

1. *Communication/marketing* – such as a mass media campaign to promote smoking cessation using adverts placed on billboards, in pharmacies, online and on television.

2. *Guidelines* – such as documentation detailing best practice for the treatment of obesity.

3. *Fiscal measures* – such as increased tax on drinks that have a high sugar content.

4. *Regulation* – such as voluntary agreement by the food industry to remove certain fats from foods.

5. *Legislation* – such as prohibition of the use of certain fats in foods.

6. *Environmental/social planning* – such as building new cycle paths.

7. *Service provision* – such as establishing clinics in pharmacies to provide advice on smoking cessation.

The types of policy categories best suited to supporting each type of intervention function can be found in Michie et al. (2014). Again, it is likely that a number of different policy categories will have been identified and the APEASE criteria (**Table 9.1**) can be used to make the final selection.

Behaviour change technique (BCT) – a 'systematic procedure included as a potentially active element of an intervention designed to change behaviour' (Michie et al., 2016). In other words, it is a specific technique thought to influence behaviour. It should also be observable, replicable and it should not be possible to break it apart into smaller components without losing its effect.

Step 7. Select behaviour change techniques

The next step in the process is to decide on the active ingredients of the intervention. This is achieved by deciding which specific **behaviour change technique** or techniques (BCTs) will be used. A wide range of different BCTs have been used in health interventions. Recently, academics have attempted to identify, define and categorise these techniques in order to aid intervention development and also to promote clearer reporting of interventions (see **Chapter 10**). At the time of writing, this programme of work has led to the identification of 93 separate BCTs that can be grouped into 16 different types (Michie et al., 2013). This taxonomy, referred to as BCT(v1), is shown in **Table 9.2**. Definitions and examples for each of the BCTs can be found in Michie et al. (2014), in the supplementary material to Michie et al. (2013) or online (see useful

Table 9.2 The BCT(v1) taxonomy which shows behaviour change techniques (BCTs) grouped according to type

Grouping and BCT	Grouping and BCT	Grouping and BCT
1. Goals and planning 1.1. Goal setting (behaviour) 1.2. Problem solving 1.3. Goal setting (outcome) 1.4. Action planning 1.5. Review behaviour goal(s) 1.6. Discrepancy between current behaviour and goal 1.7. Review outcome goal(s) 1.8. Behavioural contract 1.9. Commitment	**6. Comparison of behaviour** 6.1. Demonstration of the behaviour 6.2. Social comparison 6.3. Information about others' approval	**12. Antecedents** 12.1. Restructuring the physical environment 12.2. Restructuring the social environment 12.3. Avoidance/reducing exposure to cues for the behaviour 12.4. Distraction 12.5. Adding objects to the environment 12.6. Body changes
2. Feedback and monitoring 2.1. Monitoring of behaviour by others without feedback 2.2. Feedback on behaviour 2.3. Self-monitoring of behaviour 2.4. Self-monitoring of outcome(s) of behaviour 2.5. Monitoring of outcome(s) of behaviour without feedback 2.6. Biofeedback 2.7. Feedback on outcome(s) of behaviour	**7. Associations** 7.1. Prompts/cues 7.2. Cue signalling reward 7.3. Reduce prompts/cues 7.4. Remove access to the reward 7.5. Remove aversive stimulus 7.6. Satiation 7.7. Exposure 7.8. Associative learning	**13. Identity** 13.1. Identification of self as role model 13.2. Framing/reframing 13.3. Incompatible beliefs 13.4. Valued self-identity 13.5. Identity associated with changed behaviour
3. Social support 3.1. Social support (unspecified) 3.2. Social support (practical) 3.3. Social support (emotional)	**8. Repetition and substitution** 8.1. Behavioural practice/rehearsal 8.2. Behaviour substitution 8.3. Habit formation 8.4. Habit reversal 8.5. Overcorrection 8.6. Generalisation of target behaviour 8.7. Graded tasks	**14. Scheduled consequences** 14.1. Behaviour cost 14.2. Punishment 14.3. Remove reward 14.4. Reward approximation 14.5. Rewarding completion 14.6. Situation-specific reward 14.7. Reward incompatible behaviour 14.8. Reward alternative behaviour 14.9. Reduce reward frequency 14.10 Remove punishment
4. Shaping knowledge 4.1. Instruction on how to perform the behaviour 4.2. Information about antecedents 4.3. Re-attribution 4.4. Behavioural experiments	**9. Comparison of outcomes** 9.1. Credible source 9.2. Pros and cons 9.3. Comparative imagining of future outcomes	**15. Self-belief** 15.1. Verbal persuasion about capability 15.2. Mental rehearsal of successful performance 15.3. Focus on past success 15.4. Self-talk
5. Natural consequences 5.1. Information about health consequences 5.2. Salience of consequences 5.3. Information about social and environmental consequences 5.4. Monitoring of emotional consequences 5.5. Anticipated regret 5.6. Information about emotional consequences	**10. Reward and threat** 10.1. Material incentive (behaviour) 10.2. Material reward (behaviour) 10.3. Non-specific reward 10.4. Social reward 10.5. Social incentive 10.6. Non-specific incentive 10.7. Self-incentive 10.8. Incentive (outcome) 10.9. Self-reward 10.10. Reward (outcome) 10.11. Future punishment **11. Regulation** 11.1. Pharmocological support 11.2. Reduce negative emotions 11.3. Conserving mental resources 11.4. Paradoxical instructions	**16. Covert learning** 16.1. Imaginary punishment 16.2. Imaginary reward 16.3. Vicarious consequences

Note: See Michie et al. (2014) for definitions and examples.

Source: Michie et al. (2013). Reprinted with permission of Oxford University Press on behalf of the Society of Behavioural Medicine.

CHAPTER 9

weblinks at macmillanihe.com/tapper-health-psychology). The BCT taxonomy is likely to evolve over time as new BCTs are identified and developed. In particular, the interventions used to identify the BCTs for BCT(v1) were primarily focussed on changing the behaviour of individuals rather than on changing the behaviour of populations, which are more likely to be influenced by strategies relating to regulation, legislation and fiscal measures.

Relevant BCTs can be identified either from the intervention functions or from the theoretical domains (see Michie et al., 2014 and Cane et al., 2015, respectively). After identifying relevant BCTs you may find you have more than can realistically be included in your intervention. If so, you can once again use the APEASE criteria (**Table 9.1**) to select the best BCTs, which may include looking for evidence of the effectiveness of each of the BCTs in contexts similar to your intervention.

Step 8. Decide on the mode of delivery

The final step in the Behaviour Change Wheel approach is to decide how the intervention will be delivered. This step is only really relevant for interventions that involve some kind of communication. Policy interventions restricted to changes to guidelines, taxes, rules or laws, or changes to the physical or social environment will not necessarily need to select a mode of delivery unless the intervention also aims to increase awareness of these changes. There is a range of different ways in which an intervention can be delivered (see Michie et al., 2014). For example, it could be delivered to an entire population via posters, leaflets, social media or a mobile phone app. Or it could be delivered to individuals via a telephone helpline, a computer program or face-to-face counselling sessions. The APEASE criteria (**Table 9.1**) can be used to help select the most appropriate mode of delivery.

Limitations of the BCW approach

Whilst the Behaviour Change Wheel represents one possible approach to intervention development, there are reasons why you may decide not to use this method, or to use certain elements, but not others. First, use of the COM-B-Qv1 questionnaire (see **Box 9.1**) may mean that the main focus of the intervention is determined by the views of users or stakeholders. In some instances this may be sensible, for example where trying to change relatively simple behaviours such as cycling to work or washing hands. However, where we lack insight into the reasons for our behaviour, this approach would be less successful at identifying important determinants. For example, asking a person what it would take for them to quit smoking may elicit reasons that, when addressed, turn out to have little impact on their behaviour.

Second, the BCT taxonomy was designed to be a comprehensive list of all possible BCTs a behaviour change intervention might include, rather than a list of effective BCTs. This means that some of the BCTs it contains may be ineffective or may even be counterproductive. As such some authors have argued that, in its current form, it is not a good basis for intervention development (Kok et al., 2016).

Third, and related to the above point, it can be difficult to apply specific BCTs effectively unless one properly understands the underlying theory (Kok et al., 2016). For example, in **Chapter 6**, when we looked at implementation intentions, we also looked at factors shown to moderate their effects (such as motivation, self-regulatory ability and plan specificity). If one simply decided to use implementation intentions as a BCT (labelled as action planning in BCTv1), without an awareness of such factors, one may risk using them in ways that are unlikely to work, for example by failing to put in place measures to ensure they were formed with sufficient specificity. **Box 9.5** describes how one can test for moderation effects.

BOX 9.5 TESTING FOR MODERATION

DIG A LITTLE DEEPER

Moderation is typically assessed by looking for interaction effects (Baron & Kenny, 1986). Where the independent variable is categorical (such as whether or not someone formed an implementation intention), the proposed moderator is also categorical (such as whether a person is male or female), and the dependent variable is continuous (such as portions of fruit and vegetables consumed), analysis of variance may be used to look for an interaction between implementation intention formation and gender on portions of fruit and vegetables consumed. A significant interaction may indicate that implementation intentions are more effective for females than males (or vice versa). However, if the independent variable and/or the proposed moderator are continuous, an alternative test such as regression would need to be employed.

For example, we may want to examine the effect of stress on the efficacy of implementation intentions for promoting fruit and vegetable consumption and we may have measured stress using a questionnaire that gives us a score on a continuum between 0 and 25. Regression analyses will be able to tell us whether there is an interaction between implementation intention formation and stress, which may in turn indicate that implementation intentions become less effective at promoting fruit and vegetable consumption as a person becomes more stressed (or vice versa).

Testing for moderation gets a little more complex when we predict a non-linear effect of the moderator. For example, it may be the case that rather than having an increasingly detrimental effect on the efficacy of implementation intentions, level of stress has absolutely no detrimental effect until a certain threshold level of stress is reached (we would call this type of relationship 'stepped'). Alternatively, as relatively low levels of stress increase, so the efficacy of implementation intentions may slowly weaken. However, with increasing levels of stress, this detrimental effect may get progressively stronger (in this case the relationship would be described as 'curvilinear' or 'quadratic').

Another reason why you may choose not to use the BCT(v1) is that the BCTs have mainly been drawn from reviews of applied behaviour change interventions rather than more recent experimental studies. This means the taxonomy tends to be restricted to more established BCTs and does not really incorporate recent developments in the field. In particular it is heavily weighted toward BCTs that reflect controlled, conscious processes rather than automatic processes though, as described in **Chapter 6**, in recent years increasing emphasis has been placed on the latter. Although there will undoubtedly be revisions to BCT(v1), in its current form it has yet to reflect this shift in emphasis. For example, there are currently no BCTs identified in relation to memory, attention and decision processes. And yet in **Chapter 6** we reviewed a wide range of theories that demonstrate the importance of such processes for behaviour. We also looked at specific techniques that are being used to try to influence these types of processes, such as attentional bias modification, approach avoidance training, and inhibitory control training.

Thus, inevitably, BCT taxonomies are likely to be one step behind theory. This means that whilst BCT taxonomies may be helpful for the development of interventions that use novel combinations of BCTs or novel modes of delivery, they are unlikely to be helpful for the development of interventions using *novel BCTs*. As such, if we want to develop an intervention that uses novel BCTs, it would be better to start with theory.

An additional reason why one might want to draw more heavily on theory is because some of the BCTs in BCT(v1) are currently poorly specified. For example, BCT 11.3 is 'Conserve mental resources', defined as 'Advise on ways of minimising demands on mental resources to facilitate behavior change' (Michie et al., 2013). But what kind of advice might we provide? As discussed in **Chapter 7**, the types of tasks thought to conserve or deplete mental resources will vary depending on the theory referred to (for example, the limited resources model of self-control versus the process model of self-control). Similarly, BCT 11.2 is 'Reduce negative emotions', defined as 'Advise on ways of reducing negative emotions to facilitate performance of the behavior (includes "Stress Management")' (Michie et al., 2013). But there are several different types of negative emotion (such as stress, low mood, craving), a number of different theories of emotion regulation and numerous possible strategies for the management of negative emotions (Gross, 2015). Thus if one wanted to employ 'reduce negative emotions' as a BCT, one would really need to refer to theory for more guidance.

Finally, Abraham (2016) argues that the BCT taxonomy is less helpful for intervention development compared to some other taxonomies because the techniques are categorised according to their form, rather than the underlying mechanism they target. Abraham uses the example of implementation intentions that may be used to target quite distinct processes. For example, in some cases they may be used to develop plans of when, where and how one will perform an action, whilst in other cases they be used to help to regulate specific emotions (see **Chapter 6**).

We now turn to Intervention Mapping. Like the BCW, Intervention Mapping is a very comprehensive framework that takes a step-by-step approach to intervention development. However, slight differences in the steps taken and taxonomies employed mean it is likely to promote greater reference to and use of specific theories.

Intervention Mapping (IM)

Framework summary

Intervention Mapping (IM) was first introduced in the 1990s (Bartholomew et al., 1998) and has since undergone a number of revisions to take account of developments in the field (Bartholomew et al., 2016; Kok et al., 2016). It consists of six main steps, which should be followed in an iterative rather than linear manner. In other words, programme development may involve moving back and forth between steps. The steps should also be viewed as cumulative, so that each step builds on previous steps, and any omissions will create difficulties for subsequent steps. The steps are as follows:

1. Identify what, if anything, needs to change and for whom.

2. Identify the determinants of the relevant behaviour(s) and the beliefs that should be targeted by the intervention.

3. Find theory-based methods of behaviour change that map onto the behavioural determinants/beliefs identified in Step 2. Use these to create a list of potential techniques that could be employed in the intervention. Review the evidence for these theories and techniques. On the basis of this evidence, select or design the techniques that will be used in the intervention.

4. Develop, test and refine the intervention content, procedures and materials.

5. Decide how the intervention will be adopted and delivered. This may involve influencing the behaviour of individuals and/or groups other than those targeted by the intervention.

6. Develop an evaluation plan.

Step 1 of the IM approach is concerned with clearly identifying the behaviour that needs to change. Steps 2 to 4 are about understanding the determinants of the behaviour and using theory and evidence to develop the intervention content. In Step 2, determinants are identified by a combination of brainstorming and reviewing the literature to find relevant theoretical constructs, theories and empirical studies. Step 3 includes the use of a taxonomy of behaviour change methods grouped by type of determinant. These groupings are as follows:

(a) General methods that are applicable to all determinants

Groups of methods aimed at:

(b) Increasing knowledge

(c) Changing awareness and risk perception

(d) Changing habitual, automatic and impulsive behaviours

(e) Changing attitudes, beliefs and outcome expectations

(f) Changing social influence

(g) Changing skills, capability and self-efficacy to overcome barriers

(h) Reducing public stigma

(i) Changing environmental conditions

(j) Changing social norms

(k) Changing social support and support networks

(l) Changing organisations

(m) Changing communities

(n) Changing policy.

A number of different methods are identified within each of these groups, along with associated theories and 'parameters' (moderators that specify the conditions under which the method will be effective). Step 5 of the IM approach is mainly about intervention delivery and Step 6 concerns evaluation. **Table 9.3** provides a summary of the ways in which these steps compare with the steps of the BCW.

Table 9.3 Comparison of the different steps of the Behaviour Change Wheel (BCW) and Intervention Mapping (IM) frameworks

Purpose	BCW	IM
Identify the behaviour that needs to change (the target behaviour)	Steps 1–3	Step 1
Identify the determinants of the target behaviour	Step 4. Uses the COM-B model and, optionally, the TDF	Step 2
Use relevant theory/theoretical constructs	Steps 4 & 5. Uses the COM-B model and, optionally, the TDF	Steps 2 & 3. Uses the taxonomy of behaviour change methods
Select behaviour change techniques	Steps 5, 6 & 7. Uses the APEASE criteria and BCT taxonomy	Steps 3 & 4
Select mode of delivery	Step 8	Step 5
Evaluate effects	–	Step 6

Limitations and strengths

Michie et al. (2011) argue that IM is not as comprehensive a framework as the BCW because it will not necessarily capture all possible types of intervention. For example, when identifying the determinants of the target behaviour the COM-B model allows for a full analysis of all the conditions that need to be in place in order for the target behaviour to occur (conditions relating to capability, opportunity and motivation). By contrast, in IM, identification of determinants stems from a review of the literature to find relevant theoretical constructs, theories and empirical studies. This means that the identification of relevant determinants will be restricted to what already exists in the literature, not what is theoretically possible.

Michie et al. (2011) also argue that IM is not as coherent a framework as BCW because the taxonomies employed in IM are not always made up of categories of the same type and level of specificity. For example, the BCW has separate taxonomies relating to intervention functions and behaviour change techniques whereas IM has a taxonomy of methods for changing behaviour but this includes some methods that are quite specific, such as punishment (which is identified as a behaviour change technique in the BCW) and others that are much broader, such as persuasive communication (which is identified as an intervention function in the BCW).

Nevertheless, Kok et al. (2016) argue that the IM taxonomy of behaviour change methods is more suitable for intervention development than the BCT taxonomy because (a) the BCT taxonomy may include techniques that are not effective, or even counterproductive and (b) the BCT taxonomy does not take account of variables that may moderate the effects of the BCT. They maintain that, whilst the BCT taxonomy may be useful for coding intervention content, the IM taxonomy of behaviour change methods is more appropriate for intervention development. The IM taxonomy also makes it easier to identify and refer to specific theories of behaviour change since references to relevant theories are provided within the IM taxonomy.

However, despite its advantages, those who have used Intervention Mapping have admitted that it is elaborate, expensive, time-consuming and even tiresome (Heinen et al., 2006; Van Kesteren et al., 2006). As such, we now turn to a slightly simpler framework, MINDSPACE.

MINDSPACE

The MINDSPACE framework (Dolan et al., 2010, 2012) focusses on behaviour change that is primarily driven by automatic processes rather than by processes involving conscious decision-making. In other words, it draws more heavily on the type of literature we reviewed in **Chapter 6** as opposed to the models of behaviour change we looked at in **Chapter 5**. As such, MINDSPACE is mostly concerned with changing environmental contexts rather than 'changing minds'. It is therefore much less comprehensive compared to the BCW and IM frameworks – though also much simpler and more accessible. It was mainly designed for government policy makers to help them do three things: (a) *enhance* existing policies, (b) *introduce* new approaches and (c) *reassess* existing policies that may be inadvertently influencing behaviour in unwanted ways.

The name MINDSPACE is a mnemonic that refers to nine ways of changing behaviour (**Table 9.4**). The authors selected these nine methods on the basis of them having been repeatedly shown to have a strong influence on behaviour, primarily (though not necessarily exclusively) via automatic processes. Thus the framework is not intended to be comprehensive, but rather a useful tool that succinctly captures and summarises current evidence from the field. As you go through the techniques described in **Table 9.4**, you may find it useful to think about how they relate to the theories we looked at in **Chapters 5 and 6**.

Table 9.4 The MINDSPACE framework

MINDSPACE cue	Effects on behaviour
Messenger	We are more likely to change our behaviour in response to information that comes from someone who shares similar characteristics to us and who we perceive to be in a position of authority. We are less likely to change our behaviour if we dislike the messenger.
Incentives*	We are more likely to change our behaviour when there is an incentive for doing so. Our response to an incentive will be influenced by its relative rather than absolute size. We are more influenced by potential losses than potential gains and tend to overestimate the probability of events that are easy to imagine or recall. We mentally allocate money to different accounts and are reluctant to move money between them. Additionally, we prefer smaller, more immediate rewards to larger more distant ones.
Norms	We may change our behaviour to align with what other people, particularly people like ourselves, are doing.
Defaults	We are more likely to accept an option that comes into effect when we do not have to do anything as opposed to an option that we have to actively select.
Salience	We can only be influenced by information if we notice it (consciously or unconsciously). We are more likely to notice things that are novel, simple (easy to understand) and are situated somewhere accessible.
Priming	Our behaviour can be influenced by prior exposure to certain sights, smells or words.
Affect	A message that elicits an emotional response from us can be a very effective way of changing our behaviour.
Commitments	We are more likely to carry out a behaviour if we commit to it. The effect of a commitment on behaviour is stronger where there is a greater cost associated with failure, such as reputational damage or a failure to reciprocate (for example where two people have agreed to commit to something together).
Ego	We are motivated to view ourselves, and the groups we identify with, in a positive light. Thus we are more likely to engage in a behaviour if it improves our self-esteem or self-image. We also like our behaviours and beliefs to be consistent. This means that changing a small behaviour may lead to changes in other related behaviours as we strive for consistency.

Note: *In contrast to the BCW, the term 'incentives' is used here to refer to expectations of cost or punishment (termed 'coercion' in the BCW) as well as expectations of reward.

Source: Based on Dolan et al. (2010, 2012).

As noted above, although the MINDSPACE framework certainly has a solid basis in theory and empirical research, it was designed to be used by non-experts in the field, ideally in collaboration with experts. As such the framework itself is more focussed on effects than on theory, which in turn means its users may be at risk of ignoring important moderators that influence the outcomes of the strategies described.

Developing an intervention directly from theory

So far, we have been implicitly attempting to answer the question, 'What is the most effective way of changing this behaviour?' The best way of answering this question may indeed be by using one of the frameworks described above. However, a slightly different, but equally important question is 'What are the implications of this theory for behaviour change?' or 'How can we use this theory to help us change behaviour?' This important question allows for the discovery and development of novel strategies and behaviour change techniques (BCTs) that are likely to be missed with a framework approach, especially when the theory in question is relatively new. For example, as described above, BCT(v1) does not currently include many techniques designed to exploit attentional processes, despite the fact that we looked at a number of novel approaches to changing behaviour via attentional training in **Chapter 6**.

Thus another approach to intervention development is to start with a particular theory and use it to help inform the development of strategies and techniques (see **Case Study 1, Chapter 12,** for an example). Once such techniques have been developed, it is then a matter of establishing the type of contexts within which they may be most beneficial. For example, a technique that requires people to engage in daily attentional training is unlikely to be effective among those who are not motivated to change their behaviour (since they would be unlikely to engage in the training). The COM-B model could be employed here to help identify appropriate populations and contexts.

It is also important to note that, irrespective of how they were developed, the most successful behaviour change interventions are often those that target a range of different factors (NICE, 2007, 2014). Thus a single technique or small set of techniques developed from one quite specific theory may have a relatively small impact on behaviour if used in isolation. As such, it may be beneficial to think about how such techniques could be incorporated into existing successful interventions in order to enhance their effects. Or how they may be combined with other techniques, drawn from other theories that address different aspects of behaviour. In this regard, certain elements of the BCW and IM frameworks may be helpful. Additionally, Step 8 of the BCW can be used to select the mode of delivery and the APEASE criteria (**Table 9.1**) can help ensure that the applied utility of the intervention is considered.

Adapting an existing intervention

Another approach to intervention development is to adapt an existing, successful intervention to a new setting, population or behaviour. This has the advantage of being less labour intensive than developing an intervention from scratch, though one would still need to have a thorough understanding of the likely mediators and moderators of the intervention to ensure it was adapted appropriately (in other words, one would need to understand the underlying theory). An assessment of the target population, for example using the COM-B model or an IM needs assessment, may also be helpful to confirm that there are no other factors, not addressed by the intervention, which could limit its success. In some cases one may need to add components to an intervention to address such factors, or one could combine several different interventions.

Interventions based on practical expertise

Finally, it is possible to develop a successful intervention based on practical expertise alone, in other words, in the absence of relevant behaviour change theory. Examples of successful interventions that have taken this approach are described in **Chapter 12**. These included those based on marketing research (**Case Study 4**), motivational interviewing (that was developed on the basis of counselling experience; **Case Study 9**) and certain community interventions (informed by the experience of those living within the community; **Case Study 11**). This is not to say that such interventions could not benefit from theory. As described above, theory can help us understand how an intervention might be tailored to maximise its effects and how it could be successfully adapted for different behaviours, contexts and populations. However, one should not underestimate the importance of understanding the lived experience of those whose behaviour one is trying to change. No amount of theory can substitute for such knowledge. This is one of the reasons why stakeholder consultation and engagement is emphasised in other approaches. Ideally one would draw on both theory and practical/stakeholder expertise.

Comparison of approaches

As you can see, there are a number of different approaches to developing an intervention. The approach you choose is likely to depend on your expertise and interests (for example, theory expert versus practitioner or policy maker), your priorities (to develop an innovative new intervention or to solve a problem fast) and the time and resources available. In practice it may often be most useful to combine different elements from different approaches. **Table 9.5** summarises some of the key advantages and disadvantages of each of the six different approaches we have looked at.

Table 9.5 Advantages and disadvantages of different approaches to intervention development

Approach used	Advantage/Disadvantage			
	Expertise needed	Time and resources	Potential effectiveness	Scope for innovation
Behaviour Change Wheel	Requires training in the BCW approach and/or broad expertise in health psychology theory and intervention development.	Extensive. May also need substantial engagement from stakeholders.	High likelihood of good effectiveness.	Scope for innovation mainly restricted to BCT combinations, settings and mode of delivery.
Intervention mapping	Requires training in the IM approach and/or broad expertise in health psychology theory and intervention development.	Extensive. May also need substantial engagement from stakeholders.	High likelihood of good effectiveness.	Scope for innovation mainly restricted to BCT combinations, settings and mode of delivery.
MINDSPACE	Can be used with minimal expertise though effects may be enhanced through consultation with theory experts.	Likely to require less time and fewer resources compared to other approaches.	High likelihood of good effectiveness.	Scope for innovation mainly restricted to BCT combinations, settings and mode of delivery.
Developing an intervention directly from theory	Requires specific theoretical expertise. May also require broader expertise in intervention development.	Considerable time and resources may be required to gather evidence to refine the BCT(s). May also need substantial engagement from stakeholders.	Effectiveness likely to be less predictable but has the potential to be very high.	Scope for innovative BCTs as well as their settings and mode of delivery.
Adapting an existing intervention	Effects may be enhanced with relevant theoretical expertise. May require broad expertise in intervention development.	Likely to require less time and fewer resources compared to other approaches.	High likelihood of good effectiveness.	Scope for innovation mainly restricted to BCT combinations, settings and mode of delivery.
Developing an intervention based on practical expertise	Requires extensive experience with the target population. Effects may be enhanced through consultation with theory experts. May require broad expertise in intervention development.	Extensive time and resources may be required to obtain the practical expertise. Time and resources may be reduced where this expertise already exists.	Effectiveness likely to be less predictable but has the potential to be very high.	Scope for innovative BCTs as well as their settings and mode of delivery.

CHAPTER 9

EVALUATION FRAMEWORKS

Evaluation is an essential part of the process of developing and using behaviour change interventions. Some development frameworks, such as Intervention Mapping, incorporate evaluation whilst others, such as the Behaviour Change Wheel, do not. However, just as there are frameworks primarily focussed on intervention development, so there are also frameworks primarily focussed on intervention evaluation, some of which also incorporate elements of intervention development. We now look at some of these evaluation frameworks in order to consider the broader process of evaluation in relation to intervention development. In many instances, these frameworks can incorporate some of the different approaches we have already looked at, such as use of the Behaviour Change Wheel or Intervention Mapping. We consider the more specific details of evaluation in **Chapter 10**.

Clinical trial – a trial concerned with clinical research. Clinical research relates to the safety and effectiveness of medications, medical devices, treatment regimes or diagnostic products for use with humans. These may be for treatment, prevention, diagnosis or symptom relief. Whilst a health-related behaviour change intervention would not necessarily be considered typical of most clinical research, it may still fall within this definition and be registered as a clinical trial.

Efficacy – the extent to which an intervention produces a beneficial effect under ideal circumstances. Efficacy is assessed in explanatory trials (see **Chapter 10**).

Effectiveness – the extent to which an intervention produces a beneficial effect in real-world settings. Effectiveness is tested in pragmatic trials (see **Chapter 10**).

Clinical trial phases

In **clinical trials,** evaluation tends to follow a fairly prescribed sequence of events. The framework employed is grounded in the biomedical model (**Chapter 1**) so is best suited to the evaluation of treatments aimed at the body that exert their effects via a single mechanism. However, parts of the framework have been applied to more complex behavioural interventions, particularly Phases II and III that refer to explanatory and pragmatic trials (see **Chapter 10**). As such, it is useful to be aware of the terminology and how it fits with the rest of the framework.

The phases of a clinical trial are as follows:

- Preclinical phase – theory and/or testing on cells or animals is used to develop a new drug, device or treatment.

- Phase I – the drug/device/treatment is tested on a small number of participants to determine whether it is safe and, where relevant, obtain information about dosage. The term 'exploratory trial' is sometimes used to refer to research conducted early in this phase.

- Phase II – an explanatory trial is used to examine **efficacy** and side effects (where relevant) and may also be used to compare the effects of different versions of the drug/device/treatment.

- Phase III – a pragmatic trial is used to examine the **effectiveness** of the drug/device/treatment in a clinical setting.

- Phase IV – after a drug has been marketed, thousands of patients may be monitored to check for rare side effects. This is sometimes referred to as a 'confirmatory trial'.

Experimental Medicine (EM)

The Experimental Medicine (EM) framework was born out of the observation that, despite substantial development in theories of behaviour and behaviour change over the past three decades, these are often not effectively translated into practice. This is partly because many important questions (such as which factors moderate effects) remain unanswered. The EM framework was designed to strengthen links between theory and practice in order to accelerate progress in both areas (Sheeran et al., 2017).

Figure 9.2 The four key steps in the Experimental Medicine (EM) framework

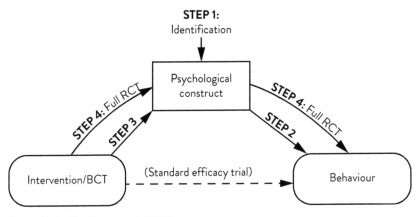

Source: Inspired by Sheeran et al. (2017).

The approach comprises four key steps. These are illustrated in **Figure 9.2** and are as follows:

1. Identification of modifiable psychological constructs (referred to as 'targets') that influence behaviour. (Examples include attitudes and self-efficacy.)

2. Development of reliable measures of these constructs. Assessment of when, how and to what extent changes in these constructs elicit changes in behaviour.

3. Identification of different intervention strategies that can maximise changes in these constructs.

4. Evaluation using a randomised controlled trial (RCT; see **Chapter 10**) to test the full model, assessing whether the intervention changes behaviour via a change in the psychological construct(s). In other words, whether the effects of the intervention on behaviour are mediated by the hypothesised psychological construct(s).

Thus by including measures of hypothesised mediators (or 'mechanisms of action'), the final evaluation is designed to ascertain not just whether the intervention works (as might typically be assessed in a standard efficacy trial), but also whether it works in the manner predicted by the relevant theory. In this way the evaluation contributes to theory development as well as practice. **Box 9.6** describes how one tests for mediation.

BOX 9.6 TESTING FOR MEDIATION

DIG A LITTLE DEEPER

In order to demonstrate that a variable mediates the relationship between two other variables, four criteria must be met (Baron & Kenny, 1986). These are as follows:

1. The independent variable (IV) must predict the dependent variable (DV). In other words, there needs to be an effect to be mediated. (In **Figure 9.2**, the intervention/BCT would be considered the IV and the behaviour the DV.)

2. The IV must predict the mediator. In other words, the intervention must influence the proposed mechanism. (In **Figure 9.2**, we can view the psychological construct as the mediator.)

3. The mediator must predict the DV. In other words, the proposed mechanism must influence the behaviour. Variability associated with the IV should be controlled for in this analysis to ensure that any link between the mediator and DV does not simply occur because both are correlated with the IV. (This will not matter if the proposed mediator is the only mediator but might matter if there are additional mechanisms responsible for the relationship between the IV and DV, see point 4).

4. When variability associated with the mediator is removed from the analysis, the relationship between the IV and DV must weaken. (In other words, if it were not for this particular mediator, there would be less of a link, or no link, between the intervention and the behaviour.) If the mediator fully mediates the relationship between the IV and the DV (in other words, it is the only mechanism via which the intervention influences the behaviour), when the variance associated with it is removed, the relationship between the IV and DV should disappear completely. However, if it only partially mediates the effect (in other words, it is one of several mechanisms) the relationship between the IV and DV should be reduced but should not disappear completely.

A common way of testing for the above relationships is using regression analyses, though researchers may also use other techniques, depending on the number of variables they are testing and the complexity of the proposed relationships.

Multiphase Optimization Strategy (MOST)

Often the most effective type of behaviour change intervention is a multi-component intervention (NICE, 2007, 2014). However, deciding which **intervention components** to use and how to implement these components can be challenging. This is because there are often far more potentially effective intervention strategies than could realistically be included in a single intervention and also because decisions will need to be made about aspects of the intervention design for which there is limited evidence (such as the order in which different components are delivered, who they are delivered by, and the intensity of these components). The difficulty for the researcher, then, is how to decide which components, in which combinations, will be most effective and also how to maximise their effects. The Multiphase Optimization Strategy (MOST) (Collins et al., 2005, 2011) is a framework specifically designed to provide researchers with the evidence they need, to make such decisions, in the most efficient way possible.

The MOST framework has five key phases as follows:

1. A relevant theoretical model(s) is identified.

2. The theoretical model(s) is used to identify a set of intervention components to be examined.

3. The effects of these components are examined using randomised experimentation (see below).

4. Additional experimental or non-experimental work may be carried out to refine the intervention.

> **Intervention component** – this term may be used in different ways by different writers. Collins et al. (2011) define an intervention component as 'any aspect of an intervention that is of interest and can be separated out for study' (p. 15). According to these authors, components may:
>
> (a) be part of the intervention
>
> (b) relate to how the intervention, or part of the intervention, is delivered
>
> (c) relate to some aspect of the environment in which the intervention takes place
>
> (d) relate to intervention adherence, or
>
> (e) relate to other aspects of the intervention associated with cost, effectiveness or efficacy.

5. A draft version of the final intervention is developed. The efficacy and/or effectiveness of this intervention can then be tested using an RCT.

The randomised experimentation will likely involve the use of a factorial study design or fractional factorial study design, since such designs are more efficient compared to a series of studies examining each component in isolation and can also provide information about interactions between components. For example, if a researcher wants to test the effects of three different BCTs (such as information about health consequences, action planning and feedback on outcomes) delivered in two different ways (telephone versus in person), this results in 16 possible intervention formats since 2 (information versus no information) $\times$ 2 (action planning versus no action planning) $\times$ 2 (feedback versus no feedback) $\times$ 2 (telephone versus in person) = 16. Whilst a series of separate studies could compare each of these components individually, this would be very time-consuming and would not provide insights into how the components interact. (For example, feedback on outcomes may be effective, but only when used in combination with information about health consequences.) A factorial design randomises participants into each of these different possible combinations, thereby making it both more efficient and more informative. However, in some instances, where a large number of different components need testing, the number of possible combinations may become unmanageable and it may make sense to use a fractional factorial design instead. Here the researcher tests a smaller number of combinations based on what are considered to be the highest priority research questions.

Sequential Multiple Assignment Randomised Trial (SMART)

A Sequential Multiple Assignment Randomised Trial (SMART) evaluation framework is useful for adaptive interventions. An adaptive intervention is a multi-component intervention in which the type or intensity of treatments used changes over time according to the needs of the individual (Almirall et al., 2014; Lei et al., 2012). It will typically involve a series of stages, with a decision taken at each stage about whether the person should continue with the existing treatment, receive a higher intensity of treatment, receive an alternative treatment or discontinue treatment. **Figure 9.3(a)** shows an example of an adaptive intervention for weight loss. Adaptive interventions are useful both because individuals may vary in their response to different treatments and also because certain treatments may become less effective over time. Additionally, an adaptive intervention can be more cost-effective as it means that more expensive, resource-intensive treatments need only be used when they are really needed, where evidence indicates that a person is unlikely to benefit from a less intensive treatment.

However, whilst this type of tailoring makes sense in principle, there may be limited evidence on which to base important design decisions, such as how long each stage should be, what criteria should be used to determine treatment type at each stage, and what treatment type would be most effective at each stage. A SMART framework can be used to gather such evidence (Almirall et al., 2014; Lei et al., 2012). This is achieved by randomly assigning participants to different intervention options at each stage of the intervention. Random assignment is used where there is a lack of existing evidence to indicate which alternative would be most effective.

Figure 9.3(b) shows how this might be used to help inform the development of an adaptive intervention for weight loss. For example, the results of this trial would help indicate whether initial treatment should be 5 or 10 sessions of individual behavioural weight loss treatment (IBT), and whether those who fail to respond to IBT would be most effectively treated by the addition of meal replacements (MR) to IBT or by switching from IBT to an alternative treatment (acceptance and commitment therapy; ACT). The results of this trial could then be used to decide between four potential adaptive interventions: short duration

Figure 9.3 (a) An example of an adaptive intervention for weight loss; (b) How a Sequential Multiple Assignment Randomised Trial (SMART) could be used to gather evidence to inform the design of this type of adaptive intervention

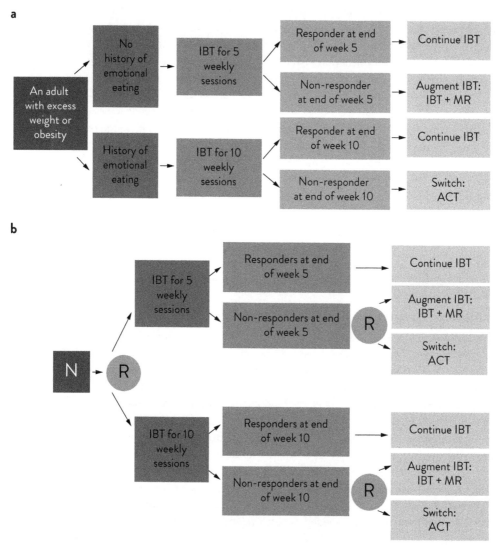

Notes: Emotional eating refers to a tendency to overeat in response to specific emotions (often negative emotions).

IBT refers to individual behavioural weight loss treatment, a treatment approach that incorporates strategies such as goal setting, self-monitoring and stimulus control.

Responders are defined as those who have lost at least 5lb of weight.

MR refers to meal replacements where the individual is provided with pre-packed foods to replace particular meals.

ACT refers to acceptance and commitment therapy, a psychotherapeutic approach that uses mindfulness-based strategies.

In (b), N refers to a specific number of participants and R indicates where participants are randomised to alternative treatments.

Source: Adapted from Almirall et al. (2014). Reprinted and adapted by permission of Oxford University Press on behalf of the Society of Behavioural Medicine.

IBT with MR augmentation for non-responders; short duration IBT with a switch to ACT for non-responders; long duration IBT with MR augmentation for non-responders; long duration IBT with a switch to ACT for non-responders. Once the most effective version of the adaptive intervention has been identified it can be evaluated against an appropriate control using a randomised controlled trial (RCT). Thus the SMART framework is used to help develop the intervention whilst the RCT is used to evaluate it (Almirall et al., 2014).

CONCLUSIONS

There are a number of different ways of developing behaviour change interventions. These place varying amounts of emphasis on theoretical versus practical/stakeholder expertise. In an ideal world, intervention development would emphasise both but, given limited time and resources, this may not always be possible. Depending on the particular situation it may be desirable to weight one more heavily than the other.

Different approaches may also allow for different degrees of novelty and creativity. Again, some situations may call for strategies that are tried and tested and promise a high likelihood of success, whilst in other circumstances there may be scope to explore more innovative methods that bring with them a higher likelihood of failure but also the possibility of improved effects. Incorporating evaluation into the intervention development process means problems can be identified at an early stage, before an intervention is rolled out to larger groups of people. We look at evaluation in more detail in **Chapter 10**. However, irrespective of the likely effectiveness of an intervention, there may still be barriers that prevent its use. We consider such barriers in **Chapter 11**.

The APEASE criteria described in this chapter (**Table 9.1**) state that it is important to consider cost-effectiveness when developing an intervention. In **Box 9.4** we also saw how one measure of intervention effectiveness might be the number of deaths prevented. But are some lives worth more than others?

THE GREAT DEBATE

When asked to decide who should receive a life-saving treatment, people are more likely to choose children and young adults than babies and older adults (Goodwin & Landy, 2014; see **Figure 9.4**). This suggests we value people's lives differently. Given limited resources, should we prioritise interventions that save the lives of children and young adults over those that save babies and older adults? What about interventions aimed at improving health more generally or increasing quality of life? And apart from age, what other factors might you take into account when allocating resources for healthcare?

Figure 9.4 The percentage of times people selected an individual of a particular age when asked to choose between one of two individuals to receive a life-saving blood transfusion of a rare blood type

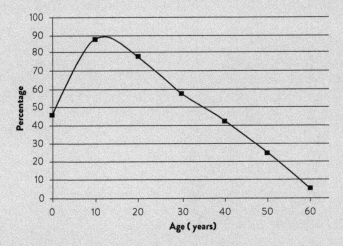

Source: Goodwin, G.P. & Landy, J.F. (2014). Valuing different human lives. *Journal of Experimental Psychology: General*, 143(2), 778. Copyright © 2014 by American Psychological Association. Adapted with permission.

Chapter Outline

New Smyrna Beach in Florida has a long expanse of white sand, gently undulating dunes and miles and miles of warm blue water. It also happens to be the shark attack capital of the world. So if you did decide to take a dip, would you be concerned about what might be lurking beneath your toes? Or would you be more worried about the car drive home?

Shark fatalities are extremely rare, killing around six people across the world every year. This is much fewer than the 45,000 who die in car accidents, the 3,300 who drown or the 760 who are killed riding their bicycles (International Shark Attack File, 2018). Of course, there are more people driving cars and riding bicycles than swimming in shark-infested seas. Nevertheless, the risk of being eaten

Image 10.1 *Sharks. Not quite as scary as they seem.*
Credit: Marcelo Cidrack.

by a shark is still pretty low. Indeed, more people die digging big holes in the sand.[1] So why are we so frightened of sharks?

One of the reasons we're more frightened of sharks than cars is that we do not evaluate and respond to information in an objective, impartial way. Instead we rely on **heuristics** and are prone to a wide range of biases. It is for this reason that we can't rely on our intuition when weighing up evidence. And it is for this reason that we need scientific methods. In this chapter we will:

> **Heuristic** – a mental shortcut used to make a judgement. Heuristics save time and effort but they also reduce accuracy.

- Explore some of the biases that influence our judgements.

- Look at the different types of research that can be used to gather evidence to help identify effective ways of changing behaviour.

- Examine the different types of study designs that can be used to evaluate the effects of an intervention.

- Think about how to measure behaviour and other important variables.

- Consider best practice for reporting research.

THE IMPORTANCE OF A SCIENTIFIC APPROACH

As discussed in **Chapter 9**, research is important throughout the entire cycle of intervention development and evaluation. Not only is it a key component of the piloting and evaluation phases, it may also feature in the development phase in relation to theory development and in the implementation phase in terms of conducting a long-term follow-up of effects. In this chapter we look at some of the different research methods used to gather evidence for an intervention and to evaluate its effects. However, we'll first take a moment to consider some of the biases that can influence our judgements.

Imagine a headteacher of a school piloting a new government scheme designed to encourage children to eat more fruit and vegetables. She may notice lots of children in the dinner hall eating apples or fruit salad for dessert, she may have parents tell her how delighted they are their children are now eating peas and carrots and she may hear children talk excitedly about kiwi and mango. To her, the evidence that the scheme has had a positive effect may seem overwhelming. Indeed, it may seem so obvious that any formal evaluation could be considered an unnecessary waste of public money. However, as humans we're prone to a number of biases and errors of judgement that mean that what we perceive, and the conclusions we draw, do not always reflect reality. In particular:

- We tend to see patterns and causal relationships where there are none (Gilovich et al., 1985; Redelmeier & Tversky, 1996; Tversky & Kahneman, 1974)

- We show a confirmation bias (Nickerson, 1998). This means we:

  » Tend to seek out information that supports rather than refutes our view

  » Are more likely to recall information that supports rather than refutes our view

  » Place more value on evidence that supports rather than refutes our view

  » Fail to consider alternative explanations that are inconsistent with our view.

---

1   If you do decide to dig a big hole in the sand, resist the temptation to crawl into it. Fatalities occur when sand collapses on top of a person.

CHAPTER 10

- We often use an availability heuristic. In other words, we evaluate the likelihood of events according to the ease with which relevant examples come to mind (Tversky & Kahneman, 1973, 1974).

- We often use an affect heuristic (Finucane et al., 2000; Kahneman, 2011; Slovic & Peters, 2006). In other words, we may use the way we feel about something to guide our judgements and decisions. We are also likely to be more influenced by information that is associated with strong emotions and visual imagery.

These heuristics and biases can help explain why we may be more afraid of sharks than cars. Relatively rare events, such as shark attacks, are more likely to be reported in the news and shared on social media compared to more common events such as car accidents. This means that when thinking about the likelihood of a shark attack, examples come readily to mind making it seem far more likely than it actually is (we are relying on an availability heuristic to assess the probability of a shark attack). The idea of a shark (or sea that might contain a shark) is also likely to elicit much stronger emotions than the idea of a car or a car drive; we have probably seen dramatised shark attacks in movies, footage of sharks attacking prey in wildlife documentaries, and pictures of menacing-looking shark teeth in magazines and on websites. Thus our concept of sharks will be associated with visual imagery and strong (negative) emotions that are more likely to influence our judgements than a series of dry statistics about the relative frequency of shark attacks. The same cannot really be said of cars, which are more likely to be linked in our minds to mundane, everyday experiences of simply getting from one place to another. Even where cars are associated with strong emotions and visual imagery (such as a coveted sports car), these will likely be positive rather than negative. These feelings guide our thinking and behaviour (we use an affect heuristic).

Returning to our example of the headteacher, who has just introduced the new scheme to promote fruit and vegetable consumption, we can see how some information (children eating apples at lunch) may be more readily available than other information (children eating fewer apples on the way home from school). We can also see how she may be more influenced by information associated with strong emotions (three parents' delight at their children now eating peas and carrots) than other information that may actually be more meaningful (uptake of peas and carrots in the canteen). Additionally, we should be aware of the fact that she may only have started looking out for evidence of fruit and vegetable consumption after the introduction of the scheme, which means she may have failed to notice (or recall) all the children eating bananas before the scheme was introduced. Finally, given the time she has invested in the scheme, and the fact that she really wants to improve the diets of her pupils, she may genuinely be less likely to notice or remember the children at lunchtime who push their broccoli to one side of their plate or throw away their apples after just one bite.

Thus we are not always very good at judging evidence. Indeed, these types of biases occur even among experts, and irrespective of the person's level of intelligence (Stanovich et al., 2013). For these reasons, we cannot simply rely on our gut feelings and impressions to tell us whether an effect has occurred or an intervention has worked – instead we need science and statistics. In the following sections we look at different methods for gathering evidence and evaluating interventions.

BOX 10.1 CRITICALLY ANALYSING THE EVIDENCE

MAKING CONNECTIONS

This chapter will give you the tools you need to critically analyse the strength of the evidence for (a) specific determinants of health and ill health (**Chapters 2–4**), (b) theories of behaviour (**Chapters 5–8**), (c) specific behaviour change techniques (**Chapter 9**) and (d) interventions designed to change behaviour (**Chapter 12**). When weighing up the evidence for these, you can use this chapter to help identify the potential weaknesses associated with particular types of evidence and research methods. This in turn can help you establish whether more research is needed, for example using more rigorous methods. In **Chapter 11** we look at bias in research and how such biases can be overcome. This information can also help you critically analyse evidence in terms of looking for possible sources of bias. But don't forget, often it's simply not possible to obtain perfect evidence – an issue we also consider in more detail in **Chapter 11**.

OBSERVATIONAL STUDY DESIGNS

Observational study designs are where a researcher observes individuals without intervening in any way or introducing any kind of manipulation (in other words, participants are *not* assigned to conditions; Grimes & Schulz, 2002a). For this reason, observational studies cannot provide conclusive evidence of causal links. However, they can be used to generate hypotheses about an area, to test theories and to look for associations that are likely to reflect causal links. Evidence for causality is strengthened where a **dose-response relationship** can be demonstrated. (Note that observational study designs should not be confused with observational measures, see section on *Measuring Behaviour Change*).

> **Dose-response relationship** – where increases in exposure to one variable are associated with consistent increases or decreases in a particular outcome. For example, increased use of cigarettes may be associated with increased rates of lung cancer.

Descriptive studies

Where an observational study has no comparison group, it is called a 'descriptive study'. These are used, often as a first step in a field of study, to describe a particular population or phenomenon (Grimes & Schulz, 2002b). They aim to build up a clearer picture of the phenomenon to help inform further research and/or preventive measures.

Case reports and case-series reports

A case report is a descriptive study that describes a particular disease in one individual whilst a case-series report describes the same occurrence across a number of individuals. Case reports and case-series reports can help identify the emergence of new diseases. For example, AIDS was first identified in 1981 by doctors in North America who noticed similar patterns of symptoms occurring in groups of gay man in Los Angeles, New York and San Francisco. More recently, a case-series report has been used to identify lung injury in people using e-cigarettes (Layden et al., 2019).

Prevalence and surveillance studies

A prevalence study looks at the occurrence of a disease or condition across a population. Prevalence studies are how we know what proportion of the world's population suffers from obesity. Surveillance studies also look at the occurrence of a disease or condition across a population but with the additional aim of directly informing preventive measures. For example, surveillance research played an important role in the eradication of smallpox (**Chapter 2**); when incidences were identified immunisation programmes targeting the surrounding community were initiated.

Analytical studies

Where an observational study has a comparison group, it is called an 'analytical study'. In medical research, an analytical study is usually one of three types: cross-sectional, cohort, or case-control. However, in psychology, prospective studies are often used to test theory in addition to cross-sectional studies (see **Box 5.3**). Prospective and cohort studies can also be referred to as 'longitudinal studies' since they take measures from the same participants over time.

Cross-sectional studies

This type of study takes measures across a range of variables at a single point in time. The data can be used to identify associations between variables that may reflect causal relationships, but the data cannot be used to confirm causal relationships or determine the direction of any causality. For example, a cross-sectional study examining physical activity and the theory of planned behaviour (**Chapter 5**) may show that positive attitudes towards physical activity are associated with higher levels of physical activity. This may be because, as predicted by the theory of planned behaviour, positive attitudes lead to an increase in behaviour. However, it could also be because higher levels of activity lead to more positive attitudes, or because another factor, such as peer group norms, leads to both positive attitudes and higher levels of activity. Though we may see a relationship between attitudes and behaviour this does not necessarily mean they are causally related. Thus cross-sectional studies can disconfirm a hypothesised relationship (for example if attitudes show no relationship to activity) or they can provide data that are consistent with a causal relationship, but they cannot be used to test causality (see also **Box 5.3**).

Prospective studies

Prospective studies are similar to cross-sectional studies except that measures are taken from the same individuals at different points in time, in line with the ways in which variables are thought to influence one another. As noted above, this is a type of longitudinal study design that is often used to test psychological theory where the researcher is interested in the relationships between a number of different continuous variables (see **Box 5.3**).

Cohort studies

A cohort study involves identifying individuals who differ on a variable of interest (but are as similar as possible in all other respects) and following them over time in order to assess the extent to which the variable of interest is associated with differences in outcomes at later points (Grimes & Schulz, 2002c). The Whitehall studies we looked at in **Chapter 3** are examples of cohort studies; the socioeconomic status of individuals was identified at the start of the study and these people were then followed over time to examine the extent to which differences in socioeconomic status predicted differences in outcomes such as cardiovascular heart disease and premature death.

- A *prospective cohort study* uses current information to form the cohorts and participants are followed forward in time. The Whitehall studies fall into this category.

- In a *retrospective cohort study* historical information is used to identify the cohort. For example, a group of older men and women may be interviewed to identify their socioeconomic status in early life. This information can then be used to group them into cohorts based on early life socioeconomic status, which can in turn be examined in relation to subsequent outcomes.

- An *ambidirectional cohort study* combines both retrospective and prospective methods. For example, a middle-aged cohort may be interviewed about their early life experiences and followed up over time to look at the relationships between socioeconomic status and ill health.

As per prospective studies, cohort studies provide stronger evidence of causality than cross-sectional studies because they give an indication of the timing of the variables of interest. For example, we know whether a person's lower socioeconomic status preceded a decline in health or vice versa. Indeed, for certain fields of health research cohort studies represent the strongest type of study design one can employ, because it is simply not possible to randomly assign people to different conditions (such as high or low socioeconomic status). However, the lack of random group assignment also means we can never be completely certain that associations between variables occurred because one directly caused the other.

Case-control studies

In a case-control study, individuals are selected because of a particular outcome of interest (Schulz & Grimes, 2002d). A control group without the outcome of interest is also identified to act as a comparison. The individuals in this control group should be matched, as far as possible, with those in the case group. The histories of individuals in the two groups are then compared (for example using questionnaires, interviews or medical records) to investigate variables of interest that might have influenced the outcome. For example, a study looking at the influence of exposure to cigarette smoke on lung cancer would identify a group of individuals with lung cancer as well as a matched control group without lung cancer. The frequency of exposure to cigarette smoke would then be compared across the two groups. Case-control studies can be more efficient than cohort studies in terms of both time and money but selection of an appropriate control group can be difficult, which means they may be more at risk of bias (Schulz & Grimes, 2002d).

EXPERIMENTAL METHODS

Experimental methods are typically used for theory development and for testing the effects of a particular treatment or behaviour change technique (BCT). An experiment tests for cause and effect by manipulating an independent variable (the cause) and carefully measuring a dependent variable (the effect), whilst controlling for other variables (extraneous variables) that might also influence the dependent variable. In psychology there are two main types of experiments: laboratory experiments and field experiments.

Laboratory experiment

These are conducted within a laboratory or other controlled environment where it is possible to take accurate measurements, exclude extraneous variables and randomly allocate participants to different conditions. These factors make the laboratory experiment an excellent test of cause and effect. However, because the experiment is conducted in an artificial setting it means the results may not necessarily be the same as what happens in real life. In other words, the results may have low ecological validity.

Field experiment

As far as possible, field experiments mimic laboratory experiments except they are conducted in a real-life setting. This means they are likely to have higher ecological validity. However, it also means it may be more difficult to control for extraneous variables, randomly allocate participants to conditions or take accurate measurements. This in turn means it may be difficult to establish cause and effect with the same level of certainty as might be achieved in a laboratory experiment. The term 'field experiment' is sometimes used to describe a randomised controlled trial (see section titled *The Randomised Controlled Trial*).

N-OF-1 TRIALS

N-of-1 trials, also known as 'single-case' or 'single-subject' designs, are a type of experimental approach where repeated measures are taken from a single individual, or a single unit (such as a family, supermarket or hospital; Kazdin, 2011; McDonald et al., 2017; Naughton & Johnston, 2014). Confidence in the effect of an intervention comes not from replicating the effect over lots of people, but rather from demonstrating its consistency in just one individual (or unit). This is achieved by taking multiple measures of an outcome over extended periods of time in both the presence and the absence of the treatment. For example, measures of the main outcome may be taken during a baseline phase, after which the intervention is introduced and another set of measures are taken. The number of measures taken will depend on the nature of the behaviour and the variability of the individual, with more measurements needed where there is more variability. The data are then examined to determine whether there is a distinction in response between the baseline and intervention phases. There are a number of different types of n-of-1 study designs, described in the sections below.

AB, ABA and ABAB designs

A design with two phases is known as an 'AB design', where A refers to the baseline phase and B to the intervention phase. This provides relatively weak evidence for an effect because it is difficult to rule out the possibility that the switch in phase occurred at the same time as something else that influenced the outcome variable. Stronger evidence for effects can be obtained from an ABA design where the treatment is subsequently withdrawn and we would expect to see the relevant outcome return to baseline levels. Other types of n-of-1 trials include ABAB designs (used to more conclusively demonstrate the effect of the manipulation, see **Figure 10.1**), alternating treatment designs (where two different versions of a treatment are tested, for example, ABCBCBC) and randomised controlled trial designs (where intervention and control conditions are randomly allocated to different time periods within individuals).

Designs where a treatment is withdrawn can be used with BCTs where effects are expected to be short-lived such as planning, goal setting, contingent reinforcement, self-monitoring and feedback (Sniehotta et al., 2012). However, for many behavioural interventions such a test is not possible because of extended carryover effects, where effects are likely to last beyond the intervention phase. For example, a person cannot be made to forget about the risks of smoking. In these types of interventions, the last phase of an ABA design may instead be used to examine the maintenance of effects over time (McDonald et al., 2017).

Multiple baseline and changing criterion designs

These designs are more suited to instances where effects are likely to be more sustained or have a longer carryover, or where it is considered unethical to withdraw a treatment.

Figure 10.1 An n-of-1 study that uses an ABAB design. This design provides more conclusive evidence of effects than AB or ABA designs

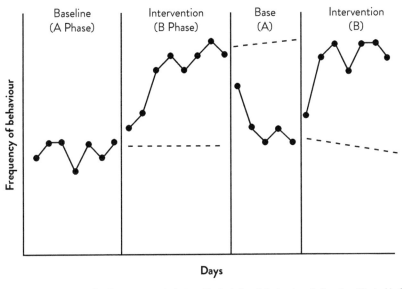

Source: Kazdin, A. E., *Single-case research designs: Methods for clinical and applied settings* (2nd ed.), Oxford University Press, New York, USA. Copyright © 2011. Reprinted with permission from Oxford University Press.

They provide much stronger evidence than an AB design. In multiple baseline designs the intervention is tested across several individuals or units but the point at which the intervention is introduced is staggered (**Figure 10.2**). For example, the effect of positioning fruit by the till at three workplace canteens might be examined using a multiple baseline design whereby the intervention (the re-positioning of the fruit) may be introduced after three weeks in the first canteen, four weeks in the second, and five weeks in the third. This would help rule out the influence of another factor being responsible for any increased uptake in fruit, for example a television programme highlighting the importance of fruit and vegetable consumption that just happened to coincide with the introduction of the intervention in the first canteen.

Changing criterion designs are useful where the aim is to produce a gradual change in the outcome. This gradual change is achieved by changing phases (usually intensifying them) when the outcome variable meets a pre-specified criterion. For example, an app that provides virtual rewards for physical activity may initially reward 1,000 steps per day. Once this has been achieved over three consecutive days the target may be increased to 2,000 steps and so on.

Data analysis for n-of-1 trials

Most n-of-1 studies use visual analysis to determine whether the intervention has an effect on behaviour (McDonald, 2017). In other words, the data are graphed to look for a distinct relationship between outcome variable and study phase, taking account of the average level of the outcome variable in each phase, the extent to which it varies, the immediacy of any change when phases are switched, the presence of any trends within phases and the consistency of data in similar phases (for example in an ABAB design; Chen et al,, 2015).

CHAPTER 10

Figure 10.2 An n-of-1 study that uses a multiple baseline design. This type of study uses staggering to test the effects of an intervention across multiple individuals or units

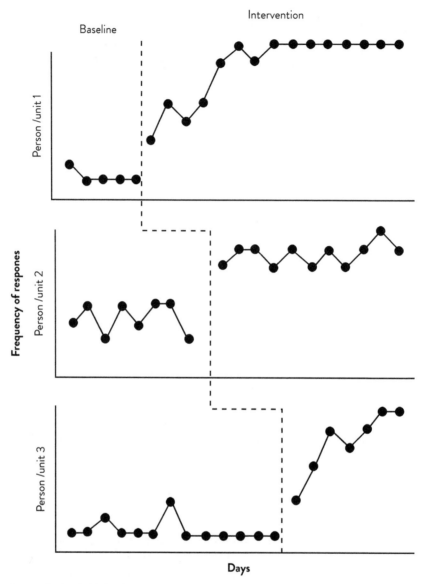

Source: Kazdin, A. E., Single-case research designs: Methods for clinical and applied settings (2nd ed.), Oxford University Press, New York, USA. Copyright © 2011. Reprinted with permission from Oxford University Press.

However, trends in the data can make interpretation difficult (for example, a trend at baseline that is in the same direction as the predicted effect of the intervention). Carryover effects can also complicate analysis and studies should be designed with intervention and control phases that are long enough to accommodate these.

There is also evidence to suggest that relying on visual analysis could sometimes introduce bias into the conclusions drawn from the data, with different researchers interpreting the same graph in different ways (Ninci et al., 2015). As such, some researchers suggest that statistical analysis can sometimes be preferable, though this may require a larger number of data points (Kazdin, 2011; McDonald, 2017). Where a particular n-of-1 protocol is employed with a group of participants it is possible to use statistical analyses such as multi-level modelling or random effects meta-analysis to also determine the extent to which findings generalise across the group and to examine variables that may moderate effects between individuals.

Advantages of n-of-1 trials

N-of-1 trials are useful because they provide information about the effect of an intervention on an individual. The same is not always true of other types of study design where effects are averaged across a large number of people and may not necessarily reflect the actual pattern of effect in any one person. For example, a study that compares an intervention and control group may show no average effect of an intervention whilst in reality it may have had a positive effect on some people and a negative effect on others. In principle such differences could be detected in a group-based design where one can identify and measure the factor that is moderating the effect (for example, perhaps the intervention has a positive effect among those with high self-efficacy and a negative effect amongst those with low self-efficacy) but such analyses still only provide estimates of average effects among larger groups of people rather than effects among individuals (or very small groups). Identifying effects at the individual level can be important in relation to theory testing; most theories of behaviour change describe the behaviour of individuals but group-based designs can disguise the fact that some people show patterns of effect that fail to support a theory, or even contradict it (Johnston & Johnston, 2013). The same applies to the trajectory of a behaviour over time; the average trajectory may not accurately reflect the true trajectory in any one person.

N-of-1 trials are also useful as they tend to include far more data points than group designs which in turn provide more information about the time course of a behaviour, for example whether it naturally rises or falls over time and the extent to which the effects of an intervention maintain or dissipate. Again this can be useful for theory testing, for example for ascertaining whether change in a particular construct (such as self-efficacy) precedes or follows a change in behaviour. Additionally, n-of-1 trials can be used with units (such as schools or supermarkets) where it may be difficult to obtain individual-level data and/or to recruit a sufficient number of units to allow them to be randomised into intervention or control groups.

Finally, n-of-1 methods can be useful for personalised medicine (see **Chapter 4**) where an intervention is tailored to an individual. For example, an n-of-1 method may be used to identify the predictors of a particular behaviour for an individual or to decide when to use different BCTs. In this way an n-of-1 approach can be used both as a type of intervention as well as a method of evaluation. This is becoming increasingly achievable with the use of smartphones and apps that allow behaviours and responses to be tracked throughout the day and BCTs to be delivered to individuals without the need for a health practitioner.

INTERRUPTED TIME-SERIES DESIGN

An interrupted time-series design can be viewed as a type of AB, n-of-1 study design. However, whilst n-of-1 study designs are often used with single individuals, and have their origins within clinical and educational settings, interrupted time-series designs tend to be applied to population-level data, for example in fields such as economics and policy. Nevertheless, the same principles apply; a particular outcome is tracked over an extended period of time in order to examine the effects of a particular intervention that is introduced part way through this period. For example, sales of sugary drinks can be monitored over time to determine whether the introduction of a sugar tax results in decreased sales (see **Chapter 12**, **Case Study 2**; also **Case Study 8** on cigarette packaging). Data are typically analysed using regression models but interpretation can be difficult where trends are non-linear, where the intervention is introduced gradually, where the variable of interest shows seasonal effects, or where the characteristics of the population change over time (Kontopantelis et al., 2015). Confidence in effects can be strengthened with a control time-series design, where the outcome of interest is also tracked in another group (for example another country or region) that does not receive the intervention.

META-ANALYSES

Advantages of meta-analyses

Meta-analyses combine the results of studies that have all looked at the same research question. They do this by taking the **effect size** for each study, weighting it by its accuracy (the sample size it was based on) and then computing an average effect size from all the studies. Meta-analyses therefore provide much stronger evidence for an effect than any one single study. They also provide a more accurate indication of the size of any effect.

> **Effect size** – a measure of the relative size of any effect. Effect size measures include Cohen's *d*, Pearson's *r*, and the odds ratio.

Potential pitfalls

Notwithstanding their advantages, caution should be used where meta-analyses examine the effects of behaviour change interventions. Peters et al. (2015) highlight a number of potential problems with these types of meta-analyses. First, if they fail to take account of relevant moderators (what they call 'parameters of effectiveness'), they may reach inaccurate conclusions about their effects. For example, implementation intentions may only be effective where people are motivated to change their behaviour. A meta-analysis that combined results of studies of implementation intentions used among both motivated and unmotivated individuals might incorrectly conclude that effects were weak or indeed absent (if there were many more studies with unmotivated than motivated individuals). Thus it is important that meta-analyses take account of potential moderators.

Second, Peters et al. (2015) state that there is often overlap between the BCTs being used in an intervention and those being used in the control group. This may occur because it is viewed as good practice to compare a new intervention with 'standard care', that is, current practice, since it would only make sense to introduce a new intervention if it was significantly better (see section on *The Randomised Controlled Trial*). However, where specific BCTs are being used in both the new intervention and the comparison group, it limits the conclusions that can be drawn about their effects. For example, suppose researchers were testing an intervention designed to improve diet among people at risk of developing diabetes, and this new intervention comprised a series of six group-based workshops using a range of different BCTs including information about health consequences, goal setting, problem solving, action planning and social support. They might compare this to standard care that may consist of three 10-minute appointments with a health professional. However, these three 10-minute appointments may also include many of the BCTs used in the new intervention. Thus, even if there was no difference between the new intervention and standard care, one could not conclude that those BCTs had no effect. Of course, the obvious solution would be to only include studies in meta-analyses where the BCT of interest was used in the intervention but not the comparison group. However, this is easier said than done since many studies do not clearly describe the exact contents of the comparison treatment (see section on *Reporting research*).

Third, Peters et al. (2015) point out that certain groups of BCTs often co-occur. For example, if use of social comparison is always accompanied by providing information about health consequences, it is not possible to know whether social comparison is effective, or whether effects are actually driven by the information about health consequences. To properly test the effects of social comparison one would need a study that compared four conditions: no BCTs; information about health consequences; social comparison; social comparison plus information about health consequences. This would allow us to establish whether social comparison worked in isolation and/or whether it enhanced the effects of providing information about health consequences. However, one generally needs twice as many participants to compare four conditions instead of two and this type of study design is rare for interventions carried out in applied settings.

Recommendations and the iterative protocol for evidence base accumulation (IPEBA)

For the above reasons, Peters et al. (2015) argue that it is difficult to draw conclusions about the effectiveness of particular BCTs from meta-analyses of heterogeneous behaviour change interventions. They call for more selective inclusion of studies in meta-analyses, using only those where a BCT has been employed appropriately (in other words, taking account of moderators) and applied differentially (that is, used in the intervention group but not the comparison group). They also call for more experimental studies testing the effects of individual BCTs (rather than behaviour change interventions that employ multiple BCTs). Such experimental studies would be better able to identify main and interaction effects of BCTs as well as identify relevant moderators. They suggest using what they refer to as an 'iterative protocol for evidence base accumulation' (IPEBA) to integrate evidence from applied interventions (that have the advantage of high external validity) with experimental studies (that have the advantage of high internal validity); see **Figure 10.3**.

Figure 10.3 The iterative protocol for evidence base accumulation (IPEBA)

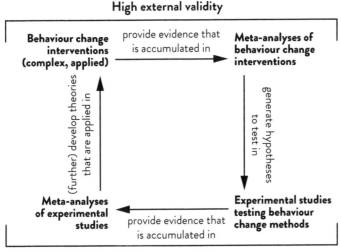

Source: Peters et al., 2015. Reprinted with permission from Taylor & Francis, www.tandfonline.com.

THE RANDOMISED CONTROLLED TRIAL

The randomised controlled trial (RCT) is considered the gold standard for evaluating behaviour change interventions (**Box 10.2**). RCTs have been the norm in medical research for over 50 years. For example, in most countries drug companies will not be given a licence to market a new drug until they have demonstrated its effects using an RCT. However, it is only more recently that they have become the standard for evaluating behaviour change interventions. An RCT has a number of important features:

- Participants are randomised to intervention and control conditions.

- Researchers should be unaware of the order in which participants are being assigned to intervention and control conditions.

- The primary outcome (the dependent variable) and any secondary outcomes (any other dependent variables of interest) should be decided upon before data collection begins and the trial should be registered with an official registry (such as ClinicalTrials.gov).

- Calculations are made to determine the sample size needed to answer the research questions. Again, this is done before data collection is started.

- Ideally, participants will be blind to group allocation (so they will not know whether they have been allocated to an experimental or control condition). However, this is not always possible, for example where it might be difficult to recruit participants to a trial without giving them some indication of the intervention content.

- Ideally, the researchers collecting the data will also be blind to participants' group allocation, though again this is not always possible, for example where it is difficult to prevent participants from revealing their group allocation to the researcher.

- Participants in intervention and control groups are treated identically with the exception of the experimental treatment.

We now look at these features in more detail as well as some other important aspects of RCTs.

BOX 10.2 WHEN DOES AN EXPERIMENT BECOME A TRIAL?

DIG A LITTLE DEEPER

In the USA, the National Institutes of Health (NIH) defines a trial as a type of experiment that examines the effects of an intervention (National Institutes of Health, 2014). But what is an intervention? The NIH states that a health intervention is any manipulation of a person or their environment designed to modify one or more health-related processes or outcomes (National Institutes of Health, 2014). These definitions mean that any piece of research that uses experimental methods to study health-related processes or outcomes should be considered a trial.

However, others have argued that we should instead distinguish between experiments and trials on the basis of their characteristics and their aims (Wiers et al., 2018). For example, whilst experiments are typically concerned with examining psychological mechanisms underlying behaviour and are usually carried out in the laboratory with healthy volunteers (who may not be motivated to change), trials are more concerned with examining the effects of an intervention in a clinical sample (who may be motivated to change) outside the laboratory.

Nevertheless, many studies combine several of these elements, for example they may look at both psychological mechanisms and effects on behaviour in a clinical population in the laboratory. Thus the labels of 'experiment' and 'trial' are best viewed as describing a continuum rather than two distinct categories.

Explanatory versus pragmatic trials

An explanatory trial is one designed to test the efficacy of an intervention and identify underlying mechanisms of action. Explanatory trials are characterised by tight methodological controls, used to ensure the results are free from bias. In other words, explanatory trials tend to have what we call high internal validity. However, high internal validity can come at the expense of external validity (also termed generalisability or applicability). External validity is the extent to which results are likely to reflect the type of results that would be obtained 'in the real world', or if an intervention were to be rolled out across the country or became part of 'usual care'.

The emphasis traditionally given to internal validity has led some to argue that external validity has been neglected (Ford & Norrie, 2016; Lobb & Colditz, 2015; Treweek & Zwarenstein, 2009). For example, it has been argued that explanatory trials often use populations, procedures or settings that bear little relation to those the intervention is ultimately intended for. This means that benefits may be overestimated, harms underestimated and implementation may prove difficult. These researchers call for more pragmatic trials that place more emphasis on external validity, and seek to establish the effectiveness of an intervention, that is, its effects when implemented in real life rather than in ideal circumstances. Pragmatic trials often aim to establish whether a new intervention is better than what is already in place (Sedgwick, 2014).

In reality, it is rarely possible to describe a trial as purely explanatory or purely pragmatic; the difference should be viewed as a continuum rather than a sharp distinction. However, when designing a trial one should think carefully about its aims, and how these aims will be met by the type of trial design employed. Often trials that are more explanatory will be more appropriate for interventions in earlier stages of development, when it is important to establish the nature of any effect and to gain a better understanding of underlying mechanisms. Pragmatic trials may be more suited to later stages of intervention development, where one is more interested in real-world utility. The PRECIS-2 tool (Pragmatic Explanatory Continuum Indicator Summary) can be used when designing a trial to help ensure it is able to answer the questions it is intended to answer (Loudon et al., 2015). Use of the tool involves deciding on the aim of the trial, whether it is primarily intended to be explanatory or pragmatic, and then considering trial design choices in nine different domains (see **Table 10.1**).

Blinding

Blinding refers to a procedure whereby study participants, investigators (those delivering the intervention) and assessors (those collecting outcome data) are kept unaware of group assignment so they are not influenced by this knowledge (Schulz & Grimes, 2002a). A single-blind trial is a trial in which just one of these groups is blinded (usually the study participants) whereas a double-blind trial typically refers to instances in which participants

Table 10.1 The nine domains that need to be considered when using the PRECIS-2 tool to assist with trial design

Domain (from Loudon et al., 2015)	Examples of a more explanatory approach	Examples of a more pragmatic approach
Eligibility – to what extent are participants in the trial similar to those who would receive this intervention if it was part of usual care?	Inclusion restricted to those most likely to benefit. Exclusion of participants who are unlikely to adhere to the intervention or for whom it may be difficult to collect data from.	Inclusion of any participant to whom the intervention may be offered if it were implemented in the real world.
Recruitment – how much extra effort is made to recruit participants over and above what would be used in the usual care setting to engage participants?	Use of press releases, newspapers advertisements, websites and other forms of media to aid recruitment. Use of incentives (that are not part of the intervention) to aid recruitment or adherence.	Recruitment using the same method via which individuals would be identified if the intervention were to be implemented in the real world.
Setting – how different are the settings of the trial from the usual care setting?	Trial conducted at just one, carefully selected site rather than multiple, different sites with diverse practices and people.	Trial conducted in a setting or sites identical to one(s) in which the intervention will eventually be used.
Organisation – how different are the resources, provider expertise, and the organisation of care delivery in the intervention arm of the trial from those available in usual care?	Provision of additional staff to deliver the intervention or additional training to staff to deliver the intervention. Provision of additional resources to facilitate intervention delivery.	Reliance on existing staff and resources.
Flexibility in delivery – how different is the flexibility in how the intervention is delivered and the flexibility anticipated in usual care?	Requirement that those delivering the intervention follow a specific procedure. Measures used to assess compliance with this procedure.	Those who are delivering the intervention allowed to make decisions about how it will be implemented.
Flexibility in adherence – how different is the flexibility in how participants are monitored and encouraged to adhere to the intervention from the flexibility anticipated in usual care?	Withdrawal of participants from the trial if they show low adherence or exclusion of their data. Use of additional procedures to address poor adherence.	No inclusion of additional procedures to promote intervention adherence (over and above what might typically be used if the intervention were to be implemented).
Follow-up – how different is the intensity of measurement and follow-up of participants in the trial from the typical follow-up in usual care?	Collection of extensive follow-up data directly from participants.	Use of follow-up measures that do not involve contacting or interacting with participants.
Primary outcome – to what extent is the trial's primary outcome directly relevant to participants?	Selection of an outcome because of its theoretical importance.	Selection of an outcome that is important to intervention users and policy makers.
Primary analysis – to what extent are all data included in the analysis of the primary outcome?	Use of per-protocol analysis, that is, only including data from participants who adhered to the intervention.	Use of intention-to-treat analysis, that is, including all participants who were recruited into the trial, even those who dropped out.

and researchers (investigators and assessors) are blinded. However, use of these terms varies, with double-blind sometimes being used to refer to instances in which just two of these groups are blinded and with some trials being referred to as triple-blind (or even quadruple-blind, where those analysing the data are unaware of which groups were which).

Since there is inconsistency in the use of these terms it is important that, when reporting the results of a trial, researchers are always clear about exactly who was blinded and how.

Blinding of participants helps control for placebo effects (see **Chapter 1**) and helps limit **demand characteristics**. Blinding of participants also means they are less likely to drop out of the study, are less likely to seek additional interventions and are more likely to adhere to study procedures (Schulz & Grimes, 2002a). However, some argue that participant blinding may be less appropriate for pragmatic trials where knowledge of treatment allocation could be considered to be part of the treatment (Sedgwick, 2014).

Blinding of investigators helps avoid bias in the way in which the investigator treats or interacts with participants. For example, consciously or unconsciously, they may end up motivating or assisting those in the intervention group more than those in the control group. They may also differ in the extent to which they encourage participants to stay in the trial, resulting in biased drop-out between trial arms, for example with participants who are less likely to change their behaviour being more likely to drop out of the intervention group and vice versa. Blinding of assessors is important in order to avoid their expectations influencing their assessments (sometimes referred to as 'information bias' or 'ascertainment bias'). This is more important when assessing variables that rely on a certain amount of judgement (such as when measuring someone's waist-to-hip ratio) and becomes less important where variables are more objective (such as when measuring someone's weight and height).

> **Demand characteristics** – where a study participant changes their behaviour in response to knowledge about how they are expected to behave. For example, they may behave in a way that conforms to the study hypothesis in order to be a 'good' participant and 'help' the experimenter. Conversely, they may attempt to prove the experimenter wrong by doing the opposite to expectations (sometimes known as the 'screw you' effect).

Allocation concealment

Allocation concealment refers to a process whereby researchers and participants are kept unaware of the schedule of assignments to intervention and control groups (Schulz & Grimes, 2002b). This is slightly different from blinding; one cannot blind without allocation concealment but one can employ allocation concealment without blinding. Specifically, the investigators delivering the intervention may be aware of which intervention they are delivering (they are not blind to group allocation) but they may still be unaware of the group allocation schedule, and will not know whether the next participant to sign up to the trial will be allocated to the intervention or control group. This is important because it prevents bias creeping into the way in which participants are assigned to groups (known as 'selection bias'). For example, if a researcher is keen to show that the intervention is effective, they may be inclined to allocate the most 'promising' looking participants to the intervention group, or to schedule appointments so they are allocated to the intervention group. Or they may exclude certain participants if they know they will be allocated to the 'wrong' group. Alternatively, they may be keen for certain participants to be allocated to a particular group if they believe they would benefit most from that treatment.

Such behaviours may be performed unconsciously or, in some instances, people may actively try to decipher the allocation schedule. For example, a common method of allocation concealment is to use sequentially numbered, opaque, sealed envelopes, each containing a group number, and each intended to be opened only after a participant has been recruited into the trial. However, it is not unheard of for practitioners to open envelopes before they're meant to or to hold them up to the light in order to see the number inside (Schulz & Grimes, 2002b). Indeed, research shows that trials without adequate allocation concealment can lead to an increase in estimates of effect size of up to 40% (Schulz, 1995; see also Kennedy et al., 2017). Such problems may be more likely where those responsible for group assignment do not fully understand the consequences of their actions or the importance of preventing bias when allocating participants to groups (Schulz, 1995). Thus efforts should be made to emphasise the importance of allocation concealment to all those involved in the trial and to ensure that allocation concealment is effective, for example by making certain that those responsible for group allocation have no involvement with participants. This can be achieved by sing an independent centralised randomisation service or a computer-assisted method with automatic assignment.

Randomisation

Whilst allocation concealment refers to the way in which an assignment schedule is implemented, randomisation describes the procedure that should be used to generate the schedule (Schulz & Grimes, 2002c). Like allocation concealment, this helps eliminate bias when assigning participants to treatment groups. It also facilitates blinding. Randomisation is not the same as alternate allocation where a researcher alternately assigns participants to different groups. Alternate allocation is inferior to randomisation as it makes both blinding and allocation concealment difficult. Thus alternate allocation to groups should never be described as random allocation.

Unrestricted randomisation

The most straightforward type of randomisation is unrestricted (or simple) randomisation. This type of randomisation is equivalent to repeated coin tossing and ensures that group allocation follows a completely unpredictable pattern. This in turn can help with allocation concealment as it makes it impossible for a researcher to spot any patterns in the schedule and guess which group the next participant will be assigned to. However, unrestricted randomisation does mean that participant numbers in each of the conditions will not necessarily be the same. Participants in each condition may also vary on certain characteristics, for example an intervention group may end up with a higher proportion of females compared to the control group. Nevertheless, as sample sizes get larger, the chances of such imbalances get smaller, such that for larger trials (those with over 100 participants per condition) the chances of significant imbalance become so small that unrestricted randomisation is likely to represent the best option (Lachin, 1988). (Though note that having a completely unpredictable assignment sequence will be of little benefit without successful allocation concealment – a trial needs both adequate sequence generation and successful allocation concealment.)

Restricted randomisation: blocking

In smaller trials, restricted randomisation methods may be used to avoid sample size imbalances between conditions. The most common of these is blocking. For example, where a trial with two conditions has a schedule with a block size of four, two participants within each block will be randomised to the intervention group and two will be randomised to the control group. However, the order of intervention and control group assignment within each block will be randomly varied. So with two conditions, A and B, a block size of four would result in six different permutations: AABB; BBAA; ABAB; BABA; ABBA; BAAB.

Block sizes can vary from very small (only two[2]) to quite large (such as twenty). However, some academics caution against using smaller block sizes since they make it

2　If you use online software such as Qualtrics to run a study, and you program it to evenly present each condition, it will employ blocked randomisation with a block size that is equivalent to the number of conditions you have. In other words, with two conditions (for example an experimental condition and a control condition), it will use a block size of two.

more likely that researchers or practitioners will guess the block size and be able to predict certain group allocations. For example, with a block size of four, every fourth allocation within a block can be predicted with perfect accuracy, and every third allocation can be accurately predicted one-third of the time (Clark et al., 2016). Indeed, there have been reports of practitioners working out that a block size of six has been used for randomisation and selection bias affecting the trial (Clark et al., 2016). Avoiding smaller block sizes (of six or less), and also randomly varying the block size, can help overcome this problem.

Restricted randomisation: random allocation rule

Another method of restricted randomisation is the random allocation rule. This is where investigators identify the total sample size before the start of the trial, and then randomly select a subset (or subsets) of the sample to be allocated to a particular condition (or conditions). For a study with 200 participants and two conditions, this would be the equivalent of placing 200 balls in a container, labelled as either intervention group or control group, and then picking each one out at random (without putting any back in again) to determine the order of allocation.

Restricted randomisation: biased coin and urn

One disadvantage of the random allocation rule is that it assumes the trial will be able to recruit the pre-specified number of participants. By contrast, biased coin and urn randomisation methods allow for a little more flexibility in total sample size since they alter allocation probabilities during the course of a trial to adjust for any imbalances that may have occurred. For example, randomisation may start with a 50:50 probability of allocating a participant to an intervention or control group, but if an imbalance between intervention and control group numbers exceed a certain threshold (such as 60% have been allocated to the intervention group and 40% to the control group), the probability is adjusted (for example to a 40:60 ratio) until the imbalance drops back below the ratio.

Stratified randomisation

However, none of the above methods guard against imbalances in the baseline characteristics of participants. This is important where certain characteristics may be related to the trial outcomes. For example, if, in a weight loss trial, participants in our intervention group have a significantly higher BMI than participants in our control group, this will make interpreting the study findings very difficult. We might find significantly higher weight loss in our intervention group, but could that simply be because these participants had higher BMIs to start with, and so had more weight to lose? We can use stratified randomisation, in combination with restricted randomisation, to ensure our groups are balanced in relation to characteristics we think may be important. For stratified randomisation investigators essentially create different allocation schedules for each of the characteristics. For example, in a weight loss trial recruiting participants with BMIs in excess of 30, we may create two strata relating to BMIs from (a) 30 to 35 and (b) 35+. If we also think gender will be important, we can divide these into four strata: (a) males 30–35, (b) males 35+, (c) females 30–35, (d) females 35+. Within each of these strata we may then use blocked randomisation to ensure that each type of participant is distributed evenly to the intervention and control groups. When a participant enters the trial, it is then a matter of identifying which stratum they fall under and following the allocation schedule for that stratum.

However, we can see that when we try to balance more than just a couple of variables, the number of strata can become unmanageable. For example, with four variables, each divided into 2 types, we would need 16 strata ($2 \times 2 \times 2 \times 2 = 16$). Likewise, we might want to divide a variable into more than two types. For example, for a weight loss trial, researchers may think that current attempts to lose weight will be important and they may divide these into supported weight loss (such as attending a slimming club), unsupported weight loss (such as dieting independently) or not attempting to lose weight. Including this variable alongside gender and BMI (30–35 versus 35+) would increase the number of strata to 12 ($2 \times 2 \times 3 = 12$). For smaller trials a large number of strata is problematic as it increases the likelihood of an imbalance in numbers between conditions (Pocock, 2006).

Minimisation

One solution to the problem of too many strata is to use a method called 'minimisation'. This is where the next participant is assigned to a condition in a way that minimises the differences between group allocations for that particular type of participant. For example, suppose for our weight loss trial we recruit a female with a BMI of over 35 who is using supported weight loss (attending a slimming club). We would refer to our recruitment records to work out the number of female supported weight loss participants with BMIs of over 35 already allocated to the intervention group, and the number already allocated to the control group. We would then assign our new participant to the group that had the lowest number, in order to minimise the differences between the intervention and control groups on these variables. (If the numbers were equal, we could allocate the participant randomly.) Strictly speaking, minimisation involves little randomisation so again it may be possible for those involved in recruitment to decipher the pattern of allocation (though see Pocock (2006) for ways to introduce greater randomisation). Minimisation is most useful in trials of less than 100 participants where there are several variables researchers want to balance (Popock, 2006). (Note that the more participants there are in a trial, the more likely the groups are to be balanced anyway, making stratification and minimisation unnecessary.)

Primary outcomes, secondary outcomes and trial registration

Another important way of avoiding bias creeping into the research literature is to ensure that the primary outcome and any secondary outcomes are identified before data collection begins. This is because trials will often collect data on a range of different outcomes. If you imagine a trial collecting data on 20 different outcomes, simply by chance alone we are likely to see a significant effect on one of these. It can then be tempting for researchers, either consciously or unconsciously, to decide that this was in fact the most important outcome and report the research as a study specifically designed to examine the effects of the intervention on this particular outcome. This introduces bias into the research literature. By stating up front what the most important outcome is, this problem is avoided. In order to ensure that this decision is made prior to data collection and analysis, and to enable others to check that the researchers have done what they said they would do, trials are registered before data collection commences. Registration involves providing details of primary and secondary outcomes as well as other information such as sample size, participant inclusion and exclusion criteria, participant recruitment methods, trial arms (conditions), measures and data analysis. This information is then time stamped and made publicly available so that when the results of the evaluation are published it is possible to confirm that the researchers have not adjusted their study or their analyses in ways that might introduce bias.

Sample size calculations and clinically significant effects

A sample size calculation, also known as a power calculation, is used to determine the number of participants needed in order to detect a statistically significant effect of the intervention treatment on the primary outcome. Sample size calculations are important to ensure the trial can properly test the hypothesis; too few participants and the study will be underpowered, making it difficult to draw any conclusions from the data. On the other hand, too many participants represent a waste of time and resources and can also be considered unethical where participants are volunteering their time and/or public money is being used to fund the trial. For these reasons, a sample size calculation should be conducted during the planning stages of a trial and should be reported in the trial registration.

To conduct a sample size calculation one first needs to decide on the type of statistical tests that are going to be used to analyse the data. One also needs to estimate the likely difference in the primary outcome between the comparison conditions (the absolute effect size), as well as the likely variability between participants on this outcome (which could stem from either true participant variability and/or from measurement error, and is represented by statistics such as standard deviations and confidence intervals). (Though note that a standardised effect size, such as Cohen's *d* or an odds ratio, takes account of variability so may be used in place of measures of absolute effect size and variability.)

These estimates may be made from pilot studies or from other studies that have used similar methods and outcome measures. Alternatively, they may be based on what would be considered a clinically significant effect. A clinically significant effect refers to an effect that is large enough to bring about a meaningful benefit. For example, experts may agree that an increase in fruit and vegetable consumption of one portion a day would be sufficient to bring about meaningful health benefits (such as a reduction in the risks of cardiovascular disease, cancer and all-cause mortality; Aune et al., 2017). However, an increase of one portion a week may be considered too small to bring about any meaningful health benefits and thus could not be used to justify the time and expense of the intervention. As such, from an applied perspective, there is little point in powering a study to detect an effect this small.

Finally, a sample size calculation should also take account of attrition, particularly where an intervention is conducted over an extended period. For example, although 100 participants may sign up to your weight loss intervention, six months later, when you want to know how much weight your participants have lost, you may find that five people have moved away and cannot be contacted and a further five have simply lost interest and do not want to take part in any more of the measures. If you needed 100 participants to detect your effect, you would now find your study underpowered. As such, when making a sample size calculation it is also important to estimate and account for likely attrition. Again, this can be estimated by looking at previous trials or pilot studies.

After completing a sample size calculation, it is not uncommon for researchers to discover they need far more participants than they anticipated. Invariably this increases the time and costs associated with the research, which may in turn make it impractical, particularly where recruitment of eligible participants is likely to be slow or challenging. Where solutions to these problems cannot be found, some authors (such as Pocock, 2006) argue that the trial should simply be abandoned before it starts because an underpowered trial will not be able to tell us anything useful about whether or not the intervention worked. However, others (such as Schulz & Grimes, 2005) argue that the results from such trials can be usefully incorporated into subsequent meta-analyses, provided the trial is methodologically strong (so unlikely to be biased) and the results are published (even where they show no effect). Indeed, Schulz and Grimes argue that a very carefully conducted underpowered trial is far more informative than a larger trial where methodological weaknesses may have introduced bias into the results.

Control group treatments

Another important decision that needs to be made when designing an RCT is what the intervention will be compared with. This decision is likely to be influenced by the extent to which the trial is explanatory versus pragmatic.

Standard care

As previously described, a pragmatic trial generally aims to establish whether a new intervention is better than current practice. As such, the new intervention is usually compared to 'standard care'. This makes sense because if we are thinking about introducing an additional intervention (that will inevitably be at additional cost) or if we are thinking about replacing an existing intervention, we need to know not just whether the new intervention is effective, but also whether it is significantly more effective than what is already being done.

For example, a patient who asks their doctor for help with quitting smoking could be randomised to standard care (which may mean being offered nicotine replacement therapy and a series of telephone support sessions) or to the intervention group (which may include a new series of group-based workshops focussing on cravings and motivation). With this type of design, it is important to think carefully about what the final intervention might comprise and what one wants to test. To illustrate, in our smoking intervention, if the aim of the group workshops was to enhance existing care, one would want to compare provision of nicotine replacement therapy and telephone support (standard care control group) with provision of nicotine replacement therapy, telephone support plus workshops (intervention group). On the other hand, if the ultimate aim was to replace the telephone support sessions with group workshops one would want to compare provision of nicotine therapy and telephone support with provision of nicotine therapy and workshops.

However, as discussed (see section on *Meta-analyses*), these types of comparisons can make it difficult to control for, and therefore draw conclusions about, the effects of particular BCTs. For example, goal setting may be used in both the telephone support sessions and the workshops. Similarly, both are likely to provide social support. Thus although this type of pragmatic trial may be ideal for testing the applied utility of an intervention and for selecting one type of intervention over another, it is not as useful for helping us to really understand the mechanisms underpinning the intervention or for advancing theory. For this we really need to use an explanatory trial where much more careful consideration is given to controlling for BCTs across conditions.

No-treatment and wait-list

For an explanatory trial, from a practical point of view the most straightforward type of control group is likely to be a no-treatment control, where participants do not receive any intervention. However, this type of approach usually rules out participant blinding. A similar solution is to have a wait-list control, where participants are offered the intervention only once the trial has finished. This may help prevent attrition within the control group and may also dissuade participants within the control group from seeking alternative treatments during the trial. However, a wait-list control usually still rules out participant blinding.

Alternative types of control group

An alternative is to provide control participants with an intervention that it is thought will have minimal effect and does not include any BCTs that are also contained in the new intervention. For example, a leaflet or booklet containing information participants are likely to already know could be used. However, because it is possible that this will have some effect on behaviour, it may be sensible to administer this treatment to the experimental group too, in order to control for any effects (assuming it is unlikely to interact with the other active elements of the intervention).

Multi-armed RCTs

Finally, in some instances it may be helpful to have more than two arms (conditions) in a trial. For example, this may be useful when comparing two different versions of an intervention or when one wants to determine whether an intervention is more effective with the addition of an extra component. This would result in a three-armed RCT, with two arms each relating to the two different versions of the intervention and one arm relating to the control condition. Where multiple versions of an intervention need to be compared, a factorial study design may also be used (see *Multiphase Optimisation Strategy*, **Chapter 9**).

Process evaluation

A process evaluation is an important part of any trial designed to evaluate a complex intervention (see page 239 for a definition of a complex intervention). It is used to assess three key aspects of the study: implementation, context and mechanisms of impact (Moore et al., 2015).

Assessing implementation

Assessing implementation is important, both for practical considerations and because it can help explain non-effects. For example, if a trial fails to show any effect of an intervention, data from a process evaluation can help provide an indication of whether this was because the intervention itself was not effective or whether this might have been because the intervention was not delivered as intended, not delivered in sufficient strength or failed to reach the target audience. A process analysis that looks at implementation may assess the following factors:

- How delivery was achieved (such as the training and resources required)
- Fidelity (the extent to which the intervention was delivered as intended)
- Dose (the 'amount' of intervention delivered)
- Reach (the extent to which the target population came into contact with the intervention)
- Adaptation (ways in which the intervention may have been adjusted).

Assessing mechanisms of impact

This may include:

- Measuring variables believed to mediate effects.
- Looking for additional, unexpected mediators and outcomes. This could include unintended outcomes that cause harm.
- Exploring user views of the intervention, for example whether it was acceptable and how they feel it might be improved.

Again, an assessment of mediators can help explain why an intervention failed to show any effects; whether this was because the BCTs failed to change the hypothesised mediators or because the hypothesised mediators had no effect on the outcome (see *Experimental medicine*, **Chapter 9**).

Assessing context

An assessment of context may include:

- Measuring variables thought to influence outcomes (moderators)
- Looking for additional potential moderators.

Moderators are sometimes called 'contextual variables' and may stem from differences between individuals in the target population (such as in age or motivation) or differences in the context within which the intervention was delivered (for example in community groups or healthcare settings).

Assessing trial procedures

In addition to the above, a process analysis may also incorporate an assessment of trial procedures, for example whether blinding was successful or whether there was contamination between trial arms (which refers to participants in one group learning about, receiving or using strategies intended for another group). Again, such information can help with the interpretation of study outcomes. For example, if a trial shows no effects this may be because participants in the control group also came into contact with the intervention. Or, if blinding was unsuccessful, there may be a risk of bias in the data.

Methods

Process evaluations typically draw on a wide range of different methodologies and tend to incorporate both quantitative and qualitative data. For example, standardised questionnaire measures may be used to assess pre-hypothesised mediators and moderators whilst qualitative interviews, conducted with a subset of participants, may be used to explore additional mechanisms of impact as well as variables that may have enhanced or limited effects (in other words, additional moderators/contextual variables). To assess intervention fidelity, intervention sessions may be video recorded, researchers may collect in situ observational data or those delivering the intervention may be asked to complete checklists. Alternatively, where intervention delivery is via a website or mobile app, these may be designed so that user engagement can be tracked (see Knittle, 2014) for further discussion of fidelity assessment).

Scope

Note that any single process evaluation may not be able to explore all the issues outlined above. The main priorities of a process evaluation are likely to vary depending on the stage of the research. For example, qualitative, exploratory data may be more important in the early stages of intervention development (such as in a feasibility or pilot study, see page 292) whilst quantitative measures assessing pre-hypothesised variables may be considered more important in a trial assessing effectiveness.

Per-protocol versus intention-to-treat analyses

Choice of approach

Two difficulties associated with RCTs are noncompliance (where a participant has not adhered to the intervention) and missing outcome data (for example, where participants have failed to return questionnaires or attend a follow-up appointment). Per-protocol and intention-to-treat analyses represent two different approaches to these problems (see also **Table 10.1**). A per-protocol analysis typically includes only those participants who both adhered to the intervention and provided complete outcome data. This is equivalent to the type of analysis one would usually employ in experimental studies. It is appropriate for trials with a more explanatory focus, aimed at establishing whether there is a causal relationship between an independent variable (such as the use of particular BCTs) and a dependent variable (the primary outcome). By contrast, an intention-to-treat analysis aims to include all participants who were recruited into the trial and randomised to treatment conditions, even those who dropped out of the intervention or failed to provide outcome data. This approach is less useful for establishing the efficacy of particular BCTs but it is useful for determining the likely effectiveness of the intervention as a whole, when implemented in a real-world context among people who may drop out, miss appointments or fail to do what they have been asked to do. In practice, for many trials it may be informative to run both per-protocol and intention-to-treat analyses.

Per-protocol analysis: defining adherence

For simple interventions, per-protocol analysis can be reasonably straightforward. However, for more complex interventions, decisions may need to be made about how adherence is defined. For example, where an intervention consists of a series of workshops delivered over several weeks or months, it may be that a relatively small percentage of participants attends them all. As such a decision would need to be made about the number (and/or type) of sessions that would need to be attended for the participant to have sufficient exposure to the intervention. Where there is drop-out, it is also important to try to establish whether this is biased between the intervention and control groups. For example, there may be greater drop-out in the intervention group among those who are less likely to change their behaviour (for example, because they are less motivated) that would bias the results in favour of the intervention. Comparing the numbers of participants who dropped out across conditions, as well as the baseline characteristics of these participants, can help assess whether this type of bias is likely to have occurred.

Intention-to-treat analysis: last observation carried forward

Intention-to-treat analysis may pose challenges in terms of how to deal with missing data. Note that since this type of analysis aims to include all participants, it is important to try to collect outcome data from all participants, even those who have dropped out of the intervention (especially as these participants may differ in some way from those who do not drop out). One of the simplest approaches to replacing ('imputing') missing outcome data is to employ what is known as 'last observation carried forward' (LOCF) whereby the missing data point is replaced by the datum from the previous observation. For example, for an intervention aimed at increasing fruit and vegetable consumption, measures might be taken at baseline, at one-month and at six-month follow-up. Missing data at six months would be replaced with data collected at one month. Where data were missing at both one month and six months, both would be replaced with data from baseline. Intuitively, such an approach seems reasonable if we expect the measure in question to remain stable over time. However, this is not always the case. For example, many interventions will result in an initial change in behaviour that dissipates over time. Likewise, some outcomes will naturally change over time, even in the absence of any intervention (such as weight, which tends to increase over time). Additionally, LOCF will underestimate the variance in a dataset. For these reasons, some researchers argue against the use of LOCF (Carpenter & Kenward, 2007; National Research Council, 2010).

CHAPTER 10

Intention-to-treat analysis: multiple imputation

An alternative to LOCF is to use something called 'multiple imputation' in which a regression model is used to predict missing values from existing scores and other relevant information and where results from a number of different estimates are combined (hence the term 'multiple'). This approach is complicated to perform but is thought to provide the most accurate estimates of missing data (Vickers & Altman, 2013). Nevertheless, it is important to note that such an approach is still unlikely to remedy biased drop-out, so it is essential to try to avoid missing data in the first place. (For further discussion of missing data, see Carpenter & Kenward, 2007 and National Research Council, 2010.)

Variations of RCT study designs

In some situations, a standard RCT can be difficult to implement. In these cases, it may be possible to modify the design, whilst still adhering to the general RCT principles outlined above. In this section we take a brief look at some of the ways in which an RCT can be adapted to suit different circumstances.

Cluster RCTs and clustering effects

A cluster RCT is used where it is not possible or desirable to randomise individual participants to intervention and control conditions, so units or groups are randomised instead (Donner & Klar, 2004). For example, in school-based interventions, where there may be changes to lesson plans, parts of the school day, or particular aspects of the school environment, it would not be feasible to try to ensure that only some pupils were exposed to these changes. So instead, whole schools are randomised to intervention and control conditions. Data analysis still uses data from the individual participant, achieved either by tracking the same participant through the study (collecting longitudinal data) or by assessing different participants at each time point (collecting cross-sectional data). However, 'clustering effects' are also accounted for in the analysis. (See **Box 10.3** for some examples of cluster RCTs.)

BOX 10.3 USING EXPERIMENTAL METHODS TO TACKLE SOCIAL PROBLEMS: A NOBEL PRIZE-WINNING APPROACH

AS AN ASIDE

In 2019 a Nobel Prize was awarded to Abhijit Banerjee, Esther Duflo and Michael Kremer 'for their experimental approach to alleviating global poverty' (The Royal Swedish Academy of Sciences, 2019). Their research has encompassed health, education, economics and agriculture. For example, in one study they looked at the effects of free school breakfasts on educational attainment in Kenya (Vermeersch & Kremer, 2004). In another study they showed that incentives (a free bag of lentils and some metal plates) significantly increased vaccination uptake in rural India. Because of the fixed costs of the vaccination clinics, this increased uptake also reduced the costs per vaccination (Banerjee et al., 2010). These studies are described as 'field experiments' by the Nobel Prize committee but are also examples of cluster RCTs. The large body of research undertaken by the prize winners has had an enormous impact on government policy around the world, for example leading to the closure of programmes that were shown to be ineffective and the reinvestment of funds into effective interventions such as remedial tutoring in India and the distribution of free medicines in low-income countries.

'Clustering' refers to the fact that individuals within a group are likely to be more similar to one another than to individuals from a different group. For example, children who go to a particular school will all come from a particular geographical location, which may be rural or urban, wealthy or deprived. These factors are likely to correlate with pupil characteristics such as diet, exercise and educational achievement. Schools will also vary in terms of the quality of teaching, the teaching methods employed, school rules and practices, the physical environment and peer group norms. Again, these factors are likely to influence the pupil. Thus if you selected a child at random from a particular school, the chances are this child would be more similar to another random child selected from the same school than to a random child selected from a different school. The extent to which individuals from the same cluster correlate with one another on a particular outcome measure is described as the 'intra-cluster correlation'. Sometimes, even where a cluster RCT is not used, it may be important to take account of clustering effects in the analysis of trial data, for example where group-based workshops are employed (where participants may influence one another) or where an intervention is delivered by a number of different health practitioners who may vary in skills and expertise.

Stepped wedge cluster RCTs

The cluster RCT design described above is sometimes referred to as a 'parallel cluster' RCT because the units (or 'clusters') are exposed to treatments in parallel with one another. An alternative is the 'stepped wedge cluster' RCT in which all clusters are exposed to the intervention but at different points in time (Hemming et al., 2015). A stepped wedge trial begins with no clusters being exposed to the intervention (all clusters are in the control condition). Individual clusters (or groups of clusters) then cross over from the control condition to the intervention condition in a series of regular intervals (or 'steps') until all clusters are in the intervention condition. The order in which the clusters cross over from intervention to control condition is randomised and assessments are taken during the baseline period (when all clusters are in the control condition), during the crossover period (when clusters are switching from control to intervention condition), and at the end of the study (when all clusters are in the intervention condition). In this way, stepped wedge designs follow a similar logic to multiple baseline designs (see *N-of-1 trials* section) except that data are analysed at the group level (rather than the individual level) and the introduction of the intervention is pre-determined (rather than being contingent upon a stable baseline).

Stepped wedge trials can be useful where key stakeholders object to the idea of a standard RCT, for example because, for political or ethical reasons, they do not want to withhold access to an intervention for any length of time. A stepped wedge trial can also be useful where, for logistical reasons, it is not possible to roll out an intervention to a large number of clusters simultaneously. However, an important disadvantage to stepped wedge trials is that intervention exposure is partially confounded with time; no clusters are exposed to the intervention at the start of the study but all clusters are receiving it at a later point in time. This means that if there is a temporal trend in the outcome of interest that is in the same direction as the anticipated effect of the intervention, it can be difficult to separate out the two to determine the actual effect of the intervention. For this reason, a standard cluster RCT is generally deemed superior to a stepped wedge RCT. (For further discussion of the pros and cons of stepped wedge trials, see Kotz et al., 2012 and Mdege et al., 2012.)

Patient preference trial

This type of trial is used where some people have a strong preference for a particular treatment (Torgerson & Sibbald, 1998). If the treatment is only available as part of a trial these people may sign up but be very unhappy if allocated to the control group and show poor adherence as a result. Whilst participants with strong preferences could be excluded, this is likely to make it more difficult to generalise from the results of the trial to the general population. For example, participants with strong preferences may be more likely to adhere to treatment procedures when allocated to the treatment of their choice. In a patient preference trial, participants' preferences are assessed at recruitment and only those who consent to randomisation are randomised. The remaining participants are assigned to their preferred treatment. This typically results in a four-arm trial: (a) randomised to experimental treatment, (b) randomised to control treatment, (c) assigned to experimental treatment based on preference and (d) assigned to control treatment based on preference. However, the analysis of data from the non-randomised arms can be problematic; the fact that these two groups of participants had strong preferences for different types of treatments suggests they are also likely to differ from one another in other ways. As such, some researchers recommend that the two non-randomised arms should be analysed as observational studies (Torgerson & Sibbald, 1998).

Crossover trial

In a crossover trial, study participants receive both treatments but the order in which they receive them varies, depending on the study arm they are randomly allocated to (Sibbald & Roberts, 1998). For example, where A refers to a control treatment and B to an experimental treatment, they would be randomised to receive either AB or BA. Because each participant is tested under both experimental and control conditions, a smaller sample size is needed to demonstrate an effect. As such, a crossover trial can be more efficient than an RCT with parallel groups. However, like n-of-1 ABA designs (see *N-of-1 trials* section), crossover designs are only suitable for testing treatments where effects are likely to be short-lived. Additionally, where there are likely to be carryover effects from one treatment to the next, these need to be taken into account in the study design, for example by including a 'washout' period between treatments (when no treatment is given) or by measuring outcomes only toward the end of each treatment period. This, together with the fact that treatments are delivered sequentially, can make the testing period much longer compared to a parallel groups design.

Feasibility and pilot studies (also known as 'exploratory studies')

A feasibility study is a study carried out before the main trial in order to answer questions the researcher may be uncertain about and to determine whether it will be possible to run the main trial as planned (Arain et al., 2010). Feasibility studies address issues such as:

- **Gatekeepers'** willingness to recruit participants
- The rate at which eligible participants can be recruited
  - Participants' willingness to be randomised
  - The utility of any new measures
  - Variability in the outcome measure of interest
  - Levels of adherence
  - Levels of attrition.

Gatekeeper – a person or organisation who controls access to participants, such as head teachers, clinicians or charitable organisations.

A feasibility study for an RCT will not always include the randomisation of participants to different groups because this may not be necessary to answer the questions of interest. It is also important to note that feasibility studies are not used to determine whether an intervention is effective, only whether it will be possible to establish this with a full trial.

By contrast, a pilot trial is a mini version of the full study, used to test all the procedures of a main study to ensure they all run smoothly (Arain et al., 2010). In some instances, a pilot trial will form the first phase of the main study, with the data from both being combined (assuming no problems arise in the pilot trial). This type of pilot is referred to as an 'internal pilot' (as opposed to an 'external pilot' where the data are analysed separately). (Note that separate aspects of a research study, such as an individual measure, can also be 'piloted'.)

MEASURING BEHAVIOUR CHANGE AND OTHER IMPORTANT VARIABLES

We've now looked at a range of different study designs that can be used to evaluate behaviour change interventions and we've argued that a carefully conducted RCT provides the most reliable evidence of effects. However, strong study design cannot compensate for weak measurement; regardless of the strength of the study design, the results will tell us very little if the method used to assess the behaviour of interest is unreliable.

A good illustration of this problem relates to the measurement of fruit and vegetable consumption in young children. School children quickly learn that in class there is often a 'right' answer. If an intervention teaches them they should be eating five portions of fruit and vegetables a day, or even that it is good to eat fruit and vegetables, they may be inclined to give what they think is the 'right' answer when asked to report on how much fruit and vegetables they eat, professing that they eat five a day (or that they eat lots). Thus an RCT evaluation that relies on young children's self-reports as its main measure may actually be evaluating what children know, rather than what they do. Here we provide an overview of different types of measures that can be used to assess behaviour as well as relevant mediators and moderators.

Self-report measures

These include measures such as questionnaires, diaries or interviews where the person reports on their own behaviour (or another variable thought to mediate or moderate effects, such as their attitude or level of self-efficacy). Self-report measures are often relatively quick and easy to administer to large numbers of people but they can result in high respondent burden (where participants have to expend a lot of time and/or effort completing the measures) which can in turn lead to poor completion rates, and/or less accurate completion. Self-reports may also be subject to recall inaccuracies, memory biases and **social desirability bias**. For these reasons it is important to be able to demonstrate the **validity** and **reliability** of any self-report measure employed. This may be

---

Social desirability bias – where a respondent answers in a way that they believe will create a good impression.

Validity (of a measure) – the extent to which an instrument measures what it is intended to measure. Types of validity include content validity (whether all aspects of the construct being measured are captured), construct validity (whether the measure correlates with other measures for which validity has already been established) and criterion validity (whether the measure correlates as expected with other related measures). Criterion validity includes predictive validity (whether the measure can predict future performance) and concurrent validity (whether the measure can be used to estimate current performance).

Reliability (of a measure) – the extent to which a measure provides scores that are reproducible. Test-retest reliability refers to whether a measure is stable over time. It is assessed by repeating the measure at two different time points (in the absence of

CHAPTER 10

any other manipulations) and looking at the extent to which the two sets of data correlate with one another. For questionnaire measures, internal consistency can also be assessed by looking at the extent to which individual items within the questionnaire correlate with one another. Finally, for observational measures, an assessment of inter-observer reliability is important. This is the extent to which two different people coding the same information produce the same data. Note that even though a measure has been shown to be reliable this does not necessarily mean it is valid.

achieved in a feasibility study. Alternatively, standardised measures may be selected for which validity and reliability have already been established.

Peer, teacher and carer report measures

These refer to instances in which someone other than the participant reports on their behaviour. For example, a parent may be asked to report on their child's eating behaviour, a teacher may be asked to report on a pupil's disruptive behaviour in the classroom, or a student may be asked to report on the smoking behaviour of their peers. Such measures can be useful for reducing social desirability bias or where a participant (such as a young child) does not have the skills needed to accurately complete a report measure. However, the respondent may be unable to provide a full report on the behaviour in question (for example a parent may not know what their child has eaten at school or at a friend's house) and such measures will still be subject to biases and inaccuracies. As such, it is again important to establish the validity and reliability of any peer, teacher or carer report measure employed.

Observational measures in the field

These are instances in which researchers observe participants' naturally occurring behaviour outside the laboratory (such as whether people take the lift or the stairs). The behaviour may be observed directly or technology such as video recordings may be employed. Observational measures will be less subject to some of the biases seen with report measures but may be very time-consuming for researchers (in other words, there is high researcher burden). Where participants become aware that their behaviour is being observed there may also be reactivity (participants may modify their behaviour). Assessing inter-observer reliability is important for observational measures to ensure that those collecting the data are recording it in the same way as one another.

Behavioural measures in the laboratory

Direct measures of behaviour can also be collected within the laboratory setting. For example, a participant's choice may be recorded (for instance whether or not they take a condom at the end of the study) or degree of behaviour may be assessed (such as how much alcohol or food they consume). Because of the disparity between intentions and behaviour (see **Chapter 5**), behavioural measures are likely to be better than simply asking participants what they intend to do. Though note this does not necessarily mean these measures will be an accurate reflection of what a participant will do outside the laboratory; behavioural measures collected in the laboratory will have lower ecological validity compared to those collected in the field. As with field-based observational measures, care also needs to be taken to avoid participant reactivity. This is sometimes achieved by not revealing the aims of the research to the participant until they have finished taking part and/or by giving the impression a task is designed to assess something different from what it is really assessing (see **Box 10.4**). As noted earlier in this chapter (see section on *Experimental methods*), laboratory studies are usually used for theory development and for testing the effects of a particular manipulation or BCT, rather than for evaluating the efficacy or effectiveness of a complete intervention.

BOX 10.4 USE OF DECEPTION IN RESEARCH

DIG A LITTLE DEEPER

Deception is where a researcher misleads participants about the purpose of the research, or the research procedures. For example, in a 'bogus taste test' participants are asked to taste and rate a number of different foods on a range of characteristics, such as their saltiness and sweetness. Unknown to the participant, the researcher is not actually interested in these ratings but rather in how much they eat. Deception is used in this instance because if someone knows the amount they eat is being measured, they tend to adjust their behaviour, rendering the measure invalid (Robinson et al., 2014c).

Deception in research should be avoided if possible. This is because there will always be a risk that participants will become upset upon learning that they have been deceived and, had they known the true purpose of the research, may not have agreed to take part. Additionally, if researchers use deception too frequently it could undermine trust in the discipline and make it more difficult for other researchers to collect valid data. As such, deception should only be used when it is essential for achieving valid data (such as amount of food eaten in the laboratory) and where the potential benefits of the research outweigh the potential harms. The participant should be informed of the true aim of the research as soon as possible (which may be before all measures have been completed) and should then be given the opportunity to provide or withhold their consent for the data that relate to the deception. They should also be given the opportunity to withdraw the rest of their data. Additionally, the researcher should put in place strategies to minimise the risk of harm, for example by verbally explaining the reason for the deception to participants.

Performance-based measures in the laboratory

As well as using behavioural and self-report measures, laboratory studies may also employ performance-based measures. For health-related research these would usually be used to assess a variable thought to mediate or moderate the effects of a particular manipulation on a health-related behaviour. For example, attentional bias (see **Chapter 6**) is often assessed in the laboratory using computer-based reaction time tasks or other methods such as eye tracking. In studies aimed at theory development and testing, such measures may be used as the main dependent variable. For example, a study may examine whether a particular manipulation reduces attentional bias for alcohol-related stimuli. The assumption may be that a reduction in attentional bias would lead to a reduction in alcohol consumption, but this behavioural outcome would not necessarily always be tested in the same study (see *Experimental medicine*, **Chapter 9**). Performance-based measures usually avoid the biases associated with report measures. They can also be used to assess processes that participants may have little insight into (such as automatic or unconscious processes). However, it can sometimes be challenging to ensure they are valid and reliable measures of the constructs they are designed to assess.

Physiological measures

Like performance-based measures, physiological measures avoid biases associated with self-report (unless participants are asked to self-report on a physiological measure, such as their weight). They may be used for a number of reasons:

- As a main outcome (for example in an intervention aimed at reducing salt intake in order to lower blood pressure)

- As a proxy for a particular behaviour or as a way of validating a self-report measure (such as blood carbon monoxide as an indicator of smoking)

- As a moderator (for example where it is anticipated that an intervention will be less effective for those with higher levels of obesity).

Physiological measures may be used in laboratory-based research or may be incorporated into RCTs.

Technology-based measures in the field

The rise of smartphones and other types of wearable sensors now make it possible to assess a range of different variables in the field in a relatively objective and unobtrusive manner. For example, pedometers and accelerometers can measure levels of physical activity, motion detectors can estimate length of sleep, and GPS codes can be used to assess exposure to particular features of an environment (such as green space or fast food restaurants). Smartphones can also be used to administer self-report and performance-based measures in the field at specific points, allowing more accurate tracking of these variables over time.

REPORTING RESEARCH

An important part of the research process is reporting findings so others can learn from them. Typically, scientific research is reported in the form of a scientific report that is submitted to a research journal and undergoes peer review before it is either accepted for publication or rejected. Peer review is where other experts in the field evaluate the manuscript to ensure the research, analysis and reporting are of a sufficient quality to warrant publication. The reviewers may request that the authors make certain adjustments to the paper before it is accepted for publication, or in some instances (usually experimental work) ask that they conduct additional studies to strengthen the conclusions that can be drawn. Alternatively, reviewers may argue that the research is not of a sufficient quality, or of sufficient importance, or they may recommend the manuscript be submitted to a different journal. The process of peer review is designed to uphold certain standards within the research literature.

However, despite the peer review processes, some research gets published with important details missing, which can in turn limit its potential contribution to knowledge within the field. For example, if certain statistical details are missing, it can make it difficult for the data to be included in later meta-analyses. Likewise, if procedural details are incomplete it can be hard to determine exactly what BCTs have been used or the extent to which the data may be subject to bias. For these reasons, international reporting guidelines have been developed to help researchers and reviewers ensure that all essential information is included in research reports. These guidelines can also be useful to refer to when planning and conducting research to ensure that best practice is employed. Some of the most widely used guidelines are listed below. Although a relevant reference is provided for each set of guidelines, in most instances there is also an associated website (see macmillanihe.com/tapper-health-psychology for weblinks). When using the guidelines, it is helpful to check the website for recent updates or extensions and to obtain copies of checklists.

- CONSORT (Consolidated Standards of Reporting Trials). These are guidelines for reporting RCTs (Schulz et al., 2010). They also include a number of extensions for different types of trials, such as cluster RCTs, pragmatic trials, n-of-1 trials and pilot and feasibility trials.

- TIDieR (Template for Intervention Description and Replication). An extension of the CONSORT guidelines, these are designed to be used in conjunction with the CONSORT guidelines when describing an intervention (Hoffmann et al., 2014).

- PRISMA (Preferred Reporting Items for Systematic Reviews and Meta-Analyses). As the name suggests, for reporting systematic reviews and meta-analyses (Moher et al., 2009).

- TREND (Transparent Reporting of Evaluations with Nonrandomised Designs). The equivalent of the CONSORT guidelines but for non-randomised trials (Des Jarlais et al., 2004).

- WIDER (Workgroup for Intervention Development and Evaluation Research). Developed specifically for behaviour change interventions and designed for use alongside other guidelines such as CONSORT (Albrecht et al., 2013).

CONCLUSIONS

To maximise our chances of successfully changing behaviour, we need to use scientific methods to identify effective strategies and to evaluate interventions. This is important because humans are not rational creatures – our thinking and judgements are influenced by a wide range of heuristics and biases. However, certain types of scientific evidence are better than others. For examples, a meta-analysis represents stronger evidence than a single study whilst a double-blinded RCT is superior to one with no blinding. For certain types of research questions, it is simply not possible to obtain the best evidence. This may be for practical or ethical reasons, or both. For example, we cannot use an RCT to evaluate the effects of socioeconomic status on longevity. Nevertheless, in many cases the evidence base for a particular effect or association could be improved. A good understanding of research methods will give you the skills you need to critically evaluate the strength of the evidence for different claims. The next time you read a research study, try using the information in this chapter to cast a critical eye over the methods. Did the authors select the strongest study design? Were there any weaknesses in the research procedures? How could the evidence for any claims be improved?

Randomised controlled trials are the norm in medicine but less common in other areas such as education, policing and social policy (see **Box 10.3**). When is it acceptable to randomise people to intervention and control conditions and when might we consider it unethical? Does it make a difference what **THE GREAT DEBATE** participants know or believe about their treatment? Or their ability to consent? Are there any other reasons why randomised controlled trials may be less commonly used in some areas than others?

Chapter Outline

Bias in Science

Addressing Bias in Science

Barriers to the Adoption and Use of Evidence-based Interventions

Conclusions

In July 2018, two nurses in Samoa accidently made up vaccines with a muscle relaxant instead of water. The two 12-month-old babies who received the vaccines died within minutes. The government temporarily suspended the vaccination programme and an anti-vaccine campaign spread rapidly on social media. As a result, vaccination rates dropped to 31% leaving many unprotected from an outbreak of measles that occurred in late 2019. Despite renewed efforts to vaccinate the population (**Image 11.1**), by January 2020, 83

Image 11.1 *A nurse administers a vaccination to a three-year-old boy in Samoa, as part of emergency efforts to control an outbreak of measles.*
Credit: © UNICEF/UNI232327/Stephen.

people had died from measles, 72 of them young children and babies. Volunteers in New Zealand donated infant-sized coffins, decorated with stars and hearts, butterflies and daisies. They placed a teddy bear in each of the caskets (Barrett, 2019; Isaacs, 2020; WHO, 2020d).

This tragic story highlights the importance of vaccination as well as the power of social media. It also underlines the need for trust, in government, scientists and the medical profession.

Vaccination programmes are evidence-based medical interventions for which there is overwhelming scientific support. This does not mean they are 100% risk free.[1] Rather, the benefits of being vaccinated significantly outweigh the risks of remaining unvaccinated (see **Chapter 12**). However, just because an intervention is evidence-based does not mean it is easy to implement. In this chapter we look at some of the barriers to evidence-based policy. We also think about some of the bias that can creep into the scientific literature which may serve to undermine trust in scientific findings. More specifically, in this chapter we will:

- Consider sources of bias in the scientific literature that could result in misleading evidence.

- Look at how these sources of bias can be addressed.

- Think about the barriers to governments implementing evidence-based policy.

- Discuss the ways in which health-related issues may be misunderstood or misinterpreted.

BIAS IN SCIENCE

In **Chapter 10** we looked at the some of the standard methods used by scientists to reduce the risk of bias in research, such as randomisation, blinding, allocation concealment and trial registration. However, despite these measures, other sources of bias can creep into the research literature. In psychology, these came under the spotlight after the publication of research that seemingly provided evidence for precognition (the ability to perceive future events; Bem, 2011; LeBel & Peters, 2011) and after researchers failed to replicate a classic, highly cited research finding on social priming (Bargh et al., 1996; Doyen et al., 2012; see also Nelson et al., 2018). In this section we look at these sources of bias and how we can start to address them.[2]

Publication bias

An essential part of the research processes is publishing research findings so others can learn from them and the field as a whole can advance. Peer review of research reports submitted to scientific journals serves a dual purpose: (a) to decide whether the research was carried out to a sufficient standard and (b) to make a judgement on the importance of the research, in other words, the extent to which it advances scientific knowledge and makes a significant contribution to the field. It is this latter judgement that is problematic because a study that shows a novel, interesting finding is likely to be weighted as more important than a study that fails to find an effect. This problem is exacerbated as more high-profile journals can afford to be more selective.

---

1   Nothing in life is 100% risk free.

2   Arguably, medicine suffers from less bias than psychology because of its longer tradition of RCTs and trial registration. Nevertheless, it is not immune. See Goldacre (2012) for an eloquent discussion of the ways in which the pharmaceutical industry can distort medical evidence.

The road from research idea to publication is usually very long and often very frustrating. As such it is no surprise that researchers who find no significant effects in a study may decide it is more sensible to move on to the next idea (that might have a better chance of being published in one of the top journals) rather than invest considerable time and effort trying to get a study reporting a null effect published in a smaller journal. This problem is compounded by the fact that career advancement for an academic depends on their publications; hence the maxim 'publish or perish'. But it is not just the number of publications that is important, it is also the kind of journals they publish in; many universities expect their faculty to be publishing in prestigious journals.

These factors lead to what is known as the 'file drawer' problem, referring to the large number of research studies that never get published which are more likely to show null effects compared to those that have been published. The wider problem for the discipline is that the research literature is likely to give a false impression of the reliability of a particular effect or, in some instances, suggest an effect exists where there is in fact none. To illustrate, imagine a particular study was repeated 20 times. Purely by chance alone one of these 20 studies may show a significant effect. But this may be the only study to be published. Thus the system within which academics work incentivises the publication of significant effects and discourages the publication of null effects, which in turn leads to bias in the literature.

Lack of replication

The same factors that work against academics publishing null effects also work against them conducting and publishing research designed to replicate other findings. Replication is essential to rule out the possibility that a significant effect is simply a spurious result. Indeed, Karl Popper, a renowned philosopher of science, stated that a scientifically true effect was one that 'can be regularly reproduced by anyone who carries out the appropriate experiment in the way prescribed' (Popper, 1959/2002, pp. 23–24). But many top-tier journals do not publish replication studies as they do not view them as making a sufficiently novel contribution to the field. Thus once again, the way in which the system works means there is little incentive for researchers to carry out replication studies, which in turn increases the risk of unreliable findings being left unchallenged in the literature.

BOX 11.1 UNDEAD THEORIES OF BEHAVIOUR CHANGE

MAKING CONNECTIONS

Ferguson and Heene (2012) argue that in the field of psychology, publication bias, together with a lack of emphasis on replication, makes it difficult to falsify theories (see also **Box 8.3**). This in turn results in what they describe as a 'vast graveyard of undead theories', theories that are popular but have little basis in fact. Could any of the theories we looked at in **Chapters 5 to 8** be described as undead theories?

P-hacking, HARKing and other 'questionable' research practices

Nelson et al. (2018) argue that bias in the literature is caused not so much by publication bias, but rather by p-hacking that turns studies that find null effects into studies that show significant effects. P-hacking is where a researcher makes decisions about data collection or data analysis that increase the chances of obtaining a statistically significant result (one where the p value is less than .05). For example, researchers might include multiple dependent measures but then focus only on the measure that found a significant effect, or they might justify the exclusion of certain data points where such exclusions push the p value over the .05 boundary. The fact that researchers have a lot of flexibility in the ways in which they can collect and analyse their data is sometimes referred to as 'researcher degrees of freedom' and this flexibility can increase their chances of obtaining a significant effect. Essentially, if there are multiple different ways of analysing a dataset the researchers get multiple shots at finding a significant effect, and with a sufficient number of different options for data analysis, chances are one will result in a significant effect. This has been demonstrated very convincingly by Simmons and colleagues who used researcher degrees of freedom to obtain 'evidence' that listening to certain songs can change a person's age (Simmons et al., 2011). In other words, at its extreme, p-hacking can be used to demonstrate just about anything.

P-hacking often goes hand in hand with HARKing (Hypothesizing After the Results are Known) (Kerr, 1998). HARKing is where a researcher forms a hypothesis based on their results and then writes up the research as if the study had been designed to test that hypothesis all along. This is at odds with the standard scientific approach of formulating a hypothesis, collecting data to test that hypothesis and then accepting or rejecting that hypothesis. Whilst there is nothing wrong with exploratory research that helps generate hypotheses, post-hoc hypotheses, presented as if they were a priori, bias the literature as they increase the probability of Type I errors occurring within the literature (in other words, results supporting a significant effect where there is no real effect).

P-hacking and HARKing are estimated to be extremely common within the scientific literature. For example, John et al. (2012) asked academic psychologists at major US universities whether they had ever engaged in ten research practices that ranged from the 'questionable' (such as failing to report all of a study's dependent measures) to the downright fraudulent (such as falsifying data). They found a surprisingly high proportion of academics answered 'yes'. However, as Nelson et al. (2018) note, most of these practices likely occur unwittingly (for example, researchers may be subject to **hindsight bias**) or they may not appreciate they are problematic. Indeed, there are many grey areas in which some of these practices may be justified (John et al., 2012). Nelson et al. suggest that very often these practices arise from researchers simply trying to make sense of their data. In some instances, instructors, reviewers or journal editors may also have inadvertently encouraged such practices by requiring that research papers 'tell a story'.

> **Hindsight bias** – the tendency for a person with knowledge of an outcome to overestimate the extent to which they would have predicted that outcome.

Selective scrutiny

Sometimes bias can stem from what appear to be very sensible practices. For example, suppose a researcher ran two experiments, one with results that supported their hypothesis and the other with results that did not. In an effort to make sense of their contradictory findings they may go back and double-check the data entry and analysis for the 'failed' experiment, only to find an error which, when corrected, leads to the study showing a significant effect. Although superficially this seems sensible, when used repeatedly by many different researchers over numerous experiments, this type of approach can introduce bias into the literature since only one type of error is corrected. Had the researcher double-checked their data and analysis for their 'successful' experiment they may have found an error that, when corrected, removed the significant effect (Chambers, 2017). This selective scrutiny, sometimes called 'biased debugging', can be viewed as a form of confirmation bias (see page 267, **Chapter 10**).

Conflicts of interest

A conflict of interest describes a situation in which those carrying out a piece of research stand to gain from obtaining a particular result. In one sense, simply being a salaried academic could be viewed as a conflict of interest given that research that shows significant effects is more likely to be published in prestigious journals (which in turn influences career progression). However, the term is generally reserved for interests scientists have beyond any desire to simply publish their findings. These typically involve situations in which the results of a study could be linked to tangible benefits or losses for any individual or organisation associated with the research. For example, an academic with shares in a weight loss company that makes meal replacement drinks would likely be hoping their research examining the effects of these drinks on body weight would show positive results as these results could then be advertised to consumers which could in turn increase sales. The same would apply to the company making the meal replacement drinks, which might be funding the research.

In public health research, conflicts of interest often relate to the tobacco, alcohol and food industries because (a) they are sufficiently wealthy to fund research, (b) directors are usually motivated to maximise profits, and (c) their profits often depend on sales that conflict with public health. In particular, both the tobacco and alcohol industries manufacture substances that are harmful to health. The food industry represents a more diverse set of products but ultimately still needs to sell food to consumers who already tend to consume too much. For example, on average we need just 2,350 calories a day, but the food industry provides us with 2,790 calories and we end up eating 2,530 calories. In wealthier countries excess calories are even higher; in the United States the food industry supplies over 4,5000 calories per person per day, with average daily consumption at 3,660 calories (Berners-Lee et al., 2018). Additionally, the foods that provide the highest profit margin for the industry tend to be highly processed, energy-dense foods that are generally worse for health compared to less profitable, unprocessed foods such as fruit and vegetables and whole grains (Brownell & Warner, 2009).

Research is important to industry because it can help companies create and improve their products and services, which can in turn increase sales and profits. However, research is also important to industry because it can add credibility to products and services by demonstrating their effectiveness. This may be better described as marketing research rather than scientific research since the aim is promotion rather than investigation (see **Box 11.2**). Industry gets involved in research, either by employing their own in-house scientists, or by collaborating with scientists at external organisations such as universities. In the latter instance the industry partner would usually provide some or all of the funds required to carry out the research, including the investigators' time.

BOX 11.2 THE (APPARENT) HEALTH BENEFITS OF RED WINE AND DARK CHOCOLATE: SCIENCE OR MARKETING?

HOT TOPIC

Flavonoids – a group of chemical compounds found in plants. These can be further divided into different types according to their precise chemical structure. They include anthocyanidins, flavonols, flavanols, flavones and flavanones. Different plants contain different levels of different types of flavonoids.

Studies suggesting red wine and dark chocolate may be good for our health are regularly featured in newspapers and magazines. After all, who doesn't like to think that their favourite indulgence could also be lowering their blood pressure, protecting their heart and boosting their memory? But why are scientists so interested in red wine and dark chocolate? And are we justified in feeling virtuous about consuming these foods?

Both red wine and dark chocolate contain high levels of **flavonoids**. Higher dietary intake of flavonoids has been associated with lower blood pressure, reduced risk of heart disease and

Image 11.2 *Newspapers may argue that a glass of red wine is good for your health, but is it really any better than a handful of berries?*
Credit: Jeff Siepman.

improved cognitive function (Cassidy et al., 2011; Wang et al., 2014; Williams & Spencer, 2012). So far so good. Except most of this research is observational in nature, in other words, it provides evidence of correlation not causation; there could be any number of alternative explanations for these associations. Whether increasing dietary flavonoids can actually lead to improvements in health is less clear (Rees et al., 2018; Wang et al., 2019).

Red wine also contains alcohol, whilst chocolate has high levels of sugar, saturated fat and calories, all of which are damaging for health when consumed in large quantities. These would likely outweigh any health benefits associated with the high flavonoid content. For example, although cocoa is very high in flavanols, most of these are destroyed in the chocolate-making process, meaning that to consume the recommended levels of flavanols one would need to eat around 750 calories of dark chocolate a day which represents over one-third of the recommended energy intake for an average person (Nestle, 2018).

Additionally, many fruits, vegetables and legumes contain flavonoids, including apples, beans, onions and berries (Haytowitz et al., 2018). These have the added advantage of also containing healthy fibre along with other vitamins and minerals. More importantly, they don't contain the high levels of sugar and saturated fat found in chocolate or the alcohol contained in red wine.

So why the interest in dark chocolate and red wine? (Or blueberries, or pomegranate juice or any other food touted as a 'superfood'?) Because companies that make large profits can afford to fund research into the health benefits of their product, issue press releases about their findings, and lobby regulatory bodies to allow them to make health claims (Nestle, 2018; Wang et al., 2019). Arguably, much research into the health benefits of single nutrients or individual foods is driven by a marketing agenda rather than a desire to improve public health.

So, sadly, chocolate and red wine are unlikely to be the secret to a long and healthy life. And although research into flavonoids could lead to the development of new drugs, when it comes to diet, the standard advice still holds true: we should eat a wide variety of foods, plenty of fruit and vegetables and limit our intake of sugar, salt and saturated fat.

From an academic's perspective, collaboration with industry provides funding. However, there are other reasons for collaborating with industry partners that go beyond the financial. In particular, scientists can sometimes be accused of living in 'ivory towers', working on abstract research questions with little relevance for the real world. Working with industry provides an opportunity to ensure knowledge and skills have tangible benefits beyond the laboratory. It is partly for this reason that politicians around the world have been advocating closer links between universities and industry (Caulfield & Ogbogu, 2015). In some instances, industry goals can also align with public health goals, for example where a food manufacturer is looking for ways to reduce sugar and salt in its products or where a supermarket is interested in increasing sales of fruit and vegetables (Aveyard et al., 2016). Additionally, some argue that it is better for independent scientists to evaluate new products and approaches, and for the findings to be in the public domain, rather than the research being conducted by the company itself (Gornall, 2015). Finally, the fact that public funding for research has declined has meant that universities, as well as individual academics, increasingly rely on industry funding to support their work (Gornall, 2015; Nestle, 2018).

However, others argue that industry funding is problematic, both because it biases the science and because it undermines public confidence in research (Aveyard et al., 2016; Besley et al., 2017; Caulfield & Ogbogu, 2015; Nestle, 2018). Industry funding can bias science in several ways. First, it can influence the results of individual research studies or the ways in which those results are presented. Specifically, research that has been funded by industry is more likely to show effects that favour the sponsoring industry's product or approach (see Litman et al., 2018; Lundh et al., 2012). And where the results of a study do not align with the interests of the sponsoring industry, they are more likely to be presented as favourable in the conclusions. In other words, conclusions in industry-funded research are less likely to be consistent with the data (see Lundh et al., 2012; Yank et al., 2007). There is little evidence to indicate that industry-funded research is methodologically weaker than non-industry-funded research, but it may be more subject to some of the biases we described previously in relation to analyses and selective reporting of outcomes. The results may also be influenced by design-related decisions that increase the chances of finding favourable effects, such as comparing a new treatment against an alternative that is known to be ineffective (Lundh et al., 2012).

Second, bias in the literature can arise because of publication bias, with some companies actively trying to supress the publication of findings that do not work in their favour. For example, as far back as the 1960s the tobacco industry knew from its own research that nicotine was addictive, but the industry went to great lengths to withhold this information from the general public. Indeed, thirty years later, in 1994, a tobacco company executive even testified in court that he did not believe that nicotine was addictive (Bero, 2005).

Finally, industry funding can bias the research agenda, in other words, the types of questions that are asked and the types of questions that are not asked. For example, food companies are more likely to fund research examining the effects of individual nutrients on health, since these can be added or removed from products to increase their health value or appeal (**Box 11.2**). They are also more likely to fund research examining the effects of individual foods on health, since findings can then be used to promote sales of that food. They are less likely to fund research that examines the effects of different types of diets, such as diets high in processed versus unprocessed foods, or research that looks at how to influence dietary choices or how to address environmental factors that lead to under- and over-nutrition (Fabbri et al., 2017; Nestle, 2018).

In some cases, this biasing of the research agenda is an explicit strategy employed by industry to divert attention away from the harmful effects of their own products, implying that the blame for particular health conditions lies elsewhere (see also **Box 11.3**). For example, in the 1980s and 1990s the tobacco industry invested substantial amounts of money into research examining the effects of diet, occupation, stress and indoor air pollutants on lung cancer. The aim was to direct attention toward these factors as a way of reducing lung cancer whilst simultaneously diverting attention away from the role of passive smoking (Bero, 2005). Similarly, in the 1960s and 1970s the Sugar Research Foundation funded research looking at how tooth decay might be reduced through the use of tooth brushing, plaque removal, fluoride treatments and vaccines; essentially anything that did not involve limiting sugar intake (Kearns et al., 2015). More recently, the soft drinks company, Coca-Cola, provided millions of dollars of funding to support research that emphasises the links between physical activity and weight control (Nestle, 2018).

BOX 11.3 THE CORPORATE PLAYBOOK: HOW BIG BUSINESS PROTECTS ITS PROFITS

HOT TOPIC

In the 1950s and 1960s the tobacco industry developed a strategy (a 'playbook') for use by all its executives, lawyers, scientists and lobbyists. The key aim was to create controversy and doubt over links between smoking and cancer in order to prevent regulation (Bero, 2005). Other big businesses have since followed the tobacco industry's lead, including drug companies, food and drinks manufacturers, the alcohol industry and corporations with a vested interest in denying climate change and environmental damage (Brownell & Warner, 2009; Goldacre, 2012; Miller & Harkins, 2010; Moodie; 2017; Nestle, 2018; Oreskes & Conway, 2011). The tactics used by these industries include the following:

- Cast doubt on the science, for example by calling it 'bad science' or using information in a misleading way.

- Fund research that is likely to serve the interests of the industry, suppress findings that do not.

- Intimidate scientists, for example by attacking their credibility or threatening to sue.

- Create front organisations, such as think tanks that appear independent or research institutions that sponsor conferences and publish journals and newsletters.

- Manufacture false debate, for example by insisting journalists give equal weight to both sides of an argument.

- Frame the issue as one of personal responsibility and freedom of choice.

- Campaign for self-regulation, develop corporate voluntary codes and introduce 'safer' or 'healthier' products.

- Fund disinformation campaigns, for example by paying celebrities and sympathetic expert witnesses or by aligning with other campaign groups.

- Influence the political agenda, for example by donating to political parties or by hiring influential politicians once they leave office.

A biased research agenda is problematic as it can influence the types of intervention approaches employed by governments and public health organisations. For example, most of the research on nutritional deficiencies has examined the effects of food fortification (the addition of particular nutrients to foods) and supplementation (the provision of vitamin and mineral supplements) rather than the effects of behavioural and environmental interventions designed to improve diet quality. Over the long term, supplementation and fortification may not be the best approach because of risks of overexposure and because they do not tackle the underlying causes of malnutrition. But there is less evidence available to inform the development of alternative intervention approaches (Lawrence et al., 2016).

Thus conflicts of interest can lead to substantial bias, both in relation to individual studies and across the entire body of research within a field. Although much industry-funded research is of a high standard and makes an important contribution to knowledge, wealthy corporations have a long history of trying to subvert scientific knowledge for the sake of profit, often at the expense of public health. In the following section we look at ways in which these and other biases might be addressed.

ADDRESSING BIAS IN SCIENCE

The evidence examined so far clearly shows that the research literature can be subject to substantial bias. Indeed, Ioannidis attempted to estimate the effects of all the different sources of bias within the literature and came to the unhappy conclusion that 'most published research findings are false' (Ioannidis, 2005, p. 696). However, these criticisms have prompted academics to think carefully about how scientific research is conducted and there are now a growing number of organisations, networks and initiatives aimed at reforming scientific practice in order to help address bias (see Chambers, 2017; Nelson et al., 2018). In this section we briefly describe some of the solutions that have been put in place and others that have been proposed.

Pre-registration

Pre-registration refers to a process where the researcher registers important details about their study before they start collecting data. These include their hypotheses, target sample size, exclusion criteria and the ways in which they intend to analyse their data. The researcher submits these details to an organisation such as the Open Science Framework where they are date stamped and deposited. When the researchers come to submit their findings for publication the registration can then be made available to reviewers so they can check whether (and how) the researchers deviated from what they originally set out to do. Note that pre-registration does not prevent researchers from changing their plans during the course of a study, or engaging in exploratory analysis, but it does ensure these changes are transparent, providing the reader with a more complete picture of the strength of the evidence for different results. For example, analysis relating to predictions made before the study started can be labelled as 'confirmatory', whilst other data analysis can be labelled as 'exploratory'. Pre-registration is equivalent to the trial registration process used for RCTs and clinical research (see **Chapter 10**) but has only been introduced for experimental studies in psychology more recently after the extent of the bias within the literature was highlighted.

Registered reports

Registered reports go one step further than pre-registration. Like pre-registration the researcher supplies important details about their study prior to any data being collected.

However, in this case the registered report is sent to a specific journal (that has agreed to accept registered reports) where it is sent out for peer review. If accepted, the journal commits to publishing the findings of the study irrespective of the results. This is a more time-consuming process than pre-registration but researchers have the advantage of obtaining valuable feedback from peers to refine their study design before they begin collecting data and have assurance that their findings will be published at the end of the study. For the research community, registered reports should lead to higher quality studies as well as reduce publication bias and other questionable practices researchers may engage in in order to get their research published.

Data sharing repositories

Researchers are meant to share their data as this can help reduce errors and discourage researchers from engaging in questionable research practices such as p-hacking. However, in practice many authors do not share their data (Wicherts et al., 2006). This may be in part because they are worried about others finding errors in their analyses but also because supplying data to others can be a time-consuming process for which there is little incentive. For older research there may also be other barriers to data sharing such as unintelligible data files or the retirement or death of the main researcher. Data sharing repositories overcome these difficulties as the researchers submit their data to an open repository at the time of publication. Repositories include the Open Science Framework and those attached to specific journals.

Bayesian analyses

In psychology, null hypothesis significance testing (NHST) is the most commonly employed approach to data analysis. NHST involves contrasting an 'experimental' hypothesis with a 'null' hypothesis. Typically, we 'reject' the null hypothesis when the likelihood of the pattern in our data occurring in repeated sampling (when the null hypothesis is correct) is less than 5% ($p < .05$). However, we cannot use NHST to establish the chances of our null hypothesis being correct. Even if we find a p value of .95 this is not the same as saying that there is a 95% chance that there is no effect or no difference. And since we can never prove that the null hypothesis is correct, we can never conclude that there is no effect. Instead, we simply 'fail to support' the experimental hypothesis.

By contrast, Bayesian statistics can be used to calculate the probability of the null hypothesis being true (as well as the probability of the experimental hypothesis being true). As such, a study that uses Bayesian analysis will be better able to conclude that there is no effect. This may make journal editors more inclined to publish the findings, which could in turn help reduce publication bias. Unlike null hypothesis testing, Bayesian analyses are also immune to bias caused by researchers periodically checking their data before deciding whether or not to collect more. Additionally, they are not biased by the researcher conducting multiple tests. For these reasons, Bayesian analyses could also help reduce the occurrence of false positives within the literature (Francis, 2012).

Addressing conflicts of interest

The most hard-line approach to tackling bias associated with conflicts of interest would be for scientists to stop accepting industry funding. For example, some journals have a policy of not publishing research funded by the tobacco industry and some universities prohibit academics from accepting tobacco industry money. This is important for reputation as well as scientific integrity. Additionally, some funding bodies will not support researchers who accept funds from tobacco companies (Cohen et al., 2009).

An alternative approach is a model that enables industry to fund research, but which limits their influence on that research. For example, certain corporations or products may be taxed, with this money being set aside for related research managed by an independent body. This type of taxation already takes place in Thailand and in California on tobacco and alcohol (Aveyard et al., 2016).

Nestle (2018) argues that academics should also think carefully before accepting industry funding; in particular about whether the proposed research qualifies as science or marketing. Where funding is accepted, data should be owned by the scientific partner who should have the freedom to publish findings irrespective of what they show. And studies should be carefully designed to control for unconscious biases.

Finally, there should be more transparency in relation to conflicts of interest. Sources of funding and competing interests should be stated clearly in any research publications. Although an increasing number of journals now require authors to submit a disclosure statement, this is not always enforced and information about conflicts of interest is still missing from many academic papers (Mandrioli et al., 2016).

Summary

To build confidence in science and scientific evidence, we need to do everything we can to eliminate bias within the literature. This is important because people will be reluctant to follow scientific advice if they feel they cannot trust scientists. The strategies outlined above should help reduce bias in the literature and restore faith in the discipline. However, even with perfect evidence, there are still a range of other factors that may prevent the use of evidence-based interventions. We explore these factors in the next section.

BARRIERS TO THE ADOPTION AND USE OF EVIDENCE-BASED INTERVENTIONS

In **Chapter 9** we drew attention to the range of different factors that need to be considered when developing an intervention, such as affordability, cost-effectiveness and acceptability (see **Table 9.1**). In this section we explore the issue of acceptability in more detail by looking at some of the reasons why important stakeholders (government and the general public) may be unwilling to adopt or utilise an otherwise effective intervention. We also look at why people may sometimes support an intervention or policy that lacks evidence. These issues help highlight the wider societal context within which health interventions take place.

Conflicting values

As discussed in **Chapter 4,** 'values' refer to very broad concepts or beliefs that help guide behaviour. However, values can conflict with one another and different people will place more or less emphasis on different values.

A good example of where values can clash is in relation to government legislation that places restrictions on the sale or consumption of health-damaging substances such as cigarettes, alcohol or certain types of foods. Whilst advocates of such legislation argue that it is an effective way of improving health, critics can accuse the government of being a 'nanny state', undermining individual freedom of choice and making it difficult for ordinary people to enjoy everyday pleasures (Capewell & Lilford, 2016; Wheeler, 2018). (Recall one of the tactics of the corporate playbook in **Box 11.3** and see further discussion in **Box 11.4**.) These types of objections can sometimes be difficult to counter because, unlike facts, values cannot be proved right or wrong. Instead, the important question is the extent to which people prioritise their health over and above their freedom to choose and their right to indulge, and also whether any gains in health would be large enough to outweigh any losses in autonomy and pleasure. The answers to these questions are likely to vary from person to person.

Another example of this type of clash in values is the US government's investment in abstinence-only-until-marriage programmes (now sometimes also called 'sexual risk avoidance programmes'; Santelli et al., 2017). These were originally developed in the 1980s by community- and faith-based organisations with strong traditional values relating to the prohibition of sex outside of marriage. Thus the main goal of these programmes is to reduce sexually transmitted diseases and unplanned pregnancies by promoting abstinence from sex outside of marriage. In theory this sounds like a reasonable approach, and there is some evidence to suggest that these programmes do reduce sexual activity (Chin et al., 2012). However, reductions in sexual activity do not necessarily translate into disease reduction (Brückner & Bearman, 2005) and the evidence for alternative comprehensive risk reduction programmes is much better (Chin et al., 2012). Comprehensive risk reduction programmes provide information about contraception as well as abstinence. Thus they can also help promote safe sex among those who fail to remain abstinent. (And evidence indicates that in practice many young people do fail to remain abstinent regardless of their intentions; Brückner & Bearman, 2005.) This contrasts with abstinence-only programmes where government funding is tied to a requirement that contraceptive methods should only be discussed to emphasise their failure rates (Santelli et al., 2017). Nevertheless, despite their much weaker evidence base, abstinence-only programmes are still used in many parts of the United States because comprehensive risk reduction programmes are viewed by some as condoning sex outside of marriage which runs counter to traditional religious values relating to abstinence.

BOX 11.4 WHEN IDEOLOGY TRUMPS SCIENCE: FROM TOBACCO SMOKE TO CLIMATE CHANGE

In the 1960s and 1970s, Frederick Seitz and Fred Singer were two of America's most distinguished scientists, renowned for **HOT TOPIC** their research in solid-state physics and satellite technology. However, from the late 1970s they began working with industry and industry-funded think tanks to challenge the scientific evidence on issues such as tobacco smoke and climate change.

Seitz and Singer are among a small number of influential scientists who, over the last four decades, have attempted to undermine scientific knowledge in order to help big business resist regulation (see also **Box 11.3**). For example, in 1992 the American Environmental Protection Agency released a report concluding that passive smoking is harmful to health. Since you cannot conduct randomised controlled trials examining the long-term effects of passive smoking on humans, inevitably, the report's conclusions were based on case-control and cohort studies that looked at associations between disease and passive smoking. Seitz exploited the uncertainties inherent in this type of research (see **Chapter 10**), claiming it could not rule out the influence of other factors, such as diet and outdoor air pollution. He dismissed it as 'junk science' (EPA, 1992; Oreskes & Conway, 2011; Singer, 1993).

We often have to rely on the weight of the scientific evidence rather than any conclusive 'proof'. Seitz and Singer would have known this, so why did they take this position? It seems likely they were motivated by ideology rather than profit. Having lived through the Cold War they were staunch believers in capitalism and the free market. And they viewed any attempt at government regulation or intervention as a slippery slope to communism. Unfortunately, their reputations as respected scientists made their tactics all the more effective; they had access to the White House and their arguments were taken seriously by journalists. As a result, government action on both second-hand smoke and climate change was delayed (Oreskes & Conway, 2011).

Competing government priorities

In some cases it is competing government priorities that represent a barrier to evidence-based policy and intervention. Although governments tend to have the same broad aims (to increase economic wealth, to keep people safe, to improve population health and to ensure citizens enjoy a good life), democratically elected governments will also be concerned about staying in power. This leads to additional priorities, unrelated to the wellbeing of the nation. In particular they need to *look* like they are doing a good job and to ensure the population are happy with the decisions they make. Some examples of competing government priorities are described below.

Avoiding policy U-turns

A central feature of scientific enquiry is the revision or rejection of prevailing theory in light of new data. Indeed, this is how scientific knowledge advances. However, this same approach, revising policy in light of new evidence, is typically viewed as a weakness for politicians and government. For example, policy 'U-turns' are described in the national press as 'humiliating' and politicians will go to great lengths to avoid or deny them (Beckford, 2011). For some reason, unlike the rest of us, politicians are expected to have all the answers up front. And because they need to look like they are doing a good job, they need to avoid bad press. This makes it difficult for them to revise or reverse a policy in light of new evidence. Henderson (2012) argues that instead of criticising politicians for U-turns we should instead make a point of praising them when they are prepared to revise their views. Likewise, when considering who to vote for, we should be asking candidates for examples of mistakes from which they have learned and we should be wary of anyone who claims to have always been right.

Doing something now

Democratically elected governments will serve for a specific term (typically four to five years) before the next election, meaning that politicians only have a limited period of time to produce results and demonstrate to citizens that they are doing a good job. Science tends to work at a much slower pace as good evidence for real-world interventions takes time to obtain. As such, government may sometimes have to implement policy in the absence of evidence, if an issue is urgent or because politicians want to be seen to be doing something now (for example, to generate positive momentum prior to a general election). The need to implement policy in the absence of perfect evidence could be viewed as an opportunity to learn something new. Policies should be viewed as experiments. In particular, it may be possible to roll out an intervention in a manner that would allow for rigorous evaluation and to commission scientists to evaluate effects (see Murphy et al., 2011). However, politicians may be disinclined to include such evaluation, in part because the timescale would likely extend beyond their term in office and in part because of negative attitudes towards policy U-turns; unfavourable results could compromise their position. Thus it is much safer to include a weaker evaluation that will likely present the new policy in a favourable light.

Keeping key voters happy

No government will enjoy support from the entire population. Party loyalties may be difficult to shift such that whatever a government does, certain groups may still be unlikely to vote for them in the next election. Thus a government may be more inclined to prioritise the views and interests of certain groups over others, such as key supporters it wants to remain loyal and 'swing voters' with a tendency to switch allegiances between parties. It may also be concerned about retaining the support of individuals or organisations that are highly influential among certain groups of voters.

Keeping donors happy

In many countries, organisations, businesses or individuals support political parties through financial donations, which can be used to help a party campaign for election. This means that a government may be wary about introducing policy or legislation that would alienate an important donor.

Misinformation

Misinformation refers to the spread of inaccurate or false information. Disinformation is a form of misinformation that is spread with deliberate intent to mislead.

From those with vested interests

As described previously, in some cases the government and general public may be deliberately misled about evidence by influential individuals or organisations whose interests or beliefs conflict with a particular policy or intervention (**Boxes 11.3** and **11.4**). These individuals or organisations may try to cast doubt on scientific evidence by exploiting the fact that there are rarely any certainties in science. This is especially true in public health where it is often not possible to randomly assign people to different groups in order to test the effects of a particular behaviour, such as smoking. Thus it is difficult for scientists to claim they have definitive proof that, for example, smoking leads to lung cancer. Instead, conclusions must rely on the weight of the evidence (which, in the case of smoking and lung cancer, one could legitimately describe as 'overwhelming').

In the news

Misinformation can also spread because of news reporters' desire to ensure that media coverage of a topic is seen as 'balanced', and to allow a forum for lively debate. However, giving equal weight to a discredited view can create the impression of controversy over a particular issue, leading the public to believe that scientists disagree and that the evidence is unclear, when in fact the very

Measles – one of the world's most infectious diseases. Measles is an airborne virus spread through saliva and nasal secretions (for example through coughing and sneezing). Symptoms include a red rash, fever, runny nose and cough. In the United States, between 1985 and 1992, death from measles occurred in around 1 in 500 of those infected. Other complications include blindness, brain damage and miscarriage in pregnant women. Before the introduction of a vaccine in 1963, global deaths from measles were around 2.6 million a year. In 2017, estimated deaths were 110,000 (CDC, 2015; WHO, 2019e).

Mumps – a viral disease spread by airborne droplets or direct contact with an infected person. Mumps affects the glands causing swelling of the neck along with fever, headache and malaise. Long-term complications, such as deafness, are very rare, and more likely to occur in adults. In the United States, between 1966 and 1971, 1 in every 5,000 people infected with mumps died (CDC, 2015).

Rubella – also known as German measles, is a contagious, airborne viral infection that causes a rash and mild fever. Although not considered dangerous in children and adults, in early pregnancy it is likely to be passed on to the foetus where it can cause miscarriage, stillbirth or congenital rubella syndrome. Children with congenital rubella syndrome can suffer from a wide range of health conditions including deafness, heart and eye defects and diabetes. They are also more likely to be diagnosed with autism. Before the development of a vaccine in 1969, 1 in every 250 babies born suffered from congenital rubella syndrome (CDC, 2015; WHO, 2018g).

large majority of scientists may be of one opinion with only a few detractors (Goldacre, 2008; Henderson, 2012).

A good example of the damaging effect of this kind of media coverage on public health is in relation to the MMR vaccination in the UK. MMR is a combined vaccine against **measles, mumps** and **rubella**, given to children in two doses when they are around 12 months old. Originally, vaccinations for these diseases were given separately (in six doses), but in 1988 they were combined to reduce the chances of infection by the diseases not immunised first and to increase vaccination coverage, especially among low-income and vulnerable groups (parents are more likely to miss vaccination appointments in a course of six rather than two). (See **Figure 11.1**.)

In 1998, ten years after the introduction of the MMR, a medic called Andrew Wakefield published a case-series report in *The Lancet* describing 12 children with both bowel and behavioural problems and reporting that the parents and doctors of 8 of these children believed their problems started after they were given the MMR vaccination. At a press conference Wakefield also questioned the safety of the MMR and said he thought it would be better to use a single vaccination for each disease. In late 2001, prompted by the prime minister refusal to say whether his infant son had been vaccinated, the story was picked up on by the media and in 2002 there was extensive reporting of the MMR vaccination. However, more than two-thirds of newspaper reports failed to mention the overwhelming evidence that the MMR vaccination is considered safe and only 11% reported that the MMR is viewed as safe in 90 other countries (Goldacre, 2008).

Figure 11.1 Change in the recorded number of cases of, and deaths from, measles in England and Wales following the introduction of a single measles vaccine in 1968 and the MMR in 1988

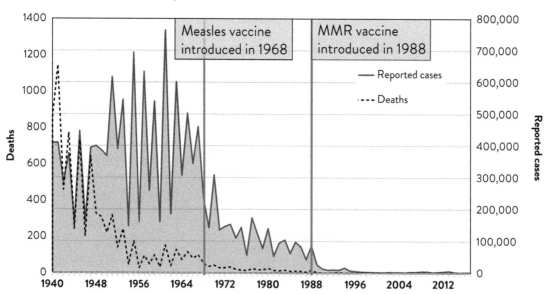

Source: Reproduced with permission from Dr Tonia Thomas, Oxford Vaccine Group. Data from Public Health England and Health Protection Agency Archive.

The original *Lancet* paper was subsequently retracted in light of the emergence of inaccuracies in the reporting of the research as well as evidence of unethical practice (Wakefield et al., 2010). There were also unreported conflicts of interest; Wakefield was involved in a patent relating to a new vaccine and was also being paid by a legal firm to help parents prepare a case against the MMR (Goldacre, 2008). Although Wakefield was eventually struck off the medical register, barring him from practising as a doctor, the damage was already done: vaccination rates in England fell from around 88% in 1988 to less than 80% in 2003, dropping to 61% in some parts of London. And cases of measles in England and Wales rose from just 56 in 1998 to 2,030 in 2012 (**Figure 11.2**). In 2006, a thirteen-year-old boy became the first child to die of measles in Britain in 14 years (Henderson, 2012; Kidd et al., 2003; Public Health England, 2018b). Wakefield now resides in Texas where he continues to campaign against the MMR through social media and public speaking engagements. In 2016, he directed a film called *Vaxxed* that claimed to expose institutional cover-ups of links between autism and MMR (Boseley, 2018). **Box 11.5** explores some of the other reasons for vaccine hesitancy.

Goldacre (2008) argues that part of the problem with media coverage of science stories is that journalists often lack expertise, meaning that there is a risk of reporting being inaccurate and subject to influence by maverick individuals. Goldacre contends that news editors do not place enough importance on science expertise, pointing out that 80% of the coverage of the MMR story was by generalist reporters rather than science specialists. Had the story been covered by journalists with scientific backgrounds, perhaps coverage would have been more accurate as they would have realised that a case-series report was insufficient evidence to make claims about causal links (see **Chapter 10**).

Figure 11.2 Change in the number of confirmed cases of measles in England and Wales following the now-retracted Wakefield paper in 1998 and misleading news reports in 2001 and 2002

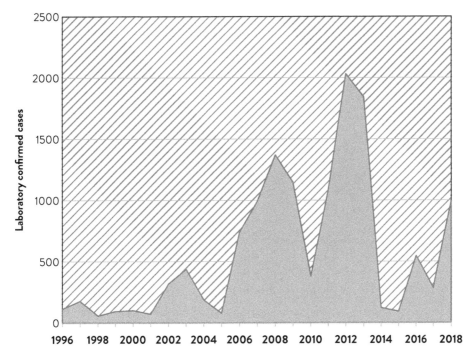

Source: Reproduced with permission from Dr Tonia Thomas, Oxford Vaccine Group. Data from Public Health England and Health Protection Agency Archive.

CHAPTER 11

BOX 11.5 ARGUMENTS AGAINST VACCINATION, NOW AND THEN

HOT TOPIC

Concerns over vaccinations are not new. People have been voicing their objections as far back as the early 1800s when Edward Jenner developed the first ever vaccination for smallpox. The decision by the British government, in 1853, to make smallpox vaccination compulsory for babies resulted in demonstrations, riots and the founding of vocal anti-vaccination groups. Objections continued until 1898, when legislation was revised to allow parents to obtain an exemption certificate – giving rise to the concept of a 'conscientious objector' (Wolfe & Sharp, 2002).

Wolfe and Sharp (2002) show the similarities between arguments against vaccination in the 1800s and today (see also Helps et al., 2018; Opel et al., 2011). These arguments centre on the following:

- Concerns that vaccines may increase the risk of other diseases

- Concerns that vaccines contain poisonous chemicals

- Beliefs that vaccines may be ineffective

- A desire to take a more 'natural' approach to promoting and maintaining good health

- Mistrust of the medical system, government or pharmaceutical industry and a concern that other interests, such as profit, are being placed over safety

- A belief that compulsory vaccination is a violation of individual liberty.

Given the persistence of these arguments over time, Wolfe and Sharp (2002) suggest that opposition to vaccination is unlikely to ever disappear completely. However, arguably the strength of opposition will wax and wane according to other influences. Larson et al. (2011) identify a number of factors that may have contributed to increasing levels of mistrust in vaccination in recent years. These include the following:

- The rise of the internet and social media which makes it easier for those who oppose vaccinations to reinforce each other's views, and disseminate information and misinformation

- A lack of familiarity with the diseases being vaccinated against (because vaccination has made them rare). This makes the disease seem less threatening

- Increasing recognition of rare genetic predispositions to certain conditions which could, in theory, increase the chances of an adverse reaction to a vaccination in a particular individual

- An increased willingness on the part of the general public to question those in authority

- An increased awareness of industry's track record of placing profit over safety (see **Box 11.3**; see also Goldacre, 2012).

Thus although arguments against vaccinations may often stem from misinformation or a misunderstanding of the risks, they can also arise, or be compounded by, other factors too. We look at vaccinations in more detail in **Chapter 12**.

On social media

The rise of social media represents an increasing threat to scientific evidence and evidence-based advice, with misinformation being forwarded on from person to person and promoted online by celebrities and influencers (**Image 11.3**). For example, in April 2020, almost half of UK adults said they had seen false or misleading information about COVID-19 during the previous week, with 40% of these saying they found it hard to know what was true or false (Ofcom, 2020). The rapid spread of vast quantities of information, much of it unverified, is described by the World Health Organization as an 'infodemic'. It is common during crises and catastrophes and can cause confusion and anxiety. It can also make people more reluctant to follow evidence-based advice (WHO, 2018f). Indeed, the example at the start of the chapter shows just how devastating an infodemic can be.

Arguably, one of the reasons why social media can be so persuasive is that it frequently relies on personal stories. As described in **Chapter 10**, emotionally charged stories can often feel more urgent and meaningful than a series of dry facts and statistics. Additionally, the information we come across on social

Image 11.3 *Social media contributes to the rapid spread of false information during crises and catastrophes.*
Credit: United Nations COVID-19 Response.

media often comes to us via family, friends or favourite celebrities. We are more inclined to be influenced by these types of people than by an unknown expert or a politician we do not like (see the theory of planned behaviour, social cognitive theory and social norms in **Chapters 5 and 6** and MINDSPACE in **Chapter 9**).

Social media companies have come under fire for their failure to tackle misinformation on their platforms, though they are now beginning to address this problem. For example, prior to 2019, if you searched for information about vaccinations on YouTube, chances are you would be directed to videos featuring upsetting stories of children supposedly harmed through vaccination and charismatic celebrities expounding the virtues of vaccine-free living (see Keelan et al., 2007). However, in 2019, YouTube adjusted their algorithms to reduce the frequency with which anti-vaccination videos appear in searches and in the 'up next' content. They also banned advertisements on videos containing anti-vaccine content. Try searching for 'anti-vax' on YouTube now, and you will be presented with a link to a Wikipedia site on vaccine controversies and a range of videos from news organisations and medics describing the science behind vaccination and addressing some of the concerns of the 'anti-vax' movement. Similarly, WhatsApp have introduced measures to prevent frequently forwarded messages from being further forwarded to multiple new chats and Facebook and Instagram now remove certain posts that have been flagged as false.

Motivated reasoning

In **Chapter 10** we saw how, as humans, we are subject to a number of errors of judgement that mean we're not always very good at weighing up evidence in an objective and unbiased way. This can also mean that our view on whether a particular policy or intervention is effective may be heavily influenced by our feelings towards it. For example, a person who is afraid of needles may be more likely to conclude that a particular vaccination is unnecessary or risky. Likewise, someone who worries about increased government intrusion into the private lives of citizens may decide that a particular piece of legislation will be ineffective at changing behaviour (see also **Box 11.4**). This type of reasoning is called 'motivated reasoning' and includes the confirmation bias and affect heuristic we described in **Chapter 10**. Motivated reasoning is likely also responsible for some of the biases we discussed earlier in this chapter in relation to scientific practice, where researchers may be heavily invested in the results of a study.

BOX 11.6 HOW CAN WE CHANGE PEOPLE'S MINDS?

MAKING CONNECTIONS

In this chapter we've seen how misinformation and motivated reasoning can lead to false beliefs with potentially devastating consequences. What's the best way of changing people's beliefs? And what types of strategies might be counterproductive? To help you answer this question, you may like to consider some of the theories we looked at in **Chapters 5 and 6** (such as protection motivation theory, social cognitive theory, evaluative conditioning and social norms). You could also look at motivational interviewing which we discuss in **Chapter 12** (**Case Study 9**).

Deep vein thrombosis (DVT) – where a blood clot develops in a deep vein, usually in the leg. If left untreated, around 1 in 10 instances of DVT will lead to a pulmonary embolism. This is where part of the clot breaks off and travels through the bloodstream to cause a blockage in one of the blood vessels in the lungs. This causes chest pain and difficulties with breathing and can be life-threatening if not treated quickly. In the UK, every year around 1 person in 1,000 develops DVT. Risk factors include being over the age of 40, being inactive for long periods, suffering from overweight or obesity and being pregnant (because pregnancy makes blood clot more easily). The hormone oestrogen, contained in some contraceptive pills, also makes blood clot more easily, which is why it increases the risk of DVT (NHS, 2016).

Misunderstanding of science and statistics

Finally, Henderson (2012) argues that few politicians have a background in science and many lack an understanding of basic scientific concepts and methods. This can mean that governments do not always give enough weight to scientific evidence or interpret it correctly. As described above, the same can be true of news reporters and of the general public. Such misunderstandings are often particularly pronounced when it comes to understanding statistics describing risks. This in turn can influence the ways in which people behave.

For example, in 1995 new research showed that a commonly used type of contraceptive pill doubled the risk of **deep vein thrombosis**. These findings were widely covered in the UK media but with no additional numerical information to clarify the risks. As such the coverage led to widespread alarm among women and many stopped using oral contraceptives. It is estimated that the scare resulted in over 10,000 extra abortions the following year (Furedi, 1999).

However, although 'double the risk' sounds alarming, this type of statistic tells us nothing about our actual risks. Double of very little is still very little. What the media coverage failed to mention were the absolute risks, which were actually still very small. In fact, the increased risks of developing deep vein thrombosis from the pill were still lower than the risks of developing it from pregnancy; pregnancy does not just double the risks of developing deep vein thrombosis, it increases it by 10 times (NHS, 2016), though the actual risk is still tiny. Had the media reported the absolute risks from the pill, that it increased the risks from 1 in 100,000 per year to 2 in 100,000 per year, the effect on behaviour may have been quite different (NHS, 2016). Thus another important barrier to evidence-based intervention is the way in which risks are communicated and understood (**Box 11.7**).

BOX 11.7 RELATIVE RISKS VERSUS ABSOLUTE RISKS

DIG A LITTLE DEEPER

Relative risk is risk compared to something else. For example, an increased risk of deep vein thrombosis from 1 in 100,000 per year to 2 in 100,000 per year is a doubling of risk, or a 100% increase in relative risk (because the size of the increase in risk is the same as the original risk). An increase to 3 per year would be expressed as a tripling of risk or a 200% increase in relative risk (because the size of the increase in risk is three times as large as the original risk). These risks might also be described as being 'twice as likely' or 'three times as likely'. Relative risks don't tell us much about our actual risks and can be quite misleading.

Absolute risk is the actual risk; for example, the increased risk of developing deep vein thrombosis from 1 in 100,000 per year to 2 in 100,000 per year. This is the absolute risk presented as natural frequencies. Absolute risk can also be expressed as percentages, for example, as an increase in risk from 0.001% to 0.002%. However, percentages tend to be more difficult to understand than natural frequencies; risks are most clearly expressed as absolute risks in natural frequencies.

Relative risks usually sound more dramatic than absolute risks, which is why they are often used in the media. A risk described as 'tripled' sounds much more important than a risk described as an increase from 0.001% to 0.003%. Unfortunately, this emphasis on attention-grabbing headlines can come at the expense of public health and wellbeing.

CONCLUSIONS

Once an effective intervention has been developed or identified, there is still no guarantee it will be adopted or used. This is evident from the outbreak of measles in Samoa that led to a number of deaths that could have been prevented through vaccination. There are a range of different reasons why evidence-based interventions and advice may not always be adopted or followed. In some cases, it may be because of competing values and priorities; health is not the only thing that is important to people and to governments and we need to view health promotion within this context. However, in other cases evidence is ignored because of misunderstandings and misinformation. Given the track records of some big corporations that have actively tried to mislead people about the scientific evidence, it is hardly surprising that people may sometimes be sceptical of the information they receive. Such mistrust may be higher where people have suffered from more exploitation in the past, for example in certain countries or among certain groups. Even for well-intentioned scientists, trust may be undermined where bias in research gives rise to misleading findings and advice. Just because a person is a scientist does not mean they are immune to bias. As scientists, we need to do everything we can to limit the extent to which our own interests and biases influence our research. We need to earn the trust of those we hope to influence.

How should we tackle medical and health misinformation on social media? How can we balance the harms caused by such misinformation with the benefits of free speech? What might be the most effective ways of changing people's minds?

THE GREAT DEBATE

CHAPTER

12 CHANGING BEHAVIOUR

Chapter Outline

This final chapter is concerned with how we actually go about changing behaviour in order to improve health (**Image 12.1**). It includes discussion of different health behaviours as well as a series of case studies describing different types of intervention. The chapter is also designed to bring together the material contained in the rest of the book and for this reason it is set out a little differently from previous chapters. In particular, certain key terms have been underlined and you are encouraged to look these up in the index to remind yourself of the theories, concepts and methods they relate to. This will help you think more critically about the interventions and how they fit into the field of health psychology.

The chapter starts by considering some of the different ways in which health interventions are described and categorised. The sections that follow are then organised around different health behaviours with accompanying case studies used to discuss

Image 12.1 *Behavioural changes, such as wearing a face mask, have been key to tackling the COVID-19 pandemic.*
Credit: Katy Tapper.

relevant interventions. These sections are not intended to be comprehensive. Rather, they are designed to highlight important or interesting issues and to reflect the broad range of approaches that can be taken to improve health. They are also designed to spark curiosity, inspire new ideas, and highlight links between different areas in this book. The concluding section draws out key issues that emerge from both this and previous chapters.

CATEGORISING BEHAVIOUR CHANGE INTERVENTIONS

There are a number of different ways of describing and categorising behaviour change interventions and you are likely to come across a range of terms in the literature. The following describe some of the most common ways in which interventions are grouped.

By type of behaviour

Interventions may be grouped according to the type of behaviour they target. At the most basic level, this could refer to the specific behaviour, such as interventions to promote fruit and vegetable consumption or to reduce binge drinking. However, interventions may also be grouped more broadly, for example, according to whether they target health-promoting behaviours (which involve doing more of something, such as eating more fruit or getting more exercise) or health-risk behaviours (which involve doing less of something, such as quitting cigarettes or cutting down on sugar). Categorising interventions in this way can be helpful because these different types of behaviours are thought to reflect different psychological processes, meaning they may require different types of strategy. In recent years, increasing attention has also been paid to maintenance behaviours that involve maintaining behavioural changes over time, such as maintaining weight loss or preventing relapse following smoking cessation. Again, categorising interventions as those that target behavioural maintenance may be helpful because behavioural maintenance requires different strategies to the short-term initiation or inhibition of behaviours.

By population or setting

Population or setting can also be a useful way of categorising an intervention since it may determine the way in which it can be delivered or the types of strategies that can be employed. Examples include school-based interventions, work-based interventions, community interventions and interventions set in primary care.

By mode of delivery

There are many different ways of grouping interventions according to their mode of delivery. At the very broadest level we can distinguish between interventions that are delivered face to face and those that are delivered from a distance. We can also distinguish between population-level interventions, that are simultaneously delivered to very large groups of people, and individual-level interventions, that are delivered to one person at a time. The latter allow for more tailoring and variability in approach.

Within these broad distinctions there are a further multitude of different delivery methods. Some interventions may be delivered by a practitioner to individuals or to groups, in person or by telephone. Mass media interventions refer to those that use technology designed to reach large audiences, such as television, magazines, billboards, the internet and, increasingly, social media. In the last two decades we have also seen the rise of interventions using digital technologies such as text messages, smartphone apps and wearable tracking devices.

By type of strategy

Sometimes health interventions are described in terms of the general type of strategy they employ. A good example of this is policy interventions. Grouping these together may be helpful since they will all require the involvement of policy makers.

By underlying psychological process or theory

Interventions may also be categorised according the types of psychological processes, constructs or theories they draw on. For example, we might talk about habits-based interventions, stage-based interventions or interventions that target social norms or attitudes. This type of grouping is most useful for meta-analyses designed to evaluate a particular theory and its utility for behaviour change.

Summary

The categories outlined above help draw attention to important intervention features. However, they are not mutually exclusive and most interventions will fall into several categories, even within the same category system. For example, a physical activity intervention may be designed to target health-risk behaviours (such as being sedentary) as well as health-promoting behaviours (such as attending an exercise class). Likewise, a multi-component intervention aimed at improving diet may combine face-to-face counselling with a self-monitoring app, or policy changes with a mass media campaign. Thus, whilst it is useful to be aware of these different descriptors, and to recognise these features in different interventions, it is not possible to neatly assign an intervention just one particular label. The interventions described in this chapter are organised according to the main type of behaviour they target. However, they have been selected to illustrate a wide range of different intervention types and you are encouraged to think about how they might relate to some of the categories described above.

HEALTHY EATING

Recommendations and relationship with health

Healthy eating involves a wide range of different behaviours and has an enormous impact on our health. For example, it is estimated that around 11 million deaths a year can be attributed to a suboptimal diet, particularly a high intake of salt and low intake of whole grains and fruit (Afshin et al., 2019). Healthy eating can be difficult because we have evolved to like many things that are bad for us when eaten in large quantities, and most of us now live in a world with constant access to such foods (**Chapter 2**). **Table 12.1** shows key healthy eating recommendations alongside reasons for these recommendations, whilst **Figure 12.1** shows what a balanced diet should look like.

Table 12.1 Key healthy eating recommendations for adults and the reasons for these recommendations

Food or nutrient	Recommendation for adults	Relationship with health	Example intakes among adults
Saturated fat	Should constitute no more than 11% of energy intake – equivalent to approximately 30g a day for men, 20g for women.[1]	Raises LDL cholesterol, which can lead to atherosclerosis, increasing the risk of cardiovascular diseases.[3]	Mean average intake in the UK constitutes 11.6% of energy intake for men and 12.2% for women.[1]
Added sugar	Should constitute no more than 5% of energy intake – approximately 30g a day, or 7 sugar cubes.[1]	Linked to tooth decay,[4] as well as higher blood pressure and higher LDL cholesterol,[5] which increase the risk of heart disease and stroke. Sugar sweetened beverages are also associated with an increased risk of type 2 diabetes.[6]	Mean average UK intake constitutes 11.1% of energy intake for men and 11.2% for women.[11]
Salt	No more than 6g a day, or one teaspoon. (Salt is sometimes labelled as sodium chloride, in which case the maximum is 2.4g a day.)[1]	Raises blood pressure, increasing the risk of heart disease and stroke.[7]	Mean average intakes in England of 9.1g for men and 6.8g for women.[12]
Red and processed meat	No more than an average of 70g a day.[1]	Likely to increase the risk of bowel cancer.[8]	Mean average UK intakes of 77g for men and 47g for women.[11]
Fruit and vegetables	At least 5 portions a day. A portion is equivalent to approximately 80g (or 30g of dried fruit). Fresh, frozen, cooked, tinned and dried fruit and vegetables all count, as well as those contained in dishes such as soups and stews. Beans and pulses count, but only as a maximum of 1 portion a day, regardless of the amount eaten. A 150ml serving of unsweetened 100% fruit or vegetable juice counts, but only as a maximum of 1 portion, regardless of the amount eaten. A smoothie containing all the edible pulped fruit or vegetable may count as more than 1 portion, depending on how it has been made. Potatoes do not count.[1]	Supply vitamins and minerals, tend to be high in fibre and low in calories. Higher consumption (up to 5 portions a day) is associated with a reduced risk of death, particularly from cardiovascular disease.[9]	Mean average UK intake of 4.2 portions a day for both men and women.[11]
Whole grains	Between 100 and 150g per day.[2]	Are a good source of fibre and B vitamins. Also contain minerals such as iron, magnesium and zinc. Associated with a lower risk of coronary heart disease, stroke, cardiovascular disease, cancer and diabetes.[10]	Median average UK intake of 20g per day.[13]

Notes: [1]NHS (2018a); see also WHO (2018d) and note that precise recommendations vary slightly across different organisations; [2]Afshin et al. (2019); [3]Food and Agriculture Organisation of the United Nations (2010); [4]Moynihan & Kelly (2014); [5]Te Morenga et al., (2014); [6]Scientific Advisory Committee on Nutrition (2015); [7]WHO (2012); [8]Scientific Advisory Committee on Nutrition (2010); [9]Wang et al. (2014); [10]Aune et al. (2016); [11]Public Health England (2018); [12]Public Health England (2016); [13]K.D. Mann et al., (2015).

Figure 12.1 The Eatwell guide: what a balanced diet looks like

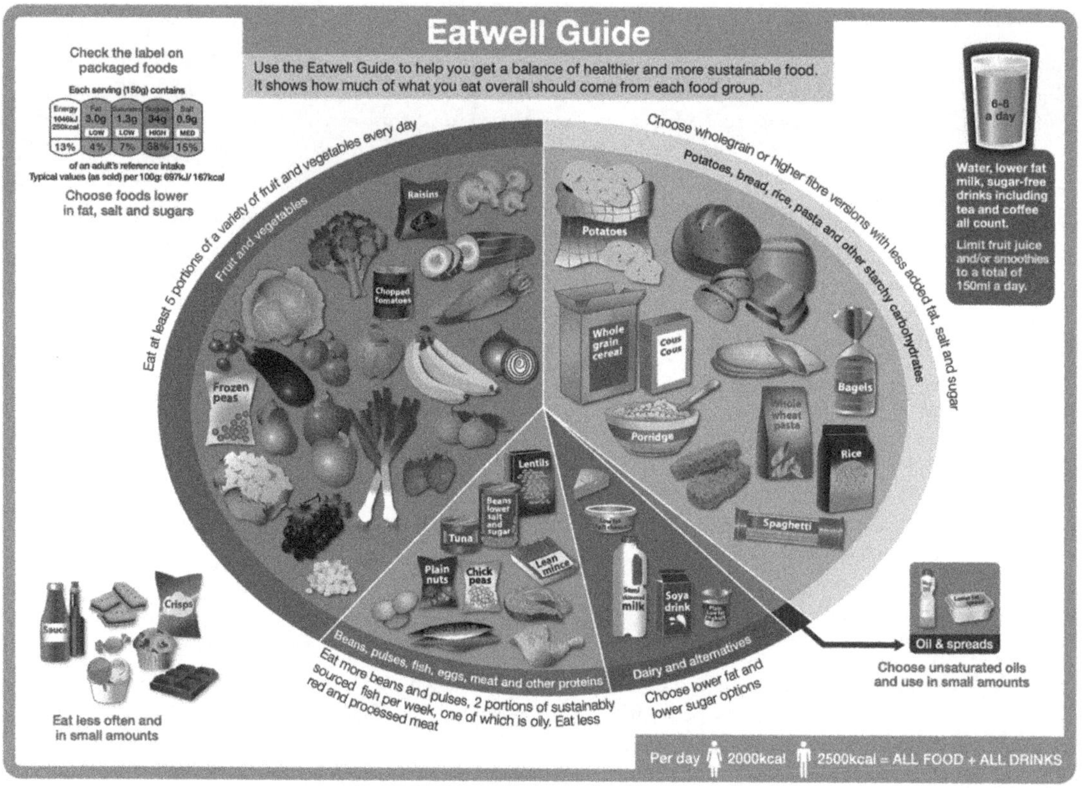

Source: Public Health England in association with the Welsh government, Food Standards Scotland and the Food Standards Agency in Northern Ireland. Crown copyright. Reproduced under the terms of the Open Government Licence.

Group differences in healthy eating

There are substantial variations in diet with nationality, gender, age and income. For example, globally, Egypt, Pakistan and Ukraine have some of the highest diet-related deaths whilst Japan, France and Spain have some of the lowest (Afshin et al., 2019). **Table 12.1** shows that in the UK, men tend to eat more salt than women, as well as more red and processed meat. Likewise, teenagers in the UK typically eat less fruit and vegetables and more added sugar compared to younger children and adults (Public Health England, 2018). Diet also varies with income. For example, in high-income countries, those from more deprived backgrounds tend to eat less fruit and vegetables and whole grains and more saturated fat, added sugar and salt (Cappuccio et al., 2015; De Irala-Estévez et al., 2000; K.D. Mann et al., 2015; Mullie et al., 2010). In **Chapter 3** we explored some of the reasons why those from poorer backgrounds tend to engage in less healthy behaviours, including misunderstanding or misinterpreting health advice or labelling (sometimes called 'health literacy'), early life experiences that lead to more impulsive behaviour, and prioritisation of other needs (such as money) that lead to reduced attentional and cognitive resources for health.

Case Studies 1 and 2 illustrate two very different interventions designed to reduce consumption of 'unhealthy' foods; the first uses individual training sessions carried out on a smartphone app whilst the second is an example of a population-level intervention that uses policy changes to try to reduce sales of sugary drinks.

CASE STUDY 1

FOODT BRAIN TRAINING APP: HELPING PEOPLE RESIST 'UNHEALTHY' FOODS

Background

Chocolate, crisps, ice cream, cakes, biscuits, burgers, chips... Many of the foods we really like are high in saturated fats, added sugars, salt and calories. Too much of these foods can be bad for our health as well as our waistline. But resisting them can be difficult, especially as they tend to capture our attention and elicit automatic motor responses toward them (**Chapter 6**). Some people show particularly strong responses to these types of foods (**Chapter 4**; see also Lawrence et al., 2012), and where this is coupled with low levels of self-control (**Chapter 7**) they are especially susceptible to overeating and weight gain. The FoodT brain training app was developed to help improve self-control among such people, by strengthening their ability to inhibit their automatic motor responses towards tempting high-calorie foods.

Intervention

The intervention consists of a series of five-minute training sessions completed on a smartphone using the FoodT app. Users are advised to complete one session a day for a week, followed by one a week for a month, preferably before meals when they are hungry. During the training a series of images appear in different parts of the screen, surrounded by a green circle or a red circle (**Image 12.2**). The user is instructed to tap on the image as fast as they can if it is in a green circle but withhold their response, and stay as still as possible, if it is in a red circle. The images consist of 'healthy' foods (such as fruit and vegetables), 'unhealthy' foods (such as crisps, biscuits and cakes) and non-food items (for example, flowers, clothing or stationery). Unhealthy foods are presented within a red circle, training the user to inhibit their motor responses toward them. Healthy foods are presented in a green circle, reinforcing an approach response. Non-food items are presented in both red and green circles. The user has the option of selecting the types of foods they would like to eat less of and more of and this determines the images that are displayed. Scores for speed and accuracy are provided within each session and users are encouraged to try to beat their previous scores each time they play. The user can also set personalised daily or weekly reminders to complete the training sessions.

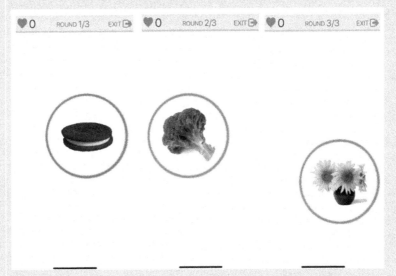

Image 12.2 *In the FoodT app users are presented with images of unhealthy foods in red circles (left) and images of healthy foods in green circles (centre) as well as non-food images in red or green circles (right). They have to click on the images in green circles as fast as they can but refrain from clicking on the images in red circles.*

Relevant theory	The FoodT app is a good example of a highly novel intervention developed directly from theory and related laboratory research (**Chapter 9**). It is informed by <u>dual-processing theories</u> of cognition and behaviour. More specifically, it uses <u>cognitive bias modification</u> (in the form of a <u>Go/No-Go</u> task) to inhibit <u>automatic action tendencies</u>. Although the researchers state that the training works by improving <u>self-control</u>, it does not appear to improve top-down inhibitory control (of the type we looked at in **Chapter 7**). Rather, it seems to reduce the extent to which foods are liked and elicit <u>cravings,</u> making it easier for individuals to exercise self-control. The researchers are still exploring the precise mechanisms underlying the effects. You might also like to think about how the intervention relates to <u>PRIME theory</u>.
Evidence	A computer-based version of the intervention was evaluated using a <u>double-blind</u> RCT with 83 adults, most of whom suffered from overweight or obesity and/or reported high levels of disinhibited eating (a tendency to overeat in response to particular cues) (Lawrence et al., 2015). Participants completed four 10-minute active (intervention group) or inactive (control group) online training sessions over a period of four days. Measures of body weight, energy intake, daily snacking and liking for the snack foods were assessed one week before and after the training. A <u>bogus taste test</u> was also administered after the training. Additionally, self-reported weight and snacking frequency were collected 1 month and 6 months after the baseline assessments, though participants were no longer <u>blind</u> to group allocation at this point. Results showed that one week after the training, those in the intervention group had lost 0.67 kg of weight, significantly more than those in the control group (whose weight increased by 0.17 kg). Compared to the control group, those in the intervention group also showed reduced energy intake and liking for the snacks but there were no group differences in daily snacking or in the amount of food consumed in the taste test. There were also no group differences in reported snacking frequency at the 1- and 6-month follow-ups and no group difference in self-reported weight at 1 month. But at 6 months, the intervention group reported a weight loss of 2.21 kg since baseline, compared to weight loss of 0.36 kg in the control group, a difference that approached statistical significance ($p = .054$).
Research in progress	As noted by the researchers, the evaluation of the computer-based version of the intervention had some weaknesses: the trial was not <u>pre-registered</u>, weight data at the 1- and 6-month follow-ups relied on <u>self-report measures</u>, and participants were not <u>blind</u> to group allocation at 1 and 6 months. Nevertheless, the findings were sufficiently promising to warrant the development of the FoodT app. At the time of writing, the app has not yet been evaluated using an <u>RCT</u> but research in this area is ongoing.
Weblinks	Background, evaluation and links to the FoodT app: www.exeter.ac.uk/foodt/

TAXING SUGARY DRINKS IN MEXICO

CASE STUDY 2

Background	Mexico has one of the highest rates of overweight and obesity in the world, with prevalence levels reaching 70% amongst adults in 2012 (Barquera et al., 2013). The Mexican population also consumes very large quantities of sugar sweetened drinks (Barquera et al., 2008; Stern et al., 2014). Consumption of sugar sweetened drinks has been linked to obesity and both obesity and sugary drink consumption showed rapid increases in Mexico between 2000 and 2012 (Barquera et al., 2008, 2013; Bes-Rastrollo et al., 2013, 2016; Stern et al., 2014). Diabetes, a condition associated with obesity, is the biggest cause of death and disability in the country (IHME, 2014; Malik et al., 2010). Sugar sweetened drinks are thought to be a key contributor to weight gain because we do not compensate for the calories contained in them. For example, if we ate 150 calories of sweets before lunch, we would likely feel a little fuller and eat a little less. This would not be the case if we drank 150 calories worth of soda. The same is also true for other high carbohydrate drinks such as fruit juices and alcohol. This may be because throughout most of our evolutionary history our main source of hydration was water and, since this contains no calories, from an evolutionary perspective it makes sense for it to be processed by our body in a way that does not supress appetite. High carbohydrate drinks are a relatively modern invention. For example, lemonade was introduced in the 1500s, Coca-Cola in 1886 and juice concentrates in the 1940s (Wolf et al., 2008).

Intervention	In January 2014 Mexico introduced an **excise tax** on drinks with added sugar (excluding dairy and alcoholic drinks). This was at a rate of 1 peso per litre. This tax was passed on from manufacturers to consumers, resulting in an equivalent increase in the price of sugar sweetened drinks (Colchero et al., 2015).	**Excise tax** – a tax paid on goods at the point of manufacture, depending on the volume manufactured. This contrasts with a sales tax or value-added tax (VAT) which is paid at the point of sale and is a percentage of the price of the goods. Strictly speaking, an excise tax is actually a duty rather than a tax since it is levied on goods rather than individuals but these terms are often used interchangeably in the literature.
Relevant theory	The increased price of sugary drinks can be seen to influence consumer <u>outcome expectancies</u> which are key components of the <u>theory of planned behaviour</u> and <u>social cognitive theory</u>. Price increases may be particularly significant for those on very low incomes because when people suffer from a severe shortage of something (such as money), information relating to this need tends to capture their attention (**Chapter 3**). Thus we might expect income to moderate the effects of such an intervention, with those on the lowest incomes showing the greatest reductions in consumption. You might also like to think about how the intervention relates to <u>social norms</u> and <u>habits.</u>	

Evaluation	Because the tax was implemented at a national level, an <u>RCT</u> was not possible. Instead, researchers employed an <u>interrupted time-series analysis</u> to examine changes in purchasing habits from January 2012 to December 2014. They estimated drinks' purchases using pantry surveys, diaries, product packaging and receipts, collected every two weeks from over 6,000 households across 53 cities. Results showed a 6% reduction in purchases of taxed drinks in early 2014 (equivalent to 12ml per person per day) that increased to a 12% reduction in December 2014. Reductions occurred across all socioeconomic groups but were highest among low socioeconomic status households where there was a reduction of 9% followed by a reduction of 17%. Purchases of untaxed beverages in December 2014 had increased by 4% (36ml), mainly driven by purchases of bottled water (Colchero et al., 2016).
Weight of the evidence	This study suggests that the excise tax was effective at bringing about a small reduction in the purchase of sugary drinks but, because of the <u>observational design</u>, the results cannot be considered conclusive. In particular, the introduction of the tax was accompanied by health education campaigns relating to sugar sweetened beverages as well as obesity reduction programmes, and it is difficult to establish the extent to which other factors such as these may have been responsible for the effects. It is difficult to avoid this type of uncertainty in situations where an RCT is not possible. As discussed in **Chapter 11**, this can sometimes lead to those with vested interests claiming that 'there is no conclusive evidence' or 'there is no proof'. But this type of interpretation misrepresents the science since conclusions should be based on the weight of the evidence. In this case the evidence indicates that the excise tax likely did reduce purchases of sugar sweetened beverages.
Elsewhere	Other countries with a sugary drinks tax include Norway, Hungary, France, Portugal, the Republic of Ireland, South Africa, United Arab Emirates, Saudi Arabia, Brunei, Thailand, Chile and certain states and cities in the United States. In the UK a sugar excise tax was introduced in April 2018, set at 18p per litre for drinks with a total sugar content of over 5g per 100 ml and 24p per litre for those over 8g per 100 ml. This was primarily aimed at encouraging manufacturers to reformulate their products to contain less sugar, rather than change consumer behaviour, and for this reason the tax was announced two years prior to its introduction. It was estimated the tax would raise over £520 million in its first year, to be spent on sports and breakfast clubs in primary schools, but because of the levels of industry reformulation this estimate was later revised to £275 million (Gauke, 2016).
Criticisms	A common criticism of these types of 'sin taxes' are that they restrict freedom of choice and represent too much interference from a 'nanny state' government (**Chapter 11**). Some also argue that the effects are too small to have any meaningful impact on health outcomes. In particular, the 12% reduction seen in Mexico would translate into a reduction of around just 10 to 12 calories a day. Objections from industry, along with economic concerns, can be a barrier too. For example, in 2011 Denmark introduced a tax on saturated fat but repealed it just 15 months later after companies complained consumers were making shopping trips to neighbouring Germany and Sweden and that Danish jobs would be at risk (Stafford, 2012). Finally, such taxes can be considered regressive in that they disproportionately affect those on lower incomes since they spend a greater proportion of their money on food. This has led some to argue that the revenue generated should be spent on initiatives specifically designed to benefit those on lower incomes (Hagenaars et al., 2017).

CHAPTER 12

Healthy eating in children

Much of the research described above relates to healthy eating among teenagers and adults. However, healthy eating is also important for children – and they have a reputation for being difficult. Whether it's a refusal to eat anything green or an aversion to food 'with bits', getting a child to eat a healthy diet can be a challenge for many parents. Compared to adults, children are less able to exercise self-control or engage in the more conscious decision-making processes so often needed to maintain a healthy lifestyle. Their environments and behaviour also tend to be more directly managed by other people. As such, the processes governing children's behaviour are slightly different from the processes governing adults' behaviour. For these reasons, we explore healthy eating in children in this separate section. Specifically, we review the determinants of children's food preferences as well as strategies that have been shown to be helpful – or unhelpful – for promoting healthy eating. The implications of this research for parents and carers are also summarised in bullet points throughout the section.

Innate predispositions

Newborns show an innate preference for sweet tastes and an innate dislike for bitter. We know this because of the characteristic facial expressions they make when given these substances (Rosenstein & Oster, 1988). This makes good evolutionary sense; sweetness tends to be a marker for calories whilst a bitter taste can indicate toxins. A preference for salt appears at around 4–6 months (Liem, 2017) and from the age of about 20 months children become increasingly neophobic, in other words, they do not like trying new things (Harris & Mason, 2017). This corresponds to the age at which they start to become more independent, so it helps protect against accidental poisoning. Food neophobia starts to decline from about 6 years of age, though this can vary considerably between children.

Tip for parents and carers:

- Get infants and toddlers used to eating a wide range of different healthy foods before they reach 1½ years and become more reluctant to try new things (**Image 12.3**).

Image 12.3 *Infants and toddlers are more receptive to trying new foods before the age of around 18 months.*
Credit: Katy Tapper.

Individual differences

On top of these more general predispositions we also see substantial individual variation. Our genes determine our ability to detect certain tastes and flavours so one person's experience of a particular food may be quite different from someone else's. For example, most people perceive coriander (cilantro) as a fresh, citrusy herb, but for around 1 in 10 people it has an unpleasant soapy, mouldy flavour (Eriksson et al., 2012). People also differ in their ability to detect bitter, sour and sweet (but not salty) tastes (Reed & Knaapila, 2010). Vegetables such as broccoli, spinach and sprouts contain bitter compounds so those who are better at detecting bitter tastes may be less likely to enjoy and eat these foods (Keller &

Adise, 2016). Around 25% of people are what are sometimes referred to as 'supertasters'. These people are especially sensitive to a bitter substance called propylthiouracil (PROP). About 50% of people are 'medium-tasters' and have some sensitivity to PROP and the remaining 25% are 'nontasters'. Sensitivity to PROP seems to relate to the person's overall responsiveness to a range of different tastes as well as the density of taste buds on their tongue (see **Box 12.1**). Some studies (but not all) have shown that adults and children who are supertasters tend to consume fewer vegetables (Keller & Adise, 2016).

As we saw in **Chapter 4**, our genes also influence a range of different physiological and behavioural traits that in turn help shape our food preferences as well as the amount of food we eat. For example, Smith et al. (2017) showed that in addition to an environmental component, there is also a hereditary component to both food fussiness (a tendency to be selective about what one eats) and food neophobia (rejection of unfamiliar foods) (see also Fildes et al., 2014). These genetic differences mean that when it comes to eating, there can be a lot of variation between different babies and children. What might be a breeze for one parent could be a minefield for another.

Tip for parents and carers:

- Don't blame yourself if your child seems to be fussier than others or seems more likely to overeat or gravitate towards foods that are high in sugar or fat. But be reassured that learning plays a large role in the development of food preferences, so these tendencies won't make healthy eating impossible, just more challenging.

BOX 12.1 ARE YOU A SUPERTASTER?

You can tell if you're a supertaster by counting the fungiform papillae on your tongue – the raised mushroom shaped structures where **TAKE THE TEST** your taste buds are located. Dye the tip of your tongue blue with some food colouring and place a sticky label with a hole on it. The hole should be 6mm diameter, like the sticky labels used to reinforce hole-punched paper. Then use a magnifying glass to count the fungiform papillae, which should look lighter than the rest of the tongue since they don't stain blue (**Image 12.4**). Less than 15 you're a 'non-taster', 16–39 you're a 'medium-taster' and 40 or more you're a 'supertaster'. If you don't like the idea of putting sticky labels and blue dye on your tongue, you can also buy little strips of paper to test your sensitivity to a bitter compound called PTC (Miller & Reedy, 1990).

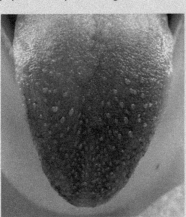

Image 12.4 *If you dye your tongue with blue food colouring the fungiform papillae will appear lighter in colour.*
Credit: Katy Tapper.

Taste exposure

Layered upon these general predispositions and trait influences come the child's unique experiences with food that also shape their likes and dislikes. One of the most important findings in this area is the concept of taste exposure, the principle that, very often, if we taste something enough times, we learn to like the flavour. For example, you can probably think of foods you didn't like as a child that you've learned to like as an adult, such as olives, spicy foods or Stilton cheese. This is an example of what is known as the 'mere exposure effect', the fact that simply being exposed to something, whether it's a painting, a piece of music, or a person, increases our liking for it (Montoya et al., 2017; Zajonc, 1968). When it comes to food, research shows that children need to taste something between 1 and 20 times (on different days) before they develop a liking for it, with more exposures needed for older and more neophobic children as well as for less intrinsically palatable foods (Cooke, 2007; Holley et al., 2017). Although the effects of exposure can sometimes be quite small, particularly when it comes to vegetables (Appleton et al., 2018), in some cases they can be strong enough to override innate predispositions. For example, Sullivan and Birch (1990) found that four- and five-year-olds who were repeatedly exposed to plain tofu came to prefer it to sweetened or salty versions (Sullivan & Birch, 1990).

Tips for parents and carers:

- Just because a child refuses something once doesn't mean it should be permanently excluded from their diet – getting a child to repeatedly taste a food on different occasions may increase their liking for that food.

- Prepare and serve food the way you would ultimately like your child to accept it – if you add sugar, salt or sauce from the start, it may subsequently be difficult to get your child to eat the food without it.

Encouraging children to eat using modelling

So far so good. We just need to get children to repeatedly try their carrots and peas and they'll learn to love them. But this is easier said than done, as anyone who has ever attempted to persuade a child to eat something knows. So how can we get children to try things? One powerful tool is modelling. Consistent with social cognitive theory, research shows that a child is more likely to eat a food if they see someone else eat it (Blissett et al., 2016; Holley et al., 2017; Houldcroft et al., 2014; Staiano et al., 2016; see also Vartanian et al., 2015). This is especially true where that person comments on how tasty the food is or how much they are enjoying it, rather than where they simply eat in silence (Hendy & Raudenbush, 2000; see also Appleton et al., 2019). Where an adult is the model, a familiar adult is likely to be more effective than a stranger (Harper & Sanders, 1975) though peers may actually be more influential than adults (Hendy & Raudenbush, 2000). However, where a peer rejects a food and makes negative comments about it, this will have a detrimental effect on consumption that may be particularly difficult to reverse (Greenhalgh et al., 2009).

Tips for parents and carers:

- It may be beneficial for parents to eat meals with their children – provided parents eat the way they'd like their child to eat. The same is true of siblings and peers.

- When eating healthy foods in front of children, make it clear how much you're enjoying them. Encourage older siblings to do the same.

Encouraging children to eat using rewards

One strategy parents often use to get their children to eat is to tell them they can only have dessert if they finish all their main course (or their peas, or their broccoli, or whatever else the parent thinks they are not eating enough of; Casey & Rozin, 1989; Moore et al., 2007, Orrell-Valente et al., 2007). This can certainly promote consumption in the short term, but what about over the long term? And how might it affect the child's liking for that food?

A series of influential studies conducted in the 1980s and 1990s suggested that rewarding a child for eating a food could have unintended, negative consequences (Birch et al., 1982, 1984; Newman & Taylor, 1992). In these studies, children between the ages of four and seven years were rewarded with play activities, verbal praise, or a snack food for consuming juice drinks, milk drinks or other types of snack food. The results showed that the child's preference for the snacks or drinks they had been rewarded for consuming declined, leading the authors to suggest that this practice could have an adverse effect on children's food preferences. However, these studies looked at the effects of reward on preference relative to other foods and drinks rather than on absolute liking or consumption. They also specifically selected foods and drinks that were initially neither liked nor disliked by the child (to allow for shifts in preference in either direction). But this scenario does not really reflect what usually happens at mealtimes, where parents typically only reward consumption of disliked foods. In contrast to these findings, subsequent studies that have looked at the effects of rewards on disliked foods have generally found that they increase both consumption and liking (Cooke et al., 2011a, 2011b; Corsini et al., 2013).

<u>Self-determination theory</u> can also help account for the contrasting effects found in these different sets of studies. According to this theory, where rewards undermine a child's feelings of autonomy, they will reduce motivation. This may be what happened in the studies that found a decline in food preference following rewards. For example, in one of these studies children were told 'Drink this juice and then you can ride the tricycle' (Birch et al., 1982). The children may have perceived this instruction as coercive, limiting their ability to decide whether and how much juice to drink. By contrast, in a study that showed increases in consumption and liking, children were told they could choose a sticker as a reward if they tasted a particular vegetable (Cooke et al., 2011b). Here, they may have felt like they had more autonomy, not just in terms of whether or not they tasted the vegetable but also in terms of which sticker they chose. This study showed that 'social rewards' in the form of verbal praise ('Brilliant, you're a great taster') also increased consumption and liking. This type of reward may have been effective because it increased feelings of competence as well as relatedness. Thus differences in the types of rewards employed, as well as the ways in which they are delivered, could be important for the kind of effect they have.

So what about the familiar parental refrain that goes something along the lines of 'Finish your peas and then you can have pudding'? Whilst food-based rewards can be an effective way of promoting consumption (Hendy, 1999; Orrell-Valente et al., 2007), they are not generally recommended by experts because they can further increase the child's liking for the food that is being used as a reward (Mikula, 1989). And this food is often one that parents would rather limit their child's intake of. (Though note that you could try enhancing liking for preferred fruits, such as strawberries and raspberries, by using them as a reward for non-eating-related activities).

Tips for parents and carers:

- Rewards can be a useful way of promoting taste exposure, liking and consumption. These could be physical rewards, tokens, access to an activity or simply verbal praise. However, care should be taken to ensure they are delivered in a way that does not undermine the child's autonomy; ideally they should instead promote feelings of competence and relatedness.

- It's best to avoid using food as a reward unless you are happy with your child showing an increased preference for that particular food.

Pressuring children to eat

Another way in which parents and carers try to encourage children to eat is by applying pressure, for example through the use of threats or by simply insisting the child eat (Moore et al., 2007, 2010; Orrell-Valente et al., 2007). This may be used to ensure a child tastes a food or eats a certain amount and seems to be more common among parents who perceive their child to be underweight (Webber et al., 2010). One concern with pressuring children to eat a certain amount of food is that it may teach them to ignore internal satiety cues and eventually lead to a tendency to overeat. For example, infants and young children are good at regulating their energy intake, but as they reach the age of two, this ability seems to diminish. Some have speculated that this may be due to parents and carers trying to control their child's food intake (Fox et al., 2006; see also Birch et al., 1987). In keeping with this interpretation, a retrospective questionnaire study found that young women who had been encouraged to 'clean their plate' as children were more likely to report overeating as adults (Brunstrom et al., 2005).

Additionally, pressuring a child to eat a certain food may reduce their liking for that food as well as their subsequent intake of it, compared to if they had not been pressured to eat it. For example, preschool children who were repeatedly asked to finish a particular type of soup made more negative comments about that soup relative to another soup they had not been pressured to eat. When their consumption of both types of soup was tested on subsequent occasions, they ate less of the soup they had been pressured to eat (though consumption of both types of soup increased relative to baseline; Galloway et al., 2006).

Tip for parents and carers:

- Try to avoid putting pressure on children to eat – it could reduce their liking for the food and, if they are not hungry, it could also encourage a tendency to ignore feelings of fullness.

Restricting what children eat

Finally, when it comes to foods that are viewed as less healthy, parents will often restrict a child's access to these, for example by not buying them, by reserving them for special occasions, by not letting them eat them, or by limiting the amount they eat (Boots et al., 2018a; Moore et al., 2007). Parents are more likely to restrict foods where they are concerned about their child being overweight (Webber et al., 2010).

However, laboratory research has shown that restricting a child's access to a particular food also increases their desire for it, as well as their intake when it is freely available (Fisher & Birch, 1999b; Jansen et al., 2008; Jansen et al., 2007; Rollins et al., 2014a). Similarly, children whose parents restrict certain snacks eat greater quantities of these foods in the laboratory when they are given free access to them (Fisher & Birch, 1999a; Jansen et al., 2007; Rollins et al., 2014b; though see Jansen et al., 2008 for a null effect). Girls have also been shown to report more negative feelings (such as guilt) after they have eaten restricted foods (Fisher & Birch, 2000).

Nevertheless, some of these effects may be limited to children with lower levels of inhibitory control (in other words, children who are more impulsive; Rollins et al., 2014a, 2014b; Anzman & Birch, 2009). As discussed in **Chapter 3**, consistent with life-history theory, children who experience harsher, more unpredictable environments before the age of five learn to respond to scarcity with more impulsive behaviours. From an evolutionary perspective this makes sense; if you do not know when you are going to be able to access a food again, it is best to make the most of it whilst you can (Nettle et al., 2017; Tapper, 2017a).

Thus whilst parents may be keen to ensure their child does not eat too many sugary, fatty or salty foods, restricting their consumption of these could actually increase their appeal. Ogden and colleagues suggest that one way to solve this dilemma may be to use what they refer to as 'covert control': strategies that restrict a child's access to certain foods but in ways that mean they are not aware of these restrictions. Such strategies include not eating unhealthy foods in front of the child, not having unhealthy foods in the house, and not taking the child to places that sell unhealthy foods (Ogden et al., 2006). Rollins and colleagues make a similar suggestion, distinguishing between restriction-based and structure-based strategies. Restriction-based strategies refer to parent-centred strategies that enforce compliance, for example by taking foods away from the child and by providing only unpredictable access determined by the parent. Structure-based strategies are more child-centred. They include predictable but flexible routines relating to when the child can access unhealthy foods and they give the child more autonomy in relation to serving sizes (Rollins et al., 2016a). Rollins and colleagues argue that whilst restriction-based strategies are counterproductive, the moderate levels of control used in structure-based strategies can help promote healthy eating whilst also supporting the development of the child's self-regulatory skills. The results of several studies provide support for the benefits of covert and structure-based strategies relative to overt restriction (Boots et al., 2018a, 2018b, 2019; Rollins et al., 2014b).

Tips for parents and carers:

- Where possible, avoid exposing children to foods you would rather they didn't eat too much of, for example by not having them in the house. This will mean you do not have to overtly limit their access to or consumption of these foods.

- Where you cannot avoid exposing children to such foods, try to develop predictable routines that restrict their consumption of them to certain times of the week. Give children some say over what and how much they eat on these occasions.

Case Study 3 looks at an intervention specifically designed to promote healthy eating among children. It is an example of a school-based intervention targeting a health promotion behaviour (increased consumption of fruit and vegetables).

CASE STUDY 3

THE FOOD DUDE HEALTHY EATING PROGRAMME IN THE UK AND IRELAND

Background	Experts recommend we eat at least five portions of fruit and vegetables a day (see **Table 12.1**). However, many children eat far fewer than this. For example, in the UK in 2017, only 18% of children aged 5–15 years were eating five or more portions a day whilst more than 1 in 10 were eating less than one portion a day (NHS, 2018b). For children, a portion is roughly the amount that fits into the palm of their hand (NHS, 2018c).
Intervention	The Food Dude Healthy Eating Programme is designed for use in schools with children aged 4 to 11 years. It has three key components: • a series of video adventures • a range of rewards • a variety of fruit and vegetables for the children to taste and eat. The video adventures feature the heroic 'Food Dudes', a group of four children aged 12 to 13 years who get their superpowers from eating fruit and vegetables (**Image 12.5**). In each episode the Food Dudes do battle against the evil Junk Punks who are trying to take over the world by depriving people of their fruit and vegetables in order to make them weak.

Image 12.5 The Food Dudes Healthy Eating Programme features the four heroic 'Food Dudes'.
Credit: Copyright © Bangor University, Wales.

Throughout each episode the Food Dudes, as well as other children, are also shown eating and enjoying a range of different fruit and vegetables. Children watch the episodes and are awarded Food Dude branded stickers and prizes for tasting or eating the fruit and vegetables that are provided to them. Each class also receives letters from the Food Dudes that are read out by the teacher. These provide praise and encouragement and remind the children of what they need to do to receive a Food Dude sticker or prize. The programme is divided into two main phases. In the first 16-day phase the children watch the episodes and receive Food Dude stickers and prizes on a daily basis. After this, the Food Dude episodes, rewards and letters are gradually phased out and the school moves towards in-house rewards such as house points and certificates (Horne et al., 2004, 2009; Lowe et al., 2004; Tapper et al., 2003).

Relevant theory	The programme was developed using social learning theory (Bandura, 1977) as well as empirical research showing the effects of repeated taste exposure on liking (Birch & Marlin, 1982; Zajonc, 1968). Social learning theory was originally developed by Bandura who later modified it and renamed it <u>social cognitive theory</u> to emphasise the role of cognition. Either version of the theory can be used to explain the effects of the Food Dude Programme. The programme can also be seen to be consistent with elements of <u>self-determination theory</u>.
Early evaluation	Evaluation of the programme in three schools found that the amount of fruit and vegetables eaten at both lunchtime and 'snacktime' (mid-morning break) showed a significant increase during the first 16-day phase of the programme (Lowe et al., 2004). A second study compared consumption in an experimental school and a control school over a longer period (Horne et al., 2004). In this study, children in the control school showed stable or declining consumption at lunchtime and snacktime, whilst children in the experimental school showed significant increases in consumption during the first phase of the programme. Four months later, lunchtime consumption had shown some decline but was still significantly higher than baseline levels (prior to the introduction of the programme), whilst consumption at snacktime had returned to baseline levels. A third study targeted lunchtime consumption of fruit and vegetables only and found significant increases in consumption over a 12-month period compared to a control school that showed no change (Horne et al., 2009). An important strength of these studies is their use of weighed and <u>observational measures</u> of food consumption, though a significant weakness is the study designs. Ideally the programme would have been evaluated using a <u>cluster RCT</u> or, alternatively, <u>a multiple baseline n-of-1</u> study or <u>interrupted time-series analysis</u>.
Later evaluation	Subsequent evaluations of the programme have produced mixed results. In a study involving 15 primary schools in deprived areas of the UK, levels of fruit and vegetable consumption measured 3 months and 6 months after the first 16-day phase were no higher than baseline (Upton et al., 2013). On the other hand, in Italy and the United States, researchers have found levels of fruit and vegetable consumption that were significantly higher than baseline, at 1 month, 3 months and 9 months after the end of the first 16-day phase (Morrill et al., 2013; Presti et al., 2013; Wengreen et al., 2013). This was also the case for a 6-year follow-up conducted in Ireland (Martin et al., 2017).

	Nevertheless, these studies generally show that the longer the follow-up, the smaller the size of the increase relative to baseline levels. In other words, the positive effects of the programme decline over time. These findings highlight the difficulties associated with the long-term maintenance of behaviour change as well as the need for assessment of <u>cost-effectiveness</u>. Additionally, the absence of effects in the UK schools underscores the challenges of preserving <u>fidelity</u> when an intervention is implemented on a wider scale and the different findings that can emerge from <u>pragmatic trials</u> versus <u>explanatory trials</u>.
Use	The Food Dude Healthy Eating Programme is currently used in schools across Ireland, with funding from the European Union and the Department of Agriculture.
Weblinks	Food Dudes in Ireland: www.fooddudes.ie Food Dude episodes: https://vimeo.com/channels/1419746

PHYSICAL ACTIVITY AND EXERCISE

Recommendations and relationship with health

Physical activity refers to any bodily movements that increase energy expenditure above resting levels, including activities carried out as part of daily life, such as cycling to work, cleaning the house or walking the dog. Exercise is a type of physical activity that is planned and has health and fitness as at least one of its objectives, such as going running, playing a sport or attending an exercise class (Garber et al., 2011).

Physical activity is important because it reduces the risk of a wide range of non-communicable diseases including heart disease, diabetes, breast cancer and colon cancer. Indeed, a lack of physical activity is estimated to be responsible for 9% of premature deaths (Lee et al., 2012). It can also help prevent bone fractures, dementia and cognitive decline as well as alleviate symptoms of anxiety and depression (Sallis et al., 2016a; WHO, 2010a). Essentially, physical activity is good for both our physical and mental health.

World Health Organization recommendations for physical activity are shown in **Table 12.2** (WHO, 2010a). These relate to aerobic activity that improves cardiovascular health, resistance exercises that strengthen muscles and bones and, for older adults, activities that improve balance. Other organisations also recommend exercises that improve flexibility to help maintain joint range of motion as well as limits to the amount of time spent in sedentary activities (Garber et al., 2011).

Table 12.2 World Health Organization recommendations for physical activity

Population	Recommendation
Children aged 5–17	• At least 60 minutes of moderate- to vigorous-intensity activity a day (that may be accumulated in shorter bouts). • Activities should include those that strengthen muscles and bones at least 3 times a week.
Adults aged 18–64	• At least 150 minutes a week of moderate-intensity aerobic activity or 75 minutes of vigorous-intensity aerobic activity (or equivalent combination of the two), performed in bouts of at least 10 minutes in duration. • For additional health benefits these durations should be increased to 300 minutes/150 minutes, respectively. • Muscle strengthening activities, including all the major muscle groups, on two or more days a week.
Adults aged 65 and over	• As per adults plus: • Those with poor mobility should perform activities to enhance balance and prevent falls at least 3 days a week. • Where health conditions limit physical activity, the individual should be as active as their abilities and conditions allow.

Group differences in physical activity

As discussed in **Chapter 2**, from an evolutionary perspective it makes sense for us to try to reduce energy expenditure by limiting physical activity. This, together with our increasingly obesogenic environment (**Chapter 2**), means we are now facing what some have described as a global pandemic in physical inactivity (Sallis et al., 2016a). For example, worldwide it is estimated that around 23% of adults and 81% of 11- to 17-year-olds fail to meet World Health Organization recommendations (Sallis et al., 2016a).

However, there are substantial variations in physical activity across different populations. For example, an estimated 4% of adults in Nepal are inactive, compared to 16% in the Netherlands, 24% in China, 37% in the UK and 61% in Saudi Arabia (Sallis et al., 2016a). In general, wealthier countries tend to be less active than poorer countries (Hallal et al., 2012).

There are also substantial within-country variations. In low- and middle-income countries, physical activity is higher in rural compared to urban areas whilst the reverse is often true in high-income countries, where city living tends to be associated with a more active lifestyle (Fan et al., 2014; Sallis et al., 2016a). The type of city you live in can make a difference too. Sallis et al. (2016b) measured physical activity in 14 cities around the world. They found that more parks, better public transport and higher residential density were all associated with higher levels of activity. They reasoned that better public transport means people are more likely to walk to a nearby bus stop or station rather than jump straight in a car, whilst higher residential density supports more local shops and services that in turn make a community more 'walkable'. Parks likely support active leisure time as well as being a destination people walk to and from. Sallis and colleagues calculated that living in a more activity-friendly city could help a person achieve around half the recommended 150 minutes of activity a week, highlighting the important role of urban planning in promoting physical activity.

Females appear to be especially influenced by the walkability of their environment, which is important since they tend to engage in less physical activity than males (Sallis et al., 2016a). Althoff et al. (2017) found that that this gender gap was more pronounced in cities that scored lower on a measure of walkability. They also found a stronger association between physical activity and obesity among females, which meant that in more walkable cities, females were more active and the overall rates of obesity were lower (**Image 12.6**). By contrast, in less walkable cities, female activity was reduced, which was in turn associated with higher levels of obesity. These data suggest that interventions designed to increase female physical activity, or improve the walkability of the local environment, could be particularly effective at both increasing overall levels of physical activity and reducing obesity. **Case Study 4** provides an example of an intervention that targets physical activity among women, though in this case it uses social marketing.

Image 12.6 In high-income countries, people who live in cities with good public transport are more physically active. This is especially true for women, who also show lower levels of obesity in more walkable cities.

Credit: World Obesity Federation.

CASE
STUDY
4

THIS GIRL CAN: INCREASING PHYSICAL ACTIVITY
AMONG WOMEN

Background	This Girl Can is a social marketing campaign designed to increase sports participation among women. It was funded by Sport England in response to their research suggesting women wanted to do more exercise but lacked time and confidence and were afraid of being judged (Sport England, 2019). The first campaign video was launched in January 2015 with subsequent videos launched in 2017 and 2018. An Australian version was released in 2018.
Intervention	The first 90-second campaign video shows women of different shapes, sizes, races and ages sweating, straining and laughing as they dance, run, swim, exercise and play team sports. The footage is overlaid with slogans such as 'I jiggle therefore I am' and 'Damn right I look hot' and plays to the sound of Missy Elliott's 'Get Ur Freak On'. The video, which was aired on television and distributed via social media, was accompanied by posters on billboards and in magazines (**Image 12.7**). There was also a website that told the stories behind the women featured in the video and provided information on a range of different sports and activities. The latest version of the website includes an app for women to create their own 'This Girl Can' poster as well as a page displaying women's #thisgirlcan Instagram images. Facebook, Instagram, Twitter and YouTube are all used to distribute relevant content and engage with the community.

Image 12.7 One of the posters from the 2015 'This Girl Can' campaign.
Source: Sport England - This Girl Can campaign.
© Sport England. Reproduced with permission.

Relevant theory	The campaign was informed by social marketing research rather than psychological theories of behaviour change. However, many of the concepts and theories covered in **Chapters 5 and 6** can be used to help account for the campaign's success. Social cognitive theory is particularly relevant given the campaign's emphasis on showing a wide range of 'real women' taking part in sport and exercise. The concepts of self-efficacy, outcome expectancies and social norms can also be used to help explain some of the effects. Additionally, you might like to think about how the campaign relates to self-determination theory and evaluative conditioning.
Evaluation	It is not generally possible to evaluate this type of mass media campaign using an RCT. Where feasible, an interrupted time-series analysis would provide the next best evidence of effects, followed by cross-sectional measures taken before and after the start of the campaign. Drawing on the latter approach, Sport England reported that one year after the introduction of the campaign, nearly 230,000 more people over the age of 16 were exercising at least once a week and that the gender gap in exercise participation had reduced from over 2 million to 1.55 million (Sport England, 2016). These estimates were based on self-report measures obtained via an annual telephone survey conducted with a random sample of around 160,000 adults.

Unintended outcomes?	By depicting real women (who are neither athletes nor models) the campaign makes a refreshing change from the unattainably slim, toned female bodies we usually see in the media. The images help challenge ideas about what most women's bodies look like when they exercise. However, in doing so the campaign may inadvertently reinforce the idea that women should be thinking about their appearance when exercising. For example, in the first video much of the footage focusses on women's buttocks, stomachs and thighs – all parts of the body women express concern over. In the video these are all reassuringly 'normal', but the connection is still made between exercise and bums, tums and thighs. (As opposed to, for example, feet, hands and arms.) Some of the slogans also reinforce the idea that women think about looking sexy when exercising ('Hot, not bothered'; 'Sweating like a pig, feeling like a fox'). So although the campaign got more women exercising, it is not clear what effect it had on preoccupation with appearance. This is important because habitual monitoring of one's bodily appearance is associated with poorer mental health (Tiggemann, 2013; Tiggemann & Williams, 2012). (Note that in the second and third videos there is much less emphasis on women's body parts and whether or not they look 'hot'.)
Weblinks	Campaign: www.thisgirlcan.co.uk Background: https://bit.ly/2JPTgWt Evaluation: https://bit.ly/3n64Nz9 Criticism: https://bit.ly/37NWSjD More criticism: https://bit.ly/2Lf7hNE Australian version: https://thisgirlcan.com.au

OBESITY

Unlike the other topics covered in this chapter, obesity refers to a health-related condition rather than a behaviour. However, it is included because of its relevance for public health and because it is so often targeted using behavioural interventions.

Obesity is where a person has a very high level of body fat, to the extent that it is generally considered a risk to their health. It is usually assessed by calculating a person's body mass index (BMI; see **Box 2.2** for discussion of BMI and alternative measures). A person is considered overweight if they have a BMI of 25 kg/m² or over, and obese if their BMI exceeds 30 kg/m².

Obesity prevalence and group differences

Since the 1980s levels of obesity have risen considerably (Ng et al., 2014). Although this increase has occurred in every single country around the world, levels of obesity, and the rate of this increase, have varied between countries. For example, countries in Australasia, North America and Western Europe have tended to show large increases; between 1980 and 2013 the percentage of adults classed as suffering from obesity rose from around 16% to 29% in Australia, 19% to 33% in the US and 15% to 25% in the UK. By contrast, other high-income countries in Asia Pacific have shown much smaller increases; for example, from 6% to 11% in Singapore, 2% to 4% in Japan, and from just under 6% to just over 6% in South Korea.

Since 2006 these increases have started to slow in high-income countries, but not in low- and middle-income countries, where nearly two-thirds of those with obesity live. The high numbers of people with obesity in some of these countries is in part due to the fact that they have some of the largest populations. For example, after the US, China and India have the second and third largest numbers of people with obesity (together accounting for 15% of the total number of people with obesity) even though they have relatively low rates of obesity (both at 4% in 2013). Some of the highest levels of obesity are in the USA, North Africa, the Middle East and Oceania. For example, in 2013 levels of obesity were at around 37% in Egypt, 37% in Saudi Arabia, 51% in Kuwait and 60% in Tonga.

Overall, women tend to show higher levels of obesity than men, and this difference is particularly pronounced in some countries. For example, in South Africa, 42% of women suffer from obesity compared to 14% of men, in Egypt the ratio is 48% to 26% and in Mexico it is 33% to 21%.

Determinants of obesity

In 2007 the UK government commissioned a large group of experts to map out the determinants of obesity. You can see the results of their efforts in **Figure 12.2**.

We have looked at some of the factors identified in **Figure 12.2** in **Chapters 2, 3 and 4**, under the very broad headings of evolutionary, environmental, social and individual determinants. These include an obesogenic environment, stressful living and working conditions, and genetics and personality. Other factors, such as the use of certain medications and economic pressures for growth and profitability, are beyond the scope of this book. However, what **Figure 12.2** illustrates is the complexity of the issue – obesity has multiple determinants all interacting in different ways with one another. Hopefully this also serves to highlight the importance of taking a multidisciplinary approach to health problems such as obesity; intervening at just one level is likely to be less effective than intervening at multiple levels, drawing on the expertise of biologists, economists and sociologists as well as psychologists.

Figure 12.2 Influences on obesity identified by the UK government's Foresight project (Butland et al., 2007)

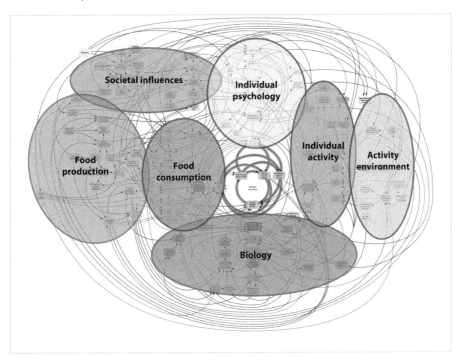

Note: The small boxes (that are barely visible) label each of the factors whilst the lines indicate the connections between them. The larger ovals categorise the broad type of determinant contained within that section of the map.

Source: © Crown copyright. Contains public sector information licensed under the Open Government Licence v3.0.

Later in this section we discuss an additional factor that has more recently been identified as a likely contributor to both weight gain and obesity – that of weight stigma.

Obesity and physical health

The link between BMI and health has been hotly debated. Prospective cohort studies show that those with BMIs of over 25 kg/m^2 are more likely to develop a range of different health problems, including diabetes, heart disease, stroke and cancer.[1] This association shows a dose-response relationship, with every increase of 5 kg/m^2 being associated with around a 30% increase in mortality (Kopelman, 2007; Whitlock et al., 2009). However, others have questioned the extent to which these associations represent causal links, arguing that they may be the result of other factors linked to both poor health and obesity, such as diet, lack of exercise and lower socioeconomic status. They have also drawn attention to the large numbers of people who suffer from overweight or obesity but who are 'metabolically healthy', for example they show no evidence of cardiometabolic abnormalities such as raised blood pressure, insulin resistance and high cholesterol (Bacon & Aphramor, 2011; Mann et al., 2015; Tomiyama et al., 2016; Wildman et al., 2008).

As discussed in **Chapter 10**, these types of observational studies cannot provide conclusive evidence of causal links. On the other hand, it is simply not possible to conduct an RCT and randomly assign people to 'obese' and 'healthy weight' conditions. Thus we have to rely on findings from observational studies, and here the weight of evidence suggests that overweight and obesity are a risk to health. For example, a prospective cohort study with over 3.5 million people showed that even among those classified as 'metabolically healthy obese', an average of five years later they were still more likely to have suffered from coronary heart disease, stroke or heart failure compared to metabolically healthy people of a normal weight. These findings could not be accounted for by differences in age, sex, smoking or socioeconomic status (Caleyachetty et al., 2017). A case-cohort study (similar to a case-control study[2]) came to a similar conclusion, showing higher incidence of coronary heart disease among metabolically healthy individuals who suffered from overweight and obesity compared to those of a healthy weight. Again, this effect remained even after controlling for age, sex, education, smoking, diet and physical activity (Lassale et al., 2018). These findings suggest that overweight and obesity are independent risk factors for poor health over and above metabolic health. Nevertheless, it is still important to consider potential unintended outcomes of any health intervention that may mean it does more harm than good; could interventions aimed at reducing overweight and obesity be detrimental to mental health?

Obesity, mental health and weight stigma

The relationship between obesity and mental health is complex. Some research shows that women with obesity (and no other health conditions) report poorer mental health compared to women of a healthy weight, but that the reverse is true for men where those with obesity actually report better mental health compared to their healthy weight counterparts (Magallares & Pais-Ribeiro, 2014). This patterning suggests there may not be anything about obesity per se that leads to poorer mental health, but rather that

---

1   Below 22.5 kg/m^2, BMI is inversely associated with mortality. In other words, the lower your BMI, the more likely you are to die. This can partly, but not fully, be explained by smoking-related diseases; smoking both suppresses appetite and is a risk factor for disease. Cancer and other lung and respiratory diseases can also cause weight loss over many years so a low BMI could occur as a result of poor health (Whitlock et al., 2009).

2   In a case-cohort study a random subcohort is used for comparison rather than matched controls.

an association can arise because of social pressures to be slim, that may be stronger for women than for men (Puhl et al., 2008; Sikorski et al., 2016).

Indeed, research shows there is a substantial **stigma** attached to obesity. For example, in the US, weight discrimination is estimated to be the fourth most common type of discrimination (after gender, race and age), with more than 1 in 10 women and nearly 1 in 20 men reporting daily or lifetime discrimination because of their weight (Puhl et al., 2008). Those suffering from obesity can face stigmatisation and discrimination from healthcare providers, employers, friends and family members, colleagues, classmates, teachers, sales clerks and the media (Flint et al., 2016; Phelan et al., 2015; Puhl & Brownell, 2006; Puhl & Heuer, 2009; Puhl et al., 2008; Rex-Lear et al., 2019). Those with obesity may also encounter frequent **microaggressions** in their daily lives, such as eye-rolling, tutting or people looking disapprovingly into their shopping baskets. Cumulatively these seemingly minor signs of disapproval can take their toll on mental health and lead to people avoiding social situations and becoming more socially isolated (Lewis et al., 2011).

> **Stigma** – the co-occurrence of labelling, stereotyping, separation, status loss and discrimination in a context in which power is exercised (Hatzenbuehler et al., 2013).

> **Microaggressions** – brief, commonplace verbal, behavioural or environmental communications that intentionally or unintentionally convey hostile, derogatory or discriminatory attitudes toward a particular group or individual.

Weight stigma can have a detrimental effect on both mental and physical health (Emmer et al., 2019; Hunger & Major, 2015; Puhl & Heuer, 2009; Tomiyama, 2014; Tomiyama et al., 2014). As described in **Chapter 2**, the threat of uncontrollable negative evaluation from others ('social-evaluative threat') is especially stressful and stress is associated with a specific physiological response, which includes raised blood pressure and the release of cortisol into the bloodstream. When stress is sustained over time, these physiological changes can damage health (Hatzenbuehler et al., 2013). Excess cortisol can lead to the body storing more energy as fat too (Björntorp, 2001).

Weight stigma can also lead to increased consumption of high-calorie foods. For example, several studies have shown that women who suffer from overweight, or who perceive themselves to be overweight, eat more calories after exposure to weight stigmatising material (Major et al., 2014; Schvey et al., 2011). Likewise, self-report data indicate that eating is one of the most commonly reported ways of coping with weight stigma (Puhl & Brownell, 2006; see also Robinson et al., 2015). In line with these findings, research shows that the more a person reports experiencing weight discrimination, the more weight they put on over time (Jackson et al., 2014). The precise mechanisms underpinning this link are unclear; some have suggested it may be because weight stigma undermines self-control (Major et al., 2014; Tomiyama, 2014; see **Chapter 7**, limited resource model) or because it provides temporary relief from psychological discomfort (so-called 'comfort eating'; Adam & Epel, 2007; Dallman et al., 2003; Jackson et al., 2014; Tomiyama, 2014). Weight stigma may also increase desire for food because high levels of cortisol can lead to activation of the brain reward system and because low mood may result in increased craving (Adam & Epel, 2007; Rudenga et al., 2013; see the elaborated intrusion theory of desire and incentive-sensitisation theory, **Chapters 7 and 8**).

Additionally, weight stigma may lead to exercise avoidance (Lewis et al., 2011; Vartanian & Shaprow, 2008; see also **Case Study 4**) as well as more disordered eating, such as binge eating, even amongst those of a healthy weight who may be worried about becoming overweight (Durso et al., 2012).

Thus interventions aimed at reducing obesity run the risk of increasing weight stigma which can be detrimental for both physical and mental health and can even lead to weight gain. Even where an intervention is successful at bringing about weight loss, its benefits

CHAPTER 12

would need to be balanced against any negative effects on mental health and wellbeing. As discussed in **Chapter 1**, health should be pursued as a means to happiness, not as an end in itself. As such, some argue that it is better to design interventions that focus on health-related behaviours (such as diet and exercise) rather than to directly target weight (for example with weight loss as an explicit aim and with regular weighing as an intervention component; Mann et al., 2015; Tomiyama et al., 2018). **Case Studies 5** and **6** provide examples of interventions that have been designed to target weight but which primarily focus on diet and exercise-related habits and behaviours.

CASE STUDY 5

TEN TOP TIPS: A HABIT-BASED INTERVENTION FOR WEIGHT MANAGEMENT

Background Overweight and obesity increase the risk of a number of different cancers, particularly those relating to the digestive organs (for example bowel cancer) and to hormones in women (for example breast cancer; Bhaskaran et al., 2014; Kyrgiou et al., 2017). Indeed, in the UK, overweight and obesity are estimated to be the second biggest preventable cause of cancer after smoking, with more than 1 in 20 cases being associated with excess weight (Brown et al., 2018). Although the reasons for the link are not yet fully understood, it is thought that fat cells produce extra growth factors and hormones that encourage cells to divide more often, increasing the chances of cancer cells being produced (Renehan et al., 2015). For these reasons, the charity Cancer Research UK focuses some of its efforts on obesity reduction. They developed the Ten Top Tips intervention in collaboration with UK academics.

Intervention The key components of the intervention are a leaflet and a logbook aimed at helping people change their eating habits (Beeken et al., 2012).

ten top tips tick sheet: Keeping track of your progress

Fill in this tick sheet every day to record whether or not you managed each tip
Keeping a record has been shown to increase people's success in developing healthy habits. Keeping track of your weight is also very useful. Daily weighing has been shown to increase successful weight control. In the notes column you can write details of how you are achieving the tips, and anything that particularly helps you use them. This information will help you plan for the next week.

ten top **tips**	m	t	w	t	f	s	s	done on 5 days or more?	**notes**
1. Keep to your meal routine									
2. Go reduced fat									
3. Walk off the weight (No. of steps)									
4. Pack a healthy snack									

Image 12.8 *The Ten Top Tips intervention includes a logbook to promote self-monitoring and habit formation.*
Source: Cancer Research UK (2011). Ten Top Tips: Weight Loss Tips Based On Scientific Evidence, Cancer Research UK.

The leaflet describes seven everyday lifestyle 'tips' for cutting calories and burning more energy, such as selecting reduced fat foods, switching high-calorie snacks for healthier alternatives and spending more time standing (for example on the bus or train). It is estimated that engaging in all these behaviours could lead to a total daily deficit of around 800 to 900 calories per day. Three additional tips (keeping to a mealtime routine, learning to read food labels, focussing on food whilst eating) are designed to promote habit formation, improve nutritional awareness and avoid unconscious slips in behaviour. The leaflet also includes some very brief information about the intervention, the possible health consequences of being overweight, and how to understand food labels, as well as answers to 'frequently asked questions'. The logbook contains a series of tables that list the ten tips alongside space for the person to keep a daily record of whether they managed each one. There is also space for them to make notes to help them plan for the following week and to record their weight (**Image 12.8**). The logbook contains 15 weeks-worth of tables as well as some additional information about habits.

Relevant theory	The intervention was developed on the basis of <u>habit theory</u>. It is designed to encourage the person to repeat each of the healthy behaviours in a consistent context over an extended period of time in order to turn them into habits. The logbook draws on <u>control theory</u> and the additional information contained in the leaflet can be seen to relate to <u>outcome expectancies</u>.
Evaluation	Following a successful <u>exploratory study</u> (Lally et al., 2008) the intervention was evaluated using an <u>RCT</u> with weight loss at 3 months as the <u>primary outcome.</u> <u>Secondary outcomes </u>included weight loss at 6, 12, 18 and 24 months (Beeken et al., 2012, 2017). To recruit the target <u>sample size</u> of 520, adults with obesity were identified from physician records at 14 general practitioner practices and a random selection of these were invited to take part. Of the 3,000 who were invited, 537 consented and were randomised to receive either the new intervention or standard care. Nurses and healthcare assistants were trained to deliver the intervention and were provided with a flip chart and script to help them do so in a consistent manner. Neither participants nor the healthcare providers were <u>blind</u> to group allocation. Participants in the intervention condition received a 30-minute session with the healthcare professional who talked them through the leaflet and logbook. They also received a wallet-sized card with guidance on food labels. Those in the control condition were referred to the practice's usual treatment. This varied from practice to practice; for example, in some practices participants were provided with an appointment with a dietician whilst in others they were referred to an external weight loss organisation. At 3 months those in the intervention group were sent a second copy of the leaflet and told they could request additional copies of the logbook. Weight was assessed by a health professional <u>blind</u> to group allocation. The results showed that those receiving the intervention lost significantly more weight at 3 months (an average of 0.87kg). This loss was maintained at 24 months but by this point was not significantly higher than those receiving standard care. <u>Intention-to-treat analysis</u> showed similar results (0.58kg at 3 months). The cost of the intervention (including both materials and time) was estimated to be £23 per person and a <u>cost-effectiveness</u> analysis showed no significant differences in cost-effectiveness at 2 years, suggesting that the intervention was neither better nor worse than standard care (Patel et al., 2018).
Mechanisms of action	The intervention was based on habit theory so we would expect it to work by increasing the extent to which targeted behaviours were carried out automatically. This was measured at baseline and 3 months using just one item from the Self-Report Habit Index for each of the targeted behaviours (such as 'Choosing reduced fat foods is something I do automatically', see **Box 6.3**). For the purposes of exploratory analysis, the researchers also included measures of self-efficacy, restraint, self-regulation and social support (Kliemann et al., 2017; Beeken et al., 2012). The researchers report that, compared to the control group, participants in the intervention group showed greater increases in both automaticity and <u>self-regulation</u> at 3 months and that these increases mediated the effects of the intervention on weight loss (Kliemann et al., 2017). Analysis of the logbooks also showed that those who engaged more with the intervention showed the greatest changes in automaticity, self-regulation and weight. These findings confirm that the intervention worked as intended, via increased automaticity of the target behaviours. The researchers also speculate that the planning and self-monitoring components of the logbook may have enhanced self-regulation. They suggest that habit formation and self-regulation may be closely linked, in that self-regulatory skills may be necessary for intentional habit formation but also that habit-based interventions could help improve self-regulation since they typically require people to set goals and to plan and monitor their behaviour.
Further developments	The Top Ten Tips intervention is now being adapted for delivery via a mobile app with a version that also includes an additional tip for dealing with cravings, based on the <u>elaborated intrusion theory of desire</u> (Kliemann et al., 2019).
Weblinks	Leaflet, logbook and other study materials (in the supplementary information): https://go.nature.com/3n7LpSv

MINDFUL EATING IN RESTAURANTS: A WEIGHT MANAGEMENT INTERVENTION FOR WOMEN

Background	Eating out in restaurants is associated with higher intakes of fat and calories and those who eat out more often tend to have higher levels of body fat (Clemens et al., 1999; McCrory et al., 1999). The Mindful Restaurant Eating intervention was designed by academics in the US to help those who frequently eat out develop skills to manage their caloric intake and prevent weight gain.
Intervention	The intervention comprises a series of six weekly two-hour group workshops with content relating to (a) weight management when eating out (such as how to limit calorie and fat intake), (b) strategies to address barriers to managing intake when eating out (including setting personal weekly goals), and (c) mindful eating exercises. The mindful eating exercises were designed to encourage participants to pay more attention to the sight, smell, taste and texture of their food and to increase awareness of feelings of hunger and satiety and cues that elicit eating. Individuals also received handouts to remind them of the course content as well as homework exercises (Timmerman & Brown, 2012).
Theory, evidence and mechanisms of action	The intervention was guided by Pender's health promotion model (Pender et al., 2006) which incorporates many of the constructs we reviewed in previous chapters (for example, see the health belief model and social cognitive theory). The constructs targeted by the intervention were perceived barriers, perceived benefits, self-efficacy and goals. The intervention also drew on empirical evidence indicating that goal setting was an effective behaviour change technique for changing dietary behaviours (Ammerman et al., 2002). The mindfulness exercises relating to food were included to help maximise enjoyment of smaller portions. The mindfulness exercises relating to hunger and satiety could work by reducing eating automaticity (habit-based eating) though this is not discussed by the researchers.
Evaluation	The evaluation is described as a pilot study and uses an RCT with 43 perimenopausal women randomly assigned to either the intervention or a wait-list control. Measures taken at baseline and immediately following the six-week intervention showed that compared to the control group, those who received the intervention reported significantly reduced intakes of calories and fat and lost significantly more weight (but did not show a significantly reduced waist circumference). They also showed greater increases in diet-related self-efficacy and reported reduced barriers to weight management when eating out (but not reduced **emotional eating**). Although these results show promise, the evaluation has some weaknesses including the lack of trial registration and participant blinding, the absence of a sample size calculation and the fact that a single primary outcome was not identified. Participant weight was also poorly matched between conditions at baseline, with those in the intervention group being substantially heavier than those in the control group.
Wider context	Mindful eating is one of the latest weight loss trends with proponents claiming it can be used to promote healthy eating as well as weight management. However, the Mindful Restaurant Eating intervention described here highlights some of the difficulties with this claim. Like most successful weight loss interventions it has multiple components. This can make it difficult to know which components are responsible for any effects and whether some components may be redundant. For example, were the mindful eating exercises important for the success of the programme or was the weight loss all down to the education and goal setting? We could try to answer this question by incorporating process measures into the evaluation, such as measures of mindful eating. These would allow us to assess the extent to which increases in mindful eating mediated the effects of the intervention. However, this introduces an additional difficulty: how to accurately assess mindful eating. Although questionnaire measures exist, the extent to which a person can accurately report on their level of **mindfulness** is unclear (Tapper, 2017b). For example, a person who is unaware

Emotional eating – eating in response to certain emotions, typically negative emotions such as stress or low mood, though the term is also used to refer to eating in response to positive emotions, for example to enhance a good mood.

Mindfulness – this has been described and defined in several different ways, though a commonly used definition is one put forward by Kabat-Zinn (2003) who states that mindfulness is 'awareness that emerges through paying attention on purpose, in the present moment, and non-judgementally to the unfolding of experience moment by moment'.

of the cues that elicit their eating may also be unaware of this fact. Likewise, a person who tries to become more aware of their food when eating may suddenly realise how often they eat without thinking.

Another difficulty with this field is the range of different practices that are labelled as mindfulness. For example, the exercises used in the Mindful Restaurant Eating intervention included paying more attention to the taste and texture of food as well as paying more attention to feelings of hunger and satiety. It would be a mistake to assume these two different practices have the same effects or that evidence for one can be taken as evidence for the other. Understanding the mechanisms underlying any effects is also important. For example, there is evidence to suggest that paying attention to one's food whilst eating can reduce the amount eaten, but this effect is inconsistent (Tapper, 2017b; Tapper & Seguias, 2020). This suggests moderation by other factors, such as type of food, context or the eating style of the individual. Until we have a better understanding of *why* paying attention to your food reduces intake, it will be difficult to know when this strategy is, and is not, likely to be helpful.

These challenges highlight the importance of experimental research. Experimental methods make it easier to isolate particular practices, or combinations of practices, and to identify mechanisms of action. This knowledge can then be used to build multi-component interventions where we have greater confidence in each element and a better understanding of their likely effects.

Weblinks   Discussion of mindful eating for weight loss: https://bit.ly/33UmfPN

BREASTFEEDING

As a species, humans have evolved to breastfeed their young (**Chapter 2**). Up until relatively recently, if a new mother was unable to breastfeed, and no **wet nurse** was available, her baby would have died. It wasn't until the mid-1800s when modern feeding bottles were invented that breastfeeding started to become optional. This was followed by the development of commercially available formula milk and a large decline in breastfeeding rates such that by the 1970s breastfeeding was often more the exception than the norm (Fomon, 2001; Stevens et al., 2009).

Wet nurse – a woman who breastfeeds someone else's baby.

The benefits of breastfeeding

Breastmilk is good for babies. It has evolved over millions of years, not just to nourish but also to protect. It has a very complex composition that varies according to the age of the baby, the time of day, the length of the feed and the pathogens the mother has been exposed to (Andreas et al., 2015). For example, colostrum, the milk produced in the first few days after birth, is particularly high in antibodies which help protect the infant from all the germs in the environment they are suddenly exposed to. Concentrations of antibodies in breastmilk gradually decline as the baby's immune system becomes stronger. The amount of fat in breastmilk gets higher as a feed gets longer and as the time since the last feed gets shorter. This makes sense; when babies are growing faster they get hungrier and want to feed more often and for longer. Levels of protein in breastmilk also fluctuate over time, matching the baby's changing nutritional needs.

Babies who breastfeed tend to be healthier. In low- and middle-income countries, where there may be more limited access to clean water and sterile bottles, breastfed babies suffer from fewer infections and episodes of diarrhoea. An estimated 823,000 deaths could be averted in these countries every year if breastfeeding became the norm. In high-income countries breastfed babies have a lower incidence of ear infections. Over the longer term, babies who are breastfed may be less likely to become overweight or develop diabetes (Victora et al., 2016). Breastfeeding has also been linked to increased intelligence (of around 2.5 to 3.5 IQ points; Horta et al., 2015, 2018).

Breastfeeding is good for the mother's health too, reducing the risk of breast cancer and possibly also ovarian cancer and diabetes. If women in high-income countries breastfed

CHAPTER 12

their babies for at least 12 months, it is estimated there would be over 22,000 fewer deaths from breast cancer every year (Victora et al., 2016).

Recommendations and group differences

The World Health Organization recommends that babies are exclusively breastfed for six months, then breastfed alongside solid food for up to two years of age or beyond (WHO, 2019a; see also Kramer & Kakuma, 2012). Over the last three decades, as the benefits of breastfeeding have become more well known, rates have gradually increased. However, they are still relatively low. Globally, less than 40% of infants aged under six months are exclusively breastfed, with rates and durations of breastfeeding being lower in high-income countries compared to low- and middle-income countries (Victora et al., 2016). There are substantial differences between individual countries too. For example, in Norway and Italy 60–70% of babies are exclusively breastfed at three months compared to less than 15% in Greece and the UK (**Figure 12.3**).

Rates of breastfeeding can also be influenced by the mother's age and socioeconomic background. In the UK, which has some of the lowest rates of breastfeeding in Europe, younger mothers and mothers from more deprived areas are less likely to breastfeed compared to their older, wealthier, better educated counterparts (**Figure 12.4**).

Reasons for not breastfeeding

Reasons for not breastfeeding are varied and range from difficulties with combining it with work, to improper latching of the baby onto the breast, which can lead to pain and poor feeding. Mothers may also be concerned they are not providing sufficient milk for their child and may be influenced by advertising for formula that portrays it as a healthy and easier

Figure 12.3 Proportion (%) of infants exclusively breastfed at 3 and 6 months in Europe, 2005–2010

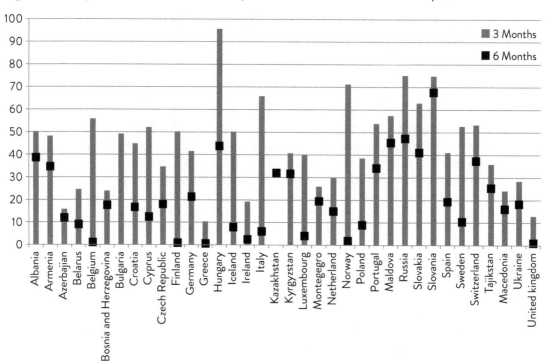

Source: Proportion (%) of children exclusively breastfed at 3 and 6 months, 2005-2010. Copenhagen: WHO Regional Office for Europe; 2013(https://www.euro.who.int/__data/assets/pdf_file/0005/190463/Proportion-of-children-exclusively-breastfed-at-3-and-6-months,-2005-2010-final.pdf, accessed 7 December 2020).

Figure 12.4 Proportion (%) of infants exclusively breastfed at 6-8 weeks in Scotland by maternal age and Scottish Index of Multiple Deprivation (SIMD) quintile, 2006–2016

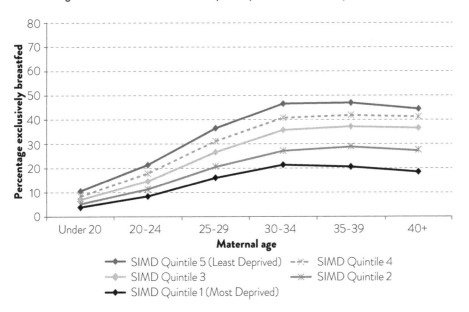

Source: ISD Scotland, CHSP Pre-School Aug 2016. Reproduced with kind permission from Breastfeeding Statistics Scotland Financial Year 2015/16 © Public Health Scotland 2016.

choice and something that can help settle fussy babies (Odom et al., 2013; Rollins et al., 2016b). Additionally, mothers may worry about breastfeeding in front of others, fearing disapproval and feelings of shame. This may lead them to feel they have to stay at home or withdraw from social situations in order to feed their baby (Johnson et al., 2018; Thomson et al., 2014). For example, Dyson and colleagues conducted focus groups with pregnant teenagers living in deprived areas of England who reported they would be too embarrassed to breastfeed in front of others and would be worried about unwanted sexual interest from strangers and sexual comments from their partners' friends. They viewed breastfeeding as morally inappropriate and did not want to be seen as 'the sort of women who would breastfeed' (Dyson et al., 2010). Similar themes were identified by Henderson et al. in focus groups with low-income men living in deprived areas of Scotland and England. Like the women, these men associated breasts with sexuality and breastfeeding with embarrassment. Many had never seen a woman breastfeeding and assumed it involved excessive public exposure. Breastfeeding women were described as 'slappers' and many said they would object to their own partner breastfeeding (Henderson et al., 2011). The authors of these studies note how these deep-seated views of breasts and breastfeeding, and a lack of exposure to breastfeeding women, make it hard to shift breastfeeding rates in these communities (**Image 12.9**).

Image 12.9 *Some people may have never seen a woman breastfeed. Mothers may feel embarrassed about breastfeeding in public and their partners may object too.*
Credit: Ksenia Makagonova.

CHAPTER 12

To help promote breastfeeding the World Health Organization (WHO, 2018a) recommends:

- Limiting marketing of formula
- Six-months paid maternity leave
- Policies that encourage women to breastfeed in the workplace and in public
- Baby-friendly initiatives in hospitals to support breastfeeding
- Community-based support and advice.

Case Study 7 provides an example of a slightly different approach to encouraging women to breastfeed.

CASE STUDY 7

NOSH: PAYING WOMEN TO BREASTFEED

Background	The NOSH (NOurishing Start for Health) scheme was designed to help reduce health inequalities (see **Chapter 3**) by increasing breastfeeding in areas of the UK with low breastfeeding rates.
Intervention	New mothers could claim up to £200 in shopping vouchers for breastfeeding their baby. These were given in £40 instalments where the mother was still breastfeeding at 2 days, 10 days, 6 weeks, 3 months and 6 months. They were claimed via an application form that was signed by the mother's midwife or health visitor. The intervention also included a website and booklet that provided information about the scheme and the benefits of breastfeeding as well as details of organisations and local groups that could provide breastfeeding advice and support.
Relevant theory	The intervention was based on empirical evidence showing that financial incentives can be an effective way of changing health-related behaviours (Giles et al., 2014). Incentives influence outcome expectancies which are important in a number of theories of behaviour change, including the theory of planned behaviour and social cognitive theory. They can also be viewed as a form of extrinsic reward. According to self-determination theory, extrinsic rewards can reduce intrinsic motivation if they undermine feelings of autonomy but increase it where they promote feelings of competence (a construct very similar to self-efficacy). You may also like to think about how this intervention relates to social norms and habits.
Evaluation	Acceptability and practicability were initially assessed in a feasibility study (Relton et al., 2014). This was followed by a cluster RCT in which 92 neighbourhoods with mean 6–8 week breastfeeding rates of 40% or less were randomised to receive either standard care or standard care plus the NOSH scheme. Results from over 10,000 women showed that at 6–8 weeks rates of breastfeeding were significantly higher in the intervention group (37.9%) compared to the control group (31.7%), with the difference between the groups increasing over time. No significant differences were found in rates of breastfeeding initiation or exclusive breastfeeding at 6–8 weeks (Relton et al., 2018). The feasibility trial and RCT also incorporated a process evaluation that included interviews with 35 women who were eligible for the scheme. These women reported that the vouchers made them feel valued for their efforts and they viewed them as compensation for the difficulties they often encountered when breastfeeding. Women did not think the scheme would influence those with strong negative or positive views about breastfeeding but could encourage those who were undecided as well as persuade women to breastfeed for longer. They also felt the scheme could help normalise breastfeeding (Johnson et al., 2018). During the feasibility study healthcare providers expressed concern that the vouchers might make women feel coerced into breastfeeding, particularly those who were struggling financially. However, in interviews conducted during the RCT they reported that this had not been the case and that the vouchers helped promote and support breastfeeding, giving it more value (Whelan et al., 2018).

Potential barriers	Although the scheme was found to be acceptable to stakeholders (local healthcare providers and eligible mothers), this did not appear to extend to the wider population. Instead, when the study was launched, it was the subject of much controversy and elicited many negative comments in the press and on social media (Giles et al., 2015; Relton et al., 2017). For example, one MP described it as 'bribery' and suggested that mothers may spend the money on 'booze and fags'. A policy adviser stated that a mother had to be motivated to breastfeed by a concern for her child, not for financial reward (Donnelly & Holehouse, 2013). One newspaper columnist described it as patronising and classist and said that what women did with their breasts should be nobody's business but their own (Ellen, 2013). Many members of the public also viewed the initiative as insulting to mothers and objected to public money being spent on what they perceived to be lifestyle choices (having children and breastfeeding). Some also felt the incentives would discriminate against mothers who were unable to breastfeed, making them feel even more guilty for not doing so (Giles et al., 2015).
Point of debate	From attacks on reproductive rights to sexual assault and harassment, there is a long history of women's bodies being treated as public property. Do interventions such as NOSH simply perpetuate this view, or can they be used to empower women?
Weblinks	Background, evaluation and intervention materials: https://bit.ly/3qKDYmo Controversy: www.bbchttps://bbc.in/37Pi7BR More controversy: https://bit.ly/3qKzuMM

SMOKING AND VAPING

Smoking damages nearly every part of the body (**Figure 12.5**), shortening life expectancy by around 11 to 12 years. Over 6 million deaths every year are thought to be caused by smoking (Gakidou et al., 2017; Jha et al., 2013; Reitsma et al., 2017; USDHHS, 2014).

The main ingredient of a cigarette is tobacco and it is this substance that causes most of the harm. Tobacco contains over 90 toxic chemicals, such as arsenic, lead and mercury (FDA, 2012). When burnt, tobacco also produces carbon monoxide and tar. Carbon monoxide displaces oxygen in the blood, meaning the heart has to work harder and the cells in the body do not get the oxygen they need. Tar is a sticky, black substance which is carcinogenic and coats the lining of the lungs, stopping them from working properly. Tobacco also contains the stimulant nicotine, which is highly addictive.

A brief history

Tobacco is native to the Americas and was first smoked by Indigenous tribes from around 1000 BC. It was discovered by Christopher Columbus in 1492 and by the 1700s was being smoked, chewed or used in snuff all around the globe. From the late 1800s cigarettes became increasingly popular, thanks in part to the invention of the Bonsack machine in 1880 that allowed them to be mass produced. By the 1950s the links between smoking and disease were well established but it was not until the 1970s that governments really started to address the issue, the delay arguably being due to the tobacco industry's efforts to counter anything that would reduce sales (see **Chapter 11**; Berridge, 2014; Musk & De Klerk, 2003).

However, 2003 represents a landmark in public health when 161 countries signed the World Health Organization Framework Convention on Tobacco Control (FCTC) (WHO,

Figure 12.5 Health consequences of smoking

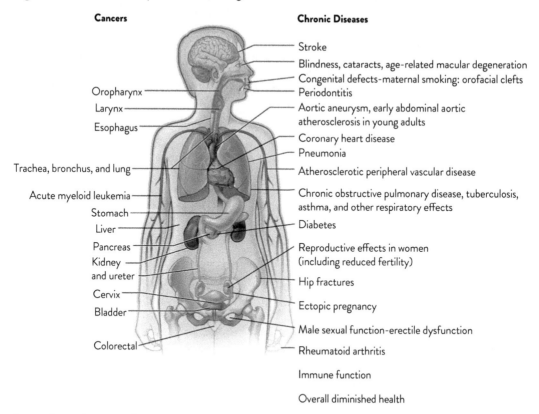

Source: Centers for Disease Control and Prevention.

2003). The FCTC was the world's very first public health **treaty**. It sets out a series of evidence-based measures to help reduce tobacco use and exposure. These include:

- Using price and tax policies to reduce sales

- Providing protection from tobacco smoke in the workplace, on public transport and in indoor public places

- Prohibiting misleading labelling on tobacco packaging

- Including large, clear, visible health warnings on tobacco packaging

- Providing access to effective educational and public awareness programmes on the health risks of tobacco

- Undertaking a ban on tobacco advertising, promotion and sponsorship

- Designing and implementing effective programmes aimed at promoting the cessation of tobacco use

- Prohibiting sales of tobacco products to minors.

By 2017 a total of 181 countries had ratified the treaty (WHO, 2017b). Six countries (including the United States) signed the treaty when it was first agreed but have yet to ratify it, whilst a further nine countries have not signed it.

In 2015 an estimated 15% of people were daily smokers; 25% of men and 5% of women. This figure represents a sizable reduction from 1980 when around 26% of people smoked. However, because of population growth, the total number of daily smokers has actually increased from around 721 million in 1980 to 967 million in 2012 (Ng et al., 2014; Reitmsa et al., 2017).

Intervention approaches

To help countries implement the FTC measures the World Health Organization has developed a package of policies and interventions (WHO, 2008). The package is titled 'MPOWER' which stands for:

- **M**onitor tobacco use and prevention policies
- **P**rotect people from tobacco smoke
- **O**ffer help to quit tobacco use (see **Table 12.3**)
- **W**arn about the dangers of tobacco
- **E**nforce bans on tobacco advertising, promotion and sponsorship
- **R**aise taxes on tobacco.

Table 12.3 Types of tobacco cessation interventions recommended by the World Health Organization

BEHAVIOURAL INTERVENTIONS	**Population level approaches**	**Brief advice**	Advice to stop using tobacco, usually taking only a few minutes, is given to all tobacco users during the course of a routine consultation and/or interaction with a physician or healthcare worker.
		Quit lines	A national toll-free quit line is a telephone counselling service that can provide both proactive and reactive counselling. A reactive quit line provides an immediate response to a call initiated by the tobacco user, but only responds to incoming calls. A proactive quit line involves setting up a schedule of follow-up calls to tobacco users to provide ongoing support.
		mTobacco cessation	Tobacco cessation interventions are delivered via mobile phone text messaging. Mobile technologies provide the opportunity to expand access to a wider population, and text messaging can provide personalized tobacco cessation support in an efficient and cost-effective manner.
	Individual specialist approaches	**Intensive behavioural support**	Behaviour support refers to multiple sessions of individual or group counselling aimed at helping people stop their tobacco use. It includes all cessation assistance that imparts knowledge about tobacco use and quitting, and provides support and resources to develop skills and strategies for changing behaviour.
		Cessation clinics	In many countries, clinics specialising in tobacco cessation services are available. These clinics offer intensive behavioural support, and where appropriate, medications or advice on the provision of medications, delivered by specially trained practitioners.
PHARMACOLOGICAL INTERVENTIONS	**Nicotine replacement therapies (NRTs)**		NRTs are available in several forms including gum, lozenges, patches, inhalers and nasal spray. These cessation tools reduce craving and withdrawal symptoms by providing a low, controlled dose of nicotine without the toxins found in cigarettes. The doses of NRT are gradually reduced over time to help the tobacco user wean off nicotine by getting used to less and less stimulation.
	Non-nicotine pharmacotherapies		These include medications such as bupropion, varenicline and cytisine. These pharmacotherapies reduce cravings and withdrawal symptoms and decrease the pleasurable effects of cigarettes and other tobacco products.

Source: WHO (2019f). Report on the Global Tobacco Epidemic, 2019. Offer to Help Quit Tobacco.

Use of the MPOWER policies varies around the world. Countries that have put in place a large number of the measures include Brazil, Turkey and Australia (WHO, 2019g). **Case Study 8** illustrates the application of one aspect of MPOWER in Australia; the use of legislation to ban advertising on tobacco packaging.

Vaping and other tobacco and nicotine products

As shown in **Table 12.4**, as well as being smoked in a cigarette, tobacco and nicotine can be consumed in a range of other forms.

Table 12.4 Some of the ways tobacco and nicotine are consumed around the world

Type	Product	Details
Smoked tobacco	Cigarette	Tobacco rolled into a paper cylinder and smoked. The smoke is inhaled. Most cigarettes contain a filter. This does not reduce the harms associated with smoking but is used by manufacturers to reduce perceptions of harm.[1]
	Beedi	A small, thin cigarette popular in India. Beedis consist of tobacco wrapped in leaves and tied with a string. They deliver more nicotine, carbon monoxide and tar compared to conventional cigarettes.
	Cigar	Tobacco wrapped in tobacco leaves. They tend to be bigger and thicker than cigarettes and last for longer. Cigar smoke is meant to be drawn into the mouth rather than inhaled.
	Pipe	Used to burn shredded tobacco that is inhaled through a stem.
	Shisha/hookah/ waterpipe/bong	A device used to heat flavoured tobacco (or cannabis or opium), usually over hot coals. The smoke is passed through water before being inhaled, typically through a long hose or pipe. Popular in the Middle East, a shisha may be shared between people at social gatherings.
Smokeless tobacco	Snuff	Ground tobacco, often scented or flavoured, that is inhaled through the nose.
	Chewing and dipping tobacco/chew/dip	Shredded or ground tobacco that is chewed or placed between the lips and gums to release the flavour and nicotine. The juices are spat out. Common in North America.
	Betal quid/gutka	A mixture that contains tobacco and betal nut as well as sweet or savoury flavourings. Popular in India, Pakistan and Asia, it is placed between the gum and cheek where it turns red as it dissolves. Paan is a similar preparation containing betal leaf but may not always contain tobacco.
	Snus	Moist, powdered tobacco that is placed against the upper gums. Used in Sweden and the US.
Heated tobacco products (HTPs)/heat-not-burn products		These heat tobacco to produce an aerosol that is inhaled. They may or may not be shaped to look like a cigarette.
Electronic cigarettes/e-cigarettes/ electronic nicotine delivery systems (ENDS)/cigalikes/vapes/e-hookahs/mods/ tanks/dab pens		These heat a liquid that contains nicotine, but not tobacco. The aerosol is then inhaled. Older models ('cigalikes') may be disposable and shaped to look like a cigarette whilst newer versions ('pod-mods') come in different shapes, sizes and colours and use a refillable pod and modifiable system. They may be shaped to look like pens, USB flash drives or other everyday items.

Note: [1]Manufacturers often design filters so they discolour during smoking, misleading smokers into thinking the filter has filtered out tar (Harris, 2011).

An increasingly popular way of consuming nicotine is through vaping. This is where an electronic cigarette (e-cigarette) is used to heat a liquid containing nicotine, a diluting agent and flavourings. Because the liquid is heated rather than burnt, aerosol is inhaled instead of smoke. And because e-cigarettes do not contain tobacco and do not produce tar or carbon monoxide, they are significantly less harmful than cigarettes (McNeill et al., 2018; Nutt et al., 2014).

However, just because vaping is less harmful than smoking does not mean it is safe. For example, in the US, where e-cigarettes are relatively unregulated, <u>observational studies</u> have been used to link vaping to a nationwide outbreak of lung injury (Blagev et al., 2019; Layden et al., 2019). Since vaping is a relatively new phenomenon it is also too early to be sure of its long-term effects.

For these reasons, e-cigarettes are controversial among those working in public health, and different countries have taken very different approaches toward their use. In the UK the focus has been on harm reduction. Smokers are encouraged to switch to vaping, or to use e-cigarettes as a smoking cessation tool. However, the content of e-cigarettes is tightly regulated, for example they cannot contain more than 20mg/mL of nicotine. Most forms of advertising are also banned, as are sales to those under the age of 18 (McNeill et al., 2018). In the US regulation varies from state to state but tends to be less strict than in the UK. For example, e-cigarettes can contain up to 59mg/mL of nicotine as well as tetrahydrocannabinol (THC; the active ingredient in cannabis). Young people have also been targeted in marketing campaigns. Other countries, such as Australia, Japan, Mexico and Switzerland have chosen to exercise more caution and ban sales of nicotine e-cigarettes altogether.

The arguments for and against e-cigarette use have been fiercely debated, both in the media and in leading medical journals (for example, *The Lancet*, 2019; Newton, 2019). These opposing views can be broadly summarised as follows.

Arguments against e-cigarettes:

- It is premature to claim that e-cigarettes are safer than cigarettes. It is too early to know about any long-term effects and an absence of evidence is not the same as an absence of harm.

- There is no good evidence to support the efficacy of e-cigarettes for smoking cessation and smokers who do switch remain dependent on e-cigarettes over the long term. This is in contrast to nicotine replacement therapy (NRT) for which there is a substantial evidence base supporting its safety and efficacy (Hartmann-Boyce et al., 2016, 2018).

- Unlike NRT, e-cigarettes are not being sold as medical products to aid smoking cessation but are instead being sold and marketed directly to the consumer.

- The high nicotine content of e-cigarettes could make them more difficult to quit than cigarettes.

- The availability of different flavours makes e-cigarettes attractive to young people. They are also being marketed to young people, for example via product placement, sponsorship of parties and sports events and payment to social media influencers. This could lead to a rise in nicotine addiction.

- E-cigarettes may act as a gateway to smoking among young people which could slow or reverse the decline in smoking in this group (Soneji et al., 2017).

- Smoking is being renormalised via e-cigarettes, especially among young people (though see Hallingberg et al. (2019) for an absence of evidence in the UK).

Arguments for e-cigarettes:

- Although the long-term effects of e-cigarettes are unknown, we can estimate likely effects and these are much lower than those of smoking (Beaglehole et al., 2019).

- Smoking cessation has a low success rate, with many smokers failing to quit, even with the help of nicotine replacement therapy (NRT). E-cigarettes, either instead of, or alongside NRT, may be more effective in helping people quit (Beard et al., 2016; Bullen et al. 2017; Hajek et al., 2019; Hartmann-Boyce et al., 2016; Notley et al., 2018; Walker et al., 2020).

- Many people never manage to quit smoking. Encouraging them to switch to e-cigarettes would bring substantial health benefits.

- Young people are mostly experimenting with e-cigarettes rather than becoming regular users (ASH, 2019; Beaglehole et al., 2019).

- Young people who are regular e-cigarette users are those who would have otherwise smoked cigarettes. For example, in the UK, less than 1% of those who use e-cigarettes are people who have never smoked regular cigarettes (McNeill et al., 2018; though see Soneji et al., 2017 for counter evidence in the US).

Some of the concerns outlined above highlight the role of marketing in the uptake of smoking and vaping, especially marketing that is targeted at young people. However, tackling marketing may be easier said than done when one is up against powerful tobacco companies[3] (see **Chapter 11**, particularly **Box 11.3**). **Case Study 8** shows how the Australian government has tried to combat tobacco marketing through legislation requiring 'plain packaging' for all cigarettes and other tobacco products.

CASE STUDY 8

PLAIN PACKAGING IN AUSTRALIA

Background	The tobacco industry spends billions on marketing every year. This has enabled them to cultivate powerful brand images, each designed to appeal to a different segment of the market. Since the 1960s, countries around the world have increasingly regulated tobacco packaging and advertising, in an attempt to counter industry marketing and reduce the harms caused by smoking. For example, in 1966 the US was the first country to require all cigarette packets to display a written health warning. In 2001, Canada ruled that these warnings include images of smoking-related disease ('graphic health warnings'). Many other countries have since followed suit. Most countries also now ban tobacco advertising in print and broadcast media (for example in newspapers and magazines and on billboards and television). But cigarette packets may still be styled to appeal to the consumer and to remind them of the brand image.
Intervention	In December 2012, Australia brought into force legislation requiring all tobacco products to be sold in 'plain' packaging, also referred to as 'standardised' packaging (Australian Government, 2011). These laws relate to all aspects of the packaging and cigarettes (**Image 12.10**). For example, the brand and variant name must be displayed in a certain position on the packaging and in a specific size, colour and font. The colour of the packaging must be Pantone 448C, a sludgy green brown that has been found to be associated with tar, dirt and death in the minds of smokers (Wells, 2012). And the cigarettes must display an alphanumeric code rather than a brand name.

The aims of the legislation were to eliminate the use of packaging as a form of advertising in order to:

1. Reduce the appeal of tobacco products
2. Reduce the potential for tobacco packaging to mislead consumers about the relative strengths of some cigarettes
3. Increase the prominence and effectiveness of health warnings.

---

3   Some, but not all, vaping brands are owned by big tobacco companies.

These were in turn intended to (a) discourage initiation, (b) encourage quitting, (c) help former smokers avoid relapse, and (d) reduce exposure to second-hand smoke (Australian DoH, 2016).

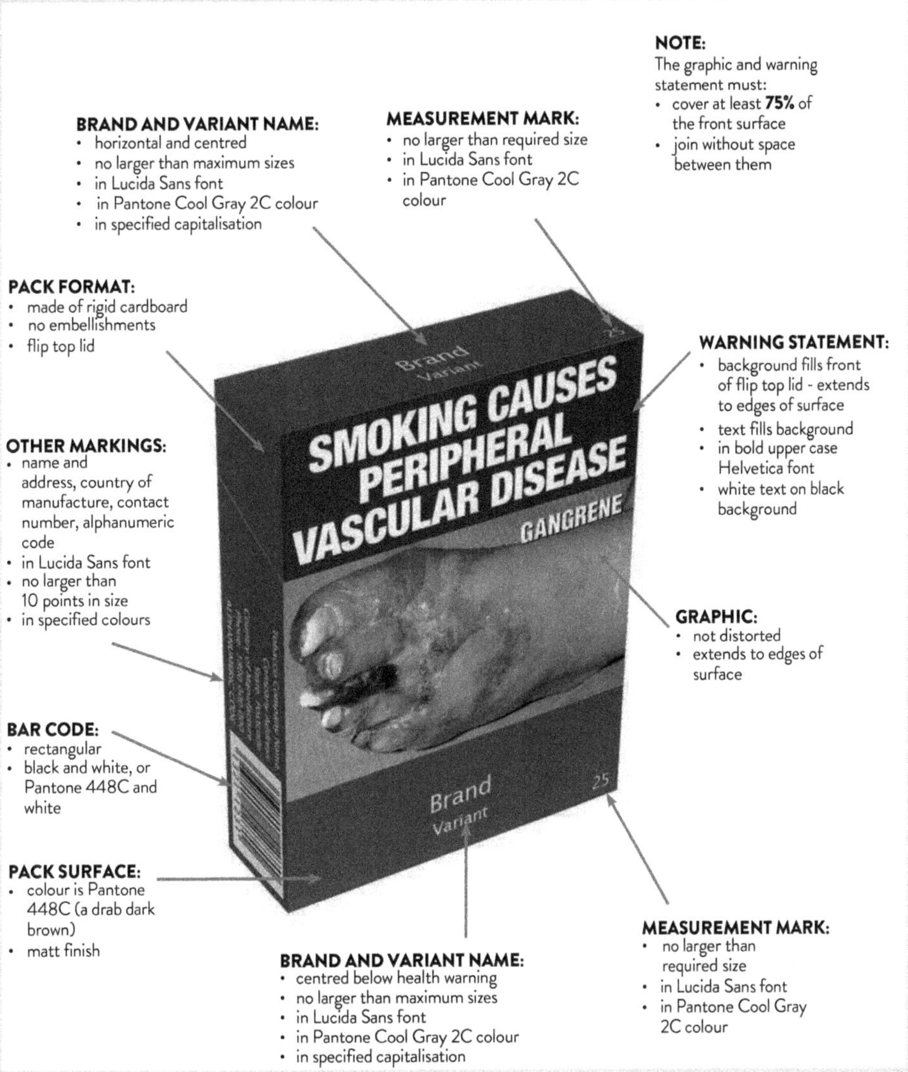

NOTE:
The graphic and warning statement must:
- cover at least **75%** of the front surface
- join without space between them

BRAND AND VARIANT NAME:
- horizontal and centred
- no larger than maximum sizes
- in Lucida Sans font
- in Pantone Cool Gray 2C colour
- in specified capitalisation

MEASUREMENT MARK:
- no larger than required size
- in Lucida Sans font
- in Pantone Cool Gray 2C colour

PACK FORMAT:
- made of rigid cardboard
- no embellishments
- flip top lid

WARNING STATEMENT:
- background fills front of flip top lid - extends to edges of surface
- text fills background
- in bold upper case Helvetica font
- white text on black background

OTHER MARKINGS:
- name and address, country of manufacture, contact number, alphanumeric code
- in Lucida Sans font
- no larger than 10 points in size
- in specified colours

GRAPHIC:
- not distorted
- extends to edges of surface

BAR CODE:
- rectangular
- black and white, or Pantone 448C and white

PACK SURFACE:
- colour is Pantone 448C (a drab dark brown)
- matt finish

BRAND AND VARIANT NAME:
- centred below health warning
- no larger than maximum sizes
- in Lucida Sans font
- in Pantone Cool Gray 2C colour
- in specified capitalisation

MEASUREMENT MARK:
- no larger than required size
- in Lucida Sans font
- in Pantone Cool Gray 2C colour

Image 12.10 Australian plain packaging requirements for the front of cigarette packs.
Source: Australian Government Department of Health (2012). © Commonwealth of Australia. Reproduced with permission.

Rationale and evidence

Internal tobacco company documents reveal that they use packaging to convey their brand image, appeal to younger adults, and mislead consumers into thinking that some cigarettes are less harmful than others (Australian DoH, 2016). For example, although certain products contain less nicotine and tar, consumers tend to compensate by smoking more of the cigarette and by taking deeper puffs, such that they do not represent a reduced risk to health (WHO, 2016b). However, describing these cigarettes as 'light' or 'mild' gives the impression they are less harmful to health. Such descriptors are now prohibited in many countries, but colour has also been shown to influence people's perceptions of risk and tobacco companies have continued to use lighter colours, for example silver and gold, to give the impression of cleaner, healthier cigarettes (WHO, 2016b). Removing such colours from tobacco packaging could help reduce these misperceptions.

People may also aspire to the qualities or lifestyle associated with a particular brand (such as 'macho', 'sophisticated' or 'fun'). The use of visual brand identifiers on the cigarette box (for example, a particular colour, graphic or font) makes the box more attractive because it reminds people of the brand and of the qualities associated with the brand. The box may also be used in social situations as a type of 'badge', to signal a person's affiliation to the brand and to the qualities it represents.

CHAPTER 12

Plain packaging excludes visual brand identifiers, so reduces the appeal of the box as well as its display in social contexts (Wakefield et al., 2008, 2012; WHO, 2016b).

Prior to the introduction of plain packaging, evidence for these potential effects came from experimental studies, focus groups and surveys. Research also suggested that plain packaging would increase the salience of health warnings (WHO, 2016b; see also Drovandi et al., 2019).

Evaluation	The full effects of plain packaging on smoking prevalence may only be evident over a longer period of time. This is because plain packaging may be most effective at reducing smoking initiation, which takes longer to be reflected in smoking prevalence statistics. The introduction of plain packaging in Australia also coincided with the introduction of enlarged and updated graphic health warnings, which makes it difficult to separate out the effects of the two. However, analysis of longitudinal survey data (using an <u>interrupted time-series design</u>) indicates that these two changes were associated with a reduction in smoking rates of over half a percent (among those aged 14 and above); smoking prevalence (defined as having smoked in the last month) was 17.21% following the changes but would likely have been 17.77% without them (Australian DoH, 2016; see also McNeill et al., 2017). Other longitudinal survey data have shown effects on a range of other outcomes thought to be associated with smoking behaviour. These include reductions in the appeal of the packaging and the extent to which smokers hold positive stereotypes about others who smoke, reduced display of cigarette packets in public places, increases in the extent to which smokers report noticing the health warnings and increased feelings of concern over smoking and thoughts about quitting (Dunlop et al., 2014; Wakefield et al., 2013, 2015; Webb et al., 2017; White et al., 2015, 2019; Yong et al., 2016; Zacher et al., 2014, 2015). Data have also shown increased quit attempts and attempts to cut down among smokers (Durkin et al., 2015; J.M. Young et al., 2014).
Relevant theory	The effects of plain packaging on behaviour relate to many of the theories we covered in earlier chapters. Tobacco industry marketing can be viewed as a form of <u>evaluative conditioning.</u> It may also exert some of its effects through <u>priming</u> and can be interpreted in light of the <u>grounded cognition theory of desire</u>. Plain packaging works to limit tobacco marketing and to substitute positive emotions with negative ones, through the use of unappealing colours, and increased prominence of health warnings and images of disease. In this way it also links to <u>protection motivation theory</u> as well as other <u>social cognitive models</u> with constructs relating to <u>attitudes</u>, <u>beliefs</u> and <u>intentions</u>. Additionally, reduced display of cigarette packets may help change smoking-related <u>social norms.</u> Finally, <u>stage models</u> (and the <u>intention-behaviour gap</u>) are relevant when considering the relationship between more immediate outcomes (such as concern, or thoughts about quitting) and smoking prevalence.
Resistance	Prior to the introduction of plain packaging, the tobacco industry engaged in several unsuccessful legal challenges (Miller et al., 2018; Greenland, 2016). They also launched a media campaign arguing that plain packaging would: • be ineffective at reducing smoking • make counterfeiting easier, increasing trade in cheaper, illicit products • push retail prices down because consumers would be less willing to pay for premium products • confuse retailers, creating delays when serving customers • put small retailers out of business due to declining sales. Research carried out since the introduction of plain packaging shows little support for these claims (Australian DoH, 2016; Scollo et al., 2015; WHO, 2016b). Following the introduction of plain packaging, tobacco companies have responded by diversifying both their brand and variant names, to help remind the consumer of their brand image, and to influence perceptions of product characteristics, including relative health. In particular, more colours have been added to brand and variant names, such as blue, white, silver and gold (Greenland, 2016). Some companies have also introduced cardboard sleeves (sold separately) designed to be placed over a cigarette box to obscure the health warnings (WHO, 2016b).
In context	Plain packaging is an initiative designed to be used in combination with other tobacco control measures. Taken in isolation, many of these measures will have limited effect on smoking prevalence, but cumulatively these effects add up (see **Figure 12.6**). We can also view different tobacco control measures as targeting different stages of behaviour change (**Chapter 5**). For example, while health warnings may help change intentions (the <u>motivational stage</u>), easy access to nicotine replacement therapy may help translate intentions to behaviour (the <u>volitional stage</u>; see **Table 12.3** for other examples).

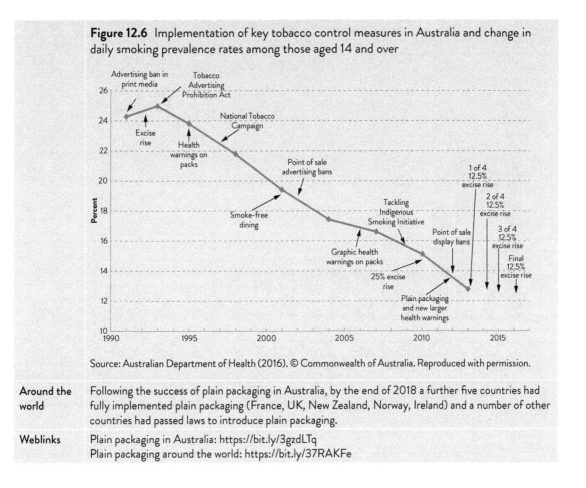

Figure 12.6 Implementation of key tobacco control measures in Australia and change in daily smoking prevalence rates among those aged 14 and over

Source: Australian Department of Health (2016). © Commonwealth of Australia. Reproduced with permission.

Around the world	Following the success of plain packaging in Australia, by the end of 2018 a further five countries had fully implemented plain packaging (France, UK, New Zealand, Norway, Ireland) and a number of other countries had passed laws to introduce plain packaging.
Weblinks	Plain packaging in Australia: https://bit.ly/3gzdLTq Plain packaging around the world: https://bit.ly/37RAKFe

ALCOHOL

In many countries alcohol use is widespread. It is partly for this reason that in 2010 it was the fifth leading risk factor for disease and ill health (after high blood pressure, tobacco smoke, household air pollution and low fruit consumption). In Eastern Europe, Andean Latin America and Southern sub-Saharan Africa, alcohol was the number one risk factor for disease and ill health (Lim et al., 2012).

Harms

Some of the harms from alcohol occur because of its effect on the body: alcohol increases the risk of a range of non-communicable diseases including cardiovascular disease, cancer and liver disease. It also suppresses the immune response, increasing the risk of infections. Drinking whilst pregnant can increase the risks of stillbirth, low birthweight and learning disabilities. Other harms relate to the effects of alcohol on behaviour: drinking increases the risk of traffic accidents, injury, violence, suicide and unsafe sex. Alcohol is also addictive so can lead to dependence and mental disorders such as depression and psychosis (Lim et al., 2012; Rehm et al., 2012, 2017; Sakar et al., 2015; WHO, 2018c). These wide-ranging effects have led some to conclude that alcohol causes more harm than a number of other legal and illegal drugs (**Figure 12.7**), whilst others state that there is no safe recommended level of alcohol consumption (**Box 12.2**).

CHAPTER 12

Figure 12.7 Expert assessment of harms to the self and others associated with a range of different legal and illegal drugs used in the UK

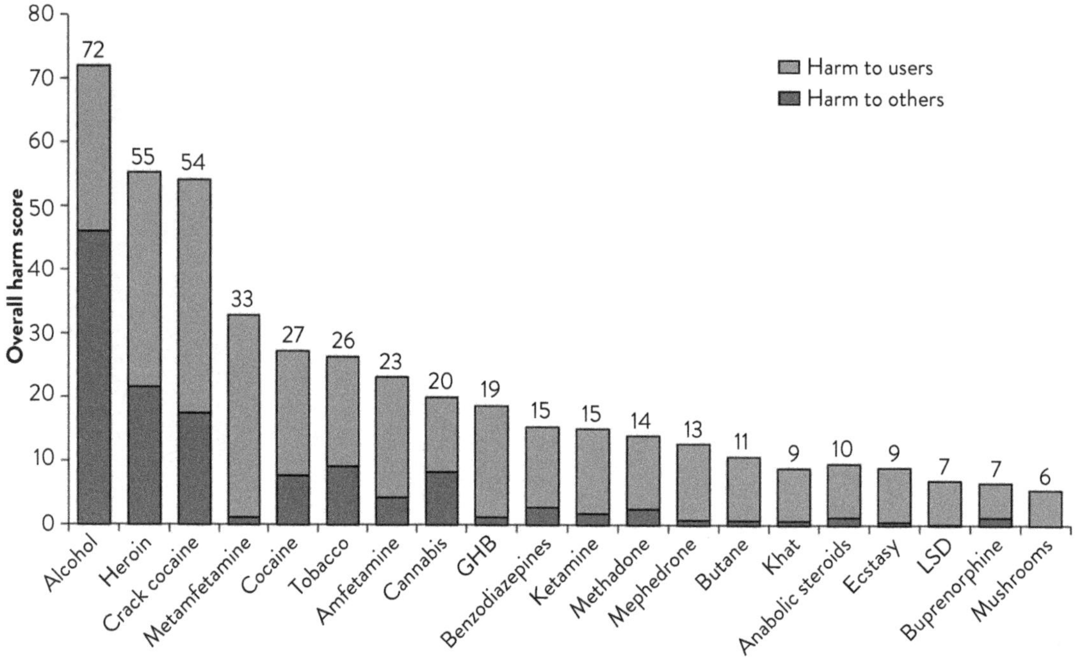

Source: Reprinted from *The Lancet*, 376(9752), Nutt, D.J., King, L.A., & Phillips, L.D., Drug harms in the UK: a multicriteria decision analysis, 1558–1565, Copyright 2010, with permission from Elsevier.

BOX 12.2 CAN ALCOHOL BE GOOD FOR YOUR HEALTH?

HOT TOPIC

You may have heard that drinking in moderation is good for your health. There is some evidence to suggest that moderate amounts of alcohol lower the risks of heart disease, stroke and diabetes. However, alcohol also increases the risks of cancer, injuries and communicable disease and a meta-analysis indicated that these risks offset any benefits. This led the authors to conclude that the level of alcohol consumption that minimises harm is zero (Griswold et al., 2018). Of course, if you are someone with a high risk of heart disease or diabetes, but a low risk of cancer, it may be that a little bit of alcohol *is* good for you. This is the type of tailored advice you might get from personalised medicine (**Chapter 4**). However, at a population level it seems that the best health message would be to reduce alcohol consumption, rather than to drink in moderation.

Group differences and recommendations

The main factors that influence alcohol use in any given country are economic wealth, religion and alcohol-related policies. Alcohol consumption tends to be higher in high-income countries. For example, both India and China were low-income countries in the 1990s but are now middle-income countries. This growth in wealth has led to more disposable income for those living there, which has in turn led to increased alcohol consumption.

However, in some high-income countries, such as Saudi Arabia and Brunei, there are low levels of alcohol consumption because, in keeping with Sharia (Islamic) law, alcohol is banned. Russia is a middle-income country but has seen significant declines in both alcohol consumption and alcohol-related disease since 2005, following the introduction of taxes and restrictions on sales and marketing (Manthey et al., 2019; WHO, 2018c).

Although alcohol consumption tends to be higher in wealthier countries, it causes more harm in poorer countries. For example, globally the highest levels of alcohol consumption are found in Europe and Australasia, but the highest levels of alcohol-related disease and injury are found in Africa. This pattern is also reflected within countries, where wealthier individuals tend to drink more but those from poorer backgrounds suffer more harm. Men also tend to drink more than women, and suffer from more alcohol-related ill health, but this gap is smaller in countries that enjoy greater gender equality (WHO, 2018c).

There is no global consensus on what constitutes safe levels of alcohol consumption (Kalinowski & Humphreys, 2016; see also **Box 12.2**). For example, in Australia and in the UK, both men and women are advised to drink no more than 14 units of alcohol a week, with a unit containing either 8g of pure ethanol (in the UK) or 10g (in Australia). This is equivalent to around 6 glasses of wine, 6 pints of beer or 14 single whiskeys. However, country definitions of what constitutes a unit (or 'standard drink') range from between 8g and 20g of pure ethanol, with most countries having no standard drink definition. Where low-risk consumption guidelines exist, these also vary widely, in terms of whether the guidelines are per day or per week, whether they differ for men and women and in terms of the actual quantities. For example, whilst the UK guidelines would be the equivalent of up to 16g per day for both men and women and the Australian guidelines would be the equivalent of up to 20g a day for both men and women, in the US, guidelines are equivalent to up to 14g a day for women and 28g a day for men (CDC, 2020).

Binge drinking

Binge drinking (or heavy episodic drinking) is where a person drinks a large amount of alcohol in a short space of time, or drinks in order to get drunk. It is defined by the World Health Organization as the consumption of 60 grams or more of pure ethanol on one occasion (WHO, 2018c). This is the equivalent of around one bottle of wine, or 7.5 shots of spirit. However, there is no worldwide agreement on what constitutes binge drinking, and the effects of alcohol will vary from one person to another. Binge drinking is particularly bad for health because the liver can only process around one unit of alcohol per hour, after which alcohol levels in the blood start to rise and the rest of the body, including the brain, becomes affected. Binge drinking increases accidents and injury as well as risky behaviours such as unsafe sex. Too much alcohol will eventually lead to unconsciousness where there is a risk a person may stop breathing, choke on their vomit or suffer from heart failure. Regular binge drinking among adolescents and young adults has also been shown to impact on brain functioning (Kuntsche et al., 2017). In 2017 an estimated 20% of adults engaged in binge drinking, which tends to peak between the ages of 20–24 years (Manthey et al., 2019; WHO, 2018c).

Intervention approaches

To reduce alcohol-related harms, the World Health Organization recommends five policy interventions (WHO, 2019g). These can be summarised using the acronym SAFER and are as follows:

- **S**trengthen restrictions on alcohol availability, such as introducing a legal minimum age for sales as well as controls on the hours and days during which alcohol may be sold.

> **Brief intervention** – an intervention that requires limited time and resources. It typically consists of one to four, 5- to 20-minute counselling sessions with a trained physician, nurse, psychologist or social worker, and would normally emphasise self-help (Nilsen et al., 2008).

- **A**dvance and enforce drink driving measures, such as introducing legal limits on blood-alcohol levels when driving and enforcing these through the use of random breath-testing and licence suspension. Complementary measures may include mass media campaigns highlighting the dangers of drink driving.

- **F**acilitate access to screening, **brief interventions** and treatment; for example, though the use of screening and brief interventions in healthcare settings, and through the provision of treatment programmes for those suffering from alcohol use disorders.

- **E**nforce bans or restrictions on alcohol advertising, sponsorship and promotion. These can prevent young people from being exposed to advertising, limit the presence of alcohol-related cues in the environment and stop industry from cultivating social norms that increase drinking (such as drinking when watching sport on television).

- **R**aise the price of alcohol through taxes and other pricing policies. These might include the prohibition of price promotions and the introduction of minimum unit pricing where drinks containing alcohol cannot be sold for less than a certain amount per gram of alcohol.

Case Study 9 describes the use of screening plus a brief intervention in a healthcare setting in South Africa.

CASE STUDY 9

REDUCING RISKY SUBSTANCE USE IN SOUTH AFRICA: A BRIEF INTERVENTION USING MOTIVATIONAL INTERVIEWING

Background	In sub-Saharan Africa much poor health is caused by communicable diseases, such as malaria, tuberculosis and HIV. However, this is starting to change, with many countries in the region seeing increased levels of non-communicable disease, such as cardiovascular disease, cancer and diabetes, the burden of which are compounded by under-resourced health systems (Gouda et al., 2019; **Chapter 3**). In South Africa the second leading cause of death is injury, most of which is driven by violence[4] and traffic accidents and often involves alcohol (Seedat et al., 2009). South Africa has a very high level of alcohol consumption with an estimated 12% of men suffering from an alcohol use disorder (WHO, 2018c). Brief interventions, delivered in hospital emergency rooms, are a potentially effective, low-cost means of targeting those at risk of alcohol misuse (Field et al., 2010; Kaner et al., 2009; Nilsen et al., 2008).
Intervention components	The intervention comprises three key components: an ASSIST-linked brief intervention, motivational interviewing, problem-solving therapy. These are described below. *1. ASSIST-linked brief intervention* ASSIST refers to the Alcohol, Smoking and Substance Involvement Screening Test, developed under the auspices of the World Health Organization as a tool for use in primary care to detect harmful substance use (WHO, 2010b). It asks about lifetime substance use and substance use over the last three months in order to provide a score that indicates risk for substance-related problems. It was developed to be brief (it takes just 5–10 minutes to administer), to assess harm rather than dependence, and to have cross-cultural relevance. It was also designed to be incorporated into a brief intervention (the ASSIST-linked brief intervention; WHO, 2010c). This intervention takes

---

4   Contributory factors are thought to include high levels of unemployment and income inequality (Seedat et al., 2009). Indeed, South Africa has the highest recorded income inequality in the world, with a Gini coefficient of 0.63 in 2014 (World Bank, 2020; **Chapter 3**).

around 3 to 15 minutes and is used after the ASSIST. It involves 10 suggested main steps (or just the first 5 for a briefer intervention):

1. ASK the client if they are interested in seeing their questionnaire scores.

2. Provide FEEDBACK to the client about their scores.

3. Give ADVICE about how they can reduce their risks.

4. Allow the client to take RESPONSIBILITY for their choices.

5. Ask the client how CONCERNED they are by their scores.

6. Weigh up the GOOD THINGS about using the substance against…

7. …the LESS GOOD THINGS about using the substance.

8. SUMMARISE AND REFLECT on the client's statements, emphasising the 'less good things'.

9. Ask the client how CONCERNED they are by the 'less good things'.

10. Give the client relevant TAKE-HOME MATERIALS.

2. Motivational interviewing (MI)

Motivational interviewing (MI) aims to increase a person's motivation to change (Miller & Rollnick, 2013; Rollnick & Miller, 1995). In order to achieve this, an interviewer will:

1. Express empathy for the client, so they feel understood and are more likely to be honest and open.

2. Support self-efficacy.

3. Avoid challenging statements made by the client that display resistance (the interviewer will 'roll with resistance').

4. Develop discrepancy between where the client is at the moment and where they want to be.

The interviewer avoids coercion or persuasion but instead tries to elicit motivation to change from the individual. They may do this by asking open-ended questions, by helping the person identify their goals and values, by encouraging them to consider the pros and cons of their behaviour and by drawing attention to instances of success. For example, an interviewer may ask 'What are the good things about using alcohol?', 'What are the less good things?' They may ask them whether the less good things concern them and about occasions when they successfully refrained from drinking. They will also summarise and reflect back the person's statements to them.

3. Problem-solving therapy (PST)

Problem-solving therapy (PST) provides individuals with a step-by-step approach to using psychosocial skills to solve life problems (D'Zurilla & Goldfried, 1971; Nezu, 2004). It has two key dimensions: problem orientation and problem-solving style. Problem orientation refers to seeing difficulties as challenges that can be overcome. Problem-solving style means applying a particular set of problem-solving skills that are more likely to lead to an effective solution. These include:

1. Identifying problems when they occur

2. Defining and understanding the problem

3. Setting goals related to the problem

4. Generating solutions

5. Evaluating and selecting a solution

6. Implementing the solution

7. Evaluating the effects of the solution and, where necessary, returning to previous steps.

The person is encouraged to take a problem-solving orientation to life and is helped to practise problem-solving skills, both within the therapy session and as homework assignments.

Intervention delivery	The intervention was delivered to patients recruited from three emergency departments in Cape Town, South Africa (Sorsdahl et al., 2015). Whilst patients were waiting to see a doctor they were asked if they were willing to complete a screening test. Those who showed moderate to high levels of substance use risk were invited to take part in a risk reduction programme. If they agreed they completed the ASSIST-linked brief intervention and, in some cases (see Evaluation) returned for a further four sessions of blended MI and PST. These latter sessions were 40 to 60 minutes, spaced approximately 1 week apart. The counsellors received 30 hours of training in MI and PST (including proficiency testing). To ensure intervention fidelity and limit intervention drift (where an intervention gradually changes over time), counsellors received three half-day booster trainings and biweekly supervision and debriefing sessions. They also received some additional training, for example in substance use risks and use of the ASSIST tool.

Theory and evidence	*ASSIST-linked brief intervention*
	The ASSIST-linked brief intervention is underpinned by the <u>transtheoretical model</u>, being designed to move people through one or more stages of change, particularly from precontemplation to contemplation or preparation. The intervention also draws on evidence showing that brief interventions that are effective tend to:
	
	• use personally relevant Feedback
	• acknowledge the client's Responsibility
	• provide clear and objective Advice
	• provide a Menu of options
	• employ Empathy
	• promote Self-efficacy.
	
	These features are summarised by the acronym FRAMES. Many of these features overlap with motivational interviewing, which the ASSIST intervention also draws on more explicitly in terms of an emphasis on reflective listening, discrepancy development and rolling with resistance (WHO, 2010c).
	
	Motivational interviewing
	MI was not developed from theory. Instead it was developed on the basis of practitioner experience of what worked in counselling sessions for substance use. Several meta-analyses have since supported its effects in relation to addictive behaviours as well as other health-related behaviours such as treatment adherence, diet and exercise (DiClemente et al., 2017; Hettema et al., 2005; Lundahl et al., 2010; Rubak et al., 2005).
	    A number of explanations have been put forward to account for the effects of MI (Magill & Hallgren, 2019; Miller & Rose, 2019). In particular there is evidence that effects are mediated by the extent to which clients talk about changing their behaviour versus not changing their behaviour; the former is associated with more behaviour change and the latter with less. Identifying such mechanisms may be useful for improving the efficacy of MI since certain interviewer behaviours (such as reflective listening and open-ended questions) have been shown to be associated with more change talk, whilst other behaviours (such as unsolicited advice and warnings) are associated with more talk about not changing (Magill et al., 2014). However, this account fails to provide a full explanation as it does not tell us why change talk is associated with behaviour change. Is it because the person is voicing a commitment to the interviewer and anticipates disapproval if they fail to stick to it? Or is it because it represents a form of <u>action planning</u>? Or does change talk simply reflect other underlying processes, such as improvements in <u>self-efficacy</u>?
	    MI can also be linked to <u>self-determination theory.</u> The interviewer can be seen to (a) support the person's autonomy by avoiding direct persuasion or coercion, (b) develop relatedness through reflective listening and empathy, and (c) promote feelings of competence by enhancing self-efficacy.
	
	Problem-solving therapy
	The orientation dimension of PST draws on concepts of <u>self-efficacy</u> and <u>outcome expectancies</u>; a person who believes they are capable of overcoming problems, and who anticipates positive outcomes from problem solving, is more likely to take steps to address difficulties in their life. The style dimension of PST can also be related to <u>social cognitive theory</u>, since guiding a client to develop skills may involve strategies such as instruction and modelling that help change <u>goals</u>, <u>outcome expectancies</u> and <u>self-efficacy</u>. Helping the client apply these skills may also lead to direct experience of success, further influencing <u>outcome expectancies</u> and <u>self-efficacy</u>. PST has been shown to be effective at reducing both mental and physical health problems (Malouff et al., 2007).

Evaluation	The intervention was evaluated using a three-armed RCT (Sorsdahl et al., 2015). Of the 2,736 patients screened, 335 met the inclusion criteria and were willing to take part. They were randomised to receive either (a) blended MI and PST (MI+PST group), (b) the first ASSIST-linked brief intervention only (MI group), or (c) a brochure on the effects of substance use (control group). Measures were taken prior to randomisation and 3 months after either the initial assessment (for control and MI groups) or the final intervention session (for the MI+PST group). Participants were given a grocery store voucher for completion of each assessment. The primary outcome was risk for substance-related problems, assessed using the ASSIST. Secondary outcomes were depression, frequency of substance-related injury, physical and verbal violence and police interaction. Results showed that ASSIST scores decreased in all three arms but were significantly lower at 3 months in the MI+PST group compared to the control and MI groups (with no significant differences between the latter). Those at risk of depression at baseline also showed significantly lower levels of depression at 3 months in the MI+PST group compared to the MI and control groups. There were no significant differences in frequency of substance-related injury, physical and verbal violence or police interaction.
Limitations and future research	Attrition in the trial was both high and biased, with only 54% of participants completing the 3-month follow-up measures (42% in the MI+PST group). Although the researchers used intention-to-treat analysis, we cannot know whether their imputed scores accurately reflected the participants who dropped out. Also, because the ASSIST scores fell in all three groups, it is possible the lower scores in the MI+PST group simply reflected a downward trajectory, given that measures in this group were taken approximately 4 months after baseline testing, as opposed to 3 months in the other two groups. It is also unclear how effects might change over time, for example whether they may diminish or grow stronger, or whether other effects, such as on injury rates, may emerge later. As the researchers note, more research is needed with longer term follow-ups and with systems in place to limit attrition (such as researchers travelling to participants to collect follow-up data rather than vice versa). Given the relatively low numbers who attended all the MI+PST sessions (41%), the researchers suggest that the number of sessions could also be reduced. Additionally, it is unclear whether the difference in effects for the MI versus the MI+PST interventions arose from differences in content or dosage. A trial that matched dosage would be needed to establish this. Finally, the equivalent decline in ASSIST scores in the MI and control arms suggests that simply screening for substance misuse may help prompt behaviour change, at least over the short term. Again, differences between these two arms might emerge over a longer timeframe, or it may be that the ASSIST-linked brief intervention was simply too brief to lead to any additional change over and above that prompted by screening. Nevertheless, the findings of this study are important because they demonstrate the feasibility and potential efficacy of brief intervention for substance misuse within an emergency department setting, in a middle-income country.
Weblinks	ASSIST: https://bit.ly/3gyz4Eu Motivational interviewing: https://motivationalinterviewing.org

VACCINATIONS

As described in **Box 11.5**, vaccinations have been used since the 1800s and are now a standard means of preventing infectious disease.

How vaccines work

A vaccine is a substance containing either a weakened **pathogen**, a killed pathogen or a small fragment of a pathogen.[5] When the vaccine is administered to an individual it stimulates their immune system to produce antibodies (proteins in the blood that bind to foreign particles in the body and kill pathogens). The immune system also creates antibody-producing memory cells. This means that if the person subsequently comes into contact with this particular

> **Pathogen** – an organism that causes a disease. A pathogen may be a bacterium, virus, fungus, protozoan or worm. Protozoa and worms that cause disease are also considered types of parasite. However, note that some would argue that a virus is not an organism because it does not meet all the criteria usually used to define something as living. For example, it does not grow and it cannot reproduce on its own (it needs to be inside the living cell of another organism in order to reproduce).

---

5 Some newer vaccines use genetic material to stimulate the body to make the relevant fragment of the pathogen.

pathogen, they are able to quickly produce the right antibodies to enable them to fight it. In other words, they have immunity. Live vaccines (containing a weakened pathogen) tend to produce a strong immune response that results in lifelong protection. By contrast, vaccines containing a killed pathogen or pathogen fragment are unable to replicate in the person's body; they generally produce a weaker immune response compared to live vaccines so several doses or 'boosters' may be needed.

Virus – a microscopic particle (smaller than a bacterium) that invades the living cells of animals, plants or bacteria. It uses the material within these cells as a source of energy and to enable it to replicate. It cannot replicate outside a living cell. Antibiotics are not effective against viruses but antiviral medicines may be used to inhibit their activity.

Bacteria – microscopic, single-celled organisms that live in a very wide range of different environments. Some bacteria are beneficial to humans, such as those that live in our gut and help us digest food (**Box 2.1**). Others are harmful and cause disease. Antibiotics can be used to treat bacterial infections, though these can kill helpful bacteria as well as harmful ones. Overuse of antibiotics also leads to antibiotic resistance, where infectious bacteria are no longer susceptible to antibiotics and disease becomes harder to treat.

Ebola – a deadly viral disease first discovered in 1976 in the Democratic Republic of Congo in a village near the Ebola river. It is spread through bodily fluids (such as blood, sweat, saliva and faeces) from those who are sick with the disease or who have died from it. Ebola leads to death in around 50% of cases (WHO, 2020b).

Vaccine development

As described in **Chapter 2**, the first ever vaccine was for the smallpox virus, developed in 1796. Since then, smallpox has been eradicated and we now have approved vaccines for more than 20 other different diseases (WHO, 2020g). These are all for diseases caused by either a **virus** (for example measles and rabies) or **bacteria** (for example tuberculosis and tetanus). Although scientists are in the process of developing vaccines for diseases caused by protozoa (including malaria) none have yet been licensed for use.

On average, it takes more than 10 years to develop a new vaccine to the point at which it can be safely rolled out to those who need it (Pronker et al., 2013). The process involves the following stages:

1. Exploratory stage – potential vaccines are developed by isolating the pathogen and finding out which parts stimulate an immune response.

2. Pre-clinical stage – tissue-cultures, cell-cultures and animals are used to test the immune response and evaluate safety. Many potential vaccines never get beyond this point.

3. Phase I human trials – these are carried out with small groups of people (typically 20–80) to evaluate efficacy, safety, side effects and tolerance to different doses.

4. Phase II human trials – conducted with hundreds of people, using randomised controlled trials, to confirm safety and establish whether and when boosters are needed.

5. Phase III human trials – thousands to tens of thousands of people take part in randomised controlled trials to further evaluate safety, efficacy and side effects. These studies are often carried out with those who are at more risk from the disease.

6. Regulatory review and approval – a licence for use is obtained by presenting all the evidence to a relevant regulatory body.

7. Mass production – the vaccine is manufactured on a larger scale and procedures are put in place to roll it out to those who need it.

8. Monitoring – batches of vaccine are continually tested for safety and purity and reporting procedures are used to capture any rare adverse side effects. Anyone can report a side effect to the relevant regulatory body, including parents, patients and healthcare providers.

During epidemics and pandemics, when the need for a vaccine is more urgent, development may be faster. For example, an **Ebola** vaccine was developed in around five years and was offered to those at high risk of infection prior to it being licensed for use (Gavi, 2020; WHO, 2018b). In this case the threat presented by the disease was balanced against an absence of evidence regarding the longer term effects of the vaccine. More recently, a vaccine for COVID-19 was developed in less than a year. However, in some cases, where a disease has been successfully contained, progress in vaccine development may be stalled or even abandoned because lower levels of the disease make it more difficult to test vaccine efficacy in Phase III trials.

Vaccination, herd immunity and vaccine hesitancy

Vaccination is the act of administering a vaccine to a person to provide them with immunity from a disease. Once a certain proportion of the population has been vaccinated, the population is also protected through herd immunity. This is where a pathogen can no longer survive in a population because there are not enough hosts left for it to infect.

The level of immunity needed to provide herd immunity varies for different pathogens, depending on their rates of transmission. For example, measles is a highly contagious disease, with each infected person going on to infect an average of 10–15 other people. This means that 90–95% of the population need to be vaccinated to provide herd immunity. For a less infectious disease, herd immunity can be achieved by vaccinating a lower proportion of the population.

Herd immunity is important because it protects people in the population who cannot safely receive vaccines, such as newborn babies, the elderly and those who have weakened immune systems, for example from cancer treatment or HIV. Though note that herd immunity only protects against diseases that are passed from person to person. It does not protect against diseases such as tetanus which is caused by bacteria in the environment (for example in soil) entering an open wound.

However, as described in **Chapter 11**, even where vaccines are readily available, some people can be reluctant to get vaccinated or to have their children vaccinated (termed 'vaccine hesitancy'). This can lead to a loss of herd immunity, meaning that those who are not vaccinated are at risk of catching the disease. Some people who have been vaccinated will also get the disease because no vaccination is 100% effective (though the proportion of vaccinated people who become infected will be much smaller than the proportion of unvaccinated people who become infected). In 2019 the World Health Organization identified vaccine hesitancy as one of the top ten threats to global health (WHO, 2020f).

There are a number of reasons why people may be reluctant to get vaccinated (see **Box 11.5**). One reason is concern over vaccine safety. Such concerns are understandable; because everyone has a unique genetic make-up, we can never entirely rule out the possibility that someone may have a serious, adverse reaction to a vaccine. Thus, in principle, if everyone else is vaccinated, the safest option for any single person is to not get vaccinated themselves but to instead rely on herd immunity. But this soon becomes the least safe option when too many people select it because the risks posed by a particular disease are always much higher than those posed by the vaccination. For example, the risk of encephalitis (life-threatening brain inflammation) from the measles vaccine is less than one in 1 million, whereas the risk of encephalitis from measles itself is 1,000 times greater at one in 1,000 (WHO, 2014).

Vaccines are described as 'safe' because of the very low risks associated with them. This is similar to the way in which we would typically describe things such flying, walking to work or eating a sandwich as 'safe'. We can never entirely rule out the possibility of accidents or allergic reactions, but the risks are too small for us to consider them 'unsafe'. Nevertheless, as discussed in **Chapter 11**, perceptions of risk can be biased by certain types of information; a frightening story in the news about someone who has suffered a rare side effect from a vaccine may weigh more heavily in decision-making than a series of dry statistics about the number of deaths the vaccine has prevented. In order to reduce feelings of fear, a person may also simply avoid thinking about vaccination, meaning they remain unvaccinated (see protection motivation theory).

Case Study 10 describes an intervention designed to address a slightly different reason for failing to get vaccinated (simply forgetting or not getting round to it), whilst **Box 12.3** considers another practice aimed at combatting infectious diseases (mask wearing among the general public).

IMPLEMENTATION INTENTIONS FOR IMMUNISATION: PROMPTING FLU VACCINATION AMONG EMPLOYEES

CASE STUDY 10

Background	Seasonal influenza (flu) is an acute respiratory infection that causes a fever, sore throat, runny nose, cough, headache, muscle and joint pain, and fatigue. Most people recover at home within 1 to 2 weeks but certain groups of people, such as the elderly and those with chronic health conditions, may suffer from complications. An estimated 290,000 to 650,000 people die from seasonal flu every year and outbreaks can also lead to high levels of school and work absenteeism (WHO, 2018e).
	Seasonal flu is caused by a virus and can be prevented with vaccination. However, because the particular types of flu viruses circulating are constantly evolving, and because a person's immunity to the virus declines over time, annual vaccination is needed. The World Health Organization continuously monitors the flu viruses circulating around the world and updates the vaccine twice a year. They recommend vaccination for anyone who is at greater risk of complications: those aged 65 or over, people with chronic medical conditions, pregnant women, and children aged between 6 months and 5 years. They also recommend the vaccination of healthcare workers to help stop the spread of the disease to vulnerable people and because healthcare workers are more likely to become infected.
	However, even where vaccines are available, many people who fall into a high-risk group still fail to get them (CDC, 2003). In some cases this may be because they have decided they do not want to be vaccinated but in other cases people may simply forget or not get round to it.
Intervention and evaluation	The intervention was designed to increase rates of seasonal flu vaccination at a US utility company among employees who were aged 50 or over or who suffered from a chronic health condition (Milkman et al., 2011).
	A total of 3,272 employees were invited to receive a flu vaccination at an onsite clinic. The employees were located at 62 different sites and clinics were held during October and November, either for a portion of a single day, a full-day or for a period of 3 days or 5 days. Employees at each location were randomly assigned to receive one of three different types of invitation. In the control condition the invitation simply informed them when and where the clinic(s) would be held. In the date planning condition the invitation additionally prompted them to write down the day and date they planned to attend the clinic, whilst in the date + time planning condition the invitation prompted them to write down the time they planned to attend the clinic as well as the day and date (**Figure 12.8**). Employees who worked at sites where clinics were available on just one day were randomised into either the control condition or the date + time planning condition. Flu vaccination was assessed using clinic records. Employees did not know they were taking part in a research study and those recording the vaccinations did not know what type of invitation employees had received. Thus the study is an example of a three-armed double-blind RCT with stratification by worksite location.

Figure 12.8 Invitations sent to employees by Milkman et al. (2011) in (a) the control condition, (b) the date planning condition and (c) the date + time planning condition

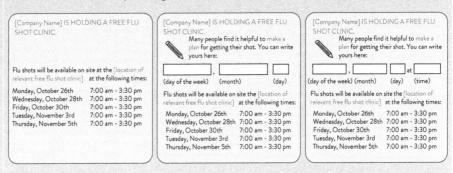

Source: Milkman, K.L., Beshears, J., Choi, J.J., Laibson, D., & Madrian, B.C. (2011). Using implementation intentions prompts to enhance influenza vaccination rates. *Proceedings of the National Academy of Sciences, 108*(26), 10415–10420. Reproduced with the permission of the Proceedings of the National Academy of Sciences.

Vaccination rates were 33.1% in the control condition, 35.6% in the date planning condition and 37.1% in the date + time planning condition. The difference between the date + time planning condition and the control condition was statistically significant. The effect of the date + time planning intervention was also higher at worksites where clinics were offered on just one day rather than on multiple days.

Interpretation and relevant theory	The planning prompts can be viewed as a type of <u>implementation intention</u>. Although they do not follow the recommended 'if-then' format, they do encourage the person to specify an external cue (the day, date and time), that is then linked in their mind to a particular behaviour (going to the clinic). Where the cue is more specific (detailing a time as well as a day), it is more effective. As discussed in **Chapter 6**, implementation intentions are thought to work by (a) increasing the cognitive accessibility of relevant situational cues and (b) by increasing the <u>automaticity</u> of the behaviour (in other words, they are <u>mediated</u> by these factors). In this intervention it is likely the implementation intentions made a particular day, date and time more accessible in employees' minds and mentally linked this day, date and time to attending the clinic. This would have meant they were more likely to notice the day, date and time when it occurred and to remember they had been planning to get vaccinated. In other words, they were less likely to forget. Increased automaticity of the behaviour in response to the cue may have meant they were also less likely to procrastinate ('I'll do it a bit later'). This may have been important because procrastination could increase the chances of someone forgetting or simply running out of time. 　　The fact that the strongest effects occurred for the date + time intervention at worksite locations that offered vaccinations on just one day is consistent with the view that implementation intentions are more effective where there is more danger of an opportunity being missed. Where there were plenty of opportunities for vaccination over multiple days, some forgetfulness or procrastination may have delayed attendance for a day or two but not prevented it completely. In other words, implementation intention efficacy was <u>moderated</u> by ease of behaviour; they were more effective in situations where the behaviour was more difficult to perform. 　　You may also like to think about how this intervention relates to <u>stage theories</u> of behaviour change (such as the <u>Rubicon model of action phases</u>), as well as the concept of a nudge (**Box 6.6**).
Weblinks	World Health Organization information on influenza: https://bit.ly/2LnYVU9 Information on influenza from the Oxford Vaccine Group: https://bit.ly/3m7ShxU

CHAPTER 12

BOX 12.3 HOW CAN WE PERSUADE PEOPLE TO WEAR FACE MASKS?

HOT TOPIC

Wearing a face mask in public can reduce the transmission of infectious diseases (Chu et al., 2020). However, prior to the COVID-19 pandemic, many people were unaccustomed to wearing a face mask and governments around the world had to engage in a range of different strategies to try to promote this practice. Could the theories we looked at in previous chapters have helped inform their approach?

A survey carried out in early 2020 indicated that people failed to wear face masks for a range of different reasons (Howard, 2020). These included:

- Difficulties obtaining a mask

- Discomfort and inconvenience

- A belief that they were unnecessary or ineffective

- Concerns about their appearance

- A belief that they were an infringement of freedom and independence.

Using the COM-B model, we can view difficulties in obtaining a mask as a barrier related to opportunity. This could be addressed by making masks easier to buy in supermarkets and local shops, for example by displaying them at the entrance or near the counter. They could also be made more readily available on public transport (for example at train stations) and in other spaces where wearing one is important.

According to the COM-B model, the other reasons for not wearing a mask predominantly reflect a lack of motivation. COM-B distinguishes between automatic motivation and reflective motivation, whilst PRIME theory predicts that automatic motivation will have stronger, more reliable effects on behaviour. So how can we increase people's automatic motivation to wear a mask?

One approach might be to associate mask wearing with positive emotions, for example using evaluative conditioning. The design and marketing of masks by companies and brands that already appeal to the target population could help achieve this (see **Case Study 8** for more information on the power of brands). Social marketing campaigns might also be helpful (see **Case Study 4**) as well as seeing public figures we like and admire wearing masks.

Another way of associating masks with strong emotions would be in terms of fear reduction (see protection motivation theory). In particular, some people may more naturally experience an automatic motivation to wear a mask because of anxiety over becoming ill, perhaps because they are part of an at-risk group and/or because they feel greater levels of health anxiety more generally. However, purposely increasing fear among the general public in order to promote mask wearing raises ethical concerns (**Box 5.7**) and may lead to unintended outcomes, for example in relation to mental health and people's willingness to engage in other important behaviours such as those relating to work and care responsibilities.

Alternative pathways to automatic motivation include habits as well as descriptive and injunctive social norms. However, habits only develop with repetition whilst descriptive norms rely on sufficient numbers of people carrying out the behaviour. Indeed, where few people wear masks, descriptive norms will further reduce mask use and may be why people report appearance-related concerns when wearing them.

Enforcing mask use, for example through legislation, could help change <u>injunctive norms</u> and also build habits and descriptive norms, though this approach may be difficult in countries where such rules are viewed as an infringement of liberties (**Chapter 11**).

According to COM-B, we can also influence behaviour via reflective motivation, for example by targeting relevant <u>attitudes</u> (beliefs) and <u>outcome expectancies</u>. This approach might draw on theories such as the <u>health belief model</u>, <u>protection motivation theory</u>,[5] the <u>theory of planned behaviour</u>, and <u>social cognitive theory</u>. For example, doubts about the necessity or effectiveness of masks could be addressed in educational campaigns and in information provided by those in positions of authority. Such an approach will be less effective where people receive inconsistent information, for example from scientists versus government or where those giving advice do not follow it themselves. The latter may also serve to undermine trust in experts and government, making people less willing to follow their advice (**Chapter 11**). However, providing consistent advice may sometimes be a challenge where clear evidence is lacking and there is no scientific consensus on an issue.

---

5 Arguably the health belief model and protection motivation theory are less relevant for mask wearing since these theories are specific to health protective behaviours whereas masks protect others more than oneself. Nevertheless, these theories are relevant to related behaviours such as handwashing and social distancing.

SAFE SEX

Types of sexually transmitted infections

Sexually transmitted infections (STIs) are caused by parasites (protozoa), bacteria or viruses and are predominantly spread through sexual contact. The risks of contracting an STI can therefore be reduced by practising safe sex, for example by using a **condom** or **dental dam**, by having fewer sexual partners, or by abstaining from sex. **Table 12.5** describes some of the most common STIs.

HIV and AIDS

HIV and AIDS represent a major global public health issue, having caused an estimated 32 million deaths to date (UNAIDS, 2019). The virus is thought to have first spread from chimpanzees to humans in the 1920s in Central Africa but it was not until 1981 that AIDS was identified in the US in a series of <u>case reports</u> describing previously healthy young, gay men living in Los Angeles (CDC, 1981; Faria et al., 2014). New HIV infections peaked in 1997, followed by a peak in AIDS-related deaths in 2004. However, rates of both new infections and deaths have since been steadily declining and more and more people are now able to access antiretroviral therapy (UNAIDS, 2019).

Condom – a thin, stretchy tube, usually made of latex, that is placed over a man's erect penis (male condom) or inside a women's vagina (female condom). The condom provides a barrier to help prevent both pregnancy and sexually transmitted infections.

Dental dam – a thin, soft square of latex or polyurethane that can be used to cover the genitals during oral sex, providing a barrier against sexually transmitted infections. (Dental dams were originally designed to block off teeth during dental surgery, hence the term 'dental'.)

CHAPTER 12

Table 12.5 Common STIs, their health effects and how they can be prevented and treated

Infection	Estimated global prevalence*	Transmission	Symptoms and effects	Treatment	Prevention
Trichomoniasis	156 million[1]	Caused by a tiny parasite (a protozoa) passed on through unprotected sex or genital contact (but not oral or anal sex).[2]	May cause abnormal discharge, soreness, itching or pain when passing urine or having sex. In pregnant women it may lead to premature birth or low birth weight. Up to half of all those infected do not develop symptoms.[2]	Antibiotics[2]	Condoms or dental dams[2].
Chlamydia	127.2 million[1]	A bacterial infection passed on through unprotected vaginal, anal or oral sex or genital contact. It can also be transmitted from mother to child during pregnancy and childbirth.[2]	Most people do not have symptoms though some may experience abnormal discharge, abdominal pain, or pain when passing urine. If left untreated, chlamydia can spread to other parts of the body, for example causing pelvic inflammatory disease, ectopic pregnancy and infertility.[2]	Antibiotics[2]	Condoms or dental dams[2].
Gonorrhoea	86.9 million[1]	Caused by bacteria passed on via unprotected vaginal, oral or anal sex. It can also be transmitted from mother to child during childbirth.[2]	Causes a thick green or yellow discharge and pain when urinating. However, around 1 in 10 men and half of women experience no symptoms. Without treatment it can spread to other parts of the body, for example causing pelvic inflammatory disease, ectopic pregnancy and infertility. In pregnant women it can cause miscarriage and premature birth, and eye infections in the newborn which, if not treated, can lead to blindness.[2]	Antibiotics[2]	Condoms or dental dams[2].

Syphilis	6.3 million[1]	Caused by a bacterial infection transmitted via unprotected vaginal, anal or oral sex. It can also be transmitted from mother to child during pregnancy and by sharing needles with a person who is infected.[2]	Early symptoms include a small, painless sore or ulcer and swollen glands. These may be followed by a rash on the hands or feet, small skin growths around the genitals, white patches in the mouth and flu-like symptoms such as headache and fever. These symptoms then disappear but, if left untreated, the infection can spread to other parts of the body, including the brain, eventually causing conditions such as meningitis, stroke, blindness and heart problems. Syphilis can also cause miscarriage and stillbirth.[2]	Antibiotics[2]	Condoms or dental dams[2].
Genital herpes	417 million[3]	Genital herpes is caused by the herpes simplex virus (HSV), the same type of virus that causes cold sores around the mouth. It is passed on through vaginal, oral or anal sex or via fingers. It can also be transmitted from mother to child during childbirth, though usually only where the mother has acquired the virus in the last 6 weeks of pregnancy.[2]	The virus causes outbreaks of small, painful blisters around the genitals, as well as tingling, burning or itching and pain when urinating. Over time outbreaks tend to get less severe and some people never have outbreaks, which means they may be unaware that they have the virus. In newborns (neonatal herpes), it can be fatal if left untreated.[2]	Like the version of the virus that causes cold sores around the mouth, there is no cure. However, antiviral medicines can shorten outbreaks and cream can be used to reduce discomfort.[2]	Condoms and dental dams reduce the chances of infection, though transmission can still occur if these do not cover the infected area.[2]
Human papillomavirus (HPV)	There are many different types of HPV. Most sexually active men and women will be infected with at least one type at some point in their lives.[4] An estimated 291 million women are currently carriers of cervical HPV.[5]	HPV is the most common type of viral infection of the reproductive tract. It is transmitted by any kind of sexual activity including touching.[2]	Most types of HPV cause no symptoms or problems.[4] However, some types cause genital warts and other types increase the risk of certain cancers. In particular, nearly 90% of cervical cancers can be attributed to just nine types of HPV.[6]	There is no cure for HPV but most infections are fought off by the body and disappear within a couple of years. Warts may be treated topically or with surgery or freezing. Cervical cancer is treated with radiotherapy, chemotherapy and/or surgery.[2]	Condoms and dental dams reduce transmission. Vaccination against the types of HPV that most often cause cervical cancer and genital warts are also available. The WHO recommends girls aged 9 to 14 years are vaccinated.[4]

(continued)

Table 12.5 (continued)

Infection	Estimated global prevalence*	Transmission	Symptoms and effects	Treatment	Prevention
Hepatitis B (HBV)	257 million[7]	Transmitted via exposure to infected blood or bodily fluids, for example from unprotected sex, shared needles, syringes and razors, or during childbirth.[7]	Hepatitis B infects the liver. Many adults who acquire the infection fight it off without developing symptoms. Others develop flu-like symptoms and **jaundice** 2 to 3 months after exposure. This type of acute hepatitis usually passes within 1 to 3 months though in some cases it may develop into chronic hepatitis. Symptoms of chronic hepatitis can be quite mild, but without treatment may eventually lead to **cirrhosis** and liver cancer. Chronic hepatitis occurs in less than 5% of cases when adults become infected but in around 90% of cases when infection occurs in infancy.[2,7]	There is no cure for hepatitis B but antivirals can slow the progression of cirrhosis and reduce the incidence of liver cancer.[7]	Vaccination is 98–100% effective. The WHO recommends all infants receive the vaccine within 24 hours of birth.[7]

Jaundice – when the skin and whites of the eyes turn yellow as a result of a build-up of bilirubin in the blood. Bilirubin is produced when red blood cells are broken down and is normally processed by the liver. Excess bilirubin could occur for a number of different reasons, including liver disease, sickle cell disease or, in newborns, simply because the liver is not quite fully developed.

Cirrhosis – scarring of the liver caused by liver damage. The scarring stops the liver from working properly and may eventually lead to liver failure. Cirrhosis may be caused by chronic hepatitis or high alcohol intake over a prolonged period of time (typically 10 years or more).

Human immunodeficiency virus (HIV)	37.9 million[8]	Acquired through the exchange of infected blood, breast milk, semen and vaginal secretions. This means it can be transmitted via unprotected sex, shared needles and syringes, pregnancy, childbirth and breastfeeding.[8]	HIV attacks the immune system, progressively weakening the person's ability to fight off infections and certain types of cancer. If left untreated it leads to acquired immunodeficiency syndrome (AIDS) within 2 to 15 years. This is where the immune system has become so damaged the person experiences life-threatening infections and illnesses.[2,8]	There is no readily available cure** though antiretroviral therapy (ART) can supress the virus to prevent the individual from getting AIDS.[2,8]	Condoms and dental dams help protect against HIV and ART prevents transmission. Antiretroviral medicine in the form of a pill can also be taken daily or before sex to prevent a person from acquiring HIV. Male circumcision reduces the risk of heterosexually acquired infection by about 60%.[8]

Notes:

1 Rowley et al. (2019); 2 NHS (2020); 3 Looker et al. (2015); 4 WHO (2019d); 5 De Sanjosé et al. (2007); 6 de Martel et al., (2017); 7 WHO (2019b); 8 WHO (2019c)

*The world's population was 7.8 billion in 2020, so 780 million represents 10% of the population, whilst 78 million represents 1%.

**Two individuals have been cured of HIV using stem-cell treatment, where stem cells from a donor with a rare gene that protects them against HIV, have been used to replace the patient's own immune cells (Gupta et al., 2020). However, this is a high-risk treatment that would be used as a last resort only, not as a replacement for antiretroviral therapy.

CHAPTER 12

Nevertheless, rates of HIV among marginalised (or 'hard-to-reach') communities can be very resistant to change. For example, compared to the general population, the risks of acquiring HIV are 22 times higher among men who have sex with men, 22 times higher among those who inject drugs, and 21 times higher among sex workers (UNAIDS, 2019). Increasing efforts to reach such communities has meant the methods employed by those working in health promotion have evolved over time (Campbell & Cornish, 2010). This changing pattern of approaches can be summarised as follows:

- *Individual-focussed approaches* – these provide information and advice in order to raise awareness of HIV and how best to avoid it. This type of approach tends to draw on social cognition models, for example targeting individual perceptions of risks, costs and benefits.

- *Peer-based approaches* – these train members of a community to disseminate skills as well as information. This type of approach can be seen to draw on elements of social cognitive theory as well as social norms.

- *Community mobilisation* – where the community is targeted to create contexts that support individual behaviour change and the development of health-enhancing group norms. One could argue that community mobilisation removes barriers that limit the success of individual- and peer-based approaches. In particular, community mobilisation aims to increase social capital (advantageous social networks, see **Chapter 3**), safe social spaces for dialogue (where new information can be discussed) and empowerment (involving community members in efforts to bring about changes that would benefit them). The latter is thought to result in **spillover effects** whereby successfully gaining control over one aspect of their lives gives people the confidence to pursue control in other areas of their lives (such as their health, see also locus of control, **Chapter 4**). Most community mobilisation initiatives take a participatory, 'bottom-up' approach, where members of the community identify their needs and are heavily involved in the design and implementation of the intervention. This is in contrast to more traditional 'top-down' approaches where interventions are developed by external 'experts' who impart their knowledge and skills to 'non-experts' (Dasgupta, 2019).

> **Spillover effect** – a term used in a range of different disciplines. In psychology it refers to instances in which changing one behaviour also brings about changes to other behaviours (Dolan & Galizzi, 2015). Spillover effects can either enhance or undermine the effects of the original behaviour. For example, going for a run may prompt a person to 'keep up the good work' by selecting something healthy to eat for tea. Or it could be used to justify sitting on the sofa all evening, eating chocolate.

- *Structural (or macro-social) interventions* – approaches that target the wider context within which community mobilisation efforts take place, specifically the material context (access to material resources), relational context (links with respected external organisations or individuals) and symbolic context (such as social status and stigmatisation). For example, policies to reduce financial insecurity, laws to help combat violence against women, increased access to non-stigmatising sexual health clinics and decriminalisation of sex work are all examples of structural interventions. Thus structural interventions address factors that are outside the control of the individual including the unequal distribution of power and resources. Health psychologists sometimes refer to such factors as distal predictors of behaviour, to contrast with more proximal predictors such as attitudes and intentions.

Whilst elements of individual- and peer-based approaches (especially information and skills) may be deemed necessary for behaviour change, they are not always sufficient. For example, peer-led interventions have had some success in more affluent communities where there is already a strong sense of identity and supportive social networks (such as gay communities in the US). However, peer-based approaches have not always been successful among more marginalised groups (for example among sex workers in South Africa). Likewise, whilst community mobilisation can be effective, it can also be very hard to achieve (Campbell & Cornish, 2010; Cornish et al., 2014). In essence, the more affluent and educated the community, the more likely it is that individual- and peer-based approaches will be effective. But among more deprived and marginalised groups, a greater range of intervention strategies will be needed to address the wider social and economic barriers these individuals face. **Case Study 11** provides an example of an intervention that started out using a peer-based approach but evolved into community mobilisation.

CASE STUDY 11

THE SONAGACHI PROJECT: COMMUNITY EMPOWERMENT FOR SEX WORKERS

Background	Female sex workers in India suffer from poverty, stigma and high rates of illiteracy. Many are struggling to support children as well as themselves and have resorted to sex work after being widowed or abandoned by their husbands. Their marginalised position makes it difficult for them to access things that might help improve their situation, such as healthcare, education or small bridging loans. For example, banks usually require official documentation such as a birth certificate or identity card, healthcare typically entails fees, and stigma can lead to women and children being made to feel unwelcome at schools and clinics or being actively excluded by staff (Gangopadhyay et al., 2005).
	Sonagachi, in Kolkata, is the largest red-light district in both India and Southeast Asia, with over 50,000 sex workers. The Sonagachi Project began in 1992 as a peer-based intervention designed to reduce HIV transmission, but it soon evolved into community mobilisation (Dasgupta, 2019; Jana et al., 2004).
Intervention	Public health funding was used to employ 12 sex workers from Sonagachi as peer outreach workers. They were given a caseload of sex workers to visit on a weekly basis where they provided information about HIV, distributed free condoms, gave free medication and antibiotics for infections, inquired about health difficulties and tried to assist with other problems. The training that was provided to the outreach workers emphasised the importance of viewing clients as peers rather than victims and of having a respectful and non-judgemental attitude. This approach was coupled with a reframing of HIV as an occupational health issue rather than a moral or criminal issue; prostitution was redefined as a legitimate way of earning money to support oneself and one's family. By implication this meant that, like other workers, sex workers could unite to fight for their rights (**Image 12.11**).
	Sexual health clinics were also established in the area and outreach workers encouraged women to attend these. In addition to sexual healthcare they provided free general healthcare for sex workers and their children. In 1995 women in Sonagachi formed a union, the Durbar Mahila Samanwaya Committee (DMSC), to fight for greater rights and to represent their interests to more powerful groups. Their activities included:

- Mediating in disputes with brothel managers and clients and helping to get women released from custody after police raids.
- Influencing journalists and politicians.
- Demanding social change, such as getting children into local schools.
- Facilitating access to registration cards for voting and to government benefits such as ration cards for subsidised food.
- Taking over a literacy programme to help sex workers and their children learn to read and write.
- Setting up a local cooperative bank to provide micro loans and to help women save money to cover emergencies or for investments such as building a home for their retirement or marrying off a daughter. The bank granted small loans with interest rates at 15%, substantially lower than the 50% rate sex workers might be charged elsewhere.
- In 1999 the DMSC took over the running of the sexual health clinic (Jana et al., 2004).

CHAPTER 12

Image 12.11 *Sex workers in Sonagachi demanding workers' rights.*
Credit: SOPA Images/LightRocket/Getty Images.

Evidence and evaluation	It is easy to see why it is not possible for this type of intervention to be evaluated using <u>RCT</u> methods. In particular, the nature of the intervention, as well as some of the important outcomes, evolved over time, rather than being identified beforehand. The timescale of these changes was also too lengthy for an RCT to have been feasible, and the community-level cluster likely too large to allow for the recruitment of a sufficient number of similar clusters. Additionally, community members may have found randomisation to trial arms unacceptable (see Bonell et al., 2006).
	Nevertheless, research examining rates of HIV infection and condom use suggest the project had a positive impact. In particular, in the late 1990s rates of HIV among sex workers in other Indian cities (Mumbai, Delhi, Chennai) were reported to be between 50% and 90%, whereas in Kolcatta they were reported to be around 11%. Condom use in Kolcatta also rose from 3% in 1992 to 90% in 1999 (Jana et al., 2004).
	A more recent systematic review of community mobilisation interventions for HIV prevention in low- and middle-income countries suggests they tend to have a positive effect amongst high-risk groups (particularly sex workers). Effects seem to be stronger where there is already a meaningful collective identity, and where they are accompanied by wider structural changes. However, the context-dependent nature of community mobilisation makes replications and RCT evaluation difficult (Cornish et al., 2014).
Relevant theory and concepts	The Sonagachi Project was not informed by theory (Jana et al., 2004). However, one can identify links with theories and concepts covered in previous chapters. For example, the use of peer educators can be linked to <u>social cognitive theory</u> and the emphasis on respect and non-judgement overlaps with some of the principles behind <u>motivational interviewing</u> and <u>self-determination theory</u>. As described above, we can also see connections with the concepts of <u>social capital</u> and <u>locus of control.</u>
	Nevertheless, the Sonagachi Project also highlights the limitations of psychological theory, and of social cognition models in particular, since these tend to predict behaviour from variables located within the individual (such as attitudes and beliefs) whilst saying little about how the social context might moderate either the effects of an intervention on such variables or the effects of such variables on behaviour.

| A sociological account of the intervention | Sociology is the study of societies, communities and groups, so many community mobilisation projects have been developed by sociologists or those working at the cross-section of psychology and sociology. A sociological account of the Sonagachi Project is provided by Campbell and Cornish (2012), who describe how it initially started out as 'technical communication' (the transfer of factual knowledge and technical skills), but subsequently evolved to include 'transformative communication' in which the community began to see their risks of infection as a result of wider political and economic factors, which in turn motivated them to address these issues. Campbell and Cornish maintain that whilst technical communication is necessary for improving the health of marginalised groups, it is not sufficient because it fails to address the power and resource inequalities that limit a person's choices. For example, if a woman has no savings and needs money to feed her child, it is difficult for her to turn away a client who wants sex without a condom, or to turn down extra money for condom-less sex. Campbell and Cornish argue that dominant groups do not voluntarily give up power or resources unless there is some personal, political or economic pressure to do so. Transformative communication helps marginalised groups work together to create such pressures, for example by organising disruptive protests or supporting particular political candidates (see also Campbell, 2019). |
| Weblinks | Website for UNAIDS, the Joint United Nations Programme on HIV and AIDS. The website includes information on HIV and AIDS as well as community-based projects around the world: www.unaids.org |

CONCLUSIONS: KEY ISSUES FOR HEALTH PSYCHOLOGY AND BEHAVIOUR CHANGE

In earlier chapters we looked at the science of behaviour change, in terms of evidence, theory and research methods. In this chapter we've used a series of case studies to take a more detailed look at behaviour change in practice. It should be apparent from these examples that there is sometimes a gap between science and practice. In this final section we consider some of the reasons for this gap as well as how the discipline might move forward.

Theory is important, but not always essential

In **Chapter 5** we emphasised the importance of theory and in **Chapter 9** we discussed the use of theory in intervention development. However, in this chapter we've looked at a number of successful interventions that were developed without any grounding in formal theory – the This Girl Can campaign (**Case Study 4**) was informed by social marketing principles; motivational interviewing (**Case Study 9**) was developed from practitioner observation; the Sonagachi Project (**Case Study 11**) grew from the community identifying its own needs. In each case, relevant expertise enabled people to recognise *what* would work, even if they couldn't fully explain *why* and *how* it would work. As discussed in **Chapter 5**, understanding why and how something works (having a theory that identifies mediators and moderators) can help us successfully adapt an intervention, or apply it to a new setting or population. This makes theory more powerful than facts. However, this does not mean theory should always come before practice. Good theory takes time to develop and health crises do not wait. So sometimes we need to work the other way around – in other words, do what seems to work and think about theory later.

We rarely have perfect evidence, so must act on the best evidence we have

In **Chapter 10** we looked at different types of evidence and thought about why evidence from randomised controlled trials (RCTs) and meta-analyses is considered the most robust. However, none of the interventions described in this chapter were underpinned by meta-analyses of RCTs. This type of conclusive evidence is especially lacking for large-scale policy interventions where a country is one of the first to implement such measures, for example the sugar tax in Mexico (**Case Study 2**) or plain tobacco packaging in Australia (**Case Study 8**). It is easy for critics to claim there is 'no good evidence' to support such approaches (**Chapter 11**), but this should not mean we default to inaction. Often, we cannot afford to wait for better evidence, so we simply have to act on the basis of the evidence we have. Likewise, it is easy for critics to argue that scientists 'got it wrong'. But science is rarely black and white or 100% certain. On the contrary, it is always a work in progress. As such, we can only make decisions and give advice according to the best evidence we have at the time and, where necessary, revise decisions and advice as more evidence becomes available. It should be okay for scientists and policy makers to change their minds. This should be viewed as a sign of progress not failure.

Context is critical, and absent from most theories of behaviour change

The things that influence our behaviour are both numerous and complex. They range from individual attitudes and predispositions to macro-level ('contextual') variables relating to the social, political and economic environment. This complexity is especially highlighted by the Sonagachi Project (**Case Study 11**) and by subsequent failures to replicate this intervention elsewhere (Campbell & Cornish, 2012). In **Chapter 1** we introduced the biopsychosocial model of health that incorporates these different types of influences, and in **Chapter 3** we examined some of the ways in which social and economic factors can affect a person's health and psychology. However, many of the theories of behaviour change we examined in **Chapters 5, 6, 7 and 8** focus on individual variables, referring to macro-level factors simply as 'barriers' (social cognitive theory) or 'demographic variables' that influence attitudes and norms (theory of planned behaviour). As such, these theories say little about how these variables might interact with other variables and moderate effects or how we might change macro-level factors in order to change behaviour. This limits the utility of these theories, particularly in contexts where people have less autonomy over their day-to-day lives.

A complete theory of behaviour change may never be possible

In principle, we could develop ever more complex theories that incorporate multiple variables of the types described in **Chapter 3** (such as social and economic variables) and **Chapter 4** (such as physiological and trait variables). However, in practice this may be hard to achieve at a rate that is useful, particularly for the types of macro-level variables touched upon in **Chapter 3**. Unlike human biology that evolves very slowly, human societies are subject to much more rapid change; contextual variables such as poverty, stigma and discrimination are in constant flux. The meanings we attach to certain things (such as breasts and breastfeeding, see **Case Study 7**) are also subject to much variation over time, place and person. This can make it difficult to extract general principles from any particular set of data, and to create theory that can be broadly applied. In a constantly changing world, theories of human behaviour may have their limits. This does not mean we should give up trying to develop good theory, rather that we should be open to other forms of evidence and recognise the value of different approaches to behaviour change, such as the more bottom-up approach taken in the Sonagachi Project (**Case Study 11**).

To tackle big issues, we need to work across disciplines

Regardless of the feasibility of a complete theory of behaviour change, the importance of interdisciplinary thinking is clear. For example, to integrate macro-level effects into models of behaviour change, we need sociologists, economists and geographers. To better understand the way individual differences moderate individual responses, we need geneticists, neuroscientists and biologists. And to develop innovative behaviour change interventions, we have much to learn from those working in marketing, computer science and the arts. As described in **Chapter 2**, over the last century we've made enormous advances in population health. By combining efforts across disciplines, we may just be able to repeat such gains over the course of the next century.

REFERENCES

Aarts, H., Dijksterhuis, A.P. & Midden, C. (1999). To plan or not to plan? Goal achievement or interrupting the performance of mundane behaviors. *European Journal of Social Psychology*, 29(8), 971–979.

Abraham, C. (2016). Charting variability to ensure conceptual and design precision: A comment on Ogden (2016). *Health Psychology Review*, 10(3), 260–264.

Abraham, C. & Sheeran, P. (2015). The health belief model. In M. Conner and P. Norman (eds.). *Predicting and Changing Health Behaviour. Research and Practice with Social Cognition Models*. Maidenhead: Open University Press.

Abraham, C.S., Sheeran, P., Abrams, D. & Spears, R. (1994). Exploring teenagers' adaptive and maladaptive thinking in relation to the threat of HIV infection. *Psychology and Health*, 9, 253–272.

Achtziger, A. & Gollwitzer, P.M. (2008). Motivation and volition in the course of action. In J. Heckenhausen and H. Heckenhausen (eds.). *Motivation and Action*. New York: Cambridge University Press.

Achtziger, A., Bayer, U.C. & Gollwitzer, P.M. (2012). Committing to implementation intentions: Attention and memory effects for selected situational cues. *Motivation and Emotion*, 36(3), 287–300.

Adam, T.C. & Epel, E.S. (2007). Stress, eating and the reward system. *Physiology & Behavior*, 91(4), 449–458.

Adriaanse, M.A., De Ridder, D.T. & De Wit, J.B. (2009). Finding the critical cue: Implementation intentions to change one's diet work best when tailored to personally relevant reasons for unhealthy eating. *Personality and Social Psychology Bulletin*, 35(1), 60–71.

Adriaanse, M.A., Oettingen, G., Gollwitzer, P.M., Hennes, E.P., De Ridder, D.T. & De Wit, J.B. (2010). When planning is not enough: Fighting unhealthy snacking habits by mental contrasting with implementation intentions (MCII). *European Journal of Social Psychology*, 40(7), 1277–1293.

Adriaanse, M.A., Vinkers, C.D., De Ridder, D.T., Hox, J.J. & De Wit, J.B. (2011). Do implementation intentions help to eat a healthy diet? A systematic review and meta-analysis of the empirical evidence. *Appetite*, 56(1), 183–193.

Afshin, A., Sur, P.J., Fay, K.A., Cornaby, L., Ferrara, G., Salama, J.S., ... & Afarideh, M. (2019). Health effects of dietary risks in 195 countries, 1990–2017: a systematic analysis for the Global Burden of Disease Study 2017. *The Lancet*, 393(10184), 1958–1972.

Ainsworth, B.E., Haskell, W.L., Whitt, M.C., Irwin, M.L., Swartz, A.M., Strath, S.J., ... & Jacobs, D.R. (2000). Compendium of physical activities: an update of activity codes and MET intensities. *Medicine and Science in Sports and Exercise*, 32(9; SUPP/1), S498–S504.

Ajzen, I. (1991). The theory of planned behavior. *Organizational Behavior and Human Decision Processes*, 50, 179–211.

Ajzen, I. (2005). *Attitudes, Personality and Behavior*. (2nd edn). Maidenhead: Open University Press.

Ajzen, I. (2014). The theory of planned behaviour is alive and well, and not ready to retire: a commentary on Sniehotta, Presseau, and Araújo-Soares. *Health Psychology Review*, 9, 131–137.

Albarracín, D., Johnson, B.T., Fishbein, M. & Muellerleile, P.A. (2001). Theories of reasoned action and planned behaviour as models on condom use: a meta-analysis. *Psychological Bulletin*, 127, 142–161.

Albrecht, L., Archibald, M., Arseneau, D. & Scott, S.D. (2013). Development of a checklist to assess the quality of reporting of knowledge translation interventions using the Workgroup for Intervention Development and Evaluation Research (WIDER) recommendations. *Implementation Science*, 8(1), 52.

Ali, M., Nelson, A. R., Lopez, A. L. & Sack, D. A. (2015). Updated global burden of cholera in endemic countries. *PLoS Neglected Tropical Diseases*, 9(6).

Allan, J.L., Sniehotta, F.F. & Johnston, M. (2013). The best laid plans: Planning skill determines the effectiveness of action plans and implementation intentions. *Annals of Behavioral Medicine*, 46(1), 114–120.

Allen, M.S., Walter, E.E. & McDermott, M.S. (2017). Personality and sedentary behavior: A systematic review and meta-analysis. *Health Psychology*, 36(3), 255.

Allom, V., Mullan, B. & Hagger, M. (2016). Does inhibitory control training improve health behaviour?

A meta-analysis. *Health Psychology Review*, 10(2), 168–186.

Almada, S.J., Zonderman, A.B., Shekelle, R.B., Dyer, A.R., Daviglus, M.L., Costa, P.T. & Stamler, J. (1991). Neuroticism and cynicism and risk of death in middle-aged men: the Western Electric Study. *Psychosomatic Medicine*, 53, 165–175.

Almirall, D., Nahum-Shani, I., Sherwood, N.E. & Murphy, S.A. (2014). Introduction to SMART designs for the development of adaptive interventions: with application to weight loss research. *Translational Behavioral Medicine*, 4(3), 260–274.

Althoff, T., Hicks, J.L., King, A.C., Delp, S.L. & Leskovec, J. (2017). Large-scale physical activity data reveal worldwide activity inequality. *Nature*, 547(7663), 336.

Alton, E.W.F.W., Armstrong, D.K., Ashby, D., Bayfield, K.J., Bilton, D., ...Wolstenholme-Hogg, P. (2015). Repeated nebulisation of non-viral *CFTR* gene therapy in patients with cystic fibrosis: a randomised, double-blind, placebo-controlled, phase 2b trial. *Lancet Respiratory Medicine*, 3, 684–691.

American Psychiatric Association (2013). *Diagnostic and Statistical Manual of Mental Disorders*. (5th edn.) Arlington, VA: American Psychiatric Publishing.

Amlung, M., Vedelago, L., Acker, J., Balodis, I. & MacKillop, J. (2017). Steep delay discounting and addictive behavior: a meta-analysis of continuous associations. *Addiction*, 112(1), 51–62.

Ammerman, A.S., Lindquist, C.H., Lohr, K.N. & Hersey, J. (2002). The efficacy of behavioral interventions to modify dietary fat and fruit and vegetable intake: a review of the evidence. *Preventive Medicine*, 35(1), 25–41.

Anderson, B.A. (2017). Going for it: The economics of automaticity in perception and action. *Current Directions in Psychological Science*, 26(2), 140–145.

Anderson, B.A., Laurent, P.A. & Yantis, S. (2011). Value-driven attentional capture. *Proceedings of the National Academy of Sciences*, 108(25), 10367–10371.

Andrade, J., Pears, S., May, J. & Kavanagh, D.J. (2012). Use of a clay modeling task to reduce chocolate craving. *Appetite*, 58(3), 955–963.

Andreas, N.J., Kampmann, B. & Le-Doare, K.M. (2015). Human breast milk: A review on its composition and bioactivity. *Early Human Development*, 91(11), 629–635.

Anselme, P. (2016). Motivational control of sign-tracking behaviour: A theoretical framework. *Neuroscience & Biobehavioral Reviews*, 65, 1–20.

Anzman, S.L. & Birch, L.L. (2009). Low inhibitory control and restrictive feeding practices predict weight outcomes. *The Journal of Pediatrics*, 155(5), 651–656.

Apolzan, J.W., Myers, C.A., Champagne, C.M., Beyl, R.A., Raynor, H.A., Anton, S.A., ... & Martin, C.K. (2017). Frequency of consuming foods predicts changes in cravings for those foods during weight loss: The POUNDS Lost Study. *Obesity*, 25(8), 1343–1348.

Appleton, K.M., Barrie, E. & Samuel, T.J. (2019). Modelling positive consequences: Increased vegetable intakes following modelled enjoyment versus modelled intake. *Appetite*, 140, 76–81.

Arain, M., Campbell, M.J., Cooper, C.L. & Lancaster, G.A. (2010). What is a pilot or feasibility study? A review of current practice and editorial policy. *BMC Medical Research Methodology*, 10(1), 67.

Arden, M.A. & Armitage, C.J. (2012). A volitional help sheet to reduce binge drinking in students: a randomized exploratory trial. *Alcohol and Alcoholism*, 47(2), 156–159.

Ariely, D. & Wertenbroch, K. (2002). Procrastination, deadlines, and performance: self-control by precommitment. *Psychological Science*, 13, 219-2–224.

Armitage, C.J. (2004). Evidence that implementation intentions reduce dietary fat intake: a randomized trial. *Health Psychology*, 23(3), 319.

Armitage, C.J. (2007). Efficacy of a brief worksite intervention to reduce smoking: the roles of behavioral and implementation intentions. *Journal of Occupational Health Psychology*, 12(4), 376.

Armitage, C.J. (2008). A volitional help sheet to encourage smoking cessation: a randomized exploratory trial. *Health Psychology*, 27(5), 557.

Armitage, C.J. (2009). Effectiveness of experimenter-provided and self-generated implementation intentions to reduce alcohol consumption in a sample of the general population: a randomized exploratory trial. *Health Psychology*, 28(5), 545.

Armitage, C.J. (2015a). Field experiment of a very brief worksite intervention to improve nutrition among health care workers. *Journal of Behavioral Medicine*, 38(4), 599–608.

Armitage, C.J. (2015b). Evidence that a volitional help sheet reduces alcohol consumption among smokers: A pilot randomized controlled trial. *Behavior Therapy*, 46(3), 342–349.

Armitage, C.J. (2016). Evidence that implementation intentions can overcome the effects of smoking habits. *Health Psychology*, 35(9), 935.

Armitage, C.J. & Arden, M.A. (2008). How useful are the stages of change for targeting interventions? Randomized test of a brief intervention to reduce smoking. *Health Psychology*, 27(6), 789.

Armitage, C.J. & Arden, M.A. (2010). A volitional help sheet to increase physical activity in people with low socioeconomic status: a randomised exploratory trial. *Psychology and Health*, *25*(10), 1129–1145.

Armitage, C.J. & Arden, M.A. (2012). A volitional help sheet to reduce alcohol consumption in the general population: a field experiment. *Prevention Science*, *13*(6), 635–643.

Armitage, C.J. & Conner, M. (2001). Efficacy of the theory of planned behaviour: a meta-analytic review. *British Journal of Social Psychology*, *40*, 471–499.

Armitage, C.J., Alganem, S. & Norman, P. (2017). Randomized Controlled Trial of a Volitional Help Sheet to Encourage Weight Loss in the Middle East. *Prevention Science*, *18*(8), 976–983.

Armitage, C.J., Harris, P.R. & Arden, M.A. (2011). Evidence that self-affirmation reduces alcohol consumption: randomized exploratory trial with a new, brief means of self-affirming. *Health Psychology*, *30*(5), 633.

Armitage, C.J., Norman, P., Noor, M., Alganem, S. & Arden, M.A. (2014). Evidence that a very brief psychological intervention boosts weight loss in a weight loss program. *Behavior Therapy*, *45*(5), 700–707.

Asaria, M., Ali, S., Doran, T., Ferguson, B., Fleetcroft, R., Goddard, M., Goldblatt, P., Laudicella, M., Raine, R. & Cookson, R. (2016). How a universal health system reduces inequalities: lessons from England. *Journal of Epidemiology and Community Health*, *70*, 637–643.

ASH (2019). Fact sheet: use of e-cigarettes among young people in Great Britain. https://ash.org.uk/wp-content/uploads/2019/06/ASH-Factsheet-Youth-E-cigarette-Use-2019.pdf

Aspen, V.A., Stein, R.I. & Wilfley, D.E. (2012). An exploration of salivation patterns in normal weight and obese children. *Appetite*, *58*, 539–542.

Astrup, A. (2011). The relevance of increased fat oxidation for body-weight management: metabolic inflexibility in the predisposition to weight gain. *Obesity Reviews*, *12*, 859–865.

Audrain-McGovern, J., Rodriguez, D., Epstein, L. H., Cuevas, J., Rodgers, K. & Wileyto, E.P. (2009). Does delay discounting play an etiological role in smoking or is it a consequence of smoking? *Drug and Alcohol Dependence*, *103*(3), 99–106.

Aune, D., Giovannucci, E., Boffetta, P., Fadnes, L.T., Keum, N., Norat, T., … & Tonstad, S. (2017). Fruit and vegetable intake and the risk of cardiovascular disease, total cancer and all-cause mortality—a systematic review and dose-response meta-analysis of prospective studies. *International Journal of Epidemiology*, *46*(3), 1029–1056.

Aune, D., Keum, N., Giovannucci, E., Fadnes, L.T., Boffetta, P., Greenwood, D.C. … & Norat, T. (2016).

Whole grain consumption and risk of cardiovascular disease, cancer, and all cause and cause specific mortality: systematic review and dose-response meta-analysis of prospective studies. *British Medical Journnal*, *353*.

Australian DoH (2016). Post-implementation review of tobacco plain packaging. https://ris.pmc.gov.au/2016/02/26/tobacco-plain-packaging

Australian Government (2011). Tobacco plain packaging regulations. www.legislation.gov.au/Details/F2013C00801/Html/Text#_Toc367282493

Australian Institute of Health and Welfare (2019). Indicators of socioeconomic inequalities in cardiovascular disease, diabetes and chronic kidney disease. www.aihw.gov.au/reports-data/behaviours-risk-factors/social-determinants/data

Avena, N.M., Rada, P. & Hoebel, B.G. (2008). Evidence for sugar addiction: behavioral and neurochemical effects of intermittent, excessive sugar intake. *Neuroscience & Biobehavioral Reviews*, *32*(1), 20–39.

Aveyard, P., Lawrence, T., Cheng, K.K., Griffin, C., Croghan, E. & Johnson, C. (2006). A randomized controlled trial of smoking cessation for pregnant women to test the effect of a transtheoretical model-based intervention on a movement in stage and interaction with baseline stage. *British Journal of Health Psychology*, *11*, 263–278.

Aveyard, P., Yach, D., Gilmore, A.B. & Capewell, S. (2016). Should we welcome food industry funding of public health research?. *British Medical Journal*, *353*, i2161.

Axon, R.N., Bradford, W.D. & Egan, B.M. (2009). The role of individual time preferences in health behaviors among hypertensive adults: a pilot study. *Journal of the American Society of Hypertension*, *3*(1), 35–41.

Bacon, L. & Aphramor, L. (2011). Weight science: evaluating the evidence for a paradigm shift. *Nutrition Journal*, *10*(1), 9.

Bailey, Z.D., Krieger, N., Agénor, M., Graves, J., Linos, N. & Bassett, M.T. (2017). Structural racism and health inequities in the USA: evidence and interventions. *The Lancet*, *389*(10077), 1453–1463.

Ball, H.L. & Volpe, L.E. (2013). Sudden infant death syndrome (SIDS) risk reduction and infant sleep location – moving the discussion forward. *Social Science and Medicine*, *79*, 84–91.

Bandura, A. (1977). *Social Learning Theory*. Englewood Cliffs, NJ: Prentice-Hall.

Bandura, A. (1986). *Social Foundations of Thought and Action: A Social Cognitive Theory*. Englewood Cliffs, NJ: Prentice-Hall.

Bandura, A. (1997). *Self-efficacy: The Exercise of Control*. New York: Freeman.

Bandura, A. (1998). Health promotion from the perspective of social cognitive theory. *Psychology and Health, 13*, 623–649.

Bandura, A. (2009). Cultivate self-efficacy for personal and organisational effectiveness. In E.A. Locke (ed.). *Handbook of Principles of Organization Behaviour.* (2nd edn) (pp. 179-200). New York: Wiley.

Banerjee, A.V., Duflo, E., Glennerster, R. & Kothari, D. (2010). Improving immunisation coverage in rural India: clustered randomised controlled evaluation of immunisation campaigns with and without incentives. *British Medical Journal, 340*, c2220.

Banning, C. (1946). Food shortage and public health, first half of 1945. *The Annals of the American Academy of Political and Social Science, 245*, 93–110.

Barefoot, J.C., Maynard, K.E., Beckham, J.C., Brummett, B.H., Hooker, K. & Siegler, I. (1998). Trust, health, and longevity. *Journal of Behavioral Medicine, 21*, 517–526.

Bargh, J.A. (1994). The four horsemen of automaticity: awareness, intention, efficiency, and control in social cognition. In R. S. Wyer & T. K. Srull (eds.). *Handbook of Social Cognition* (Vol. 1). Hillsdale, NJ: Erlbaum.

Bargh, J.A. (2016). Awareness of the prime versus awareness of its influence: implications for the real-world scope of unconscious higher mental processes. *Current Opinion in Psychology, 12*, 49–52.

Bargh, J.A., Chen, M. & Burrows, L. (1996). Automaticity of social behavior: Direct effects of trait construct and stereotype activation on action. *Journal of Personality and Social Psychology, 71*(2), 230.

Bar-Haim, Y., Lamy, D., Pergamin, L., Bakermans-Kranenburg, M.J. & Van Ijzendoorn, M.H. (2007). Threat-related attentional bias in anxious and nonanxious individuals: a meta-analytic study. *Psychological Bulletin, 133*, 1–24.

Barlow, P., Reeves, A., McKee, M., Galea, G. & Stuckler, D. (2016). Unhealthy diets, obesity and time discounting: a systematic literature review and network analysis. *Obesity Reviews, 17*(9), 810–819.

Barnicot, N.A., Bennett, F.J., Woodburn, J.C., Pilkington, T.R.E. & Antonis, A. (1972). Blood pressure and serum cholesterol in the Hadza of Tanzania. *Human Biology, 44*, 87–116.

Baron, R.M. & Kenny, D.A. (1986). The moderator-mediator variable distinction in social psychological research: Conceptual, strategic, and statistical considerations. *Journal of Personality and Social Psychology, 51*(6), 1173.

Barquera, S., Campos-Nonato, I., Hernandez-Barrera, L., Pedroza, A. & Rivera-Dommarco, J. A. (2013). Prevalence of obesity in Mexican adults 2000-2012. *Salud Publica de Mexico, 55*, S151–60.

Barquera, S., Hernandez-Barrera, L., Tolentino, M.L., Espinosa, J., Ng, S.W., Rivera, J.A. & Popkin, B.M. (2008). Energy intake from beverages is increasing among Mexican adolescents and adults. *The Journal of Nutrition, 138*(12), 2454–2461.

Barr, S. (2018, June 22). Mother bans children from eating birthday cake because 'sugar has the same effect on the brain as cocaine'. *The Independent* www.independent.co.uk/life-style/health-and-families/mother-birthday-cake-children-ban-sugar-obesity-good-morning-britain-a8411976.html

Barrett J. (2019). Decorated with butterflies, infant-sized coffins sent to measles-ravaged Samoa. www.reuters.com/article/us-health-measles-samoa/decorated-with-butterflies-infant-sized-coffins-sent-to-measles-ravaged-samoa-idUSKBN1YD01J

Barrows CH, Kokkonen GC. (1982). Dietary restriction and life extension, biological mechanisms. In G.B. Moment (ed.). *Nutritional Approaches to Aging Research.* Boca Raton, FL: CRC Press, pp. 219–243.

Barsalou, L.W. (2008). Grounded cognition. *Annual Review of Psychology, 59*, 617–645.

Barsalou, L.W. (2016). Situated conceptualization offers a theoretical account of social priming. *Current Opinion in Psychology, 12*, 6–11.

Bartholomew, L.K., Markham, C.M., Ruiter, R.A.C., Fernàndez, M.E., Kok, G. & Parcel, G.S. (2016). *Planning Health Promotion Programs: An Intervention Mapping Approach* (4th edn). Hoboken, NJ: Wiley.

Bartholomew, L.K., Parcel, G.S. & Kok, G. (1998). Intervention mapping: A process for developing theory- and evidence- based health education programs. *Health Education and Behavior, 25*(5), 545–563.

Baskin, E., Gorlin, M., Chance, Z., Novemsky, N., Dhar, R., Huskey, K. & Hatzis, M. (2016). Proximity of snacks to beverages increases food consumption in the workplace: A field study. *Appetite, 103*, 244–248.

Batterink, L., Yokum, S. & Stice, E. (2010). Body mass correlates inversely with inhibitory control in response to food among adolescent girls: an fMRI study. *Neuroimage, 52*(4), 1696–1703.

Baum, A., Garofalo, J.P. & Yali, A.M. (1999). Socioeconomic status and chronic stress. Does stress account for SES effects on health? *Annals of the New York Academy of Sciences, 896*, 131–144.

Baumeister, R.F. & Heatherton, T.F. (1996). Self-regulation failure: An overview. *Psychological Inquiry, 7*(1), 1–15.

Baumeister, R.F. & Tierney, J. (2011). *Willpower: Rediscovering the Greatest Human Strength.* New York: Penguin Books.

Baumeister, R.F. & Vohs, K.D. (2016). Strength model of self-regulation as limited resource: Assessment, controversies, update. In M.O. James & P.Z. Mark (eds.). *Advances in Experimental Social Psychology* (Vol. 54, pp. 67–127). San Diego, CA: Academic Press.

Baumeister, R.F., Bratslavsky, E. & Muraven, M. (1998). Ego depletion: Is the active self a limited resource? *Journal of Personality and Social Psychology, 74,* 1252–1265.

Baumeister, R.F., Tice, D.M. & Vohs, K.D. (2018). The strength model of self-regulation: Conclusions from the second decade of willpower research. *Perspectives on Psychological Science, 13*(2), 141–145.

Baumeister, R.F., Vohs, K.D. & Tice, D.M. (2007). The strength model of self-control. *Current Directions in Psychological Science, 16*(6), 351–355.

Baxter, B.W. & Hinson, R.E. (2001). Is smoking automatic? Demands of smoking behavior on attentional resources. *Journal of Abnormal Psychology, 110*(1), 59.

Beaglehole, R., Bates, C., Youdan, B. & Bonita, R. (2019). Nicotine without smoke: fighting the tobacco epidemic with harm reduction. *The Lancet, 394*(10200), 718–720.

Beard, E., West, R., Michie, S. & Brown, J. (2016). Association between electronic cigarette use and changes in quit attempts, success of quit attempts, use of smoking cessation pharmacotherapy, and use of stop smoking services in England: time series analysis of population trends. *British Medical Journal, 354,* i4645.

Beaver, J.D., Lawrence, A.D., van Ditzhuijzen, J., Davis, M.H., Woods, A. & Calder, A.J. (2006). Individual differences in reward drive predict neural responses to images of food. *The Journal of Neuroscience, 26,* 5160–5166.

Becattini, S., Littmann, E. R., Carter, R. A., Kim, S. G., Morjaria, S. M., Ling, L., … & Pamer, E. G. (2017). Commensal microbes provide first line defense against Listeria monocytogenes infection. *Journal of Experimental Medicine, 214*(7), 1973–1989.

Becker, D., Jostmann, N.B. & Holland, R.W. (2018). Does approach bias modification really work in the eating domain? A commentary on Kakoschke et al. (2017). *Addictive Behaviors, 77,* 293–294.

Becker, J.B., Perry, A.N. & Westenbroek, C. (2012). Sex differences in the neural mechanisms mediating addiction: a new synthesis and hypothesis. *Biology of Sex Differences, 3*(1), 14.

Becker, M.H., Haefner, D.P., Kasl, S.V., Kirscht, J.P., Maiman, L.A. & Rosenstock, I.M. (1977). Selected psychosocial models and correlates of individual health-related behaviors. *Medical Care, 15,* 27–46.

Beckford, M. (2011, June 11). David Cameron denies 'humiliating U-turn' on NHS. *The Telegraph.* www.telegraph.co.uk/news/health/news/8575172/David-Cameron-denies-humiliating-U-turn-on-NHS.html

Beedie, C.J. & Lane, A.M. (2012). The role of glucose in self-control: Another look at the evidence and an alternative conceptualization. *Personality and Social Psychology Review, 16*(2), 143–153.

Beeken, R.J., Croker, H., Morris, S., Leurent, B., Omar, R., Nazareth, I. & Wardle, J. (2012). Study protocol for the 10 Top Tips (10TT) Trial: Randomised controlled trial of habit-based advice for weight control in general practice. *BMC Public Health, 12*(1), 667.

Beeken, R.J., Leurent, B., Vickerstaff, V., Wilson, R., Croker, H., Morris, S., … & Wardle, J. (2017). A brief intervention for weight control based on habit-formation theory delivered through primary care: results from a randomised controlled trial. *International Journal of Obesity, 41*(2), 246.

Bélanger-Gravel, A., Godin, G. & Amireault, S. (2013). A meta-analytic review of the effect of implementation intentions on physical activity. *Health Psychology Review, 7*(1), 23–54.

Bell, J.F., Wilson, J.S. & Liu, G.C. (2008). Neighborhood greenness and 2-year changes in body mass index of children and youth. *American Journal of Preventive Medicine, 35,* 547–553.

Belujon, P. & Grace, A.A. (2015). Regulation of dopamine system responsivity and its adaptive and pathological response to stress. *Proceedings of the Royal Society B: Biological Sciences, 282*(1805), 20142516.

Bem, D. J. (2011). Feeling the future: experimental evidence for anomalous retroactive influences on cognition and affect. *Journal of Personality and Social Psychology, 100*(3), 407.

Bendjilali, N., Hsueh, W.C., He, Q., Willcox, D.C., Nievergelt, C.M., Donlon, T.A., Kwok, P.Y., Suzuki, M. & Willcox, B.J. (2014). Who are the Okinawans? Ancestry, genome diversity, and implications for the genetic study of human longevity from a geographically isolated population. *Journal of Gerontology Series A – Biological Sciences and Medical Sciences, 69,* 1474–1484.

Benedictow, O.J. (2004). *The Black Death 1346-1353: The Complete History.* Woodbridge: Boydell Press.

Benyamini, Y., Leventhal, E. A. & Leventhal, H. (2003). Elderly people's ratings of the importance of health-related factors to their self-assessments of health. *Social Science & Medicine, 56*(8), 1661–1667.

Beral, V., Bull, D., Doll, R., Peto, R., Reeves, G. … Thomas, D. (2001). Familial breast cancer: collaborative reanalysis of individual data from 52 epidemiological studies including 58,209 women with breast cancer and 101, 986 women without the disease. *The Lancet, 358*, 1389–1399.

Beral, V., Bull, D., Doll, R., Peto, R., Reeves, G. … van Leeuwen, F. (2002). Breast cancer and breastfeeding: collaborative reanalysis of individual data from 47 epidemiological studies in 30 countries, including 50,302 women with breast cancer and 96, 973 women without the disease. *The Lancet, 360*, 187–195.

Berger, M. & Sarnyai, Z. (2015). 'More than skin deep': stress neurobiology and mental health consequences of racial discrimination. *Stress, 18*(1), 1–10.

Berners-Lee, M., Kennelly, C., Watson, R. & Hewitt, C.N. (2018). Current global food production is sufficient to meet human nutritional needs in 2050 provided there is radical societal adaptation. *Elementa: Science of the Anthropocene, 6*(1).

Bero, L.A. (2005). Tobacco industry manipulation of research. *Public Health Reports, 120*(2), 200–208.

Berridge, K.C. (2012). From prediction error to incentive salience: mesolimbic computation of reward motivation. *European Journal of Neuroscience, 35*(7), 1124–1143.

Berridge, K.C. & Robinson, T.E. (2016). Liking, wanting, and the incentive-sensitization theory of addiction. *American Psychologist, 71*(8), 670.

Berridge, V. (2014). Electronic cigarettes and history. *The Lancet, 383*(9936), 2204–2205.

Besley, J.C., McCright, A.M., Zahry, N.R., Elliott, K.C., Kaminski, N. & Martin, J.D. (2017). Perceived conflict of interest in health science partnerships. *PloS One, 12*(4), e0175643.

Bes-Rastrollo, M., Sayon-Orea, C., Ruiz-Canela, M. & Martinez-Gonzalez, M.A. (2016). Impact of sugars and sugar taxation on body weight control: A comprehensive literature review. *Obesity, 24*(7), 1410–1426.

Bes-Rastrollo, M., Schulze, M.B., Ruiz-Canela, M. & Martinez-Gonzalez, M.A. (2013). Financial conflicts of interest and reporting bias regarding the association between sugar-sweetened beverages and weight gain: a systematic review of systematic reviews. *PLoS Medicine, 10*(12), e1001578.

Best, M. & Papies, E.K. (2017). Right here, right now: situated interventions to change consumer habits. *Journal of the Association for Consumer Research, 2*(3), 333–358.

Beutler, L.E., Moos, R.H. & Lane, G. (2003). Coping, treatment planning, and treatment outcome: discussion. *Journal of Clinical Psychology, 59*, 1151–1167.

Bhaskaran, K., Douglas, I., Forbes, H., dos-Santos-Silva, I., Leon, D.A. & Smeeth, L. (2014). Body-mass index and risk of 22 specific cancers: a population-based cohort study of 5· 24 million UK adults. *The Lancet, 384*(9945), 755–765.

Bickel, W.K., Moody, L., Quisenberry, A.J., Ramey, C.T. & Sheffer, C.E. (2014). A competing neurobehavioral decision systems model of SES-related health and behavioral disparities. *Preventive Medicine, 68*, 37–43.

Bickel, W.K., Odum, A.L. & Madden, G J. (1999). Impulsivity and cigarette smoking: delay discounting in current, never, and ex-smokers. *Psychopharmacology, 146*(4), 447–454.

Biller-Andorno, N. & Jüni, P. (2014). Abolishing mammography screening programs? A view from the Swiss Medical Board. *The New England Journal of Medicine, 370*, 1965–1967.

Binkley, J.K. & Bejnarowicz, J. (2003). Consumer price awareness in food shopping: the case of quantity surcharges. *Journal of Retailing, 79*, 27–35.

Birch, L.L. & Marlin, D.W. (1982). 'I don't like it, I never tried it': Effects of exposure on two-year-old children's food. *Appetite, 3*, 353–360.

Birch, L.L., Birch, D., Marlin, D.W. & Kramer, L. (1982). Effects of instrumental consumption on children's food preference. *Appetite, 3*(2), 125–134.

Birch, L.L., Marlin, D.W. & Rotter, J. (1984). Eating as the' means' activity in a contingency: Effects on young children's food preference. *Child Development*, 431–439.

Birch, L.L., McPhee, L., Shoba, B.C., Steinberg, L. & Krehbiel, R. (1987). 'Clean up your plate': effects of child feeding practices on the conditioning of meal size. *Learning and Motivation, 18*(3), 301–317.

Björntorp, P. (2001). Do stress reactions cause abdominal obesity and comorbidities? *Obesity Reviews, 2*(2), 73–86.

Black, C., Moon, G & Baird, J. (2014). Dietary inequalities: what is the evidence for the effect of the neighbourhood food environment? *Health and Place, 27*, 229–242.

Blagev, D.P., Harris, D., Dunn, A.C., Guidry, D.W., Grissom, C.K. & Lanspa, M.J. (2019). Clinical presentation, treatment, and short-term outcomes of lung injury associated with e-cigarettes or vaping: a prospective observational cohort study. *The Lancet, 394*(10214), 2073–2083.

Blanchard, J.J., Brown, S.A., Horan, W.P. & Sherwood, A.R. (2000). Substance use disorders in schizophrenia: review, integration, and a proposed model. *Clinical Psychology Review, 20*(2), 207–234.

Blaxter, M. (1990). *Health and Lifestyles.* London: Routledge.

Blissett, J., Bennett, C., Fogel, A., Harris, G. & Higgs, S. (2016). Parental modelling and prompting effects on acceptance of a novel fruit in 2–4-year-old children are dependent on children's food responsiveness. *British Journal of Nutrition, 115*(3), 554–564.

Blissmer, B. & McAuley, E. (2002). Testing the requirements of stages of physical activity among adults: the comparative effectiveness of stage-matched, mismatched, standard care, and control interventions. *Annals of Behavioral Medicine, 24*, 181–189.

Blum, K., Bailey, J., Gonzalez, A.M., Oscar-Berman, M., Liu, Y., Giordano, J., Braverman, E. & Gold, M. (2011). Neuro-genetics of reward deficiency syndrome (RDS) as the root cause of 'addiction transfer': a new phenomenon common after bariatric surgery. *Genetic Syndromes and Gene Therapy, S2*: 001. Doi:104172/2157-7412.S2-001.

Blum, K., Sheridan, P.J., Wood, R.C., Braverman, E.R., Chen, T.J.H., Cull, J.G. & Comings, D.E. (1996). The D2 dopamine receptor gene as a determinant of reward deficiency syndrome. *Journal of the Royal Society of Medicine, 89*, 396–400.

Blurton Jones, N.G., Hawkes, K. & O'Connell, J.F. (2002). Antiquity of postreproductive life: are there modern impacts on hunter-gatherer postreproductive life spans? *American Journal of Human Biology, 14*, 184–205.

Blurton Jones, N.G., Smith, L.C., O'Connell, J.F., Hawkes, K. & Kamuzora C.L. (1992). Demography of Hadza, an increasing and high density population of Savanna foragers. *American Journal of Physical Anthropology, 89*, 159–181.

Bogg, T. & Roberts, B.W. (2004). Conscientiousness and health-related behaviors: A meta-analysis of the leading behavioral contributors to mortality. *Psychological Bulletin, 130*, 887–919.

Bonell, C., Hargreaves, J., Strange, V., Pronyk, P. & Porter, J. (2006). Should structural interventions be evaluated using RCTs? The case of HIV prevention. *Social Science & Medicine, 63*(5), 1135–1142.

Bonevski, B., Regan, T., Paul, C., Baker, A.L. & Bisquera, A. (2014). Associations between alcohol, smoking, socioeconomic status and comorbidities: evidence from the 45 and up study. *Drug and Alcohol Review, 33*, 169–176.

Bongers, P. & Jansen, A. (2015). Emotional eating and Pavlovian learning: evidence for conditioned appetitive responding to negative emotional states. *Cognition and Emotion, 31*(2), 284–297.

Boots, S.B., Tiggemann, M. & Corsini, N. (2018a). Maternal responses to difficult food request scenarios: Relationships with feeding style and child unhealthy snack intake. *Journal of Health Psychology, 23*(13), 1732–1742.

Boots, S.B., Tiggemann, M. & Corsini, N. (2018b). 'That's enough now!': A prospective study of the effects of maternal control on children's snack intake. *Appetite, 126,* 1–7.

Boots, S.B., Tiggemann, M. & Corsini, N. (2019). Pumpkin is 'yucky'!: A prospective study of overt and covert restriction in the development of young children's food preferences. *Appetite, 135,* 54–60.

Börjeson, M. (1976). The aetiology of obesity in children. *Acta Paediatrica Scandinavica, 65,* 279–287.

Boseley, S. (2018). How disgraced anti-vaxxer Andrew Wakefield was embraced by Trump's America. *The Guardian.* www.theguardian.com/society/2018/jul/18/how-disgraced-anti-vaxxer-andrew-wakefield-was-embraced-by-trumps-america

Bosma, H., Marmot, M.G., Hemingway, H., Nicholson, A.C., Brunner, E. & Stansfeld, S.A. (1997). Low job control and risk of coronary heart disease in Whitehall II (prospective cohort) study. *British Medical Journal, 312,* 558.

Bosma, H., van de Mheen, H.D. & Mackenbach, J.P. (1999). Social class in childhood and general health in adulthood: questionnaire study of contribution of psychological attributes. *British Medical Journal, 318,* 18–22.

Boswell, R.G. & Kober, H. (2016). Food cue reactivity and craving predict eating and weight gain: A meta-analytic review. *Obesity Reviews, 17,* 159–177.

Bouchard, T.J. & Loehlin, J.C. (2001). Genes, evolution, and personality. *Behavior Genetics, 31,* 243–273.

Bradford, W.D. (2010). The association between individual time preferences and health maintenance habits. *Medical Decision Making, 30*(1), 99–112.

Bramble, D.M. & Lieberman, D.E. (2004). Endurance running and the evolution of Homo. *Nature, 432,* 345–352.

Bravata, D.M., Smith-Spangler, C., Sundaram, V., Gienger, A.L., Lin, N., Lewis, R., ... & Sirard, J.R. (2007). Using pedometers to increase physical activity and improve health: a systematic review. *Journal of the American Medical Association, 298*(19), 2296–2304.

Braveman, P.A., Cubbin, C., Egerter, S., Chideya, S., Marchi, K.S., Metxler, M. & Posner, S. (2005). Socioeconomic status in health research. One size does not fit all. *Journal of the American Medical Association, 294,* 2879–2888.

Brewer, J.A., Elwafi, H.M. & Davis, J.H. (2013). Craving to quit: Psychological models and neurobiological mechanisms of mindfulness training as treatment for addictions. *Psychology of Addictive Behaviors, 27,* 366–379.

Brewster, S.E., Elliott, M.A. & Kelly, S.W. (2015). Evidence that implementation intentions reduce drivers' speeding behavior: Testing a new intervention to change driver behavior. *Accident Analysis & Prevention, 74,* 229–242.

Brickman, A.L., Yount, S.E., Blaney, N.T., Rothberg, S.T., De-Nour, A.K. (1996). The influence of neuroticism and conscientiousness on renal deterioration in Type-1 diabetes. *Psychosomatics, 37*, 459–468.

Brickwood, K.J., Watson, G., O'Brien, J. & Williams, A.D. (2019). Consumer-based wearable activity trackers increase physical activity participation: systematic review and meta-analysis. *JMIR mHealth and uHealth, 7*(4), e11819.

Britton, A., Shipley, M., Marmot, M. & Hemingway, H. (2004). Does access to cardiac investigation and treatment contribute to social and ethnic differences in coronary heart disease? Whitehall II prospective cohort study. *British Medical Journal, 329*(7461), 318.

Brosch, T., Sander, D. & Scherer, K.R. (2007). That baby caught my eye... attention capture by infant faces. *Emotion, 7*, 685–689.

Brosch, T., Sander, D., Pourtois, G. & Scherer, K.R. (2008). Beyond fear: Rapid spatial orienting toward positive emotional stimuli. *Psychological Science, 19*(4), 362–370.

Brown, K.F., Rumgay, H., Dunlop, C., Ryan, M., Quartly, F., Cox, A., ... & Huws, D. (2018). The fraction of cancer attributable to modifiable risk factors in England, Wales, Scotland, Northern Ireland, and the United Kingdom in 2015. *British Journal of Cancer, 118*(8), 1130.

Brownell, K.D. & Warner, K.E. (2009). The perils of ignoring history: Big Tobacco played dirty and millions died. How similar is Big Food? *The Milbank Quarterly, 87*(1), 259–294.

Brückner, H. & Bearman, P. (2005). After the promise: the STD consequences of adolescent virginity pledges. *Journal of Adolescent Health, 36*(4), 271–278.

Brunstrom, J.M., Mitchell, G.L. & Baguley, T.S. (2005). Potential early-life predictors of dietary behaviour in adulthood: a retrospective study. *International Journal of Obesity, 29*(5), 463.

Bucher, T., Collins, C., Rollo, M.E., McCaffrey, T.A., De Vlieger, N., Van der Bend, D., ... & Perez-Cueto, F.J. (2016). Nudging consumers towards healthier choices: a systematic review of positional influences on food choice. *British Journal of Nutrition, 115*(12), 2252–2263.

Bui, E.T. & Fazio, R.H. (2016). Generalization of evaluative conditioning toward foods: Increasing sensitivity to health in eating intentions. *Health Psychology, 35*(8), 852.

Bullen, C., Howe, C., Laugesen, M., McRobbie, H., Parag, V., Williman, J. & Walker, N. (2013). Electronic cigarettes for smoking cessation: a randomised controlled trial. *The Lancet, 382*(9905), 1629–1637.

Burger, J.M. & Shelton, M. (2011). Changing everyday health behaviors through descriptive norm manipulations. *Social Influence, 6*(2), 69–77.

Burger, J.M., Bell, H., Harvey, K., Johnson, J., Stewart, C., Dorian, K. et al. (2010). Nutritious or delicious? The effect of descriptive norm information on food choice. *Journal of Social and Clinical Psychology, 29*, 228–242.

Burgoine, T., Forouhi, N.G., Griffin, S.J., Barge, S., Wareham, N.J. & Monsivais, P. (2016). Does neighborhood fast-food outlet exposure amplify inequalities in diet and obesity? A cross-sectional study. *American Journal of Clinical Nutrition, 103*, 1540–1547.

Burroughs, W.J. (2005). *Climate Change in Prehistory: The End of the Reign of Chaos.* New York: Cambridge University Press.

Butland, B., Jebb, S., Kopelman, P., McPherson, K., Thomas, S., Mardell, J. & Parry, V. (2007). *Tackling Obesities: Future Choices-project Report.* London: Department of Innovation, Universities and Skills. https://assets.publishing.service.gov.uk/government/uploads/system/uploads/attachment_data/file/287937/07-1184x-tackling-obesities-future-choices-report.pdf

Büttner, O.B., Wieber, F., Schulz, A.M., Bayer, U.C., Florack, A. & Gollwitzer, P.M. (2014). Visual attention and goal pursuit: deliberative and implemental mindsets affect breadth of attention. *Personality and Social Psychology Bulletin, 40*, 1248–1259.

Byrne, J.P. (2012). *Encyclopedia of the Black Death* (Vol. 1). Santa Barbara, CA: ABC-CLIO.

Cacciola, J.S., Alterman, A.I., Rutherford, M.J., McKay, J.R. & Mulvaney, F.D. (2001). The relationship of psychiatric comorbidity to treatment outcomes in methadone maintained patients. *Drug & Alcohol Dependence, 61*(3), 271–280.

Cacioppo, J.T., Petty, R.E. Feinstein, J.A. & Jarvis, W.B.G. (1996). Dispositional differences in cognitive motivation: life and times of individuals varying in need for cognition. *Psychological Bulletin, 119*, 197–253.

Caldwell, J.C. (1986). Routes to low mortality in poor countries. *Population and Development Review, 12*, 171–120.

Caleyachetty, R., Thomas, G.N., Toulis, K.A., Mohammed, N., Gokhale, K.M., Balachandran, K. & Nirantharakumar, K. (2017). Metabolically healthy obese and incident cardiovascular disease events among 3.5 million men and women. *Journal of the American College of Cardiology, 70*(12), 1429–1437.

Callesen, M.B., Scheel-Krüger, J., Kringelbach, M.L. & Møller, A. (2013). A systematic review of impulse control disorders in Parkinson's disease. *Journal of Parkinson's Disease, 3*(2), 105–138.

Cameron, D. (2009). The Big Society. https://web.archive.org/web/20120714070101/http://www.conservatives.com/News/Speeches/2009/11/David_Cameron_The_Big_Society.aspx.

Campbell, C. (2019). Social capital, social movements and global public health: Fighting for health-enabling contexts in marginalised settings. *Social Science & Medicine*, 112153.

Campbell, C. & Cornish, F. (2010). Towards a 'fourth generation' of approaches to HIV/AIDS management: creating contexts for effective community mobilisation. *AIDS Care*, 22(sup2), 1569–1579.

Campbell, C. & Cornish, F. (2012). How can community health programmes build enabling environments for transformative communication? Experiences from India and South Africa. *AIDS and Behavior*, 16(4), 847–857.

Cane, J., O'Connor, D. & Michie, S. (2012). Validation of the theoretical domains framework for use in behaviour change and implementation research. *Implementation Science*, 7(1), 37.

Cane, J., Richardson, M., Johnston, M., Ladha, R. & Michie, S. (2015). From lists of behaviour change techniques (BCTs) to structured hierarchies: Comparison of two methods of developing a hierarchy of BCT s. *British Journal of Health Psychology*, 20(1), 130–150.

Capewell, S. & Lilford, R. (2016). Are nanny states healthier states? *British Medical Journal, 355*, i6341.

Cappuccio, F.P., Ji, C., Donfrancesco, C., Palmieri, L., Ippolito, R., Vanuzzo, D., Giampaoli, S. & Strazzullo, P. (2015). Geographic and socioeconomic variation of sodium and potassium intake in Italy: results from the MINISAL-GIRCSI programme. *British Medical Journal Open*, 5, e007467.

Carmody, R.N. & Wrangham, R.W. (2009). The energetic significance of cooking. *Journal of Human Evolution*, 57, 379–391.

Carnell, S. & Wardle, J. (2008). Appetite and adiposity in children: evidence for a behavioural susceptibility theory of obesity. *American Journal of Clinical Nutrition*, 88, 22–29.

Carnell, S., Haworth, C.M.A., Polomin, R. & Wardle, J. (2008). Genetic influence on appetite in children. *International Journal of Obesity*, 32, 1468–1473.

Carpenter, C.J. (2010). A meta-analysis of the effectiveness of health belief model variables in predicting behavior. *Health Communication*, 25, 661–669.

Carpenter, J.R. & Kenward, M.G. (2007). *Missing Data in Clinical Trials - A Practical Guide*. Birmingham: National Institute for Health Research.

Carter, E.C. & McCullough, M.E. (2014). Publication bias and the limited strength model of self-control: has the evidence for ego depletion been overestimated? *Frontiers in Psychology*, 5, 823.

Carter, E.C., Kofler, L.M., Forster, D.E. & McCullough, M.E. (2015). A series of meta-analytic tests of the depletion effect: self-control does not seem to rely on a limited resource. *Journal of Experimental Psychology: General*, 144(4), 796.

Carver, C.S. & Connor-Smith, J. (2010). Personality and coping. *Annual Review of Psychology*, 61, 679–704.

Carver, C.S. & Scheier, M.F. (1982). Control theory: A useful conceptual framework for personality-social, clinical, and health psychology. *Psychological Bulletin*, 92(1), 111.

Carver, C.S., Scheier, M.F. & Weintraub, J.K. (1989). Assessing coping strategies: a theoretically based approach. *Journal of Personality and Social Psychology*, 56, 267–283.

Casey, B.J., Somerville, L.H., Gotlib, I.H., Ayduk, O., Franklin, N.T., Askren, M.K., ... & Glover, G. (2011). Behavioral and neural correlates of delay of gratification 40 years later. *Proceedings of the National Academy of Sciences*, 108(36), 14998–15003.

Casey, R. & Rozin, P. (1989). Changing children's food preferences: parent opinions. *Appetite*, 12(3), 171–182.

Caspi, A., Roberts, B.W. & Shiner, R.L. (2005). Personality development: stability and change. *Annual Review of Psychology*, 56, 453–484.

Cassidy, A., O'Reilly, É.J., Kay, C., Sampson, L., Franz, M., Forman, J.P., ... & Rimm, E.B. (2011). Habitual intake of flavonoid subclasses and incident hypertension in adults. *The American Journal of Clinical Nutrition*, 93(2), 338–347.

Castaner, O., Goday, A., Park, Y.M., Lee, S.H., Magkos, F., Shiow, S.A.T.E. & Schröder, H. (2018). The gut microbiome profile in obesity: a systematic review. *International Journal of Endocrinology*.

Caulfield, T. & Ogbogu, U. (2015). The commercialization of university-based research: Balancing risks and benefits. *BMC Medical Ethics*, 16(1), 70.

CDC (1981). Pneumocystis pneumonia – Los Angeles. *MMWR Weekly*, 30(21), 250–252.

CDC (2003). Public health and aging: Influenza vaccination coverage among adults aged > or =50 years and pneumococcal vaccination coverage among adults aged > or =65 years—United States, 2002. *MMWR Morb Mortal Wkly Rep*, 52, 987–992.

CDC (2015). *Epidemiology and Prevention of Vaccine-Preventable Diseases*. 13th ed. Washington D.C. Public Health Foundation.

CDC (2020). Alcohol and public health www.cdc.gov/alcohol/faqs.htm.

Cerasoli, C.P., Nicklin, J.M. & Ford, M.T. (2014). Intrinsic motivation and extrinsic incentives jointly predict performance: A 40-year meta-analysis. *Psychological Bulletin*, 140, 980.

Cesario, J. (2014). Priming, replication, and the hardest science. *Perspectives on Psychological Science*, 9(1), 40–48.

Chakravarthy, M.V. & Booth, F.W. (2004). Eating, exercise, and 'thrifty' genotypes: connecting the dots toward an evolutionary understanding of modern chronic diseases. *Journal of Applied Physiology, 96*, 3–10.

Chalmers, B. (1996). Western and African conceptualizations of health. *Psychology and Health, 12*(1), 1–10.

Chamberlain, K. & O'Neill, D. (1998). Understanding social class differences in health: A qualitative analysis of smokers' health beliefs. *Psychology and Health, 13*, 1105–1119.

Chambers, C. (2017). *The Seven Deadly Sins of Psychology: A Manifesto for Reforming the Culture of Scientific Practice.* Oxford: Princeton University Press.

Chandola, T., Kuper, H., Singh-Manoux, A., Bartley, M. & Marmot, M. (2004). The effect of control at home on CHD events in the Whitehall II study: gender differences in psychosocial domestic pathways to social inequalities in CHD. *Social Science and Medicine, 58*, 1501–1509.

Chapman, B.P., Roberts, B. & Duberstein, P. (2011). Personality and longevity: knowns, unknowns, and implications for public health and personalized medicine. *Journal of Aging Research*, Article ID 759170.

Charlton, S.R. & Fantino, E. (2008). Commodity specific rates of temporal discounting: does metabolic function underlie differences in rates of discounting? *Behavioural Processes, 77*(3), 334–342.

Chatzisarantis, N.L. & Hagger, M.S. (2010). Effects of implementation intentions linking suppression of alcohol consumption to socializing goals on alcohol-related decisions. *Journal of Applied Social Psychology, 40*(7), 1618–1634.

Chatzisarantis, N.L., Hagger, M.S., Biddle, S.J., Smith, B. & Wang, J.C. (2003). A meta-analysis of perceived locus of causality in exercise, sport, and physical education contexts. *Journal of Sport and Exercise Psychology, 25*, 284–306.

Chen, L.T., Peng, C.Y.J. & Chen, M.E. (2015). Computing tools for implementing standards for single-case designs. *Behavior Modification, 39*(6), 835–869.

Chen, S. & Parmigiani, G. (2007). Meta-analysis of *BRCA1* and *BRCA2* penetrance. *Journal of Clinical Oncology, 25*, 1329–1333

Chen, Z., Veling, H., Dijksterhuis, A. & Holland, R.W. (2016). How does not responding to appetitive stimuli cause devaluation: Evaluative conditioning or response inhibition? *Journal of Experimental Psychology: General, 145*(12), 1687.

Cheng, C., Cheung, M.W.L. & Lo, B.C.Y. (2016). Relationship of health locus of control with specific health behaviours and global health appraisal: a meta-analysis and effects of moderators. *Health Psychology Review, 10*, 460–477.

Chernoff, R.A. & Davison, G.C. (2005). An evaluation of a brief HIV/AIDS prevention intervention for college students using normative feedback and goal setting. *AIDS Education & Prevention, 17*(2), 91–104.

Chesson, H.W., Leichliter, J.S., Zimet, G.D., Rosenthal, S.L., Bernstein, D.I. & Fife, K.H. (2006). Discount rates and risky sexual behaviors among teenagers and young adults. *Journal of Risk and Uncertainty, 32*(3), 217–230.

Chida, Y. & Steptoe, A. (2009). The association of anger and hostility with future coronary heart disease. *Journal of the American College of Cardiology, 53*, 936–946.

Chin, H.B., Sipe, T.A., Elder, R., Mercer, S.L., Chattopadhyay, S.K., Jacob, V., ... & Chuke, S.O. (2012). The effectiveness of group-based comprehensive risk-reduction and abstinence education interventions to prevent or reduce the risk of adolescent pregnancy, human immunodeficiency virus, and sexually transmitted infections: two systematic reviews for the Guide to Community Preventive Services. *American Journal of Preventive Medicine, 42*(3), 272–294.

Cho, Y., Hong, N., Kim, K.W., Lee, M., Lee, Y.H., Lee, Y.H., ... & Lee, B.W. (2019). The effectiveness of intermittent fasting to reduce body mass index and glucose metabolism: a systematic review and meta-analysis. *Journal of Clinical Medicine, 8*(10), 1645.

Christiansen, P., Schoenmakers, T.M. & Field, M. (2015). Less than meets the eye: Reappraising the clinical relevance of attentional bias in addiction. *Addictive Behaviors, 44*, 43–50.

Christiansen, S., Oettingen, G., Dahme, B. & Klinger, R. (2010). A short goal-pursuit intervention to improve physical capacity: A randomized clinical trial in chronic back pain patients. *Pain, 149*(3), 444–452.

Chu, D.K., Akl, E.A., Duda, S., Solo, K., Yaacoub, S., Schünemann, H.J., ... & Hajizadeh, A. (2020). Physical distancing, face masks, and eye protection to prevent person-to-person transmission of SARS-CoV-2 and COVID-19: a systematic review and meta-analysis. *The Lancet, 395*, 1973–1987.

Church, T. & Martin, C.K. (2018). The obesity epidemic: a consequence of reduced energy expenditure and the uncoupling of energy intake? *Obesity, 26*(1), 14–16.

Cialdini, R.B. (2012). The focus theory of normative conduct. In P.A.M. Van Lange, A.W. Kruglanski and E.T. Higgins (eds.). *Handbook of Theories of Social Psychology.* London: Sage.

Cialdini, R.B., Demaine, L.J., Sagarin, B.J., Barrett, D.W., Rhoads, K. & Winter, P.L. (2006). Managing social norms for persuasive impact. *Social Influence*, *1*(1), 3–15.

Cialdini, R.B., Kallgren, C.A. & Reno, R.R. (1991). A focus theory of normative conduct: A theoretical refinement and reevaluation of the role of norms in human behavior. In *Advances in Experimental Social Psychology* (Vol. 24, pp. 201–234). Academic Press.

Cialdini, R.B., Reno, R.R. & Kallgren, C.A. (1990). A focus theory of normative conduct: Recyling the concept of norms to reduce littering in public places. *Journal of Personality and Social Psychology*, *58*, 1015–1026.

Clare, P., Bradford, D., Courtney, R.J., Martire, K. & Mattick, R.P. (2014). The relationship between socioeconomic status and 'hardcore' smoking over time – greater accumulation of hardened smokers in low-SES than high-SES smokers. *Tobacco Control*, *23*, e133–e138.

Clark, L.K., Fairhurst, C.M. & Torgerson, D.J. (2016). Allocation concealment in randomised controlled trials: could do better. *BMJ Open, 355*: i5663.

Clarke, D.D. & Sokoloff, L. (1998) Circulation and energy metabolism of the brain. In G. Siegel, B. Agranoff, R. Albers, S. Fisher, and M. Uhler (eds.). *Basic Neurochemistry: Molecular, Cellular, and Medical Aspects* (6th edn) (pp. 637–669). Philadelphia, PA: Lippincott Raven.

Cleland, J. (2010). The benefits of educating women. *The Lancet*, *376*, 933–934.

Clemens, J.D., Nair, G.B., Ahmed, T., Qadri, F. & Holmgren, J. (2017). Cholera. *Lancet, 390*, 1539–1549.

Clemens, L.H.E., Slawson, D.L. & Klesges, R.C. (1999). The effect of eating out on quality of diet in premenopausal women. *Journal of the American Dietetic Association*, *99*(4), 442–444.

Cobb, L.K., Appel, L.J., Franco, M., Jones-Smith, J.C., Nur, A. & Anderson, C.A.M. (2015). The relationship of the local food environment with obesity: a systematic review of methods, study quality, and results. *Obesity*, *23*, 1331–1344.

Cochran, G. & Harpending, H. (2009). *The 10,000 Year Explosion: How Civilization Accelerated Human Evolution*. New York: Basic Books.

Cohen, D.A. (2008). Obesity and the built environment: changes in environmental cues cause energy imbalances. *International Journal of Obesity*, *32*(S7), S137–S142.

Cohen, J.E., Zeller, M., Eissenberg, T., Parascandola, M., O'Keefe, R., Planinac, L. & Leischow, S. (2009). Criteria for evaluating tobacco control research funding programs and their application to models that include financial support from the tobacco industry. *Tobacco Control*, *18*(3), 228–234.

Cohen, S., Doyle, W.J. & Baum, A. (2006). Socioeconomic status is associated with stress hormones. *Psychosomatic Medicine*, *68*, 414–420.

Colchero, M.A., Popkin, B.M., Rivera, J.A. & Ng, S.W. (2016). Beverage purchases from stores in Mexico under the excise tax on sugar sweetened beverages: observational study. *British Medical Journal*, *352*, h6704.

Colchero, M.A., Salgado, J.C., Unar-Munguía, M., Molina, M., Ng, S. & Rivera-Dommarco, J.A. (2015). Changes in prices after an excise tax to sweetened sugar beverages was implemented in Mexico: evidence from urban areas. *PloS One*, *10*(12), e0144408.

Collins, L.M., Baker, T.B., Mermelstein, R.J., Piper, M.E., Jorenby, D.E., Smith, S.S., ... & Fiore, M.C. (2011). The multiphase optimization strategy for engineering effective tobacco use interventions. *Annals of Behavioral Medicine*, *41*(2), 208–226.

Collins, L.M., Murphy, S.A., Nair, V.N. & Strecher, V.J. (2005). A strategy for optimizing and evaluating behavioral interventions. *Annals of Behavioral Medicine*, *30*(1), 65–73.

Colman, R.J., Beasley, M., Kemnitz, J.W., Johnson, S.C., Weindruch, R. & Anderson, R.M. (2014). Caloric restriction reduces age-related and all-cause mortality in rhesus monkeys. *Nature Communications*, *5*, 3557.

Conner, M. & Armitage, C.J. (1998). Extending the theory of planned behavior: a review and avenues for further research. *Journal of Applied Social Psychology*, *28*, 1429–1464.

Conner, M. & Higgins, A.R. (2010). Long-term effects of implementation intentions on prevention of smoking uptake among adolescents: a cluster randomized controlled trial. *Health Psychology*, *29*(5), 529.

Conner, M. & Norman, P. (2015). Predicting and changing health behaviour: a social cognition approach. In M. Conner and P. Norman (eds.). *Predicting and Changing Health Behaviour. Research and Practice with Social Cognition Models*. Maidenhead: Open University Press.

Conner, M., Godin, G., Norman, P. & Sheeran, P. (2011). Using the question- behavior effect to promote disease prevention behaviors: Two randomized con-trolled trials. *Health Psychology*, *30*, 300–309.

Conner, M., Godin, G., Sheeran, P. & Germain, M. (2013a). Some feelings are more important: Cognitive attitudes, affective attitudes, anticipated affect, and blood donation. *Health Psychology*, *32*, 264.

Conner, M., McEachan, R., Jackson, C., McMillan, B., Woolridge, M. & Lawton, R. (2013b). Moderating effect of socioeconomic status on the relationship between health cognitions and behaviors. *Annals of Behavioral Medicine, 46,* 19–30.

Conroy, E., Degenhardt, L., Mattick, R.P. & Nelson, E.C. (2009). Child maltreatment as a risk factor for opioid dependence: Comparison of family characteristics and type and severity of child maltreatment with a matched control group. *Child Abuse & Neglect, 33*(6), 343–352.

Converse, B.A., Juarez, L. & Hennecke, M. (2019). Self-control and the reasons behind our goals. *Journal of Personality and Social Psychology, 116*(5), 860.

Cooke, L. (2007). The importance of exposure for healthy eating in childhood: a review. *Journal of Human Nutrition and Dietetics, 20*(4), 294–301.

Cooke, L.J., Chambers, L.C., Añez, E.V. & Wardle, J. (2011a). Facilitating or undermining? The effect of reward on food acceptance. A narrative review. *Appetite, 57*(2), 493–497.

Cooke, L.J., Chambers, L.C., Añez, E.V., Croker, H.A., Boniface, D., Yeomans, M.R. & Wardle, J. (2011b). Eating for pleasure or profit: the effect of incentives on children's enjoyment of vegetables. *Psychological Science, 22*(2), 190–196.

Coombes, E., Jones, A.P. & Hillsdon, M. (2010). The relationship of physical activity and overweight to objectively measured green space accessibility and use. *Social Science and Medicine, 70,* 816–822.

Cooper, C., Gross, A., Brinkman, C., Pope, R., Allen, K., Hastings, S., ... & Goode, A.P. (2018). The impact of wearable motion sensing technology on physical activity in older adults. *Experimental Gerontology, 112,* 9–19.

Cornish, F., Priego-Hernandez, J., Campbell, C., Mburu, G. & McLean, S. (2014). The impact of community mobilisation on HIV prevention in middle and low income countries: a systematic review and critique. *AIDS and Behavior, 18*(11), 2110–2134.

Corr, P.J. (2008). Reinforcement sensitivity theory (RST): Introduction. In P.J. Corr (ed.). *The Reinforcement Sensitivity Theory of Personality* (pp. 1–43). Cambridge: Cambridge University Press.

Corr, P.J. & Cooper, A.J. (2016). The reinforcement sensitivity theory of personality questionnaire (RST-PQ): development and validation. *Psychological Assessment, 28,* 1427–1440.

Corsini, N., Slater, A., Harrison, A., Cooke, L. & Cox, D.N. (2013). Rewards can be used effectively with repeated exposure to increase liking of vegetables in 4–6-year-old children. *Public Health Nutrition, 16*(5), 942–951.

Coviello, D.M., Alterman, A.I., Cacciola, J.S., Rutherford, M.J. & Zanis, D.A. (2004). The role of family history in addiction severity and treatment response. *Journal of Substance Abuse Treatment, 26*(1), 1–11.

CR Society (2020). www.crsociety.org/resources/risks

Craig, P., Dieppe, P., Macintyre, S., Michie, S., Nazareth, I. & Petticrew, M. (2008). Developing and evaluating complex interventions: the new Medical Research Council guidance. *British Medical Journal, 337,* a1655.

Criado Perez, C. (2019). *Invisible Women: Exposing Data Bias in a World Designed for Men.* London: Random House.

Cristea, I.A., Kok, R.N. & Cuijpers, P. (2016). The effectiveness of cognitive bias modification interventions for substance addictions: a meta-analysis. *PloS One, 11*(9), e0162226.

Cummins, A. & Fagg, J. (2012). Does greener mean thinner? Associations between neighbourhood greenspace and weight status among adults in England. *International Journal of Obesity, 36,* 1108–1113.

Cunningham, M.R. & Baumeister, R.F. (2016). How to make nothing out of something: Analyses of the impact of study sampling and statistical interpretation in misleading meta-analytic conclusions. *Frontiers in Psychology, 7,* 1639.

Custers, R. & Aarts, H. (2005). Positive affect as implicit motivator: on the nonconscious operation of behavioral goals. *Journal of Personality and Social Psychology, 89*(2), 129.

Cystic Fibrosis Genetic Analysis Consortium (2005) Cystic Fibrosis Mutation Database. See www.genet.sickkids.on.ca.

Dallman, M.F., Pecoraro, N., Akana, S.F., La Fleur, S.E., Gomez, F., Houshyar, H., ... & Manalo, S. (2003). Chronic stress and obesity: a new view of 'comfort food'. *Proceedings of the National Academy of Sciences, 100*(20), 11696–11701.

Dalton, A.N. & Spiller, S.A. (2012). Too much of a good thing: The benefits of implementation intentions depend on the number of goals. *Journal of Consumer Research, 39*(3), 600–614.

Daly, M., Egan, M., Quigley, J., Delaney, L. & Baumeister, R.F. (2016). Childhood self-control predicts smoking throughout life: Evidence from 21,000 cohort study participants. *Health Psychology, 35*(11), 1254.

Darke, S. (2011). *The Life of the Heroin User: Typical Beginnings, Trajectories and Outcomes.* Cambridge: Cambridge University Press.

Darke, S. (2013). Pathways to heroin dependence: time to re-appraise self-medication. *Addiction, 108*(4), 659–667.

Darke, S., Ross, J., Williamson, A., Mills, K.L., Havard, A. & Teesson, M. (2007). Patterns and correlates of attempted suicide by heroin users over a 3-year period: findings from the Australian treatment outcome study. *Drug & Alcohol Dependence, 87*(2), 146–152.

Dar-Nimrod, I. & Heine, S.J. (2011). Genetic essentialism: on the deceptive determinism of DNA. *Psychological Bulletin, 137*, 800–818.

Dar-Nimrod, I., Cheung, B.Y., Ruby, M.B. & Heine, S.J. (2014). Can merely learning about obesity genes affect eating behaviour? *Appetite, 81*, 269–276.

Dasgupta, S. (2019). Participation as a health communication strategy in HIV/AIDS intervention projects: An examination of a project targeting commercial sex workers in India. *Atlantic Journal of Communication, 27*(2), 139–151.

Daugherty, J.R. & Brase, G.L. (2010). Taking time to be healthy: Predicting health behaviors with delay discounting and time perspective. *Personality and Individual Differences, 48*(2), 202–207.

Davidson, J.R., Hughes, D.L., George, L.K. & Blazer, D.G. (1993). The epidemiology of social phobia: findings from the Duke Epidemiological Catchment Area Study. *Psychological Medicine, 23*(3), 709–718.

Davis, C. & Fox, J. (2008). Sensitivity to reward and body mass index (BMI): Evidence for a non-linear relationship. *Appetite, 50*, 43–49.

Davis, C., Patte, K., Levitan, R., Reid, C., Tweed, S. & Curis, C. (2007). From motivation to behaviour: A model of reward sensitivity, overeating, and food preferences in the risk profile for obesity. *Appetite, 48*, 12–19.

Davis, R., Campbell, R., Hildon, Z., Hobbs, L. & Michie, S. (2015). Theories of behaviour and behaviour change across the social and behavioural sciences: a scoping review. *Health Psychology Review, 9*(3), 323–344.

de Bruijn, G.J., Rhodes, R.E. & van Osch, L. (2012). Does action planning moderate the intention-habit interaction in the exercise domain? A three-way interaction analysis investigation. *Journal of Behavioral Medicine, 35*(5), 509–519.

de Cabo, R. & Mattson, M. P. (2019). Effects of intermittent fasting on health, aging, and disease. *New England Journal of Medicine, 381*(26), 2541–2551.

de Hoog, N., Stroebe, W. & de Wit, J.B.F. (2007). The impact of vulnerability to and severity of a health risk on processing and acceptance of fear-arousing communications: A meta- analysis. *Review of General Psychology, 11*, 258–285.

De Houwer, J., Baeyens, F. & Field, A.P. (2005). Associative learning of likes and dislikes: Some current controversies and possible ways forward. *Cognition & Emotion, 19*(2), 161–174.

De Irala-Estévez, J., Groth, M., Johansson, L., Oltersdorf, U., Prättälä, R. & Martínez-González, M.A. (2000). A systematic review of socio-economic differences in food habits in Europe: consumption of fruit and vegetables. *European Journal of Clinical Nutrition, 54*, 706–714.

De Jesus, M., Puleo, E., Shelton, R.C. & Emmons, K.M. (2010). Associations between perceived social environment and neighbourhood safety: health implications. *Health and Place, 16*, 1007–1013.

de Leon, J., Tracy, J., McCann, E., McGrory, A. & Diaz, F.J. (2002). Schizophrenia and tobacco smoking: a replication study in another US psychiatric hospital. *Schizophrenia Research, 56*(1), 55–65.

de Martel, C., Plummer, M., Vignat, J. & Franceschi, S. (2017). Worldwide burden of cancer attributable to HPV by site, country and HPV type. *International Journal of Cancer, 141*(4), 664–670.

De Sanjosé, S., Diaz, M., Castellsagué, X., Clifford, G., Bruni, L., Muñoz, N. & Bosch, F.X. (2007). Worldwide prevalence and genotype distribution of cervical human papillomavirus DNA in women with normal cytology: a meta-analysis. *The Lancet Infectious Diseases, 7*(7), 453–459.

de Vet, E., de Nooijer, J., de Vries, N.K. & Brug, J. (2008). Testing the transtheoretical model for fruit intake: comparing web-based tailored stage-matched and stage-mismatched feedback. *Health Education Research, 23*, 218–227.

de Vet, E., Gebhardt, W.A., Sinnige, J., Van Puffelen, A., Van Lettow, B. & de Wit, J.B. (2011a). Implementation intentions for buying, carrying, discussing and using condoms: the role of the quality of plans. *Health Education Research, 26*(3), 443–455.

de Vet, E., Oenema, A. & Brug, J. (2011b). More or better: Do the number and specificity of implementation intentions matter in increasing physical activity? *Psychology of Sport and Exercise, 12*(4), 471–477.

De Witt Huberts, J.C., Evers, C. & De Ridder, D. (2012). License to sin: Self-licensing as a mechanism underlying hedonic consumption. *European Journal of Social Psychology, 42*, 490–496

Decety, J. & Grèzes, J. (2006). The power of simulation: imagining one's own and other's behavior. *Brain Research, 1079*(1), 4–14.

Deci, E.L. & Ryan, R.M. (1985). The general causality orientations scale: Self-determination in personality. *Journal of Research in Personality, 19*, 109–134.

Deci, E.L. & Ryan, R.M. (2000). The' what' and' why' of goal pursuits: Human needs and the self-determination of behavior. *Psychological Inquiry, 11*, 227–268.

Deci, E.L. & Ryan, R.M. (2008). Facilitating optimal motivation and psychological well-being across life's domains. *Canadian Psychology, 49*, 14–23.

Deci, E.L., Koestner, R. & Ryan, R.M. (1999). A meta-analytic review of experiments examining the effects of extrinsic rewards on intrinsic motivation. *Psychological Bulletin, 125*, 627–668.

DeJong, W., Schneider, S.K., Towvim, L. G., Murphy, M.J., Doerr, E.E., Simonsen, N.R., ... & Scribner, R.A. (2009). A multisite randomized trial of social norms marketing campaigns to reduce college student drinking: A replication failure. *Substance Abuse, 30*(2), 127–140.

DeJong, W., Schneider, S.K., Towvim, L.G., Murphy, M.J., Doerr, E.E., Simonsen, N.R., ... & Scribner, R.A. (2006). A multisite randomized trial of social norms marketing campaigns to reduce college student drinking. *Journal of Studies on Alcohol, 67*(6), 868–879.

Des Jarlais, D.C., Lyles, C., Crepaz, N. & Trend Group. (2004). Improving the reporting quality of nonrandomized evaluations of behavioral and public health interventions: the TREND statement. *American Journal of Public Health, 94*(3), 361–366.

Devaux, M. & Sassi, F. (2011). Social inequalities in obesity and overweight in 11 OECD countries. *European Journal of Public Health, 23*, 464–469.

Dewey, K.G. (1997). Energy and protein requirements during lactation. *Annual Review of Nutrition, 17*, 19–36.

Dewitte, S., Verguts, T. & Lens, W. (2003). Implementation intentions do not enhance all types of goals: The moderating role of goal difficulty. *Current Psychology, 22*(1), 73–89.

Dholakia, U.M. (2010). A critical review of question-behavior effect research. *Review of Marketing Research, 7*, 145–197.

Di Lemma, L.C., & Field, M. (2017). Cue avoidance training and inhibitory control training for the reduction of alcohol consumption: a comparison of effectiveness and investigation of their mechanisms of action. *Psychopharmacology, 234*(16), 2489–2498.

Diamond, J. (1987). The worst mistake in the history of the human race. *Discover Magazine*, May, 64–66.

Diamond, J. (2003). The double puzzle of diabetes. *Nature, 423*, 599–602.

Diamond, J. (2012). *The World Until Yesterday: What Can We Learn From Traditional Societies?* London: Allen Lane.

Diamond, J. & Bellwood, P. (2003). Farmers and their languages: the first expansions. *Science, 300*(5619), 597–603.

Diamond, J.M. (1998). *Guns, Germs and Steel: A Short History of Everybody for the Last 13,000 Years.* London: Random House.

Dickerson, S.S. & Kemeny, M.E. (2004). Acute stressors and cortisol responses: a theoretical integration and synthesis of laboratory research. *Psychological Bulletin, 130*, 355–391.

Dickinson, A. (1985). Actions and habits: the development of behavioural autonomy. *Philosophical Transactions of the Royal Society of London. Series B, Biological Sciences, 67*–78.

DiClemente, C.C., Corno, C.M., Graydon, M.M., Wiprovnick, A.E. & Knoblach, D.J. (2017). Motivational interviewing, enhancement, and brief interventions over the last decade: A review of reviews of efficacy and effectiveness. *Psychology of Addictive Behaviors, 31*(8), 862.

Dijksterhuis, A. & Bargh, J. A. (2001). The perception-behavior expressway: Automatic effects of social perception on social behavior. *Advances in Experimental Social Psychology, 33*, 1–40.

Dijkstra, A., Conijn, B. & De Vries, H. (2006). A match–mismatch test of a stage model of behaviour change in tobacco smoking. *Addiction, 101*, 1035–1043.

Dijkstra, A., De Vries, H., Kok, G. & Roijackers, J. (1999). Self-evaluation and motivation to change: social cognitive constructs in smoking cessation. *Psychology and Health, 14*, 747–759.

Dijkstra, A., De Vries, H., Roijackers, J. & van Breukelen, G. (1998). Tailored interventions to communicate stage-matched information to smokers in different motivational stages. *Journal of Consulting and Clinical Psychology, 66*, 549.

Ditzen, B., Neumann, I.D., Bodenmann, G., von Dawans, B., Turner, R.A., Ehlert, U. & Heinrichs, M. (2007). Effects of different kinds of couple interaction on cortisol and heart rate responses to stress in women. *Psychoneuroendocrinology, 32*, 565–574.

Diwan, A., Castine, M., Pomerleau, C.S., Meador-Woodruff, J.H. & Dalack, G.W. (1998). Differential prevalence of cigarette smoking in patients with schizophrenic vs mood disorders. *Schizophrenia Research, 33*(1), 113–118.

DoH (1999). Saving lives: our healthier nation. www.gov.uk/government/publications/saving-lives-our-healthier-nation.

Dolan, P. & Galizzi, M.M. (2015). Like ripples on a pond: behavioral spillovers and their implications for research and policy. *Journal of Economic Psychology, 47*, 1–16.

Dolan, P., Hallsworth, M., Halpern, D., King, D. & Vlaev, I. (2010). *MINDSPACE: Influencing Behaviour for Public Policy.* London: HM Government.

Dolan, P., Hallsworth, M., Halpern, D., King, D., Metcalfe, R. & Vlaev, I. (2012). Influencing behaviour: The mindspace way. *Journal of Economic Psychology, 33*(1), 264–277.

Dombrowski, S.U., Sniehotta, F.F., Avenell, A., Johnston, M., MacLennan, G. & Araújo-Soares, V. (2012). Identifying active ingredients in complex behavioural interventions for obese adults with obesity-related co-morbidities or additional risk factors for co-morbidities: a systematic review. *Health Psychology Review, 6*(1), 7–32.

Dominy, S.S., Lynch, C., Ermini, F., Benedyk, M., Marczyk, A., Konradi, A., ... & Holsinger, L.J. (2019). Porphyromonas gingivalis in Alzheimer's disease brains: Evidence for disease causation and treatment with small-molecule inhibitors. *Science Advances*, 5(1), eaau3333.

Donnelly, L. & Holehouse, M. (2013). Mothers might not breastfeed after taking £200 NHS bribe, MP warns. *The Telegraph*. www.telegraph.co.uk/news/health/10443233/Mothers-might-not-breastfeed-after-taking-200-NHS-bribe-MP-warns.html

Donner, A. & Klar, N. (2004). Pitfalls of and controversies in cluster randomization trials. *American Journal of Public Health*, 94(3), 416–422.

Donovan, J.L., Hamdy, F.C., Lane, J.A., Mason, M., Metcalfe, C., Walsh, E., ... Neal, D.E. (2016). Patient-reported outcomes after monitoring, surgery, or radiotherapy for prostate cancer. *The New England Journal of Medicine*, 375, 1425–1437.

Doyen, S., Klein, O., Pichon, C.L. & Cleeremans, A. (2012). Behavioral priming: it's all in the mind, but whose mind? *PloS One*, 7(1), e29081.

Drobes, D.J. & Tiffany, S.T. (1997). Induction of smoking urge through imaginal and in vivo procedures: Physiological and self-report manifestations. *Journal of Abnormal Psychology*, 106(1), 15.

Drovandi, A., Teague, P.A., Glass, B. & Malau-Aduli, B. (2019). A systematic review of the perceptions of adolescents on graphic health warnings and plain packaging of cigarettes. *Systematic Reviews*, 8(1), 25.

Drummond, D.C. (2000). What does cue-reactivity have to offer clinical research? *Addiction*, 95, 129–144.

Drummond, D.C. (2001). Theories of drug craving, ancient and modern. *Addiction*, 96, 33–46.

Duckworth, A.L. & Kern, M.L. (2011). A meta-analysis of the convergent validity of self-control measures. *Journal of Research in Personality*, 45(3), 259–268.

Duckworth, A.L., Gendler, T.S. & Gross, J.J. (2016). Situational strategies for self-control. *Perspectives on Psychological Science*, 11(1), 35–55.

Duckworth, A.L., Tsukayama, E. & Kirby, T.A. (2013). Is it really self-control? Examining the predictive power of the delay of gratification task. *Personality and Social Psychology Bulletin*, 39(7), 843–855.

Duckworth, A.L., Tsukayama, E. & May, H. (2010). Establishing causality using longitudinal hierarchical linear modeling: An illustration predicting achievement from self-control. *Social Psychological and Personality Science*, 1(4), 311–317.

Dunlop, S.M., Dobbins, T., Young, J.M., Perez, D. & Currow, D.C. (2014). Impact of Australia's introduction of tobacco plain packs on adult smokers' pack-related perceptions and responses: results from a continuous tracking survey. *BMJ Open*, 4(12), e005836.

Dunn, J.R., Burgess, B. & Ross, N.A. (2005). Income distribution, public services expenditures, and all cause mortality in US states. *Journal of Epidemiology and Community Health*, 59, 768–774.

Durkin, S., Brennan, E., Coomber, K., Zacher, M., Scollo, M. & Wakefield, M. (2015). Short-term changes in quitting-related cognitions and behaviours after the implementation of plain packaging with larger health warnings: findings from a national cohort study with Australian adult smokers. *Tobacco Control*, 24(Suppl 2), ii26–ii32.

Durso, L.E., Latner, J.D. & Hayashi, K. (2012). Perceived discrimination is associated with binge eating in a community sample of non-overweight, overweight, and obese adults. *Obesity Facts*, 5(6), 869–880.

Dyson, L., Green, J.M., Renfrew, M.J., McMillan, B. & Woolridge, M. (2010). Factors influencing the infant feeding decision for socioeconomically deprived pregnant teenagers: the moral dimension. *Birth*, 37(2), 141–149.

D'Zurilla, T.J. & Goldfried, M.R. (1971). Problem solving and behaviour modification. *Journal of Abnormal Psychology*, 78(1), 107.

Earl, A. & Albarracín, D. (2007). Nature, decay, and spiraling of the effects of fear-inducing arguments and HIV counseling and testing: a meta-analysis of the short-and long-term outcomes of HIV-prevention interventions. *Health Psychology*, 26, 496–506.

Eaton, S.B. & Konner, M. (1985). Paleolithic nutrition. A consideration of its nature and current implications. *The New England Journal of Medicine*, 312, 283–289.

Eaton, S.B., Konner, M. & Shostak, M. (1988). Stone agers in the fast lane: chronic degenerative diseases in evolutionary perspective. *The American Journal of Medicine*, 84, 739–749.

Eberl, C., Wiers, R.W., Pawelczack, S., Rinck, M., Becker, E.S. & Lindenmeyer, J. (2013). Approach bias modification in alcohol dependence: do clinical effects replicate and for whom does it work best? *Developmental Cognitive Neuroscience*, 4, 38–51.

Egger, G. & Swinburn, B. (1997). An 'ecological' approach to the obesity pandemic. *British Medical Journal*, 315, 477–480.

Egger, G.J., Vogels, N. & Westerterp, K.R. (2001). Estimating historical changes in physical activity levels. *Medical Journal of Australia*, 175, 635–636.

Eigsti, I.M., Zayas, V., Mischel, W., Shoda, Y., Ayduk, O., Dadlani, M.B., ... & Casey, B.J. (2006). Predicting cognitive control from preschool to late adolescence and young adulthood. *Psychological Science*, 17(6), 478–484.

Eisenstein, M. (2020). The hunt for a healthy microbiome. *Nature, 577*(7792), S6–S8.

El Khoury, C. F., Karavetian, M., Halfens, R. J., Crutzen, R., Khoja, L. & Schols, J. M. (2019). The effects of dietary mobile apps on nutritional outcomes in adults with chronic diseases: a systematic review and meta-analysis. *Journal of the Academy of Nutrition and Dietetics, 119*(4), 626–651.

Elder, R.S. & Krishna, A. (2010). The effects of advertising copy on sensory thoughts and perceived taste. *Journal of Consumer Research, 36*(5), 748–756.

Elder, R.S. & Krishna, A. (2012). The 'visual depiction effect' in advertising: Facilitating embodied mental simulation through product orientation. *Journal of Consumer Research, 38*(6), 988–1003.

Elfeddali, I., Bolman, C., Candel, M.J., Wiers, R.W. & de Vries, H. (2012). Preventing smoking relapse via Web-based computer-tailored feedback: a randomized controlled trial. *Journal of Medical Internet Research, 14*(4).

Elgar, F.J. (2010). Income inequality, trust, and population health in 33 countries. *American Journal of Public Health, 100*, 2311–2315.

Ellen, B. (2013). Breastfeeding bribes? What a grubby little idea. *The Guardian*, www.theguardian.com/commentisfree/2013/nov/16/breastfeeding-bribes-pointless

Ellis, B.J., Figueredo, A.J., Brumbach, B.H. & Schlomer, G.L. (2009). The impact of harsh versus unpredictable environments on the evolution and development of life history strategies. *Human Nature, 20*, 204–268.

Ellis, E.M., Homish, G.G., Parks, K.A., Collins, R.L. & Kiviniemi, M.T. (2015). Increasing condom use by changing people's feelings about them: An experimental study. *Health Psychology, 34*(9), 941.

Elovainio, M., Ferrie, J.E., Singh-Manoux, A., Shipley, M., Batty, G.D., Head, J., Hamer, M., Jokela, M., Virtanen, M., Brunner, E., Marmot, M.G. & Kivimaki, M. (2011). Socioeconomic differences in cardiometabolic factors: social causation or health-related selection? Evidence from the Whitehall II cohort study, 1991-2-2004. *American Journal of Epidemiology, 174*, 779--789.

Emmer, C., Bosnjak, M. & Mata, J. (2019). The association between weight stigma and mental health: A meta-analysis. *Obesity Reviews*, 1–13.

Engel, G. L. (1977). The need for a new medical model: a challenge for biomedicine. *Science, 196*(4286), 129–136.

EPA (1992). Respiratory health effects of passive smoking: Lung cancer and other disorders. www.epa.gov/indoor-air-quality-iaq/respiratory-health-effects-passive-smoking-lung-cancer-and-other-disorders

Epstein, L.H., Paluch, R. & Coleman, K.J. (1996). Differences in salivation to repeated food cues in obese and nonobese women. *Psychosomatic Medicine, 58*, 160–164.

Epstein, S. (1994). Integration of the cognitive and the psychodynamic unconscious. *American Psychologist, 49*(8), 709.

Eriksson, N., Wu, S., Do, C.B., Kiefer, A.K., Tung, J.Y., Mountain, J.L., Hinds, D.A. & Francke, U. (2012). A genetic variant near olfactory receptor genes influences cilantro preference. *Flavour, 1*(1), 22.

Ernst, E. (2019). *Alternative Medicine: A Critical Assessment of 150 Modalities*. Switzerland: Springer.

Ertelt, T.W., Mitchell, J.E., Lancaster, K., Crosby, R.D., Steffen, K.J. & Marina, J.M. (2008). Alcohol abuse and dependence before and after bariatric surgery: a review of literature and report of a new data set. *Surgery for Obesity and Related Diseases, 4*, 647–650.

Estabrooks, P.A., Lee, R.E. & Gyurcsik, N.C. (2003). Resources for physical activity participation: does availability and accessibility differ by neighborhood socioeconomic status? *Annals of Behavioral Medicine, 25*, 100–104.

Estruch, R., Ros, E., Salas-Salvadó, J., Covas, M.I., Corella, D. et al. (2013). Primary prevention of cardiovascular disease with a Mediterranean diet. *The New England Journal of Medicine, 368*, 1279–1290.

Eurofound (2015a). *First Findings: Sixth European Working Conditions Survey*. Luxembourg: Publications Office of the European Union.

Eurofound (2015b). *Improving Working Conditions in Occupations with Multiple Disadvantages*. Luxembourg: Publications Office of the European Union.

Evans, A.H., Pavese, N., Lawrence, A.D., Tai, Y.F., Appel, S., Doder, M., ... & Piccini, P. (2006). Compulsive drug use linked to sensitized ventral striatal dopamine transmission. *Annals of Neurology, 59*(5), 852–858.

Evans, D. (2004). *Placebo: Mind Over Matter in Modern Medicine*. New York: HarperCollins.

Evans, D.R., Boggero, I.A. & Segerstrom, S.C. (2016). The nature of self-regulatory fatigue and 'ego depletion' lessons from physical fatigue. *Personality and Social Psychology Review, 20*(4), 291–310.

Evans, J.S.B. (2006). The heuristic-analytic theory of reasoning: extension and evaluation. *Psychonomic Bulletin & Review, 13*(3), 378–395.

Evans, J.S.B. (2008). Dual-processing accounts of reasoning, judgment, and social cognition. *Annual Review of Psychology, 59*, 255–278.

Fabbri, A., Chartres, N., Scrinis, G. & Bero, L.A. (2017). Study sponsorship and the nutrition research agenda: analysis of randomized controlled trials included in systematic reviews of nutrition interventions to address obesity. *Public Health Nutrition, 20*(7), 1306–1313.

Fan, J.X., Wen, M. & Kowaleski-Jones, L. (2014). Rural-urban differences in objective and subjective measures of physical activity: findings from the National Health and Nutrition Examination Survey (NHANES) 2003-2006. *Preventing Chronic Cisease, 11*, E141–E141.

Faria, N.R., Rambaut, A., Suchard, M.A., Baele, G., Bedford, T., Ward, M.J., ... & Posada, D. (2014). The early spread and epidemic ignition of HIV-1 in human populations. *Science, 346*(6205), 56–61.

Farooqi, I.S. & O'Rahilly, S. (2005). Monogenic obesity in humans. *Annual Review of Medicine, 56*, 443–458.

FDA (2012). Harmful and potentially harmful constituents in tobacco products and tobacco smoke; established list. www.fda.gov/tobacco-products/products-ingredients-components/harmful-and-potentially-harmful-constituents-hphcs

Feil, J. & Hasking, P. (2008). The relationship between personality, coping strategies and alcohol use. *Addiction Research and Theory, 16*, 526–537.

Ferguson, C.J. & Heene, M. (2012). A vast graveyard of undead theories: Publication bias and psychological science's aversion to the null. *Perspectives on Psychological Science, 7*(6), 555–561.

Fergusson, D.M., Boden, J.M. & Horwood, L.J. (2009). Tests of causal links between alcohol abuse or dependence and major depression. *Archives of General Psychiatry, 66*(3), 260–266.

Festinger, L. (1957). *A Theory of Cognitive Dissonance.* London: Tavistock.

Field, C.A., Baird, J., Saitz, R., Caetano, R. & Monti, P.M. (2010). The mixed evidence for brief intervention in emergency departments, trauma care centers, and inpatient hospital settings: what should we do? *Alcoholism: Clinical and Experimental Research, 34*(12), 2004–2010.

Field, M. & Eastwood, B. (2005). Experimental manipulation of attentional bias increases the motivation to drink alcohol. *Psychopharmacology, 183*(3), 350–357.

Field, M., Eastwood, B., Bradley, B.P. & Mogg, K. (2006). Selective processing of cannabis cues in regular cannabis users. *Drug and Alcohol Dependence, 85*(1), 75–82.

Field, M., Kiernan, A., Eastwood, B. & Child, R. (2008). Rapid approach responses to alcohol cues in heavy drinkers. *Journal of Behavior Therapy and Experimental Psychiatry, 39*(3), 209–218.

Field, M., Werthmann, J., Franken, I., Hofmann, W., Hogarth, L. & Roefs, A. (2016). The role of attentional bias in obesity and addiction. *Health Psychology, 35*(8), 767.

Fildes, A., van Jaarsveld, C.H., Llewellyn, C.H., Fisher, A., Cooke, L. & Wardle, J. (2014). Nature and nurture in children's food preferences. *The American Journal of Clinical Nutrition, 99*(4), 911–917.

Finkel, E.J., DeWall, C.N., Slotter, E.B., Oaten, M. & Foshee, V.A. (2009). Self-regulatory failure and intimate partner violence perpetration. *Journal of Personality and Social Psychology, 97*(3), 483.

Finucane, M.L., Alhakami, A., Slovic, P. & Johnson, S.M. (2000). The affect heuristic in judgments of risks and benefits. *Journal of Behavioral Decision Making, 13*(1), 1–17.

Fishbein, M. & Ajzen, I. (1975). *Belief, Attitude, Intention, and Behavior: An Introduction to Theory and Research.* Reading, MA: Addison-Wesley.

Fishbein, M. & Ajzen, I. (2010). *Predicting and Changing Behavior: The Reasoned Action Approach.* New York: Psychology Press.

Fisher, J.O. & Birch, L.L. (1999a). Restricting access to foods and children's eating. *Appetite, 32*(3), 405–419.

Fisher, J.O. & Birch, L.L. (1999b). Restricting access to palatable foods affects children's behavioral response, food selection, and intake. *The American Journal of Clinical Nutrition, 69*(6), 1264–1272.

Fisher, J.O. & Birch, L.L. (2000). Parents' restrictive feeding practices are associated with young girls' negative self-evaluation of eating. *Journal of the American Dietetic Association, 100*(11), 1341–1346.

Flint, S.W., Hudson, J. & Lavallee, D. (2016). The portrayal of obesity in UK national newspapers. *Stigma and Health, 1*(1), 16.

Floyd, D.L., Prentice-Dunn, S. & Rogers, R.W. (2000). A meta-analysis of research on protection motivation theory. *Journal of Applied Social Psychology, 30*, 407–429.

Fomon, S. J. (2001). Infant feeding in the 20th century: formula and beikost. *The Journal of Nutrition, 131*(2), 409S–420S.

Food and Agriculture Organisation of the United Nations (2010). Fats and fatty acids in human nutrition. Report of an expert consultation. http://foris.fao.org/preview/25553-0ece4cb94ac52f9a25af77ca5cfba7a8c.pdf

Ford, G. (2006). *The New Contended Little Baby Book: The Secret to Calm and Confident Parenting.* London: Random House.

Ford, I. & Norrie, J. (2016). Pragmatic trials. *New England Journal of Medicine, 375*(5), 454–463.

Förster, J., Liberman, N. & Friedman, R. S. (2007). Seven principles of goal activation: A systematic approach to distinguishing goal priming from priming of non-goal constructs. *Personality and Social Psychology Review, 11*(3), 211–233.

Forwood, S.E., Ahern, A.L., Hollands, G.J., Ng, Y.L. & Marteau, T.M. (2015). Priming healthy eating. You can't prime all the people all of the time. *Appetite*, *89*, 93–102.

Foverskov, E. & Holm, A. (2016). Socioeconomic inequality in health in the British household panel: tests of the social causation, health selection and the indirect selection hypothesis using dynamic fixed effects panel models. *Social Science and Medicine*, *150*, 172–183.

Fox, M.K., Devaney, B., Reidy, K., Razafindrakoto, C. & Ziegler, P. (2006). Relationship between portion size and energy intake among infants and toddlers: evidence of self-regulation. *Journal of the American Dietetic Association*, *106*(1), 77–83.

Foxcroft, D.R., Moreira, M.T., Almeida Santimano, N.M. & Smith, L.A. (2015). Social norms information for alcohol misuse in university and college students. *Cochrane Database Syst Rev*, *1*.

Franca, L.R., Dautzenberg, B., Falissard, B. & Reynaud, M. (2010). Peer substance use overestimation among French university students: a cross-sectional survey. *BMC Public Health*, *10*(1), 169.

Francis, G. (2012). Too good to be true: Publication bias in two prominent studies from experimental psychology. *Psychonomic Bulletin & Review*, *19*(2), 151–156.

Franken, I.H.A. & Muris, P. (2006). Personality characteristics and college students' substance use. *Personality and Individual Differences*, *40*, 1497–1503.

Franklin, T.R., Wang, Z., Li, Y., Suh, J.J., Goldman, M., Lohoff, F.W., … & Berrettini, W. (2011). Dopamine transporter genotype modulation of neural responses to smoking cues: confirmation in a new cohort. *Addiction Biology*, *16*(2), 308–322.

Franssen, W.M., Franssen, G.H., Spaas, J., Solmi, F. & Eijnde, B.O. (2020). Can consumer wearable activity tracker-based interventions improve physical activity and cardiometabolic health in patients with chronic diseases? A systematic review and meta-analysis of randomised controlled trials. *International Journal of Behavioral Nutrition and Physical Activity*, *17*(1), 1–20.

Freire, R. (2020). Scientific evidence of diets for weight loss: different macronutrient composition, intermittent fasting, and popular diets. *Nutrition*, *69*, 110549.

French, D.P. (2013). The role of self-efficacy in changing health-related behaviour: cause, effects or spurious association? *British Journal of Health Psychology*, *18*, 237–243.

Friedman, H.S., Tucker, J.S., Schwartz, J.E., Martin, L.R., Tomlinson-Keasey, C., Wingard, D.L. & Criqui, M.H. (1995). Child conscientiousness and longevity: health behaviors and cause of death. *Journal of Personality and Social Psychology*, *68*, 696–703.

Friedman, M. & Rosenman, R.H. (1959). Association of specific overt behaviour pattern with blood and cardiovascular findings; blood cholesterol level, blood clotting time, incidence of arcus senilis, and clinical coronary artery disease. *Journal of the American Medical Association*, *169*, 1286–1296.

Fries, J.F. (1983). The compression of morbidity. *The Milbank Memorial Fund Quarterly. Health and Society*, 397–419.

Friese, M., Loschelder, D.D., Gieseler, K., Frankenbach, J. & Inzlicht, M. (2019). Is ego depletion real? An analysis of arguments. *Personality and Social Psychology Review*, *23*(2), 107–131.

Frisch, R.E. & McArthur, J.W. (1974). Menstrual cycles: fatness as a determinant of minimum weight for height necessary for their maintenance or onset. *Science*, *185*, 949–951.

Fujita, K. (2011). On conceptualizing self-control as more than the effortful inhibition of impulses. *Personality and Social Psychology Review*, *15*(4), 352–366.

Fujita, K., Gollwitzer, P.M. & Oettingen, G. (2007). Mindsets and pre-conscious open-mindedness to incidental information. *Journal of Experimental Social Psychology*, *43*, 48–61.

Funcke, J.B., von Schnurbein, J., Lennerz, B., Lahr, G., Debatin, K.M., Fischer-Posovszky, P. & Wabitsch, M. (2014). Monogenic forms of childhood obesity due to mutations in the leptin gene. *Molecular and Cellular Pediatrics*, *1*: 3.

Funder, D.C. (2001). Personality. *Annual Review of Psychology*, *52*, 197–221.

Furedi, A. (1999). Social consequences. The public health implications of the 1995 'pill scare'. *Human Reproduction Update*, *5*(6), 621–626.

Gage, T.B. (2005). Are modern environments really bad for us?: Revisiting the demographic and epidemiologic transitions. *Yearbook of Physical Anthropology*, *48*, 96–117.

Gage, T.B. Dewitte, S.N. & Wood, J.W. (2012). Demography part 1: mortality and migration. In S. Stinson, B. Bogin & D. O'Rourke (eds.). *Human Biology: An Evolutionary and Biocultural Perspective*, 2nd edn. Hoboken, NJ: John Wiley & Sons.

Gagné, F.M. & Lydon, J.E. (2001). Mind-set and close relationships: When bias leads to (in)accurate predictions. *Journal of Personality and Social Psychology*, *81*, 85–96.

Gailliot, M.T. & Baumeister, R.F. (2007). The physiology of willpower: Linking blood glucose to self-control. *Personality and Social Psychology Review*, *11*, 303–327.

Gailliot, M.T., Baumeister, R.F., DeWall, C.N., Maner, J.K., Plant, E.A., Tice, D.M., … & Schmeichel, B.J. (2007a). Self-control relies on glucose as a limited energy source: willpower is more than a metaphor. *Journal of Personality and Social Psychology, 92*(2), 325.

Gailliot, M.T., Plant, E.A., Butz, D.A. & Baumeister, R.F. (2007b). Increasing self-regulatory strength can reduce the depleting effect of suppressing stereotypes. *Personality and Social Psychology Bulletin, 33*, 281–294.

Gakidou, E., Afshin, A., Abajobir, A.A., Abate, K.H., Abbafati, C., Abbas, K.M., ... & Abu-Raddad, L.J. (2017). Global, regional, and national comparative risk assessment of 84 behavioural, environmental and occupational, and metabolic risks or clusters of risks, 1990–2016: a systematic analysis for the Global Burden of Disease Study 2016. *The Lancet, 390*(10100), 1345–1422.

Gakidou, E., Cowling, K., Lozano, R. & Murray, C.J.L. (2010). Increased educational attainment and its effect on child mortality in 175 countries between 1970 and 2009: a systematic analysis. *The Lancet, 376*, 959–974.

Gale, C.R., Batty, D. & Deary, I.J. (2008). Locus of control at age 10 years and health outcomes and behaviors at age 30 years: the 1970 British cohort study. *Psychosomatic Medicine, 70*, 397–403.

Galizzi, M.M. & Whitmarsh, L. (2019). How to measure behavioral Spillovers: a methodological review and checklist. *Frontiers in Psychology, 10*, 342.

Galloway, A.T., Fiorito, L.M., Francis, L.A. & Birch, L.L. (2006). 'Finish your soup': counterproductive effects of pressuring children to eat on intake and affect. *Appetite, 46(3)*, 318–323.

Gangopadhyay, D.N., Chanda, M., Sarkar, K., Niyogi, S.K., Chakraborty, S., Saha, M.K., ... & Detels, R. (2005). Evaluation of sexually transmitted diseases/ human immunodeficiency virus intervention programs for sex workers in Calcutta, India. *Sexually Transmitted Diseases, 32*(11), 680.

Garber, C.E., Blissmer, B., Deschenes, M.R., Franklin, B.A., Lamonte, M.J., Lee, I.M., ... & Swain, D.P. (2011). Quantity and quality of exercise for developing and maintaining cardiorespiratory, musculoskeletal, and neuromotor fitness in apparently healthy adults: guidance for prescribing exercise. *Medicine and Science in Sports and Exercise, 43*(7),1334–1359.

Gardner, B. (2015). A review and analysis of the use of 'habit' in understanding, predicting and influencing health-related behaviour. *Health Psychology Review, 9*(3), 277–295.

Gardner, B. & Tang, V. (2014). Reflecting on non-reflective action: An exploratory think-aloud study of self-report habit measures. *British Journal of Health Psychology, 19*(2), 258–273.

Gardner, B., Abraham, C., Lally, P. & de Bruijn, G. J. (2012b). Towards parsimony in habit measurement: Testing the convergent and predictive validity of an automaticity subscale of the Self-Report Habit Index. *International Journal of Behavioral Nutrition and Physical Activity, 9*(1), 102.

Gardner, B., de Bruijn, G.J. & Lally, P. (2011). A systematic review and meta-analysis of applications of the self-report habit index to nutrition and physical activity behaviours. *Annals of Behavioral Medicine, 42*(2), 174–187.

Gardner, B., de Bruijn, G.J. & Lally, P. (2012a). Habit, identity, and repetitive action: A prospective study of binge-drinking in UK students. *British Journal of Health Psychology, 17*(3), 565–581.

Garn, S.M., Bailey, S.M., Solomon, M.A. & Hopkins, P. (1981). Effect of remaining family members on fatness prediction. *The American Journal of Clinical Nutrition, 34*, 148–153.

Gauke D. (2016). *Budget*. London: HM Treasury.

Gavi (2020). The race to develop an Ebola vaccine. www.gavi.org/vaccineswork/race-develop-ebola-vaccine

Gay, N.J. (2004). The theory of measles elimination: implications for the design of elimination strategies. *The Journal of Infectious Diseases, 189*, S27–35.

Gay-Reese, J., Pank, G., Bell, P. (Producers) & Kapadia, A. (Director). (2015). *Amy* [Motion Picture]. United Kingdom: Altitude Film Distributio, A24.

Gearhardt, A.N., Grilo, C.M., DiLeone, R.J., Brownell, K.D. & Potenza, M.N. (2011a). Can food be addictive? Public health and policy implications. *Addiction, 106(7)*, 1208–1212.

Gearhardt, A.N., Yokum, S., Orr, P.T., Stice, E., Corbin, W.R. & Brownell, K.D. (2011b). Neural correlates of food addiction. *Archives of General Psychiatry, 68*(8), 808–816.

Gellert, P., Ziegelmann, J.P. & Schwarzer, R. (2012). Affective and health-related outcome expectancies for physical activity in older adults. *Psychology and Health, 27*, 816–828.

Ghaemi, S. N. (2009). The rise and fall of the biopsychosocial model. *The British Journal of Psychiatry, 195*(1), 3–4.

Gibbons, F.X., Gerrard, M. & Lane, D J. (2003). A social reaction model of adolescent health risk. In J. M. Suls & K.A. Wallston (eds.). *Social Psychological Foundations of Health and Illness* (pp. 107–136). Oxford: Blackwell.

Gibbons, F.X., Gerrard, M., Stock, M.L. & Finneran, S.D. (2015). The prototype/willingness model. In M. Conner and P. Norman (eds.). *Predicting and Changing Health Behaviour. Research and Practice with Social Cognition Models*. Maidenhead: Open University Press.

Gidlow, C., Johnston, L.H., Crone, D., Ellis, N. & James, D. (2006). A systematic review of the relationship between socio-economic position and physical activity. *Health Education Journal, 65*(3).

Giles, E.L., Holmes, M., McColl, E., Sniehotta, F.F. & Adams, J.M. (2015). Acceptability of financial incentives for breastfeeding: thematic analysis of readers' comments to UK online news reports. *BMC Pregnancy and Childbirth, 15*(1), 116.

Giles, E.L., Robalino, S., McColl, E., Sniehotta, F.F. & Adams, J. (2014). The effectiveness of financial incentives for health behaviour change: systematic review and meta-analysis. *PloS One, 9*(3), e90347.

Gillan, C.M., Otto, A.R., Phelps, E.A. & Daw, N.D. (2015). Model-based learning protects against forming habits. *Cognitive, Affective & Behavioral Neuroscience, 15*(3), 523–536.

Gilovich, T., Vallone, R. & Tversky, A. (1985). The hot hand in basketball: On the misperception of random sequences. *Cognitive Psychology, 17*(3), 295–314.

Giner-Sorolla, R. (2001). Guilty pleasures and grim necessities: affective attitudes in dilemmas of self-control. *Journal of Personality and Social Psychology, 80*, 206.

Giordano, G.N. & Lindström, M. (2016). Trust and health: testing the reverse causality hypothesis. *Journal of Epidemiology and Community Health, 70*, 10–16.

Glanz, K. & Bishop, D.B. (2010). The role of behavioral science theory in development and implementation of public health interventions. *Annual Review of Public Health, 31*, 399–418.

Glasman L.R. & Albarracín, D. (2006). Forming attitudes that predict future behaviour: a meta-analysis of the attitude-behavior relation. *Psychological Bulletin, 132*, 778–822.

Godin, G., Sheeran, P., Conner, M. & Germain, M. (2008). Asking questions changes behavior: Mere measurement effects on frequency of blood donation. *Health Psychology, 27*, 179–184.

Godin, G., Sheeran, P., Conner, M., Bélanger-Gravel, A., Gallani, M.C.B. & Nolin, B. (2010). Social structure, social cognition, and physical activity: A test of four models. *British Journal of Health Psychology, 15*, 79–95.

Goldacre, B. (2008). *Bad Science*. London: Fourth Estate.

Goldacre, B. (2012). *Bad Pharma: How Medicine is Broken, and How We Can Fix It*. London: HarperCollins.

Goldenberg, J.L. & Arndt, J. (2008). The implications of death for health: A terror management health model for behavioral health promotion. *Psychological Review, 115*, 1032–1053.

Goldfield, G.S. & Epstein, L.H. (2002). Can fruits and vegetables and activities substitute for snack foods?. *Health Psychology, 21*(3), 299.

Goldin, J. & Homonoff, T. (2013). Smoke gets in your eyes: cigarette tax salience and regressivity. *American Economic Journal: Economic Policy, 5*, 302–336.

Goldstein, C.M., Thomas, J.G., Wing, R.R. & Bond, D.S. (2017). Successful weight loss maintainers use health-tracking smartphone applications more than a nationally representative sample: comparison of the National Weight Control Registry to Pew Tracking for Health. *Obesity Science & Practice, 3*(2), 117–126.

Gollwitzer, P.M. (1993). Goal achievement: The role of intentions. In W. Stroebe & M. Hewstone (eds.). *European Review of Social Psychology* (Vol. 4, pp. 141–185). Chichester: Wiley.

Gollwitzer, P.M. (1996). The volitional benefits of planning. In P.M. Gollwitzer & J. Bargh (eds.). *The Psychology of Action: Linking Cognition and Motivation to Behavior* (pp. 287–312). New York: Guilford Press.

Gollwitzer, P.M. (1999). Implementation intentions: Strong effects of simple plans. *American Psychologist, 54*(7), 493.

Gollwitzer, P.M. & Brandstätter, V. (1997). Implementation intentions and effective goal pursuit. *Journal of Personality and Social Psychology, 73*(1), 186.

Gollwitzer, P.M. & Kinney, R.F. (1989). Effects of deliberative and implemental mind-sets on illusion of control. *Journal of Personality and Social Psychology, 56*, 531–542.

Gollwitzer, P.M. & Sheeran, P. (2006). Implementation intentions and goal achievement: A meta-analysis of effects and processes. *Advances in Experimental Social Psychology, 38*, 69–119.

Gollwitzer, P.M., Bayer, U.C. & McCulloch, K.C. (2005). The control of the unwanted. In R.R. Hassin, J.S. Uleman & J.A. Bargh (eds.). *The New Unconscious* (pp. 485–516). Oxford: Oxford University Press.

Gong, Y., Gallacher, J., Palmer, S. & Fone, D. (2014). Neighbourhood green space, physical function and participation in physical activities among elderly men: the Caerphilly prospective study. *International Journal of Behavioral Nutrition and Physical Activity, 11*, 40.

Goodwin, G.P. & Landy, J.F. (2014). Valuing different human lives. *Journal of Experimental Psychology: General, 143*(2), 778.

Goodwin, R. & Hamilton, S.P. (2002). Cigarette smoking and panic: the role of neuroticism. *American Journal of Psychiatry, 159*, 1208–1213.

Gordon-Larsen, P., Nelson, M.C., Page, P. & Popkin, B.M. (2006). Inequality in the built environment underlies key health disparities in physical activity and obesity. *Pediatrics, 117*, 417–424.

Gore, S.M., Bird, A.G., & Ross, A.J. (1996). Prison rights: mandatory drugs tests and performance indicators for prisons. *British Medical Journal, 312*(7043), 1411–1413.

Goren-Inbar, N., Alperson, N., Kislev, M.E., Simchoni, O., Melamed, Y., Ben-Nun, A. & Werker, E. (2004). Evidence of hominin control of fire at Gesher Benot Ya'aqov, Israel. *Science, 304*, 725–727.

Gornall, J. (2015). Sugar: spinning a web of influence. *British Medical Journal, 350*, h231.

Gostin, L. O., DeBartolo, M. C. & Friedman, E. A. (2015). The International Health Regulations 10 years on: the governing framework for global health security. *Lancet, 386*(10009), 2222–2226.

Gouda, H.N., Charlson, F., Sorsdahl, K., Ahmadzada, S., Ferrari, A.J., Erskine, H., ... & Mayosi, B.M. (2019). Burden of non-communicable diseases in sub-Saharan Africa, 1990–2017: results from the Global Burden of Disease Study 2017. *The Lancet Global Health, 7*(10), e1375–e1387.

Gould, R.A. (1980). *Living Archeology*. Cambridge: Cambridge University Press.

Graham, J.D., Bray, S.R. & Ginis, K.A.M. (2014). 'Pay the piper': It helps initially, but motivation takes a toll on self-control. *Psychology of Sport and Exercise, 15*(1), 89–96.

Gralnek, I.M., Dulai, G.S., Fennerty, M.B. & Spiegel, B.M.R. (2006). Esomeprazole versus other proton pump inhibitors in erosive esophagitis: a meta-analysis of randomized clinical trials. *Clinical Gastroenterology and Hepatology, 4*, 1452–1458.

Grant, B.F., Goldstein, R.B., Chou, S.P., Huang, B., Stinson, F.S., Dawson, D.A., ... & Ruan, W.J. (2009). Sociodemographic and psychopathologic predictors of first incidence of DSM-IV substance use, mood and anxiety disorders: results from the Wave 2 National Epidemiologic Survey on Alcohol and Related Conditions. *Molecular Psychiatry, 14*(11), 1051.

Gray, J.A. (1982). *The Neuropsychology of Anxiety: An Enquiry into the Functions of the Septo-Hippocampal System*. Oxford: Oxford University Press.

Gray, J.A. & McNaughton, N. (2000). *The Neuropsychology of Anxiety: An Enquiry into the Functions of the Septo-Hippocampal System*. Oxford: Oxford University Press.

Greaves, C.J., Sheppard, K.E., Abraham, C., Hardeman, W., Roden, M., Evans, P. H. & Schwarz, P. (2011). Systematic review of reviews of intervention components associated with increased effectiveness in dietary and physical activity interventions. *BMC Public Health, 11*, 119.

Green, L., Fry, A.F. & Myerson, J. (1994). Discounting of delayed rewards: A life-span comparison. *Psychological Science, 5*(1), 33–36.

Greenhalgh, J., Dowey, A.J., Horne, P.J., Lowe, C.F., Griffiths, J.H. & Whitaker, C.J. (2009). Positive-and negative peer modelling effects on young children's consumption of novel blue foods. *Appetite, 52*(3), 646–653.

Greenland, S.J. (2016). The Australian experience following plain packaging: the impact on tobacco branding. *Addiction, 111*(12), 2248–2258.

Grekin, E.R., Sher, K.J. & Wood, P.K. (2006). Personality and substance dependence symptoms: modelling substance-specific traits. *Psychology of Addictive Behaviors, 20*, 415–424.

Gresky, J., Batieva, E., Kitova, A., Kalmykov, A., Belinskiy, A., Reinhold, S. & Berezina, N. (2016). New cases of trepanations from the 5th to 3rd millennia BC in Southern Russia in the context of previous research: Possible evidence for a ritually motivated tradition of cranial surgery? *American Journal of Physical Anthropology, 160*(4), 665–682.

Grier, S. & Bryant, C. A. (2005). Social marketing in public health. *Annual Review of Public Health, 26*, 319–339.

Grimes, D.A. & Schulz, K.F. (2002a). An overview of clinical research: the lay of the land. *The Lancet, 359*(9300), 57–61.

Grimes, D.A. & Schulz, K.F. (2002b). Descriptive studies: what they can and cannot do. *The Lancet, 359*(9301), 145–149.

Grimes, D.A. & Schulz, K.F. (2002c). Cohort studies: marching towards outcomes. *The Lancet, 359*(9303), 341–345.

Grimm, J.W., Hope, B.T., Wise, R.A. & Shaham, Y. (2001). Neuroadaptation: incubation of cocaine craving after withdrawal. *Nature, 412*(6843), 141.

Griskevicius, V., Ackerman, J.M., Cantú, S.M., Delton, A.W., Robertson, T.E., Simpson, J.A., Thompson, M.E. & Tybur, J.M. (2013). When the economy falters, do people spend or save? Responses to resource scarcity depend on childhood environments. *Psychological Science, 24*, 197–205.

Griswold, M.G., Fullman, N., Hawley, C., Arian, N., Zimsen, S.R., Tymeson, H.D., ... & Abate, K.H. (2018). Alcohol use and burden for 195 countries and territories, 1990–2016: a systematic analysis for the Global Burden of Disease Study 2016. *The Lancet, 392*(10152), 1015–1035.

Gross, J.J. (ed.) (2015). *Handbook of Emotion Regulation*. New York: Guilford Press.

Gross, M. (2017). How our diet changed our evolution. *Current Biology*, 27, R731–R745.

Grucza, R.A., Wang, J.C., Stitzel, J.A., Hinrichs, A.L., Saccone, S.F., ... Bierut, L.J. (2008). A risk of allele for nicotine dependence in CHRNA5 is a protective allele for cocaine dependence. *Biological Psychiatry*, 64, 922–929.

Gupta, R.K. et al. (2020). Evidence for HIV-1 cure after *CCR5Δ32/Δ32* allogeneic haemopoietic stem-cell transplantation 30 months post analytical treatment interruption: a case report. *Lancet HIV*, S2352–3018.

Gurven, A.D., Blackwell, A.D., Rodriguez, D.E., Stieglitz, J. & Kaplan, H. (2012). Does blood pressure inevitably rise with age? *Hypertension*, 60, 25–33.

Hagenaars, L.L., Jeurissen, P.P.T. & Klazinga, N.S. (2017). The taxation of unhealthy energy-dense foods (EDFs) and sugar-sweetened beverages (SSBs): an overview of patterns observed in the policy content and policy context of 13 case studies. *Health Policy*, 121(8), 887–894.

Hagger, M.S. & Chatzisarantis, N.L. (2011). Causality orientations moderate the undermining effect of rewards on intrinsic motivation. *Journal of Experimental Social Psychology*, 47, 485–489.

Hagger, M.S. & Chatzisarantis, N.L. (2013). The sweet taste of success: The presence of glucose in the oral cavity moderates the depletion of self-control resources. *Personality and Social Psychology Bulletin*, 39(1), 28–42.

Hagger, M.S. & Chatzisarantis, N.L.D. (2015). Self-determination theory. In M. Conner and P. Norman (eds.). *Predicting and Changing Health Behaviour: Research and Practice with Social Cognition Models.* Maidenhead: Open University Press.

Hagger, M.S., Chatzisarantis, N.L., Alberts, H., Anggono, C.O., Batailler, C., Birt, A.R., ... & Calvillo, D.P. (2016). A multilab preregistered replication of the ego-depletion effect. *Perspectives on Psychological Science*, 11(4), 546–573.

Hagger, M.S., Lonsdale, A. & Chatzisarantis, N.L. (2012a). A theory-based intervention to reduce alcohol drinking in excess of guideline limits among undergraduate students. *British Journal of Health Psychology*, 17(1), 18–43.

Hagger, M.S., Lonsdale, A., Koka, A., Hein, V., Pasi, H., Lintunen, T. & Chatzisarantis, N.L. (2012b). An intervention to reduce alcohol consumption in undergraduate students using implementation intentions and mental simulations: A cross-national study. *International Journal of Behavioral Medicine*, 19(1), 82–96.

Hagger, M.S., Wood, C., Stiff, C. & Chatzisarantis, N.L. (2010). Ego depletion and the strength model of self-control: a meta-analysis. *Psychological Bulletin*, 136(4), 495.

Hahesy, A.L., Wilens, T.E., Biederman, J., Van Patten, S.L. & Spencer, T. (2002). Temporal association between childhood psychopathology and substance use disorders: findings from a sample of adults with opioid or alcohol dependency. *Psychiatry Research*, 109(3), 245–253.

Hajek, P., Phillips-Waller, A., Przulj, D., Pesola, F., Myers Smith, K., Bisal, N., ... & Ross, L. (2019). A randomized trial of e-cigarettes versus nicotine-replacement therapy. *New England Journal of Medicine*, 380(7), 629–637.

Hall, W., Carter, A. & Forlini, C. (2015). The brain disease model of addiction: is it supported by the evidence and has it delivered on its promises? *The Lancet Psychiatry*, 2(1), 105–110.

Hallal, P.C., Andersen, L.B., Bull, F.C., Guthold, R., Haskell, W., Ekelund, U. & Lancet Physical Activity Series Working Group. (2012). Global physical activity levels: surveillance progress, pitfalls, and prospects. *The Lancet*, 380(9838), 247–257.

Hallingberg, B., Maynard, O.M., Bauld, L., Brown, R., Gray, L., Lowthian, E., ... & Moore, G. (2019). Have e-cigarettes renormalised or displaced youth smoking? Results of a segmented regression analysis of repeated cross sectional survey data in England, Scotland and Wales. *Tobacco Control*, doi: 10.1136/tobaccocontrol-2018-054584.

Hamilton, J., Fawson, S., May, J., Andrade, J. & Kavanagh, D.J. (2013). Brief guided imagery and body scanning interventions reduce food cravings. *Appetite*, 71, 158–162.

Hammond, K.R. (1996). *Human Judgment and Social Policy.* New York: Oxford University Press.

Hampson, S.E. (2012). Personality processes: mechanisms by which personality traits 'get outside the skin'. *Annual Review of Psychology*, 63, 315–339.

Hankonen, N., Absetz, P., Kinnunen, M., Haukkala, A. & Jallinoja, P. (2013). Toward identifying a broader range of social cognitive determinants of dietary intentions and behaviors. *Applied Psychology: Health and Wellbeing*, 5, 118–135.

Hardeman, W., Johnston, M., Johnston, D., Bonetti, D., Wareham, N.J. & Kinmounth, A.L. (2002). Application of the theory of planned behaviour in behaviour change interventions: a systematic review. *Psychology and Health*, 17, 123–158.

Hardman, C.A., Herbert, V.M., Brunstrom, J.M., Munafò, M.R. & Rogers, P.J. (2012). Dopamine and food reward: Effects of acute tyrosine/phenylalanine depletion on appetite. *Physiology & Behavior, 105*(5), 1202–1207.

Harper, L.V. & Sanders, K.M. (1975). The effect of adults' eating on young children's acceptance of unfamiliar foods. *Journal of Experimental Child Psychology, 20*(2), 206–214.

Harris, B. (2011). The intractable cigarette 'filter problem'. *Tobacco Control, 20* (Suppl 1), i10–i16.

Harris, D.R. (2007). Agriculture, cultivation, and domestication: exploring the conceptual framework of early food production. In: T.P. Denman, J. Iriarte, and L. Vrydaghs (eds.). *Rethinking Agriculture: Archaeological and Ethnoarchaeological Perspectives.* Walnut Creek: CA: Left Coast Press, pp. 16–35.

Harris, G. & Mason, S. (2017). Are there sensitive periods for food acceptance in infancy? *Current Nutrition Reports, 6*(2), 190–196.

Harris, J.B., LaRocque, R.C., Qadri, F., Ryan, E.T. & Calderwood, S.B. (2012). Cholera. *Lancet, 379,* 2466–2476.

Harris, J.W.K. (1983). Cultural beginnings: Plio-Pleistocene archaeological occurrences form the Afar, Ethiopia. In N. David (ed.) *African Archaeological Review.* Cambridge: Cambridge University Press.

Harrison, J.A., Mullen, P.D. & Green, L.W. (1992). A meta-analysis of studies of the health belief model with adults. *Health Education Research, 7,* 107–116.

Hartmann-Boyce, J., Chepkin, S.C., Ye, W., Bullen, C. & Lancaster, T. (2018). Nicotine replacement therapy versus control for smoking cessation. *Cochrane Database of Systematic Reviews, 5.* Art. No.: CD000146. DOI: 10.1002/14651858.CD000146.pub5.

Hartmann-Boyce, J., McRobbie, H., Bullen, C., Begh, R., Stead, L.F. & Hajek, P. (2016). Electronic cigarettes for smoking cessation. *Cochrane Database of Systematic Reviews,* (9).

Harvey, K., Kemps, E. & Tiggemann, M. (2005). The nature of imagery processes underlying food cravings. *British Journal of Health Psychology, 10*(1), 49–56.

Hasking, P.A. (2006). Reinforcement sensitivity, coping, disordered eating and drinking behaviour in adolescents. *Personality and Individual Differences, 40,* 677–688.

Hastings, G., Stead, M. & Webb, J. (2004). Fear appeals in social marketing: Strategic and ethical reasons for concern. *Psychology & Marketing, 21,* 961–986.

Hatzenbuehler, M.L., Phelan, J.C. & Link, B.G. (2013). Stigma as a fundamental cause of population health inequalities. *American Journal of Public Health, 103*(5), 813–821.

Haytowitz, D. B., Wu, X. & Bhagwat, S. (2018). USDA database for the flavonoid content of selected foods, Release 3.3. US Department of Agriculture: Beltsville, MD, USA.

Health and Safety Executive (2016). Statistics on Fatal Injuries in the Workplace In Great Britain 2016. Crown Copyright.

Heather, N. (2016). On defining addiction. In N. Heather and G. Segal (eds.). *Addiction and Choice: Rethinking the Relationship.* Oxford: Oxford University Press.

Heffernan, K., Cloitre, M., Tardiff, K., Marzuk, P.M., Portera, L. & Leon, A.C. (2000). Childhood trauma as a correlate of lifetime opiate use in psychiatric patients. *Addictive Behaviors, 25*(5), 797–803.

Heinen, M.M., Bartholomew, L.K., Wensing, M., van de Kerkhof, P. & van Achterberg, T. (2006). Supporting adherence and healthy lifestyles in leg ulcer patients: systematic development of the Lively Legs program for dermatology outpatient clinics. *Patient Education and Counseling, 61*(2), 279–291.

Heinrichs, M., Baumgartner, T., Kirschbaum, C. & Ehlert, U. (2003). Social support and oxytocin interact to suppress cortisol and subjective responses to psychosocial stress. *Biological Society, 54,* 1389–1398.

Helps, C., Leask, J. & Barclay, L. (2018). 'It just forces hardship': impacts of government financial penalties on non-vaccinating parents. *Journal of Public Health Policy, 39*(2), 156–169.

Heminsley, A. (2014). *Running Like a Girl.* London: Windmill Books.

Hemming, K., Haines, T.P., Chilton, P.J., Girling, A.J. & Lilford, R.J. (2015). The stepped wedge cluster randomised trial: rationale, design, analysis, and reporting. *British Medical Journal, 350,* h391.

Henderson, L., McMillan, B., Green, J.M. & Renfrew, M.J. (2011). Men and infant feeding: Perceptions of embarrassment, sexuality, and social conduct in white low-income British men. *Birth, 38*(1), 61–70.

Henderson, M. (2012). *The Geek Manifesto: Why Science Matters.* London: Bantam.

Hendrikse, J.J., Cachia, R.L., Kothe, E.J., McPhie, S., Skouteris, H. & Hayden, M.J. (2015). Attentional biases for food cues in overweight and individuals with obesity: a systematic review of the literature. *Obesity Reviews, 16,* 424–432.

Hendy, H.M. (1999). Comparison of five teacher actions to encourage children's new food acceptance. *Annals of Behavioral Medicine, 21*(1), 20.

Hendy, H.M. & Raudenbush, B. (2000). Effectiveness of teacher modeling to encourage food acceptance in preschool children. *Appetite, 34*(1), 61–76.

Henry, A.G., Brooks, A.S. & Piperno, D.R. (2011). Microfossils in calculus demonstrate consumption of plants and cooked foods in Neanderthal diets (Shanidar III, Iraq; Spy I and II, Belgium). *Proceedings of the National Academy of Sciences of the USA*, 108, 486-491.

Herbert, B.M., Blechert, J., Hautzinger, M., Matthias, E. & Herbert, C. (2013). Intuitive eating is associated with interoceptive sensitivity. Effects on body mass index. *Appetite*, *70*, 22–30.

Herbert, B.M., Muth, E.R., Pollatos, O. & Herbert, C. (2012). Interoception across modalities: on the relationship between cardiac awareness and the sensitivity for gastric. *PLoS ONE*, *7*, e36646.

Hettema, J., Steele, J. & Miller, W.R. (2005). Motivational interviewing. *Annual Review of Clinical Psychology*, *1*, 91–111.

Hewlett, B.S., van de Koppel, J.M.H. & van de Koppel, M. (1986). Causes of death among Aka Pygmies of the Central African Republic. In L.L. Cavalli-Sforza (ed.). *African Pygmies*. New York: Academic Press, pp. 45–63.

Hien, D.A., Jiang, H., Campbell, A.N., Hu, M.C., Miele, G.M., Cohen, L.R., ... & Suarez-Morales, L. (2009). Do treatment improvements in PTSD severity affect substance use outcomes? A secondary analysis from a randomized clinical trial in NIDA's Clinical Trials Network. *American Journal of Psychiatry*, *167*(1), 95–101.

Higgins, A. & Conner, M. (2003). Understanding adolescent smoking: The role of the Theory of Planned Behaviour and implementation intentions. *Psychology, Health & Medicine*, *8*(2), 173–186.

Higgs, S (2015). Social norms and their influence on eating behaviours. *Appetite*, *86*, 38–44.

Hilbert, A. (2016). Weight stigma reduction and genetic determinism. *PLoS ONE*, *11*, e0162993.

Hill, J.O., Wyatt, H.R., Reed, G.W.,& Peters, J.C. (2003). Obesity and the environment: where do we go from here? *Science*, *299*, 853–855.

Hillman, C.H., Pontifex, M.B., Raine, L.B., Castelli, D.M., Hall, E.E. & Kramer, A.F. (2009). The effect of acute treadmill walking on cognitive control and academic achievement in preadolescent children. *Neuroscience*, *159*(3), 1044–1054.

Ho, K.J., Mikkelson, B., Lewis, L.A., Feldman, S.A. & Taylor, C.B. (1972). Alaskan arctic Eskimos: response to a customary high fat diet. *American Journal of Clinical Nutrition*, *25*, 737–745.

Hoffmann, T.C., Glasziou, P.P., Boutron, I., Milne, R., Perera, R., Moher, D., ... & Lamb, S.E. (2014). Better reporting of interventions: template for intervention description and replication (TIDieR) checklist and guide. *British Medical Journal*, *348*, g1687.

Hofmann, W., De Houwer, J., Perugini, M., Baeyens, F. & Crombez, G. (2010). Evaluative conditioning in humans: a meta-analysis. *Psychological Bulletin*, *136*(3), 390.

Hofmann, W., Friese, M. & Wiers, R. W. (2008). Impulsive versus reflective influences on health behavior: A theoretical framework and empirical review. *Health Psychology Review*, *2*(2), 111–137.

Hollander, K., Heidt, C., Van der Zwaard, B.C., Braumann, K.M. & Zech, A. (2017). Long-term effects of habitual barefoot running and walking: a systematic review. *Medicine & Science in Sports & Exercise*, *49*(4), 752–762.

Hollands, G.J. & Marteau, T.M. (2016). Pairing images of unhealthy and healthy foods with images of negative and positive health consequences: Impact on attitudes and food choice. *Health Psychology*, *35*(8), 847.

Hollands, G.J., Bignardi, G., Johnston, M., Kelly, M.P., Ogilvie, D., Petticrew, M., ... & Marteau, T.M. (2017). The TIPPME intervention typology for changing environments to change behaviour. *Nature Human Behaviour*, *1*(8), 1–9.

Hollands, G.J., Marteau, T.M. & Fletcher, P.C. (2016). Non-conscious processes in changing health-related behaviour: a conceptual analysis and framework. *Health Psychology Review*, *10*(4), 381–394.

Hollands, G.J., Shemilt, I., Marteau, T.M., Jebb, S.A., Kelly, M.P., Nakamura, R., ... & Ogilvie, D. (2013). Altering micro-environments to change population health behaviour: towards an evidence base for choice architecture interventions. *BMC Public Health*, *13*(1), 1218.

Holley, C.E., Farrow, C. & Haycraft, E. (2017). A systematic review of methods for increasing vegetable consumption in early childhood. *Current Nutrition Reports*, *6*(2), 157–170.

Holloszy, J.O. & Fontana, L. (2007). Caloric restriction in humans. *Experimental Gerontology*, *42*, 709–712.

Holmes, T. H. & Rahe, R. H. (1967). The social readjustment rating scale. *Journal of Psychosomatic Research*, *11*, 213–218.

Holt-Lunstad, J., Smith, T.B. & Layton, J.B. (2010). Social relationships and mortality risk: a meta-analytic review. *PLoS Medicine*, *7*, e1000316.

Hooper, L. V., Littman, D. R. & Macpherson, A. J. (2012). Interactions between the microbiota and the immune system. *Science*, *336*(6086), 1268–1273.

Horne, B.D., Muhlestein, J.B. & Anderson, J.L. (2015). Health effects of intermittent fasting: hormesis or harm? A systematic review. *The American Journal of Clinical Nutrition*, *102*, 464-470.

Horne, P.J., Hardman, C.A., Lowe, C.F., Tapper, K., Le Noury, J., Madden, P., ... & Doody, M. (2009). Increasing parental provision and children's consumption of lunchbox fruit and vegetables in Ireland: the Food Dudes intervention. *European Journal of Clinical Nutrition*, 63(5), 613.

Horne, P.J., Tapper, K., Lowe, C.F., Hardman, C.A., Jackson, M.C. & Woolner, J. (2004). Increasing children's fruit and vegetable consumption: a peer-modelling and rewards-based intervention. *European Journal of Clinical Nutrition*, 58(12), 1649.

Horta, B.L., Hartwig, F.P. & Victora, C.G. (2018). Breastfeeding and intelligence in adulthood: due to genetic confounding? *The Lancet Global Health*, 6(12), e1276–e1277.

Horta, B.L., Loret de Mola, C. & Victora, C.G. (2015). Breastfeeding and intelligence: a systematic review and meta-analysis. *Acta Paediatrica*, 104, 14–19.

Houben, K., Havermans, R.C., Nederkoorn, C. & Jansen, A. (2012). Beer à No-Go: Learning to stop responding to alcohol cues reduces alcohol intake via reduced affective associations rather than increased response inhibition. *Addiction*, 107(7), 1280–1287.

Houldcroft, L., Haycraft, E. & Farrow, C. (2014). Peer and friend influences on children's eating. *Social Development*, 23(1), 19–40.

House, J.S., Landis, K.R. & Umberson, D. (1988). Social relationships and health. *Science*, 241, 540–545.

Howard, D.H. (2007). Producing organ donors. *Journal of Economic Perspectives*, 21(3), 25–36.

Howard, M.C. (2020). Understanding face mask use to prevent coronavirus and other illnesses: Development of a multidimensional face mask perceptions scale. *British Journal of Health Psychology*, DOI:10.1111/bjhp.12453

Howell, N. (2000). *Demography of the Dobe !Kung*. 2nd edn. New York: Aldine De Gruyter.

Hsu, A., Yang, J., Yilmaz, Y.H., Haque, M.S., Can, C. & Blandford, A.E. (2014, April). Persuasive technology for overcoming food cravings and improving snack choices. In *Proceedings of the SIGCHI Conference on Human Factors in Computing Systems* (pp. 3403–3412). ACM.

Huber, M., Knottnerus, J. A., Green, L., van der Horst, H., Jadad, A. R., Kromhout, D., ... & Schnabel, P. (2011). How should we define health? *British Medical Journal*, 343, d4163.

Hughes, J.R., Hatsukami, D.K., Mitchell, J.E. & Dahlgren, L.A. (1986). Prevalence of smoking among psychiatric outpatients. *American Journal of Psychiatry*, 143(8), 993–997.

Hughes, J.R., Keely, J.P., Fagerstrom, K.O. & Callas, P.W. (2005). Intentions to quit smoking change over short periods of time. *Addictive Behaviors*, 30, 653–662.

Hunger, J.M. & Major, B. (2015). Weight stigma mediates the association between BMI and self-reported health. *Health Psychology*, 34(2), 172.

Hutchinson, J.C., Sherman, T., Martinovic, N. & Tenenbaum, G. (2008). The effect of manipulated self-efficacy on perceived and sustained effort. *Journal of Applied Sport Psychology*, 20, 457–472,

Hutchison, K.E., Haughey, H., Niculescu, M., Schacht, J., Kaiser, A., Stitzel, J., ... & Filbey, F. (2008). The incentive salience of alcohol: translating the effects of genetic variant in CNR1. *Archives of General Psychiatry*, 65(7), 841–850.

Huvenne, H. & Dubern, B. (2014). Monogenic forms of obesity. In C. Nobrega & R. Rodriguez-Lopez (eds.). *Molecular Mechanisms Underpinning the Development of Obesity*. New York: Springer.

Hyde, J., Hankins, M., Deale, A. & Marteau, T.M. (2008). Interventions to increase self-efficacy in the context of addiction behaviours: a systematic literature review. *Journal of Health Psychology*, 13, 607–623.

IHME (2014). Mexico global burden of disease. www.healthdata.org/mexico

IHME (2020). GBD compare. https://vizhub.healthdata.org/gbd-compare/

Ilic, D., Neuberger, M.M., Djulbegovic, M. & Dahm, P. (2013). Screening for prostate cancer. *Cochrane Database of Systematic Reviews*, 1, Article Number CD004720.

International Shark Attack File. (2018). www.floridamuseum.ufl.edu/shark-attacks/yearly-worldwide-summary/ and www.floridamuseum.ufl.edu/shark-attacks/odds/compare-risk/death/ and www.floridamuseum.ufl.edu/shark-attacks/odds/compare-risk/sand-holes/

Inzlicht, M. & Berkman, E. (2015). Six questions for the resource model of control (and some answers). *Social and Personality Psychology Compass*, 9(10), 511–524.

Inzlicht, M. & Schmeichel, B.J. (2012). What is ego depletion? Toward a mechanistic revision of the resource model of self-control. *Perspectives on Psychological Science*, 7(5), 450–463.

Inzlicht, M. & Schmeichel, B.J. (2016). Beyond limited resources. Self-control failure as the product of shifting priorities. In K.D. Vohs & R.F. Baumeister (eds.). *Handbook of Self-Regulation: Research, Theory, and Applications*. New York: Guilford Press.

Inzlicht, M., Schmeichel, B.J. & Macrae, C.N. (2014). Why self-control seems (but may not be) limited. *Trends in Cognitive Sciences*, 18(3), 127–133.

Ioannidis, J.P. (2005). Why most published research findings are false. *PLoS Medicine, 2*(8), e124.

Isaacs, D. (2020). Lessons from the tragic measles outbreak in Samoa. *Journal of Paediatrics and Child Health, 56*(1), 175-175.

Jackson, S.E., Beeken, R.J. & Wardle, J. (2014). Perceived weight discrimination and changes in weight, waist circumference, and weight status. *Obesity, 22*(12), 2485-2488.

James, W.P.T. (1995). A public health approach to the problem of obesity. *International Journal of Obesity, 19*, S37-46.

Jana, S., Basu, I., Rotheram-Borus, M.J. & Newman, P.A. (2004). The Sonagachi Project: a sustainable community intervention program. *AIDS Education and Prevention, 16*(5), 405-414.

Jang, K.L., Thordarson, D.S., Stein, M.B., Cohan, S.L. & Taylor, S. (2007), Coping styles and personality: a biometric analysis. *Anxiety, Stress, and Coping, 20*, 17-24.

Janis, I.L. (1967). Effects of fear arousal on attitude change: Recent developments in theory and experimental research. *Advances in Experimental Social Psychology, 3*, 166-224.

Janis, I.L. & Feshbach, S. (1953). Effect of fear-arousing communications. *The Journal of Abnormal and Social Psychology, 48*, 78-92.

Jansen, A., Boon, B., Nauta, H. & Van den Hout, M. (1992). Salivation discordant with hunger. *Behaviour Research and Therapy, 30*(2), 163-166.

Jansen, A., Havermans, R.C. & Nederkoorn, C. (2011). Cued overeating. In V.R. Preedy, R.R. Watson & C.R. Martin (eds.). *Handbook of Behavior, Food and Nutrition.* New York: Springer-Verlag.

Jansen, A., Schyns, G., Bongers, P. & van den Akker, K. (2016). From lab to clinic: Extinction of cued cravings to reduce overeating. *Physiology & Behavior, 162*, 174-180.

Jansen, E., Mulkens, S. & Jansen, A. (2007). Do not eat the red food!: prohibition of snacks leads to their relatively higher consumption in children. *Appetite, 49*(3), 572-577.

Jansen, E., Mulkens, S., Emond, Y. & Jansen, A. (2008). From the Garden of Eden to the land of plenty: Restriction of fruit and sweets intake leads to increased fruit and sweets consumption in children. *Appetite, 51*(3), 570-575.

Janz, N.K. & Becker, M.H. (1984). The health belief model: A decade later. *Health Education Quarterly, 11*, 1-47.

Jen, M.H., Sund, E.R., Johnston, R. & Jones, K. (2010). Trustful societies, trustful individuals, and health: an analysis of self-rated health and social trust using the World Value Survey. *Health and Place, 16*, 1022-1029.

Jenkins, D.W. & Cauthon, D.J. (2011). Barefoot running claims and controversies. A review of the literature. *Journal of the American Podiatric Medical Association, 101*, 231-246.

Jha, P., Ramasundarahettige, C., Landsman, V., Rostron, B., Thun, M., Anderson, R.N., ... & Peto, R. (2013). 21st-century hazards of smoking and benefits of cessation in the United States. *New England Journal of Medicine, 368*(4), 341-350.

Ji, M.F. & Wood, W. (2007). Purchase and consumption habits: not necessarily what you intend. *Journal of Consumer Psychology, 17*(4), 261-276.

Job, V., Bernecker, K., Miketta, S. & Friese, M. (2015a). Implicit theories about willpower predict the activation of a rest goal following self-control exertion. *Journal of Personality and Social Psychology, 109*(4), 694.

Job, V., Dweck, C.S. & Walton, G.M. (2010). Ego depletion—Is it all in your head? Implicit theories about willpower affect self-regulation. *Psychological Science, 21*(11), 1686-1693.

Job, V., Walton, G.M., Bernecker, K. & Dweck, C.S. (2013). Beliefs about willpower determine the impact of glucose on self-control. *Proceedings of the National Academy of Sciences, 201313475*.

Job, V., Walton, G.M., Bernecker, K. & Dweck, C.S. (2015b). Implicit theories about willpower predict self-regulation and grades in everyday life. *Journal of Personality and Social Psychology, 108*(4), 637.

John, L.K., Loewenstein, G. & Prelec, D. (2012). Measuring the prevalence of questionable research practices with incentives for truth telling. *Psychological Science, 23*(5), 524-532.

Johnson, E.J. & Goldstein, D. (2003). Do defaults save lives? *Science, 302*, 1338-1339.

Johnson, M., Whelan, B., Relton, C., Thomas, K., Strong, M., Scott, E. & Renfrew, M.J. (2018). Valuing breastfeeding: a qualitative study of women's experiences of a financial incentive scheme for breastfeeding. *BMC Pregnancy and Childbirth, 18*(1), 20.

Johnson, P.M. & Kenny, P.J. (2010). Dopamine D2 receptors in addiction-like reward dysfunction and compulsive eating in obese rats. *Nature Neuroscience, 13*(5), 635.

Johnston, D.W. & Johnston, M. (2013). Useful theories should apply to individuals. *British Journal of Health Psychology, 18*(3), 469-473.

Jokela, M., Hintsanen, M., Hakulinen, C., Batty, G.D., Nabi, H., Singh-Manoux, A. & Kivimäki, M. (2013). Association of personality with the development and persistence of obesity: a meta-analysis based on individual-participant data. *Obesity Reviews, 14*, 315-323.

Jones, A., Di Lemma, L.C., Robinson, E., Christiansen, P., Nolan, S., Tudur-Smith, C. & Field, M. (2016). Inhibitory control training for appetitive behaviour change: A meta-analytic investigation of mechanisms of action and moderators of effectiveness. *Appetite, 97*, 16–28.

Jones, A., Hardman, C.A., Lawrence, N. & Field, M. (2017). Cognitive training as a potential treatment for overweight and obesity: A critical review of the evidence: Proposal for special issue in appetite: Executive function training & eating behaviour. *Appetite, 124*, 50–67.

Jones, C.R., Fazio, R.H. & Olson, M.A. (2009). Implicit misattribution as a mechanism underlying evaluative conditioning. *Journal of Personality and Social Psychology, 96*(5), 933.

Jones, C.R., Olson, M.A. & Fazio, R.H. (2010). Evaluative conditioning: The 'how' question. In *Advances in Experimental Social Psychology* (Vol. 43, pp. 205-255). Academic Press.

Judah, G., Gardner, B. & Aunger, R. (2013). Forming a flossing habit: an exploratory study of the psychological determinants of habit formation. *British Journal of Health Psychology, 18*(2), 338–353.

Judge, K. (1995). Income distribution and life expectancy: a critical appraisal. *British Medical Journal, 311*, 1282.

Kabat-Zinn, J. (2003). Mindfulness-based interventions in context: Past, present, and future. *Clinical Psychology: Science and Practice, 10*, 144–156.

Kahneman, D. (2011). *Thinking, Fast and Slow*. London: Penguin Books.

Kahneman, D. & Tversky, A. (1982). The psychology of preferences. *Scientific American, 246*(1), 160–173.

Kakoschke, N., Kemps, E. & Tiggemann, M. (2017). Approach bias modification training and consumption: A review of the literature. *Addictive Behaviors, 64*, 21–28.

Kakoschke, N., Kemps, E. & Tiggemann, M. (2018). What is the appropriate control condition for approach bias modification? A response to commentary by Becker et al. (2017). *Addictive Behaviors, 77*, 295–6.

Kalinowski, A. & Humphreys, K. (2016). Governmental standard drink definitions and low-risk alcohol consumption guidelines in 37 countries. *Addiction, 111*(7), 1293–1298.

Kaner, E.F., Dickinson, H.O., Beyer, F., Pienaar, E., Schlesinger, C., Campbell, F., ... & Heather, N. (2009). The effectiveness of brief alcohol interventions in primary care settings: a systematic review. *Drug and Alcohol Review, 28*(3), 301–323.

Kaplan, G.A., Pamik, E.R., Lynch, J.W., Cohen, R.D. & Balfour, J.L. (1996). Inequality in income and mortality in the United States: analysis of mortality and potential pathways. *British Medical Journal, 312*, 999.

Kappes, H.B. & Morewedge, C.K. (2016). Mental simulation as substitute for experience. *Social and Personality Psychology Compass, 10*(7), 405–420.

Karasek, R.A & Theorell, T. (1990). *Healthy Work: Stress, Productivity, and the Reconstruction of Working Life*. New York: Basic Books.

Karremans, J.C., Stroebe, W. & Claus, J. (2006). Beyond Vicary's fantasies: The impact of subliminal priming and brand choice. *Journal of Experimental Social Psychology, 42*(6), 792–798.

Kasser, T. & Ryan, R.M. (1996). Further examining the American dream: Differential correlates of intrinsic and extrinsic goals. *Personality and Social Psychology Bulletin, 22*, 280–287.

Kavanagh, D.J., Andrade, J. & May, J. (2005). Imaginary relish and exquisite torture: The elaborated intrusion theory of desire. *Psychological Review, 112*, 446–467.

Kavanagh, D.J., May, J. & Andrade, J. (2009). Tests of the Elaborated Intrusion Theory of craving and desire: Features of alcohol craving during treatment for an alcohol disorder. *British Journal of Clinical Psychology, 48*, 241–254.

Kawachi, I. & Kennedy, B.P. (1997). Socioeconomic determinants of health: health and social cohesion: why care about income inequality? *British Medical Journal, 314*, 1037.

Kawachi, I., Kennedy, B.P., Lochner, K. & Prothrow-Stith, D. (1997). Social capital, income inequality, and mortality. *Public Health, 87*, 1491–1498.

Kazdin, A.E. (2011). Single-case research designs: Methods for clinical and applied settings (2nd edn). New York: Oxford University Press.

Kearns, A., Bailey, N., Gannon, M., Livingston, M. & Leyland, A. (2014). 'All in it together'? Social cohesion in a divided society: attitudes to income inequality and redistribution in a residential context. *Journal of Social Policy, 43*, 453–477.

Kearns, C.E., Glantz, S.A. & Schmidt, L.A. (2015). Sugar industry influence on the scientific agenda of the National Institute of Dental Research's 1971 National Caries Program: a historical analysis of internal documents. *PLoS Medicine, 12*(3), e1001798.

Keatley, D., Clarke, D. & Hagger, M. S. (2013). The predictive validity of implicit measures of self-determined motivation across health-related behaviours. *British Journal of Health Psychology, 18*, 2–17.

Keelan, J., Pavri-Garcia, V., Tomlinson, G. & Wilson, K. (2007). YouTube as a source of information on immunization: a content analysis. *Journal of the American Medical Association, 298*(21), 2482–2484.

Keller, H. (2007). *Cultures of Infancy*. Mahwah, NJ: Erlbaum.

Keller, H., Yovsi, R., Borke, J., Kärtner, J., Jensen, H. & Papaligoura, Z. (2004). Developmental consequences of early parenting experiences: Self-recognition and self-regulation in three cultural communities. *Child Development*, 75(6), 1745–1760.

Keller, K.L. & Adise, S. (2016). Variation in the ability to taste bitter thiourea compounds: implications for food acceptance, dietary intake, and obesity risk in children. *Annual Review of Nutrition*, 36, 157–182.

Keller, L. & Gollwitzer, P.M. (2017). Mindsets affect risk perception and risk-taking behavior. *Social Psychology*, 43, 135–147.

Kemps, E. & Tiggemann, M. (2007). Modality-specific imagery reduces cravings for food: An application of the elaborated intrusion theory of desire to food craving. *Journal of Experimental Psychology: Applied*, 13(2), 95.

Kemps, E. & Tiggemann, M. (2013). Hand-held dynamic visual noise reduces naturally occurring food cravings and craving-related consumption. *Appetite*, 68, 152–157.

Kemps, E., Tiggemann, M. & Christianson, R. (2008). Concurrent visuo-spatial processing reduces food cravings in prescribed weight-loss dieters. *Journal of Behavior Therapy and Experimental Psychiatry*, 39(2), 177–186.

Kendler, K.S., Heath, A.C., Neale, M.C., Kessler, R.C. & Eaves, L.J. (1993). Alcoholism and major depression in women: a twin study of the causes of comorbidity. *Archives of General Psychiatry*, 50(9), 690–698.

Kendler, K.S., Prescott, C.A., Myers, J. & Neale, M.C. (2003). The structure of genetic and environmental risk factors for common psychiatric and substance use disorders in men and women. *Archives of General Psychiatry*, 60(9), 929–937.

Kennedy, A.D., Torgerson, D.J., Campbell, M.K. & Grant, A.M. (2017). Subversion of allocation concealment in a randomised controlled trial: a historical case study. *Trials*, 18(1), 204.

Kennedy, B.P., Kawachi, I. & Prothrow-Stith, D. (1996). Income distribution and mortality: cross sectional ecological study of the Robin Hood index in the United States. *British Medical Journal*, 312, 1004.

Kern, M.L. & Friedman, H.S. (2008). Do conscientious individuals live longer? A quantitative review. *Health Psychology*, 27, 505–512.

Kerr, N. (1884) President's Inaugural Address. *Proceedings of the Society for the Study and Cure of Inebriety*, 1(1), 2–17.

Kerr, N.L. (1998). HARKing: Hypothesizing after the results are known. *Personality and Social Psychology Review*, 2(3), 196–217.

Kerst, W.F. & Waters, A.J. (2014). Attentional retraining administered in the field reduces smokers' attentional bias and craving. *Health Psychology*, 33(10), 1232.

Kessels, L.T., Ruiter, R.A., Wouters, L. & Jansma, B.M. (2014). Neuroscientific evidence for defensive avoidance of fear appeals. *International Journal of Psychology*, 49, 80–88.

Kessels, L.T.E., Ruiter, R.A.C. & Jansma, B.M. (2010). Increased attention but more efficient disengagement: Neuroscientific evidence for defensive processing of threatening health information. *Health Psychology*, 29, 346–354.

Kessels, L.T.E., Ruiter, R.A.C., Brug, J. & Jansma, B.M. (2011). The effects of tailored and threatening nutrition information on message attention: Evidence from an event-related potential study. *Appetite*, 56, 32–38.

Khamis, R.Y., Ammari, T. & Mikhail, G.W. (2016). Gender differences in coronary heart disease. *Heart*, 102(14), 1142–1149.

Khantzian, E.J. (1997). The self-medication hypothesis of substance use disorders: a reconsideration and recent applications. *Harvard Review of Psychiatry*, 4(5), 231–244.

Kidd, C., Palmeri, H. & Aslin, R.N. (2013). Rational snacking: Young children's decision-making on the marshmallow task is moderated by beliefs about environmental reliability. *Cognition*, 126(1), 109–114.

Kidd, I.M., Booth, C.J., Rigden, S.P., Tong, C.W. & MacMahon, E.M. (2003). Measles-associated encephalitis in children with renal transplants: a predictable effect of waning herd immunity? *The Lancet*, 362(9386), 832.

Kivimäki, M., Nyberg, S.T., Batty, G.D., Fransson, E.I., Heikkilä, K. et al. (2012). Job strain as a risk factor for coronary heart disease: a collaborative meta-analysis of individual participant data. *The Lancet*, 380, 1491–1497.

Klein, S. L. & Flanagan, K. L. (2016). Sex differences in immune responses. *Nature Reviews Immunology*, 16(10), 626.

Kliemann, N., Croker, H., Johnson, F. & Beeken, R.J. (2019). Development of the Top Tips Habit-Based Weight Loss App and Preliminary Indications of Its Usage, Effectiveness, and Acceptability: Mixed-Methods Pilot Study. *JMIR MHealth and UHealth*, 7(5), e12326.

Kliemann, N., Vickerstaff, V., Croker, H., Johnson, F., Nazareth, I. & Beeken, R.J. (2017). The role of self-regulatory skills and automaticity on the effectiveness of a brief weight loss habit-based intervention: secondary analysis of the 10 top tips randomised trial. *International Journal of Behavioral Nutrition and Physical Activity*, 14(1), 119.

Knäuper, B., Pillay, R., Lacaille, J., McCollam, A. & Kelso, E. (2011). Replacing craving imagery with alternative pleasant imagery reduces craving intensity. *Appetite*, 57(1), 173–178.

Knittle, K. (2014). Fidelity in intervention delivery: A rough field guide. *European Health Psychologist*, 16(5), 190–195.

Knyazev, G.G., Slobodskaya, H.R., Kharchenko, I.I. & Wilson, G. D. (2004). Personality and substance use in Russian youths: The predictive and moderating role of behavioral activation and gender. *Personality and Individual Differences*, 37, 827–843.

Koebnick, C., Strassner, C., Hoffmann, I. & Leitzmann, C. (1999). Consequences of a long-term raw food diet on body weight and menstruation: results of a questionnaire survey. *Annals of Nutrition and Metabolism*, 43, 69–79.

Kok, G., Gottlieb, N.H., Peters, G.J.Y., Mullen, P.D., Parcel, G.S., Ruiter, R.A., ... & Bartholomew, L.K. (2016). A taxonomy of behaviour change methods: an Intervention Mapping approach. *Health Psychology Review*, 10(3), 297–312.

Kondo, N., Sembajwe, G., Kawachi, I., van Dam, R.M., Subramanian, S.V. & Yamagata, Z. (2009). Income inequality, mortality, and self rated health: meta-analysis of multilevel studies. *British Medical Journal*, 339, b4471.

Konner, M. & Eaton, S.B. (2010). Paleolithic nutrition. Twenty-five years later. *Nutrition in Clinical Practice*, 25, 594–602.

Kontopantelis, E., Doran, T., Springate, D.A., Buchan, I. & Reeves, D. (2015). Regression based quasi-experimental approach when randomisation is not an option: interrupted time series analysis. *British Medical Journal*, 350, h2750.

Kootte, R. S., Levin, E., Salojärvi, J., Smits, L. P., Hartstra, A. V., Udayappan, S. D., ... & Knop, F. K. (2017). Improvement of insulin sensitivity after lean donor feces in metabolic syndrome is driven by baseline intestinal microbiota composition. *Cell Metabolism*, 26(4), 611–619.

Kopelman, P. (2007). Health risks associated with overweight and obesity. *Obesity Reviews*, 8, 13–17.

Kosslyn, S.M., Ganis, G. & Thompson, W.L. (2001). Neural foundations of imagery. *Nature Reviews Neuroscience*, 2(9), 635.

Kotov, R., Gamez, W., Schmidt, F. & Watson, D. (2010). Linking 'big' personality traits to anxiety, depressive, and substance use disorders: a meta-analysis. *Psychological Bulletin*, 136, 768–821.

Kotz, D., Spigt, M., Arts, I.C., Crutzen, R. & Viechtbauer, W. (2012). Use of the stepped wedge design cannot be recommended: a critical appraisal and comparison with the classic cluster randomized controlled trial design. *Journal of Clinical Epidemiology*, 65(12), 1249–1252.

Kramer, A. (1977). Effect of storage on nutritive value of food. *Journal of Food Quality*, 1, 23–55.

Kramer, M.S. & Kakuma, R. (2012). Optimal duration of exclusive breastfeeding. *Cochrane Database of Systematic Reviews*, (8), Art. No.: CD003517.

Kraus, S.J. (1995). Attitudes and the prediction of behaviour: a meta-analysis of the empirical literature. *Personality and Social Psychology Bulletin*, 21, 58–75.

Krause, N.M. & Jay, G.M. (1994). What do global self-rated health items measure? *Medical Care*, 930–942.

Krishna, A., Morrin, M. & Sayin, E. (2014). Smellizing cookies and salivating: A focus on olfactory imagery. *Journal of Consumer Research*, 41(1), 18–34.

Kröger, H., Pakpahan, E. & Hoffmann, R. (2015). What causes health inequality? A systematic review on the relative importance of social causation and health selection. *European Journal of Public Health*, 25, 951––960.

Krpan, D., Galizzi, M.M. & Dolan, P. (2019). Looking at spillovers in the mirror: Making a case for 'behavioral spillunders'. *Frontiers in Psychology*, 10, 1142.

Kumari, V. & Postma, P. (2005). Nicotine use in schizophrenia: the self medication hypotheses. *Neuroscience & Biobehavioral Reviews*, 29(6), 1021–1034.

Kunst, A.E., Groenhof, F., Mackenbach, J.P. & EU Working Group on Socioeconomic Inequalities in Health. (1998). Occupational class and cause specific mortality in middle aged men in 11 European countries: comparison of population based studies. *British Medical Journal*, 316, 1636–1642.

Kuntsche, E., Kuntsche, S., Thrul, J. & Gmel, G. (2017). Binge drinking: Health impact, prevalence, correlates and interventions. *Psychology & Health*, 32(8), 976–1017.

Kuper, H. & Marmot, M. (2003). Job strain, job demands, decision latitude, and risk of coronary heart disease within the Whitehall II study. *Journal of Epidemiology and Community Health*, 57, 147–153.

Kurzban, R. (2010). Does the brain consume additional glucose during self-control tasks? *Evolutionary Psychology*, 8(2), 244–259.

Kyrgiou, M., Kalliala, I., Markozannes, G., Gunter, M.J., Paraskevaidis, E., Gabra, H., ... & Tsilidis, K.K. (2017). Adiposity and cancer at major anatomical sites: umbrella review of the literature. *British Medical Journal*, 356, j477.

Lachin, J.M. (1988). Properties of simple randomization in clinical trials. *Controlled Clinical Trials*, 9(4), 312–326.

Lachowycz, K. & Jones, A.P. (2011). Greenspace and obesity: a systematic review of the evidence. *Obesity Reviews, 12*, 183–189.

Laing, B.Y., Mangione, C.M., Tseng, C.H., Leng, M., Vaisberg, E., Mahida, M., ... & Bell, D.S. (2014). Effectiveness of a smartphone application for weight loss compared with usual care in overweight primary care patients: a randomized, controlled trial. *Annals of Internal Medicine, 161*(10_Supplement), S5–S12.

Lally, P. & Gardner, B. (2013). Promoting habit formation. *Health Psychology Review, 7*, S137–S158.

Lally, P., Chipperfield, A. & Wardle, J. (2008). Healthy habits: efficacy of simple advice on weight control based on a habit-formation model. *International Journal of Obesity, 32*(4), 700.

Lally, P., Van Jaarsveld, C.H., Potts, H.W. & Wardle, J. (2010). How are habits formed: Modelling habit formation in the real world. *European Journal of Social Psychology, 40*(6), 998–1009.

Lamm, B., Gudi, H., Fassbender, I., Freitag, C., Graf, F., Goertz, C., ... & Schwarzer, G. (2015). Rural NSO and German middle-class mothers' interaction with their 3-and 6-month-old infants: A longitudinal cross-cultural analysis. *Journal of Family Psychology, 29*(4), 649.

Lamm, B., Keller, H., Teiser, J., Gudi, H., Yovsi, R.D., Freitag, C., ... & Vöhringer, I. (2018). Waiting for the second treat: developing culture-specific modes of self-regulation. *Child Development, 89*(3), e261–e277.

Lancet Infectious Diseases, The (2020). COVID-19, a pandemic or not? *The Lancet Infectious Diseases, 20*, 393.

Lancet, The (2014) Prescribing antibiotics: a battle of resistance (Editorial). *The Lancet, 384*(9943), 558.

Lancet, The (2019). E-cigarettes: time to realign our approach? *The Lancet, 394*, 1297.

Land, M.A., Webster, J., Christoforou, A., Johnson, C., Trevena, H., Hodgins, F., Chalmers, J., Woodward, M., Barzi, F., Smith, W., Flood, V., Jeffery, P., Nowson, C. & Neal., B. (2014). The association of knowledge, attitudes and behaviours related to salt with the 24-hour urinary sodium excretion. *International Journal of Behavioral Nutrition and Physical Activity, 11*, 47.

Langebeek, N., Gisolf, E.H., Reiss, P., Vervoort, S.C., Hafsteinsdóttir, T.B., Richter, C., Sprangers, A.G. & Nieuwkerk, P.T. (2014). Predictors and correlates of adherence to combination antiretroviral therapy (ART) for chronic HIV infection: a meta-analysis. *BMC Medicine, 12*, 142.

Lara, J., Evans, E.H., O'Brien, N., Moynihan, P.J., Meyer, T.D., Adamson, A.J., ... & Mathers, J.C. (2014). Association of behaviour change techniques with effectiveness of dietary interventions among adults of retirement age: a systematic review and meta-analysis of randomised controlled trials. *BMC Medicine, 12*(1), 177.

Larabie, L.C. (2005). To what extent do smokers plan quit attempts? *Tobacco Control, 14*, 425–428.

Larkins, J.M. & Sher, K.J. (2006). Family history of alcoholism and the stability of personality in young adulthood. *Psychology of Addictive Behaviors, 4*, 471–477.

Larson, H.J., Cooper, L.Z., Eskola, J., Katz, S.L., & Ratzan, S. (2011). Addressing the vaccine confidence gap. *The Lancet, 378*(9790), 526–535.

Larson, J.S. (1999). The conceptualization of health. *Medical Care Research and Review, 56*(2), 123–136.

Larson, N.I., Story, M.T. & Nelson, M.C. (2009). Neighborhood environments – disparities in access to healthy foods in the U.S. *American Journal of Preventive Medicine, 36*, 74–81.

Lassale, C., Tzoulaki, I., Moons, K.G., Sweeting, M., Boer, J., Johnson, L., ... & Wennberg, P. (2017). Separate and combined associations of obesity and metabolic health with coronary heart disease: a pan-European case-cohort analysis. *European Heart Journal, 39*(5), 397–406.

Lawrence, M., Wingrove, K., Naude, C. & Durao, S. (2016). Evidence synthesis and translation for nutrition interventions to combat micronutrient deficiencies with particular focus on food fortification. *Nutrients, 8*(9), 555.

Lawrence, N.S., Hinton, E.C., Parkinson, J.A. & Lawrence, A.D. (2012). Nucleus accumbens response to food cues predicts subsequent snack consumption in women and increased body mass index in those with reduced self-control. *Neuroimage, 63*(1), 415–422.

Lawrence, N.S., O'Sullivan, J., Parslow, D., Javaid, M., Adams, R.C., Chambers, C.D., ... & Verbruggen, F. (2015). Training response inhibition to food is associated with weight loss and reduced energy intake. *Appetite, 95*, 17–28.

Lawton, R., Conner, M. & McEachan, R. (2009). Desire or reason: predicting health behaviors from affective and cognitive attitudes. *Health Psychology, 28*, 56.

Layden, J.E., Ghinai, I., Pray, I., Kimball, A., Layer, M., Tenforde, M., ... & Haupt, T. (2019). Pulmonary illness related to e-cigarette use in Illinois and Wisconsin: preliminary report. *New England Journal of Medicine*, DOI: 10.1056/NEJMoa1911614.

Lazarus, R.S. & Folkman, S. (1984). *Stress, Appraisal, and Coping.* New York: Springer.

LeBel, E.P. & Peters, K.R. (2011). Fearing the future of empirical psychology: Bem's (2011) evidence of psi as a case study of deficiencies in modal research practice. *Review of General Psychology, 15*(4), 371.

Lee, I.M., Shiroma, E.J., Lobelo, F., Puska, P., Blair, S.N., Katzmarzyk, P.T. & Lancet Physical Activity Series Working Group. (2012). Effect of physical inactivity on major non-communicable diseases worldwide: an analysis of burden of disease and life expectancy. *The Lancet, 380*(9838), 219–229.

Lee, N.M., Lucke, J., Hall, W.D., Meurk, C., Boyle, F.M. & Carter, A. (2013). Public views on food addiction and obesity. Implications for policy and treatment. *PLoS ONE, 8*(9), e74836.

Lefevre, M., Redman, L.M., Heilbronn, L.K., Smith, J.V., Martin, C.K., Rood, J.C., Greenway, F.L., Williamson, D.A., Smith, S.R. & Ravussin, E. (2009). Caloric restriction alone and with exercise improves CVD risk in healthy non-obese individuals. *Atherosclerosis, 203*, 206–213.

Legget, K.T., Cornier, M.A., Rojas, D.C., Lawful, B. & Tregellas, J.R. (2015). Harnessing the power of disgust: a randomized trial to reduce high-calorie food appeal through implicit priming. *The American Journal of Clinical Nutrition, 102*(2), 249–255.

Lei, H., Nahum-Shani, I., Lynch, K., Oslin, D. & Murphy, S.A. (2012). A 'SMART' design for building individualized treatment sequences. *Annual Review of Clinical Psychology, 8*, 21–48.

Leonard, W.R. (2012). Human nutritional evolution. In S. Stinson, B. Bogin & D. O'Rourke (eds.). *Human Biology: An Evolutionary and Biocultural Perspective*, 2nd edn. New York: John Wiley & Sons.

Lepper, M.R., Greene, D. & Nisbett, R.E. (1973). Undermining children's intrinsic interest with extrinsic reward: A test of the 'overjustification' hypothesis. *Journal of Personality and Social Psychology, 28*, 129.

Lerman, C., Caporaso, N.E., Audrain, J., Main, D., Boyd, N.R. & Shields, P.G. (2000). Interacting effects of the serotonin transporter gene and neuroticism in smoking practices and nicotine dependence. *Molecular Psychiatry, 5*, 189–192.

Levesque, C. & Pelletier, L.G. (2003). On the investigation of primed and chronic autonomous and heteronomous motivational orientations. *Personality and Social Psychology Bulletin, 29*, 1570–1584.

Levine, J.A. (2003). Non-exercise activity thermogenesis. *Proceedings of the Nutrition Society, 62*, 667–679.

Levine, J.A. (2004). Non-exercise activity thermogenesis (NEAT). *Nutrition Reviews, 62*(suppl_2), S82–S97.

Levine, J.A., Eberhardt, N.L. & Jensen, M.D. (1999). Role of nonexercise activity thermogenesis in resistance to fat gain in humans. *Science, 283*, 212–214.

Levine, J.A., Lanningham-Foster, L.M., McCrady, S.K., Krizan, A.C., Olson, L.R., Kane, P.H., Jensen, M.D. & Clark, M.M. (2005). Interindividual variation in posture allocation: possible role in human obesity. *Science, 307*, 584–586.

Levy, A., Polman, R. & Clough, P. (2008). Adherence to sport injury rehabilitation programs: an integrated psycho-social approach. *Scandinavian Journal of Medicine and Science in Sports, 18*, 798–809.

Lewis, D.M. (2011). WHO definition is still valid. *British Medical Journal, 343*, 435.

Lewis, S., Thomas, S.L., Blood, R.W., Castle, D.J., Hyde, J. & Komesaroff, P.A. (2011). How do obese individuals perceive and respond to the different types of obesity stigma that they encounter in their daily lives? A qualitative study. *Social Science & Medicine, 73*(9), 1349–1356.

Lewis, Z.H., Lyons, E.J., Jarvis, J.M. & Baillargeon, J. (2015). Using an electronic activity monitor system as an intervention modality: a systematic review. *BMC Public Health, 15*(1), 585.

Leyton, M., Casey, K.F., Delaney, J.S., Kolivakis, T. & Benkelfat, C. (2005). Cocaine craving, euphoria, and self-administration: a preliminary study of the effect of catecholamine precursor depletion. *Behavioral Neuroscience, 119*(6), 1619.

Li, M.D. & Burmeister, M. (2009). New insights into the genetics of addiction. *Nature Reviews Genetics, 10*, 225–231.

Li, R., Montpetit, A., Rousseau, M., Wu, S.Y.M., Greenwood, C.M.T., Spector, T.D., Pollak, M., Polychronakos, C. & Richards, J.B. (2014). Somatic point mutations occurring early in development: a monozygotic twin study. *Journal of Medical Genetics, 51*, 28–34.

Liebenberg, L. (2006). Persistence hunting by modern hunter-gatherers. *Current Anthropology, 47*, 1017–1026.

Lieberman, D.E., Venkadesan, M., Werbel, W.A., Daoud, A.I., Andrea, S.D., Davis, I.S., Mang'Eni, R.O. & Pitsiladis, Y. (2010). Foot strike patterns and collision forces in habitually barefoot versus shod runners. *Nature, 463*, 531–536.

Liem, D.G. (2017). Infants' and children's salt taste perception and liking: a review. *Nutrients, 9*(9), 1011.

Liem, D.G., Miremadi, F., Zandstra, E.H. & Keast, R.S. (2012). Health labelling can influence taste perception and use of table salt for reduced-sodium products. *Public Health Nutrition, 15*(12), 2340–2347.

Lim, S.S., Vos, T., Flaxman, A.D., Danaei, G., Shibuya, K., Adair-Rohani, H., ... & Aryee, M. (2012). A comparative risk assessment of burden of disease and injury attributable to 67 risk factors and risk factor clusters in 21 regions, 1990–2010: a systematic analysis for the Global Burden of Disease Study 2010. *The Lancet, 380*(9859), 2224–2260.

Litman, E.A., Gortmaker, S.L., Ebbeling, C.B. & Ludwig, D.S. (2018). Source of bias in sugar-sweetened beverage research: a systematic review. *Public Health Nutrition, 21*(12), 2345–2350.

Llewellyn, C.H., Trzaskowski, M., van Jaarsveld, C.H.M., Plomin, R. & Wardle, J. (2014). Satiety mechanisms in genetic risk of obesity. *Journal of the American Medical Association Pediatrics, 169*, 338–344.

Llewellyn, C.H., van Jaarsveld, C.H.M., Boniface, D., Carnell, S. & Wardle, J. (2008). Eating rate is a heritable phenotype related to weight in children. *American Journal of Clinical Nutrition, 88*, 1560–1566.

Lobb, R. & Colditz, G.A. (2013). Implementation science and its application to population health. *Annual Review of Public Health, 34*, 235–251.

Looker, K.J., Magaret, A.S., Turner, K.M., Vickerman, P., Gottlieb, S.L. & Newman, L.M. (2015). Global estimates of prevalent and incident herpes simplex virus type 2 infections in 2012. *PloS One, 10*(1).

Loudon, K., Treweek, S., Sullivan, F., Donnan, P., Thorpe, K.E. & Zwarenstein, M. (2015). The PRECIS-2 tool: designing trials that are fit for purpose. *British Medical Journal, 350*, h2147.

Lovibond, P.F. & Shanks, D.R. (2002). The role of awareness in Pavlovian conditioning: empirical evidence and theoretical implications. *Journal of Experimental Psychology: Animal Behavior Processes, 28*(1), 3.

Lowe, C.F., Horne, P.J., Tapper, K., Bowdery, M. & Egerton, C. (2004). Effects of a peer modelling and rewards-based intervention to increase fruit and vegetable consumption in children. *European Journal of Clinical Nutrition, 58*(3), 510.

Loxton, N.J. & Dawe, S. (2001). Alcohol abuse and dysfunctional eating in adolescent girls: The influence of individual differences in sensitivity to reward and punishment. *International Journal of Eating Disorders, 29*, 455–462.

Lundahl, B.W., Kunz, C., Brownell, C., Tollefson, D. & Burke, B.L. (2010). A meta-analysis of motivational interviewing: Twenty-five years of empirical studies. *Research on Social Work Practice, 20*(2), 137–160.

Lundh, A., Sismondo, S., Lexchin, J., Busuioc, O.A. & Bero, L. (2012). Industry sponsorship and research outcome. *Cochrane Database of Systematic Reviews*, Issue 12. Art. No.: MR000033.

Luo, D., Smith, J.A., Meadows, N.A., Schuh, A., Manescu, K.E., Bure, K., Davies, B., Horne, R., Kope, M., DiGiusto, D.L. & Brindley, D.A. (2016). A quantitative assessment of factors affecting the technological development and adoption of companion diagnostics. *Frontiers in Genetics, 6*: 357.

Luszczynska, A. & Schwarzer, R. (2015). Social cognitive theory. In M. Conner and P. Norman (eds.). *Predicting and Changing Health Behaviour: Research and Practice with Social Cognition Models*. Maidenhead: Open University Press.

Lutz, W. & Kebede, E. (2018). Education and health: redrawing the Preston curve. *Population and Development Review, 44*(2), 343.

Lynch, C., Bird, S., Lythgo, N. & Selva-Raj, I. (2020). Changing the physical activity behavior of adults with fitness trackers: A systematic review and meta-analysis. *American Journal of Health Promotion, 34*(4), 418–430.

Lynch, J., Smith, G.D., Hillemeier, M., Shaw, M., Raghunathan, T. & Kaplan, G. (2001). Income inequality, the psychosocial environment, and health: comparisons of wealthy nations. *The Lancet, 358*, 194–200.

Macacu, A., Autier, P., Boniol, M. & Boyle, P. (2015). Active and passive smoking and risk of breast cancer: a meta-analysis. *Breast Cancer Research Treatment, 154*, 213–224.

Machulska, A., Zlomuzica, A., Rinck, M., Assion, H.J. & Margraf, J. (2016). Approach bias modification in inpatient psychiatric smokers. *Journal of Psychiatric Research, 76*, 44–51.

Mackenbach, J.P. (2002). Income inequality and population health. *British Medical Journal, 324*, 1–2.

MacKillop, J. & Kahler, C. W. (2009). Delayed reward discounting predicts treatment response for heavy drinkers receiving smoking cessation treatment. *Drug and Alcohol Dependence, 104*(3), 197–203.

Maes, S. & Gebhardt, W. (2000). Self-regulation and health behavior: the health behavior goal model. In M. Boekaerts, P.R. Pintrich and M. Zeidner (eds.). *Handbook of Self-Regulation: Theory, Research and Applications* (pp. 343–268). San Diego, CA: Academic Press.

Magallares, A. & Pais-Ribeiro, J.L. (2014). Mental health and obesity: A meta-analysis. *Applied Research in Quality of Life, 9*(2), 295–308.

Magill, M. & Hallgren, K.A. (2019). Mechanisms of behavior change in motivational interviewing: do we understand how MI works?. *Current Opinion in Psychology, 30*, 1–5.

Magill, M., Gaume, J., Apodaca, T.R., Walthers, J., Mastroleo, N.R., Borsari, B. & Longabaugh, R. (2014). The technical hypothesis of motivational interviewing: A meta-analysis of MI's key causal model. *Journal of Consulting and Clinical Psychology, 82*(6), 973.

Maher, J.P. & Conroy, D.E. (2015). Habit strength moderates the effects of daily action planning prompts on physical activity but not sedentary behavior. *Journal of Sport and Exercise Psychology, 37*(1), 97–107.

Maillard, A.M., Hippolyte, L., Rodriguez-Herreros, B., Chewner, S.J.R.A., Dremmel, D. et al. (2015). 16p11.2 locus modulates response to satiety before the onset of obesity. *International Journal of Obesity*, *40*, 870–876.

Maiman, L.A. & Becker, M.H. (1974). The health belief model: Origins and correlates in psychological theory. *Health Education & Behavior*, *2*, 336–353.

Mainvil, L.A., Lawson, R., Horwath, C.C., McKenzie, J.E. & Reeder, A.I. (2009). Validated scales to assess adult self-efficacy to eat fruits and vegetables. *American Journal of Health Promotion*, *23*, 210–217.

Maio, G.R. & Esses, V.M. (2001). The need for affect: individual differences in the motivation to approach or avoid emotions. *Journal of Personality*, *69*, 584–615.

Maio, G.R., Haddock, G. & Verplanken, B. (2019). *The Psychology of Attitudes and Attitude Change*. London: Sage.

Major, B., Hunger, J.M., Bunyan, D.P. & Miller, C.T. (2014). The ironic effects of weight stigma. *Journal of Experimental Social Psychology*, *51*, 74–80.

Malik, V.S., Popkin, B.M., Bray, G.A., Després, J.P., Willett, W.C. & Hu, F.B. (2010). Sugar-sweetened beverages and risk of metabolic syndrome and type 2 diabetes: a meta-analysis. *Diabetes Care*, *33*(11), 2477–2483.

Malouff, J.M., Thorsteinsson, E.B. & Schutte, N.S. (2007). The efficacy of problem solving therapy in reducing mental and physical health problems: a meta-analysis. *Clinical Psychology Review*, *27*(1), 46–57.

Mancia, G., Fagard, R., Narkiewicz, K., Redon, J., Zanchetti, A., Bohm, M. et al. (2013). 2013 ESH/ESC guidelines for the management of arterial hypertension. *European Heart Journal*, *34*, 2159-2219.

Mandrioli, D., Kearns, C.E. & Bero, L.A. (2016). Relationship between research outcomes and risk of bias, study sponsorship, and author financial conflicts of interest in reviews of the effects of artificially sweetened beverages on weight outcomes: a systematic review of reviews. *PloS One*, *11*(9), e0162198.

Mani, A., Mullainathan, S., Shafir, E. & Zhao, J. (2013). Poverty impedes cognitive function. *Science*, *341*, 976–980.

Mann, K.D., Pearce, M.S., McKevith, B., Thielecke, F. & Seal, C. J. (2015). Low whole grain intake in the UK: results from the National Diet and Nutrition Survey rolling programme 2008–11. *British Journal of Nutrition*, *113*(10), 1643–1651.

Mann, T., Tomiyama, A.J. & Ward, A. (2015). Promoting public health in the context of the 'obesity epidemic' false starts and promising new directions. *Perspectives on Psychological Science*, *10*(6), 706–710.

Manthey, J., Shield, K.D., Rylett, M., Hasan, O.S., Probst, C. & Rehm, J. (2019). Global alcohol exposure between 1990 and 2017 and forecasts until 2030: a modelling study. *The Lancet*, *393*(10190), 2493–2502.

Marissen, M.A., Franken, I.H., Waters, A.J., Blanken, P., Van Den Brink, W. & Hendriks, V.M. (2006). Attentional bias predicts heroin relapse following treatment. *Addiction*, *101*(9), 1306–1312.

Marlowe, F.W. (2010). *The Hadza. Hunter-Gatherers of Tanzania*. Berkeley and Los Angeles, CA: University of California Press.

Marmot, M.G. & Shipley, M.J. (1996). Do socioeconomic differences in mortality persist after retirement? 25 year follow up of civil servants from the first Whitehall study. *British Medical Journal*, *313*, 117.

Marmot, M.G., Bosma, H., Hemingway, H., Brunner, E. & Stansfeld, S. (1997). Contribution of job control and other risk factors to social variations in coronary heart disease incidence. *The Lancet*, *350*, 235–239.

Marmot, M.G., Shipley, M.J. & Rose, G. (1984). Inequalities in death – specific explanations of a general pattern? *The Lancet*. 1003–1006.

Marteau, T.M., French, D.P., Griffin, S.J., Prevost, A.T., Sutton, S., Watkinson, C., Attwood, S. & Hollands, G.J. (2010). Effects of communicating DNA-based disease risk estimates on risk-reducing behaviours. *Cochrane Database of Systematic Review*, *10*, Article number CD 007275.

Marteau, T.M., Ogilvie, D., Roland, M., Suhrcke, M. & Kelly, M.P. (2011). Judging nudging: can nudging improve population health? *British Medical Journal*, *342*, 263–265.

Martin, C., Concannon, M., Bel-Serrat, S., Heinen, M. & Murrin, C.M. (2017). The long-term impact of the Food Dudes Healthy Eating Programme on Irish primary school aged children. *Proceedings of the Nutrition Society*, *76*(OCE3), E93.

Martin, J., Sheeran, P., Slade, P., Wright, A. & Dibble, T. (2011). Durable effects of implementation intentions: reduced rates of confirmed pregnancy at 2 years. *Health Psychology*, *30*(3), 368.

Martins, S.S., Keyes, K.M., Storr, C.L., Zhu, H. & Chilcoat, H.D. (2009). Pathways between nonmedical opioid use/dependence and psychiatric disorders: results from the National Epidemiologic Survey on Alcohol and Related Conditions. *Drug & Alcohol Dependence*, *103*(1), 16–24.

Martiny-Huenger, T., Martiny, S.E., Parks-Stamm, E.J., Pfeiffer, E. & Gollwitzer, P.M. (2017). From conscious thought to automatic action: A simulation account of action planning. *Journal of Experimental Psychology: General*, *146*(10), 1513.

Masicampo, E.J. & Baumeister, R.F. (2008). Toward a physiology of dual-process reasoning and judgment: Lemonade, willpower, and expensive rule-based analysis. *Psychological Science, 19*(3), 255–260.

Matarazzo, J.D. (1980). Behavioral health and behavioral medicine: frontiers for a new health psychology. *American Psychologist, 35*(9), 807–817

Matarazzo, J.D. (1984). Behavioral health: a 1990 challenge for the health sciences professions. In J.D. Matarazzo et al. (eds.) *Behavioural Health: A Handbook of Health Enhancement and Disease Prevention.* New York: Wiley, pp. 3–40.

Matthews, K.A. (1988). Coronary heart disease and type A behaviors: update on and alternative to the Booth-Kewley and Friedman (1987) quantitative review. *Psychological Bulletin, 104*, 373–380.

Matthews, K.A., Gallo, L.C. & Taylor, S.E. (2010). Are psychosocial factors mediators of socioeconomic status and health connections? *Annals of the New York Academy of Sciences, 1186*, 146–173.

Mattison, J.A., Roth, G.S., Beasley, T.M., Tilmont, E.M., Handy, A.M., Herbert, R.L. et al. (2012). Impact of caloric restriction on health and survival in rhesus monkeys from the NIA study. *Nature, 489*, 318–322.

Maude-Griffin, P. & Tiffany, S.T. (1996). Production of smoking urges through imagery: The impact of affect and smoking abstinence. *Experimental and Clinical Psychopharmacology, 4*(2), 198.

Maxmen, A. (2012). Calorie restriction falters in the long run. Genetics and healthy diet matter more of longevity. *Nature, 488*, 569.

May, J., Andrade, J., Kavanagh, D.J. & Hetherington, M. (2012). Elaborated intrusion theory. A cognitive-emotional theory of food craving. *Current Obesity Reports, 1*, 114–121.

May, J., Andrade, J., Panabokke, N. & Kavanagh, D. (2004). Images of desire: cognitive models of craving. *Memory, 12*(4), 447–461.

May, J., Kavanagh, D.J. & Andrade, J. (2015). The elaborated intrusion theory of desire: A 10-year retrospective and implications for addiction treatments. *Addictive Behaviors, 44*, 29–34.

McAlaney, J. & McMahon, J. (2007). Normative beliefs, misperceptions, and heavy episodic drinking in a British student sample. *Journal of Studies on Alcohol and Drugs, 68*(3), 385–392.

McCarty, D. (1981). Changing contraceptive usage intentions: A test of the Fishbein model of intention. *Journal of Applied Social Psychology, 11*, 192–211.

McCay, C.M., Crowell, M.F. & Maynard, L.A. (1935). The effect of retarded growth upon the length of life span and upon the ultimate body size. *The Journal of Nutrition, 10*, 63–79.

McCrae, R.R. & Costa, P.T. (1987). Validation of the Five-Factor Model of Personality across instruments and observers. *Journal of Personality and Social Psychology, 52.* 81–90.

McCrae, R.R. & Costa, P.T. (2008). The Five-Factor Theory of Personality. In O.P. John, R.W. Robins & L.A. Pervin (eds.). *Handbook of Personality: Theory and Research.* New York: Guilford.

McCrory, M.A., Fuss, P.J., Hays, N.P., Vinken, A.G., Greenberg, A.S. & Roberts, S.B. (1999). Overeating in America: association between restaurant food consumption and body fatness in healthy adult men and women ages 19 to 80. *Obesity Research, 7*(6), 564–571.

McDonald, S., Quinn, F., Vieira, R., O'Brien, N., White, M., Johnston, D.W. & Sniehotta, F.F. (2017). The state of the art and future opportunities for using longitudinal n-of-1 methods in health behaviour research: a systematic literature overview. *Health Psychology Review, 11*(4), 307–323.

McDougall, C. (2010). *Born to Run: the Hidden Tribe, the Ultra-Runner, and the Greatest Race the World Has Never Seen.* London: Profile Books.

McEachan, R.R.C., Conner, M., Taylor, N.J. & Lawton, R.J. (2011). Prospective prediction of health-related behaviours with the theory of planned behaviour: A meta-analysis. *Health Psychology Review, 5*, 97–144.

McGonigal, K. (2012). *The Willpower Instinct: How Self-Control Works, Why It Matters, and What You Can Do to Get More of It.* New York: Penguin Books.

McGowan, P.O., Saaki, A., D'Alessio, A.C., Dymov, S., Labonté, B., Szyf, M., Turecki, G. & Meaney, M.J. (2009). Epigenetic regulation of the glucocorticoid receptor in human brain associates with childhood abuse. *Nature Neuroscience, 12*, 342–348.

McKeown, T. (1976). *The Modern Rise of Population.* New York: Academic Press.

McLean, R. & Hoek, J. (2014). Sodium and nutrition labelling: a qualitative study exploring New Zealand consumers' food purchasing behaviours. *Public Health Nutrition, 17*, 1138–1147.

McLellan, A.T., Lewis, D.C., O'Brien, C.P. & Kleber, H.D. (2000). Drug dependence, a chronic medical illness: implications for treatment, insurance, and outcomes evaluation. *Journal of the American Medical Association, 284*, 1689–1695.

McMahon, A.J. & Scheel, M.H. (2010). Glucose promotes controlled processing: Matching, maximizing, and root beer. *Judgment and Decision Making, 5*(6), 450.

McMillan, B., Conner, M., Green, J., Dyson, L., Renfrew, M. & Woolridge, M. (2009). Using an extended theory of planned behaviour to inform interventions aimed at increasing breastfeeding uptake in primiparas experiencing material deprivation. *British Journal of Health Psychology, 14*, 379–403.

McNeill A., Brose, L.S., Calder R., Bauld, L. & Robson, D. (2018). *Evidence Review of e- cigarettes and Heated Tobacco Products 2018*. A report commissioned by Public Health England. London: Public Health England.

McNeill, A., Gravely, S., Hitchman, S.C., Bauld, L., Hammond, D. & Hartmann-Boyce, J. (2017). Tobacco packaging design for reducing tobacco use. *Cochrane Database of Systematic Reviews*, (4).

McPherson, K., Steel, C.M. & Dixon, J.M. (2000). Breast cancer – epidemiology, risk factors, and genetics. *British Medical Journal, 321*, 624–628.

McSweeney, F.K. & Swindell, S. (1999). General-process theories of motivation revisited: the role of habituation. *Psychological Bulletin, 125*(4), 437.

Mdege, N.D., Man, M.S., Taylor, C.A. & Torgerson, D.J. (2012). There are some circumstances where the stepped-wedge cluster randomized trial is preferable to the alternative: no randomized trial at all. Response to the commentary by Kotz and colleagues. *Journal of Clinical Epidemiology, 65*(12), 1253.

Meador, C. K. (1992). Hex death: voodoo magic or persuasion? *Southern Medical Journal, 85*(3), 244–247.

Mehling, W. E., Price, C., Daubenmier, J. J., Acree, M., Bartmess, E. & Stewart, A. (2012). The multidimensional assessment of interoceptive awareness (MAIA). *PloS One, 7*(11), e48230.

Meijer, M., Rohl, J., Bloomfield, K. & Grittner, U. (2012). Do neighborhoods affect individual mortality? A systematic review and meta-analysis of multilevel studies. *Social Science and Medicine, 74*, 1204–1212.

Meisel, S.F., Beeken, R.J., van Jaarsveld, C.H.M. & Wardle, J. (2015). Genetic susceptibility testing and readiness to control weight: results from a randomized controlled trial. *Obesity, 23*, 305–312.

Menni, C., Lin, C., Cecelja, M., Mangino, M., Matey-Hernandez, M. L., Keehn, L., ... & Chowienczyk, P. (2018). Gut microbial diversity is associated with lower arterial stiffness in women. *European Heart Journal, 39*(25), 2390–2397.

Metcalfe, J. & Mischel, W. (1999). A hot/cool-system analysis of delay of gratification: dynamics of willpower. *Psychological Review, 106*(1), 3.

Michaelson, L.E. & Munakata, Y. (2016). Trust matters: Seeing how an adult treats another person influences preschoolers' willingness to delay gratification. *Developmental Science, 19*(6), 1011–1019.

Michels, K.B., Mohllajee, A.P., Roset-Bahmanyar, E., Beehler, G.P. & Moysich, K.B. (2007). Diet and breast cancer. A review of the prospective observational studies. *Cancer, 109*, 2712–2749.

Michie S., Johnston M. & Carey R. (2016) Behavior change techniques. In: M. Gellman and J. Turner (eds.). *Encyclopedia of Behavioral Medicine*. New York: Springer.

Michie, S. & Prestwich, A. (2010). Are interventions theory-based? Development of a theory coding scheme. *Health Psychology, 29*(1), 1.

Michie, S., Abraham, C., Whittington, C., McAteer, J. & Gupta, S. (2009). Effective techniques in healthy eating and physical activity interventions: a meta-regression. *Health Psychology, 28*(6), 690.

Michie, S., Atkins, L. & West, R. (2014). *The Behaviour Change Wheel: A Guide to Developing Interventions*. London: Silverback Publishing.

Michie, S., Dormandy, E. & Marteau, T.M. (2004). Increasing screening uptake amongst those intending to be screened: the use of action plans. *Patient Education and Counseling, 55*(2), 218–222.

Michie, S., Richardson, M., Johnston, M., Abraham, C., Francis, J., Hardeman, W., ... & Wood, C.E. (2013). The behavior change technique taxonomy (v1) of 93 hierarchically clustered techniques: building an international consensus for the reporting of behavior change interventions. *Annals of Behavioral Medicine, 46*(1), 81–95.

Michie, S., Van Stralen, M.M. & West, R. (2011). The behaviour change wheel: a new method for characterising and designing behaviour change interventions. *Implementation Science, 6*(1), 42.

Michie, S., West, R., Campbell, R., Brown, J. & Gainforth, H. (2014). *ABC of Behaviour Change Theories*. Sutton: Silverback Publishing.

Mikula, G. (1989). Influencing food preferences of children by 'if-then' type instructions. *European Journal of Social Psychology, 19*(3), 225–241.

Miles, E., Sheeran, P., Baird, H., Macdonald, I., Webb, T.L. & Harris, P.R. (2016). Does self-control improve with practice? Evidence from a six-week training program. *Journal of Experimental Psychology: General, 145*(8), 1075.

Miliband, E. (2010). What this country needs is a Labour with a new vision. *The New Statesman*. www.newstatesman.com/uk-politics/2010/08/labour-movement-society-party

Milkman, K.L., Beshears, J., Choi, J.J., Laibson, D. & Madrian, B.C. (2011). Using implementation intentions prompts to enhance influenza vaccination rates. *Proceedings of the National Academy of Sciences, 108*(26), 10415–10420.

Miller Jr, I.J. & Reedy Jr, F.E. (1990). Variations in human taste bud density and taste intensity perception. *Physiology & Behavior, 47*(6), 1213–1219.

Miller, C.L., Brownbill, A.L., Dono, J. & Ettridge, K. (2018). Presenting a strong and united front to tobacco industry interference: a content analysis of Australian newspaper coverage of tobacco plain packaging 2008–2014. *BMJ open, 8*(9), e023485.

Miller, D. & Harkins, C. (2010). Corporate strategy, corporate capture: food and alcohol industry lobbying and public health. *Critical Social Policy, 30*(4), 564–589.

Miller, D.T. & Prentice, D.A. (2016). Changing norms to change behavior. *Annual Review of Psychology, 67*, 339–361.

Miller, N.S. & Gold, M.S. (1994). Dissociation of 'conscious desire'(craving) from and relapse in alcohol and cocaine dependence. *Annals of Clinical Psychiatry, 6*(2), 99–106.

Miller, T.Q., Smith, T.W., Turner, C.W., Guijarro, M.L. & Hallet, A.J. (1996). A meta-analytic review of research on hostility and physical health. *Psychological Bulletin, 119*, 322–348.

Miller, W.R. & Rollnick, S. (2013). *Motivational Interviewing: Helping People Change* (3rd edn). New York: Guilford Press.

Miller, W.R. & Rose, G.S. (2009). Toward a theory of motivational interviewing. *American Psychologist, 64*(6), 527.

Milne, S., Orbell, S. & Sheeran, P. (2002). Combining motivational and volitional interventions to promote exercise participation: Protection motivation theory and implementation intentions. *British Journal of Health Psychology, 7*(2), 163–184.

Milne, S., Sheeran, P. & Orbell, S. (2000). Prediction and intervention in health-related behavior: A meta-analytic review of protection motivation theory. *Journal of Applied Social Psychology, 30*, 106–143.

Milton, K. (1999). Nutritional characteristics of wild primate foods: do the diets of our closest living relatives have lessons for us? *Nutrition, 15*, 488–498.

Milton, K. (2000). Back to basics: why foods of wild primates have relevance for modern human health. *Nutrition, 16*, 480–483.

Milyavskaya, M. & Inzlicht, M. (2017). What's so great about self-control? Examining the importance of effortful self-control and temptation in predicting real-life depletion and goal attainment. *Social Psychological and Personality Science, 8*(6), 603–611.

Mindell, J.A., Sadeh, A., Wiegand, B., How, T.H. & Goh, D.Y. (2010). Cross-cultural differences in infant and toddler sleep. *Sleep Medicine, 11*(3), 274–280.

Mischel, W. (1961). Father-absence and delay of gratification. *The Journal of Abnormal and Social Psychology, 63*(1), 116.

Mischel, W. & Baker, N. (1975). Cognitive appraisals and transformations in delay behavior. *Journal of Personality and Social Psychology, 31*(2), 254.

Mischel, W., Shoda, Y. & Peake, P.K. (1988). The nature of adolescent competencies predicted by preschool delay of gratification. *Journal of Personality and Social Psychology, 54*(4), 687.

Mischel, W., Shoda, Y. & Rodriguez, M.I. (1989). Delay of gratification in children. *Science, 244*(4907), 933–938.

Mitchell, C.J., De Houwer, J. & Lovibond, P.F. (2009). The propositional nature of human associative learning. *Behavioral and Brain Sciences, 32*(2), 183–198.

Mittal, C. & Griskevicius, V. (2014). Sense of control under uncertainty depends on people's childhood environment: a life history theory approach. *Journal of Personality and Social Psychology, 107*, 621–637.

Mitteroecker, P., Huttegger, S.M., Fischer, B. & Pavlicev, M. (2016). Cliff-edge model of obstetric selection in humans. *Proceedings of the National Academy of Sciences, 113*(51), 14680–14685.

Moeller, S.J., Parvaz, M.A., Shumay, E., Beebe-Wang, N., Konova, A.B., Alia-Klein, N., ... & Goldstein, R.Z. (2013). Gene× abstinence effects on drug cue reactivity in addiction: multimodal evidence. *Journal of Neuroscience, 33*(24), 10027–10036.

Moffitt, T.E., Arseneault, L., Belsky, D., Dickson, N., Hancox, R.J., Harrington, H., ... & Sears, M.R. (2011). A gradient of childhood self-control predicts health, wealth, and public safety. *Proceedings of the National Academy of Sciences, 108*(7), 2693–2698.

Mogg, K., Field, M. & Bradley, B.P. (2005). Attentional and approach biases for smoking cues in smokers: an investigation of competing theoretical views of addiction. *Psychopharmacology, 180*(2), 333–341.

Moher, D., Liberati, A., Tetzlaff, J., Altman, D.G. & The PRISMA Group (2009). *Preferred Reporting Items for Systematic Reviews and Meta-Analyses:* The PRISMA Statement. *British Medical Journal, 339*, b2535.

Molden, D.C., Hui, C.M., Scholer, A.A., Meier, B.P., Noreen, E.E., D'Agostino, P.R. & Martin, V. (2012). Motivational versus metabolic effects of carbohydrates on self-control. *Psychological Science, 23*(10), 1137–1144.

Molitoris, J., Barclay, K. & Kolk, M. (2019). When and where birth spacing matters for child survival: an international comparison using the DHS. *Demography, 56*(4), 1349–1370.

Monninkhof, E.M., Elias, S.G., Vlems, F.A., van der Tweel, I., Schuit, A.J., Voskuil, D.W. & van Leeuwen, F.E. (2007). Physical activity and breast cancer. A systematic review. *Epidemiology, 18*, 137–157.

Montoya, R.M., Horton, R.S., Vevea, J.L., Citkowicz, M. & Lauber, E.A. (2017). A re-examination of the mere exposure effect: The influence of repeated exposure on recognition, familiarity, and liking. *Psychological Bulletin, 143*(5), 459.

Moodie, A. R. (2017). What public health practitioners need to know about unhealthy industry tactics. *American Journal of Public Health, 107*, 1047–1049.

Moore, G.F., Audrey, S., Barker, M., Bond, L., Bonell, C., Hardeman, W., ... & Baird, J. (2015). Process evaluation of complex interventions: Medical Research Council guidance. *British Medical Journal, 350*, h1258.

Moore, G.F., Williams, A., Moore, L. & Murphy, S. (2013). An exploratory cluster randomised trial of a university halls of residence based social norms marketing campaign to reduce alcohol consumption among 1st year students. *Substance Abuse Treatment, Prevention, and Policy, 8*(1), 15.

Moore, S.N., Tapper, K. & Murphy, S. (2007). Feeding strategies used by mothers of 3–5-year-old children. *Appetite, 49*(3), 704–707.

Moore, S.N., Tapper, K. & Murphy, S. (2010). Feeding strategies used by primary school meal staff and their impact on children's eating. *Journal of Human Nutrition and Dietetics, 23*(1), 78–84.

Moors, A. & De Houwer, J. (2006). Automaticity: a theoretical and conceptual analysis. *Psychological Bulletin, 132*(2), 297.

Mora, R.J. (1999). Malnutrition: organic and functional consequences. *World Journal of Surgery, 23*(6), 530–535.

Morewedge, C.K., Huh, Y.E. & Vosgerau, J. (2010). Thought for food: Imagined consumption reduces actual consumption. *Science, 330*(6010), 1530–1533.

Morrill, B.A., Madden, G.J., Wengreen, H.J., Fargo, J.D. & Aguilar, S.S. (2016). A randomized controlled trial of the Food Dudes program: tangible rewards are more effective than social rewards for increasing short-and long-term fruit and vegetable consumption. *Journal of the Academy of Nutrition and Dietetics, 116*(4), 618–629.

Morse, S.J. (2016). Addiction, choice, and criminal law. In N. Heather and G. Segal (eds.). *Addiction and Choice: Rethinking the Relationship.* Oxford: Oxford University Press.

Moskowitz, J.T., Hult, J.R., Bussolari, C. & Acree, M. (2009). What works in coping with HIV? A meta-analysis with implications for coping with serious illness. *Psychological Bulletin, 135*, 121–141.

Mosley, M. & Spencer, M. (2013). *The Fast Diet.* London: Short Books.

Moynihan, P.J. & Kelly, S.A.M. (2014). Effect on caries of restricting sugars intake: systematic review to inform WHO guidelines. *Journal of Dental Research, 93*(1), 8–18.

Mroczek, D.K. & Spiro, A. (2007). Personality change influences mortality in older men. *Psychological Science, 18*, 371–376.

Mroczek, D.K., Spiro, A. & Turiano, N. (2009). Do health behaviors explain the effect of neuroticism on mortality? Longitudinal findings from the VA normative ageing study. *Journal of Research in Personality, 43*, 653–659.

Mullainathan, S. & Shafir, E. (2013). *Scarcity. The True Cost of Not Having Enough.* London: Penguin Books.

Muller, A. (2002). Education, income inequality, and mortality: a multiple regression analysis. *British Medical Journal, 324*, 23.

Mullie, P., Clarys, P., Hulens, M. & Vansant, G. (2010). Dietary patterns and socioeconomic position. *European Journal of Clinical Nutrition, 64*, 231–238.

Muraven, M. (2010a). Practicing self-control lowers the risk of smoking lapse. *Psychology of Addictive Behaviors, 24*(3), 446.

Muraven, M. (2010b). Building self-control strength: Practicing self-control leads to improved self-control performance. *Journal of Experimental Social Psychology, 46*(2), 465–468.

Muraven, M. & Slessareva, E. (2003). Mechanisms of self-control failure: Motivation and limited resources. *Personality and Social Psychology Bulletin, 29*(7), 894–906.

Muraven, M., Baumeister, R.F. & Tice, D.M. (1999). Longitudinal improvement of self-regulation through practice: Building self-control strength through repeated exercise. *The Journal of Social Psychology, 139*(4), 446–457.

Muraven, M., Tice, D.M. & Baumeister, R.F. (1998). Self-control as a limited resource: Regulatory depletion patterns. *Journal of Personality and Social Psychology, 74*(3), 774.

Murberg, T.A., Bru, E. & Stephens, P. (2002). Personality and coping among congestive heart failure patients. *Personality and Individual Differences, 32*, 775–784.

Murgraff, V., White, D. & Phillips, K. (1996). Moderating binge drinking: is it possible to change behaviour if you plan it in advance. *Alcohol and Alcoholism, 31*(6), 577–582.

Murphy, S., Moore, G., Tapper, K., Lynch, R., Raisanen, L., Desousa, C. & Moore, L. (2011). Free healthy breakfasts in primary schools: a cluster randomised controlled trial of a policy intervention in Wales, UK. PHN-2009-003631R. *Public Health Nutrition, 14*, 219–226.

Murray, C.J.L., Rosenfeld, L.C., Lim, S.S., Andrews, K. G., Foreman, K.J., Haring, D., Fullman, N., Lozano, R. & Lopez, A.D. (2012). Global malaria mortality between 1980 and 2010: a systematic analysis. *The Lancet, 379*, 413–431.

Murtagh, S., Rowe, D. A., Elliott, M. A., McMinn, D. & Nelson, N. M. (2012). Predicting active school travel: The role of planned behavior and habit strength. *International Journal of Behavioral Nutrition and Physical Activity, 9*(1), 65.

Musk, A.W. & De Klerk, N.H. (2003). History of tobacco and health. *Respirology, 8*(3), 286–290.

Mutch, D.M. & Clément, K. (2006). Unraveling the genetics of human obesity. *PLoS Genetics, 2*, e188.

Myrtek, M. (2001). Meta-analyses of prospective studies on coronary heart disease, type A personality, and hostility. *International Journal of Cardiology, 79*, 245–251.

Nagy, K. & Milton, K. (1979). Aspects of dietary quality, nutrient assimilation and water balance in wild howler monkeys. *Oecologia, 30*, 249–258.

Nandi, A., Glymour, M.M. & Subramanian, S.V. (2014). Association among socioeconomic status, health behaviors, and all-cause mortality in the United States. *Epidemiology, 25*, 170–177.

Narevic, E. & Schoenberg, N.E. (2002). Lay explanations for Kentucky's 'Coronory Valley'. *Journal of Community Health, 27*, 53–62.

National Institutes of Health (2014). www.nidcd. nih.gov/research/clinical-studies/researchers-professionals/clinical-trials-definition

National Research Council (2010). *The Prevention and Treatment of Missing Data in Clinical Trials.* Washington, DC: The National Academies Press. https://doi.org/10.17226/12955.

Naughton, F. & Johnston, D. (2014). A starter kit for undertaking n-of-1 trials. *European Health Psychologist, 16*(5), 196–205.

Neal, D.T., Wood, W. & Drolet, A. (2013). How do people adhere to goals when willpower is low? The profits (and pitfalls) of strong habits. *Journal of Personality and Social Psychology, 104*(6), 959.

Neal, D.T., Wood, W., Labrecque, J. S. & Lally, P. (2012). How do habits guide behavior? Perceived and actual triggers of habits in daily life. *Journal of Experimental Social Psychology, 48*(2), 492–498.

Neal, D.T., Wood, W., Wu, M. & Kurlander, D. (2011). The pull of the past: When do habits persist despite conflict with motives?. *Personality and Social Psychology Bulletin, 37*(11), 1428–1437.

Neighbors, C., Dillard, A.J., Lewis, M.A., Bergstrom, R.L. & Neil, T.A. (2006). Normative misperceptions and temporal precedence of perceived norms and drinking. *Journal of Studies on Alcohol, 67*(2), 290–299.

Neighbors, C., Larimer, M.E. & Lewis, M.A. (2004). Targeting misperceptions of descriptive drinking norms: efficacy of a computer-delivered personalized normative feedback intervention. *Journal of Consulting and Clinical Psychology, 72*(3), 434.

Nelson, L. D., Simmons, J. & Simonsohn, U. (2018). Psychology's renaissance. *Annual Review of Psychology, 69*, 511–534.

Nestle, M. (2018). *Unsavoury Truth: How Food Companies Skew the Science of What We Eat.* New York: Basic Books.

Neter, E. & Brainin, E. (2012). eHealth literacy: extending the digital divide to the realm of health information. *Journal of Medical Internet Research, 14*: e19.

Nettle, D. (2010). Why are there social gradients in preventative health behaviour? A perspective from behavioural ecology. *PLoS ONE, 5*, e13371.

Nettle, D., Andrews, C. & Bateson, M. (2017). Food insecurity as a driver of obesity in humans: The insurance hypothesis. *Behavioral and Brain Sciences, 40*, e105, doi:10.1017/S0140525X16000947.

Newman, J. & Taylor, A. (1992). Effect of a means-end contingency on young children's food preferences. *Journal of Experimental Child Psychology, 53*(2), 200–216.

Newton, J.N. (2019). Time for *The Lancet* to realign with the evidence on e-cigarettes? *The Lancet, 394*(10211), 1804–1805.

Nezu, A.M. (2004). Problem solving and behavior therapy revisited. *Behavior Therapy, 35*(1), 1–33.

Ng, J.Y., Ntoumanis, N., Thøgersen-Ntoumani, C., Deci, E.L., Ryan, R.M., Duda, J.L. & Williams, G.C. (2012). Self-determination theory applied to health contexts: A meta-analysis. *Perspectives on Psychological Science, 7*, 325–340.

Ng, M., Fleming, T., Robinson, M., Thomson, B, Graetz, N., Margono, C. ... Gakidou, E. (2014). Global, regional, and national prevalence of overweight and obesity in children and adults during 1980–2013: a systematic analysis for the Global Burden of Disease Study 2013. *The Lancet, 384*, 766–781.

Ng, M., Freeman, M.K., Fleming, T.D., Robinson, M., Dwyer-Lindgren, L., Thomson, B., ... & Murray, C.J. (2014). Smoking prevalence and cigarette consumption in 187 countries, 1980-2012. *Journal of the American Medical Association, 311*(2), 183–192.

NHS (2015). Health survey for England, 2014. https://digital.nhs.uk/data-and-information/publications/statistical/health-survey-for-england/health-survey-for-england-2014.

NHS (2016). Deep vein thrombosis. www.nhs.uk/conditions/deep-vein-thrombosis-dvt

NHS (2018a). Eat well. www.nhs.uk/live-well/eat-well/

NHS (2018b). Health survey for England 2017. https://digital.nhs.uk/data-and-information/publications/statistical/health-survey-for-england/2017

NHS (2018c). 5 A Day FAQs. www.nhs.uk/live-well/eat-well/5-a-day-faqs/

NHS (2020). Health conditions. www.nhs.uk/conditions/

NICE (2007). *Behaviour change at population, community and individual levels.* London: National Institute for Health and Clinical Excellence.

NICE (2014). *Behaviour change: Individual approaches.* London: National Institute for Health and Clinical Excellence.

Nichols, P.D., Petrie, J. & Singh, S. (2010). Long-chain omega-3 oils – an update on sustainable sources. *Nutrients, 2*(6), 572–585.

Nicholson, J.K., Holmes, E., Kinross, J., Burcelin, R., Gibson, G., Jia, W. & Pettersson, S. (2012). Host-gut microbiota metabolic interactions. *Science, 336*(6086), 1262–1267.

Nickerson, R.S. (1998). Confirmation bias: A ubiquitous phenomenon in many guises. *Review of General Psychology, 2*(2), 175.

Niemiec, C.P., Ryan, R.M. & Deci, E.L. (2009). The path taken: Consequences of attaining intrinsic and extrinsic aspirations in post-college life. *Journal of Research in Personality, 43*, 291–306.

Nilsen, P., Baird, J., Mello, M.J., Nirenberg, T., Woolard, R., Bendtsen, P. & Longabaugh, R. (2008). A systematic review of emergency care brief alcohol interventions for injury patients. *Journal of Substance Abuse Treatment, 35*(2), 184–201.

Ninci, J., Vannest, K.J., Willson, V. & Zhang, N. (2015). Interrater agreement between visual analysts of single-case data: A meta-analysis. *Behavior Modification, 39*(4), 510–541.

Noar, S.M., Benac, C.N. & Harris, M.S. (2007). Does tailoring matter? Meta-analytic review of tailored print health behavior change interventions. *Psychological Bulletin, 133*(4), 673.

Norman, C.D. & Skinner, H.A. (2006). eHealth literacy: essential skills for consumer health in a networked world. *Journal of Medical Internet Research, 8*, e9.

Norman, P., Boer, H., Seydel, E.R. & Mullan, B. (2015). Protection motivation theory. In M. Conner and P. Norman (eds.). *Predicting and Changing Health Behaviour: Research and Practice with Social Cognition Models.* Maidenhead: Open University Press.

Notley, C., Ward, E., Dawkins, L. & Holland, R. (2018). The unique contribution of e-cigarettes for tobacco harm reduction in supporting smoking relapse prevention. *Harm Reduction Journal, 15*(1), 31.

Nutt, D.J., King, L.A. & Phillips, L.D. (2010). Drug harms in the UK: a multicriteria decision analysis. *The Lancet, 376*(9752), 1558–1565.

Nutt, D.J., Phillips, L.D., Balfour, D., Curran, H.V., Dockrell, M., Foulds, J., ... & Ramsey, J. (2014). Estimating the harms of nicotine-containing products using the MCDA approach. *European Addiction Research, 20*(5), 218–225.

Nyberg, S.Y., Fransson, E.I., Heikkilä, K., Alfredsson, L., Casini, A. et al. (2013). Job strain and cardiovascular disease risk factors: meta-analysis of individual-participant data from 47,000 men and women. *PLoS ONE, 8*, e67323.

O'Connor, D.B., Armitage, C.J. & Ferguson, E. (2015). Randomized test of an implementation intention-based tool to reduce stress-induced eating. *Annals of Behavioral Medicine, 49*(3), 331–343.

O'Connor, R.M., Stewart, S. H. & Watt, M.C. (2009). Distinguishing BAS risk for university students' drinking, smoking, and gambling behaviors. *Personality and Individual Differences, 46*, 514–519.

O'Dea, K. (1991). Traditional diet and food preferences of Australian Aboriginal hunter-gatherers. *Philosphical Transactions: Biological Sciences, 334*, 233–241.

O'Sullivan, S.S., Evans, A.H. & Lees, A.J. (2009). Dopamine dysregulation syndrome. *CNS Drugs, 23*(2), 157–170.

Oaten, M. & Cheng, K. (2006a). Improved self-control: The benefits of a regular program of academic study. *Basic and Applied Social Psychology, 28*(1), 1–16.

Oaten, M. & Cheng, K. (2006b). Longitudinal gains in self-regulation from regular physical exercise. *British Journal of Health Psychology, 11*(4), 717–733.

O'Brien, C.P., Testa, T., O'Brien, T.J., Brady, J.P. & Wells, B. (1977). Conditioned narcotic withdrawal in humans. *Science, 195*(4282), 1000–1002.

Odom, E.C., Li, R., Scanlon, K.S., Perrine, C.G. & Grummer-Strawn, L. (2013). Reasons for earlier than desired cessation of breastfeeding. *Pediatrics, 131*(3), e726–e732.

Odum, A.L. (2011). Delay discounting: trait variable?. *Behavioural Processes, 87*(1), 1–9.

Oettingen, G. (2012). Future thought and behaviour change. *European Review of Social Psychology, 23*(1), 1–63.

Oettingen, G., Hönig, G. & Gollwitzer, P.M. (2000). Effective self-regulation of goal attainment. *International Journal of Educational Research, 33*(7), 705–732.

Ofcom (2020). Half of UK adults exposed to false claims about coronavirus. www.ofcom.org.uk/about-ofcom/latest/features-and-news/half-of-uk-adults-exposed-to-false-claims-about-coronavirus

Office for National Statistics (2016) Adult smoking habits in Great Britain: 2014. www.ons.gov.uk/peoplepopulationandcommunity/healthandsocialcare/healthandlifeexpectancies/bulletins/adultsmokinghabitsingreatbritain/2014

Ogden, J., Reynolds, R. & Smith, A. (2006). Expanding the concept of parental control: a role for overt and covert control in children's snacking behaviour? *Appetite, 47*(1), 100–106.

Oh, S. & Lewis, C. (2008). Korean preschoolers' advanced inhibitory control and its relation to other executive skills and mental state understanding. *Child Development, 79*(1), 80–99.

Okuda, N., Nishi, N., Ishikawa-Takata, K., Yoshimura, E., Horie, S., Nakanishi, T., Sato, Y. & Takimoto, H. (2014). Understanding of sodium content labeled on food packages by Japanese people. *Hypertension Research, 37*, 467–471.

Olander, E.K., Fletcher, H., Williams, S., Atkinson, L., Turner, A. & French, D.P. (2013). What are the most effective techniques in changing obese individuals' physical activity self-efficacy and behaviour: a systematic review and meta-analysis. *International Journal of Behavioral Nutrition and Physical Activity, 10*, 29.

Omran, A.R. (1971). The epidemiologic transition: a theory of the epidemiology of population change. *The Milbank Quarterly, 83*, 731–757.

Opel, D.J., Mangione-Smith, R., Taylor, J.A., Korfiatis, C., Wiese, C., Catz, S. & Martin, D.P. (2011). Development of a survey to identify vaccine-hesitant parents: the parent attitudes about childhood vaccines survey. *Human Vaccines, 7*(4), 419–425.

Orbell, S. & Sheeran, P. (1998). 'Inclined abstainers': a problem for predicting health-related behaviour. *British Journal of Social Psychology, 37*, 151–165.

Oreskes, N. & Conway, E. (2011). *Merchants of Doubt. How a Handful of Scientists Obscured the Truth on Issues from Tobacco Smoke to Global Warming.* London: Bloomsbury.

Orrell-Valente, J.K., Hill, L.G., Brechwald, W.A., Dodge, K.A., Pettit, G.S. & Bates, J.E. (2007). 'Just three more bites': an observational analysis of parents' socialization of children's eating at mealtime. *Appetite, 48*(1), 37–45.

Osler, M., Prescott, E., Gronbaek, M., Christensen, U., Due, P. & Engholm, G. (2002). Income inequality, individual income, and mortality in Danish adults: analysis of pooled data from two cohort studies. *British Medical Journal, 324*, 13–16.

Ouellette, J.A. & Wood, W. (1998). Habit and intention in everyday life: The multiple processes by which past behavior predicts future behavior. *Psychological Bulletin, 124*, 54.

Painter, R.C., de Rooij, S.R. Bossuyt, P.M., Simmers, T.A., Osmond, C., Barker, D.J., Bleker, O.P. & Roseboom, T.J. (2006). Early onset of coronary artery disease after prenatal exposure to the Dutch famine. *American Journal of Clinical Nutrition, 84*, 322–327.

Painter, R.C., Osmond, C., Gluckman, P., Hanson, M., Phillips, D.I.W. & Roseboom, T.J. (2008). Transgenerational effects of prenatal exposure to the Dutch famine on neonatal adiposity and health in later life. *BJOG. An International Journal of Obstetrics and Gynaecology, 115*, 1243–1249.

Pakpour, A.H., Gholami, M., Gellert, P., Yekaninejad, M.S., Dombrowski, S.U. & Webb, T.L. (2016). The effects of two planning interventions on the oral health behavior of Iranian adolescents: a cluster randomized controlled trial. *Annals of Behavioral Medicine, 50*(3), 409–418.

Papies, E.K. (2016a). Goal priming as a situated intervention tool. *Current Opinion in Psychology, 12*, 12–16.

Papies, E.K. (2016b). Health goal priming as a situated intervention tool: how to benefit from nonconscious motivational routes to health behaviour. *Health Psychology Review, 10*(4), 408–424.

Papies, E.K. & Aarts, H. (2016). Automatic self-regulation: from habit to goal pursuit. In K. Vohs & R. Baumeister (eds.). *Handbook of Self regulation: Research, Theory, and Applications* (3rd edn). New York: Guilford Press.

Papies, E.K. & Barsalou, L.W. (2015). Grounding desire and motivated behavior: A theoretical framework and empirical evidence. In W. Hofmann & L. Nordgren (eds.). *The Psychology of Desire*. New York: Guilford Press.

Papies, E.K. & Hamstra, P. (2010). Goal priming and eating behavior: enhancing self-regulation by environmental cues. *Health Psychology, 29*(4), 384.

Papies, E.K., Aarts, H. & De Vries, N.K. (2009). Planning is for doing: Implementation intentions go beyond the mere creation of goal-directed associations. *Journal of Experimental Social Psychology, 45*(5), 1148–1151.

Papies, E.K., Best, M., Gelibter, E. & Barsalou, L.W. (2017). The role of simulations in consumer experiences and behavior: Insights from the grounded cognition theory of desire. *Journal of the Association for Consumer Research, 2*(4), 402–418.

Papies, E.K., Potjes, I., Keesman, M., Schwinghammer, S. & Van Koningsbruggen, G.M. (2014). Using health primes to reduce unhealthy snack purchases among overweight consumers in a grocery store. *International Journal of Obesity, 38*(4), 597–602.

Papies, E.K., Pronk, T.M., Keesman, M. & Barsalou, L.W. (2015). The benefits of simply observing: Mindful attention modulates the link between motivation and behaviour. *Journal of Personality and Social Psychology, 108*, 148–170.

Paradies, Y., Ben, J., Denson, N., Elias, A., Priest, N., Pieterse, A., ... & Gee, G. (2015). Racism as a determinant of health: a systematic review and meta-analysis. *PloS One, 10*(9), e0138511.

Paravidino, V. B., Mediano, M. F. F., Hoffman, D. J. & Sichieri, R. (2016). Effect of exercise intensity on spontaneous physical activity energy expenditure in overweight boys: a crossover study. *PloS One, 11*(1).

Parks-Stamm, E.J., Gollwitzer, P.M. & Oettingen, G. (2010). Implementation intentions and test anxiety: Shielding academic performance from distraction. *Learning and Individual Differences, 20*(1), 30–33.

Patel, N., Beeken, R.J., Leurent, B., Omar, R.Z., Nazareth, I. & Morris, S. (2018). Cost-effectiveness of habit-based advice for weight control versus usual care in general practice in the Ten Top Tips (10TT) trial: economic evaluation based on a randomised controlled trial. *BMJ Open, 8*(8), e017511.

Pavlov, I.P. (1927). *Conditioned Reflexes.* (G.V. Anrep, translation.) London: Oxford University Press.

Paz-Fiho, G., Wong, M.L. & Licinio, J. (2011). Ten years of leptin replacement therapy. *Obesity Reviews, 12,* 315–323.

Pearce, L.R., Atanassova, N., Banton, M.C., Bottomley, B., van der Klaauw, A.A. et al. (2013). *KSR2* mutations are associated with obesity, insulin resistance, and impaired cellular fuel oxidation. *Cell, 155,* 765–777.

Peirce, J. M. & Alviña, K. (2019). The role of inflammation and the gut microbiome in depression and anxiety. *Journal of Neuroscience Research, 97*(10), 1223–1241.

Pelchat, M.L. (2002). Of human bondage: Food craving, obsession, compulsion, and addiction. *Physiology & Behavior, 76,* 347–352.

Pembrey, M.E., Bygren, L.O., Kaati, G., Edvinsson, S., Northstone, K., Sjöström, M., Golding, J. and The ALSPAC Study Team. (2006). Sex-specific, males-line transgenerational responses in humans. *European Journal of Human Genetics, 14,* 159–166.

Pender, N.J., Murdaugh, C.L., Parsons, M.A. & Ann, M. (2006). *Health Promotion in Nursing Practice.* Upper Saddle River, NJ: Prentice Hall.

Penley, J.A., Tomaka, J. & Wiebe, J.S. (2002). The association of coping to physical and psychological health outcomes: a meta-analytic review. *Journal of Behavioral Medicine, 25,* 551–603.

Perkins, H.W., Linkenbach, J.W., Lewis, M.A. & Neighbors, C. (2010). Effectiveness of social norms media marketing in reducing drinking and driving: A statewide campaign. *Addictive Behaviors, 35*(10), 866–874.

Perry, G.H., Dominy, N.J., Claw, K.G., Lee, A.S., Fiegler, H., Redon, R., Werner, J. et al. (2007). Diet and the evolution of human amylase gene copy number variation. *Nature Genetics, 39,* 1256–1260.

Peters, G.J.Y., De Bruin, M. & Crutzen, R. (2015). Everything should be as simple as possible, but no simpler: towards a protocol for accumulating evidence regarding the active content of health behaviour change interventions. *Health Psychology Review, 9*(1), 1–14.

Peters, G.J.Y., Ruiter, R.A. & Kok, G. (2013). Threatening communication: a critical re-analysis and a revised meta-analytic test of fear appeal theory. *Health Psychology Review, 7,* S8–S31.

Petrescu, D.C., Hollands, G.J., Couturier, D.L., Ng, Y.L. & Marteau, T.M. (2016). Public acceptability in the UK and USA of nudging to reduce obesity: the example of reducing sugar-sweetened beverages consumption. *PLoS One, 11*(6), e0155995.

Petticrew, M.P., Lee, K. & McKee, M. (2012). Type A behavior pattern and coronary heart disease: Philip Morris's 'crown jewel'. *American Journal of Public Health, 102*(11), 2018–2025.

Phelan, S.M., Burgess, D.J., Yeazel, M.W., Hellerstedt, W.L., Griffin, J.M. & van Ryn, M. (2015). Impact of weight bias and stigma on quality of care and outcomes for patients with obesity. *Obesity Reviews, 16*(4), 319–326.

Piacenza, F., Malavolta, M., Basso, A., Costarelli, L., Giacconi, R., Ravussin, E., Redman, L.M., Mocchegiani, E. (2015). Effect of 6-month caloric restriction on Cu bound to ceruloplasm in adult overweight subjects. *Journal of Nutritional Biochemistry, 26,* 876–882.

Plassmann, H., O'Doherty, J., Shiv, B. & Rangel, A. (2008). Marketing actions can modulate neural representations of experienced pleasantness. *Proceedings of the National Academy of Sciences, 105*(3), 1050–1054.

Plataforma SINC (2008). Medical textbooks use white, heterosexual men as a 'universal model. *Science Daily.* www.sciencedaily.com/releases/2008/10/081015132108.htm

Plotnikoff, R.C., Lippke, S., Trinh, L., Courneya, K.S., Birkett, N. & Sigal, R.J. (2010). Protection motivation theory and the prediction of physical activity among adults with type 1 or types 2 diabetes in a large population sample. *British Journal of Health Psychology, 15,* 643–661.

Plotnikoff, R.C., Rhodes, R.E. & Trinh, L. (2009a). Protection motivation theory and physical activity: a longitudinal test among a representative population sample of Canadian adults. *Journal of Health Psychology, 14,* 1119–1134.

Plotnikoff, R.C., Trinh, L., Courneya, K.S., Karuamuni, N. & Sigal, R.J. (2009b). Predictors of aerobic physical activity and resistance training among Canadian adults with type 2 diabetes: an application of the protection motivation theory. *Psychology of Sport and Exercise, 10*, 320–328.

Pocock, S.J. (2006). *Clinical Trials. A Practical Approach.* Chichester: John Wiley & Sons.

Pontzer, H. (2018). Energy constraint as a novel mechanism linking exercise and health. *Physiology, 33*(6), 384–393.

Pontzer, H., Durazo-Arvizu, R., Dugas, L. R., Plange-Rhule, J., Bovet, P., Forrester, T. E., ... & Luke, A. (2016). Constrained total energy expenditure and metabolic adaptation to physical activity in adult humans. *Current Biology, 26*(3), 410–417.

Pontzer, H., Raichlen, D.A., Wood, B.M., Mabulla, A.Z., Racette, S.B., & Marlowe, F.W. (2012). Hunter-gatherer energetics and human obesity. *PloS One, 7*(7), e40503.

Pontzer, H., Raichlen, D.A., Wood, B.M., Thompson, M.A., Racette, S.B., Mabulla, A.Z.P. & Marlowe, F.W. (2015). Energy expenditure and activity among Hadza hunter-gatherers. *American Journal of Human Biology, 27*, 628–637.

Pool, E., Brosch, T., Delplanque, S. & Sander, D. (2016). Attentional bias for positive emotional stimuli: A meta-analytic investigation. *Psychological Bulletin, 142*, 79–106.

Poolman, E.M. & Galvani, A.P. (2016). Evaluating candidate agents of selective pressure for cystic fibrosis. *Journal of the Royal Society Interface, 4*, 91–98.

Poortinga, W. (2006). Social relations or social capital? Individual and community health effects of bonding social capital. *Social Science and Medicine, 63*, 255-2–270.

Poortinga, W. (2012). Community resilience and health: the role of bonding, bridging, and linking aspects of social capital. *Health and Place, 18*, 286–295.

Popko, L. (2018). Some notes on Papyrus Ebers, Ancient Egyptian treatments of migraine, and a crocodile on the patient's head. *Bulletin of the History of Medicine, 92*(2), 352–366.

Popper, K. (1959/2002). *The Logic of Scientific Discovery.* New York: Routledge.

Porter, R. (1999). *The Greatest Benefit to Mankind: A Medical History of Humanity from Antiquity to the Present.* London: Fontana Press.

Posner, M.I., Rothbart, M.K., & Sheese, B.E. (2007). Attention genes. *Developmental Science, 10*(1), 24–29.

Powell, L.M., Slater, S., Chaloupka, F.J. & Harper, D. (2006). Availability of physical activity-related facilities and neighborhood demographic and socioeconomic characteristics: a national study. *American Journal of Public Health, 96*, 1676–1680.

Powell, L.M., Szczypka, G., Chaloupka, F.J. & Braunschweig, C.L. (2007). Nutritional content of television food advertisements seen by children and adolescents in the United States. *Pediatrics, 120*(3), 576–583.

Prentice, M.B. & Rahalison, L. (2007). Plague. *The Lancet, 369*, 1196–1207.

Prescott, C.A., Aggen, S.H. & Kendler, K.S. (2000). Sex-specific genetic influences on the comorbidity of alcoholism and major depression in a population-based sample of US twins. *Archives of General Psychiatry, 57*(8), 803–811.

Presti, G., Cau, S., Oppo, A. & Moderato, P. (2015). Increased classroom consumption of home-provided fruits and vegetables for Normal and overweight children: results of the food dudes program in Italy. *Journal of Nutrition Education and Behavior, 47*(4), 338–344.

Prestwich, A. & Kellar, I. (2014). How can the impact of implementation intentions as a behaviour change intervention be improved? *Revue Européenne de Psychologie Appliquée/European Review of Applied Psychology, 64*(1), 35–41.

Prestwich, A., Kellar, I., Parker, R., MacRae, S., Learmonth, M., Sykes, B., Taylor, N. & Castle, H. (2013). How can self-efficacy be increased? Meta-analysis of dietary interventions. *Health Psychology Review, 8*, 270–285.

Prestwich, A., Lawton, R. & Conner, M. (2003). The use of implementation intentions and the decision balance sheet in promoting exercise behaviour. *Psychology and Health, 18*(6), 707–721.

Prestwich, A., Perugini, M. & Hurling, R. (2009). Can the effects of implementation intentions on exercise be enhanced using text messages? *Psychology and Health, 24*(6), 677–687.

Prestwich, A., Sheeran, P., Webb, T.L. & Gollwitzer, P.M. (2015). Implementation intentions. In M. Conner and P. Norman (eds.). *Predicting and Changing Health Behaviour: Research and Practice with Social Cognition Models.* Maidenhead: Open University Press.

Prestwich, A., Sniehotta, F.F., Whittington, C., Dombrowski, S.U., Rogers, L. & Michie, S. (2014). Does theory influence the effectiveness of health behavior interventions? Meta-analysis. *Health Psychology, 33*(5), 465.

Prochaska, J.O. & DiClemente, C.C. (1983). Stages and processes of self-change of smoking: toward an integrative model of change. *Journal of Consulting and Clinical Psychology, 51*, 390–395.

Prochaska, J.O. & Velicer, W.F. (1997). The transtheoretical model of health behavior change. *American Journal of Health Promotion, 12*, 38–48.

Prochaska, J.O., DiClemente, C.C. & Norcross, J.C. (1992). In search of how people change: applications to addictive behaviors. *American Psychologist, 47,* 1102–1114.

Prochaska, J.O., Redding, C.A. & Evers, K. (2008). The transtheoretical model and stages of change. In K. Glanz, B.K. Rimer and K. Viswanth (eds.). *Health Behavior and Health Education: Theory, Research, and Practice.* (pp. 97–121). San Francisco: Jossey-Bass.

Pronker, E.S., Weenen, T.C., Commandeur, H., Claassen, E.H. & Osterhaus, A.D. (2013). Risk in vaccine research and development quantified. *PloS One, 8*(3), e57755.

Public Health England (2016). *National Diet and Nutrition Survey: Assessment of Dietary Sodium in Adults (19 to 64 years) in England, 2014.* London: Public Health England. https://assets.publishing. service.gov.uk/government/uploads/system/uploads/ attachment_data/file/773836/Sodium_study_2014_ England_Text_final.pdf

Public Health England (2018a). Confirmed cases of measles, mumps and rubella in England and Wales: 1996 to 2017. www.gov.uk/government/publications/ measles-confirmed-cases/confirmed-cases-of- measles-mumps-and-rubella-in-england-and-wales- 2012-to-2013

Public Health England (2018b). *National Diet and Nutrition Survey. Results from Year 7 and 8 (combined) of the Rolling Programme (2014/2015 to 2015/2016).* London: Public Health England. www.gov.uk/ government/statistics/ndns-results-from-years-7- and-8-combined

Puca, R.M. (2001). Preferred difficulty and subjective probability in different action phases. *Motivation and Emotion, 25,* 307–326.

Puhl, R.M. & Brownell, K.D. (2006). Confronting and coping with weight stigma: an investigation of overweight and obese adults. *Obesity, 14*(10), 1802–1815.

Puhl, R.M. & Heuer, C.A. (2009). The stigma of obesity: a review and update. *Obesity, 17*(5), 941–964.

Puhl, R.M., Andreyeva, T. & Brownell, K.D. (2008). Perceptions of weight discrimination: prevalence and comparison to race and gender discrimination in America. *International Journal of Obesity, 32*(6), 992.

Quinlan, K.B. & McCaul, K.D. (2000). Matched and mismatched interventions with young adult smokers: testing a stage theory. *Health Psychology, 19,* 165–171.

Quinn, J.M., Pascoe, A., Wood, W. & Neal, D.T. (2010). Can't control yourself? Monitor those bad habits. *Personality and Social Psychology Bulletin, 36*(4), 499–511.

Rabinovich, R., Gaudzinski-Windheuser, S. & Goren-Inbar, N. (2008). Systematic butchering of fallow deer (Dama) at the early middle Pleistocene

Acheulian site of Gesher Benot Ya-aqov (Israel). *Journal of Human Evolution, 54,* 134–149.

Raisi-Estabragh, Z., McCracken, C., Bethell, M. S., Cooper, J., Cooper, C., Caulfield, M.J., … & Petersen, S.E. (2020). Greater risk of severe COVID-19 in Black, Asian and Minority Ethnic populations is not explained by cardiometabolic, socioeconomic or behavioural factors, or by 25 (OH)-vitamin D status: study of 1326 cases from the UK Biobank. *Journal of Public Health , 42*(3), 451-460.

Ramachandrappa, S. & Farooqi, I.S. (2011). Genetic approaches to understanding human obesity. *The Journal of Clinical Investigation, 121,* 2080–2086.

Ramchand, R., Ahluwalia, S.C., Xenakis, L, Apaydin, E., Raaen, L. & Grimm, G. (2017). A systematic review of peer-supported interventions for health promotion and disease prevention. *Preventive Medicine, 101,* 156–170.

Ravelli, A.C.J., van der Meulen, J.H.P., Michels, R.P.J., Osmond, C., Barker, D.J.P. Hales, C.N. & Bleker, O.P. (1998). Glucose tolerance in adults after prenatal exposure to famine. *The Lancet, 351,* 173–177

Ravelli, G.P., Stein, Z.A. & Susser, M.W. (1976). Obesity in young men after famine exposure in utero and early infancy. *New England Journal of Medicine, 12,* 349-353.

Ravndal, E., Lauritzen, G., Frank, O., Jansson, I. & Larsson, J. (2001). Childhood maltreatment among Norwegian drug abusers in treatment. *International Journal of Social Welfare, 10*(2), 142–147.

Reardon, S. (2015). Gene-editing wave hits clinic. *Nature, 527,* 146–147.

Rebbeck, T.R., Friebel, T., Lynch, H.T., Neuhausen, S.L., van't Veer, L. … Weber, B.L. (2004). Bilateral prophylactic mastectomy reduces breast cancer risk in BRCA1 and BRCA2 mutation carries: the PROSE study group. *Journal of Clinical Oncology, 22,* 1055–1062.

Reber, A.S. (1993). *Implicit Learning and Tacit Knowledge.* Oxford: Oxford University Press.

Redelmeier, D.A. & Tversky, A. (1996). On the belief that arthritis pain is related to the weather. *Proceedings of the National Academy of Sciences, 93*(7), 2895–2896.

Reed, D.R. & Knaapila, A. (2010). Genetics of taste and smell: poisons and pleasures. *Progress in Molecular Biology and Translational Science, 94,* 213–240.

Rees, A., Dodd, G. & Spencer, J. (2018). The effects of flavonoids on cardiovascular health: a review of human intervention trials and implications for cerebrovascular function. *Nutrients, 10*(12), 1852.

Rees, D.C., Williams, T.N. & Gladwin, M.T. (2010). Sickle-cell disease. *The Lancet, 376,* 2018–2031.

Rehm, J., Shield, K.D., Joharchi, N. & Shuper, P.A. (2012). Alcohol consumption and the intention to engage in unprotected sex: Systematic review and meta-analysis of experimental studies. *Addiction, 107*(1), 51–59.

Reid, A.E. & Aiken, L.S. (2013). Correcting injunctive norm misperceptions motivates behavior change: A randomized controlled sun protection intervention. *Health Psychology, 32*(5), 551.

Reimers, S., Maylor, E.A., Stewart, N. & Chater, N. (2009). Associations between a one-shot delay discounting measure and age, income, education and real-world impulsive behavior. *Personality and Individual Differences, 47*(8), 973–978.

Reitsma, M.B., Fullman, N., Ng, M., Salama, J.S., Abajobir, A., Abate, K.H., ... & Adebiyi, A.O. (2017). Smoking prevalence and attributable disease burden in 195 countries and territories, 1990–2015: a systematic analysis from the Global Burden of Disease Study 2015. *The Lancet, 389*(10082), 1885–1906.

Relton, C., Strong, M., Thomas, K.J., Whelan, B., Walters, S. J., Burrows, J., ... & Fox-Rushby, J. (2018). Effect of financial incentives on breastfeeding: a cluster randomized clinical trial. *JAMA Pediatrics, 172*(2), e174523-e174523.

Relton, C., Umney, D., Strong, M., Thomas, K. & Renfrew, M.J. (2017). Challenging social norms: Discourse analysis of a research project aiming to use financial incentives to change breastfeeding behaviours. *The Lancet, 390*, S75.

Relton, C., Whelan, B., Strong, M., Thomas, K., Whitford, H., Scott, E. & van Cleemput, P. (2014). Are financial incentives for breastfeeding feasible in the UK? A mixed methods field study. *The Lancet, 384*, S5.

Renehan, A.G., Zwahlen, M. & Egger, M. (2015). Adiposity and cancer risk: new mechanistic insights from epidemiology. *Nature Reviews Cancer, 15*(8), 484.

Revedin, A., Aranguren, B., Becattini, R., Longo, L., Marconi, E., Lippi, M.M., Skakun, N., Sinitsyn, A., Spiridonova, E. & Svoboda, J. (2010). Thirty thousand-year-old evidence of plant food processing. *Proceedings of the National Academy of Sciences of the USA, 107*, 18818–18819.

Rex-Lear, M., Jensen-Campbell, L.A. & Lee, S. (2019). Young and biased: Children's perceptions of overweight peers. *Journal of Applied Biobehavioral Research*, e12161.

Rhodes, R.E. & de Bruijn, G.J. (2010). Automatic and motivational correlates of physical activity: Does intensity moderate the relationship? *Behavioral Medicine, 36*(2), 44–52.

Rhodes, R.E. & Smith, N.E.I. (2006). Personality correlates of physical activity: a review and meta-analysis. *British Journal of Sports Medicine, 40*, 958–965.

Rhodes, R.E., Courney, K.S. & Hayduk, L.A. (2002). Does personality moderate the theory of planned behavior in the exercise domain? *Journal of Sport and Exercise Psychology, 24*, 120–132.

Rice, T., Unruh, L.Y., Rosenau, P., Barnes, A.J., Saltman, R.B. & van Ginnekin, E. (2014). Challenges facing the United States of America in implementing universal coverage. *Bulletin of the World Health Organization, 92*, 894–902.

Richards, C.E., Magin, P.J. & Callister, R. (2009). Is your prescription of distance running shoes evidence-based? *British Journal of Sports Medicine, 43*, 159–162.

Rivis, A. & Sheeran, P. (2003). Descriptive norms as an additional predictor in the theory of planned behaviour: A meta-analysis. *Current Psychology, 22*(3), 218-233.

Rivis, A. & Sheeran, P. (2013). Automatic risk behavior: direct effects of binge drinker stereotypes on drinking behavior. *Health Psychology, 32*(5), 571.

Rizza, W., Veronese, N. & Fontana, L. (2014). What are the roles of calorie restriction and diet quality in promoting healthy longevity? *Ageing Research Reviews, 13*, 38–45.

Roberts, B.W., Kuncel, N.R., Shiner, R., Caspi, A. & Goldberg, L.R. (2007). The power of personality. The comparative validity of personality traits, socioeconomic status, and cognitive ability for predicting important life outcomes. *Perspectives on Psychological Science, 2*, 313–345.

Roberts, B.W., Luo, J., Briley, D. A., Chow, P. I., Su, R. & Hill, P. L. (2017). A systematic review of personality trait change through intervention. *Psychological Bulletin, 143*(2), 117.

Roberts, B.W., Walton, K.E. & Viechtbauer, W. (2006). Patterns of mean-level change in personality traits across the life course: A meta-analysis of longitudinal studies. *Psychological Bulletin, 132*, 1–25.

Robinson, E., Fleming, A. & Higgs, S. (2014a). Prompting healthier eating: Testing the use of health and social norm based messages. *Health Psychology, 33*(9), 1057.

Robinson, E., Hunger, J.M. & Daly, M. (2015). Perceived weight status and risk of weight gain across life in US and UK adults. *International Journal of Obesity, 39*(12), 1721.

Robinson, E., Kersbergen, I., Brunstrom, J.M. & Field, M. (2014c). I'm watching you. Awareness that food consumption is being monitored is a demand characteristic in eating-behaviour experiments. *Appetite, 83*, 19–25.

Robinson, E., Thomas, J., Aveyard, P. & Higgs, S. (2014b). What everyone else is eating: a systematic review and meta-analysis of the effect of informational eating norms on eating behavior. *Journal of the Academy of Nutrition and Dietetics, 114*(3), 414–429.

Robinson, M.J. & Berridge, K.C. (2013). Instant transformation of learned repulsion into motivational 'wanting'. *Current Biology, 23*(4), 282–289.

Robinson, T.E. & Berridge, K.C. (1993). The neural basis of drug craving: an incentive-sensitization theory of addiction. *Brain Research Reviews, 18*(3), 247–291.

Robinson, T.E. & Berridge, K.C. (2001). Incentive-sensitization and addiction. *Addiction, 96*(1), 103–114.

Robinson, T.E. & Berridge, K.C. (2003). Addiction. *Annual Review of Psychology, 54*, 25–53.

Robinson, T.E. & Berridge, K.C. (2008). The incentive sensitization theory of addiction: some current issues. *Philosophical Transactions of the Royal Society B: Biological Sciences, 363*(1507), 3137–3146.

Rodrigues, A.M., O'Brien, N., French, D.P., Glidewell, L. & Sniehotta, F.F. (2015). The question–behavior effect: Genuine effect or spurious phenomenon? A systematic review of randomized controlled trials with meta-analyses. *Health Psychology, 34*, 61.

Roesch, S.C., Adams, L., Hines, A., Palmores, A., Vyas, P., Tran, C., Pekin, S. & Vaughn, A.A. (2005). Coping with prostate cancer: a meta-analytic review. *Journal of Behavioral Medicine, 28*, 281–293.

Rogers, P.J. (2017). Food and drug addictions: Similarities and differences. *Pharmacology Biochemistry and Behavior, 153*, 182–190.

Rogers, R.W. (1975). A protection motivation theory of fear appeals and attitude change. *The Journal of Psychology, 91*, 93–114.

Rogers, R.W. (1983). Cognitive and physiological processes in fear appeals and attitude change: a revised theory of protection motivation. In J.T. Cacioppo and R.E. Petty (eds.). *Social Psychophysiology: A Source Book*. New York: Guilford Press.

Rollins, B.Y., Loken, E., Savage, J.S. & Birch, L.L. (2014a). Effects of restriction on children's intake differ by child temperament, food reinforcement, and parent's chronic use of restriction. *Appetite, 73*, 31–39.

Rollins, B.Y., Loken, E., Savage, J.S. & Birch, L.L. (2014b). Maternal controlling feeding practices and girls' inhibitory control interact to predict changes in BMI and eating in the absence of hunger from 5 to 7 y. *The American Journal of Clinical Nutrition, 99*(2), 249–257.

Rollins, B.Y., Loken, E., Savage, J.S. & Birch, L.L. (2014c). Measurement of food reinforcement in preschool children. Associations with food intake, BMI and reward sensitivity. *Appetite, 72*, 21–27.

Rollins, B.Y., Savage, J.S., Fisher, J.O. & Birch, L.L. (2016a). Alternatives to restrictive feeding practices to promote self-regulation in childhood: a developmental perspective. *Pediatric Obesity, 11*(5), 326–332.

Rollins, N.C., Bhandari, N., Hajeebhoy, N., Horton, S., Lutter, C.K., Martines, J.C., ... & Group, T.L.B.S. (2016b). Why invest, and what it will take to improve breastfeeding practices? *The Lancet, 387*(10017), 491–504.

Rollnick, S. & Miller, W.R. (1995). What is motivational interviewing? *Behavioural and Cognitive Psychotherapy, 23*(4), 325–334.

Rosa-Díaz, I.M. (2004). Price knowledge: effects of consumers' attitudes towards prices, demographics, and socio-cultural characteristics. *Journal of Product and Brand Management, 13*, 406–428.

Roseboom, T.J., van der Meulen, J.H.P., Osmond, C., Barker, D.J.P., Ravelli, A.C.J., Schroeder-Tanka, J.M., van Montfrans, G.A., Michels, R.P.J. & Bleker, O.P. (2000). Coronary heart disease after prenatal exposure to the Dutch famine, 1944–45. *Heart, 84*, 595–598.

Rosenman, R.H., Brand, R.J., Sholtz, R.I. & Friedman, M. (1976). Multivariate prediction of coronary heart disease during 8.5 year follow-up in the western collaborative group study. *The American Journal of Cardiology, 37*, 903–910.

Rosenstein, D. & Oster, H. (1988). Differential facial responses to four basic tastes in newborns. *Child Development*, 1555–1568.

Rosenstock, I.M. (1974). Historical origins of the health belief model. *Health Education Monographs, 2*, 328–335.

Rosenstock, I.M., Strecher, V.J. & Becker, M.H. (1988). Social learning theory and the health belief model. *Health Education Quarterly, 15*, 175–183.

Roser, M. & Ortiz-Ospina, E. (2018). Literacy. https://ourworldindata.org/literacy#all-charts-preview

Roser, M. & Ortiz-Ospina, E. (2020). Primary and secondary education. Published online at OurWorldInData.org. https://ourworldindata.org/primary-and-secondary-education

Roser, M., Ritchie, H. & Ortiz-Ospina, E. (2019). World Population Growth. https://ourworldindata.org/world-population-growth#all-charts-preview

Rosling, H. (2018). *Factfulness*. London: Hodder & Stoughton.

Ross, D. (2002). *Ireland: History of a Nation*. New Lanark: Geddes & Grosset.

Rossow, I. & Lauritzen, G. (2001). Shattered childhood: a key issue in suicidal behavior among drug addicts? *Addiction, 96*(2), 227–240.

Rothbart, M.K. (2007). Temperament, development, and personality. *Current Directions in Psychological Science, 16*, 207–212.

Rothbart, M.K. & Derryberry, D. (1981). Development of individual differences in temperament. In M.E. Lamb & A. Brown (Eds.), *Advances in Developmental Psychology* (Vol. 1, pp. 37–86). Hillsdale, NJ: Erlbaum.

Rotter, J.B. (1966). Generalized expectancies for internal versus external control of reinforcement. *Psychological Monographs: General and Applied, 80,* 1–28.

Rovniak, L.S., Anderson, E.S., Winett, R.A. & Stephens, R.S. (2002). Social cognitive determinants of physical activity in young adults: a prospective structural equation analysis. *Annals of Behavioral Medicine, 24,* 149–156.

Rowley, J., Vander Hoorn, S., Korenromp, E., Low, N., Unemo, M., Abu-Raddad, L.J., ... & Thwin, S.S. (2019). Chlamydia, gonorrhoea, trichomoniasis and syphilis: global prevalence and incidence estimates, 2016. *Bulletin of the World Health Organization, 97*(8), 548.

Royal Swedish Academy of Sciences, The (2019). www.nobelprize.org/prizes/economic-sciences/2019/press-release/

Rozin, P., Scott, S., Dingley, M., Urbanek, J. K., Jiang, H. & Kaltenbach, M. (2011). Nudge to nobesity I: Minor changes in accessibility decrease food intake. *Judgment and Decision Making, 6*(4), 323.

Rubak, S., Sandbæk, A., Lauritzen, T. & Christensen, B. (2005). Motivational interviewing: a systematic review and meta-analysis. *British Journal of General Practice, 55*(513), 305–312.

Ruddock, H.K. & Hardman, C.A. (2017). Food addiction beliefs amongst the lay public: What are the consequences for eating behaviour? *Current Addiction Reports, 4*(2), 110–115.

Ruddock, H.K., Dickson, J.M., Field, M. & Hardman, C.A. (2015). Eating to live or living to eat? Exploring the causal attributions of self-perceived food addiction. *Appetite, 95,* 262–268.

Rudenga, K.J., Sinha, R. & Small, D.M. (2013). Acute stress potentiates brain response to milkshake as a function of body weight and chronic stress. *International Journal of Obesity, 37*(2), 309.

Ryan, R. (2009). Self determination theory and well being. *Social Psychology, 84,* e848.

Ryan, R.M. & Deci, E.L. (2000). Self-determination theory and the facilitation of intrinsic motivation, social development, and well-being. *American Psychologist, 55,* 68–78.

Sabbagh, M.A., Xu, F., Carlson, S.M., Moses, L.J. & Lee, K. (2006). The development of executive functioning and theory of mind: A comparison of Chinese and US preschoolers. *Psychological Science, 17*(1), 74–81.

Saddawi-Konefka, D., Baker, K., Guarino, A., Burns, S.M., Oettingen, G., Gollwitzer, P.M. & Charnin, J.E. (2017). Changing resident physician studying behaviors: A randomized, comparative effectiveness trial of goal setting versus use of WOOP. *Journal of Graduate Medical Education, 9*(4), 451–457.

Sadr, K. (2003). The Neolithic of southern Africa. *The Journal of African History, 44*(2), 195–209.

Saelens, B.E. & Epstein, L.H. (1996). Reinforcing value of food in obese and non-obese women. *Appetite, 27,* 41–50.

Sakar, D., Jung, M.K. & Wang, H.J. (2015). Alcohol and the immune system. *Alcohol Research: Current Reviews, 37*(2), 153.

Sakkou, M., Wiedmer, P., Anlag, K., Hamm, A., Seuntjens, E., Ettwiller, L., Tschöp, M.H. Treier, M. (2007). A role for brain-specific homeobox factor Bsx in the control of hyperphagia and locomotory behaviour. *Cell Metabolism, 5,* 450–463.

Sallis, J.F., Bull, F., Guthold, R., Heath, G.W., Inoue, S., Kelly, P., ... & Lancet Physical Activity Series 2 Executive Committee. (2016a). Progress in physical activity over the Olympic quadrennium. *The Lancet, 388*(10051), 1325–1336.

Sallis, J.F., Cerin, E., Conway, T.L., Adams, M.A., Frank, L. D., Pratt, M., ... & Davey, R. (2016b). Physical activity in relation to urban environments in 14 cities worldwide: a cross-sectional study. *The Lancet, 387*(10034), 2207–2217.

Salvy, S.J., Nitecki, L.A. & Epstein, L.H. (2009). Do social activities substitute for food in youth? *Annals of Behavioral Medicine, 38*(3), 205–212.

Samuelson, W. & Zeckhauser, R. (1988). Status quo bias in decision making. *Journal of Risk and Uncertainty, 1*(1), 7–59.

Sander, D., Grandjean, D. & Scherer, K.R. (2005). A systems approach to appraisal mechanisms in emotion. *Neural Networks, 18*(4), 317–352.

Sanders, T. (2015). Greener neighbourhoods, slimmer children? Evidence from 4423 participants aged 6 to 13 years in the longitudinal study of Australian children. *International Journal of Obesity, 39,* 1224–1229.

Santelli, J.S., Kantor, L.M., Grilo, S.A., Speizer, I.S., Lindberg, L.D., Heitel, J., ... & Heck, C.J. (2017). Abstinence-only-until-marriage: An updated review of US policies and programs and their impact. *Journal of Adolescent Health, 61*(3), 273–280.

Savani, K. & Job, V. (2017). Reverse ego-depletion: Acts of self-control can improve subsequent performance in Indian cultural contexts. *Journal of Personality and Social Psychology, 113*(4), 589.

Schachar, R., Logan, G.D., Robaey, P., Chen, S., Ickowicz, A. & Barr, C. (2007). Restraint and cancellation: multiple inhibition deficits in attention deficit hyperactivity disorder. *Journal of Abnormal Child Psychology, 35*(2), 229–238.

Schaller, M. (2011). The behavioural immune system and the psychology of human sociality. *Philosophical Transactions of the Royal Society B, 366,* 3418–3426.

Schaller, M. & Murray, D.R. (2008). Pathogens, personality, and culture: disease prevalence predicts worldwide variability in sociosexuality, extraversion, and openness to experience. *Journal of Personality and Social Psychology, 95,* 212–221.

Schlam, T.R., Wilson, N.L., Shoda, Y., Mischel, W. & Ayduk, O. (2013). Preschoolers' delay of gratification predicts their body mass 30 years later. *The Journal of Pediatrics, 162*(1), 90–93.

Schlebusch, C. M., Malmström, H., Günther, T., Sjödin, P., Coutinho, A., Edlund, H., ... & Lombard, M. (2017). Southern African ancient genomes estimate modern human divergence to 350,000 to 260,000 years ago. *Science, 358*(6363), 652–655.

Schmeichel, B.J., Harmon-Jones, C. & Harmon-Jones, E. (2010). Exercising self-control increases approach motivation. *Journal of Personality and Social Psychology, 99,* 162–173.

Schmitt, D.P., Allik, J., McCrae, R.R., Benet-Martínez, V., Alcalay, L., Ault, L., ... Poels, K. (2007). The geographic distribution of big five personality traits. Patterns and profiles of human self-description across 56 nations. *Journal of Cross-Cultural Psychology, 38,* 173–212.

Schnall, P.L., Landsbergis, P.A. & Baker, D. (1994). Job strain and cardiovascular disease. *Annual Review of Public Health, 15,* 381–411.

Schneider, W. & Shiffrin, R. M. (1977). Controlled and automatic human information processing: I. Detection, search, and attention. *Psychological Review, 84*(1), 1.

Schnohr, P., O'Keefe, J. H., Marott, J. L., Lange, P. & Jensen, G. B. (2015). Dose of jogging and long-term mortality: the Copenhagen City Heart Study. *Journal of the American College of Cardiology, 65*(5), 411–419.

Schnorr, S.L., Candela, M., Rampelli, S., Centanni, M., Consolandi, C., Basaglia, G., ... & Fiori, J. (2014). Gut microbiome of the Hadza hunter-gatherers. *Nature Communications, 5,* 3654.

Schork, N.J. (2015). Time for one-person trials. *Nature, 520,* 609–611.

Schreier, H.M.C. & Chen, E. (2013). Socioeconomic status and the health of youth: a multilevel, multidomain approach to conceptualizing pathways. *Psychological Bulletin, 139,* 606–654.

Schröder, F.H., Hugosson, J., Roobol, M.J., Tammela, T.L.J., Ciatto, S., Nelen, V., ...Auvinen, A. (2009). Screening and prostate-cancer mortality in a randomized European study. *The New England Journal of Medicine, 360,* 1320–1328.

Schultz, P.W., Khazian, A.M. & Zaleski, A.C. (2008). Using normative social influence to promote conservation among hotel guests. *Social Influence, 3,* 4–23.

Schultz, P.W., Nolan, J.M., Cialdini, R.B., Goldstein, N.J. & Griskevicius, V. (2007). The constructive, destructive, and reconstructive power of social norms. *Psychological Science, 18*(5), 429–434.

Schultz, W., Dayan, P. & Montague, P.R. (1997). A neural substrate of prediction and reward. *Science, 275,* 1593–1599.

Schulz, K.F. (1995). Subverting Randomization. *Journal of the American Medical Association, 274,* 1456–1458.

Schulz, K.F. & Grimes, D.A. (2002a). Blinding in randomised trials: hiding who got what. *The Lancet, 359*(9307), 696–700.

Schulz, K.F. & Grimes, D.A. (2002b). Allocation concealment in randomised trials: defending against deciphering. *The Lancet, 359*(9306), 614–618.

Schulz, K.F. & Grimes, D.A. (2002c). Generation of allocation sequences in randomised trials: chance, not choice. *The Lancet, 359*(9305), 515–519.

Schulz, K.F. & Grimes, D.A. (2002d). Case-control studies: research in reverse. *The Lancet, 359*(9304), 431–434.

Schulz, K.F. & Grimes, D.A. (2005). Sample size calculations in randomised trials: mandatory and mystical. *The Lancet, 365*(9467), 1348–1353.

Schulz, K.F., Altman, D.G., Moher, D. for the CONSORT Group. (2010). CONSORT 2010 Statement: updated guidelines for reporting parallel group randomised trials. *British Medical Journal, 340,* c332.

Schumacher, S., Kemps, E. & Tiggemann, M. (2017). Acceptance-and imagery-based strategies can reduce chocolate cravings: A test of the elaborated-intrusion theory of desire. *Appetite, 113,* 63–70.

Schüz, B., Wiedemann, A. U., Mallach, N. & Scholz, U. (2009). Effects of a short behavioural intervention for dental flossing: randomized-controlled trial on planning when, where and how. *Journal of Clinical Periodontology, 36*(6), 498–505.

Schvey, N.A., Puhl, R.M. & Brownell, K.D. (2011). The impact of weight stigma on caloric consumption. *Obesity, 19*(10), 1957–1962.

Schwabe, L. & Wolf, O. T. (2013). Stress and multiple memory systems: from 'thinking' to 'doing'. *Trends in Cognitive Sciences, 17*(2), 60–68.

Schwartz, G.E. (1982). Testing the biopsychosocial model: The ultimate challenge facing behavioral medicine? *Journal of Consulting and Clinical Psychology, 50*(6), 1040.

Schwartz, S.H. (1992). Universals in the content and structure of values: Theoretical advances and empirical tests in 20 countries. *Advances in Experimental Social Psychology, 25,* 1–65.

Schwartz, S.H., Cieciuch, J., Vecchione, M., Davidov, E., Fischer, R., Beierlein, C., ... & Dirilen-

Gumus, O. (2012). Refining the theory of basic individual values. *Journal of Personality and Social Psychology, 103*(4), 663.

Scientific Advisory Committee on Nutrition (2010). Iron and health. London: TSO. www.gov.uk/government/publications/sacn-iron-and-health-report

Scientific Advisory Committee on Nutrition (2015). Carbohydrates and health. London: TSO. https://assets.publishing.service.gov.uk/government/uploads/system/uploads/attachment_data/file/445503/SACN_Carbohydrates_and_Health.pdf

Scollo, M., Zacher, M., Coomber, K. & Wakefield, M. (2015). Use of illicit tobacco following introduction of standardised packaging of tobacco products in Australia: results from a national cross-sectional survey. *Tobacco Control, 24*(Suppl 2), ii76–ii81.

Scott, S.E., Walter, F.M., Webster, A., Sutton, S. & Emery, J. (2013). The model of pathways to treatment: conceptualization and integration with existing theory. *British Journal of Health Psychology, 18*, 45–65.

Sedgwick, P. (2014). Explanatory trials versus pragmatic trials. *British Medical Journal, 349*, g6694.

Seedat, M., Van Niekerk, A., Jewkes, R., Suffla, S. & Ratele, K. (2009). Violence and injuries in South Africa: prioritising an agenda for prevention. *The Lancet, 374*(9694), 1011–1022.

Seeley, E.A. & Gardner, W.L. (2003). The 'selfless' and self-regulation: The role of chronic other-orientation in averting self-regulatory depletion. *Self and Identity, 2*(2), 103–117.

Seeyave, D.M., Coleman, S., Appugliese, D., Corwyn, R.F., Bradley, R.H., Davidson, N.S., ... & Lumeng, J.C. (2009). Ability to delay gratification at age 4 years and risk of overweight at age 11 years. *Archives of Pediatrics & Adolescent Medicine, 163*(4), 303–308.

Segal, G. (2016). Ambiguous terms and false dichotomies. In N. Heather and G. Segal (eds.). *Addiction and Choice: Rethinking the Relationship.* Oxford: Oxford University Press.

Selinger, J.C., O'Connor, S.M., Wong, J.D. & Donelan, J.M. (2015). Humans can continuously optimize energetic cost during walking. *Current Biology, 25*, 1–5.

Sellen, D.W. (2007). Evolution of infant and young child feeding: implications for contemporary public health. *Annual Review of Nutrition, 27*, 123–148.

Sellen, D.W. & Mace, R. (1997). Fertility and mode of subsistence: a phylogenetic analysis. *Current Anthropology, 38*, 878–889.

Sellen, D.W. & Mace, R. (1999). A phylogenetic analysis of the relationship between sub-adult mortality and mode of subsistence. *Journal of Biosocial Science, 31*, 1–16.

Serre, F., Fatseas, M., Swendsen, J. & Auriacombe, M. (2015). Ecological momentary assessment in the investigation of craving and substance use in daily life: A systematic review. *Drug and Alcohol Dependence, 148*, 1–20.

Shah, A.K., Mullainathan, S. & Shafir, E. (2012). Some consequences of having too little. *Science, 338*, 682–685.

Shah, J.Y., Friedman, R. & Kruglanski, A.W. (2002). Forgetting all else: on the antecedents and consequences of goal shielding. *Journal of Personality and Social Psychology, 83*(6), 1261.

Shanks, D.R. (2010). Learning: From association to cognition. *Annual Review of Psychology, 61*, 273–301.

Shariff, A.F., Willard, A.K., Andersen, T. & Norenzayan, A. (2016). Religious priming: A meta-analysis with a focus on prosociality. *Personality and Social Psychology Review, 20*(1), 27–48.

Sharma, S. & Tripathi, P. (2019). Gut microbiome and type 2 diabetes: where we are and where to go? *The Journal of Nutritional Biochemistry, 63*, 101–108.

Sheeran, P., Gollwitzer, P.M. & Bargh, J. A. (2013). Nonconscious processes and health. *Health Psychology, 32*, 460.

Sheeran, P., Klein, W.M. & Rothman, A.J. (2017). Health behavior change: Moving from observation to intervention. *Annual Review of Psychology, 68*, 573–600.

Sherman, S.J. (1980). On the self-erasing nature of errors of prediction. *Journal of Personality and Social Psychology, 39*, 211.

Shibuya, K., Hashimoto, H. & Yano, E. (2002). Individual income, income distribution, and self rated health in Japan: cross sectional analysis of nationally representative sample. *British Medical Journal, 324*, 16–19.

Shilton, T., Sparks, M., McQueen, D., Lamarre, M.C. & Jackson, S. (2011). *British Medical Journal, 343*, 435.

Shipley, B.A., Weiss, A., Der, G., Taylor, M.D. & Deary, I.J. (2007). Neuroticism, extraversion, and mortality in the UK health and lifestyle survey: a 21 –year prospective cohort study. *Psychosomatic Medicine, 69*, 923–931.

Shoda, Y., Mischel, W. & Peake, P.K. (1990). Predicting adolescent cognitive and self-regulatory competencies from preschool delay of gratification: Identifying diagnostic conditions. *Developmental Psychology, 26*(6), 978.

Sibbald, B. & Roberts, C. (1998). Understanding controlled trials Crossover trials. *British Medical Journal, 316*(7146), 1719–1720.

Siegel, R.L., Miller, K.D. & Jemal, A. (2016). Cancer Statistics, 2016. *CA-A Cancer Journal for Clinicians*, *66*, 7–30.

Siegler, I.C., Feaganes, J.R. & Rimer, B.K. (1995). Predictors of adoption of mammography in women under age 50. *Health Psychology*, *14*, 274.

Sienkiewicz-Jarosz, H., Scinska, A., Swiecicki, L., Lipczynska-Lojkowska, W., Kuran, W., Ryglewicz, D., ... & Bienkowski, P. (2013). Sweet liking in patients with Parkinson's disease. *Journal of the Neurological Sciences*, *329*(1), 17–22.

Sieverding, M., Decker, S. & Zimmermann, F. (2010). Information about low participation in cancer screening demotivates other people. *Psychological Science*, *21*(7), 941–943.

Sikorski, C., Spahlholz, J., Hartlev, M. & Riedel-Heller, S.G. (2016). Weight-based discrimination: an ubiquitary phenomenon? *International Journal of Obesity*, *40*(2), 333.

Silverman, M.N. & Deuster, P.A. (2014). Biological mechanisms underlying the role of physical fitness in health and resilience. *Interface Focus*, *4*(5), 20140040.

Simmons, J.P., Nelson, L.D. & Simonsohn, U. (2011). False-positive psychology: Undisclosed flexibility in data collection and analysis allows presenting anything as significant. *Psychological Science*, *22*(11), 1359–1366.

Simpson, J.A., Griskevicius, V., Kuo, S.I., Sung, S. & Collins, W.A. (2012). Evolution, stress, and sensitive periods: the influence of unpredictability in early versus late childhood on sex and risky behavior. *Developmental Psychology*, *48*, 674–686.

Singer, S.F. (1993). Junk Science at the EPA. Legacy Tobacco Documents Library. www.industry documents.ucsf.edu/docs/jjlb0175

Sisson, S.B., Camhi, S.M., Tudor-Locke, C., Johnson, W.D. & Katzmarzyk, P.T. (2012). Characteristics of step-defined physical activity categories in U.S. adults. *American Journal of Health Promotion*, *26*, 152–159.

Skinner, M.D. & Aubin, H.J. (2010). Craving's place in addiction theory: Contributions of the major models. *Neuroscience and Biobehavioral Reviews*, *34*, 606–623.

Skorka-Brown, J., Andrade, J. & May, J. (2014). Playing 'Tetris' reduces the strength, frequency and vividness of naturally occurring cravings. *Appetite*, *76*, 161–165.

Skorka-Brown, J., Andrade, J., Whalley, B. & May, J. (2015). Playing Tetris decreases drug and other cravings in real world settings. *Addictive Behaviors*, *51*, 165–170.

Sloman, S.A. (1996). The empirical case for two systems of reasoning. *Psychological Bulletin*, *119*(1), 3.

Slovic, P. & Peters, E. (2006). Risk perception and affect. *Current Directions in Psychological Science*, *15*(6), 322–325.

Smith, A.D., Herle, M., Fildes, A., Cooke, L., Steinsbekk, S. & Llewellyn, C.H. (2017). Food fussiness and food neophobia share a common etiology in early childhood. *Journal of Child Psychology and Psychiatry*, *58*(2), 189–196.

Smith, C.T., Dang, L.C., Cowan, R.L., Kessler, R.M. & Zald, D.H. (2016). Variability in paralimbic dopamine signaling correlates with subjective responses to d-amphetamine. *Neuropharmacology*, *108*, 394–402.

Smith, K.F., Goldberg, M., Rosenthal, S., Carlson, L., Chen, J., Chen, C. & Ramachandran, S. (2014). Global rise in human infectious disease outbreaks. *Journal of The Royal Society Interface*, *11*(101), 20140950.

Smith, R. (1996). The big idea. *British Medical Journal*, *312*, 7036.

Smith, T.W., Glazer, K., Ruiz, J.M. & Gallo, L.C. (2004). Hostility, anger, aggressiveness, and coronary heart disease: an interpersonal perspective on personality, emotion, and health. *Journal of Personality*, *72*, 1217–1270.

Snel, M., Jonker, J.T., Hammer, S., Kerpershoek, G., Lamb, H.J., Meinders, A.E., Pijl, H., de Roos, A., Romijn, J.A., Smith, J.W.A. & Jazet, I.M. (2012). Long-term beneficial effect of a 16-week very low calorie diet on pericardial fat in obese type 2 diabetes mellitus patients. *Obesity*, *20*, 1572–1576.

Snelgrove, J.W., Pikhart, H. & Stafford, M. (2009). A multilevel analysis of social capital and self-rated health: evidence from the British Household Panel Survey. *Social Science and Medicine*, *68*, 1993–2001.

Sniehotta, F.F. (2009). Towards a theory of intentional behaviour change: Plans, planning, and self-regulation. *British Journal of Health Psychology*, *14*, 261–273.

Sniehotta, F.F. & Presseau, J. (2012). The habitual use of the self-report habit index. *Annals of Behavioral Medicine*, *43*(1), 139–140.

Sniehotta, F.F., Gellert, P., Witham, M.D., Donnan, P.T., Crombie, I.K. & McMurdo, M.E.T. (2013). Psychological theory in an interdisciplinary context: How do social cognitions predict physical activity in older adults alongside demographic, health-related, social, and environmental factors. *International Journal of Behavioral Nutrition and Physical Activity*, *10*, 106.

Sniehotta, F.F., Presseau, J. & Araujo-Soares, V. (2014). Time to retire the theory of planned behaviour. *Health Psychology Review*, *8*, 1–7.

Sniehotta, F.F., Presseau, J., Hobbs, N. & Araújo-Soares, V. (2012). Testing self-regulation interventions to increase walking using factorial randomized N-of-1 trials. *Health Psychology*, *31*(6), 733.

Sniehotta, F.F., Scholz, U. & Schwarzer, R. (2006). Action plans and coping plans for physical exercise: A longitudinal intervention study in cardiac rehabilitation. *British Journal of Health Psychology, 11*(1), 23–37.

Sniehotta, F.F., Schwarzer, R., Scholz, U. & Schüz, B. (2005). Action planning and coping planning for long-term lifestyle change: theory and assessment. *European Journal of Social Psychology, 35*(4), 565–576.

Snowdon, C. (2010). *The Spirit Level Delusion: Fact Checking the Left's New Theory of Everything*. London: Little Dice.

Snyder-Mackler, N., Sanz, J., Kohn, J.N., Brinkworth, J.F., Morrow, S., Shaver, A. O., ... & Barreiro, L. B. (2016). Social status alters immune regulation and response to infection in macaques. *Science, 354*(6315), 1041–1045.

Sogg, S. (2007). Alcohol misuse after bariatric surgery: epiphenomenon or 'Oprah' phenomenon? *Surgery for Obesity and Related Diseases, 3*, 366–368.

Sohal, R.S. & Forster, M.J. (2014). Caloric restriction and the aging process: a critique. *Free Radical Biology and Medicine, 73*, 366–382.

Sohl, S.J. & Moyer, A. (2007). Tailored interventions to promote mammography screening: a meta-analytic review. *Preventive Medicine, 45*, 252–261.

Sokol, R. & Fisher, E. (2016). Peer support for the hardly reached: a systematic review. *American Journal of Public Health, 106*, e1–e8.

Soler, R.E., Leeks, K.D., Buchanan, L.R., Brownson, R.C., Heath, G.W., Hopkins, D.H. & Task Force on Community Preventive Services. (2010). Point-of-decision prompts to increase stair use: A systematic review update. *American Journal of Preventive Medicine, 38*, S292–S300.

Solomon, R.L. (1980). The opponent-process theory of acquired motivation: the costs of pleasure and the benefits of pain. *American Psychologist, 35*(8), 691.

Solomon, R.L. & Corbit, J.D. (1974). An opponent-process theory of motivation: I. Temporal dynamics of affect. *Psychological Review, 81*(2), 119.

Soneji, S., Barrington-Trimis, J.L., Wills, T.A., Leventhal, A.M., Unger, J.B., Gibson, L.A., ... & Spindle, T.R. (2017). Association between initial use of e-cigarettes and subsequent cigarette smoking among adolescents and young adults: a systematic review and meta-analysis. *JAMA Pediatrics, 171*(8), 788–797.

Sorsdahl, K., Stein, D.J., Corrigall, J., Cuijpers, P., Smits, N., Naledi, T. & Myers, B. (2015). The efficacy of a blended motivational interviewing and problem solving therapy intervention to reduce substance use among patients presenting for emergency services in South Africa: A randomized controlled trial. *Substance Abuse Treatment, Prevention, and Policy, 10*(1), 46.

Sport England (2016). Record number of women get active. www.sportengland.org/news-and-features/news/2016/december/8/record-numbers-of-women-getting-active/

Sport England (2019). This Girl Can. www.sportengland.org/our-work/women/this-girl-can/

Spurk, D. & Abele, A.E. (2014). Synchronous and time-lagged effects between occupational self-efficacy and objective and subjective career success: findings from a four-wave and 9-year longitudinal study. *Journal of Vocational Behavior, 84*, 119–132.

Stadler, G., Oettingen, G. & Gollwitzer, P.M. (2010). Intervention effects of information and self-regulation on eating fruits and vegetables over two years. *Health Psychology, 29*(3), 274.

Stafford, M., Chandola, T. & Marmot, M. (2007). Association between fear of crime and mental health and physical functioning. *American Journal of Public Health, 97*, 2076–2081.

Stafford, N. (2012). Denmark cancels 'fat tax' and shelves 'sugar tax' because of threat of job losses. *British Medical Journal, 345*, e7889.

Staiano, A.E., Marker, A.M., Frelier, J.M., Hsia, D.S. & Martin, C.K. (2016). Influence of screen-based peer modeling on preschool children's vegetable consumption and preferences. *Journal of Nutrition Education and Behavior, 48*(5), 331–335.

Stamatakis, E., Zaninotto, P. Falaschetti, E., Mindell, J. & Head, J. (2010). Time trends in childhood and adolescent obesity in England from 1995 to 2007 and projections of prevalence to 2015. *Journal of Epidemiology and Community Health, 64*, 167–174.

Stanovich, K.E. & West, R. F. (2000). Individual differences in reasoning: Implications for the rationality debate? *Behavioral and Brain Sciences, 23*(5), 645–665.

Stanovich, K.E., West, R.F. & Toplak, M.E. (2013). Myside bias, rational thinking, and intelligence. *Current Directions in Psychological Science, 22*(4), 259–264.

Starling, A.P. & Stock, J.T. (2007). Dental indicators of health and stress in early Egyptian and Nubian agriculturalists: a difficult transition and gradual recovery. *American Journal of Physical Anthropology, 134*, 520–528.

Stern, D., Piernas, C., Barquera, S., Rivera, J.A. & Popkin, B.M. (2014). Caloric beverages were major sources of energy among children and adults in Mexico, 1999–2012. *The Journal of Nutrition, 144*(6), 949–956.

Stevens, E. (2010). Raw Food Diet FAQ. www.thebestofrawfood.com/raw-food-diet.html

Stevens, E.E., Patrick, T.E. & Pickler, R. (2009). A history of infant feeding. *The Journal of Perinatal Education, 18*(2), 32.

Stevenson, D.R. (1999) Blood pressure and age in cross-cultural perspective. *Human Biology, 71*, 529–551.

Stewart, B.W. & Wild, C.P. (2014). *World Cancer Report 2014.* https://publications.iarc.fr/Non-Series-Publications/World-Cancer-Reports/World-Cancer-Report-2014

Stice, E., Burger, K.S. & Yokum, S. (2013). Relative ability of fat and sugar tastes to activate reward, gustatory, and somatosensory regions. *American Journal of Clinical Nutrition, 98*, 1377–1384.

Stice, E., Lawrence, N.S., Kemps, E. & Veling, H. (2016). Training motor responses to food: A novel treatment for obesity targeting implicit processes. *Clinical Psychology Review, 49*, 16–27.

Stocks, N.P., Ryan, P., McElroy, H. & Allan, J. (2004). Statin prescribing in Australia: socioeconomic and sex differences. A cross-sectional study. *MJA, 180*, 229–231.

Strack, F. & Deutsch, R. (2004). Reflective and impulsive determinants of social behavior. *Personality and Social Psychology Review, 8*(3), 220–247.

Stringhini, S., Berkman, L., Dugravot, A., Ferrie, J.E., Marmot, M., Kivimaki, M. & Singh-Manoux, A. (2012). Socioeconomic status, structural and functional measures of social support, and mortality. *American Journal of Epidemiology, 175*, 1275–1283.

Stringhini, S., Dugravot, A., Shipley, M., Goldberg, M., Zins, M., Kivimäki, M., Marmot, M., Sabia, S. & Singh-Manoux, A. (2011). Health behaviours, socioeconomic status, and mortality: further analyses of the British Whitehall II and the French GAZEL prospective cohorts. *Plos Medicine, 8*, e1000419.

Stringhini, S., Sabia, S., Shipley, M., Brunner, E., Nabi, H., Kivimaki, M. & Singh-Manoux, A. (2010). Association of socioeconomic position with health behaviors and mortality. *Journal of the American Medical Association, 303*, 1159–1166.

Stroebe, W., Mensink, W., Aarts, H., Schut, H. & Kruglanski, A. W. (2008). Why dieters fail: Testing the goal conflict model of eating. *Journal of Experimental Social Psychology, 44*(1), 26–36.

Stubbe, J.H., Boomsma, D.I., Vink, J.M.V., Cornes, B.K., Martin, N.G., Skytthe, A. et al. (2006). Genetic influences on exercise participation in 37.051 twin pairs from seven countries. *PLoS ONE, 1*(1): e22.

Sturm, R. & Gresenz, C.R. (2002). Relations of income inequality and family income to chronic medical conditions and mental health disorders: national survey in USA. *British Medical Journal, 324*, 20

Sullivan, S.A. & Birch, L.L. (1990). Pass the sugar, pass the salt: Experience dictates preference. *Developmental Psychology, 26*(4), 546.

Suls, J. & Martin, R. (2005). The daily life of the garden-variety neurotic: reactivity, stressor exposure, mood spillover, and maladaptive coping. *Journal of Personality, 73*, 1–25.

Suls, J. & Rothman, A. (2004). Evolution of the biopsychosocial model: prospects and challenges for health psychology. *Health Psychology, 23*(2), 119.

Sutton, S. (1994). The past predicts the future: Interpreting behaviour-behaviour relationships in social psychological models of health behaviour. In D.R. Rutter & L. Quine (eds.). *Social Psychology and Health: European Perspectives* (pp. 71–88). Aldershot: Avebury.

Sutton, S. (2001). Back to the drawing board? A review of applications of the transtheoretical model to substance use. *Addiction, 96*, 175–186.

Sutton, S. (2015). Stage theories. In M. Conner and P. Norman (eds.). *Predicting and Changing Health Behaviour. Research and Practice with Social Cognition Models.* Maidenhead: Open University Press.

Tang, S.H. & Hall, V.C. (1995). The overjustification effect: a meta-analysis. *Applied Cognitive Psychology, 9*, 365–404.

Tangney, J.P., Baumeister, R.F. & Boone, A.L. (2004). High self-control predicts good adjustment, less pathology, better grades, and interpersonal success. *Journal of Personality, 72* (2), 271–324.

Tannenbaum, M.B., Hepler, J., Zimmerman, R.S., Saul, L., Jacobs, S., Wilson, K. & Albarracín, D. (2015). Appealing to fear: a meta-analysis of fear appeal effectiveness and theories. *Psychological Bulletin, 141*, 1178–1204.

Tapper, K. (2017a). Children respond to food restriction by increasing food consumption. *Behavioral and Brain Sciences, 40*(e129).

Tapper, K. (2017b). Can mindfulness influence weight management related eating behaviors? If so, how? *Clinical Psychology Review, 53*, 122–134.

Tapper, K. (2018). Mindfulness and craving: effects and mechanisms. *Clinical Psychology Review, 59*, 101–117

Tapper, K. & Seguias, L. (2020). The effects of mindful eating on food consumption over a half-day period. *Appetite, 145*.

Tapper, K. & Turner, A. (2018). The effect of a mindfulness-based decentering strategy on chocolate craving. *Appetite, 130*, 157–162.

Tapper, K., Baker, L., Jiga-Boy, G., Haddock, G. & Maio, G.R. (2015). Sensitivity to reward and punishment: associations with diet, alcohol consumption, and smoking. *Personality and Individual Differences, 72*, 79–84.

Tapper, K., Horne, P.J. & Lowe, C.F. (2003). The Food Dudes to the rescue. *The Psychologist*, *16*(1), 18–21.

Tapper, K., Jiga-Boy, G.M., Haddock, G., Maio, G.R. & Valle, C. (2012). Motivating health behaviour change: provision of cognitive support for health values. *The Lancet*, *380*, S71.

Tapper, K., Jiga-Boy, G., Maio, G.R., Haddock, G. & Lewis, M. (2014). Development and preliminary evaluation of an internet-based healthy eating program: randomized controlled trial. *Journal of Medical Internet Research*, *16*(10), e231.

Tapper, K., Pothos, E.M. & Lawrence, A.D. (2010). Feast your eyes: Hunger and trait reward drive predict attentional bias for food cues. *Emotion*, *10*(6), 949–954.

Tavares, L.S., Plotnikoff, R.C. & Loucaides, C. (2009). Social-cognitive theories for predicting physical activity behaviours of employed women with and without young children. *Psychology, Health & Medicine*, *14*, 129–142.

Taylor, N., Conner, M. & Lawton, R. (2012). The impact of theory on the effectiveness of worksite physical activity interventions: a meta-analysis and meta-regression. *Health Psychology Review*, *6*(1), 33–73.

Taylor, S.E. (2006). Tend and befriend. Biobehavioral bases of affiliation under stress. *Current Directions in Psychological Science*, *15*, 273–277.

Taylor, S.E. & Gollwitzer, P.M. (1995). Effects of mindset on positive illusions. *Journal of Personality and Social Psychology*, *69*, 213–226.

Taylor, S.E. & Seeman, T.E. (1999). Psychosocial resources and the SES-health relationship. *Annals of the New York Academy of Sciences*, *896*, 210–225.

Taylor, S.E., Klein, L.C., Lewis, B.P., Gruenewald, T.L., Gurung, R.A.R. & Updegraff, J.A. (2000). Biobehavioral responses to stress in females: tend-and-befriend, not fight-or-flight. *Psychological Review*, *2000*, 411–429.

Te Morenga, L.A., Howatson, A.J., Jones, R.M. & Mann, J. (2014). Dietary sugars and cardiometabolic risk: systematic review and meta-analyses of randomized controlled trials of the effects on blood pressure and lipids. *The American Journal of Clinical Nutrition*, *100*(1), 65–79.

Teachman, B.A., Gapinski, K.D., Brownell, K.D., Rawlins, M. & Jeyaram, S. (2003). Demonstrations of implicit anti-fat bias: the impact of providing causal information and evoking empathy. *Health Psychology*, *22*, 68–78.

Teixeira, P.J., Carraça, E.V., Markland, D., Silva, M.N. & Ryan, R.M. (2012). Exercise, physical activity, and self-determination theory: a systematic review. *International Journal of Behavioral Nutrition and Physical Activity*, *9*, 78.

Teixeira, P.J., Carraça, E.V., Marques, M.M., Rutter, H., Oppert, J.M., De Bourdeaudhuij, I., Lakerveld, J. & Brug, J. (2015). Successful behavior change in obesity interventions in adults: a systematic review of self-regulation mediators. *BMC Medicine*, *13*, 84.

Terracciano, A., Löckenhoff, C.E., Zonderman, A.B., Ferrucci, L. & Costa, P.T. (2008). Personality predictors of longevity: activity, emotional stability, and conscientiousness. *Psychosomatic Medicine*, *70*, 621–627.

Thaler, R.H. & Sunstein, C. (2008). *Nudge: Improving Decisions About Health, Wealth and Happiness*. New Haven, CT: Yale University Press.

Theeuwes, J. (1994). Endogenous and exogenous control of visual selection. *Perception*, *23*(4), 429–440.

Theeuwes, J. (2010). Top–down and bottom–up control of visual selection. *Acta Psychologica*, *135*(2), 77–99.

Thivel, D., Aucouturier, J., Metz, L., Morio, B. & Duche, P. (2014). Is there spontaneous energy expenditure compensation in response to intensive exercise in obese youth?. *Pediatric Obesity*, *9*(2), 147–154.

Thomas, J.M., Ursell, A., Robinson, E.L., Aveyard, P., Jebb, S.A., Herman, C.P. & Higgs, S. (2017). Using a descriptive social norm to increase vegetable selection in workplace restaurant settings. *Health Psychology*, *36*(11), 1026.

Thompson, I.M., Pauler, D.K., Goodman, P.J., Tangen, C.M., Lucia, M.S., Parnes, H.L.P., … Coltman, C.A. (2004). Prevalence of prostate cancer among men with a prostate-sepcific antigen level <4.0 ng per millilitre. *The New England Journal of Medicine*, *350*, 2239–2246.

Thompson, R. & Haddock, G. (2012). Sometimes stories sell: when narrative appeals most likely to work? *European Journal of Social Psychology*, *42*, 92–102.

Thomson, G., Ebisch-Burton, K. & Flacking, R. (2015). Shame if you do–shame if you don't: women's experiences of infant feeding. *Maternal & Child Nutrition*, *11*(1), 33–46.

Tice, D.M., Baumeister, R.F., Shmueli, D. & Muraven, M. (2007). Restoring the self: Positive affect helps improve self-regulation following ego depletion. *Journal of Experimental Social Psychology*, *43*(3), 379–384.

Tiffany, S.T. (1990). A cognitive model of drug urges and drug-use behavior: Role of automatic and nonautomatic processes. *Psychological Review*, *97*, 147–168.

Tiffany, S.T. (1999). Cognitive concepts of craving. *Alcohol Research and Health*, *23*(3), 215–224.

Tiffany, S.T. & Carter, B.L. (1998). Is craving the source of compulsive drug use? *Journal of Psychopharmacology*, *12*(1), 23–30.

Tiffany, S.T. & Conklin, C.A. (2000). A cognitive processing model of alcohol craving and compulsive alcohol use. *Addiction, 95,* S145–153.

Tiffany, S.T. & Wray, J.M. (2012). The clinical significance of drug craving. *Annals of the New York Academy of Sciences, 1248,* 1–17.

Tiggemann, M. (2013). Objectification Theory: Of relevance for eating disorder researchers and clinicians? *Clinical Psychologist, 17*(2), 35–45.

Tiggemann, M. & Williams, E. (2012). The role of self-objectification in disordered eating, depressed mood, and sexual functioning among women: A comprehensive test of objectification theory. *Psychology of Women Quarterly, 36*(1), 66–75.

Timmerman, G.M. & Brown, A. (2012). The effect of a mindful restaurant eating intervention on weight management in women. *Journal of Nutrition Education and Behavior, 44*(1), 22–28.

Toates, F. (2006). A model of the hierarchy of behaviour, cognition, and consciousness. *Consciousness and Cognition, 15*(1), 75–118.

Tobacman, J.K. (2003). Does deficiency of arylsulfatase B have a role in cystic fibrosis? *Chest, 123,* 2130–2139.

Tobias, R. (2009). Changing behavior by memory aids: a social psychological model of prospective memory and habit development tested with dynamic field data. *Psychological Review, 116*(2), 408.

Tomiyama, A.J. (2014). Weight stigma is stressful. A review of evidence for the Cyclic Obesity/Weight-Based Stigma model. *Appetite, 82,* 8–15.

Tomiyama, A.J., Carr, D., Granberg, E.M., Major, B., Robinson, E., Sutin, A.R. & Brewis, A. (2018). How and why weight stigma drives the obesity 'epidemic' and harms health. *BMC Medicine, 16*(1), 123.

Tomiyama, A.J., Epel, E.S., McClatchey, T.M., Poelke, G., Kemeny, M.E., McCoy, S.K. & Daubenmier, J. (2014). Associations of weight stigma with cortisol and oxidative stress independent of adiposity. *Health Psychology, 33*(8), 862.

Tomiyama, A.J., Hunger, J.M., Nguyen-Cuu, J. & Wells, C. (2016). Misclassification of cardiometabolic health when using body mass index categories in NHANES 2005–2012. *International Journal of Obesity, 40*(5), 883.

Tomporowski, P.D. (2003). Effects of acute bouts of exercise on cognition. *Acta Psychologica, 112*(3), 297–324.

Torgerson, D.J. & Sibbald, B. (1998). Understanding controlled trials. What is a patient preference trial? *BMJ: British Medical Journal, 316*(7128), 360.

Townsend Centre for International Poverty Research (1999). Health Inequalities. www.bristol.ac.uk/poverty/healthinequalities.html

Treweek, S. & Zwarenstein, M. (2009). Making trials matter: pragmatic and explanatory trials and the problem of applicability. *Trials, 10*(1), 37.

Tsukayama, E., Toomey, S. L., Faith, M.S. & Duckworth, A.L. (2010). Self-control as a protective factor against overweight status in the transition from childhood to adolescence. *Archives of Pediatrics & Adolescent Medicine, 164*(7), 631–635.

Tulloch, H., Reida, R., D'Angeloa, M.S., Plotnikoff, R.C., Morrina, L., Beatona, L., Papadakisa, S. & Pipe, A. (2009). Predicting short and long-term exercise intentions and behaviour in patients with coronary artery disease: A test of protection motivation theory. *Psychology and Health, 24,* 255–269.

Turiano, N.A., Chapman, B.P., Gruenewald, T.L. & Mroczek, D.K. (2015). Personality and the leading behavioural contributors of mortality. *Health Psychology, 34,* 51–60.

Turnbaugh, P.J., Ley, R.E., Mahowald, M.A., Magrini, V., Mardis, E.R. & Gordon, J.I. (2006). An obesity-associated gut microbiome with increased capacity for energy harvest. *Nature, 444*(7122), 1027.

Tversky, A. & Kahneman, D. (1973). Availability: A heuristic for judging frequency and probability. *Cognitive Psychology, 5*(2), 207–232.

Tversky, A. & Kahneman, D. (1974). Judgment under uncertainty: Heuristics and biases. *Science, 185*(4157), 1124–1131.

Tversky, A. & Kahneman, D. (1992). Advances in prospect theory: Cumulative representation of uncertainty. *Journal of Risk and Uncertainty, 5*(4), 297–323.

UNAIDS (2019). Global HIV and AIDS statistics – 2019 fact sheet. www.unaids.org/en/resources/fact-sheet

UNESCO (2019). *Global Education Monitoring Report – Gender Report: Building Bridges for Gender Equality.* Paris, UNESCO. https://unesdoc.unesco.org/ark:/48223/pf0000368753?posInSet=1&queryId=6ea71640-5f7f-49aa-8883-42321ef6323c%C2%A0

Ungar, P.S. (2007). Limits to knowledge on the evolution of hominin diet. In Ungar, P.S. (ed.). *Evolution of the Human Diet.* New York: Oxford University Press.

Ungar, P.S., Grine, F.E. & Teaford, M.F. (2006). Diet in early Homo: a review of the evidence and a new model of adaptive versatility. *Annual Review of Anthropology, 35,* 209–228.

Unicef (2015). The investment case for education and equity. www.unicef.org/reports/investment-case-education-and-equity

Unicef (2019). Research on bed sharing, infant sleep and SIDS. www.unicef.org.uk/babyfriendly/news-

and-research/baby-friendly-research/infant-health-research/infant-health-research-bed-sharing-infant-sleep-and-sids/

United Nations (2015). www.un.org/en/development/desa/population/theme/trends/dem-comp-change/animated-figures/index.html

United Nations (2018). World Urbanization Prospects 2018. https://population.un.org/wup/Download/

United Nations (2019). World Population Prospects 2019. https://population.un.org/wpp/Download/Standard/Population/

United States Census Bureau. (2019). Health insurance coverage in the United States: 2018. www.census.gov/library/publications/2019/demo/p60-267.html

Upton, D., Upton, P. & Taylor, C. (2013). Increasing children's lunchtime consumption of fruit and vegetables: an evaluation of the Food Dudes programme. *Public Health Nutrition, 16*(6), 1066–1072.

USDHHS (2014). The Health Consequences of Smoking: 50 Years of Progress. A Report of the Surgeon General. Atlanta, GA: U.S. Department of Health and Human Services. www.hhs.gov/surgeongeneral/reports-and-publications/tobacco/index.html

Vachon-Presseau, E., Berger, S. E., Abdullah, T. B., Huang, L., Cecchi, G. A., Griffith, J. W., ... & Apkarian, A. V. (2018). Brain and psychological determinants of placebo pill response in chronic pain patients. *Nature Communications, 9*(1), 3397.

van 't Riet, J. & Ruiter, R.A. (2013). Defensive reactions to health-promoting information: an overview and implications for future research. *Health Psychology Review, 7,* S104–S136.

van 't Riet, J., Sijtsema, S.J., Dagevos, H. & De Bruijn, G.J. (2011). The importance of habits in eating behaviour. An overview and recommendations for future research. *Appetite, 57*(3), 585–596.

van den Akker, K., Jansen, A., Frentz, F. & Havermans, R.C. (2013). Impulsivity makes more susceptible to overeating after contextual appetitive conditioning. *Appetite, 70,* 73–80.

Van Duyn, M.A.S., Kristal, A.R., Dodd, K., Campbell, M.K., Subar, A.F., Stables, G., Nebeling, L. & Glanz, K. (2001). Association of awareness, intrapersonal and interpersonal factors, and stage of dietary change with fruit and vegetable consumption: a national survey. *American Journal of Health Promotion, 16,* 69–78.

Van Kesteren, N.M., Kok, G., Hospers, H.J., Schippers, J. & Wildt, W.D. (2006). Systematic development of a self-help and motivational enhancement intervention to promote sexual health in HIV-positive men who have sex with men. *AIDS Patient Care & STDs, 20*(12), 858–875.

Van Mechelen, W. (1992). Running injuries. A review of the epidemiological literature. Sports Medicine, 14, 320–335.

Van Nood, E., Vrieze, A., Nieuwdorp, M., Fuentes, S., Zoetendal, E. G., de Vos, W. M., ... & Speelman, P. (2013). Duodenal infusion of donor feces for recurrent Clostridium difficile. *New England Journal of Medicine, 368*(5), 407–415.

van Osch, L., Lechner, L., Reubsaet, A. & Vries, H. D. (2010). From theory to practice: An explorative study into the instrumentality and specificity of implementation intentions. *Psychology and Health, 25*(3), 351–364.

van Osch, L., Lechner, L., Reubsaet, A., Wigger, S. & Vries, H. (2008a). Relapse prevention in a national smoking cessation contest: effects of coping planning. *British Journal of Health Psychology, 13*(3), 525–535.

van Osch, L., Reubsaet, A., Lechner, L. & de Vries, H. (2008b). The formation of specific action plans can enhance sun protection behavior in motivated parents. *Preventive Medicine, 47*(1), 127–132.

Vansteenkiste, M., Lens, W. & Deci, E.L. (2006). Intrinsic versus extrinsic goal contents in self-determination theory: another look at the quality of academic motivation. *Educational Psychologist, 41,* 19–31.

Vartanian, L.R. & Shaprow, J.G. (2008). Effects of weight stigma on exercise motivation and behavior: a preliminary investigation among college-aged females. *Journal of Health Psychology, 13*(1), 131–138.

Vartanian, L.R., Spanos, S., Herman, C.P. & Polivy, J. (2015). Modeling of food intake: a meta-analytic review. *Social Influence, 10*(3), 119–136.

Vaughn, L. M., Jacquez, F. & Bakar, R. C. (2009). Cultural health attributions, beliefs, and practices: Effects on healthcare and medical education. *The Open Medical Education Journal, 2*(1).

Vedhara, K., Gill, S., Eldesouky, L., Campbell, B.K., Arevalo, J.M.G., Ma, J. & Coles, S.W. (2015). Personality and gene expression: do individual differences exist in the leukocyte transcriptome? *Psychoneuroendocrinology, 52,* 72–82.

Veenendaal, M.V.E., Painter, R.C., de Rooij, S.R., Bossuyt, P.M.M., van der Post, J.A.M., Gluckman, P.D., Hanson, M.A. & Roseboom, T.J. (2013). Transgenerational effects of prenatal exposure to the 1944–45 Dutch famine. *BJOG. An International Journal of Obstetrics and Gynaecology, 120,* 548–554.

Veling, H., Lawrence, N.S., Chen, Z., van Koningsbruggen, G.M. & Holland, R.W. (2017). What is trained during food go/no-go training? A review focusing on mechanisms and a research agenda. *Current Addiction Reports, 4*(1), 35–41.

Veltkamp, M., Aarts, H. & Custers, R. (2008). On the emergence of deprivation-reducing behaviors: Subliminal priming of behavior representations turns deprivation into motivation. *Journal of Experimental Social Psychology, 44*(3), 866–873.

Verhoeven, A.A., Adriaanse, M.A., de Ridder, D.T., de Vet, E. & Fennis, B.M. (2013). Less is more: The effect of multiple implementation intentions targeting unhealthy snacking habits. *European Journal of Social Psychology, 43*(5), 344–354.

Vermeersch, C. & Kremer, M. (2004). School meals, educational achievement and school competition: evidence from a randomized evaluation. Policy Research Working Paper; No. 3523. World Bank, Washington, DC.

Verplanken, B. & Aarts, H. (1999). Habit, attitude, and planned behaviour: is habit an empty construct or an interesting case of goal-directed automaticity? *European Review of Social Psychology, 10*(1), 101–134.

Verplanken, B. & Orbell, S. (2003). Reflections on past behavior: a self-report index of habit strength. *Journal of Applied Social Psychology, 33*(6), 1313–1330.

Verplanken, B. & Wood, W. (2006). Interventions to break and create consumer habits. *Journal of Public Policy & Marketing, 25*(1), 90–103.

Verplanken, B., Aarts, H. & Van Knippenberg, A. (1997). Habit, information acquisition, and the process of making travel mode choices. *European Journal of Social Psychology, 27*(5), 539–560.

Verplanken, B., Walker, I., Davis, A. & Jurasek, M. (2008). Context change and travel mode choice: combining the habit discontinuity and self-activation hypotheses. *Journal of Environmental Psychology, 28*(2), 121–127.

Veugelers, P.J. & Yip, A.M. (2003). Socioeconomic disparities in healthcare use: does universal coverage reduce inequalities in health? *Journal of Epidemiology and Community Health, 57*, 424–428.

Vickers, A.J. & Altman, D.G. (2013). Statistics notes: missing outcomes in randomised trials. *British Medical Journal, 346*, f3438.

Victora, C.G., Bahl, R., Barros, A.J., França, G.V., Horton, S., Krasevec, J., ... & Group, T.L.B.S. (2016). Breastfeeding in the 21st century: epidemiology, mechanisms, and lifelong effect. *The Lancet, 387*(10017), 475–490.

Vilà, I., Carrero, I. & Redondo, R. (2017). Reducing fat intake using implementation intentions: A meta-analytic review. *British Journal of Health Psychology, 22*(2), 281–294.

Vinkers, C.D., Adriaanse, M.A., Kroese, F.M. & de Ridder, D.T. (2015). Better sorry than safe: Making a Plan B reduces effectiveness of implementation intentions in healthy eating goals. *Psychology & Health, 30*(7), 821–838.

Vohs, K.D., Baumeister, R.F. & Schmeichel, B.J. (2012). Motivation, personal beliefs, and limited resources all contribute to self-control. *Journal of Experimental Social Psychology, 48*(4), 943–947.

Voigt, D.C., Dillard, J.P., Braddock, K.H., Anderson, J.W., Sopory, P. & Stephenson, M.T. (2009). Carver and White's (1994) BIS/BAS scales and their relationship to risky health behaviours. *Personality and Individual Differences, 47*, 89–93.

Vrba, E.S, Denton, G.H, Partridge, T.C & Gurkle, L.H. (1995). (eds.). *Palaeoclimate and Evolution with Emphasis on Human Origins*. New Haven, CT: Yale University Press.

Wakefield, A.J., Murch, S.H. & Anthony, A. (2010). Ileal-lymphoid-nodular hyperplasia, non-specific colitis, and pervasive developmental disorder in children (Retraction of vol 351, pg 637, 1998). *The Lancet, 375*(9713), 445–445.

Wakefield, M., Coomber, K., Zacher, M., Durkin, S., Brennan, E. & Scollo, M. (2015). Australian adult smokers' responses to plain packaging with larger graphic health warnings 1 year after implementation: results from a national cross-sectional tracking survey. *Tobacco Control, 24*(Suppl 2), ii17–ii25.

Wakefield, M., Germain, D., Durkin, S., Hammond, D., Goldberg, M. & Borland, R. (2012). Do larger pictorial health warnings diminish the need for plain packaging of cigarettes? *Addiction, 107*(6), 1159–1167.

Wakefield, M.A., Germain, D. & Durkin, S.J. (2008). How does increasingly plainer cigarette packaging influence adult smokers' perceptions about brand image? An experimental study. *Tobacco Control, 17*(6), 416–421.

Wakefield, M.A., Hayes, L., Durkin, S. & Borland, R. (2013). Introduction effects of the Australian plain packaging policy on adult smokers: a cross-sectional study. *BMJ Open, 3*(7), e003175.

Walker, N., Parag, V., Verbiest, M., Laking, G., Laugesen, M. & Bullen, C. (2020). Nicotine patches used in combination with e-cigarettes (with and without nicotine) for smoking cessation: a pragmatic, randomised trial. *The Lancet Respiratory Medicine, 8*(1), 54–64.

Walsh, E.M. & Kiviniemi, M.T. (2014). Changing how I feel about the food: experimentally manipulated affective associations with fruits change fruit choice behaviors. *Journal of Behavioral Medicine, 37*(2), 322–331.

Wan, E.W. & Sternthal, B. (2008). Regulating the effects of depletion through monitoring. *Personality and Social Psychology Bulletin, 34*(1), 32–46.

Wang, G.J., Volkow, N.D., Logan, J., Pappas, N.R., Wong, C.T., Zhu, W., Netusil, N. & Fowler, J.S.

(2001). Brain dopamine and obesity. *The Lancet, 357,* 354–357.

Wang, X., Ouyang, Y.Y., Liu, J. & Zhao, G. (2014). Flavonoid intake and risk of CVD: a systematic review and meta-analysis of prospective cohort studies. *British Journal of Nutrition, 111*(1), 1–11.

Wang, X., Ouyang, Y., Liu, J., Zhu, M., Zhao, G., Bao, W. & Hu, F.B. (2014). Fruit and vegetable consumption and mortality from all causes, cardiovascular disease, and cancer: systematic review and dose-response meta-analysis of prospective cohort studies. *British Medical Journal, 349,* g4490.

Wang, X.T. & Dvorak, R.D. (2010). Sweet future: Fluctuating blood glucose levels affect future discounting. *Psychological Science, 21,* 183–188.

Wang, Y., Feltham, B., Suh, M. & Jones, P.J. (2019). Cocoa flavanols and blood pressure reduction: Is there enough evidence to support a health claim in the United States? *Trends in Food Science & Technology, 83,* 203–210.

Wansink, B. & Chandon, P. (2014). Slim by design: Redirecting the accidental drivers of mindless overeating. *Journal of Consumer Psychology, 24*(3), 413–431.

Wardle, J., Carnell, S., Haworth, C.M.A., Farooqi, S., O'Rahilly, S. & Plomin, R. (2008). Obesity associated genetic variation in FTO is associated with diminished satiety. *The Journal of Clinical Endocrinology and Metabolism, 93,* 3640–3643.

Wasim, M., Awan, F.R., Najam, S.S., Khan, A.R. & Khan, H.N. (2016). Role of leptin deficiency, inefficiency, and leptin receptors in obesity. *Biochemical Genetics, 54,* 565–575.

Watts, T.W., Duncan, G.J. & Quan, H. (2018). Revisiting the marshmallow test: A conceptual replication investigating links between early delay of gratification and later outcomes. *Psychological cience, 29*(7), 1159–1177.

Weaver, I.C.G., Cervoni, N., Champagne, F.A., D'Alessio, A.C., Sharma, S., Seckl, J.R., Dymov, S., Szyf, M. & Meaney, M.J. (2004). Epigenetic programming by maternal behavior. *Nature Neuroscience, 7,* 847–854.

Weaver, I.C.G., Meaney, M.J. & Szyf, M. (2006). Maternal care effects on the hippocampal transcriptome and anxiety-mediated behaviors in the offspring that are reversible in adulthood. *Proceedings of the National Academy of Sciences, 103,* 3480–3485.

Webb, H., Jones, B. M., McNeill, K., Lim, L., Frain, A. J., O'Brien, K. J., ... & Cruwys, T. (2017). Smoke signals: The decline of brand identity predicts reduced smoking behaviour following the introduction of plain packaging. *Addictive Behaviors Reports, 5,* 49–55.

Webb, T. L., Sheeran, P. & Luszczynska, A. (2009). Planning to break unwanted habits: Habit strength moderates implementation intention effects on behaviour change. *British Journal of Social Psychology, 48*(3), 507–523.

Webb, T.L. & Sheeran, P. (2008). Mechanisms of implementation intention effects: the role of goal intentions, self-efficacy, and accessibility of plan components. *British Journal of Social Psychology, 47*(3), 373–395.

Webb, T.L., Joseph, J., Yardley, L. & Michie, S. (2010). Using the internet to promote health behavior change: A systematic review and meta-analysis of the impact of theoretical basis, use of behavior change techniques, and mode of delivery on efficacy. *Journal of Medical Internet Research, 12,* e4.

Webber, L., Hill, C., Cooke, L., Carnell, S. & Wardle, J. (2010). Associations between child weight and maternal feeding styles are mediated by maternal perceptions and concerns. *European Journal of Clinical Nutrition, 64*(3), 259.

Weidemann, G., Satkunarajah, M. & Lovibond, P.F. (2016). I think, therefore eyeblink: The importance of contingency awareness in conditioning. *Psychological Science, 27*(4), 467–475.

Weindruch, R., Walford, R.L., Fligiel, S. & Guthrie, D. (1986). The retardation of aging in mice by dietary restriction: longevity, cancer, immunity and lifetime energy intake. *The Journal of Nutrition, 116,* 641–651.

Weingarten, E., Chen, Q., McAdams, M., Yi, J., Hepler, J. & Albarracín, D. (2016). From primed concepts to action: A meta-analysis of the behavioral effects of incidentally presented words. *Psychological Bulletin, 142*(5), 472.

Weinstein, N.D., Rothman, A.J. & Sutton, S.R. (1998). Stage theories of health behavior: conceptual and methodological issues. *Health Psychology, 17,* 290–299.

Weinstein, N.D., Sandman, P.M. & Blalock, S. (2008). The precaution adoption process model. In K. Glanz, B.K. Rimer & K. Viswanth (eds.). *Health Behavior and Health Education: Theory, Research, and Practice.* (4th edn, pp. 123–147). San Francisco, CA: Jossey-Bass.

Welch, H.G. & Passow, H.J. (2014). Quantifying the benefits and harms of screening mammography. *Journal of the American Medical Association Internal Medicine, 174,* 448–453.

Wells, R. (2012). Does this colour turn you off? *The Sydney Morning Herald.* www.smh.com.au/national/does-this-colour-turn-you-off-20120816-24bf4.html

Welton, S., Minty, R., O'Driscoll, T., Willms, H., Poirier, D., Madden, S. & Kelly, L. (2020). Intermittent fasting and weight loss: systematic review. *Canadian Family Physician, 66*(2), 117–125.

Wendling, A. & Wudyka, A. (2011). Narcotic addiction following gastric bypass surgery – a case study. *Obesity Surgery, 21*, 680–683.

Wengreen, H.J., Madden, G.J., Aguilar, S.S., Smits, R.R. & Jones, B.A. (2013). Incentivizing children's fruit and vegetable consumption: results of a United States pilot study of the Food Dudes Program. *Journal of Nutrition Education and Behavior, 45*(1), 54–59.

Wentzel, K.R. (1991). Relations between social competence and academic achievement in early adolescence. *Child Development, 62*(5), 1066–1078.

West, R. (2005). Time for a change: putting the transtheoretical (stages of change) model to rest. *Addiction, 100*, 1036–1039.

West, R. (2006). The transtheoretical model of behaviour change and the scientific method. *Addiction, 101*, 774–778.

West, R. & Brown, J. (2013). *Theory of Addition.* (2nd edn). Oxford: Wiley Blackwell.

West, R. & Sohal, T. (2006). 'Catastrophic' pathways to smoking cessation: findings from national survey. *British Medical Journal, 332*, 458–460.

West, R., Michie, S., Rubin, G.J. & Amlôt, R. (2020). Applying principles of behaviour change to reduce SARS-CoV-2 transmission. *Nature Human Behaviour*, 1–9.

Wheeler, B. (2018). Are we living in a 'nanny state'? *BBC News.* www.bbc.co.uk/news/uk-politics-45356189

Whelan, B., Relton, C., Johnson, M., Strong, M., Thomas, K.J., Umney, D. & Renfrew, M. (2018). Valuing breastfeeding: health care professionals' experiences of delivering a conditional cash transfer scheme for breastfeeding in areas with low breastfeeding rates. *SAGE Open, 8*(2), 2158244018776367.

Whelton, P.K. (1994). Epidemiology of hypertension. *Lancet, 344*, 101–106.

White, V., Williams, T. & Wakefield, M. (2015). Has the introduction of plain packaging with larger graphic health warnings changed adolescents' perceptions of cigarette packs and brands? *Tobacco Control, 24*(Suppl 2), ii42–ii49.

Whitehead, M., Pennington, A., Orton, L., Nayak, S., Petticrew, M., Sowden, A. & White, M. (2016). How could differences in 'control over destiny' lead to socio-economic inequalities in health? A synthesis of theories and pathways in the living environment. *Health and Place, 39*, 51–61.

Whitlock, G., Lewington, S, Sherliker, P, Clarke, R., Emberson, J., Halsey, J. … Peto, R. Prospective Studies Collaboration. (2009). Body-mass index and cause-specific mortality in 900,000 adults: collaborative analyses of 57 prospective studies. *Lancet, 373*, 1083–1096.

WHO (1948). Constitution of the World Health Organization. www.who.int/governance/eb/who_constitution_en.pdf

WHO (2003). WHO Framework Convention on Tobacco Control. https://apps.who.int/iris/bitstream/handle/10665/42811/9241591013.pdf;jsessionid=6291A42D664B591CFBD7AF740D6727C0?sequence=1

WHO (2008). MPower. A policy package to reverse the tobacco epidemic. www.who.int/tobacco/mpower/package/en/

WHO (2009a). Pandemic influenza preparedness and response. www.who.int/influenza/resources/documents/pandemic_guidance_04_2009/en/

WHO (2009b). WHO Guidelines on Hand Hygiene in Health Care. www.who.int/gpsc/5may/tools/9789241597906/en/

WHO (2010a). Global recommendations on physical activity for health. www.who.int/dietphysicalactivity/publications/9789241599979/en/

WHO (2010b). The Alcohol, Smoking and Substance Involvement Screening Test (ASSIST). www.who.int/management-of-substance-use/assist

WHO (2010c). The ASSIST-linked brief intervention for hazardous and hharmful substance use. www.who.int/management-of-substance-use/assist

WHO (2011). Report on the burden of endemic health care-associated infection worldwide. www.who.int/gpsc/country_work/en/

WHO (2012). Guideline: Sodium intake for adults and children. https://apps.who.int/iris/bitstream/handle/10665/77985/9789241504836_eng.pdf?sequence=1

WHO (2014). Observed rate of vaccine reactions. www.who.int/vaccine_safety/initiative/tools/MMR_vaccine_rates_information_sheet.pdf

WHO (2015a). Health in 2015 from Millennium Development Goals to Sustainable Development Goals.

WHO (2015b). World Health Organization Best Practices for the Naming of New Human Infectious Diseases. www.who.int/topics/infectious_diseases/naming-new-diseases/en/

WHO (2016a). Obesity and overweight. www.who.int/mediacentre/factsheets/fs311/en/

WHO (2016b). Plain packaging of tobacco products. Evidence, design and implementation. www.who.int/tobacco/publications/industry/plain-packaging-tobacco-products/en/

WHO (2016c). World Health Statistics 2016. Monitoring Health for the SDG. www.who.int/gho/publications/world_health_statistics/2016/en/

WHO (2017a). Diarrhoeal disease. www.who.int/en/news-room/fact-sheets/detail/diarrhoeal-disease

WHO (2017b). Parties to the WHO Framework on Tobacco Control. www.who.int/fctc/signatories_parties/en/

WHO (2018a). Breastfeeding: Global targets 2025. www.who.int/mediacentre/events/2016/world-breastfeeding-week/en/

WHO (2018b). Ebola vaccine frequently asked questions. www.who.int/emergencies/diseases/ebola/frequently-asked-questions/ebola-vaccine

WHO (2018c). Global status report on alcohol and health 2018. www.who.int/substance_abuse/publications/global_alcohol_report/en/

WHO (2018d). Healthy diet. Factsheet no. 394. https://www.who.int/en/news-room/fact-sheets/detail/healthy-diet

WHO (2018e). Influenza (seasonal). www.who.int/en/news-room/fact-sheets/detail/influenza-(seasonal)

WHO (2018f). Managing epidemics. Key facts about major deadly diseases. www.who.int/emergencies/diseases/managing-epidemics/en/

WHO (2018g). Rubella. www.who.int/news-room/fact-sheets/detail/rubella

WHO (2019a). Breastfeeding. www.who.int/topics/breastfeeding/en/

WHO (2019b). Hepatitis B. www.who.int/news-room/fact-sheets/detail/hepatitis-b

WHO (2019c). HIV/AIDS. www.who.int/news-room/fact-sheets/detail/hiv-aids

WHO (2019d). Human papillomavirus (HPV) and cervical cancer. www.who.int/news-room/fact-sheets/detail/human-papillomavirus-(hpv)-and-cervical-cancer

WHO (2019e). Measles. www.who.int/news-room/fact-sheets/detail/measles

WHO (2019f). Report on the global tobacco epidemic, 2019. Offer to Help Quit Tobacco. https://apps.who.int/iris/bitstream/handle/10665/326043/9789241516204-eng.pdf?ua=1

WHO (2019g). The SAFER technical package: five areas of intervention at national and subnational levels. www.who.int/publications-detail/the-safer-technical-package

WHO (2020a). Diabetes. www.who.int/health-topics/diabetes#tab=tab_1

WHO (2020b). Ebola virus disease. www.who.int/health-topics/ebola#tab=tab_1

WHO (2020c). Life expectancy. www.who.int/gho/mortality_burden_disease/life_tables/situation_trends/en/

WHO (2020d). Measles outbreaks in the Pacific. www.who.int/westernpacific/emergencies/measles-outbreaks-in-the-pacific

WHO (2020e). Raised cholesterol. www.who.int/gho/ncd/risk_factors/cholesterol_text/en/

WHO (2020f). Ten threats to global health in 2019. www.who.int/news-room/spotlight/ten-threats-to-global-health-in-2019

WHO (2020g). Immunization, vaccines and biologicals. www.who.int/teams/immunization-vaccines-and-biologicals/diseases

WHO (2020h). WHO Coronavirus Disease (COVID-19) Dashboard. https://covid19.who.int

Wicherts, J.M., Borsboom, D., Kats, J. & Molenaar, D. (2006). The poor availability of psychological research data for reanalysis. *American Psychologist, 61*(7), 726.

Widman, L., Noar, S.M., Choukas-Bradley, S. & Francis, D.B. (2014). Adolescent sexual health communication and condom use: a meta-analysis. *Health Psychology, 33*, 1113.

Wiebe, D.J., Drew, L.M. & Croom, A. (2010). Personality, health and illness. In D. French, K. Vedhara, A.A. Kaptein & J. Weinman (eds.). *Health Psychology* (2nd edn). Chichester: Blackwell Publishing.

Wiedemann, A.U., Lippke, S. & Schwarzer, R. (2012). Multiple plans and memory performance: Results of a randomized controlled trial targeting fruit and vegetable intake. *Journal of Behavioral Medicine, 35*(4), 387-392.

Wiedemann, A.U., Lippke, S., Reuter, T., Ziegelmann, J.P. & Schüz, B. (2011). The more the better? The number of plans predicts health behaviour change. *Applied Psychology: Health and Well-Being, 3*(1), 87–106.

Wiers, R.W., Boffo, M. & Field, M. (2018). What's in a trial? On the importance of distinguishing between experimental lab studies and randomized controlled trials: The case of cognitive bias modification and alcohol use disorders. *Journal of Studies on Alcohol and Drugs, 79*(3), 333–343.

Wiers, R.W., Rinck, M., Kordts, R., Houben, K. & Strack, F. (2010). Retraining automatic action-tendencies to approach alcohol in hazardous drinkers. *Addiction, 105*(2), 279–287.

Wilding, S., Conner, M., Sandberg, T., Prestwich, A., Lawton, R., Wood, C., Miles, E., Godin, G. & Sheeran, P. (2016). The question-behaviour effect: A theoretical and methodological review and meta-analysis. *European Review of Social Psychology, 27*, 196–230.

Wildman, R.P., Muntner, P., Reynolds, K., McGinn, A.P., Rajpathak, S., Wylie-Rosett, J. & Sowers, M.R. (2008). The obese without cardiometabolic risk factor clustering and the normal weight with cardiometabolic risk factor clustering: prevalence and correlates of 2 phenotypes among the US population (NHANES 1999-2004). *Archives of Internal Medicine, 168*(15), 1617–1624.

Wilkins, J., Schoville, B.J., Brown, K.S. & Chazan, M. (2012). Evidence for early hafted hunting technology. *Science, 338*, 942–945.

Wilkinson, R.G. (1990). Income distribution and mortality: a 'natural' experiment. *Sociology of Health and Illness, 12*, 391–412.

Wilkinson, R.G. (1992). Income distribution and life expectancy. *British Medical Journal, 304*, 165–168.

Wilkinson, R.G. & Pickett, K.E. (2006). Income inequality and population health: a review and explanation of the evidence. *Social Science and Medicine, 62*, 1768–1784.

Wilkinson, R.G. & Pickett, K.E. (2010). *The Spirit Level: Why Equality is Better for Everyone*. London: Penguin Books.

Willcox, B.J., Willcox, D.C., Todoriki, H., Fujiyoshi, A., Yano, K., He, Q., Curb, J.D. & Suzuki, M. (2007). Caloric restriction, the traditional Okinawan diet, and healthy aging. The diet of the world's longest-lived people and its potential impact on morbidity and life span. *Annals of the New York Academy of Sciences, 1114*, 434–455.

Williams, D.M., Anderson, E.S. & Winett, R.A. (2005). A review of the outcome expectancy construct in physical activity research. *Annals of Behavioral Medicine, 29*, 70–79.

Williams, R.J. & Spencer, J.P. (2012). Flavonoids, cognition, and dementia: actions, mechanisms, and potential therapeutic utility for Alzheimer disease. *Free Radical Biology and Medicine, 52*(1), 35–45.

Williams, S.L. & French, D.P. (2011). What are the most effective intervention techniques for changing physical activity self-efficacy and physical activity behaviour-and are they the same? *Health Education Research, 26*, 308–322.

Williams, T.N., Mwangi, T.W., Wambua, S., Alexander, N.D., Kortok, M., Snow, R.W. & Marsh, K. (2005). Sickle cell trait and the risk of *Plasmodium falciparum* malaria and other childhood diseases. *The Journal of Infectious Diseases, 192*, 178–186.

Williams-Piehota, P., Pizarro, J., Schneider, T.R. Mowad, L. & Salovey, P. (2005). Matching health messages to monitor-blunter coping styles to motivate screening mammography. *Health Psychology, 24*, 58–67.

Williams-Piehota, P., Schneider, T.R., Pizarro, J., Mowad, L. & Salovey, P. (2004). Matching health messages to health locus of control beliefs for promoting mammography utilization. *Psychology and Health, 19*, 407–423.

Wilmore, J.H., Costill, D.L. & Kenney, W.L. (2008). *Physiology of Sport and Exercise*. Champaign, IL: Human Kinetics.

Wilper, A.P., Woolhandler, S., Lasser, K.E., McCormick, D., Bor, D.H. & Himmelstein, D.U. (2009). Health insurance and mortality in US adults. *American Journal of Public Health, 99*, 2289–2295.

Withrock, I.C., Anderson, S.J., Jefferson, M.A., McCormack, G.R., Mlynarczyk, G.S., Nakama, A., ... & Lind, M.S. (2015). Genetic diseases conferring resistance to infectious diseases. *Genes & Diseases, 2*(3), 247–254.

Witte, K. (1992) Putting the fear back into fear appeals: the extended parallel process model. *Communication Monographs 59*, 329–349.

Witte, K. & Allen, M. (2000). A meta-analysis of fear appeals: implications for effective public health campaigns. *Health Education and Behavior, 27*, 591–615.

Wiuf, C. (2001). Do ΔF508 heterozygotes have a selective advantage? *Genetic Research, 78*, 41–47.

Wolf, A., Bray, G.A. & Popkin, B.M. (2008). A short history of beverages and how our body treats them. *Obesity Reviews, 9*(2), 151–164.

Wolf, A.M.D., Wender, R.C., Etzioni, R.B., Thompson, I.M., D'Amico, A.V., Volk, R.J., ...Smith, R.A. (2010). American Cancer Society guideline for the early detection of prostate cancer. Update 2010. *CA: A Cancer Journal for Clinicians, 60*, 70–98.

Wolfe, R.M. & Sharp, L.K. (2002). Anti-vaccinationists past and present. *British Medical Journal, 325*(7361), 430–432.

Wood, F., Robling, M., Prout, H., Kinnersley, P., Houston, H. & Butler, C. (2010). A question of balance: a qualitative study of mothers' interpretations of dietary recommendations. *Annals of Family Medicine, 8*, 51–57.

Wood, W. (2017). Habit in personality and social psychology. *Personality and Social Psychology Review, 21*, 389–403.

Wood, W. & Neal, D.T. (2007). A new look at habits and the habit-goal interface. *Psychological Review, 114*(4), 843.

Wood, W. & Neal, D.T. (2009). The habitual consumer. *Journal of Consumer Psychology, 19*(4), 579–592.

Wood, W. & Rünger, D. (2016). Psychology of habit. *Annual Review of Psychology, 67*, 289–314.

Wood, W., Quinn, J.M. & Kashy, D.A. (2002). Habits in everyday life: thought, emotion, and action. *Journal of Personality and Social Psychology, 83*(6), 1281–1297.

World Bank (2019). World Bank Open Data. https://data.worldbank.org

World Bank (2020a). GINI index.https://data.worldbank.org/indicator/SI.POV.GINI?end=2014&locations=ZA&start=2014&view=map

World Bank (2020b). World Bank country and lending groups. https://datahelpdesk.worldbank.org/knowledgebase/articles/906519-world-bank-country-and-lending-groups

Wrangham, R. (2013). The evolution of human nutrition. *Current Biology, 23*, 354–355.

Wrangham, R. & Carmody, R. (2010). Human adaptation to the control of fire. *Evolutionary Anthropology, 19*, 187–199.

Wrangham, R. & Conklin-Brittain, N. (2003). Cooking as a biological trait. *Comparative Biochemistry and Physiology Part A, 136*, 35-46.

Wrangham, R.W. (2006). The cooking enigma. In: P. Ungar (ed.). *Early Hominin Diets: The Known, The Unknown, and The Unknowable.* New York: Oxford University Press, pp. 308–323.

Wroblewski, L.E., Peek, R.M. & Wilson, K.T. (2010). Helicobacter pylori and gastric cancer: factors that modulate disease risk. *Clinical Microbiology Reviews, 23*(4), 713–739.

Wu, G.D., Chen, J., Hoffmann, C., Bittinger, K., Chen, Y.Y., Keilbaugh, S.A., ... & Sinha, R. (2011). Linking long-term dietary patterns with gut microbial enterotypes. *Science, 334*(6052), 105–108.

Wu, N.S., Schairer, L.C., Dellor, E. & Grella, C. (2010). Childhood trauma and health outcomes in adults with comorbid substance abuse and mental health disorders. *Addictive Behaviors, 35*(1), 68–71.

Wu, Y., Antony, S., Meitzler, J. L. & Doroshow, J. H. (2014). Molecular mechanisms underlying chronic inflammation-associated cancers. *Cancer Letters, 345*(2), 164–173.

Wyvell, C.L. & Berridge, K.C. (2000). Intra-accumbens amphetamine increases the conditioned incentive salience of sucrose reward: enhancement of reward 'wanting' without enhanced 'liking' or response reinforcement. *Journal of Neuroscience, 20*(21), 8122–8130.

Wyvell, C.L. & Berridge, K.C. (2001). Incentive sensitization by previous amphetamine exposure: increased cue-triggered 'wanting' for sucrose reward. *Journal of Neuroscience, 21*(19), 7831–7840.

Yank, V., Rennie, D. & Bero, L.A. (2007). Financial ties and concordance between results and conclusions in meta-analyses: retrospective cohort study. *British Medical Journal, 335*(7631), 1202–1205.

Yeomans, M.R., Chambers, L., Blumenthal, H. & Blake, A. (2008). The role of expectancy in sensory and hedonic evaluation: The case of smoked salmon ice-cream. *Food Quality and Preference, 19*(6), 565–573.

Yong, E. (2012). Bad copy. *Nature, 485*(7398), 298.

Yong, H.H., Borland, R., Hammond, D., Thrasher, J.F., Cummings, K.M. & Fong, G.T. (2016). Smokers' reactions to the new larger health warning labels on plain cigarette packs in Australia: findings from the ITC Australia project. *Tobacco Control, 25*(2), 181–187.

Young, J.M., Stacey, I., Dobbins, T.A., Dunlop, S., Dessaix, A.L. & Currow, D.C. (2014). Association between tobacco plain packaging and Quitline calls: a population–based, interrupted time-series analysis. *Medical Journal of Australia, 200*(1), 29–32.

Young, L.R. & Nestle, M. (2012). Reducing portion sizes to prevent obesity. A call to action. *American Journal of Preventive Medicine, 43*, 565–568.

Young, M.D., Plotnikoff, R.C., Collins, C.E., Callister, R. & Morgan, P.J. (2014). Social cognitive theory and physical activity: a systematic review and meta-analysis. *Obesity Reviews, 15*, 983–995.

Zacher, M., Bayly, M., Brennan, E., Dono, J., Miller, C., Durkin, S., ... & Wakefield, M. (2014). Personal tobacco pack display before and after the introduction of plain packaging with larger pictorial health warnings in A ustralia: an observational study of outdoor café strips. *Addiction, 109*(4), 653–662.

Zacher, M., Bayly, M., Brennan, E., Dono, J., Miller, C., Durkin, S., ... & Wakefield, M. (2015). Personal pack display and active smoking at outdoor café strips: assessing the impact of plain packaging 1 year postimplementation. *Tobacco Control, 24*(Suppl 2), ii94–ii97.

Zajonc, R.B. (1968). Attitudinal effects of mere exposure. *Journal of Personality and Social Psychology, 9*(2p2), 1.

Zakrzewski, S.R. (2003). Variation in ancient Egyptian stature and body proportions. *American Journal of Physical Anthropology, 121*, 219–229.

Zakrzewski, S.R. (2006). Human skeletal diversity in the Egyptian Nile valley. In M. Chlodnicki, M. Kobusiewicz & K. Kroeper. (eds.). *Archaeology of early Northeastern Africa.* Poznan: Poznan Archaeological Museum Press.

Zampieri, F. (2017). The impact of modern medicine on human evolution. In M. Tibayrenc & F.J. Ayala (eds.). *On Human Nature: Biology, Psychology, Ethics, Politics, and Religion.* (pp. 707–727). London: Academic Press.

Zhang, J., Liu, H., Luo, S., Chavez-Badiola, A., Liu, Z., Yang, M., Munne, S., Konstantinidis, M., Wells, D. & Huang, T. (2016). First live birth using human oocytes reconstituted by spindle nuclear transfer for mitochondrial DNA mutation causing Leigh syndrome. *Fertility and Sterility, 106*, e375–e376.

Ziegelmann, J.P., Lippke, S. & Schwarzer, R. (2006). Adoption and maintenance of physical activity: Planning interventions in young, middle-aged, and older adults. *Psychology & Health, 21*(2), 145–163.

Zimmerman, B.J. (1995). Self-efficacy and educational development. In A. Bandura (ed.). *Self-Efficacy in Changing Societies*. Cambridge: Cambridge University Press.

Zimmerman, R.S. & Vernberg, D. (1994). Models of preventative health behavior: comparison, critique, and meta-analysis. *Advances in Medical Sociology, 4,* 45–67.

Zuckerman, J.N., Rombo, L. & Fisch, A. (2007). The true burden and risk of cholera: implications for prevention and control. *The Lancet Infectious Diseases, 7*(8), 521–530.

Zuk, M. (2013). *Paleofantasy. What Evolution Really Tells us About Sex, Diet, and How We Live*. New York: W.W. Norton & Company.

INDEX

Key terms are indicated in **bold**